-ition might be essentially true or false descriptions of this historical flux.

I have got a clearer notion, I think, that I had when we talked in Athens, of what makes my way of seeing things puzzling to you — a mystery, you called it. You expect to look at everything as I look on the things I don't believe in — religious myths, e.g. — which can have, of course, a symbolic or pragmatic truth. My nature, on the other hand, compels me to believe in something in quite a different sense, and this something is, in my view, double — material nature with its animation on the one hand, and logical or mathematical forms on the other. These are discovered by us, starting from sensation, and, in the first case, are tested by pragmatic standards. But we look to them in order to understand the origin of our experience (or its standard in signification) and I, for one, heartily accept them in that rôle. So I embrace materialism on pragmatic grounds — and on transcendental grounds also. The prohibition to believe which, in some expressions of it, pragmatism seems to impose, as if every opinion had to be symbolic and had to be superseded, is what

[left margin, vertical:] I object to. It is too Hegelian. History, at least, must have a definite constitution, apart from the pragmatic value of knowing it. With these qualifications I always agree.

The Works of George Santayana

Volume V, Book One

Herman J. Saatkamp Jr., General Editor
William G. Holzberger, Textual Editor
Marianne S. Wokeck, Editor
Kristine W. Frost, Associate Editor
Joshua B. Garrison, Assistant Editor

To the memory of
Daniel and Margot Cory

A charcoal sketch by Andreas Andersen, 1897.
By permission of the Houghton Library, Harvard University
(MS Am 1371.6).

The Letters of George Santayana

Book One, [1868]–1909

Edited and with an Introduction by
William G. Holzberger

The MIT Press, Cambridge, Massachusetts, and London, England

This publication has been supported by the National Endowment for the Humanities, a federal agency which supports the study of such fields as history, philosophy, literature, and languages.

Additional funding was provided by Corliss Lamont, Emil Ogden, and the Comité Conjunto Hispano-Norteamericano para la Cooperación Cultural y Educativa.

The endpapers are facsimiles of a letter from Santayana to William James, dated 27 July 1905. Publication is by permission of the Houghton Library, Harvard University (bMS Am 1092.9 [594–609]).

COMMITTEE ON
SCHOLARLY EDITIONS

AN APPROVED EDITION

MODERN LANGUAGE
ASSOCIATION OF AMERICA

A selected edition of *The Letters of George Santayana* was published by Scribner's in 1955. Other letters written by Santayana have been published previously in books and periodicals. All information concerning previous publications is included in the textual notes.

Manufactured in the United States of America

Library of Congress Cataloging-in-Publication Data

Santayana, George, 1863–1952.
    [Correspondence]
    The letters of George Santayana / G. Santayana; edited and with an introduction by William G. Holzberger,–Santayana ed.
        p. cm.–(The works of George Santayana; v.5)
    Includes bibliographical references and index.
    ISBN 0-262-19457-0 (hardcover: alk. paper)
    1. Santayana, George, 1863–1952–Correspondence.   2. Philosophers–United States–Correspondence.   I. Holzberger, William G.   II. Title.

B945.S2   1986 vol. 5
[B945.S24 A4]
191–dc21   00–048978

The paper used in this publication meets the minimum requirements of American National Standards for Information Sciences–Permanence of Paper for Printed Library Materials. ANSI Z39.48 1984. ⊚™

The Santayana Edition

Herman J. Saatkamp Jr., General Editor
William G. Holzberger, Textual Editor
Marianne S. Wokeck, Editor
Kristine W. Frost, Associate Editor
Joshua B. Garrison, Assistant Editor

Editorial Board

The Works of George Santayana

I *Persons and Places: Fragments of Autobiography*, 1986
II *The Sense of Beauty: Being the Outlines of Æsthetic Theory*, 1988
III *Interpretations of Poetry and Religion*, 1989
IV *The Last Puritan: A Memoir in the Form of a Novel*, 1994
V *The Letters of George Santayana, Book One*, 2001

Contents

Book One, [1868]–1909

Preface

Book One, [1868]–1909

Except for the first letter in this collection, sent by Santayana to his sisters Susan and Josephine when he was only about six years old, this first book of Santayana's letters includes correspondence written during the years 1882 through 1909, a period of twenty-eight years, or from Santayana's nineteenth through his forty-sixth year. The considerably longer period of time covered by this book of Santayana's correspondence over the subsequent books reflects the fact that the early letters are naturally the most difficult to obtain. A great many of them have doubtless been destroyed or otherwise lost. Despite the obvious brilliance of Santayana's early letters they were not yet the letters of a famous author, and for that reason not automatically preserved by many of their recipients. The letters constituting Book One, therefore, doubtless represent only a fraction of all the letters that Santayana wrote during this period.

Jorge Agustín Nicolás Ruiz de Santayana, who later called himself George Santayana, was born in Madrid on 16 December 1863 and spent the first years of his life in Ávila, the medieval walled town in old Castile. In 1872, when he was eight and a half years old, he was brought by his father to Boston to be reunited with his mother, Josefina Borrás Sturgis, his two half sisters, Susan (called Susana) and Josephine, and half brother, Robert. In Boston, the young Santayana, who upon arrival knew not a word of English, first attended a kindergarten and afterwards a public elementary school before transferring to the Boston Public Latin School in 1874. After spending eight years at the Latin School, where he was relatively happy and successful and recognized for his exceptional intellectual abilities, he graduated in 1882 and in the fall of that year matriculated at Harvard College.

The second-earliest extant letter is that of 21 August 1882 to John Galen Howard, written not long after the two young men had graduated from the Latin School. This letter presents some interesting insights into the uncompromising and apparently supreme self-confidence of the eighteen-year-old Santayana. One letter remains from his undergraduate years at Harvard, that to Professor Charles Eliot Norton, written in 1885 during Santayana's junior year, and then the succession of extant letters commences in earnest with those of the later summer and autumn of 1886, following upon his graduation from Harvard and his journey to Europe to pursue graduate study in philosophy in Germany. The letters from Germany of 1886–88 to his Harvard classmates Henry Ward Abbot and William Morton Fullerton and to his mentor in the Harvard philosophy department, William James, describe his experiences as a traveling student sharing the Walker Fellowship with another Harvard classmate, Charles Augustus Strong. They also exhibit the young Santayana's remarkably insightful and sophisticated mind, razor-sharp sardonic wit, and power of expression, as well as his fiercely independent and self-directed spirit.

Rather than attempt to complete a doctoral dissertation in German at a German university, which he felt incapable of doing successfully, Santayana returned to America in July 1888 to write his doctoral dissertation in English and take his degree from Harvard. He settled down in his mother's house in Roxbury and worked diligently on his dissertation on the philosophy of Rudolf Hermann Lotze, which he completed the following year, receiving both the M.A. and Ph.D. degrees from his alma mater. In the fall of that year, 1889, he was hired by the Harvard philosophy department as a part-time instructor. This was the beginning of his teaching career at Harvard which would end some twenty-three years later with his letter of resignation to President Abbott Lawrence Lowell of 6 June 1912.

Though valued by his former teachers–Josiah Royce, William James, and George Herbert Palmer–now his colleagues in the philosophy department, and appreciated by his students, Santayana was never liked by the all-powerful Harvard president, Charles William Eliot. Eliot, the father of the modern American university, evidently disliked Santayana for several reasons. While Eliot was busy building Harvard, the great University, Santayana was regretting the disappearance of the Harvard College that he had known and enjoyed: the small, intimate school remote from the hustle and bustle of America of the Gilded Age. Eliot disliked Santayana for what he regarded as his aloofness and detachment: Santayana eschewed participation in faculty meetings and refused to serve on committees. Also, there is some indication that the Puritanical Eliot looked with disapproval upon Santayana's failure to marry and at his habit of choosing his friends and companions from among the undergraduate men, rather than from among his faculty colleagues and their wives. He therefore kept Santayana at the rank of lecturer for an inordinately long time, eight years, before promoting him, with staunch support from his departmental colleagues, to the rank of assistant professor in 1898, with a salary of two thousand dollars per year.

During those early years of his teaching career at Harvard, Santayana wrote mainly poetry, which he published in *The Harvard Monthly,* the student-edited journal that he had helped found. His first published book, *Sonnets and Other Verses* appeared in 1894. Thus, in the early part of Santayana's professional career at Harvard, he was identified with William Vaughn Moody, Robert Morss Lovett, Hugh McCullogh and the other "Harvard (or Neo-Traditionalist) Poets." This, however, would not do for a career as a professor of philosophy, and Santayana's first prose book, *The Sense of Beauty: Being the Outlines of Aesthetic Theory,* was developed from the course in aesthetics that he was then offering at Harvard. This first philosophical book was Santayana's response to the pressure from his department and the university administration for a professional book. *The Sense of Beauty* was published by Charles Scribner's Sons in 1896, marking the beginning of Santayana's lifelong association with the House of Scribner. Scribner's in New York and Constable in London remained Santayana's principal publishers.

Santayana's letters of the 1880s were to his college classmates and to his mentor William James. In the 1890s, he continued to write to classmates like Henry Ward Abbot and Boylston Beal, to several publishers, including Stone and Kimball (who brought out his early books of poetry) and Scribner's, but now also to younger friends that he made among the undergraduates, like Guy Murchie and W. Cameron Forbes. Many of these early letters are written from foreign places, for from the time of his first return visit to his father in Ávila, during the summer of 1883, when he was nineteen, Santayana was an inveterate traveler. During the years of Harvard teaching, he lived economically in bachelor rooms in the Harvard Yard, or with his mother in Roxbury, saving his earnings in order to spend the summers living and traveling in Europe.

During the 1890s, Santayana continued to write poetry and in 1899 published his long and elaborate verse drama called *Lucifer: A Theological Tragedy.* The work is complicated and problematical, combining as it does characters from several different mythopoetic traditions, including the Hebrew, Christian, and Greek. It was ignored by the critics (though Santayana himself authored an anonymous review that appeared in an issue of *The Harvard Monthly*), and it was never performed. *Lucifer* was followed a year later by Scribner's publication of *Interpretations of Poetry and Religion*. This book, a collection of essays and reviews, places Santayana in the tradition of Matthew Arnold in England and contemporary thinkers on the Continent who, while rejecting a conception of religion as literally true, nevertheless valued religion for its moral and aesthetic importance and tried to protect it from its own zealous advocates who persisted in leading religion upon a devastating collision course with the natural sciences. The following year, 1901, Santayana's final volume of new poems, *A Hermit of Carmel and Other Poems,* was published, marking the end of his career as a poet. From then on, though always writing in an essentially and intensely poetic style, Santayana concentrated on writing prose and succeeding as a professional philosopher. But it was not until publication of his early masterwork, *The Life of Reason, or the Phases of Human Progress,* in five volumes during 1905–6, that Santayana's reputation as a professional thinker of wide learning and penetrating insight was finally established.

The publication of *The Life of Reason* made it impossible for President Eliot to continue to ignore Santayana's distinction and importance, and in 1907 he promoted him from assistant to full professor and doubled his salary to four thousand dollars per annum. During this first decade of the twentieth century, while Santayana was building his professional career at Harvard, we see him corresponding with the doyenne of Boston society, Isabella Stewart Gardner, at whose Venetian palace in Boston he was a frequent guest; with fashionable young friends like Lawrence Smith Butler, nephew of Stanford White, the distinguished American architect; with his young teaching assistant, Horace Meyer Kallen; and with his elder half sister Susana, an enormous influence in his life. In 1902 Susana had married a former Spanish beau, Celedonio Sastre, a widower, and had gone to live with him and his six children in Ávila. A rich correspondence with Susana followed, which lasted until her death in 1928, and includes some of the most interesting and revealing of all of Santayana's letters.

A measure of Santayana's achievement as a writer and intellectual was his election in 1909 to membership in the National Institute of Arts and Letters, later known as the American Academy and Institute of Arts and Letters.

William G. Holzberger

Acknowledgments

This comprehensive edition of Santayana's personal and professional correspondence has been over thirty years in the making, and a great number of persons in many different walks of life have contributed to it. It was begun by Daniel Cory in the late 1960s as a two-volume sequel to his 1955 Scribner's edition of two hundred ninety-six letters by Santayana. I began collaborating with Cory on the project in 1971. After his sudden death by heart attack on 16 June 1972, I worked on the letters with the assistance of his widow, Mrs. Margot Cory, who was his successor as the Santayana literary executor. I continued to work on the preparation of a comprehensive edition of Santayana's letters until I joined the project to produce a multi-volume critical edition of Santayana's works headed by Herman J. Saatkamp Jr., General Editor. As textual editor of *The Works of George Santayana* it was necessary to deflect my attention substantially from the letters in order to help prepare the first four volumes of the edition for publication.[1] In 1988 Professor Saatkamp and I decided to incorporate the letters into the comprehensive edition of Santayana's writings as the fifth volume, and work on the letters resumed. At that time, however, the staff of the Santayana Edition was concentrating on preparation of the text of Volume IV, Santayana's novel, *The Last Puritan,* and the focus of attention and principal resources had to be directed toward completion of work on that volume, which was published in 1994. Since publication of the novel, however, the focus of the editorial staff has been on completion of the letters volume.

Included in the host of persons who have, over an exceptionally long period of time, contributed in many different ways to this large and complicated project are both private individuals as well as representatives of libraries and other institutions. Many of these persons no longer occupy the positions they did when they contributed to this project, and others are no longer alive. While it is impossible to acknowledge here everyone who helped make this edition of Santayana's letters a reality, we wish at least to mention those persons and institutions whose contributions were absolutely vital to the successful completion of the project.

Foremost, perhaps, among these individuals is the late Margot Cory. Margaret Degen Batten Cory was born in England on 27 November 1900 and, after many years' residence in Italy, died in England on 30 March 1995. As the Santayana literary executrix and heir to her late husband's ownership of Santayana's literary properties, Margot Cory owned the copyright in Santayana's letters. Not only did Mrs. Cory agree to the continuation of work on this edition after her husband's death, but she aided and encouraged its realization in many significant ways. In the early stages she made typewritten transcriptions of hundreds of letters, both to her husband and to others. Indeed, many letters to various individuals could not have been included had not Mrs. Cory, in an age before photocopying machines, first made handwritten copies of letters lent to her husband which she later recopied on the typewriter. Mrs. Cory's interest in this project was extremely keen, and it is our deep regret that she did not have the satisfaction of seeing the letters volume published during her lifetime.

The names of private persons who possess letters by George Santayana are given in the list of Manuscript Locations, and we are very grateful to these individuals for providing, often as gifts, photocopies of their letters. I wish to thank especially those who also contributed valuable information and who aided this project in other ways as well. Foremost is Richard Colton Lyon. Not only has Professor Lyon supplied copies of his own substantial and valuable correspondence, but he has been of great assistance in locating other letters. It was through the kind cooperation of Professor Lyon that I learned the whereabouts of the late Mrs. David M. Little, formerly Mrs. George Sturgis, the wife of Santayana's nephew. With help from Professor Lyon, Mrs. Little provided copies of letters that Santayana had written to her former husband, who had for many years served as Santayana's financial manager. Mrs. Little, before her death on 17 February 1976, was of unique service to this project by supplying information about the Sturgis family, and a great many footnotes to the letters are the result of information that she provided. Rosamond Thomas Bennett Sturgis Little was devoted to "Uncle George" both during and after his lifetime in a way that might be expected of few nieces by marriage. Mrs. Little's son, Robert Sturgis, a Boston architect, is also warmly thanked for permitting inclusion of his letters from his granduncle, for arranging for the deposit of Santayana's letters in the Sturgis Family Papers in Harvard's Houghton Library, and for his interest in the comprehensive edition of Santayana's writings and his continued helpfulness to the editors.

The late Dr. Corliss Lamont, a distinguished humanist and author and a life-long admirer of Santayana, was, over the years, a constant friend to this project. His direct financial aid to the Santayana Edition, together with his concern and assistance with various problems, were always much appreciated. The extensive collection of Santayana manuscripts and other materials in Columbia University's Butler Library constitute Dr. Lamont's gift to Santayana scholarship. Other private owners who have been particularly helpful include Mr. Guy Murchie Jr., whose glosses on the letters to his father have provided information for footnotes to those letters. Professors Justus Buchler and Peter Viereck also supplied helpful information about their letters from Santayana.

Several individuals have personally supported this project with generous financial gifts, professional advice, and scholarly research. These include Morris Grossman, Professor Emeritus, Fairfield University; John Lachs, Centennial Professor of Philosophy, Vanderbilt University; Emil Ogden, Ogden Resources Corporation, College Station, Texas; John McCormick, Professor Emeritus, Rutgers University; Henny Wenkart, Professor and Editor, New York City; and Excmo. Sr. D. Francisco Javier Jiménez-Ugarte Hernandez, Spanish Ambassador to Greece, who helped arrange the grant from the Comité Conjunto Hispano-Norteamericana.

Santayana Edition Board members who have continuously assisted the project in many and various ways are: Willard Arnett, Hugh Dawson, Morris Grossman, Angus Kerr-Lawson, John Lachs, Richard C. Lyon, Douglas MacDonald, John Michelsen, Andrew Reck, Beth J. Singer, Timothy Sprigge, and Henny Wenkart.

Many learned and distinguished scholars have contributed directly to the making of this edition. Among my Bucknell colleagues are several who have provided help with editorial tasks. Perhaps our greatest debt is due Professor Mills Fox Edgerton Jr., who has given most generously of his time, energy, and thoroughgoing knowledge of Romance languages. Not only has he translated the Spanish letters to José and Isabel Sastre, and provided numerous translations of words and phrases, but he has searched for Santayana letters during his travels through Spain. On one occasion he acted as my emissary to Santayana's grandnephew, the late Don Eduardo Sastre Martín, of Madrid and Ávila, in an effort to learn the whereabouts of any Santayana manuscripts or other materials extant in Spain. We are grateful to Professor James M. Heath of the Bucknell Classics Department who has continually and unstintingly given of his time and specialized knowledge in assisting the editors with the transcribing and translating of Greek and Latin words and phrases and the tracing to their origins of quotations in these ancient languages. Mark W. Padilla, Associate Professor of Classics and Associate Dean of the College of Arts and Sciences, has also helped with translations of Latin words and phrases. Professor John Gale of the Modern Languages and Linguistics Department has rendered much the same sort of assistance with French words and phrases, and Professor Marianna M. Archambault and her husband, Professor Paul Archambault of Syracuse University, have also been helpful with questions relating to the French and Italian languages. A friend and colleague in the Bucknell English Department, Professor James F. Carens, member of the Harvard class of 1949, has helped in a variety of ways: by discussing the edition with me, making valuable suggestions based upon his own experience as an editor of letters, by serving as a guide to and about Harvard University, and by reading drafts of the Introduction to this volume and making suggestions for revision that I not only adopted but believe have significantly improved the quality of the Introduction. Peter Hinks, Associate Editor with the Frederick Douglass Papers, Yale University, collated letters at the Beinecke Library. English Department chairmen who have aided in important ways are Harry R. Garvin, the late John W. Tilton, Michael D. Payne, Dennis Baumwoll, and John Rickard. Bucknell University officers who have supported this project by supplying funds for materials and travel, allowing me released time from teaching duties, and providing office space, equipment, and supplies specifically for work on the letters are Wendell I. Smith, former Provost, Larry Shinn, former Vice President for Academic Affairs, Daniel Little, current Vice President for Academic Affairs, Eugenia P. Gerdes, Dean of the College of Arts and Sciences, and former Associate Deans Barbara A. Shailor and S. Jackson Hill. To all of these colleagues I extend deep and sincere gratitude.

Texas A&M University officers and faculty who supported our work over many years include John J. McDermott, Distinguished Professor of Philosophy and Humanities, who directed the project during the transition from Texas to Indiana; Woodrow Jones, Dean of the College of Liberal Arts; Ben M. Crouch, Executive Associate Dean; Charles Stoup, Senior Academic Business Administrator; Robin Smith, Professor and Head, Department of Philosophy and Humanities; Kenneth M. Price, Professor of English; Robert A. Calvert, Professor of History, and Scott Austin, Professor of Philosophy.

Special thanks to Sherman D. Frost for his ongoing support of the work of the Edition. His help with computer-related questions, development of the Santayana Edition web page, and assistance with the physical relocation of the project have been a significant contribution to our progress toward publication of the letters.

Since its move to Indiana University-Purdue University, Indianapolis (IUPUI), the Edition has had the unconditional support of the University and the School of Liberal Arts. In particular, we must acknowledge the diligent work of the two newest members of the Santayana Edition. Marianne S. Wokeck, Editor, and Joshua B. Garrison, Assistant Editor, who have become completely involved with the final preparation of the letters for publication. Special thanks to the entire staff of the Dean's office who have assisted with our day-to-day work since the decision to relocate. Noteworthy support has come from Gerald L. Bepko, Vice President for Long-Range Planning and Chancellor of IUPUI; William M. Plater, Executive Vice Chancellor and Dean of the Faculties; Mark Brenner, Vice Chancellor for Research and Graduate Education; Curtis R. Simic, President, Indiana University Foundation; Nathan Houser, Director and General Editor, Peirce Edition Project; Paul R. Bippen, Dean, Indiana University-Purdue University Columbus; Janet Feldmann, Director, Library and Media Services, IUPU Columbus; and Steven J. Schmidt, University Library, IUPUI.

An eminent textual scholar who has contributed to this edition in significant ways is G. Thomas Tanselle, Textual Editor of *The Writings of Herman Melville* (a critical edition in fifteen volumes) and a foremost authority on editorial scholarship. Professor Tanselle has been very helpful in responding to queries about editorial matters and his writings on textual scholarship have served as a fundamental guide to the editors of the Santayana Edition. Thanks to Joseph M. Thomas for conducting the inspection of Book One of the letters for the Committee on Scholarly Editions of the Modern Language Association of America, and to Robert H. Hirst, chair of this committee, for his guidance and support. Mr. Harold Kulungian has given me several useful hints and suggestions. He ascertained the correct date of Santayana's letter to B. A. G. Fuller of 11 January 1905 (misdated in Cory's 1955 edition as 1904). Hugh J. Dawson of the English Department of the University of San Francisco and a member of the Editorial Board of the Santayana Edition has been a valuable source of information on the location of letters and has made many other notable contributions to this project. His frequent travels and researches in Europe have resulted in the acquisition of copies of three letters to the late Professor Enrico Castelli, whom Professor Dawson interviewed at his home in Rome in 1976. Our thanks also to Professor R. W. B. Lewis, the distinguished biographer of Edith Wharton, and to Dr. Marion Mainwaring, a professional researcher, who attempted to locate additional letters to Santayana's Harvard classmate William Morton Fullerton that—in addition to the four letters to Fullerton included in this edition— were believed to exist. I am very grateful to the late Richard Ellmann, the noted biographer and editor, Fellow of New College and Goldsmiths' Professor of English Literature in Oxford University. During the sabbatical year I spent at Oxford working on the letters edition (1975–76), Professor Ellmann was particularly helpful in discussing the plan for the edition and making suggestions regarding every aspect of the project. Indeed, his edition of the letters of James Joyce, together with the edition of Oscar Wilde's letters by Rupert Hart-Davis, were the earliest models for this edition of Santayana's letters.

A special note of thanks is due to Professor J. Albert Robbins, of Indiana University, who served as Chairman of the Committee on Manuscript Holdings of the American Literature Section of the Modern Language Association of America, in charge of gathering information for the updated edition of *American Literary Manuscripts,* an invaluable source of information regarding library manuscript holdings. Professor Robbins and his staff responded to my request, early in 1976, for additional information regarding the location of Santayana holograph letters in library collections, by undertaking a "hand search" of file data before their material was computerized sufficiently to make such a search less laborious. The result of their efforts was the locating and acquiring of a substantial number of letters, the existence of which had not previously been suspected. Yet another friend from the beginning is James Ballowe of Bradley University. An accomplished poet, critic, author and a distinguished Santayana scholar and editor, Professor Ballowe is warmly acknowledged here for his continual interest in and encouragement of this project and for his willingness to be helpful in every way. We are grateful to the late Paul G. Kuntz, Professor Emeritus of Philosophy at Emory University, for the work he did in collating our transcriptions of Santayana's letters to Mrs. Bernard Berenson against the originals in the Berensons' Villa I Tatti (now owned by Harvard University) in Settignano, Italy.

Special thanks are due individuals who sent copies or gave permission for their Santayana letters to be photocopied by the libraries in which they are held. These include: Robert Lowell (Houghton Library, Harvard University); Robert Fitzgerald; Mrs. Ann P. Howgate (letters to her late husband, George Washburn Howgate, who, in 1938, became Santayana's first biographer); Mrs. Christina M. Welch, daughter of John P. Marquand, and Mr. Carl D. Brandt (Houghton Library, Harvard University); Mrs. Arthur Davison Ficke (Beinecke Library, Yale University); Dr. Cecil Anrep, of Villa I Tatti, at Settignano, Italy, letters to Bernard and Mary Berenson; and Lino S. Lipinsky de Orlov. Max Schwartz, brother of the late Benjamin Schwartz who, in 1936, with Justus Buchler, edited *Obiter Scripta: Lectures, Essays and Reviews,* searched through his brother's papers in an effort to discover additional Santayana correspondence. Mrs. Max Eastman (Lilly Library, Indiana University); Horace M. Kallen (YIVO Institute for Jewish Research in New York City and the American Jewish Archives, Hebrew Union College, Cincinnati, Ohio); Lewis Mumford; Milton K. Munitz; and Paul Arthur Schilpp (founder and editor of *The Library of Living Philosophers,* the second volume of which was devoted to the philosophy of Santayana). Sidney Hook gave permission for the inclusion here of his Santayana letters published in *The American Scholar* (Winter 1976–77). George Knox helped locate the letters to Carl Sadakichi Hartmann. (University of California, Riverside). Father Ceferino Santos Escudero, of the University of Madrid, who compiled a bibliography of Santayana's writings, supplied copies of the two letters in Spanish to Miguel de Unamuno and J. L. Ochoa; the English translations of these letters were done for this edition by Mr. Henry C. Reed.

I am particularly grateful to the late Spanish poet, Jorge Guillén, for permission to receive a copy of his letter from Santayana in the Houghton Library, and to Mary de Rachewilz, curator of the Ezra Pound Archive in Yale's Beinecke Library, who allowed librarians to check our transcriptions of letters to her father against the original holograph letters before the Archive was officially opened. I wish also to thank Mme. de Rachewilz for her kindness and hospitality to my family and me during visits to Brunnenburg, at Tirolo di Merano, where, in the early stages of the letters edition, I conferred with Mrs. Cory on the project. I am grateful to the late Don Eduardo Sastre Martín, Santayana's grandnephew, for the interviews in his home in Madrid that he gave to my colleague Professor Mills F. Edgerton Jr. and for his help in obtaining copies of letters in Spanish to his parents, José and Isabel Sastre. Thanks also to Pedro García Martín, Emilio Santos Sastre, and Ana Sastre Moyano who provided copies of letters and postcards written to Santayana's sister and brother-in-law and other members of the Sastre family. The late Mr. Hy Oppenheim, a retired lawyer and an avid student of Santayana's writings, is remembered with thanks for his frequent informative communications and for his gifts of copies of Santayana's works. Thanks, too, to Mr. David Wapinsky, a devoted student of Santayana's writings, for sharing with us the fruits of his researches into the existence of undiscovered Santayana manuscript materials.

Realization of a project of this magnitude would be impossible without the cooperation of a host of librarians, archivists, and technical members of the staffs of a great number of libraries. Many of the personnel who contributed remain anonymous to us. Still others were persons whose names we learned through our correspondence with them and their institutions twenty or thirty years ago. Doubtless many of these persons are no longer associated with the libraries with which they were once connected. For this reason, and because space is necessarily limited in an edition of this size, we are prevented from listing here the names of the scores of dedicated staff on whose conscientious and generous assistance this edition has been so utterly dependent. But I wish to express the profound thanks of the editors to each and every one of these colleagues.

We must, however, acknowledge here individually a few persons upon whose cooperation and assistance this project has fundamentally depended. These are the principal librarians at libraries containing major collections of Santayana manuscript materials. Mr. Kenneth A. Lohf, Librarian for Rare Books and Manuscripts of the Butler Library at Columbia University, has had responsibility for the largest and most important collection of Santayana materials. Mr. Lohf and staff, including Bernard Crystal, Rudolph Ellenbogen, and Jean Ashton, have been a never-failing source of cooperation and assistance to the editors, for which we are very grateful. Harvard's Houghton Library, as would be expected, is another treasure trove for Santayana scholars. I know that Daniel Cory counted the Librarian of the Houghton, Mr. William H. Bond, as a valued personal friend, and we deeply appreciate his kind assistance. Other persons at the Houghton who have been particularly helpful to us are Leslie A. Morris, Elizabeth A. Falsey, Rodney Dennis, Jennie Rathbun, Mrs. Richard B. Currier, and Ms. Deborah B. Kelley. The Charles Scribner's Sons Archive, in the Princeton University Library, is a huge and invaluable collection of the correspondence of many prominent authors whose works have been published by the house of Scribner. The late Charles Scribner IV has the gratitude of scholars generally for continuing the policy of his company of preserving all correspondence with authors. I am personally in Mr. Scribner's debt for his unfailingly kind attention to my questions and requests pertaining to publication by his company of Santayana's writings, for permission to receive photocopies of letters from the Scribner Archive and to reproduce and publish them in this edition. Librarians at Princeton who so effectively assisted us in the acquisition of photocopies are Alexander P. Clark, Jean F. Preston, and Don C. Skemer, Curators of Manuscripts; Margaret M. Sherry, Archivist; and Mrs. Mardel Pacheco and Mrs. Michael Sherman of the Manuscripts Division. At the Alderman Library of the University of Virginia we wish to thank Michael Plunkett and Anne Freudenberg, Curators of Manuscripts, Adrienne Cannon, Special Collections, and assistants Elizabeth Ryall and Gregory A. Johnson. At the Humanities Research Center of the University of Texas at Austin, Cathy Henderson, Barbara Smith-LaBorde, Mary M. Hirth, and June Moll, Librarians, have been particularly cooperative in aiding our work, as have Thomas F. Staley and Mr. F. W. Roberts, Directors of the Center, and staff including Sally Leach, David Farmer, and John R. Payne. Mr. Thomas M. Whitehead, Head of the Special Collections Department of the Samuel Paley Library at Temple University, was most cooperative in enabling us to acquire copies of the large collection of Santayana letters in the archive of the London publishing firm of Constable and Company, Ltd. Special thanks are also due to several librarians at the Beinecke Rare Book and Manuscript Library at Yale University for their continuous cooperation and valuable services over many years including: Ms. Dorothy Bridgewater, formerly Acting Head of the Reference Department; Ms. Carol Park of the Reference Department; Mr. Kenneth Nesheim, formerly Acting Curator, Collection of American Literature; Mr. Donald Gallup, Curator of American Literature; Mr. Peter Dzwonkowski, Assistant to the Curator, who very helpfully collated our transcriptions of Santayana's letters to Ezra Pound against the originals in the then unopened Pound Archive; and Mr. Robert O. Anthony, adviser to the Walter Lippmann Papers Collection.

The Rockefeller Archive Center houses the majority of Santayana's letters to Charles Augustus Strong (368). David Rockefeller, Alice Victor, Darwin Stapleton, and Thomas Rosenbaum were extremely generous in providing copies of these letters to the Edition on very short notice.

Librarians of specialized collections who have been particularly helpful to us are Ms. Fanny Zelcer of the American Jewish Archives; Mr. James Lawton of the Boston Public Library; Mr. Monte Olenick of the Brooklyn Public Library; Mr. John C. Broderick, Chief, The Library of

Congress; Mr. Andrew Berner and Ms. Susan Grant, the University Club
Library, New York City; Doña Dolores Gomez Molleda, Director, Casa-
Museo Unamuno, University of Salamanca, Spain; Mr. Ezekiel Lifschutz,
Archivist, and Mr. Marek Web, Archives Department, YIVO Institute for
Jewish Research, New York City.

Librarians of the Ellen Clarke Bertrand Library at Bucknell University
have provided aid in several important ways, and I wish to thank especially Mr. George Jenks and Mrs. Ann de Klerk, former Directors of the
Library who provided a room in the Library specifically for work on the
letters edition. Other librarians of the Bertrand Library that must be
acknowledged here for their special assistance are Mrs. Helena Rivoire,
Head of Technical Services; Ms. Patricia J. Rom, Head of the Reference
Department; and Mr. Ronald B. Daniels, Head of Public Services. I am
also much obliged to the librarians and staff of the Bodleian Library and
the English Faculty Library of Oxford University for allowing me the continued use of the resources of those fine institutions while working on the
edition during my residence at Oxford from September 1975 to July 1976.

We are very grateful to the institutions that have provided the financial
support on which the completion of this project depended. First and foremost is the National Endowment for the Humanities. The award of a
Research Fellowship for 1975–76 enabled me to devote a full year to getting the project underway. Since 1976 the Endowment has underwritten
the comprehensive edition of Santayana's *Works,* in which the letters edition is included. Officers and staff members to whom we are especially
indebted for their indispensable support are James Herbert, Director,
Division of Research Programs, Margot Backas, Michael Hall, George
Lucas, Douglas Arnold, Stephen Veneziani, and Alice Hudgins. Other
organizations that have contributed importantly to the completion of the
letters edition are The John Simon Guggenheim Memorial Foundation
for granting a Fellowship for work on the letters edition to Daniel Cory in
1972; the American Council of Learned Societies for awarding me two
separate grants for work on the project; and to the Committee on
Scholarly Development of Bucknell University for the award of grants
that allowed me to devote several summers to work on the letters edition.

We wish also to acknowledge the student assistants who, over the many
years of work on this collection of Santayana's letters, have labored along-
side the editors with much-appreciated dedication, performing tasks
essential to the completion of this project. The first student editorial assistant to work on the letters project was Keith Washburn, a graduate student

in English at Bucknell who helped during the initial stages in 1972. Mrs. Robin Hummel Kenner worked on the project from September 1972 until January 1978, beginning during her undergraduate years and continuing on after graduation. Mrs. Kenner, in a pre-computer era, made most of the original typewriter transcriptions of the letters. Kristine Dane worked on the project from July 1991 through May 1997, beginning as an undergraduate and continuing to work on the project while pursuing graduate studies. Her contributions to the letters edition were many and various. The other Bucknell students who worked on this edition of Santayana's letters are listed here in chronological order of their connection with the project, from earliest to latest: Laurie Russell, Karen Hoffnagle, Elizabeth Smith, Kathy Bittner, Afsaneh Bahar, Hugh Bailey, Roberta Visaggio, Jeanne Wiggers, Caroline Keller, Cherri Lee Smith, Beth Lynn Davis, Lori Fraind, Wendy Van Wyck, Michael Wardell, and Jennifer Beck. Let us thank here also Mrs. Ruth Snyder, formerly secretary to the Classics and History departments at Bucknell, who, in the mid-1980s, made our original typewritten transcriptions of the letters from Santayana to Scribner's editor John Hall Wheelock of the period 1946–52 which had just then been made available.

At Texas A&M University graduate assistants involved with the project include Karen Antell, Ann T. Butler, John Cavin, Matthew Caleb Flamm, Luis Guadaño, Kara Kellogg, Nakia S. Pope, Robert Renzetti, Wayne Riggs, Clay Davis Splawn, James Dan Unger. Special thanks to Denise Johnston Barrychuck, Jodine Thomas, Lori Moore, Margaret B. Yergler, Anne Divita, and Connie Chavez, students and staff who worked with the Edition for extended periods of time.

At the University of Tampa, special thanks are given to editorial assistants Shirley Cueto and John W. Jones, and to research assistants Austria M. Lavigne, Jodi Lerner, and Nina Mollica.

Finally, I wish to acknowledge the persons with whom I have worked very closely for a long time on this edition of Santayana's letters and whose collaboration has made possible its completion. First, I want to thank especially my friend and colleague of many years, the General Editor of *The Works of George Santayana* and Associate Editor of this edition of the letters, Herman J. Saatkamp Jr., with whom I have had the pleasure of coediting the four earlier volumes of the Critical Edition. Not only has Professor Saatkamp been responsible for overseeing and directing all phases of the *Works* edition, including this volume of letters, but in his frequent travels through this country and indeed all over the world he has sought everywhere and frequently found previously unknown or unlocated Santayana correspondence. During those travels he has also spent countless hours in numerous libraries making sight collations of our transcriptions (taken from Xerox copies of Santayana's handwritten letters) against the original holograph letters. This edition of Santayana's correspondence owes a very great deal to the boundless energy and enthusiasm for Santayana's writings that Professor Saatkamp has brought to it, and I am sure that, like me, Santayanans everywhere are very grateful to him.

Another person who made a very significant contribution to this letters edition is Donna Hanna-Calvert, who was for several years the Associate Editor of *The Works of George Santayana* at the Texas A&M University headquarters of the project. Ms. Hanna-Calvert was always a most astute, congenial, and helpful colleague, and I am indebted to her both for her assistance with the letters project as well as for her collaboration on earlier volumes of the edition. I owe her much for making my working visits to the editorial offices at Texas A&M very pleasant, comfortable, efficient, and productive.

To the current Associate Editor of *The Works of George Santayana* (and also of this edition of the letters specifically), Kristine W. Frost, this letters volume and I are very heavily indebted. Ms. Frost has had the responsibility of coordinating and executing the multiple tasks of preparing the text of the letters edition for publication. She has assisted the General Editor and me in every conceivable aspect of the preparation of this letters edition while simultaneously organizing and carrying out collation schedules for future volumes of the *Works* edition that are currently in preparation, and directly supervising the activities of our student helpers and other editorial assistants. I wish also to express here to Kristine Frost what I know all of us on the edition especially appreciate in working with her: I mean her invariably equable temperament, her unshakable good nature. Working with her is always a pleasure.

I want to thank especially my wife, Annegret, for her many years of service to this letters edition (as well as to earlier volumes of *The Works of George Santayana*) as editorial assistant. She has supported my work on this project in every conceivable way. The help and companionship she provided on the numerous and extensive travels that this work has entailed often transformed difficulty, inconvenience, and hard labor into achievement and adventure. I am grateful to her for all the effort, encouragement, and patience that she has contributed to the completion of this enterprise.

Our other editorial assistant on the letters edition, Brenda Bridges, at Texas A&M, also richly deserves recognition here and the gratitude of the editors for effectively carrying out many important and demanding tasks, including researching the information for much of the footnote annotation to the letters. Thanks to Ms. Bridges's astuteness and unflagging perseverance, the extensive and exceptionally valuable collection of letters by Santayana to Charles Augustus Strong—long believed lost or destroyed—were located and copies acquired for this edition.

Therefore, to all these kind, cooperative, expert, and industrious persons and magnanimous institutions that have contributed so materially and indispensably to the production of this edition of Santayana's letters, I extend my deep gratitude.

William G. Holzberger
Professor of English Emeritus
Bucknell University

[1]Volumes published to date: I *Persons and Places: Fragments of Autobiography* (1986); II *The Sense of Beauty: Being the Outlines of Aesthetic Theory* (1988); III *Interpretations of Poetry and Religion* (1989); IV *The Last Puritan: A Memoir in the Form of a Novel* (1994).

Introduction

William G. Holzberger

George Santayana (1863–1952) was one of the most learned and culti-vated men of his time. Born in Spain and educated in America, he taught philosophy at Harvard University for twenty-two years before returning permanently to Europe at age forty-eight to devote himself exclusively to writing. He knew several languages, including Latin and Greek. Besides his mastery of English, he was at home in Spanish and French (though he modestly down-played his knowledge of those languages). As a young man, Santayana studied Italian in order to read Dante, Cavalcanti, Michelangelo, and other Italian Platonizing poets in their own language; and, in later life, as a result of his long residence in Rome, he acquired facility in speaking Italian.[1] While a graduate student in Germany during 1886–88, Santayana lived with Harvard friends in an English-speaking boardinghouse in Berlin, thereby missing an opportunity to learn to speak German properly. However, he could read the original versions of German literary and philosophical works. He also knew the world, hav-ing lived for protracted periods in Spain, America, Germany, England, France, and Italy. A true cosmopolitan, Santayana nevertheless always regarded himself as a Spaniard and kept his Spanish passport current. He possessed many talents and had a multifaceted personality, and each of those facets is reflected vividly in his letters. World famous as a philoso-pher, he was also a poet, essayist, dramatist, literary critic, autobiogra-pher, and author of a best-selling novel. The numerous letters referring to *The Last Puritan,* his novel begun in 1889 and completed over a period of forty-five years on 31 Aug 1934,[2] describe the way in which a modest story of college life evolved into a major study of American culture and modern civilization. The letters incorporate a thoroughgoing statement of Santayana's own critical interpretation of *The Last Puritan.*

Santayana's letters represent the full range of his interests, knowledge, and achievements, and students of English prose style will encounter in them superb examples of epistolary writing. They are of supreme value to the biographer. Some letters are important for establishing dates of significant events in Santayana's life and career. For instance, the 13 Oct 1933 letter to Daniel Cory describes Santayana's discovery of the philosophy of Martin Heidegger and the similarity of his own theory of essences to Heidegger's ontology. Other letters illuminate Santayana's philosophical system. The 1 Mar 1949 letter to Richard C. Lyon is an excellent example of the "philosophical" letters. In it Santayana states his views on matter, idea, the self, intuition, and other perennial philosophical issues, relative to the views of philosophers such as Plato, Descartes, Kant, Berkeley, Fichte, Kierkegaard, Bergson, and Russell. The second paragraph of the 21 Sep 1917 letter to Charles Augustus Strong constitutes a succinct and very clear expression of Santayana's controversial theory of essences; and the huge collection of Santayana's letters to Strong is in itself a treasure-trove of revelations of the development of Santayana's philosophical system.[3] In fact, we find in Santayana's letters not only a distillation of his philosophy but also a multitude of new perspectives on the published work. The responses to his correspondents are filled with spontaneous comments on and restatements of his fundamental philosophical ideas and principles. Because Santayana's philosophy was not for him a thing apart, but rather the foundation of his existence, the letters indicate the ways in which his entire life was permeated and directed by that philosophy. Essential to Santayana's position is the Greek ideal of the "life of reason," a conception of the good life as requiring a continual commitment to the pursuit of self-knowledge, discipline, and an unromantic determination to harmonize rather than indulge the passions. It is the ideal of *sophrosune* or moderation venerated by classical philosophers like Aristotle and despised by modern ones like Bertrand Russell.

The fullest expression of Santayana's philosophical system, which we may observe developing in his letters, is in the four volumes of *Realms of Being,* published over a period of fourteen years (1927 to 1940). Santayana devotes a volume to each of the four realms: essence, matter, truth, and spirit. These realms are not so much regions or elements of being as they are kinds or representations thereof. Santayana's formulation of the realm of essence caused him, in the view of several of his critics, to be allied with Platonic idealism; however, Santayana's essences, unlike those of Plato, are not the ultimate reality. For Santayana essences are merely an infinite number of real though non-existent passive forms. The unconscious and unformed realm of matter is the sole source of power and existence. In Santayana's view, the embodiment of essences by matter results in the substantial physical world. Unlike Plato, for whom spirit or consciousness exists eternally and independently of matter, Santayana conceived of spirit as conscious self-awareness generated by matter when the vital physical organism (or psyche, in Santayana's terms) achieves a certain level of organization, as in a human being.

Spirit, for Santayana, reluctantly shares the career of the body that has generated it. If it were free to do so, spirit would range impartially over the spectacle of existence. But, because of its ineluctable identification with the career of a specific individual organism, spirit is pulled away from its natural tendency to disinterested observation by the necessity of attending to the requirements of the organism to which it is bound. In Santayana's letters we see dramatic representations of the predicament of the philosopher whose spirit, in its effort to seek and comprehend the truth of things, necessarily strives to transcend the confinements and limitations of particular perspectives, personal or national allegiances, or historical contexts and observe things impartially under the aspect of eternity. But, because the philosopher is nevertheless an individual and mortal person, subject to the conditions of his environment and physical organism, he must, however reluctantly, be called back to the never permanently escapable present personal, social, political, material reality.

That Santayana was keenly aware of this dichotomy is made perfectly clear in his published writings, in his personal life, and in his letters. His striving for a transcendental perspective devoid of personal, national, or ideological bias is seen in his perennial effort to stand aloof from social, political, or professional organizations that would demand of him an allegiance to their particular agendas and make impossible, even intermittently, the perspective of eternity. At the same time, we can see his recognition of the limitations and obligations placed upon every human individual by one's nationality, genetic inheritance, and psychological conditioning. This recognition is reflected in the fact that Santayana always identified himself as a Spanish citizen, and (despite the ultimately atheistic character of his philosophical principles) a Roman Catholic. It is reflected also in the record of loyalty and devotion to family and friends that we observe in the letters. Perhaps the greatest problem for Santayana, as manifested in the letters, was the life-long effort of the philosopher to reconcile his inclination to live in the eternal with the necessity of the individual human being to live in the here and now.

A succinct statement of his positions on religion, science, and poetry is found in the 31 Aug 1951 letter to Ira D. Cardiff. In that letter Santayana attempts to explain his unbifurcated view of religion and naturalism, and he indicts positivism for unimaginativeness. Because Santayana's philosophy is one of materialism and naturalism, wherein everything—including spirit or consciousness—has a material basis, there can be no personal immortality of the kind traditionally conceived of by religion. The individual spirit is contingent upon the continued existence of the physical organism or psyche that generated it. At the dissolution of that organism in death, the spirit, as a consequence of that disorganization of matter, is annihilated. Except, therefore, where consciousness is temporarily allied to some physical organism, nature is unconscious and indifferent to human interests. There are, therefore, no supernatural beings, no disembodied spirits, no gods. Thus religion does not describe an actual otherworldly realm but rather only this world idealized and represented mythopoetically. For Santayana religion—and even science—is a kind of poetry.

Other letters tell us much about Santayana's literary method and the achievement of his apparently effortless style. We learn from many letters that the effect of spontaneous flow in his published writing is actually the result of a method involving several drafts and much revision leading to the finished work. In the letter of 13 Dec 1949 to Mrs. David (Rosamond) Little, he quotes the compositional principle of Boileau as representing his own method: "Polish it continually, and repolish it; add occasionally, and delete often."[4] He frequently had two or three compositions going forward simultaneously, moving from one to another as inspiration and interest guided him. Sometimes he used material pruned from one project for the substance of another (for example, the incorporation of the surplus of his Spinoza lecture, "Ultimate Religion," in his book, *The Realm of Spirit,* as described in the 14 May 1932 letter to Cory). And, apropos of Cory, the detailed criticisms that Santayana makes of the drafts of essays that Cory sent to him for comment constitute a sort of concise manual for writers, and they reveal Santayana's unremitting quest, through continuous review and revision, for perfection of diction and form in his own writing.

Some letters (for instance, that to the literary scholar and critic William Bysshe Stein of 1 Sep 1949) reveal that Santayana conceived of the practice of literary criticism as stating the critic's personal taste rather than making objective evaluations. The letters also document Santayana's subordination of aesthetics to ethics and his view of the relativism of the latter. Still other letters, like the 15 Mar 1946 one to Rosamond Sturgis (later Mrs. Little), express Santayana's traditionalist views on education and

American education in particular. In addition to illuminating his ideas, views, and accomplishments as thinker and writer, Santayana's letters are especially important in revealing the personal side of the famous author. Nowhere else–not even in his autobiography, *Persons and Places*–does he express so directly and succinctly his fundamental attitudes and convictions or reveal more intimately the characteristics of his complex personality.

Each reader of the letters doubtless will relish in them what he or she is most interested in knowing about Santayana's life and thought; and many persons will use this edition to consult specific letters as these pertain to certain ideas, persons, or historical events. But anyone who reads extensively in this collection will see emerge the distinctive personality of the writer, in a kind of verbal self-portrait. There are, to be sure, other documents available in which a portrait of Santayana may appear, including the many fine articles and books about him, especially John McCormick's recent critical biography and Santayana's inimitable autobiography.[5] These descriptions of Santayana's personality and experience are extremely valuable in fleshing out our image of him as a person and writer. Private letters usually represent the most spontaneous and unguarded form of written expression,[6] and, by focussing on Santayana's letters as illustrative of their author's personality and character, we discover in them a concentrated and revealing self-portrait. This verbal self-portrait, produced partly by unconscious revelations, contributes significantly to our conception of the sort of individual that Santayana was and, therefore, to our understanding of his writings.

That Santayana was a precocious genius is evident from even a cursory reading of his early letters. Among the most interesting are those written in 1886 to his Harvard classmate, Henry Ward Abbot, while Santayana was pursuing graduate studies in philosophy in Germany. The maturity of view, intellectual acuteness, and power of expression in these letters are remarkable. Santayana's perennial emphasis on the crucial importance of the Socratic principle of self-knowledge and the ethical doctrine of moral relativism[7] characteristic of his most mature writings are nowhere more perfectly expressed than in the 6 Oct 1886 letter to Abbot written from Berlin when Santayana was not quite twenty-three years old. In response to Abbot's indecision about going into business–as his family evidently wanted–or pursuing instead some other career, Santayana wrote:

> To do right is to know what you want. Now when you are
> dissatisfied with yourself, it's because you are after some-

thing you don't want. What objects are you proposing to
yourself? are they the objects you really value? If they are
not, you are cheating yourself. I don't mean that if you
chose to pursue the objects you most value, you would
attain them; of course not. Your experience will tell you
that. ... but success in getting after much labour what you
really don't care for is the bitterest and most ridiculous
failure.

Santayana had several other close friends among his Harvard classmates, and the fact that he was socially active during his undergraduate
years (or at least as active as his very modest means would permit) is now
well known. He had drawn cartoons for and served on the editorial board
of the *Harvard Lampoon;* he was president of the Philosophical Club and
took part in Hasty Pudding Club theatricals. But Santayana seems always
to have been a rather formal person who resented what he considered
undue familiarity. In the 21 Aug 1882 letter to John Galen Howard, written following their graduation from the Boston Public Latin School,
Santayana expressed his unwillingness to be patronized even by the ven-
erable headmaster, Dr. Moses Merrill:

> ... I hope he has not had the impudence of addressing all
> the fellows by their first names, as he has done me. If he
> supposed I would be flattered by being treated with inti-
> macy by him, he was greatly mistaken. If I did not deem
> it unwise to forfeit anyone's good opinion merely for the
> pleasure of speaking out one's mind plainly, I should
> have answered him and addressed him as "my dear
> Moses."

Forty-six years later, on 4 May 1928, Santayana wrote to his nephew
and business manager, George Sturgis, that he had received a letter from
a William C. Sturgis (a member of the prominent Boston family to which
Santayana's mother's first husband had belonged) of whom Santayana
had never heard:

> He calls me George", but I don't know who he can be.
> Will you enlighten me? ... When you reply please tell me
> whether he is habitually called William, Will, Willy, Billy,
> or Bill, so that I may live up to our relationship.

Santayana was, of course, on a first-name basis with members of his
immediate family, addressing his sister Susan as "Dear Susie," and he was

not so stiff as not to be on a first-name basis with other persons as well. In letters to the intimate friends of his youth—for instance, his Harvard classmates—he addressed Henry Ward Abbot, Boylston Adams Beal, and Robert Burnside Potter as "Harry," "Boylston," or "Bob." In later letters written to close male friends usually the person is addressed by the last name only, in the manner more common among men in an earlier time than it is today. Goldsworthy Lowes Dickinson, Horace Meyer Kallen, and Logan Pearsall Smith are addressed as "Dickinson," "Kallen," or "Smith." The Russell brothers (John Francis Stanley, the second Earl Russell, and his younger brother, Bertrand) are each addressed simply as "Dear Russell." Daniel Cory was undoubtedly Santayana's closest friend during the last twenty-five years of his life, yet he is never addressed in any of the hundreds of pieces of correspondence that Santayana wrote to him in any way but as "Dear Cory."[8] In writing or speaking about Santayana, Cory referred to him simply as "Santayana" (though in conversation he sometimes referred to him as "the Master," in the manner of Henry James's disciples and scholars). In *Santayana: The Later Years,* Cory describes his arrival at Santayana's bedside in Rome, shortly before the latter's death, saying, "I'm here, Santayana," so we may assume that once their friendship had been established Cory addressed his elderly friend simply as "Santayana."[9] (We do know that in Santayana's last years his relationship with the young poet, Robert Lowell, became so friendly that Lowell, thanking Santayana for helping him financially, humorously addressed him in one letter as "My dear Uncle.")[10] Santayana's editors at Constable and Scribner's—Otto Kyllmann and John Hall Wheelock, respectively—are always addressed as Mr. Kyllmann and Mr. Wheelock, as is Mr. Scribner when Santayana writes directly to the head of the New York publishing house. Even close women friends of many years—like Mrs. Crawford (Nancy) Toy, Mrs. Robert (Elizabeth) Potter, and Mrs. Frederick (Mary) Winslow—are addressed in the letters as "Mrs. Toy," "Mrs. Potter," or "Mrs. Winslow."

The impression of Santayana as an essentially formal man is reinforced by the language of his letters, in which there is a notable absence of slang or obscenity. This is so much the case that one is a little startled to encounter in a few letters even such mild imprecations as "damn" or "damned." As in his published writings, Santayana's diction in the letters might be described the way critics have characterized that of Hawthorne and Henry James: "formal but alive."

Santayana's formal style, however, in no way inhibited the expression of his formidable wit. There is little or no broad humor in Santayana's letters, not much in the way of comedy or fun (except perhaps for the 31 Aug 1887 "Rabelaisian" letter to William Morton Fullerton and the 25 Nov and 10 Dec 1904 "Arabian Nights" letters to Mrs. Bernard Berenson), but there is plenty of wit: dry, ironical commentary that is often paradoxical and ingenious and invariably in the service of some point that he is making.

A typical example of Santayana's irony and wit is found in the letter of 2 Apr 1923 to George Sturgis, in which Santayana comments on the recent appearance of the Scribner's edition of his *Poems*:

> ... a copy Scribner has sent me looks so mean and poverty-stricken that I am afraid they are doing it on the cheap, in order to make money. Money out of poems! I received $1.87 for the first two editions, and was thankful, the publisher having failed in the interval, as was to be expected.[11]

In another letter to George Sturgis two years later, Santayana comments on "the instability of the female will," describing his own present dependence upon the decisions of several women friends and relatives as to where and when he may be traveling. He mentions that his friend Charles Augustus Strong is enjoying the electric heating that Strong's daughter, Margaret, had installed in her father's Paris apartment against his will, and writes:

> ... probably I shall go to a hotel [instead of joining Strong in the Avenue de l'Observatoire apartment], as Margaret herself may turn up at any moment—another case of La donna è mobile, especially with an auto-mobile, if you will excuse an Italian pun. For Margaret has one of her own much better than her father's.[12]

In the summer of 1928 Santayana's friend, the Yale English professor and popular literary critic, William Lyon Phelps, and his wife were planning a trip to Spain, about which Santayana wrote:

> I admire your courage and that of Mrs. Phelps in going to Madrid in August. We might apply to it a story Strong likes to tell about a delegate's description of the summer breezes of Chicago: that not content with coming out of the very mouth of hell, they had first blown over the State

of Texas. For Texas read the plains of La Mancha, and
you will know what awaits you.[13]

A final example of the mordant irony of which Santayana was capable
is in the 27 Mar 1939 letter to George Sturgis regarding Bertrand Russell,
who, Santayana believed, like Russell's elder brother, had wasted his
genius through personal and political folly:

> Not that his philosophy would have been sound: he is a
> born heretic or genial madman, like John Knox or
> Giordano Bruno: yet he is preternaturally intelligent,
> penetrating, and radical; so that the more wrong he is the
> clearer he makes the wrongness of his position; and what
> more can you expect a philosopher to prove except that
> the views he has adopted are radically and eternally
> impossible? If every philosopher had done that in the
> past, we should now be almost out of the wood.

As we encounter Santayana's wit in the letters, we may occasionally
find ourselves laughing out loud, but more often our amused response is
of a quieter kind. Santayana's sense of humor—or, more precisely, his
witty and ironic cast of mind—is much akin to that of Henry James (with
whom he shares not only a formal style but also other qualities and characteristics)[14] and not at all like that of Mark Twain.

Concomitant with Santayana's ironical view of the world was his own
capacity for laughter. He likened himself to Democritus, "the laughing
philosopher," and said that his friends told him that he laughed too much.
Yet most of the photographs of Santayana depict him as very grim. He did
not like being photographed and thought the typical grinning snapshot a
very inaccurate representation of someone. Thus, almost all of the extant
photos of Santayana—with the exception of a group taken in the Blue
Sisters' nursing-home in Rome toward the end of his life—portray him as
an unsmiling and somber man. The same is true of the drawings made
from photographs to illustrate the dust jackets of several of his books, one
of which, he complained to Scribner's, made him look "cross-eyed and
ferocious."[15] These somber or hostile-looking pictures, combined with his
political conservatism and reputation for avoiding society, have contributed to a widespread notion that Santayana was remote and forbid-
ding; "cold-blooded" is a term sometimes applied to him. It is true that
the Santayana represented in the letters is unsentimental and tough-
minded, and his love of solitude and his philosophic resignation give the

impression that he was more indifferent and detached from human life and feeling than are most people. But the letters provide considerable evidence that Santayana was capable of profound emotional attachments.

So far as we know, Santayana never had a romantic relationship with a woman, though there were several women with whom he enjoyed close friendship and lifelong correspondence. Mrs. Toy, Mrs. Potter, and Mrs. Winslow fit this description. And, until her death in 1928, Santayana's elder half sister Susan was, in complex ways, the beloved woman in his life. However, Santayana—like Schopenhauer and Nietzsche—saw women as fundamentally different from men, as is illustrated by a 17 Feb 1887 letter to Henry Ward Abbot:

> A woman, for example, is despised in so far as she is a human individual competing with others for life, especially because her methods of competing are small and mean; but she is loved and even worshiped as the complement of man, as something filling out his life without sharing his qualities.

Feminists, with some justification, condemn Santayana as a sexist who characterized women as inferior. Santayana believed that, compared to men, women are generally not as intelligent, interesting, or physically fine; men are the superior gender. This exaltation of the masculine may be derived from Santayana's own sexual nature. From his letters, from the events of *The Last Puritan* and his remarks about the novel in the letters, and from the conversation about A. E. Housman reported by Cory,[16] it seems clear that Santayana's sexual orientation was not conventional. The early letters to his Harvard classmate, Henry Ward Abbot, are particularly significant in this regard. On 23 Apr 1887 Santayana wrote:

> … I hate my own arrogance and would worship the man who should knock it out of me. Says a Spanish song:
>
> > I am searching land & ocean
> > For the man that I might love,
> > And whenever my heart finds him
> > Then he will have found his slave.
>
> Man or thing—it makes no difference—but heaven grant it be no woman. … Of course all girls aren't foolish—some are charming and I am tender on two or three myself; but if I ever humbug a woman into marrying me, it will be a

piece of selfishness on my part, depend upon it, and not
a conquest on hers.

The comments of the young Santayana in this letter about women and
marriage are common in the banter of young men, but the general tone
here is not heterosexual, and, for this reason and in light of Santayana's
other writings, we are disinclined to take seriously the statement about his
being "tender" on two or three girls.

A year earlier, in the spring of 1886 (his senior year at Harvard),
Santayana had met the tall, athletic, good-looking, cultivated, and
supremely self-confident Earl Russell and he evidently fell in love with
the young aristocrat. His letters to Abbot of 1887 reveal his complete
infatuation:

> ... Russell is the ablest man, all round, that I have ever
> met. You have no idea what a splendid creature he is, no
> more had I till I had seen a great deal of him. He isn't
> good, that is he is completely selfish and rather cruel,
> although I fancy I made too much of his heartlessness at
> first. But then both practically and intellectually he is
> really brilliant. ... I know I am making a fool of myself in
> writing about him ... but I send a note of his so that you
> may judge for yourself and also have some idea of the
> men I am seeing here. Pass the note on to Herbert Lyman
> and let him keep it or send it back to me. I am going to-
> morrow to stay with Russell again, for he is laid up and
> wants company. ... Don't tell this round, I beg of you, but
> I tell you because I am telling you everything to-day. I
> make an exception of Herbert, because I should have to
> tell him sooner or later, and he won't chuckle over it as if
> it were a joke merely, which it isn't.[17]

In a letter to Abbot written a week later, Santayana reveals the abject
character of his relationship with Russell:

> ... what I call my "fall from grace and self-control" ... is
> simply this. Russell has a way of treating people which is
> insufferably insolent and insulting. Never for a moment
> did I imagine I could allow anyone to treat me in such a
> way. But I find that instead of caring for my own dignity
> and independence ... I find that I don't care a rap for my
> interest in myself or my ways of doing things, but that I
> am quite willing to stand anything, however outrageous,

that comes from a certain quarter. This is what has happened to me. I am a fool to say a word about it—especially when people think that I am talking about trifles. ... don't imagine I am referring to "country matters".[18]

The revelations of these letters to Abbot are franker expressions of Santayana's willingness to abase himself and accept abuse from Russell than are found in *Persons and Places,* including the episode he relates there about accidentally pulling the young earl into the Thames and being violently abused verbally by him for clumsiness.[19] And Santayana's willingness to swallow his pride and suffer indignities from Russell seems to have been unending. In the autumn of 1923, when he was almost sixty and planning a trip to England to deliver the Herbert Spencer Lecture at Oxford, he wrote to Russell saying that he hoped there would be a chance to see him. Russell's reply was: "Do as you like," and Santayana responded as follows:

> If you leave it to me, I will certainly come [to Russell's house in Hampshire]. I don't believe that anything has really happened to alter our relations to one another which were always tacit and expressed in conduct rather than words. You now say more than you ever <u>said</u> to me, even in our young days, about being "attached to me"; you <u>must</u> have been, in some way which in spite of my cold-blooded psychology I don't pretend to understand. In that case, why drop me now, when certainly there has been no change on my side except that involved in passing from twenty to sixty? Let me come, anyhow once, and we can judge better whether everything is as usual or whether the barrier you speak of—which certainly is not "Elizabeth" or her affairs—really exists.
> Shall it be next Tuesday, and if so, what train shall I take?
> Yours ever,[20]

Santayana did visit Russell, who was indifferent, even frequently mistaking his name and calling him "Sargeaunt," the name of another of Russell's friends, a Latin master at Westminster.[21]

As in the cases of Henry James and A. E. Housman there is no evidence that Santayana was an active or practicing homosexual or that his youthful relationship with Russell (or anyone else, for that matter) was homosexual in a physical sense. Indeed, the Hamlet echo of his warning to Abbot not to construe his attachment to Russell as involving "country matters" might indicate that Santayana regarded his devotion as transcending the merely physical.[22]

Only a deep emotional attachment could have enabled Santayana to continue for so many years to tolerate Russell's unpleasantness and indifference; yet Santayana appears always to have been aware of Russell's faults. This insuperable critical faculty doubtless sobered Santayana's affections for other persons about whom he felt less strongly: he had no illusions about people. For instance, he appreciated his nephew, George Sturgis, for his able stewardship of his financial properties, as he had George's father—Santayana's half brother Robert—for performing the same service. He frequently closed letters to George Sturgis with "Yours affectionately," and even signed one to him of 1927: "With much love." But other letters reveal that he did not care for his nephew any more than he had for George's father; he found both men lacking in sensitivity and sympathetic imagination.[23] But the letters show that Santayana was genuinely affectionate toward several persons. He was very well disposed toward George Sturgis's first wife, Rosamond, with whom he carried on a long correspondence.

Santayana appreciated Rosamond's thoughtfulness and kindness in sending him packages of food and clothing, after the war in Italy had ended and supplies in Rome remained short. He regularly signed his letters to her "Your affectionate Uncle George." He was also very fond of George's and Rosamond's eldest son, Robert ("Bob") Shaw Sturgis, who had visited him several times in Rome in 1944 when Bob was there in the U.S. Air Force. His letters to Bob after the war, when the latter was a Harvard undergraduate studying architecture (the field that Santayana had once thought seriously of making his profession), are full of unfeigned interest in the young man's activities and plans. The grandfatherly affection that the octogenarian felt for his good-looking, intelligent, and artistic young grandnephew is unmistakable in both the letters Santayana wrote to Rosamond and those to Bob himself.

If Santayana's affection for young Bob Sturgis was grandfatherly, his feeling for the young Daniel Cory was fatherly. Santayana first met Cory in April 1927, when Cory was twenty-two and Santayana sixty-three, and a long, intimate friendship began. Cory, who first encountered Santayana's writings at Columbia University, had left college before completing a degree and had gone to live and work in London. Impressed with an essay that the young man had written on his philosophy and sent to him, Santayana offered to pay Cory's expenses for a visit to Rome. He was pleased by Cory's critical acumen, his interest in and grasp of Santayana's philosophy, and engaged the young man to assist him in arranging the manuscript of *The Realm of Matter* for publication. This was the beginning of a friendship and professional association that lasted for twenty-five years, until Santayana's death in 1952.

Initially, Santayana did not think of Cory's position of literary assistant or secretary as becoming permanent.[24] But Cory, while working for Santayana, made the acquaintance of Santayana's friend, the American epistemologist Charles Augustus Strong, who also wanted someone to help him prepare his writings for publication, and Cory became Strong's assistant or secretary as well. Both Strong and Santayana paid Cory a modest monthly allowance. This combined income enabled Cory to live separately, usually in England; but he spent protracted periods living near Strong, either in Paris or at Le Balze ("The Cliffs"), Strong's villa at Fiesole, near Florence. Cory also made infrequent visits to Santayana in Rome, helping him with his writing projects. For the most part, during their long association, Cory lived far from Santayana, usually in another country, and sometimes several years passed without the two men seeing one another. Despite the separation, however, Santayana continued to send Cory his monthly allowance, with special supplements for medical bills, clothing, and travel. Though he never expected Cory's dependency upon him to become permanent, Santayana eventually realized that it had and accepted responsibility for supporting Cory as long as he could do so. Before the mail between Italy and the United States was cut off by World War II, he arranged with Scribner's for Cory to receive the royalties on his books, so that the latter might not be left without resources.

In the beginning, Santayana's appreciation of Daniel Cory was based largely upon Cory's solid understanding and sincere advocacy of Santayana's philosophy, as shown in the 21 May 1928 letter to Cory:

> ... you understand the <u>true inwardness</u> of it, and your
> ways of expressing it are enough your own for me to feel
> sure that it is not a casual adoption of a technical theory,
> but a true participation in the Idea.

Later, Santayana's admiration and affection for Cory was increased by Cory's considerable charm, his talent for reading aloud (a valuable skill in the revision of manuscripts and something that Santayana felt he himself could not do well), his enterprise in addressing himself to the task of propagating Santayana's views by writing articles on his philosophy for publication in professional journals, and his representation of Santayana in communication with the editors of leading periodicals—such as T. S. Eliot of *The Criterion* and Henry Seidel Canby of *The Saturday Review of Literature*—about publication of Santayana's writings in their magazines. He also believed that Cory was someone he could depend on in a personal emergency, someone who would assist him if he became seriously ill. And it was, indeed, Cory who traveled from England to Rome to be with Santayana during the final weeks of his life and who made the difficult arrangements for Santayana's funeral and burial in the Campo Verano Cemetery in Rome.[25]

Despite his affection for Cory and his appreciation of Cory's personal loyalty and devotion to his philosophy, Santayana did not hesitate to criticize him—both in letters to Cory and to others—on several counts: for being a spendthrift; lacking initiative; failing to complete independent literary projects that he had begun (such as Cory's unfinished autobiographical novel, *Michael*); repeating to him unpleasant things that C. A. Strong had said about him (Santayana), thereby exacerbating his always difficult relations with Strong;[26] and for wasting "the best years of his life playing golf."[27]

The affectionate side of Santayana revealed in the letters contrasts with the cold-bloodedness of which he has been accused (and of which he even accuses himself). This conception of Santayana—as lacking in human warmth and sympathy—may well derive, in part, from his political views and his tendency to perceive things *sub specie aeternitatis.* He was a true modern in terms of the bleakness of his outlook and in his chronic detachment. There is also something very Spanish in the essential starkness of his view of life. In 1917, during World War I, Santayana wrote a letter to Bertrand Russell that Russell quoted from in his autobiography to demonstrate Santayana's lack of feeling:

> As for deaths and loss of capital, I don't much care. The young men killed would grow older if they lived, and then they would be good for nothing; and after being good for nothing for a number of years they would die of catarrh or a bad kidney or the halter or old age—and would that be less horrible?[28]

This letter suggests that Santayana did not consider the anguish suffered by the families, sweethearts, and comrades of the soldiers killed in the war, or indeed the loss of life to the soldiers themselves. However it is evident from numerous other letters that Santayana wrote during the period

1914–18 that he was profoundly distressed by the terrible events of this war and especially by the appalling loss of life on all sides. The letters show, in fact, that he was so depressed by these events that he found it difficult to think or write. Twenty-seven years later, writing to Andrew J. Onderdonk on 20 Jan 1945, he was less discomfited by the horrific events of World War II:

> Perhaps the years since we last saw each other, and the many since we saw each other often–34!–have made me more inhuman than ever; but public and private tragedies move me now much less than they did. I think of all the empires reduced to filthy little heaps of ruins; of all the battles and sieges in the histories, and all the horrible fates of potentates, tyrants, patriots, and saints; and what now happens to us seems almost a matter of course.

Santayana believed that, in order to understand the world, the observer must not be too closely attached to it or too actively engaged in it. The social activism of a Bertrand Russell or a Jean-Paul Sartre was anathema to him. His detachment could, on occasion–as in his comments on the two world wars–appear as sheer lack of interest in human well-being. In October 1928 Horace M. Kallen wrote asking Santayana to "sponsor" Kallen's new book on "the Sacco and Vanzetti letters" or to join a committee that Kallen was forming to protest the way in which the case of the two Italian anarchists had been handled. In a 22 Oct 1928 letter Santayana refused Kallen's request, making the following comment:

> I don't know whether those men were condemned for what, morally, wasn't a crime, or whether they were innocent altogether: in any case, it was a scandal to put off their execution so long, and then to execute them. It shows the weakness, confusion, and occasional cruelty of a democratic government: it is more merciful to the condemned, and more deterrent to others, to execute them at once, as do my friends the Bolsheviks and the Fascists. But that, I imagine, is not what your book is intended to prove.

Santayana, somewhat chillingly, places the emphasis not upon the possibility that two innocent men were condemned and executed, but rather that they were not executed more quickly once the American court had pronounced them guilty. In several other letters he uniformly refuses requests to participate in public demonstrations to endorse or denounce either side of a particular moral or political issue.

Santayana's conservative politics—he described himself as a Tory[29]—sometimes caused him to take positions that seem mean-spirited. In 1940 Rosamond Sturgis was assisting a young working-class college student with his expenses. In a 10 Oct 1940 letter to her Santayana authorized Rosamond to have George Sturgis withdraw a hundred dollars from his account to be added to the fund for the student, but he included this comment:

> ... to tell you the whole truth, I don't like to give in charity to the deserving; it only encourages them to make greater demands on life, to strain, and to increase the half-educated proletariate [sic]; whereas the undeserving merely get a drink, are happy for half an hour, and no worse afterwards than they were before. However, it may be the American ideal to increase the half-educated proletariat until it includes everybody; but would that be a happy result?

Again, the apparent callousness and cynicism of Santayana's remarks in this letter are disconcerting: we wonder at the smug injustice of a social philosophy that accepts the accident of birth as the sole determiner of opportunity and privilege for some and denial and deprivation for others.

Santayana frequently has been accused of anti-Semitism, and in several letters we do find unpalatable statements about Jews and Jewishness. On 12 Aug 1936 he wrote to George Sturgis that he was reconciled to the necessary transitoriness of things, that all conservatisms were doomed because nothing could be kept up permanently, and for example added:

> The Jews, for instance, aren't in the least like Abraham or King Solomon: they are just sheenies.

And in a 1 May 1938 letter to Mrs. Toy about Walter Lippmann, Sidney Hook, and Irwin Edman, he wrote:

> Are the Jews going to repent of being <u>anti</u>'s, for fear that soon there should be nothing left to be <u>anti</u> against? After all they have made themselves very comfortable in Christendom, and if nothing but an international proletariat remained, it would not offer them such brilliant careers as professors and prime minister and newspaper proprietors.

Mrs. Toy's response to this letter evidently recommended that Santayana avoid anti-Semitism, for in his 12 Aug 1938 letter to her he observed:

> I ought to love the Jews, as they seem to be my only
> friends intellectually, beginning with Edman–not to go
> back to Spinoza.

These remarks of Santayana's, though critical and contemptuous of what he perceived to be ancient and modern Jewish attitudes, did not prevent his appreciation of virtuous individual Jews. Ironically, Baruch Spinoza was Santayana's acknowledged master, and there was no philosopher for whom he had greater respect. He appreciated the keen interest in his own philosophy taken by Morris Cohen and Irwin Edman, and he appears to have been fond of his former graduate assistant at Harvard, Horace M. Kallen, to whom, after his retirement from Harvard, he had given his doctoral cap and gown and to whom he wrote numerous warm, friendly letters,[30] frequently complimenting Kallen on his publications. To George Sturgis on 31 Jan 1941 Santayana wrote that his doctor in Rome (Luigi Sabbatucci, who served as his physician from 1935 until Santayana's death in 1952) had, like himself, never heard of *lire miste* (evidently a form of Italian wartime currency) "although he is a Jew, and a very nice person." But Santayana's most redeeming statement on the matter of racial prejudice is probably that found in his 23 Sep 1926 letter to John Jay Chapman, an American bigot who had offered Santayana the presidency of "The Aryan Society":

> Against whom is the Aryan Society directed? Against the
> Arabians, the Jews, the Chinese, and the blameless
> Ethiopians? I confess that I don't like the Jewish spirit,
> because it is worldly, seeing God in thrift and success,
> and I know nothing of the blacks; but the Arabs and the
> Chinese seem to me in some ways, apart from the cos-
> tume, nearer to the Greeks than we are in Europe and
> America: they have taken the measure of life more
> sanely. Might it not turn out, then, that the Aryan Society,
> if it stood for the life of reason, was especially directed
> against the Aryans? Races, like nations, seem an unfortu-
> nate class of units to identify with moral ideas.

If, therefore, Santayana's comments in his letters and other writings are perceived by some readers as repugnantly anti-Semitic, others today–including a number of Jewish scholars–argue that such a view is an exaggeration and reject the charge that Santayana was truly anti-Semitic. At the very least, the quotation from the letter to Chapman indicates that he was not a racist.

Charles Loeser, Santayana's classmate at Harvard, was from a prosperous Jewish family. Santayana enjoyed Loeser's company and admired his mastery of foreign languages and expert knowledge of art, which Santayana thought even greater than Bernard Berenson's. The two young men traveled together and afterward remained friends for many years.

The young Santayana also enjoyed the forays he made into Boston society, but most especially he relished the company of other sophisticated or cultivated young men. In some letters we find the elderly philosopher reminiscing about the bachelor dinner parties of the 1890s in Cambridge that had given him some of the most pleasant moments of his life. As he got older, however, Santayana more and more preferred to be alone, and a correlate of this love of solitude was his dislike of controversy, a rather surprising characteristic in a philosopher. On 6 Jun 1939 he wrote to Mrs. Toy: "I don't like mental fierceness, even on my own side in philosophy. ..." Many years earlier, during the summer following his retirement from Harvard, Santayana had written (on 2 Aug 1912) to his former colleague and department chairman, George Herbert Palmer, that he expected to benefit from conversations in Cambridge, England, with his friends Bertrand Russell and G. E. Moore:

> ... whose views are near enough to mine to be stimulating to me, while the fact that they live in an atmosphere of controversy (which for myself I hate) renders them keenly alive to all sorts of objections and pitfalls which I need to be warned of, in my rather solitary and unchecked reasonings.

If Santayana enjoyed occasionally discussing philosophical issues with friends (and, in the last part of his life, with many of the persons who visited him at the nursing home in Rome), he decidedly did not enjoy professional conferences. In the 23 Sep 1932 letter to Mrs. Toy in which he reported on his recent participation in the *Domus Spinozana* conference at The Hague (6–10 Sep 1932), Santayana described the meetings as being "like all meetings and international conferences, rather tiresome and futile"; "in the end," he had written to his sister Susan on 1 Oct 1913, "every philosopher has to walk alone." And in the 18 Jul 1913 letter to the poet Arthur Davison Ficke, Santayana echoed Socrates' remark to Crito in Plato's dialogue of the same name:

> ... what does it matter what <u>other people</u> think? If we
> care too much about persuading them we may disturb
> their peaceful conventions to no good purpose, since
> they will never get anything straight, while we blunt the
> edge of truth in our own words.

Santayana believed that if his auditors or readers could comprehend intu-
itively the truth of his views, they would accept them; but if they could
not do so, there was no point in attempting to badger people into agreement. One must catch the spark if concurrence is to be genuine and
meaningful. Agreement in intellectual matters, he felt, came about more
through sympathetic understanding than through debate.

Just as he did not like the gatherings of professors at professional meetings, neither did Santayana—with few exceptions—like individual professors; and he didn't like being one himself. On 6 Jun 1912, at the time of
his retirement from Harvard, he wrote to President Abbott Lawrence
Lowell that "although fond of books and of young men, I was never altogether fit to be a professor." Three years later, on 4 Aug 1915, he wrote to
his former graduate student, B. A. G. Fuller, who was then on the
Harvard philosophy faculty, about his disillusionment with teaching philosophy:

> ... I can't take the teaching of philosophy seriously in
> itself, either as a means of being a philosopher or of
> teaching the young anything solid: they merely flirt with
> that for a year or two instead of flirting with something
> else. Philosophy is not a science; it might be a life or a
> means of artistic expression, but it is not likely to be
> either at an American college.

Contrary to the present-day practice of calling every college or university teacher of philosophy—from the greenest assistant professor to the
hoariest veteran—a "philosopher," Santayana made a significant distinction between a "philosopher" and what he referred to as a "mere professor" of philosophy.[31] For Santayana the teaching of philosophy was a
profession like any other; but, for the true philosopher, philosophy was
not only a profession but also a vocation or way of life. In a humorous
vein, he wrote to George Sturgis, his nephew and new financial manager,
on 14 Aug 1921:

> In respect to money-matters, I am a <u>true</u> philosopher (not
> a mere professor of Phil. 10, 12, etc) and my one wish is

not to hear about them, but to cash cheques and be happy.

More seriously, he says in a 1926 letter to Lewis Mumford regarding Mumford's discussion of him in *The Golden Day*:

> ... I feel that you are thinking of me—quite naturally—as just a Harvard professor, author of a book called "The Life of Reason". Your appreciation seems absolutely just, as directed upon that semi-public personage: but I never felt myself to be identical with that being, and now much less than ever.[32]

In a 16 Jun 1934 letter to Harry Austryn Wolfson, Santayana uses his favorite, Spinoza, to make clear his distinction between the philosopher and the "mere professor" of philosophy:

> I believe there is another reason also why Spinoza seems to me so pre-eminent: that in spite of being traditional, or because he was not distracted by side issues, he was an entire and majestic mind, a singularly consecrated soul. All these trite dogmas and problems lived in him and were the natural channels for his intuitions and emotions. That is what I feel to make a real <u>philosopher</u> and not, what we are condemned to be, <u>professors</u> of the philosophy of other people, or of our own opinions.

Spinoza had been excommunicated by the rabbis in 1656 and banished from Amsterdam for his heretical ideas; living on the outskirts of the city, he earned a meager subsistence as a lens-grinder. Several years later, in order to maintain his intellectual independence, Spinoza turned down the offer of a chair of philosophy at Heidelberg. Santayana believed that, by retiring as soon as he could from Harvard, he had achieved a comparable independence. He expressed this idea of the necessary freedom of the philosopher in the 9 Jun 1937 letter to Cory saying: "you are now a recognised free lance in philosophy, as all philosophers ought to be. ..."

While avowedly not fond of professors, Santayana nevertheless moved among them all his life, as many of his correspondents and many of his visitors during the years that he lived in hotels in Rome were professors. In fact, almost all of Santayana's friends and associates were individuals of either social or intellectual stature, or both. In some of his letters he distinguishes between what he calls "nice" people (the well-bred, well-educated, and well-to-do) and common or ordinary people. His habit of choosing his friends from among socially prominent Americans and aristocratic Europeans led to accusations of sponging, social climbing, and snobbery. Santayana responds to the latter charge in the 8 Sep 1920 letter to William Lyon Phelps:

> I protest against being called a snob; what I love is what
> is simple, humble, easy, what ought to be common, and
> it is only the bombast of false ambitions and false superi-
> ority, that I abhor.

There is no indication that Santayana, whatever his preferences for the well-born and well-bred, was ever anything but courteous to and considerate of persons in humble positions. In his letters, Santayana refers to the waiters in the restaurants he frequented as being his friends, and there are references to the servants in the hotels or private houses that he stayed in that express Santayana's consideration of them and his desire to do the right thing and be thought well of by them. Perhaps Santayana received a certain satisfaction from the names distinguished by European aristocratic titles in some of the lists of persons he sent to his publishers to receive complimentary copies of his books, but there is no evidence of Santayana ever fawning on any Boston Brahmin or European aristocrat— not even Bertrand Russell's elder brother, where the matter was complicated far beyond mere snobbery.

One purpose of this introduction is to suggest the ways in which Santayana's letters reveal various characteristics of his personality, how a self-portrait emerges from the letters. That portrait is both fascinating and invaluable in giving us a better understanding of the complex personality of someone who was a profound thinker, gifted artist, and sophisticated man of the world. By thus illuminating more subtly and fully Santayana's personality and character, the letters can deepen our insight into his philosophical and literary works. (And many of the letters address directly the principal ideas and themes of those works.) But though remarkably interesting and informative, the letters make no sensational revelations about Santayana's personal life. It is not at all the case with him—as it often is with celebrities—that the private individual differs dramatically from the public persona. On the contrary, the evidence of the letters is that Santayana was a person of exceptional integrity, a man with a clear conception of who and what he was and what he ought to be, and one who tried to live a life of reason in accord with this conception of himself.

Nevertheless, the personality reflected in the letters is complicated and paradoxical. Some letters reveal Santayana as a political reactionary, complacent about arbitrary inequalities of opportunity in society, approving of ruthlessly repressive forces like Mussolini and the Italian and Spanish fascists, and–in terms of his remarks about the Jews–insensitive about racial slurs. Yet the letters also show him as someone who rejected totalitarianism on principle, disapproved of capitalism on moral grounds, advocated a kind of state socialism, and was sympathetic to Bolshevism.[33] They depict a thinker who aided and abetted creative expression in others even when that expression clashed with his own opinions. They show a man tolerant of irritating traits in family and friends, who frequently suffered annoyance and inconvenience in order to accommodate persons to whom he felt a debt of loyalty. They show us an honest man, generous with his money and time, often contributing to the financial support of relatives, friends, and needy strangers, and taking the time and trouble to write conscientious appraisals of works sent to him by other writers. All in all, the portrait of Santayana that emerges from the letters is that of a man devoted to his work, one who valued friendship and loyalty highly, was considerate and polite, but who quickly comprehended a situation and was never reluctant to speak his mind. We invariably find him giving his correspondents his frank opinions, irrespective of their own views. There is nothing of the boor or bully in this candor, but rather only a desire to be truthful.

Santayana's letters depict a person of rare gifts and remarkable accomplishments, a very private individual, neither curmudgeonly nor arrogant. They reveal a man endowed with great intellectual powers, living detached from and "above" the world, who was nonetheless thoroughly human.

Notes

[1]Most of Santayana's correspondence is in English. However, he wrote in Spanish to relatives and friends in Spain, and the 29 Apr 1945 letter (to Dino Rigacci) is in Italian.
[2]Per 6 Sep 1934 to Cory.
[3]The collection of 373 pieces of correspondence from Santayana to his Harvard classmate, life-long friend, and fellow professional philosopher, C. A. Strong (1862–1940), over the half-century from 1889 to 1939, is second only in size to the collection of correspondence from Santayana to Daniel Cory (over the quarter-century from 1927 to 1952) totaling 400 items. Until recently, only a few items of Santayana's correspondence to Strong had been located, and it was feared that the rest had been destroyed when German soldiers occupied the latter's Villa le Balze, at Fiesole, Italy, during the Second World War. Fortunately, however, the rest was discovered, early in 1999,

housed in the Rockefeller Archive Center, Sleepy Hollow, New York. Strong's wife, Elizabeth, was the daughter of John D. Rockefeller, and the letters were deposited in the Archive by Elizabeth Cuevas, Strong's granddaughter, a couple of years earlier.

[4]The letter reads: "Polissez-le toujours, et le repolissez, / Ajoutez quelquefois et souvent effacez."

[5]See especially Margaret Münsterberg, "Santayana at Cambridge," *American Mercury* 1 (1924): 69–74; George W. Howgate, *George Santayana* (Philadelphia: University of Pennsylvania Press; London: Oxford University Press, 1938); *Dialogue on George Santayana* (New York: Horizon Press, 1959), ed. Corliss Lamont; Bruno Lind, *Vagabond Scholar: A Venture into the Privacy of George Santayana* (New York: Bridgehead Books, 1962); John McCormick, *George Santayana: A Biography* (New York: Alfred A. Knopf, 1987); and George Santayana, *Persons and Places: Fragments of Autobiography,* Critical Edition, ed. William G. Holzberger and Herman J. Saatkamp Jr. (Cambridge: The MIT Press, 1986). (Further references to the autobiography are to the Critical Edition.) For a concise biography of Santayana as poet see Holzberger, "Introduction" to *The Complete Poems of George Santayana* (Lewisburg: Bucknell University Press; London: Associated University Presses, 1979), 23–82. Daniel Cory, in *Santayana: The Later Years, A Portrait with Letters* (New York: George Braziller, 1963), makes specific use of his letters from Santayana to illustrate aspects of Santayana's character and personality.

[6]Even in his personal correspondence, so careful and deliberate a writer as Santayana was never wholly spontaneous and unguarded.

[7]"Moral relativism," as Santayana uses the term, must be understood to include more than mere arbitrary choice of behavior. For Santayana, morals are relative to the individual and the specific situation, and the natural sanctions which determine acceptable behavior are immediate and absolute.

[8]The letter of 18 Dec 1928 begins, without salutation: "Of course, dear Cory"; and within the letters to Cory of 21 May 1928, 1 Jul 1937, and 23 Jan 1940 we find the phrases "My dear Cory", "For heaven's sake, dear Cory", and "Now, dear Cory", respectively. But in the 352 letters to Cory that begin with a salutation it is uniformly "Dear Cory".

[9]*The Later Years,* 321. Cory's part of the correspondence is unlocated; Santayana usually discarded letters after reading them.

[10]Letter from Lowell to Santayana of 8 Jan [1950]. Santayana kept Lowell's letters, which are in the Humanities Research Center, The University of Texas at Austin.

[11]The first book of Santayana's poems was *Sonnets and Other Verses* (Cambridge: Stone and Kimball, 1894). A revised, expanded edition was published in 1896.

[12]14 May 1925.

[13]15 Jul 1928.

[14]Grattan Freyer, the late Irish literary critic, said to me that *The Last Puritan* was "like the best of Henry James."

[15]"And why has my photo been redrawn so as to make me cross-eyed and ferocious? I know that self-knowledge is often self-deception, but I feel not at all as this personage looks." (1 Feb 1936 to Wheelock)

[16]"I suppose Housman was really what people nowadays call 'homosexual,' [said Santayana]."

"Why do you say that?" I [Cory] protested at once.

"Oh, the sentiment of his poems is unmistakable, [Santayana replied]."

There was a pause, and then he added, as if he were primarily speaking to himself, "I think I must have been that way in my Harvard days—although I was unconscious of it at the time." (*The Later Years,* 40)

[17]20 May 1887.

[18]27 May 1887.

[19]*Persons,* 297–98.

[20]5 Sep 1923 and undated letter written between 20 Sep and 24 Oct 1923. "Elizabeth" refers to the Countess Russell, the earl's third wife, who had left him in 1918.

[21]*Persons,* 517.

[22]There is no evidence that Santayana ever had a physical sexual relationship with either a man or a woman. This suggests perhaps that whatever sexual promptings he may have experienced were sublimated to his thought and art and found expression in his writings. It is also possible that Santayana deliberately embraced the tradition of celibacy advocated by the Roman Catholic Church for members of the clergy (and by the religions of India and China for holy-men and wisemen). He had a great respect for the traditions of the Church and frequently refers to himself in the letters as monk-like, saying that he could live happily in a monastery.

[23]In a 30 Sep 1938 letter to Cory, Santayana described George Sturgis as "a nice person, but not very perceptive"; and in a 31 Dec 1944 letter to Rosamond Sturgis, from whom George recently had been divorced before his sudden death on 20 Dec 1944, Santayana wrote: "George never gave me any explanation of the estrangement that had arisen between you, and of course I respected his discretion and asked no questions. But I could well imagine that, like his father, he might prove hard to live with in the long run. In fact, when you came to Rome, I couldn't help wondering how you ever decided to marry him. He was very good, very useful, and very able in many ways, and for me he proved a treasure (literally) in the management of my affairs, as his father had been too. But there was never a resposive [*sic*] chord."

[24]For example, in the 2 Aug 1944 letter to George Sturgis, Santayana wrote: "Cory has been a problem for Strong and me for many years. He too is not a business man, and between us three we managed to land him, at the age of nearly forty, in no man's land. I feel a certain responsibility for him, as it was as my disciple and secretary that he first turned to philosophy: but I never meant to make our connection permanent."

[25]*The Later Years,* 325–27.

[26]"… perhaps you would do better not to report to either of us any nasty thing that the other may say, or do, in regard to his good old friend. It makes it harder to keep up the amicable tone of our relations. … Do help us to remain friends." (11 Nov 1931 to Cory)

[27]5 Feb 1936 to Rosamond Sturgis.

[28][Dec 1917].

[29]In the 12 May 1946 letter to David Page, Santayana says, while he is well aware that others regard his political views as "Fascism and Phalangism," that he regards them as "Toryism."

[30]See, for instance, 15 and 25 Sep 1926 to Kallen.

[31]This attitude of Santayana's was more common in an earlier time. I recall Paul Arthur Schilpp espousing this view in class at Northwestern University during the 1950s. Schilpp made a point of reserving the term "philosopher" for the great figures of the history of philosophy and for contemporary theorists of international reputation.

[32]16 Dec 1926, Lewis Mumford, *The Golden Day* (New York: Boni and Liveright, 1926).

[33]"Something in me tells me that the Russian Bolsheviks are right—not in their conduct, which has been scandalous and silly—but in their sense for values, in their equal hostility to every government founded on property and privilege." (6 Apr 1918 to Mrs. Winslow); "I think [Soviet Russian communism] is a splendid experiment. Lenin is as good as Lycurgus or Pythagoras. Let him have his way!" (6 Apr 1930 to Kallen); "I am

not a <u>modern</u> or <u>liberal</u> socialist: but I feel in my bones that our form of industrial society is very precarious, and that it will disappear, perhaps rather soon, as completely as the mediaeval or the Graeco-Roman civilizations have disappeared." (4 Oct 1931 to George Sturgis); "I ... agree with ... [Karl Marx's] low opinion of capitalism. ... To my own mind, absurd as capitalism is—I live on invisible and unearned money myself, I don't know why or how—it seems to be only a technical device accompanying industrialism: and the latter is the radical evil." (15 Apr 1933 to Hook); "I prefer the Bolschies [to the current British government]; and perhaps everywhere, through one approach or another, it is to State socialism that we are bound" (19 Oct 1935 to R. S. Barlow); "But my ideal would be a communistic public life, as in the Spartan upper class or as in a monastery, if it went with perfect liberty in thought and in the arts, like painting or writing. And I should limit all the luxuries to public gardens, libraries, churches, theatres and clubs, where each member might satisfy his own taste and develop his own vocation. I have lived myself as far as possible on that plan, and found it satisfactory. But I dread <u>uniformity</u> imposed upon mankind; that is a waste of opportunities and a dull slavery. That is what I dislike in democracy and social pressure." (9 May 1945 to Rosamond Sturgis)

List of Letters

Book One, [1868]–1909

[1895 or 1896]	Gertrude Stein
28 February 1895	Charles Eliot Norton
2 May 1895	Macmillan and Co.
4 June 1895	Herbert Stone and Hannibal Kimball
18 June 1895	William Cameron Forbes
19 June 1895	Macmillan and Co.
3 September 1895	Guy Murchie
[1895–96?]	Lawrence Smith Butler
Monday [1895–96?]	Lawrence Smith Butler
Thursday [1895–96]	Lawrence Smith Butler
3 October 1895	Macmillan and Co.
10 November 1895	Charles Augustus Strong
1 December 1895	Guy Murchie
12 March 1896	Guy Murchie
19 March 1896	Charles Scribner's Sons
23 March 1896	Herbert Stone and Hannibal Kimball
[Spring 1896]	William Cameron Forbes
5 May 1896	Charles Scribner's Sons
20 June 1896	Charles Scribner's Sons
27 June 1896	Guy Murchie
26 July 1896	Charles Scribner's Sons
11 August 1896	Conrad Hensler Slade
13 August 1896	Guy Murchie
20 August 1896	Hannibal Ingalls Kimball
29 September 1896	Charles Scribner's Sons
10 October 1896	Boylston Adams Beal
15 October [1896]	James Edwin Creighton
17 October 1896	Josiah Royce
22 October 1896	Charles Scribner's Sons
1 November 1896	William Cameron Forbes
11 November 1896	Carlotta Russell Lowell
19 November 1896	Henry Ward Abbot
21 December 1896	Charles Scribner's Sons
14 January 1897	Susan Sturgis de Sastre
31 January 1897	Hannibal Ingalls Kimball
1 February 1897	Charles Scribner's Sons
23 April 1897	Josiah Royce
17 July 1897	Guy Murchie
16 September 1897	Hugo Münsterberg

Letters: [1868]–1909

To Susan and Josephine Sturgis

[1868] • Ávila, Spain   (MS: Sastre)

Querida Susana[1,2]

he recibido tu carta que era escrita en Londres Lo que han dicho tus tíos
que yo soy guapo eso no es verdad. Dice papá[3] que te ponga que tu si que
eres guapa y Josefina tambien; pero yo digo que esas son guasas, pero lo
que si es verdad es que te quiere mucho tu hermano y ahijado

Jorge

Mi querida Josefina. No te es olvide escribirme cuando llegues á Boston y
estes desocupada.

Yo tambien te escribiré mientras pueda para que tengas siempre pre-
senta á tu hermano que se acuerda mucho de ti y de tus cuentos

Jorge

[1]Translation:

Dear Susan

I have received your letter written in London. What your aunt and uncle said, that I
am good-looking, that isn't true. Papa says that I should write to you that you are good-
looking and Josephine too; but I say that that's teasing, but what is true is that your
brother and godson loves you very much

My dear Josephine. Don't forget to write to me when you get to Boston and have nothing to do.

I will write you too when I am able so that you will always have in your thoughts
your brother who remembers you and your stories a lot

[2]Santayana was five when he wrote this to his half sisters, Susan (1851–1928) and
Josephine (1853–1930), who were en route with their mother, via London, to Boston.
His half brother, Robert (1854–1921), had been sent to Boston earlier to attend school.
George remained in Spain with his father.

[3]A retired colonial official, Agustín Ruiz de Santayana y Reboiro (1814–93), married
Josefina Borrás y Carbonell (1826–1912) about 1863; their son, "George" Jorge Agustín
Nicolás Ruiz de Santayana y Borrás, was born later that year. See *Persons,* 11–50.

To John Galen Howard

21 August 1882 • Roxbury, Massachusetts   (MS: Berkeley)

Roxbury, Aug. 21st 1882.

My dear Howard.[1]

I address myself to you again, not because there is anything which I can
impart in the way of interesting information, but partly in order to thank
you for your very kind letter which I received some time ago, and partly

to ask you to let me know what are your plans, so that if you return to Boston I may have the pleasure of seeing you. It appears from repeated consultation of the calendar that the summer is coming to an end, to say nothing of the chilly weather which has come to enforce the fact through the evidence of the senses. Hence it occurs to me that you may soon be returning to town.

I suppose you have been the happy recipient of a letter from Mr. Merrill similar to the one I have received from him. I doubt, however, that he has put into yours the amount of gush and eloquence and unction he has lavished on mine. At least I hope he has not had the impudence of addressing all the fellows by their first names, as he has done me. If he supposed I would be flattered by being treated with intimacy by him, he was greatly mistaken. If I did not deem it unwise to forfeit anyone's good opinion merely for the pleasure of speaking out one's mind plainly, I should have answered him and addressed him as "my dear Moses."

I have kept busy this summer principally by reading. I have nearly concluded Dante's Inferno.[2] I thought to have read the whole Comedia this summer, but I find it takes quite long to read a page with my imperfect knowledge of Italian. First I read four or five lines in the original, then the same in a translation, and then reread the Italian to see that I take in the force of each word. Thus I proceed slowly till I get to the end of the Canto when I once more reread the whole. I find it for more beautiful even than I imagined. I have translated some parts for myself in verse like the original in structure, but like all translations it is very unlike the original in effect.

Hoping to hear from you, and also to see you before long, I remain

Sincerely yours,

George Santayana.

<hr />

[1]John Galen Howard (1864–1931) and Santayana were classmates at the Boston Public Latin School during the headmastership of Moses Merrill, Ph.D. (1833–1902). They graduated in the spring of 1882. Howard wrote poetry and became an architect. He later lived in the Berkeley area and worked on the University of California buildings.

[2]Dante Alighieri (1265–1321), born in Florence, was the first important author to write in Italian. His idealized love for the Florentine Beatrice Portinari (1266–90) was the inspiration for many of his works. His *Divina Commedia* (The Divine Comedy) (1321) is an epic poem of the progress of the individual soul toward God and of the political and social progress of mankind toward peace on earth. *Inferno* (Hell) is part one, in which Vergil conducts Dante through the region of damnation, where souls suffer eternal punishments appropriate to their sins. Santayana's analysis of this work constitutes section three of *Poets*.

To Charles Eliot Norton

9 June [1885] • Cambridge, Massachusetts   (MS: Virginia)

Dear Mr. Norton.[1]

Allow me to thank you for your kind note, in the name of the others who wish to study Dante, as well as in my own. We appreciate very much your kindness in being willing to undertake this additional work for us, and only hope it may not cause you serious inconvenience.

Very respectfully yours,
George Santayana.

19 Hollis.

June 9th.

[1]Santayana had been an undergraduate pupil of Charles Eliot Norton (1827–1908), a member of the Harvard class of 1846. Norton was professor of art history there and a Dante scholar. He was cousin to Charles William Eliot, Harvard's president from 1869 to 1909.

To Henry Ward Abbot

16 August 1886 • Göttingen, Germany   (MS: Columbia)

Göttingen, Aug 16th 1886.
P. Adr. Fräulein Schlote.
16 D Obere Karspüle.

Dear Abbot.[1]

I had some hopes of getting a letter from you while I was yet in Spain, but I do not wonder at all at your not having written, for I know by experience what a bother letter writing often is. I am now comparatively comfortable and quiet, waiting for my landlady's toothache to allow her to give me German lessons.[2] My trunk and I arrived here without injury some five days ago. We had had rather a hard time on the way from Spain, getting shaken up a good deal and very dirty; but at Paris we managed to get put to rights again, and we started in very good trim for Cologne. I stopped there a day, admiring the cathedral and the yellow-haired barbarians. The women are ugly, but the men before they grow fat are lusty and fine looking after their species. I think, however, that you Americans are all the better for being a mixture of several nationalities, just as the English are in a great measure. These purer races seem to pay for the distinctness of the type which they preserve by missing some of the ordinary attributes of humanity. For example, the Germans as far as I know have no capacity for being bored. Else I think the race would have become extinct long ago through self-torture.

I hope to hear that you remain in Europe for the present. As I have told you I think more than once, it would be a pity, from my point of view, if you should go into business in Boston and make up your mind not to live for anything but what most men live for, namely, their business and their family. Now I have no quarrel with this state of things as far as the world at large is concerned; I don't want the community to spend its time meditating on poetry and religion. But there are always a few men whose main interest is ~~in~~ to note the aspects of things in an artistic or philosophical way. They are rather useless individuals, but as I happen to belong to the class, I think them much superior to the rest of mankind. Now it seems to me that you ought to belong to the brotherhood theoretical also. Perhaps you would not be willing to go the length I am going, and start out avowdedly with no other purpose but that of living in order to observe life. In that case it would not be well for you to study art and insist on Bohemianizing as I suggested to you that you might do. But still, without going to that extreme, why couldn't you keep as near as possible to the theoretical field? Why couldn't you study law? That is what your brother-in-law Stimson has done, and you see how it has not at all interfered with his artistic work.[3] But what I should be sorry to hear is that you are going to let your interest in painting and philosophy drop out gradually, just as a man drops his school friends and his classics. One is glad to come across them afterwards, but it is always a sort of surprise when one does. But the beauty of the thing is to be at home in the world of ideas and to remain subject to the fascination of studying the aspects of things. In one way a lawyer or political man has a better change of doing this than a professor or artist, because in the case of the latter love of theory often degenerates into marriage. And when a man has the right of property ~~of~~ over a thing it sinks for him into the world of practical business reality, while conceptions, whether artistic or philosophical, have no reality exce~~pts~~t in the world of imagination. So that the artist or professor is apt to be a ridiculous person—a sort of lunatic; for to treat an idea like a thing is like seeing ghosts—the result of mistaking a fact of imagination for a fact of experience. Therefore it may be quite as desirable, even from my point of view, that you should not study art; although if you feel that you can do something in that direction, why on earth don't you try? But it astonishes me that you Bostonians resist so much anything that takes you out of your town, when that is precisely what does you most good. I am wrestling with Herbert Lyman on this point and find it very hard to convince [across] him.[4] But I take for granted that you perceive the necessity of having heard something besides the Unitarian insipidities. Although I have preached you so long a sermon, my real object in beginning to write was to get a letter from you in reply, so as to know what you propose to do and how you are enjoying the season. I myself have spent a moderately agreeable month in Avila, and expect to spend a couple more here struggling against the confusion of tongues. Then I go to Berlin, where Strong is already settled.[5] Houghton is here now, rolling in luxury and waxing strong in pessimism.[6] My room is also very comfortable, but the house is a tower of Babel, inhabited by about a dozen females of different nationalities, each more anxious to teach her own language than to learn that of the others.

Write soon and believe me

Very sincerely yours

George Santayana.

[1]A member of Santayana's Harvard class of 1886.

[2]According to *Persons* (253), Frau Pastorin Schlote's elderly daughter gave Santayana German lessons. In *Puritan*, the hero's German governess was named Irma Schlote.

[3]Frederic Jesup Stimson (1855–1943) was a lawyer, diplomat, and author. He received his A.B. (1876) in philosophy and LL.B. (1878) and LL.D. (1922) from Harvard, where he taught comparative legislation from 1902 to 1915. He served as ambassador to Argentina and Brazil. He wrote fiction under the pseudonym of J. S. of Dale.

[4]Herbert Lyman (1864–1941) was a member of the Harvard class of 1886 and of a prominent Boston family. See *Persons*, 224–25 and 254–56.

[5]Charles Augustus Strong (1862–1940), an American philosopher and psychologist, was Santayana's longtime friend from Harvard. They lived together off and on for many years. Strong and Santayana were sharing the Walker Fellowship, which was awarded jointly for postgraduate study of philosophy in Germany. From 1887 to 1889 Strong taught philosophy part-time at Cornell University. Later he taught psychology at the University of Chicago and at Columbia. See *Persons*, 239–42.

[6]Alanson Bigelow Houghton (1863–1941) originated *The Harvard Monthly* in 1885, became a congressman from New York, and later served as ambassador to Germany and then to England. [D. C.]

To Ward Thoron
16 August 1886 • Göttingen, Germany   (MS: Houghton)

9   Göttingen, Aug 16th 1886.
Dear Ward.[1,2]

                    Affectionately yours
                    George Santayana

P.S. My further sentiments may be expressed in · · · · · · · · ·

            A Psalm of Travel,
    or what the soul of the young man said to
                his grandmother.

I like to leave my house and home
And spew my insides in the sea,
With just one trunk on earth to roam,
That is the height of bliss for me;
To roam alone without my trunk—
That is the depth of misery.

I cannot part from what I prize
For all I prize is in my head;
My fancies are the fields and skies
I will not change till I am deed,
Unless indeed I lose my wits
Or (what is much the same thing,) wed.

That freedom cheats us with a word
Which sets up knaves and murders kings.
We are not free till we have stirred.
So cut your mother's apron strings
And putting money in your purse
Fly off on the express train's wings.

I'll stay at home when I am lame
And coppers give when I have gold,
I'll modest be when known to fame,
I will be chaste when I am old.
Then all the angels will rejoice
To bring a lost-sheep to the fold.

This is my only chance to taste
The sweet and bitter fruit of earth,
And in the struggle and the haste
I needn't ask what all is worth.
It isn't wasting very much
To waste the time 'twixt death and birth.

"Lieee down as if to pleasant dreams
When you lie down among the dead"[3]
So says a poet: but it seems
That it were better to have said:
As if to pleasant dreams arise
Before the time to dream is fled.

So let us dream of changing skies
Of rushing streams and windy weather:
Though we are bound by fortune's ties
We'll to the outmost stretch the tether,
And be it gay or be it sad,
We'll dream our little dream together.

In the course of which, by the way, an occasional letter from you would
be a pleasant incident.
Address. P.Adr. Fräulein Schlote

16 D Obere Karspüle

Göttingen.

[1]Ward Thoron (1867–1938), "destined to be [Santayana's] closest friend while [they]
were undergraduates," graduated with Harvard's class of 1886. A business executive
for nearly fifty years, he retired in 1932 and turned to literary work. He edited *The
Letters of Mrs. Henry Adams* (1936). See *Persons,* 221–24.

[2]On the first page of this letter, Santayana drew sketches and labeled them:
Grandmother Sch., Schlote (Land lady), American Girls, Irish Ditto., English Old
maid., German Ditto., French Ditto. (?), ʄRussian; Greek, Servant girls., Wörterbuch.
[dictionary], View of Göttingen, Bier., Constitutional.

[3]Santayana probably had in mind the closing of William Cullen Bryant's
"Thanatopsis" (1817), which exhorts the reader to approach death "Like one who
wraps the drapery of his couch / About him, and lies down to pleasant dreams."

To Henry Ward Abbot
27 August 1886 • Göttingen, Germany   (MS: Columbia)

> Göttingen, Aug 27ᵗʰ 1886.
> Address.
> Care of Frau Sturm.
> Werder Strasse 6
> Dresden

Dear Abbot.

I must thank you at once for your letter. Of course I take an interest in you; what else should I take an interest in except in the doings and think-ings of people who have more or less my own point of view and my own interests, and especially of those among them whom I happen to have met and liked? As you say, we haven't been great friends in college; but that has an easy explanation. At first I had no friends at all, and after a while, when I could have made many acquaintances, I found the damnable worldliness and snobbishness prevalent at Harvard relegated me to a sort of limbo, the sphere of those who, though they might have committed no actual sin, had not been baptized in the only true Church. Of course such a limbo contained a good many souls; and among them I found some very good friends indeed, whom I by no means would change for others. At the same time, if college society were a little more simple and disinterested, I could have made friends not only in limbo, but also in heaven and hell. In hell I did make some friends, because that, of course, is always possible; but in heaven–unless Herbert Lyman be a cherub–I made no friends at all till the very last; for Ward Thoron must be counted among the fallen angels. You mustn't think that I am a sorehead, or that I think any fellows intentionally turned me the cold shoulder, because I had little cash and wasn't in a fashionable set: I know very well that I have a great many tricks that can make people dislike me, and that I lack all the qualities that go to make a popular fellow. I have never had any ambition to be a popular fel-low: what I complain of is that a certain artificial state of things at Harvard makes it impossible for a man who is not a popular fellow to have those fellows for his friends who would have been his friends at school, and would be his friends in the world. So that the fact that there has been no "ease of fellowship" as you say, between us at college, is no reason what-ever for my not taking an interest in you or for concluding that we really belong to different spheres. Certainly, after reading your letter, I am sure that you are just the man with whom I should like to talk things over. You have, whatever you may say, the contemplative disease; and what ₍is₎ more, you are able to escape the conclusions which people agree to be the proper one's to arrive at, although I fancy you feel a little wicked for doing so. For instance, what you say of your family, although the effort you make to say it perhaps leads you to exaggerate, shows that you can open your eyes to ~~see~~ look at those truths which it is considered wrong to see. It is wrong to see that right and truth may be subjective, imaginary things, or that one's family may be very much in one's way; yet you are willing to consider these heresies. But although your letter confirms my belief that you ought to go into the idea business rather than into any other, I see that you can't do so now. Of course a man shouldn't quarrel with ~~ones~~ his bread and butter, nor with his family even if he had his own bread and butter already. But if you go into business to please your mother or your grandfather, it is a great deal better than if you went into business to please yourself; you will in all probability not lose your taste for intellectual things, nor get very much absorbed in your employment. I myself would not hesitate to go into business if circumstances made it necessary for me to do so; nor would I think I was ~~gi~~selling my birthright for my mess of potage. For after all our birthright is our love of observing; and a man can study the world in one place as well as in ~~on~~another. If you have an ambition to write novels, you lose nothing by going to an office every morning, where the values of men can be learned as well as the values of cotton and sugar.

So, although I am awfully sorry you can't be within reach of me this winter, I see no reason why you should regret your situation. Of course it is not ideal, since you are ₍not₎ as free as one likes to be—not as free, perhaps, as I am; because my family, having nothing to bribe me with, are very willing that I should follow my inclinations, and even help me as much as they are able. But your mother was not mistaken when she thought me an ungrateful son: I am ungrateful; because the amount of space occupied in my mind by my family and my obligations to them is infinitesimal compared with the amount occupied by [*illegible*]my own ambitions. My father, who is very shrewd and cynical, and my mother who is determined and unselfish, ₍&₎ always ready to face fortune, both perceive this, and acquiesce in it. They know perfectly well that I like to be away from home, because I tell them so; but of course they also see that it is good for me. I am not the most comforting and loving of sons—but naturally they can't blame me for existing or being more or less as I am.—But although you are not as free as one likes to be, you probably will have leisure enough to read a little, and a good opportunity of seeing the world. Besides, as some o/ld Roman said, to know well the ways of men, one house is enough. So I shall be expecting your first novel, as well as the news of your engagement to that divine creature which you so generously assign to me. By the way, I do not expect that either you /nor I can do as much as Stimson, whom I admire very much; but we can help make that atmosphere in which Stimsons bloom, and perhaps even greater men. We can't expect to be geniuses (and I believe Stimson has the quality, in what degree we cannot yet tell) but we can be lovers of the things of which geniuses are masters; we can be, like Norton, maggots in the big men's cheese. And for myself, being a supercilious and ¢Epicurean maggot, I like cheese better than Philistine potatoes.

In a week I leave Göttingen and go to Dresden, to be with Herbert Lyman.[1] We are to have a room together, and I expect to have a delightful time, with the pictures and music, and the German books I expect to read. Herbert is a man whom I think as much of as my theory of human nature allows me to think of anyone. I am looking forward to being with him with real pleasure, but I am afraid he is going home for the winter. I shall be reduced to such men as Strong and Houghton, who to be sure, have a great deal to say that is interesting, but who are not wholly satisfactory. Nevertheless, I hope to pass the winter pleasantly, occupied with some new aspects of the same old questions. I am not insensible to the sincere compliment you pay me by giving me your confidence to the extent you do; but for God's sake, no compliments of any other kind. I don't know how much water there may be in my stream; but I am sure that many a sluggish river has more. I have not had the chance to stagnate; I have been shut in and forced down in one single direction, and much of my force comes from my limitations. I have as much to admire in you or in anyone (for I am not flattering) as you or anyone can have to admire in me. I am a slightly different specimen—more or less curious—a little rare, perhaps, because an imported article. But if you think it worth while to write to me, why, I shall be very glad, very glad indeed, to write to you, and preach your patience out. You may be able to be a little franker with me than with most people, because being an antimoralist in sympathies as well as in theory, I will not think any the worse of you for telling me what is psychologically (or, as in Ward's case, physiologically) true of you. I know before hand that at the bottom of things spiritual is darkness, and at the bottom of things physical, filth; but I think it a pleasant thing for a few persons (and there have always been such) to say it to each other in a decent way. It will also be a great pleasure for me to hear through you about other fellows, and when the time comes, about the woman to be deeply and sincerely loved–by you.

Very sincerely yours
George Santayana

[*across*]

P.S. I have read this interminable letter over. Don't think from its damned tone that I don't see and value your handsome way of treating me. I hope you won't be sorry you have trusted me in this matter. Yet I haven't answered half the things in your letter, so you may hear from me again before long.

[1]Lyman brought Santayana (who did not stay for commencement) his degree in Germany. They were together several weeks early in the autumn of 1886 in Dresden; Lyman was to spend a year or two in Germany studying music and Santayana two years studying philosophy at Göttingen and Berlin.

To William Morton Fullerton

9 September 1886 • Dresden, Germany   (MS: Texas)

Dresden, Sept 9<u>th</u> 1886.

My dear Fullerton.[1]

I was lounging on the soft and luxurious brown flowered damask sofa of one of the pleasant apartments on the first floor of a Dresden boarding house or "pension", as people call such an abode in this eastern and more anciently civilized part of the earth–the seat of a riper and more aesthetically developed culture than that of even that noblest of American institutions, our beloved and but recently relinquished Alma Mater, dear old grassy, elm-shaded Harvard University[2]–and I was suffering my summer noontide fancies to be dissipated into the thin and fleecy flakes of a disintegrating and dissolving mist of lazy and listlessly vagrant day-dream phantasy, when, by what happy and opportune inspiration of Providence I scarcely venture to conjecture, our common friend Lyman, with whom, by the way, I am now relishing the sweets of European existence, read me, with that unobtrusive and neverfailing thoughtful∧ness∧ and solicitude for others' pleasure which characterizes him in so remarkable a degree, a delightfully easy and charmingly artistic composition of yours–a letter you addressed to him not long ago, whose beauties produced such a vivid and

lively impression upon me, and so irresistably brought to my mind the rec-
ollection of those happy college days, which, to be sure, are not yet lost in
the pink and purple glory of the western sky, and of such of them in particular as furnished me an opportunity of enjoying your graceful and abun-
dant erudition, that I could not withstand the impulse to send you a word
of greeting across the restless billows of the blue-green Atlantic Ocean,
although I knew beforehand that the rustic vulgarity of my coarse and ple-
beian mental idiosyncrasies would render it hopeless and utterly impracticable for me to rival the elegance and refined, and copious, and
Ciceronian flow of your composition,[3] because I hoped that you would
forgive the shortcomings of such poor imitation as I could pretend to produce in view of the always flattering evidence of the attempt; and furthermore that you might be interested to hear about the wanderings of two of
your whilome friends and classmates, to whom your epistle had furnished
so much instruction and entertainment, and who would willingly induce
you to take up the pen once more and to comit to the invaluable and
humanizing agency of ink and paper some of the stray thoughts of your
less busily and productively occupied hours, for the delectation and exu-
beration of both, but especially of

Your sincerely admiring friend
George Santayana.

[across]
Address, Care of C. A. Strong, Schiffbauerdamm 3[II]. Berlin.

[1]William Morton Fullerton (1865–1952), member of the Harvard class of 1886,
became a journalist and spent most of his life in Paris. He was a member of the international literary society. Fullerton had numerous love affairs with both men and
women and awakened the dormant sexuality of such notable writers as Henry James
and Edith Wharton. (See Marion Mainwaring's *Mysteries of Paris: The Quest for Morton
Fullerton* [Hanover, NH: University Press of New England, 2000].)
[2]In June 1886 Santayana graduated (A.B.) *summa cum laude* from Harvard (*in absentia*,
sailing for Germany without waiting for the result of his last examination).
[3]Marcus Tullius Cicero (106–43 B.C.) was a Roman orator, statesman, and man of letters. He created the smooth and rhetorically powerful Hellenized style of prose. A master of oratory, Cicero was also a student of literary criticism, an authority on Stoic
philosophy, and a brilliant letter writer.

To Henry Ward Abbot
6 October 1886 • Berlin, Germany   (MS: Columbia)

Berlin, Oct. 6$^{\underline{th}}$ 1886.
Schiffbauerdamm 3$^{\underline{II}}$

Dear Abbot.

I said, I believe, in my last letter that I would write before long again, because I had more to say in answer to all you told me than I could put into one letter. I have put off writing all this time partly because I thought I might possibly hear from you, and partly because I was afraid of making myself a nuisance. But I have felt like writing to you very many times. You asked why I take an interest in you, which after all it is natural I should take; but since that time I have been forced to wonder myself why I take so <u>much</u> interest in you. And as far as I can see the reason is this. I suspect you are going through a critical period, and I feel that you are dissatisfied with yourself. Why are you dissatisfied with yourself? Another man, I for instance, would be satisfied to be as you are. You are not dissatisfied with yourself because you can't do what other people do and what is expected of a man, but because you imagine you can't do something very excellent which you feel somehow drawn to do. Now I am interested in seeing if you are going to attempt this something excellent, or not; whether you are going to prefer to live on moodily, taking refuge more or less in dissipation, or whether you are going to start out in some direction where you see something you really value. It isn't at all a question of what you can accomplish; it is only a question of what attitude you are going to take, what sort of things you are going attend to. Now you know that I am as willing that people ~~if~~ should worship the devil as that they should worship God; I only ask in whose service will they live more smoothly, gracefully, and intelligently. It's all prejudice and point of view to say that one sort of life is better than another, because it pursues different objects. All that an emancipated man asks is which objects attract him most, and what are the means of attaining those objects. To do right is to know what you want. Now when you are dissatisfied with yourself, it's because you are after something you don't want. What objects are you proposing to yourself? are they the objects you really value? If they are not, you are cheating yourself. I don't mean that if you chose to pursue the objects you most value, you would attain them; of course not. Your experience will tell you that. Therefore a wise man won't value anything much. But this wise indifference, this safeguard against disʃappointment, would come too soon if it came before a man had started in the direction of his true satisfactions. Indifference is quite premature if it leads a man to misunderstand his own desires. In the first place there is always some small chance of success; but success in getting after much labor what you really don't care for is the bitterest and most ridiculous failure. And in the second place, to have before one admired objects, and hopes of true satisfaction, is itself a very pleasant and ennobling thing. So if, as I suspect, you are wavering a little in regard to the direction you will start out in, I hope you will think this over; because, as I am not a moralist, nor a minister, nor an old man, nor anyone with a right to preach and gɤ[*illegible*]ive advice, I may possibly have struck the truth. I trust you will not be offended at my writing to you as I do. Gossip and jokes have I not, but that which I have I give you; don't doubt that I am "with the greatest respect" your sincere friend

GeorgeSantayana

[*across*]
P.S. When you see Ward, please give him an affectionate scolding from me.

To Henry Ward Abbot
1 November 1886 • Berlin, Germany   (MS: Columbia)

Berlin, Nov. 1ˢᵗ 1886.

Dear Abbot.

I will not delay in answering your letter of Oct. 20ᵗʰ which I got yesterday and with which I am vastly delighted–delighted with everything except with the news about Stimson. That is distressing. I knew nothing about his being sick or overworked, and I still hope your fears about his not living long are exaggerated. It would be a pitiful thing that he should die so young. Take warning, you say very properly; but warning not to do what? Not to work? Surely not, but rather not to trust in anything good. I see, however, that you are not inclined to trust in anything good, at least as far as human sentiments are concerned; for you say, with really excessive cynicism, "He has your sympathies I am sure, for he thought you" etc, as if you thought a man incapable of caring for another who doesn't happen to care for him. That is not true. We can see what is fine and beautiful in a man, and value it for itself. We can deplore the constant frustration of everything good in this world.

There is not much to describe in my way of eating, walking, and sleeping at Berlin. I am at a boarding house on the river, with a pleasant view and an unpleasant landlady. My food is far from appetizing, but as it seems to accomplish its purpose, we ought to pronounce it good. I go every morning to the University and hear lectures for three or four hours;[1] in the afternoon I take a walk, read a little, and write letters. Finally I go to bed between two feather mattresses.

The lectures I have heard so far have given me a very favorable impression of the professors. There is a wholesome thoroughness and anti-Hegelianism about them.[2] They all seem to be talking about the world we live in. I mean to hear something besides philosophy—some politics and anatomy, and Grimm's lectures on modern art.[3] I take a course in Kant[4] given by a follower of Schopenhauer,[5] named Deussen, and a course in Ethics by Paulsen, a moderated and humanized Kantian. I also hear a psychophysical course by a robust, somewhat brutal, and very suggestive man, Ebbinghaus.[6]

The most remarkable thing at the University is the monotonous deformity of the students. A recitation room at Harvard is an assembly of the Olympian gods compared with a roomful of Berliners. I make it a practice to sit in the front row at lectures quite as much to avoid the sight of the students as to succeed in hearing the professor. I find the lectures pretty easy to understand.

There are many Americans here, but I see little of them. As you know, I believe, I am at the same house with Strong, to whom a second cousin has lately annexed himself–a vulgar Presbyterian minister from Rochester N.Y. Houghton is at a reassuring distance—more than a mile; that poor fellow, Boylston Beal, is about as far off.[7] He has a diplomatic friend with whom he dines daily at the Kaiserhof, and the consciousness of expense and the imagination of swellness make him perfectly happy. Herbert Lyman was good enough to come to Berlin for a couple of days before going to London, on his way home. I was very glad to see him, but he is gone now.

You challenge me to defend the various contradictions you discover in my letters, on pain of not believing me a sound adviser. I might refuse the challenge, since I am not bound to explain contradictions away, because I do not pretend to think only on one hypothesis. I might also refuse on the ground that I am not a dogmatic right-and-wrong fulminator, and therefore can hardly pretend to be an adviser at all. My advice is all given in the spirit of the common phrase: That's what I would do if I were you. And I think it is hardly worth while to go back and explain what I mean by this and that in letters written hastily and impetuously. Nevertheless I can easily make my general position more clear by a parable. Suppose a mustard seed asked advice of an oak how it should grow, and that the oak (being a fanatic) said: Young seed, unless you grow up into an oak and bear acorns you will be a worthless and immoral plant. God's rain will not fall on you and his lightning will strike you,–or if (by the mercy of a long-suffering God) you should prosper for a time, do not deceive yourself. You may rest assured that in the end the devil will fell you and make a fire of you that will never burn down. But, dearly belovèd seed, if you do what is right and grow up into a good oak tree, you will never be cut down, but you will remain fresh and green forever and ever. And suppose further the mustard seed asked advice also of an elm, which said: My little seed, consider yourself and study your own nature, till you discover what kind of a seed you are. Then look for the ground where your species grows best, and plant yourself there. In this way you will have the best chance of growing up into a good and beautiful tree. But if you plant yourself in ground unfit for you, you may never spring up, or if you do, you will live with pain and difficulty, and be a shrunken and feeble plant. Yet if you should make a mistake, do not be too much troubled; for in the end all trees alike must perish, and the time will soon come when neither green boughs nor dry branches will be remembered.

Now if our mustard seed came from Boston and had always heard people call what they do right and what they don't do wrong, it might reason with itself thus: "The oak is a righteous tree and is giving me moral advice: for he knows what ~~it~~ is right and, behold! he does it. But the elm is a hypocrite whose life contradicts his doctrine, for ~~it~~ he is ~~itself~~ ‸himself‸ an elm and yet says it makes no difference what sort of a tree I become. How can ~~it~~ he think it right to be anything else but an elm? Or if he thinks it right to be anything, why doesn't he become anything, instead of being always just an elm." Yet if our Boston mustard seed ever outgrows its native superstitions it will perceive that the oak was blind, and made a bigoted blunder, threatened imaginary evils and promised impossible goods. The elm on the other hand gave sound, disinterested counsel, founded on observation of the realities of life and sympathy for his fellow beings. What an absurdity to accuse the poor elm of contradiction because it said it was right to be anything, and at the same time dared to be something itself! What an injustice to accuse it of hypocrisy because, although confined by nature to one place and one form, it was willing to respect interests it could not share and admire beauties it could not possess!

I should think this would be enough to show you what I mean; but in case the notion is too new for you I will express it in a more abstract form. I am here so much on my own ground and feel it so safe under me, that I delight in ~~retracing~~ going over it in every direction. To say that all standards of value are arbitrary is not to say that you have none—that you have given up the practice of estimating the relative worth of things. All you have done is to admit that this worth depends on a standard proper to you, and that the same things have a different value according to other standards. To perceive that your ideal is one of many which are actual, and of numberless ideals which are possible, is not equivalent to giving it up. The unemancipated are like the children who think the little angels talk English: but there is no contradiction in going on talking English when you discover that the little angels don't. English doesn't become less necessary when it becomes less heavenly. So I go on using my moral language—talking about good, bad, beautiful, ugly, right and wrong. I suppose you to understand my language: if you don't, why, you are a foreigner, and I will respect you as such and wish I could understand you better. I take for granted that my good is your good: should your good happen to be my evil, why, I will say you worship the devil,—and admit your perfect right to do so, else I should be authorizing you to deny my right to worship God. You may say that what you worship is God also; and you will be right. For, to paraphrase Spinoza,[8] we do not worship a being because he is God, but he is God because we worship him. So that if there is a power A in the world, which I worship, and an opposite power B, which you worship, so long as I live A will be God and B devil, and so long as you live A will be devil and B God. While we both live A and B will be each God and devil at once. One need not be a Manichaean to see that;[9] it is enough to observe two Saints of hostile religions. For you mustn't suppose I am inventing a merely possible example; didn't the pagan gods actually figure as Christian devils? Devils and Gods aren't persons so much as offices; and for the same potentate to be both at once, it is not necessary he should have a double nature; all that is needed is an old woman to pray to him and a young woman to pray to get rid of him.

But you didn't quite understand what I meant by saying it would be better for you to go into business to please your family than to go in to please yourself. I had a malicious notion that in that case you would be less apt to stick to it. We will let that go, however, and suppose I was singing the praises of dutifulness and unselfishness. Why on earth shouldn't I? Do you suppose I have made up my mind not to praise anything? Far from it. I prefer my family to other people's, because it is mine, and my verses to other people's, because they are mine, and for the same reason I would prefer my country, if I had one, to other people's. I by no means propose to become Brahma so soon: I like my humanity better. If it is contradictory and hypocritical to have tastes and prejudices, I must give up logic and sincerity. But it seems to me that when one sees the arbitrariness of all ideals, the à priori[10] equality of all aims, one can stick to one's own with all the better conscience. That is what I had in mind when I said that to do right is to know what you want: if you try to discover your own needs and aspirations, i.e. to specify the objects that can satisfy them, you will do better than if you start out on the Quixotic and hopeless search of the needs and aspirations you ought to have. In the case of needs, the absurdity of asking what they ought to be is glaring enough: it is no less real in the case of aspirations. The only obligation possible appears when your needs and aspirations are given and you ask what you ought to do to satisfy them. Then it ⸗ceases to be nonsense to talk of mistakes, successes, right and wrong conduct, wisdom, and folly. Only one thing has to be guarded against: the psychological error of supposing that a man's needs and aspirations cannot have an object beyond his own body and soul. Nature can put needs and aspirations in us which tend to our own destruction. E.g. the sexual instinct, the ascetic aspirations, and such instincts as the insects and birds have, to make life possible for their offspring. All such instincts are in a real sense unselfish. But whether the selfish man is better than the unselfish man or worse, depends on whether you, who make the judgment, have the need and aspiration of finding unselfish men in the world. From all this you can easily see that in my opinion suicide may easily be justified: for instance if you take the absence of pain as your ideal you make it the duty of every man woman and child to commit suicide without delay—and murder, also, for the matter of that, in ~~the~~ case of anyones ~~asking for~~ ‸taking‸ too much time about it. For evidently, absence of pain can be secured only in the grave. But of course your thinking it right and proper has nothing to do with your ability to kill yourself. You may know that you will probably do no good in the world and that the stomach ache and the heart-ache are your most faithful friends, but it's no use. There is the instinct of self preservation in the way [across] and also one's interest in life. One would rather have a bad time than not see the show, just as a

lover will go to see the woman, ∧even∧ if the sight of her makes him suffer. The power of instinct and impulse is far greater than that of self interest. But the trouble with Joe Gardner[11] was plainly that he cared too much
for something, namely, for animal culae.

Your sincere friend,

George Santayana

[1]The University of Berlin.

[2]Georg Wilhelm Friedrich Hegel (1770–1831) was a German philosopher and proponent of idealism. His system is presented in *Phenomenology of Mind* (1807), *Science of Logic*
(1812–16), *Encyclopedia of the Philosophical Sciences* (1817), and *Philosophy of Right* (1821).
Hegel rejected the existence of finite objects in space and time, establishing instead a
rational unity, the Absolute. The quest for understanding the Absolute proceeds
according to the Hegelian dialectic in which positing something (thesis), denying it
(antithesis), and combining the partial truths in each (synthesis) results in a new thesis.

[3]Herman Friedrich Grimm (1828–1901) taught at the University of Berlin.

[4]Immanuel Kant (1724–1804), German philosopher, is best known for his three
Critiques. In the *Critique of Pure Reason* (1781) Kant sets out to determine the cognitive
powers of reason. His task is to ascertain what knowledge is possible through pure reason, i.e., reason independent of any other human faculty. His transcendental arguments as well as his distinction between appearances (phenomena) and
things-in-themselves (noumena) are developed in this work. Kant's ethical considerations are the subject of the *Critique of Practical Reason* (1788) in which he develops his
conception of moral imperatives and human freedom. The *Critique of Judgment* (1790)
focuses on the beautiful and sublime.

[5]Arthur Schopenhauer (1788–1860) was a German philosopher whose principle work
is *The World as Will and Idea* (1818). His philosophy opposes the Cartesian primacy of
intellect in man and the mechanistic model of nature. Following Kant, Schopenhauer
rejected metaphysical theorizing based on rational deduction but claimed that humans
cannot avoid metaphysical wonder. For every human the will is evident as the 'in-itself'
of individual being. The will is an arational force without ultimate purpose or design.
There is no dualism. The mutual resistance of various wills causes strife, and the individual cannot satisfy the want of his will and therefore lives in pain. The only escape
is the negation of will, but temporary escape can be found in science and art.

[6]Paul Deussen (1845–1919) was a German philologist and philosopher, a lecturer at
Berlin (1881–99), a professor at Kiel, a follower of Schopenhauer, and a scholar of
Indian thought. Friedrich Paulsen (1846–1908) began teaching in the Berlin philosophy department in 1871. Herman Ebbinghaus (1850–1909) was *Privatdozent* at Berlin
(1880–94) and subsequently professor at Freiburg and Halle. See *Persons,* 256–60.

[7]Boylston Adams Beal (1865–1944) was a member of Santayana's Harvard class of
1886 and one of his closest friends during the 1890s. Santayana moved into the pension in Berlin kept by an Englishwoman, where Beal was living. This cost Santayana
the opportunity to learn to speak German, a language which he read easily but in
which he could never converse effectively. (See *Persons,* 226–27 and 260.) Beal was one
of the "pure and intense Bostonians of the old school." (*Persons,* 224)

[8]Baruch (or Benedict) Spinoza (1632–77) was a rationalist philosopher of Jewish
descent. He was expelled from the synagogue for his unorthodoxy in 1656, and in 1673
he refused the chair of philosophy at Heidelberg because he was unwilling to give up
his independence and tranquility. He earned his living by grinding lenses. Spinoza's

philosophy finds its fullest expression in his most famous work, *Ethics* (1677). Spinoza maintains one cannot understand the world without understanding it as a whole, a single system that has two names, God and Nature. Together with Plato and Aristotle, Spinoza is one of the chief sources of Santayana's philosophic inspiration. At the time of his graduation, Santayana published his essay, "The Ethical Doctrine of Spinoza," in *The Harvard Monthly* 2 (June 1886): 144–52. Later, he wrote an introduction to Spinoza's *Ethics and "De intellectus emendatione"* (London: Dent, 1910, vii–xxii). See *Persons*, 233–36.

[9]Manichaeism was a religion founded by a third-century Persian named Mani. He announced himself a prophet in 242, was driven into exile under Zoroastrian pressure, and after his return was flayed to death. His religion, however, spread over the Roman Empire and Asia. Manichaeism took the dualism of Zoroastrianism and spiritualized the struggle between light and dark into warfare between good and evil. The teaching was strongly ascetic, and the 'elect' or 'perfect' practiced celibacy and austerity; they were assured of immediate happiness after death. This widespread religion was opposed successfully by Christianity and died out around 500.

[10]The phrase *a priori* is used in philosophy to mean knowledge which is independent of experience.

[11]Unidentified.

To Herbert [Lyman]

9 November 1886 • Berlin, Germany   (MS: Unknown)

November 9, 1886

Dear Herbert,
    While you sail across the ocean,
Wafted by duty and your own sweet will,
Into my head has come a little notion
To reach your hermitage on Beacon Hill.[1]
Though lacking other means of locomotion,
I can bestride a Pegasean[2] quill,
And when that hobby-horse begins to amble
O'er all the world it's pretty sure to ramble.

I mean to gas a little now and then
About my life at German universities,
About the books I notice and the men,
And about all their comical perversities.
These frequently will lead my talk again
To life in general, and what a curse it is;
On which sad theme when weary of enlarging,
I'll draw a little picture in the margin.

And I will write in dear Byronic[3] rhyme,
Hoping the husk may hide the want of kernel,
And while my tent is pitched in this far clime,
I'll send you my epistolary journal.
Perhaps it may in coming wintry time,
When we are stiffening in the frost eternal,
From the heart's embers time's cold ashes blow
And make the boyish flame a moment glow.

　　　At Dresden we were taken in
　　　By penniless Frau Sturm,
　　　A woman uglier than sin
　　　And than the Siegfried Wurm.[4]

　　　She gave us food that we could bite
　　　But that we couldn't chew,
　　　And fed us morning, noon, and night
　　　On variegated gou.

　　　The head of madam's eldest loon
　　　Was like the O of Giotto,[5]
　　　Like shadows in the afternoon
　　　Were the long legs of Otto.

　　　I hate the silly nervous smirk
　　　Of pallid, lean Lilie,
　　　But feel some slight suspicion lurk
　　　That Lieschen[6] pleases me.

　　　Young Alex was all skin and hair,
　　　The dirty little shrimp;
　　　The trousers that you used to wear
　　　Now clothe that evil imp.

　　　And now, perhaps, while thus we chide,
　　　On their piano stuck,
　　　We smile in effigy beside
　　　That handsome English buck.

Frau Sturm was gifted with the gift of lungs
To celebrate the days of her prosperity,
And, though unskilful with the modern tongues,

She used her old one with extreme dexterity.
The story of her glories and her wrongs
She said would teach us German with celerity,
If we would wrestle with her till we fled
To wrestle with her German feather bed.

> Pray heaven you may know enough
> To learn on no such plan
> For to teach any kind of stuff
> Herr Richter[7] is the man.

> Herr Richter gives good music lessons,
> He teaches French and Dutch,
> Of English furnishes the essence,
> And doesn't charge too much.

> Good stories and the court affairs
> Are also in his line:
> You'll find him up three flights of stairs—
> Herr! how your face will shine!

> The portraits of himself and wife
> Of golden frames can boast,
> And you can't tell, to save your life,
> Which frame to pity most.

> There we would sit and yawn and grin
> Till five or thereabout,
> When a small boy came marching in,
> And we went strolling out.

We also went to see the mellow pictures
Of Virgins, Venuses, Christs, Saints, and satyrs.
And I must make a few religious strictures
On the old masters and their imitators
For painting chestnuts from the Holy Scriptures.
To vice rather than virtue, beauty caters,
And naked angels shouldn't kick and tussle
Nor saints raise such a quantity of muscle.

Chastity shrinks from the Italian school
And Rubens[8] is a danger to virginity

(Though baggy Venuses make passion cool
Till corsets reestablish their divinity.)
It's wrong for cherubs to display a t___
Since they must sing soprano to infinity,
And reformed Magdalenes[9] should wear some clothes
And read their Bibles in a modest pose.

I grant, in subjects drawn from heathen fable
A little freedom serves religion's need,
And shows the world that morals are unstable
Unless well founded on a Christian creed.
To paint the orgies at the satyrs' table
Or the nymphs dancing to the shepherd's reed
Is proper—but too far have painters gone
In representing Leda and the Swan.[10]

In truth the German is the school of virtue
And turns the youthful mind from immorality.
To gaze on kitchen furniture won't hurt you
And painted robes are full of spirituality.
A martyr's nakedness will not pervert you
When she has lost all signs of animality
And is so stark and ludicrously thin,
The more she shows, the less you want to sin.

Upon the whole, I doubt the advisability
Of sending girls abroad upon a tour
To run through the museums with agility
And eye antiques and pictures so impure,
Then chatter with idiotic volubility
About the culture which they thus procure,—
For nobody's so often heard to cry Oh, Ah,
As Pinky Jones of Cattleboro', I owe.

Besides, I have myself a great objection
To have a bonnet thrust before my eyes
When I have aimed my glass in the direction
Of a Madonna sitting in the skies.
With Italy's old masters a collection
Of Vassar's modern pupils hardly vies,
Because although their faces may be painted

Their souls can never possibly be sainted.

Of all the places for the female tourist
The ladies' railway carriage is the best,
For while they're there, your peace of mind is surest,
And till you reach a station, you may rest.
But of all spots, a gallery's the poorest
In which to fall a victim to the pest;
They gabble, gape, laugh, question, pass, repass,
Now want your catalogue, now want your glass.

But they behave much better at the play
And being prettier than pure Teutonics,
They are quite welcome at a nice café
Combined with Bairisch and with philharmonics.
It's entertaining there to watch the way
That Mars and Venus practice their platonics,
I mean, how the refulgent warrior twirls
His blonde moustache at stylish foreign girls.

In the foyer the same thing is occurring
Whenever Wagner's[11] operas are sung,
During the pauses in the 'cello's purring
The fiddle's wheazle and the brasses' bung,
When you have clapped the Gudehus unerring,
The Rieser's stomach and the Malten's lung,
And make an upward move, to take an airing
And stretch your legs, and do a little staring.

December 22, 1886

Well, well (but this "well, well" is optimistic,
And is a sign of rank Philistinism,
"So, so" is rather more characteristic
Of this dull world, itself a vulgarism)
I will today continue my sophistic,
But promise to attempt no witticism,
For Thanksgiving and Christmas disagree
With a dyspeptic reprobate like me.

And just in this most uncongenial season,
My birthday—heaven help me!—chanced to come,

Thus giving me another weighty reason,
When all the world is merry, to be glum.
On a day meant to pray, and feast, and freeze in,
Into life's pudding dropped this little plum,
Which, after three and twenty years of boiling,
Wonders what keeps the mess so long a-spoiling.

Some say it is a Cook who takes the trouble
To mix this witches' caldron of a dish,
Oh! not for food, but just to see it bubble
With living toads and flies and flesh and fish.
When these fall out, the flames their pain redouble,
Except a few, whom by a special wish,
The Cook at last picks out: "<u>Well done</u>," says he,
"Now for unending ages look at Me!"

And yet it is but proper to be thankful
Since the gods send us all the good we get,
Be it a drop of comfort or a tankful
Which for the thirsty human heart they set.
I think the blustering biped is a <u>blank</u> fool
Who says he doesn't owe the gods a debt,
Because, although his life may be a curse,
Would not the loss of good things make it worse?

I like to say "the gods," not "God," because
I mean those powers congenial, tutelary,
From whom our human life its virtue draws,—
Jehovah, Phoebus, Bacchus,[12] Jesus, Mary,—
And not that frightful universal cause
A theory inflicts on the unwary.
God is a monster, if God means the whole,
But the soul thanks the part that helps the soul.

    I'm thankful that, as matters go,
    I neither toil nor spin,
    But read the dear old wits, heigh ho!
    And like their death's heads grin.

    That I need neither reap nor sow
    Nor gather into barn,

But live ~~in Berlin town~~ among my books, heigh ho!
And ~~hear professors' yarns~~ spin the learned yarn.

That I, the human heart to know,
Was born into the old
One, Roman, Catholic, heigh ho!
And Apostolic fold.

And that, to learn how fateful flow
Our thoughts and institutions,
I turned up in the age, heigh ho!
Of E- and re-volutions.

That then I spent four years or so
At great old Harvard College,
To see the ~~worth~~ might of life, heigh ho!
And ~~worthlessness~~ the impotence of knowledge.

And found there is no vice so low
But nature lurks therein,
Nor any love so high, heigh ho!
But has a taint of sin.

And felt the warm and warmer glow
Of brotherly communion,
And learned to smile at fate, heigh ho!
In friendship's blessed union.

Let this but last till death's wind blow
And till my bones are rotten,
Then let the world sail on, heigh ho!
And let me be forgotten.

So, then, I went to a Thanksgiving feast,
In which a ball was added to a dinner,
And so I mean, on Christmas day at least,
To go to mass, like any pious sinner.
By thirteen marks my wealth was thus decreased,
Nor do I hope of grace to be the winner;
Alas! after I've prayed, and drunk, and flirted,
I'm not in love, nor tipsy, nor converted.

May, 1887 †Written in part earlier.†

Alas, this verse is woefully belated
And Germany seems, oh, so far away!
Yet if what is forgot were not narrated
What would our memoir-writers have to say?
And we digest bread better if we've waited,
After it leaves the oven, for a day—
At least, so say my aunts, and there's no question
That fresh-baked truth is bad for the digestion.

Else why should new convictions mean a colic
And old ones be a syrup to the soul,
Or prophets spend a youth so melancholic
With yearning bowels and with eyes that roll,
But in their later days begin to frolic
And find sin providential on the whole;
Or why have socialists delirious hair,
Or why do visions follow close on prayer?

Because,—unless you know a better reason,—
Truth-hunters often gulp their prey down raw,
Forgetting that the flesh they ought to season
And that the bones are fatal to the jaw
And that to drink God's living blood is treason
Against the human stomach's civil law,
And that, when all is spiced and boned and blooded,
The art of mastication must be studied.

Truly the love of wisdom means sobriety
Since truth, boiled down, is but a starving diet
Although of dressings there is such variety
That you like nothing else, if once you try it,
And are insured for life against satiety.
Philosophy—but who can justify it?
I'll leave it, just as God left the creation
And Milton[13] God, without justification.

I am the last who would deny the vanity
Of asking questions of the stars forever
Vain is the very knowledge that humanity
In seeking truth has made a vain endeavor
And vain the sad and sceptical urbanity

Which from these studies it is hard to sever—
And yet this vain urbanity and knowledge
Is just the thing for which we went to college.

That all is vanity is undeniable,
But joy is no less joy for being vain
And evils to which everything is liable
Are evils of which nothing should complain.
The facts are fixed, our mood alone is pliable
And call it dew or drizzle, rain is rain,
And by the proof that life is an inanity
We cannot change the fortunes of humanity.

The facts are fixed; and granting the fatality
That gives divine philosophy dominion,
I wish you would compare with impartiality
Her telescope with the poetic pinion
Or the balloon of faith's conventionality,
And tell me truly which, in your opinion,
Is the most proper to delight our vision
With pleasant vistas into fields Elysian.[14]

The poet's flight is upward like the lark's
His zenith always lies above his nest
And of the heavens' wonders all he marks
Is what can still the longing of his breast.
When on the working world he disembarks
He brings no comfort from his dreamy quest,
For fancy must be rather energetic
To make a wife and critic seem poetic.

And whither the balloon of faith will take us
Turns on the weather and the winds that blow
Which sometimes lost amid the clouds forsake us
And sometimes headlong on the desert throw.
Besides the best balloon that faith can make us
Sooner or later to the ground must go,
As is made certain by the earthly perch
Of every once aeronautic Church.

But if upon your house's upper story

Safe, ornamental, and at slight expense,
You build a little glass observatory
And mount therein a philosophic lens
And in the midnight quiet scan the glory
Of all that circles in the void immense,
You run no risks, you taste a noble pleasure,
And learn to run your round and keep your measure.

To mention midnight and an upper story
Reminds me of a certain German spree.
'Twas in a precinct half way up to glory
Where climbers find the opposite of glee,
In other words, the place was purgatory.
I went to a professor's house to tea
Up five flights at the south end of the city,—
However, the professor's wife was pretty.

Her office—German fashion—was to wait
Upon the men, and with an indescribable
Conglomerate of gou to pile each plate
(The wine, I'm glad to mention, was imbibable)
And to her seat just opposite her mate
She had to hurry back, whene'er contrivable,—
To eat, you think? Gott, nein! to—else I'm blest!—
Peel oranges and apples for the rest.

In this Arcadia[15] of fifth-floor simplicity
I lingered for the space of four full hours
Afraid of sinning 'gainst polite rusticity
By being first to quit the festive bowers.
I counted twelve score minutes of felicity
Then sleep quite overcame my counting powers,
And, turning to some use my nodding head,
I bowed adieu, and hurried home to bed.

———

The newspapers have lately been compiling
A list of the best hundred books to read.
Methinks the times are little fit for piling
A hundred articles on any creed.
So many oracles give cause for smiling

When ten commandments are so hard to heed,
Yet let me say the Bible should be read
And Shakespere in addition, not instead.

On Homer and Lucretius nature lays
With all her strength the seal of her authority;
Cervantes and Molière for the world's ways
Over all life's observers take priority
And Goethe and poor Byron paint our days
And by their failings show our inferiority,
While in Spinoza and in Schopenhauer
Is found the picture of the ruling power.

That's what my conscience says, for you must know
I have that article in my possession
And feel an inward satisfaction glow
Whene'er I see another man's transgression.
Did genial Hot-Scotch down my plumbing flow
I couldn't wear a happier expression
Than when all other feelings are subdued
By the sweet consciousness of being good.

Men cannot live without a conscience long
For nought so much the life within us smothers
As ignorance that other men are wrong.
You think your aims no better than another's
And hardly have the courage to be strong
In fighting for the earth against your brothers,
Till conscience, showing you alone are right,
Gives you a holy eagerness for fight.

Before I had a conscience I would cry:
Infinite pity, all-pursuing sorrow,
Eternal laughter of the hollow sky!
We fight today, our children fight to-morrow
Victors and vanquished in the battle die!
Ye gods, the life you lend I will not borrow;
Put not your cruel strength in my right arm,
But leave me weak, that I do little harm!

But now I have a conscience I cry out:

O blessed chance to smite the evildoer,
To rule the godless nations round about
And for their false faith substitute my truer!
I'll carry my election with a shout,
And I'll supplant my mistress' other wooer:
Gods of my fathers, all your blessings give
Since for your glory and my good I live.

Hail, Conscience! firm amid the wreck of creeds,
Bulwark of Saints, who human laws neglected,
Progressive too, since to fit growing needs
Thy oracles are readily corrected,—
By walking in thy ways a man succeeds,
By thee are all our interests protected,
And then the bliss of God thou givest us,
Who's always good, no matter what he does!

May 30, 1887

Why is it sweet to hear these church bells ringing
As if for me they had a message still?
The old bells question not why they are swinging
But feel their ancient music's iron thrill;
Without mistrust the tender blades are springing,
The birds at singing season sing their fill,
The morning sun is without reason there,
And why should my stirred bosom stifle prayer!

Though I lack faith to love, I have compassion
In sight of things so tragically fair
And feel the bitter wrong that God should fashion
An instrument for idle winds to tear
And wake tumultuous rhapsodies of passion
To die insulted in the vacant air,—
Or does God catch the sweet delirious notes
That thrill in little love-birds' swelling throats?

Almost—almost I think I might believe it,
And trust the echoes of these ancient walls,
For to a heart too willing to receive it
The tender promise of the ages calls.

Count I faith's loss a loss? Why not retrieve it,
Since fatal logic logically falls
And that proud reason from its base is hurled
That makes one vast unreason of the world?

Oh, if salvation were a trick of reason,
How easily would all the world be saved!
But roses bloom not in the winter season
Nor hope of heaven in a heart enslaved.
To break the bond with earth were easy treason
If it were God alone the bosom craved,
But we have chosen love and chosen rest
And with our wings' plucked feathers built our nest.

And from a high-walled garden, rich in flowers,
Upon the driving clouds I like to look
That cast their pleasant shadow on my bowers
And feed the trickling fountain and the brook.
Nor should I tremble if the gusty showers
Fell on my blossoms, or if thunder shook
My fragant arbors and their leafy gloom,
And with the things I love bestrewed my tomb.

But if I sickened of my hidden pleasure
And shuddered at the all-enclosing void,
If my heart pined for some excessive treasure
In whose fruition it were never cloyed,
Or, doting on existence over measure,
If I should hate the Maker who destroyed,
Then I should leave my garden to decay
Nor notice if my fountain ceased to play.

But putting idle thoughts of ease behind me
Forth I should wander to the windswept moor
And bid the mountains and the sea remind me
Of perfect goods that should like them endure,
And no false joy, no length of toil should blind me
To the exceeding wealth that made me poor
And more were my unbroken spirit blest
By heaven hoped for than by earth possessed.

Is there within the breast of the Eternal
A sanctuary left for banished joy
Where aureoled in golden splendor vernal
The angel of my dream is still a boy,
Saved from oblivion and the pit infernal,
From love's apostasy and shame's annoy,
Saved from his own tide's ebbing, silent, fair,
Benignant, holy, and forever there?

O bright ideal, lead the unsuspecting
To pluck their berries among thorns and briers,
And teach them the hard lesson of detecting
What fate will yield of all the heart's desires.
But spare me now, and pardon my neglecting
To cast my reason in thy quenchless fires.
Ablaze with mad saints' hearts: How wise a sin
To smile at the vain torment they are in!

So let me bless the alms the minutes proffer
And bask a happy beggar in the sun,
And hold at churches' gate my little coffer
And snatch the dropping pennies, one by one.
Within, the faithful may petitions offer
And pardon crave for sins that they have done.
But I am merry if I lose or win
Nor deem possession of my nature sin.

Oh, it is very pleasant to be small,
Making our step no longer than our tether,
And without languishing for wings, to crawl
And love the fragrance of our native heather.
Oh peace, to scan our fate and say: that's all!
Oh happiness, to meet that fate together!
Oh crowning joy, to die in fitting time,
And seal the poem with a noble rhyme!

[*Unsigned*]

[1]Boston was built on three hills, Beacon, Copp's, and Fort. Beacon, once a rigid peak sustaining the beacon for which it was named, has now a rounded top approached by a gentle rise from the waterfront. The state capitol dominates the landscape.
[2]In Greek mythology Pegasus was the winged horse of the Muses.

[3]George Gordon Noel Byron, sixth baron Byron (1788–1824), was an English romantic poet. Handsome, athletic (despite a clubfoot), brilliant, and magnetic, Byron was himself the model for the 'Byronic heroes' of his verse narratives. He was Santayana's first and lasting literary hero. Santayana relished *Don Juan* (1819–24), Byron's epic satire, and many of Santayana's early verses were written in imitation of Byron's meter and manner. The detachment, humor, wit, and satiric character of Santayana's mature style owes much to this early influence.

[4]Siegfried is the hero of the medieval epic, *Das Nibelungenlied*, upon which Wagner based his operatic tetrology, *Der Ring des Nibelungen*. Siegfried slays a dragon (Wurm) who is really a giant; a drop of the dragon's blood on Siegfried's tongue allows him to understand the birds.

[5]Giotto di Bondone (c. 1266–1337) was a great Italian painter. When asked by the pope for a sample of his work, the artist sent only a perfect circle painted with a free movement of his arm from the elbow.

[6]Diminutive form of the name.

[7]Unidentified.

[8]Peter Paul Rubens (1577–1640), foremost painter of the Flemish school, did many paintings for the Spanish and French courts, notably a series of twenty-four paintings of the life of Marie de' Medici (Louvre). He was one of the most popular and prolific artists of all time.

[9]Mary Magdalene may have been the harlot whom Jesus rescued from her evil life. She is identified by the name of her home town, Magdala, famous for its immorality.

[10]In Greek mythology, Leda was the mother by Zeus (who came to her in the shape of a swan) of two eggs, from one of which came Castor and Clytemnestra, and from the other Polydeuces and Helen. The subject of Leda and the Swan has been a favorite with artists, including Paul Veronese, Correggio, and Michelangelo.

[11]Richard Wagner (1813–83) was a German composer, conductor, and author famous for his operas. Most of his work is based on Teutonic and Nordic myths. His greatest work is *Der Ring des Nibelungen* (1869, 1870, 1876). Gudehus, Rieser, and Malten were opera singers.

[12]Phoebus is an epithet of Apollo, in his quality as the god of light. The name stands for the sun personified. Bacchus was, in the classic Greek view, a handsome young man and a powerful god (Dionysus). The fat, drunken Bacchus familiar from Renaissance paintings was a later concept. In the *Lusiad* (1572) of Camoëns, Bacchus is the guardian power of Islam and an evil demon of Zeus.

[13]John Milton (1608–74) was an English poet and prose writer, most respected in English literature. *Paradise Lost* (1667) is among his prolific writings.

[14]In Greek religion Elysian fields were the happy otherworld for heroes favored by the gods.

[15]Arcadia, a region of ancient Greece in mid-Peloponnesus, was inhabited by a pastoral people.

To Henry Ward Abbot
12 December 1886 • Berlin, Germany   (MS: Columbia)

Berlin, Dec 12$\underline{th}$ 1886.

Dear Abbot.

Thank you very much for your letter and the accompanying copy of the Sentimental Calendar.[1] I have read the stories with great pleasure, and lent the book to Houghton. I think I like "In a Garret" best of all. "Mrs Knollys" and "the Bells of Avalon" are also very touching. The play is good, but I think Stimson is at his best in the pathetic. His pathos is true— not false, moralizing pathos like Dickens'[2]—but the simple feeling of the pity of it all—of the helplessness and failure of our plans. You notice in "In a Garret" the ultimate lesson of experience and philosophy, namely Fate, or the feeling that the world isn't run in our interest or with any reference to our needs—you notice this, I say, used as a <u>motif</u>. It is interesting to see how what made the best old tragedies also makes the best modern stories. I think Stimson has a wonderful faculty of idealizing—of giving the essence of a situation. Take as an example the description of the old lady's world at the North-West End in "In a Garret" or the friendship of the two fellows in "Two Passions and a Cardinal Virtue." But in Stimson's fantastic writing there is for me something unaccountable and wilful. I don't see the point, for instance, of all the incantations of the necromancer, although the story is interesting. This is pro*f*bably owing to a defect in me, for I confess aimless fancy doesn't appeal to me in any shape, from "Midsummer Night's Dream" to "Alice in Wonderland". Art, it seems to me, must be more real than nature, or it loses its raison d'être. By more real, I mean more primitive, simple, and clear. A passion, feeling, or character must be presented more according to its inner essence and tendency than it can appear in the world owing to disturbing accidents. A composition which is nothing but a mass of accidents is worse than the truth, uglier than the reality. Why should one take the trouble of producing such a thing? Nature does it all too frequently; but she seldom succeeds in bringing a single seed or tendency to full development without distorting it and crippling it by some foreign influence. That is why she leaves room for art.

I go almost daily to the Museum here where there is a beautiful collection of Greek marbles and also a lot of early German and Italian paintings. I cannot pass from those statues to those pictures without feeling that I am passing from art to caricature. And nothing could be plainer than that the

ancients conceived art as simplification—elimination of accidents, and
expression of the soul as it would express itself in the most favorable possible environment. The Christians, on the contrary, in the service of religion, express the thwarting of the natural tendency of the soul, the
crushing of spontaneous life by the pressure of overwhelming external
power. This early Christian art is hideous—poor starved, crooked, cowed
creatures, in which the attempt at humanity seems to be about given up.
And it is interesting to trace the gradual recovery of the human type in the
pictures of the renaissance. I notice the same thing in the streets. Among
the Germans there are Mediaeval types and types almost classical. Among
the peasants and mechanics one sees frequently the bandy legged, big
headed, heavy nosed figures of the early paintings, and among the better
class one sees the tall, stolid, robust, καλὸς καὶ μέγας[3] type of the
ancients. Of course the fine Germans are coarser and sleepier than the fine
Greeks; but the resemblance is noticeable and shows, as it seems to me,
how the soul, such as it was or is, succeeds in expressing itself under favorable circumstances. The English aristocracy and the American too, are further examples of the same thing.

Excuse my delivering a treatise after this fashion, but whereof the heart
is full, the pen writeth. I am of course wrong and anti-Nortonian,[4] but I
hate sentimentalism and pre-Raphaelitism[5] with all my soul. It is not true
that deformity expresses the spirit—it only expresses the sad plight of the
spirit that can't express itself.

I am amused at the fun you poke at me, and at the advice Barrett
Wendell[6] gives me. I respect Scott for thinking me an ass, because it shows
a certain robust healthiness of judgment.[7] He doubtless sees the good and
bad in me with tolerable impartiality, for Scott is a sensible fellow, and usually hits the mark in what he says. I do not pretend that he has much deli-
cacy of judgment, but he is sound, and naturally values soundness above
other things. Droppers, however, if I understand him, comes to the same
conclusion in an other way.[8] With him it isn't a spontaneous judgment of
one man meeting another; he is biased by his crude dogmas and vulgar
standards. I submit that his tribunal has no jurisdiction in my case. But
every unsophisticated man is competent to judge any other, as a man; that
your table should think me a poor sort of creature is perfectly natural and
perfectly right. As ∧far as I am∧ a student, of course they have nothing to
say in the matter. Ward's case is less easily explained. And here let me
once for all say that what I write about other people, I am perfectly willing they should see or hear. If not, I shouldn't say it. If they are foolish

enough to get mad, it is they ∧who are∧ concerned. What I said about Ward's being a fallen angel was perfectly harmless and true, although perhaps not clear. But the unjust way in which the fellows at college treat Ward is to be regretted. It is owing to the prodigious social intolerance and narrow-mindedness which prevails in those parts; because Ward, if one takes him for what he is, and not for what Boston infallibility decrees everyone should pretend to be, is a delightful fellow. He has more virtues, too, than people give him credit for. But Harvard society judges people on a utilitarian standard; on the use they are to Harvard society as swipes or circus riders.

I proposed not to bore you with any more of my metaphysics or ethics, but I will say a word by way of conclusion. If you want any more, go to Spinoza and Schopenhauer, where I get mine. I don't think Royce's[9] argument against absolute relativity is a mere quibble. But it is not what he makes it, a proof of the existence of one absolute, either in truth or ∧right∧ conduct. Truly the assertion of anything implies the absolute truth of something—viz. of itself. Likewise when we desire something we imply the absolute value of something—viz. of the thing desired. Further, thinking means the taking of some idea for true, and acting the taking of some aim for choiceworthy. There is then an evident contradiction in saying that you take nothing for true or in acting and saying that you think nothing worth having. Because to take something to be true is but a definition of thinking, and to think something worth having is but a definition of desire (or the tendency to act.) But it doesn't follow that what is taken for granted is always the same truth, or the same aim: on the contrary history and memory report that the standards in both cases are variable. Royce's conclusion rests in fact on the idealistic dogma that knowledge of objects is but modification of the subject and therefore that truth cannot be a relation of similarity between the thought and the object, but must be a relation of congruity within a single thought (whatever such a thing may mean.) Put this together with the observation that a truth must always be assumed in thinking, and you get his conclusion that a single thought—the same and not the same as mine—is always assumed. All this mystification arises from the impossibility of being a thoroughgoing idealist, because just as all thought implies a truth, and all desire ∧a∧ value, so all consciousness of any kind implies the existence of something not itself outside of itself. If I started as Royce does with the doctrine that there is but one real thought and one real aim, I should of course believe that there was an absolute true and good; but Royce himself would grant that if there were many separate thoughts and aims, there would be just as many separate absolute truths and goods. He too is an enemy of dogmatism, until he formulates his own dogma.

Your sincere friend   GeorgeSantayana

[1]J. S. of Dale [Frederic Jesup Stimson], *The Sentimental Calendar, being twelve funny stories* (New York: Charles Scribner's Sons, 1886).
[2]Charles Dickens (1812–70) was a famous English novelist. His writing is noted for its direct style, remarkable descriptions of character, and sentimental crusades against social evils. Among his works are *Oliver Twist* (1837–39), *Bleak House* (1852–53), and *A Tale of Two Cities* (1859).
[3]Handsome and tall.
[4]Against the aesthetic preferences of Professor Charles Eliot Norton. [D. C.]
[5]Pre-Raphaelitism was practiced by the Pre-Raphaelite Brotherhood, a group of artists and poets formed in London in 1848. This group stressed rejection of academism which they traced to Raphael and the High Renaissance; they had a religious and moralizing cast.
[6]Barrett Wendell (1855–1921) was a member of the Harvard class of 1877, a founder of the *Lampoon*, and later an English professor at Harvard. He gave the first course of Harvard exchange lectures (1904–1905) at the Sorbonne, funded by the James Hazen Hyde Foundation. See *Persons*, 405–6.
[7]Presumably Samuel Mathewson Scott, class of 1886.
[8]Presumably Garrett Droppers, class of 1887.
[9]Josiah Royce (1855–1916), Santayana's dissertation director, was an English instructor at Berkeley (1878–82) and philosophy professor at Harvard (1882–1916). Influenced by the German idealists, Royce held that the world exists only insofar as beings with minds know it and the finite self knows truth only because the individual mind is part of the world-mind. Among his works are *The Spirit of Modern Philosophy* (1892), *The World and the Individual* (1900–1901), and *The Philosophy of Loyalty* (1908). Here Santayana condemns the logic of idealism, the prevailing philosophy of the time. See *Character*, 97–138.

To William James
9 January 1887 • Berlin, Germany   (MS: Houghton)

Berlin, Jan 9th 1887.

Dear Prof. James.[1]

I was delighted to get your letter[2] this morning, and hope you will forgive my not having written. The truth is I was ashamed to do so, because I have done those things which I ought not to have done, and I have not done those things which I ought to have done, and there is no science in me. But I have been having a good quiet time, picking up some German, and finding out which way the philosophical wind blows in these parts. On the whole, I think this semester has done me good, although I have not carried out the plan about doing laboratory work. Strong, to whom I have handed your letter, has probably told you that we have taken Prof. Ebbinghaus' psychology and Prof. Paulsen's ethics. These with some public courses I hear go over the ground covered in the philosophical courses at Harvard; and they have served to get my notions in shape and to convince me that it is high time to turn to something less general.

We have been several times to see Prof. Gizycki, who has been very kind and hospitable, lent us books and invited us to tea.[3] We have not yet taken any courses with him, but I like his method and point of view very much, and admire his penetration. Prof. Ebbinghaus has also asked me to dinner (Strong was away) and made it very pleasant for me. He has a very pretty wife and a fat baby one year old, and seems to entertain students a good deal. He asks me to give you his regards, and says he owes you a letter.

I find it pretty hard to make friends among the Germans, although they are good, simple-hearted people. The Americans are so much more lively that I always find myself going with them. There are a great many here, studying everything and nothing. I have been to some American dinners and Kneipes,[4] but otherwise I have poked comfortably at home, reading Goethe,[5] with whom I am in love. I find no difficulty in reading, and understanding lectures, but I am helpless when it comes to talk.

We still propose to take up physiology, but I am afraid as far as I am concerned I shall do little in that direction. I do not know how to work. I think, apart from the spelling book and the Greek grammar, I have never studied anything except for pleasure and with enthusiasm; and I find it terribly hard to peg at things that I don't seem to grasp. I recognize that all this is an additional reason for trying to get a feeling for the severe, minute way of handling things, and I shall try to do something in that direction. But my vocation ∧is∧ toward the human, political problems. Even the metaphysical and ethical puzzles appear to me rather as obstacles to be cleared than as truths to be attained. I feel now as if I could pass beyond them into the real world. And as far as the world we live in—I mean the social world—is to be got at by study, it strikes me it is to be found in history and political economy (not counting literature.) It is in this direction that I am drawn. Of course, if one could study everything, it would be very nice to understand the physical world too: but isn't it a fact that popular and second hand science, bad as it is, is less treacherous than popular Pol. Econ. and history? I can better afford to be misled about chemistry or physiology than about free trade or the Reformation. That is why I am anxious to look into these subjects for myself.

Strong is looking well, and seems to feel up to things once more. He is very reticent about all personal matters, so that I know less about what has been troubling him than you probably do. I am afraid I am not a sympathetic fellow for him to be with. Houghton is now in this house, and we have very lively discussions on all sorts of things.

I am awfully sorry about your wakefulness. I hoped to see your book before long. Perhaps your having less to attend to this year is a good thing for it. Loeser writes me that the philosophical club is much less active now, which I suppose means that '87 has few philosophers in it.[6] I look back on our discussions there with great pleasure. Indeed, Cambridge stands in my mind for everything that cozy and homelike.

With best regards to Mrs. James,[7] I am

Most sincerely yours

George Santayana.

[1]William James (1842–1910) and his brother Henry were sons of Henry James Sr., a wealthy American theologian. William studied art in Paris and pursued scientific studies in Germany. Harvard awarded him the M.D. in 1869.

James began teaching at Harvard in 1873 as instructor in anatomy and physiology. In 1876 he began teaching psychology and set up the first American psychological laboratory. His search for a metaphysical basis for his speculations about human consciousness and behavior led him to study philosophy, which he began to teach in 1879. At his retirement in 1907 he was recognized as the foremost American philosopher. His books include *Principles of Psychology* (1890) and *Pragmatism* (1907). James's relationship with his pupil, Santayana, was one of mutual respect for one another's intellect, philosophical disagreement, and temperamental antithesis.

[2]On 26 Dec 1886 James wrote to Santayana: "I can imagine no happier phase in an intellectual man's life than to be, at your age, turned loose into Germany to absorb all he can. And I doubt not you'll make the most of it. 'To thine own self be true.'" [D. C.]

[3]Georg von Gizycki (1851–95) was a professor of philosophy at the University of Berlin and a founder of the German Society for Ethical Culture. [D. C.]

[4]Beer parties.

[5]Johann Wolfgang von Goethe (1749–1832) was a German poet, dramatist, novelist, and scientist. Sources for his work included Greek mythology and German legends. Goethe was, for Santayana, one of the great philosophical poets, that is, poets who effectively express the dominant world view of their era. See *Poets*, 139–99, and *Egotism*, 43–53. Goethe's lifework was the drama *Faust* (1808, 1831).

[6]Charles Alexander Loeser (1864–1928), Santayana's first college friend, was the son of a wealthy Jewish merchant in Brooklyn. He had been to school in Switzerland, knew French and German well, and was at home in Europe; he later lived in Florence. Loeser was a learned art critic, but he wrote nothing and thus attained no reputation. See *Persons*, 215–21.

[7]Alice Gibbens James (1849–1922).

To Henry Ward Abbot
16 January 1887 • Berlin, Germany   (MS: Columbia)

Berlin, Jan 16th 1887.

Dear Abbot.

I can hardly tell you how much you amuse me. If you must guard against my influence, why do you answer my letters immediately? Then you talk about yourself as inspecting the universal joke of things from the point of view of the grave, and wondering what is the use of taking life in the unsophisticated and primitive way you attribute to me. At the same time you blame yourself for lack of energy, and give me your paternal blessing, trusting my illusions may not be shaken too rudely. But I should like to know how the path of least resistance has led you to the point of view of the grave, ₍pun apart₎, which according to my naive notion of things lies decidedₗy inₐ the direction of the greatest resistance. What you call the point of view of the grave is what I should call the point of view of the easy chair. From that the universal joke is indeed very funny. But a man in his grave is not only apathetic, but also invulnerable. That is what you forget. Your dead man is not merely amused, he is also brave, and if his having nothing to gain makes him impartial his having nothing to lose makes him free. "Is it worth while after all?" you ask. What a simple-hearted question! Of course it isn't worth while. Do you suppose when God made up his mind to create this world after his own image, he thought it was worth while? I wouldn't make such an imputation on his intelligence. Do you suppose he existed there in his uncaused loneliness because it was worth while? Did ₥Nothing ask God, before God existed, whether he thought it would be worth while to try life for a while? or did ₥Nothing have to decide the question? Do you suppose the slow, painful, nasty, bloody process, by which things in this world grow, is worth having for the sake of this perfection of a moment? Did you come into this world because you thought it worth while? No more do you stay in it because you do. The idea of demanding that things should be worth doing is a human impertinence. That things are to be done is settled first: when things are all full grown, it comes into the foolish head of a little insect buzzing about among the flowers, to ask if things were worth having, and he settles the question according to the quantity of honey he finds. That is to say he decides whether it is worth while to live and buz on the assumption that it is worth while to get honey—and the more convinced he is of the unalterable worth of honey the more forward will he be to proclaim the worthlessness of life. When he stops buzzing and worshiping honey—when he takes the point of view of the grave—he will stop asking for the worth of things.

The point of view of the grave is not to be attained by you or me every time we happen not to want anything in particular. It is not gained except by renunciation. Pleasure must first cease to attract and pain to repel, and this, you will confess, is no easy matter. But meantime, I beg of you, let us remember that the joke of things is one at our expense. It is very funny, but it is exceedingly unpleasant.

You have decidedly the best of the argument about art, and yet I think I meant something by what I said. Greek statues say so much more to me than any other form of art, and the Greek view of life and nature appeals to me so strongly, that I am unjust to other forms. The hapless word essence—bastard in its birth, overburdened during its life, and dishonored in its grave—seems to have made my sayings still more objectionable. I will venture on another formula, and say that all art should be characterization, not accumulation. Ancient art characterized natural tendencies, while modern art characterizes situations. But selection and the elimination of what doesn't help the characterization is as necessary in one case as in the other. I offer the humblest apologies for my rashness in regard to Stimson's story—I never looked for the moral! I see now what it means, but the way of expressing it still strikes me as a little wild. As I told you before, I am not a competent critic of the fantastic, being, so to speak, ghost-and-faery-blind.

You say you are a hero-worshiper. I have always felt an unsatisfied long-ing to be one—but I could find no hero. Tell me what is necessary to bring a man into the category of heroes—of course I don't mean what qualities in him, but what effects on the worshiper. I always have found a great diffi-culty in feeling the glow of admiration and the glow of loyalty towards the same persons. Admiration comes from qualities, and loyalty from obliga-tions. What one admires are abstractions and sides of character, but one is loyal to the whole man, as to one who is knit into one's own life. Perhaps I ought to confess that I worship one hero, although as a man out of his-tory he oughtn't to count. I mean Byron. Toward Byron, I do feel a com-bination of admiration and loyalty; I admire what he is in himself, and I ₐamₐ full of recognition for what he has been to me. For you must know, Byron is my first friend among the poets, and my favorite.

I don't propose to return to the metaphysics of my last letter. Still, I must accept your challenge for a definition of the terms. By absolute I understand that which is self-existent–that which might exist if everything else disappeared. Now, I didn't pretend to say that each man is an absolute being: I conceive that only the universe is an absolute being. But I meant that each man's standard of truth and worth was absolute–i.e. that it could exist without the existence of the other standards. Of course, if the man is not absolute, his standard could not have existed unless the whole world related to the man had existed; and so the standard, <u>as a psychological fact,</u> is relative to everything else in the world. But as a standard, it is absolute. We could not have the metric system unless the whole world was what it is: but as a standard the meter is absolute, and does not derive its value from its relation to the yard.

As you say, before claiming to understand and much more to condemn a man, one must know what sense he gives to his words. His definitions are often harder to understand than all the rest of his system–as, e.g. in Spinoza. The book is here the definition of the meaning of the words. As a general thing I find it works pretty well ∧to∧ begin by accepting a man's conclusions, and taking for granted they express the well-known facts, to work back from them to his premises. Thus one can often get at an author's starting point, and be better prepared to judge his logic. For instance, you hear a man declare that all men do and must act in the pursuit of pleasure. Accept the conclusion and see to what a definition of pleasure it will lead. You will have to grant that the pursuit may take place before the pleasure has ∧ever∧ been experienced. The pleasure therefore is not an image, not a memory, but a result. You will also have to grant that the pleasure pursued is not always attained. Thus you will arrive at the moderately true description of the facts which consists in saying that men must act in the pursuit of something of which they may have no idea and which they may never attain. Whether this uncertain something is a sensation or an action will be of no consequence. The difference between the hedonists and the naturalists will thus be reduced to an original difference in their observations.[1] If a man believes that men usually know what they are about, he will like the hedonists: if he thinks men usually don't, he will like the naturalists. I like the naturalists.

Hartmann is thought very little of in these parts.[2] He seems to belong to the dreaming rather than to the talking school of philosophers. I have hardly read him; what I have read has seemed to me rather futile. I think the talking philosophers alone are worth hearing: they come to you as one

man to another, on the basis of everyday facts and life. That is what makes
Aristotle so much the safest and wisest of men.[3] The dreaming philosophers should be read as one reads the confessions of converts and the
plaints of lyric poets. It may be very beautiful and very profound, but it
has only the interest of autobiography. To find out what may be known
about the world common to us all, we must go to those who have thought
it worth their while to talk about it.

Strong is back, and says he is all right. It is evident, however, that he is
still rather restless and unsatisfied. Tantum religio potuit suadere malorum.
By the way, do you ever read Lucretius?[4] If you don't, I should advise you
to try him. He fills me with the greatest enthusiasm and delight. The arguments are often childish, but the energy, the flow, the magnificence and
solidity are above everything. I am now reading St. Augustine's De
Civitate Dei, another splendid book.[5] It is historico-lyrical, like the Bible,
full of curious knowledge and broad lights thrown on the nature of the
forces that made Christianity. It is not technical, except here and there,
and so full of soul and divine madness that even the theology is never dull.
And then the glory of the Latin, so majestic, so clear, so sonorous! I tell
you ŗhour modern languages are mean and cramped in comparison.

Have you not seen Herbert Lyman? Tell me something about Ward, not
what he says of me.

Your dangerous friend

George Santayana

[1]In ethical theory, the view that the meanings of value judgments are equivalent to
statements about the natural world is called naturalism. Hedonism is the ethical position that the 'good' is definable only in terms of pleasure.

[2]Karl Robert Eduard von Hartmann (1842–1906) was a German philosopher whose
theory combining pantheism and panlogism was expressed in his *The Philosophy of the
Unconscious* (1869).

[3]Aristotle (384–322 B.C.), born in the Ionian city of Stagira, entered Plato's Academy
about 367 B.C. and remained until Plato's death in 347. For three years he supervised
the education of Alexander the Great and eventually founded the Lyceum in 335. He
combined brilliant intelligence with encyclopedic knowledge and was a prolific writer
on logic, ethics, psychology, natural science, natural history, politics, metaphysics, and
art. His naturalism led him to reject Plato's Theory of Forms and postulate instead his
hylomorphic conception of substance. Besides his enormous influence on Western
thought, Aristotle was the primary influence on the ideas expounded in Santayana's
Reason.

[4]Titus Lucretius Carus (c. 98–55 B.C.) was the Roman author of the unfinished *De
Rerum Natura* (On the Nature of Things), a didactic poem in six books which set forth
a complete science of the universe based on the philosophies of Democritus and
Epicurus. The central theme was that all things operate according to their own laws

and are not influenced by supernatural powers. Lucretius hoped to free men from the yoke of religious superstition and the fear of death. Santayana quotes from *De Rerum Natura*, 1.101: "So potent was religion in persuading to evil deeds."

[5]Saint Augustine (354–430) was reared a Christian but became a Manichaean. Later he reverted to Christianity. In 396 he was made bishop of Hippo Regius. St. Augustine utilized his immense learning in both apologetics of Christian doctrine and polemics against the Manichaeans, Donatists, and Pelagians. Catholics as well as Protestants consider him a master of theology. *The City of God* (413–27), in twenty-two volumes, is an apology for Christianity against the accusation that the Church was responsible for the decline of the Roman Empire.

To Henry Ward Abbot

5 February 1887 • Berlin, Germany   (MS: Columbia)

Berlin, Feb. 5th 1887.

Dear Abbot.

I am afraid I can't save you from solipsism[1] by argument, but I don't regret it much, since it is easy for you to save yourself from it by action. Philosophy, after all, is not the foundation of things, but a late and rather ineffective activity of reflecting men. It is not the business of philosophy to show that things exist. You must bring your bullion to the mint, then reason can put its stamp upon it and make it legal tender. But if you don't bring your material, if you don't give reason your rough and precious experience, you can get nothing from her but counterfeit bills—nostrums and formulas and revelations. Now a man's stock of experience, his inalienable ideas, are given facts. His reason for holding on to them is that he can't get rid of them. Why do we think at all, why do we talk about world, and ideas, and self, and memory, and will, except because we must? You say that you are will, and that your existence as such is given by immediate intuition. That is a rather complicated fact to be foundation of knowledge. If however it is a fact which you cannot doubt, it is a perfectly good foundation. Any fact you cannot doubt is—any inevitable idea is true. Now, if you imagine a being whose stock consists of this intuition of itself as will and of a world as ideas, I think you will be unable to make that being believe in other wills. That being would not rebel against solipsism; anything else would be impossible for it. It happens that we are not such beings; our inevitable ideas are not a self as will and as a reservoir of images. This notion is at best a possible one for us—possible together with innumerable other notions. If you find, however, that you can actually get rid of all other ideas and live merely on this stock, nothing can prevent your trying the experiment. Be a solipsist. Say "My own existence as will and the existence of a world of ideas in my mind—these I cannot doubt. But this is all that I find it necessary to believe. ⱥWith this faith I can do my business, make love to my sweetheart, write to my friends, and sing in tune with the spheres." If you can do that, what possible objection is there to your solipsism? Surely none coming from a sincere and disinterested philosophy. But <u>can</u> you do it? That is the question. I suspect that your business and letterwriting, your love and the music of the spheres, would fill your mind with other notions besides those first inevitable ones, and make these other notions no less ine[*illegible*]vitable. They would increase your inalienable stock of ideas and make your philosophy unsatisfactory, not because it had not accounted for the ideas you brought originally, but because you had more ideas now which it would need a different philosophy to account for. You must keep one thing always in mind if you want to avoid hopeless entanglements: we do not act on the ideas we ₐpreviouslyₐ have, but we acquire ideas as the consequence of action and experience. If you habitually treat these visions of other men as if they were your equals, you will <u>therefore</u> believe that they have will and intelligence like yourself. Now, your own survival in the world depends on your social relations, so that solipsism is a practically impossible doctrine. It could not flourish except among isolated beings, and man is gregarious.

So much for the practical difficulties of solipsism. Abstractly the theory cannot be disproved—what theory can?—yet I think it is not without its arbitrariness. Not that it is more arbitrary than any other which does not express our normal mental habits; all I mean is that it has no more reasonableness than any other imagined, artificial system. For what do you mean by <u>self</u>? What do you mean by existence <u>in the mind</u>? So long as you believe in a self-existent world of objects in space, you know what you mean by the objects in the mind. You mean those objects which are not self-existent in space. If, however, you abandon (or think you abandon, for I think the argument proves you have not really done so) the notion of objects self-existent in space, your phrase "objects in the mind" loses its meaning, since there is no longer any contrast between two modes or places of existenⱦce, one the mind and the other external space. Objects now do not come into the mind, they merely come into existence. Ideas, if they have no real objects, are real objects themselves. The quality of independence, unaccountableness, imperiousness which belonged to the things now belongs to the ideas. They are yours—they are in you—no more than the objective world was before. This is what makes idealists invent a universal consciousness in which the ideas eternally lie: if this world is to be an idea it has to be an independent, objective one. For see what the alternative is: There shall be only my own personal ideas—but how far do I reach? Did the world begin with the first sensation I had in my mother's womb? Evidently my foetus is an idea in my mind quite as foreign to me as you are. Did the world begin with the first idea I can remember I had? But in that case the world has begun at different points, since sometimes I can remember an event which happened when I was four, but then I could remember what happened when I was ~~one~~ three. Or shall the ideas in existence be only those I have at this moment? But this moment is nothing—it is a limit, it contains no ideas at all. Ideas are alive, they grow and change, they are not flashed ready made into the darkness. My ideas are therefore indeterminate in quantity and duration. As impossible as it is to say where one ˄of˄ them stops and another begins, so impossible is it to say where my consciousness becomes different from that of my mother, or wherein it is different from that of other men now. When in a crowd, in a contagion of excitement, we do not think in ourselves only but in other people at the same time. The bodies are separate but the consciousness is not. The result is that I have more ideas than I know; I can't trace them downward to there depth and full content, nor outward to their limits. In what sense, then, are my ideas mine? Only as the left side of a street is to the left; I only can talk of myself because I think of you, of my ideas because I postulate yours. If I existed alone, I should have no self, as the theologians very well saw when to save the personality of God the made him three persons. That is about all I have thought about solipsism. You say, or hint, that you are resigned to being an egotist and egoist, but not to be a solipsist. The things are but two sides of the same; it is harder to deny the existence of other men in thinking than in willing, be cause in thinking we depend so much on words, and books, and education—all social things, while in willing we are more independent, at least we feel more independent, for in reality we are perhaps less so. The more fundamental part of us is where we have more in common, and where influences are more easily exercised. It is more easy to influence than to persuade.

Strong and I propose to go to England about the first of March, so that when you write again you had better address care of Brown, Shipley & Co.[2] It is possible I may stay in England the rest of this year, but I cannot tell until I have seen the place. I naturally have to go with Strong, as our partnership is of mind and pocket; he is rather sick of this place because one is so isolated in it. Bad thing for a would be philosopher to complain

of isolation. Poor Strong! he is like a man up to his middle in cold water who hasn't the courage to duck. The cold water is the antitheological stream.   Hoping all this is nothing but your idea
                    I am sincerely your friend   G.S.

[1]As a metaphysical doctrine, solipsism is the view that nothing other than oneself exists. It originated with the Cartesian method of doubt and was (perhaps unknowingly) helped along by Locke's empiricism. Though Kant thought the theoretical plausibility of solipsism a "scandal to philosophy," his own views are also potentially open to it. Santayana would address this problem later in *Scepticism*, chapter III.
[2]Santayana's London bank which he used as a permanent address.

To Henry Ward Abbot
17 February 1887 • Berlin, Germany   (MS: Columbia)

Berlin, Feb. 17th 1887.

Dear Abbot.

Here is your brilliant letter of the 2nd which I will answer at once as usual, and instead of metaphysics, as in my last, we shall indulge in a little psychology. I see that we are apt to miss the point of each others arguments, but I don't mind that particularly so long as we catch each other's ideas.

The first subject of psychological analysis will be myself. You say that I turn out to have opinions contrary to those which it would be natural for me to have (1) habitually (2) in disparaging the dreaming philosophers (3) in having already reached the third or positivistic stage of thought, according to Comte, when in reality I am far removed from being a positivist.[1] (1) and (2) I will leave for you to explain. But in regard to my conversion to Positivism I will make a little confession and trust you will not refuse me absolution considering my sincere sorrow and firm purpose of amendment (Vide, Catholic Catechism) To be sure, I began as Comte says, with the theological stage. I found solutions satisfactory to myself for the supposed contradictions in the Trinity, the origin of evil, eternal punishment, and transsubstantiation. Having accomplished this little task, I began to take an interest in other things beside theology, because I had given up my original faint desire of being pious and holy. I then began metaphysics, but this second stage never took with me the shape of a belief in the authority of reason, i.e. of my own opinion. My own opinion usually satisfies me pretty well, but I hardly think it the necessary centre of universal tru̶and eternal truth. I have never believed in God, or the freedom of the will, or immortality, or a universal consciousness, or an absolute right and wrong, except in the Orthodox Catholic sense and for strictly devotional and ecclesiastical reasons. Once give up your attachment to religion and to the Church, and you give up the only reason for maintaining those dogmas. I have always seen that; so that I may well say that I have really skipped the metaphysical stage in the Comtian evolution. Spinoza was the man I believed in always, as the alternative to Catholicism. And it is only in Spinoza's manner that I am a positivist at all. I believe in the real world, in the world of thought and extension, of psychology and physics. God or substance with Spinoza equals reality; and this reality, which may have countless forms, we find only in space and in (other men's) consciousness. I say in other men's, because Spinoza was too sane to care to discuss anything from the point of view of subjective idealism. When one prints a book to convince other people, one oughtn't to discuss in it whether they exist. But this is all by the way, although some other day I will discuss with you the question of Spinoza's hedonism. If you care to know what I think about it in general, you can find it in my paper on Spinoza in the Monthly,[2] if you still have that [*illegible*]around.

The second subject of psychological analysis will be you. Your soul is a very good sensitive plate, but it has been underexposed, and the picture is blurred. You feel quickly and finely, but you don't grasp firmly, you let go and let slip (a new case of <u>laissez faire et passer.</u>)[3] You must try to think your thoughts whole and think them through, also your desires. For example you tell me when you remember yourself you envy a hero, when you forget yourself you worship him. Think that through, and you have all any man needs in the way of moral doctrine. You wish to be like the thing you worship—that is surely the height of moral ambition. But you don't hold on to this exalted ambition of yours; you let it float through your imagination, to make you aesthetic and pessimistic, but you don't let it grow upon you enough to make you act. I admit that your ideal moral ambition seems to me a bit high, and your practical ambition a bit dormant. Why should a man envy what he worships? Envy and worship seem hardly to belong to the same object. I will be exceedingly bold and attempt to tell you what you really feel. You worship or rather love the courageous will that rises up refreshed by blows—that is your complement. But you do not envy that at all, because that is not an object of your own will, but a different kind of will from yours which reveals itself to you as beauty and perfect action. What you envy is something else, something which is an object of your own desire, the living down the conflict between the real and the ideal, the sense of having found your place in nature, and of possessing that "continuous, supreme, and unending blessedness" which comes from making peace with the reality. Now if you will make this separation between what you worship and what you envy, you will straightway begin to pursue the enviable and to be satisfied without possession of the divine. That which we worship, that which we love with wonder and joy, is precisely that which is quite out of the sphere of our own attainments—the qualities of the opposite sex, of nature, and of the gods. You say that worship comes when we do not think of ourselves. That is true enough, yet the worship all the same arises from the relation of that divine thing to ourselves. A divine thing might be defined as that which enters into our life, but not as a competitor. A woman, for example, is despised in so far as she is a human individual competing with others for life, especially because her methods of competing are small and mean; but she is loved and even worshiped as the complement of man, as something filling out his life without sharing his qualities. Now when it comes to a hero, of course it is not so easy to separate the qualities in him which are beyond our sphere and those which are necessary to us in order to find our own place in the world. To make this separation is the whole problem of life. You know Goethe says that right living is founded on renunciation, that is, on seeing precisely what lies beyond our sphere and ceasing to desire that, except as an object of contemplation. At the same time all that lies on this side of that limit, is perceived to be attainable, to belong to us potentially. If we are without it, we shall rebel against this state of things, and with reasonable hope (since the thing is by us attainable) we shall begin to strive after it. When it is attained we shall have reached Spinoza's blessedness, and shall say to our last moment ₐof lifeₐ, as Faust did "Linger still, thou art so fair."[4] But all this rapturous optimism, you must remember, comes after renunciation—after we desire nothing that we can't get. Satisfaction is then evidently inevitable.

The third subject of psychological analysis would be Ward; but I wrote him a long letter yesterday in which I expatiated a good deal on that subject, so I will take Herbert instead now. True that he has broadened very much in the last years, but I have had no more to do with it than with the ripening of a sound apple on a sound tree. The only man in college whom I have really improved is Loeser, and that because (both in the good and bad sense) he was eminently capable of improvement. But Herbert has had more influence on me than I on him, because more than any other of my friends he has the virtues which are outside of my sphere, and in which consequently I can take a pure, objective satisfaction. He is that uncommon creature, a man with all the ordinary virtues and none of the ordinary vices. His understanding, as you say, is good—good in quantity but especially good in quality, for he is open to truths without being puzzled by problems. A perplexed mind is an unhealthy mind, and the philosophy perplexed minds think out is always sick. To be at home with your own truth and at peace with it, is the right condition in which to sally forth in search of foreign truth. That is why my heart loathes and my reason despises all your sect-founders and sect-changers, and all your people who want to begin to make everything afresh. Not having any eyes for what is near and present, nor any love for it, they have no understanding for what is to come, which must necessarily come out of the present and be built upon it. But nothing appeals to me so much as the people who live quietly and unhesitatingly on their own ressources—spiritual and social—without feeling called upon to abandon their natural possessions to run after all kinds of novelties and crudities. Now Herbert is an excellent example of a man with a right appreciation and attachment for his natural surroundings—with a wholesome willingness to live under the conditions in which he finds himself. As you may imagine, the type of character and life which is represented by Americans among men and Bostonians among Americans and the Lymans among Bostonians, is hardly my ideal. It is a self-checking, horrified, narrow-minded, sweet-saliva sort of existence, unbearable to a man and an animal. Yet see how gently, how considerately Herbert has grown out of it, without breaking with its forms, and without repudiating it in his heart for a moment. That seems admirable to me. The thing was good in its way, and wisdom consisted in not giving it up, except in the sense in which one gives up what takes a subordinate place in one's life. It is this sort of action that prevents a man's getting upset; and it has given Herbert his reliability, his sweetness, and his faculty of doing right naturally.

You ask for a long letter, so I will begin another sheet, and fill it with a little psychology of a more general sort. And first I will say that a certain lack of mutual understanding between you and me on the subject of ˄the˄ point of view of the grave and of the busy bee, seems to arise from the fact that I look at the things as psychological events, and you more as logical or moral necessities. Now I maintain that all logical and moral necessity is simply a psychological fact—to be accounted for by psychological laws. Whether the joke of things is funny at three score years and ten, is for me a purely psychological question. As a matter of fact you will admit, I suppose, that most old men, perhaps because they <u>have</u> had such a disagreeable time of it, look back on their lives with a foolish satisfaction, and wouldn't like to hear about the veil of Mâyâ[5] having generously made fools of them, or about their having stultified themselves with a wife and children, to say nothing of the effects of beer, ~~on~~ to which subject they would consider all allusions impertinent. They would on the contrary declare that they had seldom been deceived, that they had done a great deal more for the world than people gave them credit for, and that as to the joke of things, their own affairs were too momentous to be funny, and their approaching loss anything but a joke. It seems to me therefore that the vanity of life is less visible from the point of view of the grave in the sense of the end of an old man's life, than even from the point of view of the mortified or will-overcoming man which I took up in my other letter. The old man's attitude toward life is like his attitude toward his own children, who represent life for him henceforth—namely, fatuous and fond. The saint's attitude is one of indifference to the prizes of life accompanied with readiness to share its struggles and sorrows. The saint is precisely in the position of your damned fool; he buzzes without expecting honey. And the reason is that if you really give up desire, you give up preferences: peace and war, pain and pleasure become the same. You may not understand this state of mind, but it is approached by some people. And you cannot deny that in the absence of preferences it is just as wise or foolish to act as not to act. The saint does not feel that he is wise and prudent in his willingness to act; he feels that the reason or cause of his action is outside of him—that it is God that acts in him. He is in the position of my busy bee, if in the recognized absence of honey or of desire for it, it should know itself to be made to buzz by physical causes. ~~He~~ It would not resist these physical causes, even if you said that they were making a damned fool of it, because ~~he~~ it has given up all desire for honey, which wisdom also is. If nothing is desirable or satisfactory in this world, why is wisdom better than folly? Readiness to act under divine (i.e. physical) compulsion is a consequence, not a contradigtion, of the doctrine of vanity. I am not sure that you will not call this also sophistry and Spencerian unknowables;[6] know, however, that it is what orthodox mystics and pessimists have always taught. Cf. Ecclesiastes, Thomas à Kempis, Deutsche Theologie, St. John of the Cross, St. Theresa, etc.[7]

The psychology of your dogmatic pessimism of your pessimism that says we <u>ought not</u> to live, is not hard to explain. Given a man full of naive desires; let him be so favorably situated that his naive desires are for the most part satisfied, and he begins a search for refined and unmixed pleasures. He thereupon becomes blasé, and sings with Solomon,[8] when not overpowered by the demands of his eight or nine hundred concubines, that all is vanity. If, unlike Solomon, he is not also a wise man, he will reason with himself thus. "I wanted pleasures, continuous and unmixed–that is the only object I had in life, ergo, the only object which anyone not a damned fool can have. This object is unattainable. There is then no object to make life worth living: ergo, no one <u>ought</u> to live." This last of course is on the supposition that we oughtn't to do what isn't worth doing–an undeniable maxim when it is question of a means to an end, but an impossible one when it is question of ultimate ends. For if our ultimate end must be worth choosing, ~~it~~ we ʌmust have a further standard by which we can measure its worth, that is, it must not be ultimate. Ultimate objects are facts needing no justification: if you try to justify them you are in the position of the Indian who made the earth rest on the elephant, or of the European who made it hang on God. The latter had the disadvantage, by the way, of not knowing about the tortoise. The confusion in all these cases arises from the attempt to apply to the whole what by its nature applies only to the part–rationality, worth, damned foolishness, weight, and causality, being all relations between parts, which the whole cannot have simply because it is not a part of something bigger, nor ~~an object~~ ʌa meansʌ to any ulterior object.

I have hardly left myself room to say that I am going to England for six weeks or more, and that my address is Brown, Shipley & Co.

Your sincere friend
George Santayana

---

[1]Auguste Comte (1798–1857) was a French philosopher and social theorist. His doctrine, positivism, postulated that all sciences go through three stages of development: theological, metaphysical, and positive. He thought that human society goes through similar stages. His philosophical system is presented in *The Positive Philosophy of Auguste Comte*, 2 vols. (1853).

[2]*The Harvard Monthly* was founded in 1885 by A. B. Houghton and was dedicated to the publication of the best work by the Harvard student body and faculty. Santayana was a member of the original editorial board, and many of his early works first appeared there.

[3]To allow something to pass one by unhindered or unexamined.

[4]Part Two, *Britannica Great Books* 45, 155.

[5]In Hinduism the veil of Maya is the illusory world of the senses as opposed to the unitary mystical world of truth.

[6]Herbert Spencer (1820–1903) was an Englishman who applied the study of natural sciences and psychology to philosophy, finding in the doctrine of evolution the unifying principle of knowledge and applying it to all phenomena. He did not deal with the "unknowable" but instead dealt with those things which could be compared with and related to other things.

[7]Ecclesiastes is a book of the Old Testament believed to be written by Solomon. A somewhat cynical essay, it begins with the theme that "all is vanity" but eventually praises hard work, wisdom, and mercy. Thomas à Kempis (c. 1380–1471) was a German monk who was author or copyist of the devotional work *The Following* (or *Imitation) of Christ*. *Eine deutsche Theologie* is a historical account of German mystics by an unknown author. Saint John of the Cross (San Juan de la Cruz) is the religious name of Juan de Yepes y Alvarez (1542–91), who was a Spanish mystic and poet. He took an active part in Saint Theresa's efforts to reform the Carmelite order. Saint Theresa (Teresa de Cepeda y Ahumada) (1515–82) was a Spanish Carmelite nun and mystic who was born near Ávila. She became Mother Superior and founded seventeen convents.

[8]Solomon (d. c. 932 B.C.) was the son and successor of David, King of Israel. During the first part of Solomon's reign, the Israelites experienced great prosperity and peace. The latter portion was characterized by discontent over heavy taxation and increasing dissatisfaction amongst the northern tribes. The splendor of the court and Solomon's enormous building projects were part of the cause.

To William James
21 February 1887 • Berlin, Germany   (MS: Houghton)

Berlin, Feb 21[st]1887.

Dear Professor James.

I am very much obliged to you for your articles on Habit and on the Perception of Space[1]. I have read them with great interest—all the more because they go over some of the points you brought out in Phil. 2 and 9. I remember how much the idea of the nervous system as a sort of recording angel struck me at that time. It touches one of my pet questions, the sanction of Ethics, the supposed disappearance of which alarms Mr. Lilly and his school.[2] I can't help feeling that if people were more inclined to look for the sanction of morals in the facts, they would stop worrying about the future of morality.

The tone of the philosophers here is good-humoredly positivistic. Christianity and Hegelianism are mildly spoken of, and accounted for as historal movements. Some of the professors are transcendentalists,[3] it is true, but hardly in the interests of theology. Dr. Deussen, for instance, is a thoroughgoing Schopenhauerians while Prof. Paulsen is a Spinozist, with

tendencies toward state socialism. Prof. Ebbinghaus calls himself a materialist <u>im besseren Sinne</u>.[4] But everybody (with the possible exception of Dr.
Deussen, who will not hear of disbelief in the τὸ ὄντως ὄγ[5]) is calm and
benevolent, and thinks philosophy was made for man and not man for philosophy.

Strong and I intend to spend the coming vacation in England, where we
find we can go very cheaply by way of Hamburg. My address will therefore be care of Brown, Shipley & Co, and anything sent to me for Strong
will reach him. He is looking well and says he feels very much better. He
has been working two hours a day over Lotze's psychology and hearing
lectures with me.[6] He seems to be a little afraid of himself in view of the
probability of his getting a chance to teach at Cornell next winter. I tell him
he is well prepared enough and should thank his stars that he can begin to
learn in a practical way by teaching. Still, considering what good friends
we are, Strong tells me astonishingly little about himself, perhaps because
he thinks I don't understand how he feels about things, or perhaps because
he is naturally reserved. But the fact is I have no idea what has been the
matter with him this winter, except that evidently he has not been at ease.

I myself have done very little tangible work, although I have been reading all sorts of things, especially Goethe. I don't think my time has been
wholly wasted, as I have gathered a good many impressions besides a
working knowledge of German—enough, that is, to read and understand,
but not enough to talk connectedly. I ought to have got along much better
with the language, but I have really had very little occasion to speak it, and
the pronunciation is so abominably hard that I hardly trust myself with
more than a syllable at a time. I enjoy hearing it, however, especially in
the hearty, honest native way. On the whole I am very glad I came to
Germany, although the superiority of the place from the student's point of
view is not so great as I had imagined. In health too, I am feeling well, better a great deal than last year when, as you may remember, I was a little
under the weather. In Spain, too, during the summer my stomach became
refractory, but this cooler and moister climate made everything all right
again. For a while I had some trouble with the complicated cooking here
in vogue—but custom can make one swallow any dish, even if it contains
thirty nine articles.[7]

In England I expect to have a very good time, as I have never been
there for any length of time. In London, too, there are several members of
our—i.e. the Sturgis—family, whom I shall enjoy meeting.[8] Socially I have
had a dull time here, as the Germans are rather impossible to get at, and

when gotten at not very entertaining, while the Americans are often far from pleasant. I have missed my college friends very much, although they have been very good in writing to me. In fact, I find myself with a rather formidable correspondance to carry on, with my family in Spain, and my family in America, and my friends at present scattered in the four quarters of the globe. The fellows that have just graduated seem for the most part to be very much exercised on the subject of themselves and their future, as is natural enough. What I enjoy most here is the Museum, where I go almost daily. The ancient statues are the most beautiful things I have ever seen.

Hoping you will find time to write to me again, I am

Most sincerely yours

George Santayana

[1]Probably chapters in *Principles of Psychology* (1890).

[2]William Samuel Lilly (1840–1919) was a controversial English writer and champion of the Catholic Church. [D. C.]

[3]Transcendentalists were high-minded and idealistic, stressing individualism, self-reliance, and social reform. Their system held that there are modes of being beyond the reach of mundane experience.

[4]In a better sense.

[5]That which really is.

[6]Santayana wrote his dissertation on Rudolph Hermann Lotze (1817–81), a German metaphysician who was highly regarded in his day but who has since fallen into obscurity. Philosophically, Lotze supported precise investigation and experimentation yet also appreciated the influence of feeling. He thought these two could not be separated in the total life of an individual. His works include *Logic* (1841) and *Metaphysic* (1843).

[7]The Thirty-Nine Articles are the articles of faith of the Church of England, the acceptance of which is obligatory on its clergy.

[8]See *Persons*, 51–53.

To Henry Ward Abbot

23 March 1887 • London, England   (MS: Columbia)

London, March 23ᵈ '87.

Dear Harry,

I think it is better we should indulge in first names, if you have no objection, because we are really friends on personal and not on business grounds. Your last letter, like all the others, interests me exceedingly, although I confess your view of Catholicism and orthodoxy in general is pitiful. Allow me to tell you that you don't know what you are talking about. I say this simply because it is what I think, and not because I am angry or provoked, and I will let the matter rest, without attempting to explain to you why religion is fit for other people ~~than~~ ˄besides˄ whores and servant girls. I am sure that you say this absurdity impulsively and that you wouldn't maintain it in the face of history and daily experience. Yet I can't let you tell me things of that sort without protesting against them as vigorously as possible. I like myself to ridicule religion. There is nothing in the world which seems to me ˄to be˄ without absurdity of some sort in it, and I see no reason why we should not enjoy the ludicrous wherever we see it as much as we enjoy the beautiful. We are surely exercising a faculty on its appropriate object. But when you deny to religion the right to awaken any other feeling but that of scorn, you ˄are˄ depriving yourself of some of your noblest faculties, by depriving them of their only object. And what is worse, you are insulting those better equipped mortals who possess the religious organ, which you call an excrescence because you don't know how to use it. Pray try to look at the matter otherwise.

I have been two weeks in London now, and enjoyed myself very much. I like the place, and above all I like the people. They are handsome, gentle, manly, and courteous. There may be machinery all over this cathedral, but it is a cathedral still. This beautiful English temper is what has been gained by not breaking with the past, but by keeping up every institution until it absolutely refused to be kept up. I have found a boarding house at Notting Hill, N.W. from the Park, where I get good food cheap, and where there are a number of fellows, one of them exceedingly nice. He is a Scotchman from Dundee, who is in business here, and belongs to the Artillery Volunteers and is also fond of pictures. I talk with him of an evening over a cup of coffee by the dining room fire,–for theatres are dear. I have already seen the main sights, but as you know I care little ∅for "places of interest" unless there is something beautiful or impressive about them. I like the Tower, and Westminster Abbey, but I don't like the British Museum. Perhaps the best sight is London itself, which I always imagined I should like. It is more like an American than like a European city, and makes me feel safe and comfortable again. There was a certain isolation for me at Berlin, on account of the language and the barbarism of the inhabitants; here I stand on my own feet, and can go into things if I like. Most probably I shall stay here until the summer–in England, I mean. Strong is much inclined to go to Cambridge for a term, and I will go too.

<u>March 25</u>ᵗʰ You see by this interruption how differently I am situated here from the way I was at Berlin. There I could sit down to a letter and

not get up till it was finished even if it carried me into the small hours of the night. It was very pleasant to write to old friends in the quiet time, with the bedroom door securely locked against all the actual and present world. I hope in a week or two to be living again in the student fashion, and to have my days ~~made~~ ‸cut‸ out of whole cloth. Then I may undertake your cure, as you demand, although if you expect me to cure you of pessimism you have struck the wrong man. "Eat, drink, and die" is precisely my motto, only it has come to seem to me a very comforting one. Our demands, especially our emotional demands, are easily changed. That hope and belief we are deprived of are not necessary for us; we can substitute something else for them. Belief in God and in the monstrous importance of our own condition is rather a source of unhappiness and unhealthy strain than of consolation. The one consolation is the "vanitas"— the voice of judgment crying "All's well" through the dark silence following the extinction of the world. All is finite, all is to end, all is bearable—that is our comfort. And while it lasts, we can enjoy what we find to enjoy, running our scales as merrily as possible between hunger and satiety. We are souls bereaved, to be sure, but we can be easily comforted. Off with the old love and on with the new, if you have any sap in you. If you haven't, of course you will mope and whine, and lament the loss of your first and only love. As for me, I confess I am happier without religion of the optimistic sort—the belief in a Providence working for the best. Disbelief leaves one freer to love the good and hate the bad. One stands frankly on one's own ground (as the English government does in its foreign policy, where it stands virtuously in defense of its own supposed interests) and judges all things boldly according as they help or thwart one's desires. "That is a sensible man," I say when I see one of this stamp, "and it is a pleasure to do business with him."

But while I say that I get on better with this new love, that she cooks my dinner and darns my stockings better than yonder angel, why should I insult my old love and call her a whore fit only for sailors and drunken knaves? That is what you want me to do. The fact is Christianity is still a possible system, seeing that intelligent men are still able to believe it. If you or I are not able, what a piece of foolish arrogance it is in us to vituperate those fortunate mortels whose mental kalleidoscope still presents the old and beautiful pattern. And how vain it is to wish to disturb them, when we know that the least shock will destroy that vision, and that probably we may turn and turn forever without finding it again. The trouble with you, my dear fellow, is that your are still a dogmatist, and believe that nobody has a right to have a picture different from yours. This seems to me the vainest of all superstitions. You look back at all the conceptions of the race; you see their causes, historical, physiological, and geographical; and yet—mirabile dictu![1]—you put your own conceptions outside your own system of the world. Your views are not caused, it would seem, by historical, physiological, or geographical conditions. They are absolute and eternal, and only servant girls and prostitutes can have others. Don't you see that your own conceptions are precisely on a par with all the others, according to your own doctrine, and that their value cannot consist in anything but their necessity here and now and for you? You say: These and these causes produce conviction in men. And you should add: I am only a man, and the fact that the said causes have produced convictions in me also, is a confirmation of my doctrine. You will have convictions ∧in your head∧ but you will have them as you have hair upon it, and it will be as absurd for you to quarrel with men for differing from you in belief as for having a flaxen or a woolly crop. You have no obligation to like theologians, any more than to marry niggers, but you must fight them in a pitched battle, pitting your resources against theirs, and the event will show—not who is right, for ~~their~~ there is no "right" in our system—but who is to survive, and which view is to be held hereafter with conviction, until some change, historical, physiological, or geographical cause the advent of a new orthodoxy.

This, unless I am much mistaken, is the result of knowing a little geology, as you put it. So far from showing any absurdity or contradiction in Catholicism, it shows the absurdity and contradiction of abusing Catholicism as if it were not a perfectly normal and inevitable condition of mind, produced by causes similar to those which produced all beliefs—including our own—and therefore as fit to be held by men as any other system. And if you had abused some new fangled, impossible sect, whose capacity to produce illusion and govern life was very doubtful, one might excuse your contempt: but such a tone is foolish when it is question of Christianity, on which our civilization is mainly built, and whose destruction means almost the destruction of our world.

I have run on in this way, although I said at the beginning of this letter that I would leave the subject for the present. Still, no harm is done. I have very little to say about what has been going on. Boylston Beal has shown me one or two very interesting letters of yours. Royce's novel[2] will be curious reading—I don't know at all what to expect. Of course it will be in the haec fabula docet[3] style, but I have no idea how he will present the moral. I have been reading Fullerton's letters to "My dear Evnard[4]". Highly amusing, and sometimes not half bad. Any news you can send me about the fellows is always welcome. Is there no chance of my seeing you over here? They tell me it is possible Ward may come—I do wish he would.

Sincerely yours
George Santayana

[1]Wonderful to say!

[2]*The Feud of Oakfield Creek: A Novel of California Life* (Boston and New York: Houghton Mifflin and Co., 1887).

[3]This story teaches.

[4]William Fullerton wrote book reviews for the *Boston Record Advertiser* for a while between leaving Harvard and going to London and Paris and sometimes signed himself Zadoc Everard. Santayana and a few other classmates were in on the hoax. (per Marion Mainwaring)

To Henry Ward Abbot
23 April 1887 • Oxford, England   (MS: Columbia)

Oxford, April 23ᵈ '87

Dear Harry.

I came here from London the day before yesterday, and am settled with Strong in a rather pleasant house. We have a sitting room downstairs and two clean bedrooms, and, according to the custom of the place, keep house for ourselves—the landlady cooks and we pay the market and grocer's bills. The arrangement is cheap and convenient—I live on less than two pounds a week all told and much more comfortably than at Harvard. I shall stay four weeks at least, and then wend my way to Avila, via Paris, to await further developments.

I am going to go on reading German while I am here, and when I get home, where there are no books, I hope to do some writing. I have a number of chaotic notebooks and loose sheets, scribbled last winter in my Berlin hermitage, out of which I shall try to bring order. That is what I have before me for the present.

While at Oxford I hope to meet some more specimens of the English race, thanks to Lord Russell, who has been a godsend to me.[1] I don't tell you anything about my adventures with him because I have to maintain with you my reputation as a philosopher, and in this respect I have quite lost my reason. When I am safely in Spain again, and can treat the matter objectively, I will make a full confession of my fall—from grace and self-control I mean and not into the Thames, although this also is mortifying enough.[2] Herbert Lyman can tell you about it, if you care to know.

Your letter of to-day is very strong–on a higher plane altogether from your last one. I am not sure that I do know your weakness; I think it is your strength that I am discovering. You have the real truth on your side when you say that I go too far in my psychological treatment of belief. It is impossible to abandon the postulate of one eternal and objective truth–I fully admit that and should have said so in my argument. Truth is the form of our judging imagination just as space and time are forms of our perceptive imagination. It is as impossible to make a statement without postulating a real objective truth, as to conceive a figure without implying indefinite space. But it is precisely on account of this necessity of postulating truth, that I claim respect for such systems as Christianity–not mere courtesy, but the sincere recognition that it stands on the same footing as our own system. I protest against the solipsism of creeds. I demand that just as ∧a∧ sane ~~men~~ ∧man∧ recognize∧s∧ that ~~their~~ ∧his∧ neighbors are centres of reality for themselves just as much as he is a centre of reality for himself, and that he appears to them as a mere object with as good right as they are objects to his own consciousness; so I say should ∧a∧ system∉ recognize that it appears as a psychological fact in other systems <u>with as much justice</u> as other systems appear as psychological facts to itself. I do not propose that we should give up the postulate of absolute truth (although I may sometimes seem to say so, owing to the difficulty of expressing oneself): I only propose that we should abandon the assertion, implied in any claim of the <u>exclusive right</u> of our own system to be considered true, that absolute truth is postulated once only–in one consciousness–instead of being postulated in many separate acts. This is not clear–I can't make it clear. But my conception is that we must believe our beliefs to be absolutely true, just as we believe ~~ourselves~~ ∧our feelings∧ to be perfectly real; but that this necessity no more excludes our admitting other beliefs as absolutely true for themselves–from their own point of view–than our belief in the reality and subjectivity of our feelings excludes our belief in the reality and subjectivity of other people's. The advantage which you try to give beliefs founded on "reason and logic" is illusory, as it seems to me, because reason and logic are internal to systems, not external to them. You don't get your convictions through reason and logic, but build reason and logic on your convictions. The coercive force of logic depends on the similarity of the structure of human minds, on which the necessity of logical axioms also depends. The sanction of logic is in psychology, not vice versa. That reasons must be given is a fact, but there can be no reason why facts, why the world at all, should be given. As a matter of fact, I agree with you that Christianity is becoming untenable, because the firm and unshakable convictions in our minds are no longer Christian doctrines, but scientific ones. You may be able to argue a man out of his Orthodoxy because you may find in his own mind your own convictions latent, and by your fanning there you may make them consume and dissipate his orthodox beliefs. Hence the very just opposition of the Church to lay education—to the storing of the mind with convictions unassociated with her creed, so that the latter may subsequently be dropped out of the man's thinking without serious disorganization of ~~the~~ his mind. It is for this reason that I believe in the strength of empirical philosophy as opposed to subjective systems. There are certain convictions which cannot be exiled from the mind, convictions about everyday practical matters, about history, and about the ordinary passions of men. A system starting from these universal convictions has a foothold in every mind, and can coerce that mind to accept at least some of its content. The same is not true of systems founded on extraordinary and exceptional experiences, because these simply may cease to exist, in which case the system loses its hold. This is what is happening to Christianity. So I should say that the criterion by which one system is judged to be more tenable than another is not logic byut necessity—not the greater reasonableness of believing its facts but the greater impossibility of disbelieving them.

You are not appreciative enough, it seems to me, of the virtues of English people. This magnificent humanity of theirs is something which I honor more than amiability or freedom from prejudice. They treat one contemptuously perhaps, but haven't they a cause? aren't they cleaner, and richer, and more high bred than other people? I like a man to feel his worth, just as I like a man to feel his beauty, otherwise the splendor is taken out of both. But at the same time he should be humble, i.e. glad to recognize his shortcomings. Nothing is more exhilirating than to see the fit man ∧come to the front∧ in full consciousness of his divine right to lead; and nothing is more edifying than to see the unfit, conscious of their incapacity, look up to the leader with loyalty and gratitude. Such a thing reconciles one with the imperfection and weakness of man. The absurdity of conceit comes when a man is not willing to yield where others are able to conquer. The word conceit suggests the criticism of me you quote from Marcus Kimball.[3] It's quite true that I trust myself too much, especially in matters of opinion and judgment. But I really believe in myself less than you think. If I were asked whether I ∧would rather∧ awake tomorrow morning as myself or as Marcus Kimball, for example, I should be willing to toss up for it—more than he would say, I fancy. I can't help my philosophical passion. If I were not to generalize and preach I should have to stop thinking. If Charlie Minot knew me he would know how sincerely I agree with him about myself.[4] I am certainly mediocre as a whole, and in the important human qualities—courage, serviceableness, and honesty—sadly deficient. I have of course my strong side—a strip of greatness, as it were—but I am altogether too poor a specimen of humanity for this to tell in the long run. Don't bet anything on my turning out well. I don't care enough about it myself to work for success. What I crave is not do great things but to see great things. And I hate my own arrogance and would worship the man who should knock it out of me. Says a Spanish song:

I am searching land & ocean
For the man that I might love,
And whenever my heart finds him
Then he will have found his slave.

Man or thing—it makes no difference—but heaven grant it be no woman. I should like very much to have you and Ward stay with me at my wife's—even in the face of possible infidelities—but I shouldn't enjoy staying at her house myself. Of course all girls aren't foolish—some are charming and I am tender on two or three myself; but if I ever humbug a woman into marrying me, it will be a ~~peice~~ piece of selfishness on my part, depend upon it, and not a conquest on hers. I don't say she wouldn't manage me after all, but it would be by taking advantage of my sloth and weaknesses, not by my honorable surrender.

I have not yet got Royce's novel which is doubtless at Brown Shipley & Co.'s. Books always get delayed, but I hope I shall get it soon. I am sorry it is not good. One couldn't expect anything delicate and fine from Royce: the Mephistopheles[5] become benevolent couldn't be more than strong and significant. I shall read the book with interest anyway, and with me it is bound to be a least a <u>succès d'estime</u>.[6]

Write again soon. You can't imagine what comfort and pleasure I get from you.

Sincerely yours
George Santayana

[1]John Francis Stanley, second earl Russell, (1865–1931) was the grandson and heir of Lord John Russell, the reforming prime minister; son of Lord and Lady Amberley; and elder brother of Bertrand Russell.

Santayana met Russell in 1886 when Russell visited Harvard after having been sent down from Balliol College, Oxford. Santayana's emotional bond to Russell, the "most extraordinary of all my friends," was strong. Their friendship continued throughout the vicissitudes of Russell's public and private life. At the time of his death at Marseilles, Russell was an undersecretary in the Labour government. See *Persons*, 290.

[2]Santayana describes this fall into the Thames (and the accidental pulling in after him of the earl Russell) in *Persons*, 296–97.

[3]Marcus Morton Kimball was a member of Santayana's Harvard class of 1886.

[4]Charles Henry Minot (d. 1887), a member of Harvard's class of 1886, committed suicide.

[5]Mephistopheles is the demonic tempter in the Faust legend. He inherits his varying form and personality from both the Christian system of demonology in which he is one of the seven chief devils, and from the pagan Germanic tradition of the kobold, or mischievous familiar spirit. Thus he is never identified with the Devil who is the fallen angel Lucifer, although he resembles him; Mephistopheles is more the pure fiend of pagan superstition in earlier stories, and later the fiendish sneerer at all values with an air of urbane sophistication.

[6]An indifferent success.

To Ward Thoron
24 April 1887 • Oxford, England   (MS: Virginia)

April 24$^{\underline{th}}$ '87[1]

At last, dear Ward, I take a rhyming quill:
From its cleft point there springs an inky rill
Whose twisted stream, with intersecting flow,
Shall trace the ways my feet & fancies go.
They do not go together, for my feet
Wear the gray flagstones of an Oxford street
And wake the ivy-muffled echoes thrown
From great walls' crumbling honeycomb of stone,
Or press the rich moist fields that sweep between
Long hedgerows budding into joyous green.
But what can Oxford's halls or hedgerows be,
Or outraged lingering sanctities, to me?
Not of ~~this one more~~ ₍another₎ springtime have I need
Nor of this cradle of a still-born creed,
But of bold spirit kindred to the powers
That reared these cloisters & that piled these towers.
     ₍Of₎ Some ~~splendid~~ ₍wide₎ vision and determined will
With charm to captivate and strength to kill.
The world is ~~rich:~~ ₍wide:₎ it is not flesh and bone

And sun and moon, and thunderbolt alone.
It is imagination swift and high
Creating in a dream its earth & sky–
Why then gape idly at external laws
When we ourselves have faculty to cause?
Build rather on your nature, when you can,
And bid the human spirit rule the man,
Nay, not the man, but all the world as well,
Till man be god of heaven & of hell.
Come, mad ambition, come, divine conceit,
That bringest nature down at fancy's feet,
Alone creative, capable alone
Of giving mind the sceptre, man the throne
Build us more pyramids & minsters still
On thine own regal cornerstone: <u>I will</u>!

[*Unsigned*]

[1]This poem could be a parody of the prevailing German philosophy, as exemplified in Schopenhauer's *The World as Will and Idea*. [D. C.]

To Henry Ward Abbot
30 April 1887 • Oxford, England   (MS: Columbia)

Oxford, April 30th '87

Dear Harry.

I have read Royce's book, which I received a few days ago. I am glad to have it, and read it with interest if hardly with pleasure. It is indeed linked dulness long drawn out. It is intolerably diffuse. When a man has something to say he begins by telling you what the situation is, what objects he has in view in speaking to you, and what he proposes to say. He then says it. When he is through he informs you ∧of∧ what he has said, and of his reasons for saying it, and concludes with a hopeful ∧re∧view of the whole matter.

Apart from this and from the vileness of some of the words and phrases (e.g. "lonesome", "I don't just perceive why") I like the style. The absence of cleverness is a praiseworthy self abnegation on the part of a clever man.

I honor his desire to see books solidly and honestly written, although I must deplore his attempt at writing one himself.

As you will doubtless have anticipated, I disapprove of the moral, at least of the doctrines involved in it. What business has anyone to call the rather weak affection a wife retains for her husband unworthy? Aren't husbands ₐ& wivesₐ to love each other after they cease to think each other perfect? There is, too, a ludicrous inadequacy in the "crime" the unfortunate little fool committed, ~~and~~ to bring about such dreadful tragedies. Royce shows his inexperience. One must laugh at the notion of what's her name's chastity on the ground that her husband had once got entangled with a girl foolish enough to go mad of disappointment. If at least he had seduced the creature, or made love to her after he was married, or been engaged to both at once–but as it was the hullabaloo is absurd. Nothing is really so immoral as an extravagant morality. Royce's theories of love and marriage disgust me. They show what nonsense we talk when we ~~lose~~ ₐloseₐ respect for experience, tradition, and authority.

I like the old Alonzo, Bertha Boscowitz,[1] and the fight that closes the story. Royce might write a story of adventure, I should think, in which all the characters should be rough and vulgar. But he has no idea how a lady feels, much less how she expresses her feelings. I am curious to see how the papers treat the book.

I am being entertained with breakfasts and lunches here, thanks to my introductions from his lordship.[2] I find it up hill work to talk to the English fellows, although they are remarkably at home in all sorts of things. They won't say what they are thinking about, but keep always thinking about what they ɣshall say. The result is that with my love of laying down the law, I do most of the talking and doubtless appear an intolerable damned fool. By the way, Catholicism is in high favor in these parts, and conversions are continual. All this, according to you, would be impossible if they had only taken N.H.4.[3]

I have been meaning every time I write to ask you to send me your picture, which you never gave me. But as I usually work myself up to a fine frenzy in writing to you, I forget the thing.

Sincerely yours

G.S.

---

[1]Santayana uses the name Boscovitz for a family of characters in *Puritan.*
[2]John Francis Stanley Russell.
[3]Natural History 4.

To William James
11 May 1887 • Oxford, England   (MS: Houghton)

Oxford,
May 11<u>th</u> 1887.

Dear Prof. James.

It's some time since I got your kind letter, including a card for Mr. Hodgson,[1] and a few days ago I received the second part of your essay on space perception, for which I am very much obliged. Mr. Hodgson has been very kind in asking me to all the meetings of the Aristotelian Society. I have been to three and found them truly interesting, not so much perhaps because the discussions were brilliant as because ~~it~~ they gave me such a good chance to observe the state of the English mind. I find that the empiricists are decidedly on the offensive at present, and that the Hegelians are anxious to minimize their claims. Mr. Alexander[2] read a most interesting paper on Hegel's "Rechtsphilosophie" in which he maintained that Hegelianism rightly understood was and intended to be nothing but a description, a method of treating and classifying the facts of experience, and by no means an organon of discovery.[3]

Here in Oxford I have not met many professors or fellows as yet, but I have seen a great many students who ∧are∧ far more intelligent and well-informed than we at Harvard. On coming to England I looked up our friend the young Earl Russell who has been overwhelmingly kind to me; it is through him that I have come to meet all these men. I find them charming, with a gentle seriousness and self-possession I have seen nowhere else. Russell himself is not here but is studying engineering and navigation, and getting a yacht ready for the summer cruise. He is exceedingly clever and versatile, and hardly to be blamed (being an Irish landlord) for being at present disgusted with politics.

Strong who has naturally come in for a share in my gaiety seems nevertheless to be bored he∧re∧ in Oxford, and is going off to Paris to meet his friend Mc Donnald,[4] taking Cambridge and London on the way. He has been working steadily on Mill's[5] logic, etc. in preparation for his next year's work. I have no doubt that when he has a definite and inevitable task before him he will find it easy and pleasant; but he seems to lack the faculty of intellectual delight, so that study is hard for him if it has no definite purpose. This is rather an American trait, isn't it? I've often noticed that my friends wanted to have an objective point, in their walks as well as in their work, and I wondered how on that principle they reconciled themselves either with life or philosophy.

I myself have been reading a good deal, but I don't find the lectures here interesting, with a few exceptions. The inferiority to Germany is very marked in this respect. I shall therefore leave Oxford somewhat before the end of the term, and go directly to Avila where I shall have complete seclusion and independence. I hope to put some unfinished papers I have lying about into some order while I am there. Avila is an excellent place for writing, being an impossible one for reading as I carry no books with me.

Hoping all is well at

Harvard   I am   Sincerely yours

George Santayana

[1]James wrote to Santayana on 15 Mar 1887, including a card of introduction to Shadworth Holloway Hodgson (1832–1912), an English metaphysician and epistemologist.
[2]Samuel Alexander (1859–1938) was an Australian-born philosopher who studied mathematics, classics, and philosophy at Oxford, and later psychology at Freiburg. He opposed the prevalent idealistic systems. His realist epistemology was spelled out in *Space, Time, and Deity*, 2 vols. (1920). He held that knowledge consists in the 'compresence' of a mental act and an object. The world therefore contains a mind-independent reality.
[3]*Grundlinien der philosophie des Rechts* (The Philosophy of Right) (Berlin: In der Nicolaischen Buchhandlung, 1821).
[4]Unidentified.
[5]John Stuart Mill (1806–73) was an English philosopher and economist who formed the Unitarian Society. He was a member of Parliament who advocated women's suffrage. His philosophical reputation was established with the publication of *System of Logic* (1843). *Utilitarianism* (1863) expounds his alterations to Benthamism and includes his distinction between types of pleasure. Mill followed in the empiricist tradition but avoided the skepticism of Hume and theology of Berkeley by positing a theory about how knowledge of the external world is generated. This led him to conclude that matter is nothing more than a permanent possibility of sensation.

To George Pierce Baker
17 May 1887 • Oxford, England   (MS: Beinecke)

Oxford, May 17, 87.

Dear Baker.[1]

I'm so sorry that Baldwin[2] has acted in this unreasonable way about the Monthly. Surely he should have handed you the books and money at once. I had no idea that anything of the kind was happening, for you didn't mention it in your previous letter, which I have just reread to see if I could have been stupid enough not to answer at once on a matter so important to the life and reputation of the <u>Monthly</u>. As to dividing the surplus from last year among ourselves, I have always opposed the idea (except in joking, you understand) and would refuse to have anything to do with a division of spoils. I shall write to Baldwin this morning and tell him so. I am especially ashamed of this affair, because I am a friend and believer in Baldwin and never wished to admit that his erratic tendencies would lead to serious trouble.

You have made a great success of the <u>Monthly</u> this year, and improved it greatly. I hoped to see more of your own work in it, but I suppose you had enough with the management. Berenson[3] writes good articles—not without faults, to be sure, but with splendid qualities. But I should discourage his verse. The extracts from Leahy's Tragedy had good lines in them. Why doesn't Sanford produce anything, or is his work poor?[4] Yet your great success has been undoubtedly the graduate articles. They have been very interesting. Bôcher's, however, was too short, and read like a note to longer paper.[5]

Royce's novel! Good heavens, what a failure! I'm so sorry for him, poor man; he knows so much about the universal consciousness that he has forgotten what individual consciousness is like, especially in women. And thus I have no patience with the false, inexperienced morality of the book, which shows private judgment (on the subject of what is seriously wrong and what is excusable) run wild. And the tedium of it.

I am having a delicious time in Oxford, such as no mortal has a right to expect in any part of this wretched earth. I am being dined lunched and breakfasted, and have met a lot of nice fellows, who are sweet, gentle, and good besides being learned and athletic—in fact, walking ideals. Of course the town is charming, and the fields emerald green. I feed, read, go to some lectures, walk, talk, and loaf. Perfectly happy for the time being, but looking forward to a stupid summer at Avila, where I propose to do some solid work, pleasure being out of the question. My future depends mainly on the Harvard-fellowship-dispensing-bureau. If they wisely decide to contribute to the patriotic work of keeping me alive, I shall probably be in Berlin again next winter.[6]

You tell me nothing about your plans, or about the doings of other fellows. Loeser has written me some most interesting letters, but I have not heard from him for a long time now. What has become of Morton? And of the Lamb crowd generally? If you hear of any fellows I know coming abroad next winter, pray let me know, for the sight of a Harvard man is balm to my soul. Lyman and I saw Michael at Dresden on September last. Beal writes me from Berlin that Ames and Peabody '86 have just gone through there on their way round the world. I have heard from Carpenter, who seems pleased with Paris. Strong has just left me (being in a restless and fidgety mood—and of course you have heard he is to instruct in Phil. at Cornell next year, price $1000) and gone to Paris too, to see a friend of his McDonnald, a queer fish. Amused to hear that the three Billies (exclusive of the postman) have come to matrimonial or extramatrimonial grief—Allen, Barnes and Hearst. And poor Simms.[7]

Excuse my frivolity & believe me   Sincerely yours

George Santayana

[across]

Address, Brown, Shipley & Co till June 15—then Avila.

[1]George Pierce Baker (1866–1935) was a member of the Harvard class of 1887 and founded the 47 Workshop, a graduate course in practical theater in which students wrote, directed, acted, and produced their plays before a handpicked academic audience. Baker transferred the Workshop from Harvard to Yale in 1925 after a disagreement with President Abbott Lawrence Lowell and the Harvard Corporation over a new theater.

[2]Thomas "Tommy" Tileston Baldwin (d. 1923), a Southerner and member of the intimate group of Harvard undergraduates in the class of 1886 to which Santayana belonged, produced the *Harvard Lampoon* and *The Harvard Monthly.*

[3]Born in Lithuania, Bernard Berenson (1865–1959), who met Santayana at Boston Latin School, was a member of the Harvard class of 1887. He was an art critic and an authority on Italian art, especially of the Renaissance.

[4]Probably William Augustine Leahy, a member of Harvard's class of 1888, and William Sanford Barnes (d. 1910), a member of Harvard's class of 1886.

[5]Ferdinand Bôcher (1832–1902) was professor of modern languages who taught French at Harvard (1870–1902).

[6]The Walker Fellowship Committee at Harvard renewed Santayana's fellowship in Germany for a second year.

[7]Members of Santayana's class of 1886 included: Johnson Morton (d. 1922); Charles Estus Lamb (d. 1905); Oliver Ames (d. 1929); George Lee Peabody (d. 1911); George Rice Carpenter (1863–1909) taught at Harvard (1888–90) and was a professor of rhetoric and English composition at Columbia (1893–1909); William Lothrop Allen; and William Randoph Hearst (1863–1951) was a journalist and publisher who founded a news empire. Michael is possibly Francis Michael (Harvard's class of 1887), and Simms is unidentified.

To Henry Ward Abbot
20 May 1887 • Oxford, England   (MS: Columbia)

Oxford, May 20, 1887.

Dear Harry.

So glad to get your interesting letter today, as I am off again tomorrow and may not have a chance of writing for some time. I also have a letter from Ward at last, which I have just answered. I do not see any real cause for Herbert Lyman's despairing tone about Ward. He isn't ruined yet, on the contrary I should say he seems to be improving and that they have made excellent plans for him. He is to go into an office and study at the same time, as you doubtless know. And Washington is a good place for him, as people there won't discourage him with their frowns and by ignoring the serious side in him on account of his flightiness. We shall see.

I wonder what Henry Grew[1] told you about my father, (or was it about my mother ∧or her first husband,∧[2] by any chance?) For surely nothing Quixotic has ever come to light about my father, at least to my knowledge. But he is an interesting man, and I shall be glad to tell you about him. It will help you, too, to understand where I get my genuine epicurianism and my faculty of living well on next to nothing a year. My father studied law at Valladolid, and on graduating went to Madrid, without a penny, for his father was dead and his mother and numerous brothers and sisters living ,(and they were humble people at best, my grandfather[3] having been a government employee) and made friends there of all sorts. He had a good hand and a fondness for books and for painting and had translated ∧some of∧ Seneca's plays[4] into Spanish verse, etc. so that he found protectors easily and was sent to Manila. There in addition to his government employment he practised law to some extent—but never succeeded, being inconceivably lazy and dilatory. He returned three times to Spain to recover his health which was ruined by the climate and way of life of Manila, finally, I believe in '59, when he retired on a pension and a very small capital. He had been supporting most of his family in Spain, but they had died off to a great extent by that time. One of his brothers, his favorite one, was shot in the first Carlist war,[5] and this is one of the sources of the bitter hatred my father has for the clergy and all their doings, a hatred which in his old age has become a mania.

And now it becomes necessary to say that my father had met my mother in her romantic days when she was a Virginia without a Paul[6] in one of the smaller Philippines, supporting herself by trading at the age of seventeen, and living entirely among the Indians. In fact it was the coming of my father and one or two other Spaniards to the island that drove my mother from it, as of course she couldn't live alone where ~~their~~ there were white men. I don't know how much truth there may be in the story that there was a love episode at this time between them, but I believe ~~it~~ the ‸story‸ is a later growth which has sprung up in the light of subsequent events. It surely was nothing ‸at most‸ but a flirtation, for I am glad to say that neither my father nor my mother have ever been in love either with each other or with anybody else. I know this not only on authority but also through intuition. And if what Henry Grew told you was the fable which some of the Sturgises have invented that my father romantically refused to get married for love of my mother and waited till she became a widow— the notion is deliciously absurd, since my father has no illusions on the subject of women—least of all about my mother—and lives comfortably enough without her after marriage. And then, to put on the finishing touch, the Sturgises ought to know that no one lives in Manila without a mistress, even if he isn't a priest. Besides my father first knew my mother well after she was married to Mr. Sturgis, who was one of my father's friends at Manila, and liked him for being more intellectual and rational than most of the Spaniards in the place. In fact he once made a 90 days voyage to Boston with my mother and Mr. Sturgis, at the latter's suggestion that he might thus get to Spain quicker—which was the fact. And when long after Mr. Sturgis's death my mother met him at Madrid again, the marriage that was arranged was surely not romantic. My mother was independent, anti-religious, and an old friend—thus no unpleasant complications were to be feared, and a home and interests for one's old age might be formed. But they were married with the agreement that my mother was to return to America, where my father could never dream of living.

I see I have told you more about my father's history than about himself. Well, he is now over seventy. His first and overmastering concern is his ꬶdigestion—which is weak. His next is I dare say what becomes of me, and his almost exclusive subject of conversation is the ruin wrought by the Church. He is very anxious to live many years. He has read and thought a good deal, and writes admirably. His talk is also very interesting and even eloquent—full of cynicism and contempt for human nature together with a strange reverence for material success and prosperity. His philosophy is that of Voltaire minus the Deism, which he considers an insincerity on Voltaire's part.[7] My father believes a great deal in people's insincerity and ill will. I think he doesn't give them enough credit for their stupidity and irrationality and utter helplessness physical and moral. Still in particular cases where we have disagreed I must confess he has turned out to be in the right, and that farfetched as his suspicions appeared to me, they were quite justified. It is a strange effect that my father's character and opinions have on me. I never feel inclined to combat what he says although I would often say the opposite myself, for it is so well reasoned, so clearly logical, simple, and compact that all I ∧can∧ do is to listen in silence, while my imagination is filled with all the things he is leaving out, and my heart is going out to all the things he ~~does not~~ doesn't value.–I respect him and yet I pity him.

For the second time in this letter you refer to what you call my "pluck". Now I like to be flattered, and encourage anyone willing to do so, but I like to be flattered judiciously. In what does my "pluck" consist? Anyone would think I was working my way through dreadful trials in hopes of benefiting my fellow-man. The fact is I am living comfortably, travelling about Europe, going precisely where I like, reading when I want to, writing when I feel like it, making friends, both of old acquaintances and of new, with a fair prospect of keeping this up for a time, and with no aim or purpose at all except such as I ~~chose~~ choose to put before myself–and I am doing this at other people's expense without incurring any uncomfortable obligations. How is the "pluck" then shown? It is true that I haven't much to spend but I find what I have enough for all necessary things–among which the chief is dressing and living apparently like other people. Of course, I don't live like other people really, because I leave out all the little expenses, but I do so from habit not with any conscious economy. My economy comes in when I plan what I shall do and how I shall do it–I forget all about economy in carrying out my plan. So that really I don't find poverty at all a burden, but rather a stimulant. Besides I sponge systematically and on principle, not feeling my dignity compromised thereby anymore than if I were a monk or a soldier. For instance you mention what Loeser has done for me. Well, I think it was very good of him, and not only very good but very wise since he is no poorer in consequence and we had very good times together. I think you will believe me, even if other people don't, when I say that I didn't go to see him or keep up with him all through college because he treated me a great deal, any more than I keep up with him now from gratitude. I don't feel any gratitude, or any other uncomfortable sensation. But I'm fond of the man, from having had a good time with him often, talking over things and going to the theatre; and

I am interested in him, and in what he has to say, for he is no fool. No more by the way is Russell, in fact a great deal less for Russell is the ablest man, all round, that I have ever met. You have no idea what a splendid creature he is, no more had I till I had seen a great deal of him. He isn't good, that is he is completely selfish and rather cruel, although I fancy I made too much of his heartlessness at first. But then both practically and intellectually he is really brilliant. Leaving the practical side apart in which direction you may say I am easily dazzled, he is up on every subject from Greek tragedy to common law and from smutty stories to Buddhism. I know I am making a fool of myself in writing about him—it's quite different from writing about one's father about whom one doesn't of course care—but I send a note of his[8] so that you may judge for yourself and also have some idea of the men I am seeing here. Pass the note on to Herbert Lyman and let him keep it or send it back to me. I am going to-morrow to stay with Russell again, for he is laid up and wants company. It is Ward's malady, so you see I have the requisite experience for nurse. Don't tell this round, I beg of you, but I tell you because I am telling you everything to-day. I make an exception of Herbert, because I should have to tell him sooner or later, and he won't chuckle over it as if it were a joke merely, which it isn't.

I like Stimson's fable exceedingly. It is perfectly true, but I think you are mistaken in treating it as a protest. It is merely a description. Why shouldn't we acquiesce in the normal state of things, and if we prefer to be Poets be Poets bravely and with the consciousness that we are but the light topmost spray of the heaving sea?

As to Fullerton's bosh, it isn't worth writing about. He is an ass, but will doubtless succeed in the end, "owing to the prevalence of fools."

Here is a long letter with no metaphysics! I am really becoming sane in this English atmosphere.   Good bye.

George Santayana

[1]Henry Sturgis Grew, Harvard class of 1896, was a rich relative of Santayana. See *Persons*, 59–62.

[2]Santayana's mother married the American-born George Sturgis (1817–57) in Manila in 1849. See *Persons*, 39–41.

[3]Don Nicolás Ruiz de Santayana of Badumès in the province of Santander was married to Doña María Antonia Reboiro of Zamora.

[4]Lucius Annaeus Seneca (c. 3 B.C.–A.D. 65) was a Roman Stoic philosopher and playwright who was born in Spain. His extant works include nine tragedies. Seneca saw philosophy as a therapeutic enterprise, designed for moral edification.

[5]Ultrareactionaries, the Carlists were partisans of Don Carlos, second son of Charles IV of Spain, and of his successors, who claimed the Spanish throne under the Salic law. Carlos's brother, Ferdinand VII, had abrogated the law of male succession in favor of his daughter, Isabella II. In the bloody civil war of 1836–39 Isabella's forces defeated the Carlists (who, a century later, supported Franco).

[6]Santayana refers to *Paul et Virginie* (1788) by Jacques-Henri Bernardin Saint-Pierre (1737–1814), the story of two French children, Virginia and Paul, brought up as brother and sister according to nature's law. Living on an island, they are reared by their mothers in a simple life free of religious superstition, social prejudice, and fear of authority. Virginia goes to Paris to be educated so she may assume her aunt's fortune. Returning to the island years later, she refuses to undress to save herself and drowns when her ship founders on a reef in sight of land. Paul and the two mothers then die of grief.

[7]François Marie Arouet de Voltaire (1694–1778) became the leader of the Enlightenment, arguing for freedom and toleration. Voltaire disseminated the ideas of Locke and Newton in a land dominated by Cartesianism and the speculative metaphysics of Leibniz. Most of these observations are in his *Letters Concerning the English Nation* (1733), the work responsible for bringing the social and political ideals of the English to the continent. His *Candide* (1759) attacks Leibniz's optimism. Though a militant theist, Voltaire opposed Christianity.

Deism, a doctrine of natural religion, was a popular religious view in the late 17th and early 18th centuries. Deists typically held that while reason proves that there is a God, there is no further evidence that God actively participates in the world. This belief leads to a rejection of Christianity and Judaism.

[8]Unlocated.

To Henry Ward Abbot

27 May 1887 • Oxford, England   (MS: Columbia)

Oxford, May 27, 87.

Dear Harry,

A word today to tell you that you have put a very fanciful and astonishing meaning on my "fall from grace". I didn't discover it from your own enigmatical references to it, but this morning comes a letter from the good and outspoken Herbert which announces that I have been batting[1] with Russell. If you ~~chose~~ choose to believe it, I am perfectly willing and shouldn't mind your knowing it if it were true—for I shouldn't be in the least ashamed of it. But it doesn't happen to be true. If you reread my letter you will see that what I had in mind was what I had already written to Herbert Lyman about—namely my running after Russell in a senseless and absurd fashion. Now don't put an ignoble and unworthy interpretation on this also, or I shall think that you are blind to everything that enters into my life. "My running after Russell" means "my thoughts running after him"; so, after believing that I have been bumming with him, don't imagine that I have been sniping him. He has taken me up because he has chosen to do so, and after his fashion has been overwhelmingly kind. But the trouble, from my point of view, what I call my "fall from grace and self-control" (I think I said self-control also) is simply this. Russell has a way of treating people which is insufferably insolent and insulting. Never for a moment did I imagine I could allow anyone to treat me in such a way. But I find that instead of caring for my own dignity and independence—instead of subordinating ∧to∧ my interest in myself and ∧to∧ my ways of doing things, all other interests and ways of doing things—instead of this old habit of mine, I find that I don't care a rap for my interest in myself or my ways of doing things, but that I am quite willing to stand anything, however outrageous, that comes from a certain quarter. This is what has happened to me. I am a fool to say a word about it—especially when people think that I am talking about trifles. Is it actually possible that you ~~beleive~~ believe me capable of making a fuss and feeling unhappy because I had been off on a bat? You insist on not believing what I say when I tell you that such things are of absolutely no importance or interest for me, except as they may effect health and get a man into trouble. When I write about gay things [*across*] I will write gaily—when I write in this serious fashion don't imagine I am referring to "country matters".[2]   Sincerely G.S.

P.S. I need hardly say that this letter as well as the last one ~~are~~ is not intended for Droppers & Co. I returned last night from Russell's, leaving him convalescent. You see he has a better judgment than you and Herbert about the objects for which I make expeditions.

[1]A "bat" can mean a prostitute (a bat house is a brothel) or a spree (such as a drinking bout), carousal, or binge. Batter means to copulate, and battered means given up to debauchery.
[2]Implying sexual experiences (quoted from *Hamlet*, III.ii.117).

To Henry Ward Abbot
29 May 1887 • Oxford, England   (MS: Columbia)

Oxford, May 29ᵗʰ '87.

Dear Harry,
    I am afraid I sent you a rather ill-tempered note yesterday. It was natural that you should have understood me as you did, although I didn't like

it because my present mood is so decidedly the contrary one to what you imagined.

I have your note of May 12ᵗʰ and like your new view of absolute truth. But are you sure that this solves the question we were discussing? What you now say is that there are many absolutely (or perfectly) true judgments. Our problem was rather whether the reality is not equally well represented by various conceptions. I incline to the opinion that our intelligence has essentially a relative and partial function in the world and that its acquaintance with things is therefore partial and relative. No thought we are even potentially capable of would exhaust the reality and take it all up within itself. Our conceptions are of course part of the reality, but ~~their~~ there is an infinite plus. My notion differs from Spencer's in this, that he makes an unknowable underlying matter and mind, so that the unknowable lies as it were within the known to explain it. This seems to me idle and vain. My unintelligible is simply the part of reality with which our intelligence ~~do~~ is not fit to deal, for I believe that our intelligence is not at the centre of things, but ~~is~~ only at one point on their circumference. But if by knowledge be meant any mode of actual palpitating presence, however different from our own life, then I should maintain (inevitably enough) that all reality was knowable and known.

[*across*]

I inclose some verses, since you ask for them.[1] There is nothing in them, however, which you have not heard a hundred times. Sincerely

G. S.

Oxford, May, 1887.

In England, splendid land of ilk and money,
A pleasant torpor permeates the brain,
The cool is luscious and the mist is sunny,
And dreamy blood runs thick in every vein,
While sentimental feelings which it's funny
One ever should have come to have again
Melt the sick fancy to the sappy mood
Of wishing to be loving, meek, and good.

Almost, almost I think I might believe it
And trust the echoes of these ancient walls,
For to a heart too willing to receive it
The tender promise of the ages calls.

Count I faith's loss a loss? Why not retrieve it,
Since fatal logic logically falls,
And that proud reason from its base is hurled
That makes one vast unreason of the world?

Oh, if salvation were a trick of reason,
How easily would all the world be saved!
But roses bloom not in the winter season
Nor hope of heaven in a heart enslaved.
To break the bond with earth were easy treason
If it were only God the bosom craved,
But we have chosen love and chosen rest,
And with our breast's ~~lost~~ plucked feathers ~~made~~ built ₄our nest.

And from a high walled garden, rich in flowers,
Upon the driving clouds I like to look
That cast their pleasant shadow on my bowers
And feed the trickling fountain and the brook.
Nor should I tremble if the gusty showers
Fell on my blossoms, or if thunder shook
My fragrant arbors and their leafy gloom
And ₄with₄ the things I love bestrewed my tomb.

Yet if I sickened of my secret pleasures
And shuddered at the all-enclosing void,
If my heart pined for some excessive treasure
In whose fruition it were never cloyed,
Or, doting on existence over measure,
If I should hate the Maker who destroyed,
Then I should leave my garden to decay
Nor notice if my fountain ceased to play.

And putting idle thoughts of ease behind me
Forth I should wander to the windswept moor,
And bid the mountains and the sea remind me
Of perfect good that should like them endure.
And no false joy, no length of toil should blind me
To the exceeding wealth that made me poor,
And more were my unbroken spirit blest
By heaven hoped for than by earth possessed.

Though I lack faith to love, I have compassion
In sight of things so tragically fair,
And feel the bitter wrong that God should fashion
An instrument for idle winds to tear,
And wake tumultuous rhapsodies of passion
To die insulted in the vacant air,–
Or does God catch the sweet delirious notes
That thrill in little love-birds' swelling throats?

Is there within the breast of the eternal
A sanctuary left for banished joy,
Where aureoled in golden splendor vernal
The angel of my dream is still a boy,
Saved from oblivion and the pit infernal
And love's apostasy and shame's annoy,
Saved from his own tide's ebbing, silent, fair,
Benignant, holy, and forever there?

O bright ideal, lead the unsuspecting
To pluck their berries among thorns and briers
And teach them the hard lesson of detecting
What fate will yeild of all the heart's desires.
But spare me now, and pardon my neglecting
To cast my reason in thy quenchless fires
Ablaze with mad saints' hearts: the wiser sinner
In the embers of his passion cooks his dinner.

So I will snatch the alms the minutes offer
And bask a happy beggar in the sun,
And fill at Churches' gate my little coffer
And bless the dropping pennies, one by one.
Within, the faithful may petitions proffer,
And pardon crave for sins that they have done,
But I am merry if I lose or win,
Nor deem possession of my nature sin.

Oh, it is very pleasant to be small,
~~And~~ Makᶜing our step no longer than our tether,
And, without languishing for wings, to crawl
And love the fragrance of our native heather.
O peace, to scan our fate and say: That's all!

O happiness, to meet that fate together!
O crowning joy, to die in fitting time,
And seal the poem with a noble rhyme!

[1]The text of these verses is the earliest of three holograph versions of "At the Church Door," a poem that remained unpublished during Santayana's lifetime. See *Complete Poems*, 418–21.

To Henry Ward Abbot
18 June 1887 • London, England   (MS: Columbia)

London, June 18th 1887.

Dear Harry,

Have your excited letter of the 4th You don't tell me clearly what you think of my father, as far as you can judge from what I told you. I wish you would. You take me, I suspect, much too seriously. Nothing matters so very much, not even whether a man wastes his life, and is a humbug. But if the thing seems so momentous to you, why haven't you the courage of your convictions, and why don't you dare to break off from your present surroundings? Are you afraid of poverty? Fine reason for an idealist, who thinks greatness worth having! What is greatness?

Oh, it is sweet to wander with no hope
Along life's labyrinthine, beaten way,
Without impatience at the steep's delay
Nor sorrow at the swift descended slope!
Why this inane curiosity to grope
In the dim dust for gems' unmeaning ray,
And fell ambition that compels to pray
For a stage broader than the heaven's cope?
Farewell, my burden! no more will I bear
The foolish load of love and dead despair,
But trip the idle race with careless feet.
The crown of laurel let another wear,
It is my crown to mock the runner's heat
With gentle wonder and with laughter sweet.[1]

G. S.

[1]A later version of this poem became Sonnet XIII of his Sonnets First Series in *Sonnets*, 15. See *Complete Poems*, 97.

To William Morton Fullerton
10 July 1887 • Ávila, Spain

(MS: Texas)

Avila, July 10, 87.

Dear Fullerton—

Although I never received any answer to a letter I wrote you ever so long ago, I have read so many lately penned by you that I almost feel I owe you an acknowledgement. Truly I cannot pretend to possess Mr. Evnard's wonderful erudition and eloquence, but I may say that I fully share his admiration for Mr. William Morton Fullerton's genius, and I remember I had the privilege of being that celebrated critic's classmate and even ₐhisₐ humble partner in college journalism.[1] I therefore have some hope that he will not pass this second letter of mine ₐbyₐ unnoticed, especially as I am informed that he has some notion of coming to Europe and perhaps even to Berlin next winter. Is that so, dear Fully? You don't know how glad I should be to see you there. As you probably know the faculty has done the first sensible act in ~~their~~ ₐitsₐ history, and voted to contribute ſto my support.[2] The result is that I shall return to Germany next winter, and continue reading and hearing lectures. Fain would I dwell in England, best of earthly abodes. But duty—whose voice I listen to, in spite of a debauched conscience—compels me, by the tender inducement of $500 per annum, to relinquish that Capua[3] of philosophers, and do battle on Teutonic ground. Lo! I have on my table (of which the famous advertizer critic also makes occasional mention) a copy of Kant, not sent to me, as is the case with the great man just referred to, by the author or publisher pining for a favorable notice, but alas! sent to me for the vile condiseration of one and sixpense from Trübrur & Co of Ludgate Hill, London. E.C. This, together with Lucretius, Swinburne, Musset, Goethe, and Walt Whitman, make up my library.[4] I am glad, by the way, you give Walt the protection of your powerful influence. How I like that think of his where he talks of the necessity of having "aplomb in the midst of irrational things!"![5] Things are so irrational, dear Fullerton, and I know very well you inwardly think so too, only having gone in for success you can't afford to say so or to think so explicitly. But it is jolly to have old Walt so frank and open, and so willing to live like an animal accidentally finding himself partly rational and rather emotional. "Aplomb in the midst of irrationel things"—that's my motto!

Don't think of getting mad because I say that having gone in for success you can't afford to say what you inwardly think. Who knows what he really thinks? What every intelligent fellow knows is what he can best defend and what on the whole it is easiest and most respectable to say. If he isn't a fool he says that and damns what he may inwardly thinks, as even to himself undiscoverable.

I am at present here, like the prudent ant in the fable, laying up a store of tin for the winter. Weather warm, but not insufferable; rather more bearable in fact that Boston in summer. Nothing to do but read and write when the spirit moves. Queer old brokendown hidalgo here, yclept Don Pelayo like the founder of the Spanish monarchy, to which he is firmly attached.[6] In fact his attachment to the throne and the card-table are heroic, and the ingratitude of both shocking and pitiful. This worthy gentleman was educated at the great University of Salamanca and feels the natural wonder of the wise man of that place to understand why the earth, instead of revolving about the sun, doesn't fall down to the ground. He also wants to know if the Andes are visible from Boston. Besides learning much from this prodigy of wisdom, I listen to my father's invectives against the clericals and Carlists and to some account of his experiences in the East Indies. Sic transit tempus.[7]

Now if it is true that you are coming abroad, let me advise you on the strength of recent experience at Berlin, at Oxford, and at Cambridge, as well as on various accounts coming from Paris, to choose Berlin as the seat of your labors. The lectures there are incalculably the best, and although the students are not so charming as the English nor the city so gay as Paris, yet this sacrifice of pleasure is well compensated by the delight of ₍the₎ sincerity, strength, soundness, and maturity characteristic of German scholarship. They have an independence there enjoyed no where else—not even at Harvard. Besides, I hope it would not be the opposite of an inducement that we are to be there—Houghton, Lyman, and myself, besides Beal and a lot of American you would soon get to know. Place also cheap. Do write.   Yours ever

George Santayana.

[across]
    Address, Avila, Spain for 2 months
permanently, Brown Shipley & Co, London.

[1]As an undergraduate, Santayana contributed to *The Harvard Monthly* and the *Harvard Lampoon.*
[2]By awarding him half of the Walker Fellowship.

[3]The luxury of this ancient city in southern Italy is proverbial.

[4]Algernon Charles Swinburne (1837–1909) was an English poet whose work represents a blending of classical theme with flamboyant romanticism. His literary criticism helped popularize older English dramatists.

Alfred de Musset (1810–57) was a French poet, novelist, and dramatist. His early poetry probes introspectively into the ecstasies and despairs of love. His affair with George Sand [Amantine Lucile Aurore Dupin Baronne Dudevant] ended disastrously; his subsequent life and work were darker.

Walter Whitman (1819–92) was an American poet whose themes include love, death, nationalism, and democracy. His most famous work is *Leaves of Grass* (1855). Santayana was influenced by Whitman, calling him and Browning barbarians in his essay, "The Poetry of Barbarism." Yet Santayana composed two poems subtitled "after Walt Whitman." "Had I the Choice" and "You tides with ceaseless swell" were published in *Complete Poems*, 404–5 and 410–11.

[5]Santayana quotes "Me Imperturbe" from *Leaves of Grass*.

[6]A cleric, Don Pelayo was Santayana's father's only friend in Ávila. See *Persons*, 201–3.

[7]Thus passes time.

To William Morton Fullerton
31 August 1887 • Ávila, Spain   (MS: Texas)

Avila, Aug 31, 87.

Dear Fullerton—

Thanks very much for your interesting letter, which I read in bed this morning, being at present convalescent from a little bilious attack that has recently turned me inside out. This biliousness of mine will give you optimist a chance to attribute any disagreeable and unsightly truth I may hereafter mention to the stock cause, viz, to indigestion. Men having generally turned their eyes to more profitable uses than seeing, when ever they discover anything it is supposed to be by means of that larger organ called the liver. Were we bilious people not here in rather large numbers, to enlighten the world, to what depths of superstition and infatuation would not you comfortable hypocrites have brought it!

I confess I am overwhelmed by the catalogue of ₍your collection₎ honors and glories. I tremble in addressing such a high and famous authority. I marvel at his having deigned to write me a sixteen-page letter. I am going to have it framed in four nickle frames (until the times turn golden) between tøwo plates of glass, ɏso that both sides may be legible. These four tablets I shall hand down to my nephews (for like the Pope I shall have only nephews) as the main part of their inheritance (indeed, they won't get much else.) Meantime I shall treasure them in an ar¢k, modelled on the ar¢k of the covenant, and for this purpose I write by this mail to the British and Foreign Bible Society for a Bible, in order to inform myself on the subject of ar¢k-architecture. Alas! my own Bible, that my mother gave me with tears in her eyes,[1] begging me never to part with it, has disappeared in the most tragic and lamentable manner. Being often in Popish and other heathen countries, I naturally carried my Bible jealously in my breeches pocket, lest the Inquisition or some tribe of cannibals should confiscate it and desecrate it, incidentally wasting and eating me as a Christian and a brother. But sad and strange experience has convinced me that the reason why in these godless countries there are no Bibles is not because the Devil, therein supreme, prohibits them, lest men should believe and be saved. The reason why Bibles are not found is because there is an alarming scarcity of paper, none being to be found even in water-closets. Now, as I am unfortunately a great frequenter of these establishments, on account of biliousness, diarrhoea, indigestion, dyspepsia, and colic; and as at the same time, mindful of my dear and sainted mother's last wishes,[2] I always carry my Bible in my breeches' pocket; I have found myself in a cruel dilemma. Godliness said "Treasure thy Bible, and on no account tear out the leaves thereof." But cleanliness answered "Did not David eat the consecrated bread when he was ahungered, and did not the Lord justify David? Tear thou then out likewise the leaves of thy Bible, and wipe thine ass therewith for thy need is as pressing as Davids, nay more." And when I considered that since I was in England I have given up the use of drawers, and that the British and Foreign Bible Society might not be willing to send me a clean pair of trousers, even if I told them in what sacred cause I had sacrificed th¢ose I possessed,—when I considered those things I always decided in favor of cleanliness. I was careful, however,—I must say this in my own justification,—to begin by tearing out the Song of Solomon, and the passage about Loch's daughters, and Ecclesiastes, and the pages descriptive of Sodom and Gomorrah, and such others as I thought godliness wouldn't much care about. Still, as time went on, and my visits to water closets unprovided with paper continued, more and more of my Bible has disappeared, and now, I regret to say, only the upper half of the first page of the Gospel according to St. John remains. That is why I have to send to the British and Foreign Bible Society to for a new copy in which to learn how the ark was built. When it comes, I assure you your letter shall be worthily enshrined.

It is evident that you are now one of the most influencial and courted of our literary men. This intimacy with the leading men of the time, ~~som~~ which you seem to take so unassumingly and unconsciously, is something ~~w~~that would turn another fellow's head. But I suppose you are so well up to all these great people in ability and influence, that you feel yourself in your native element among them. Nay, since in spite of this refulgent sunrise of yours (I wax poetic and fancy you are Apollo himself–by the way, you only mention your intellectual and professional successes, and keep a modest silence about your <u>succès de beauté</u>)[3] ~~(~~in spite of all this glory, I say, you complain of intellectual loneliness, and hint, with an excess of flattery that confuses me, that I might have contributed to dispel it. Evidently your genius is so unapproachable and soaring in its conceptions and destiny that, even among the leading men of the day, you feel alone. I am aware that this is not what you said–you are too modest to perceive it–but it is the conclusion I am forced to draw. Your offhand mention of your first novel naturally excites my curiosity. When may we hope to see it? Of course, when you are planning a novel, you must have had some experience of the tender passion. If you are engaged, or expect to be so, of course I cannot ask for any confidences, but if your loves have been less serious, or if unfortunately they have been unhappy, why don't you tell me something about them? You know I am very prudent and sympathetic (I think I can say that without arrogance) and although I haven't the genius, etc. of your new friends, I can FEEL! Besides as I have always been an admirer of yours, and not of your intellect alone, I have some right to be treated with confidence. I therefore think you might tell me something, when you next find time to write to me, about the inner side of all this full life of yours. All these great friends of yours have daughters, and all of these daughters have eyes, and some of them, at least, hearts. Ergo, when a handsome and fascinating young man, with the most brilliant prospects, appears upon the scene as if by magic, and carries everything before him, it is not credible that these maidens should all prove insensible. Something must have happened.

I am sorry that you aren't coming abroad this winter, for my own sake, but I see that you couldn't do better for yourself than to remain where you are. Perhaps a little more quiet and time to think would be good for you, as you must be bewildered by such a rush of business. Thus it is necessary for you to read French and German and to be able to appreciate the fine points in those languages. I suppose you read them already, but to have seen the people and the ways of foreign countries seems essential to a good comprehension of their spirit. That is why so few people, in reading the classics, understand the tone and temper of the ancient mind.

Houghton has treated me in an unaccountable way, not acknowledging two letters and a book I sent him, (the latter at his request.) I have heard that he was visible in May or June in the streets of Berlin in company with a German-looking man and a woman of irresponsible appearance. I have not heard from him since I left Berlin in March.

The day after to-morrow I start for Gibraltar, where I am to join my sister[4] who comes from America. We intend to take a little turn in Southern Spain and then return here for a few weeks. I shall then leave for Germany. My plans are not yet wholly formed, as I want to make some satisfactory arrangement with Herbert Lyman, who says he is going to get off. I hope so.

Don Pelayo is woebegone. Still he has a new pair of boots, rather too long for him, which serve also as feelers when he is about to run into a heap of stones. For he is blind, or (as he says) near sighted. Talking of this Don reminds me of something that I have learned with regret, viz, that you don't care for the Don, that is, Don Quixote.[5] You must reform yourself in that respect, or else expect a sermon or two from me at some future occasion. Today I write no more, being still rather used up with too much bile. Do write again, else I will.

Yours ever

George Santayana

Address

B. S. & Co. London.

[1]Santayana's mother was indifferent to religion. See *Persons*, 49.
[2]She did not die until 1912.
[3]Conquests or love affairs.
[4]Susan, the second child of Josefina Borrás and her first husband, George Sturgis, was born in Manila, in the Philippine Islands, on 5 June 1851, and christened Susan Parkman Sturgis, after her father's mother, Susan Parkman of Boston. The family, however, did not like the name Susan, and called her "Susana" or "Susie." Her father, an American businessman in Manila, died in 1857, at the age of forty. She was then taken to Boston and remained there, with her mother and younger brother (Robert) and sister (Josephine) until 1861, when her mother returned with the children to Madrid. There her mother married Agustín Ruiz de Santayana, father of George Santayana (who was born in Madrid on 16 Dec 1863). Several years later, about 1868, Josefina returned to Boston with her three living Sturgis children (two children, Pepín, the first, and Victor, the last by her first husband, had died in infancy). After spending her young adult life in Boston and leaving a convent in which she had been a novice, Susana returned to Ávila. In 1892, at the age of forty-one, she married Celedonio Sastre, a lawyer and small landowner, then a widower with six children. Her relation-

ship with Santayana remained very close; for years he was a summer guest in her Ávila home. She lived to be seventy-seven years of age and died on 10 Feb 1928. In a letter to Daniel Cory (24 Feb 1939) Santayana said Susana was "certainly the most important influence in my life."

[5]Don Quixote is the title character of Miguel de Cervantes's classic work (1605). Quixote's chivalric romanticism is contrasted by his traveling companion Sancho Panza's practical realism. Though *Don Quixote* is a satire on the exaggerated chivalry of the 17th century, some critics have interpreted it as an idealist being continually mocked and defeated in a materialistic world. Others have taken it as an attack on the Catholic church or on contemporary Spanish politics.

To William James
18 December 1887 • Berlin, Germany   (MS: Houghton)

Potsdamerstr. 123[III].
Berlin, Dec. 18. 87.

Dear Prof. James.

I have been here since the first of November, going much the same rounds as last year. I have discovered a Privatdocent, Dr. Simmel,[1] whose lectures interest me very much. I am also taking Prof. Gizycki's Übungen[2] on Kant's "Practical Reason." He gives them at his own house on Monday evenings, and I find them interesting and Prof. Gizycki's vigorous Utilitarianism[3] exhilirating. I am taking some history with Prof. Bresslau,[4] and hearing a pleasant ornamental course of Prof. Grimm's on the XVIII century.

Being under obligations to do something and not to waste my time in occasional reading and theorizing, I have tried to become methodical. I read with notebook in hand, and have one volume destined to contain the pearls of ethical and another the nuts of metaphysical wisdom. If I am expected to send something to Harvard as evidence of work not seen, I will try to bring a paper together out of some of these jottings. I do not do it for my own satisfaction, because as a matter of fact I am far from satisfied with ~~their~~ these results of my reading. I want more time and more experience to sift them and show me where my real sympathies carry me. For on one point I am satisfied with my conclusions, and that is that it is our sympathies that must guide our opinions. I believe you interpret‸ed‸ something I wrote to you last year in the sense that I was disgusted with philosophy. There was certainly a change at that time in my attitude toward my studies but hardly a change in the studies themselves. In fact since I have been in Germany I have become optimistic about the prospects in philosophy. If philosophy were the attempt to solve a given problem, I should see reason to be discouraged about its success; but it strikes me that it is rather an attempt to express a half-undiscovered reality, just as art is, and that two different renderings, if they are expressive, far from cancelling each other add to each other's value. The great bane of philosophy is the theological animus which hurries a man toward final and intolerant truths as towards his salvation. Such truths may be necessary to men but philosophy can hardly furnish them. It can only interpret nature, in parts with accuracy, in parts only with a vague symbolism. I confess I do not see why we should be so vehemently curious about the absolute truth, which is not to be made or altered by our discovery of it. But philosophy seems to me to be its own reward, and its justification lies in the delight and dignity of the art itself.

Prof. Gizycki often speaks of you and of Mr. Salter.[5] He is interested to know whether we may soon hope to see your book on the human mind.[6] I hear nothing this year about Harvard affairs. Loeser, who used to keep me well informed, has not written for a long time, and I do not even know where he is. Strong writes me that he is busy and contented, and is expounding Sir W. Hamilton[7] to classes of two and three. There are a great many Harvard men here this winter, Gates, Hildreth (85) Webster the mathematician, Carpenter, Beal, Bullard, Wateman, Von Klenze of my own class,[8] and some '87 men.

I expect to leave Berlin about the middle of March and go to some smaller University for the summer semester. My address at present is as above, but C/o Brown Shipley & Co London is always safer. I hope you will find time to drop me a line and tell me if I am expected to write something as holder of a fellowship. Wishing you and Mrs. James a very happy new year   I am sincerely

George Santayana

[1]Georg Simmel (1858–1918), a German vitalist philosopher and sociologist, became a founding father of sociology. His philosophical work focused on the dichotomy of life and form: life being a continual process and unknowable while form is stable and can be known. He suggested that the tension between such opposing poles was a permanent part of the functioning world.

[2]Seminar.

[3]Utilitarianism is a moral doctrine which defines proper and improper actions by the amount of utility or disutility the action produces. Generally, right actions are those that produce pleasure or minimize pain, while wrong actions cause pain or detract from pleasure.

[4]Heinrich Bresslau was professor of history at the University of Berlin. [D. C.]

⁵William Mackintire Salter (1853–1931) was Mrs. James's brother-in-law who was an authority on the thought of Nietzsche. [D. C.]

⁶*Principles of Psychology*, 2 vols., 1890.

⁷Sir William Hamilton (1788–1856) was a Scottish philosopher who argued that perception gives immediate, direct knowledge of objects. Yet this knowledge is not absolute but relative on account of three factors: the knowledge is purely phenomenal, the objects which we perceive are modified by the various senses, thinking of something is necessarily thinking of it under certain conditions. The objects of our knowledge are always conditioned and therefore relative.

⁸Possibly Lewis Edwards Gates (d. 1924), who received his A.B. (1884) in philosophy; Henry Theodore Hildreth received his A.B. (1885) and Ph.D. (1895); Arthur Gordon Webster (1863–1923), class of 1885, was a physicist whose lectures on mathematical physics at Clark University were unsurpassed; George Rice Carpenter; Francis Bullard (1862–1913), a nephew of Charles Eliot Norton, became an intimate friend of Santayana (see *Persons*, 224–26); possibly Walter Bowen Waterman (d. 1927) (there was no Wateman in Santayana's class); Camillo von Klenze (1865–1943), class of 1886, taught German literature at the University of Chicago, Brown University, and CUNY, and was honorary professor of American literature in Munich.

To William Morton Fullerton

28 December 1887 • Berlin, Germany   (MS: Texas)

Berlin, Dec. 28, '87.

Dear Fullerton–

I am astonished at your wanting me to send you more stuff à la Rabelais;¹ I certainly can do no such thing professionally and on demand, but only at the call of nature, as it were, or when the spirit (or bowels) may move. But as to your prohibition to be serious, I consider it an insult to a philosopher. I am always serious. It is a great mistake to suppose I am ever in fun. It is the thing that jokes, not I. If this world, seriously and solemnly described, makes people laugh, is it my fault? I am not to blame for the absurdities of nature.

You want my opinion on the axiom that "in a world of squat things a toad would be beautiful". Well, there is a fraction of an idea in it. It is not the shape or quality of things in itself that makes them beautiful, but the relation of this quality to something else. But to what? Your axiom says, to the quality of the real world–"If things <u>were</u> squat" it says. Now that is wrong. If all things were squat the flatness of the world would be neither a beauty nor a fault. If the world were accidentally less flat than the creative impulse or formative idea would naturally have made it, then things squat would be beautiful indeed. See what I mean? There is a certain ideal dwelling in each of us, which the growth of our minds and bodies under the most favorable circumstances would fulfil. But the circumstances are not favorable ₌as₌ a rule. Therefore the actual result differs from what it strives to be and naturally would be but for external obstacles. Hence ugliness and beauty, as well as all forms of good and bad The difference between beauty and good in the general and all-inclusive sense, is that beauty is the excellence or perfection of the <u>expression</u> of a thing: It is the adequate presentation of the ideal impulse, whereas virtue is its adequate existence. Therefore virtue is beautiful when represented, but beauty is not virtuous. For beauty being in the image or expression of things, these things need not exist to produce beauty, but only their image need exist—Verbum sat.[2]

Now, having expatiated sufficiently in answer to your question, let me put one to you in turn. What is one to do with one's amatory instincts? Now, for heaven's sake, don't be conventional and hypocritical in the answer you give yourself and me. If you are, you won't take me in. I know that you don't really believe that the ordinary talk on such subjects is satisfactory. Let me describe the real situation. A boy lives to his twelfth or fifteenth year, if he is properly brought up, in a state of mental innocence—I don't say he should not know where he came from when he reached ~~the~~ this world, and on which track he travelled thither, nor that he should never have seen dogs stuck together; what I say is that, unless he has been currupted, these things have no meaning and no attraction for him. But soon it is otherwise. He grows more and more uncomfortable, his imagination is more and more occupied with obscene things. Every scrap of medical or other knowledge he hears on this subject he remembers. Some day he tries experiments with some girl, or with some other boy. This is, I say, supposing he has not been corrupted intentionally and taken to whorehouses in his boyhood, as some are, or fallen a victim to paiderastia, as is the lot of others. But in some way or other, sooner or later, the boy gets his first experience in the art of love. Now, I say, what is a man to do about it? It is no use saying that he should be an angel, because he isn't. Even if he holds himself in, and only wet dreams violate his virginity, he is not an angel, because angels don't have wet dreams. He must choose among the following

<u>Amatory attitudes</u>.

1. Wet dreams and the fidgets.
2. Mastibation.
3. Paiderastia.

4. Whoring.

5. Seductions or a mistress.

6. Matrimony.

I don't put a mistress as a separate heading because it really comes under 4, 5, or 6, as the case may be. A man who takes his mistress from among prostitutes, shares her with others, and leaves her soon, is practically whoring. A man whose mistress is supposed to be respectable is practically seducing ~~him~~ her. A man who lives openly with his mistress and moves in her sphere is practically married. Now I see fearful objections to every one of these six amatory attitudes. 1 and 6 have the merit of being virtuous, but it is their only one. 2 has nothing in its favor. The discussion is therefore confined to 3, 4, & 5. 4 has the disavantage of ruining the health. 5 has the disadvantage of scenes and bad social complications—children, husbands at law, etc. On̸e hardly wants to spend one's youth ˄en˄acting modern French dramas. 3 has therefore been often preferred by impartial judges, like the ancients and orientals, yet our prejudices against it are so strong that it hardly comes under the possibilities for us. What shall we do? Oh matrimony, truly thou art an inevitable evil!

As you perceive, I do not consider sentimental love at all in my pros and cons. It is only a disturbing force, as far as the true amatory instincts are concerned. Of course it has the same origin, but just as insanity may spring from religion, so sentimental love may spring from the Sexual instinct. The latter, however, being intermittent, which religion is not, the insanity produced is temporary. Here is a serious letter for you: now answer it like a man and a Christian—(in the better sense of the word, which is "a fellow such as I approve of".)

The world continues to wag away much as usual. Snow—Christmas over (thank God!) new year coming. Tell me about the suicides which I hear are prevalent at Harvard. I was sorry about Charlie Minots death. As you know, he was no particularl friend of mine, being too swell for your humble servant, but he seemed to be a nice fellow and was better situated than most rascals are who have to live on.

I can't imagine what you mean by ˄the˄ sarcasm in my last letter. True, I don't remember all I said in it, by I know à priori that there could be no sarcasm in it. I am incapable of such a thing.   Ever yours

G. Santayana.

¹François Rabelais (c. 1490–1553) was the French author of the satirical romances *Gargantua and Pantagruel*. A Benedictine monk and teacher of medicine, Rabelais wrote the first two books of his history of the giant Gargantua and his son Pantagruel during a stay in Lyons from 1532 to 1534. The third and fourth books followed in 1546–52. There is a fifth book of dubious authenticity. The work is a satire against the vulgarity and abuses of society delivered in burlesque humor that often conceals his serious discussions of education, politics, and philosophy.

²Usually *verb. sap.* (abbreviation of *Verbum sapienti sat est*): a word to the wise is sufficient.

To William James
28 January 1888 • Berlin, Germany   (MS: Houghton)

Potsdamerstr. 123^{III}
Berlin, Jan. 28. 88.

Dear Prof. James—

I am much obliged for your letter¹, as well as for your article of the perception of time which I received soon after. I understand perfectly what you say about my not profiting as much as I should from the Walker Fellowship. I keep myself tolerably busy, to be sure, but I hardly work with the energy and singlemindedness which one associates with the idea of a man living on a scholarship. And what I shall write will certainly not smack so much of a professorship of philosophy as if it were on the normal jerk of the knee-pan. But then it is very doubtful that I should ever get a professorship of philosophy anyway, and I hardly care to sacrifice my tastes to that bare possibility. I mean to ask for the fellowship for one more year, but of course I shouldn't expect to get it if there is a more thorough student who wants it. I am quite at ease about the duties that my supposed ability imposes on me, and by no means give myself up as a bad job. But you must understand perfectly how uncertain my future is, and my preparations cannot be very definite until I know what I am to prepare for. Philosophy itself is now-a-days a tolerably broad field.

Simmel is a young man of sallow and ascetic look who lectures on pessimism and on compory philosophy in its relation with the natural sciences. He knows his subject like a German, and likes to go into the fine points. I go in to some lectures of Ebbinghaus's but am not taking anything with him regularly this term. Last year I took two courses with him, his psychology and his history of the same. I think him an excellent man, very clear and sound.

I had a short letter from Strong in answer to a very long one of mine, but have no recent news of him. I met his <u>fiancée</u> in London last Spring as well as her family. She is very amiable and rather pretty, and it seems to be a very nice thing all round.[2]

Hoping to hear from you again I am

Very sincerely yours

G. Santayana

[1]James wrote on 2 Jan 1888 and told Santayana what was expected of him if his Walker fellowship was to be renewed: "I know your ability, and also your way of talking small about yourself. But your ability imposes arduous duties. It seems to me that for a Walker fellow you are not profiting quite as much as you might by the resources of Berlin in the Philosophical line. … I can hardly defend your cause in the Committee, if on the whole you do not seem pretty definitely working on the lines which lead to philosophical professorships. For that is the way in which the Walker fellowship is construed by those who administer it." [D. C.]

[2]Elizabeth "Bessie" Rockefeller (1866–1906), eldest child of John D. and Laura Rockefeller, married Strong on 22 Mar 1889. Santayana met the Rockefellers in London at the June 1887 Jubilee of Queen Victoria. See *Persons*, 372–74.

To William James

3 July 1888 • Ávila, Spain   (MS: Houghton)

Avila, July 3. 88.

Dear Prof. James.

I am glad to know that I have been reappointed to the Walker Fellowship, as that seems to show that I have not yet quite lost my reputation. I have left Germany, however, without any desire to go back there, nor do I think that I should learn or study much if I returned. I had thought of Paris as a possible resting place, but on the whole it seems to offer few advantages for me. I therefore intend to return to America. I have reached the stage where I must work by myself; but I have not enough motive force within me to accomplish anything without encouragement and stimulation from without. And it seems to me that I could employ the fellowship better at Harvard than anywhere else, since there I should have more people to talk with, and an atmosphere less favorable to apathy. Then the advantage of a library managed on rational principles is not to be despised. I hope you will write to me soon and tell me what you think of my plan. If you have any other to suggest that seems to you better, I hope you will do so. But I dare say you will agree with me that I could make as good use of

my time at Harvard as anywhere. Three terms of Berlin have fully convinced me that the German school, although it is well to have some
acquaintance with it, is not one to which I can attach myself. After the first
impression of novelty and freedom, I have become oppressed by the
scholasticism of the thing and by the absurd pretension to be scientific. In
fact, my whole experience, since I left college and even before, has been
a series of disenchantments. First I lost my faith in the kind of philosophy
that Prof. Palmer[1] and Royce are interested in; and, then, when I came to
Germany, I also lost my faith in psycho-physics, and all the other attempts
to discover something very momentous. A German professor like Wundt[2]
seems to me a survival of the alchymist. What is the use of patience and
ingenuity, when the fundamental aim and intention is hopeless and perverse? I might as well stick to Kant's Critique of the Practical Reason, or
take at once to dogmatic theology. Indeed, the whole thing has sometimes
seemed to me so wrong and futile, that I have suspected that I had made
a mistake in taking up philosophy at all, since all the professors of it
seemed to be working along so merrily at problems that to me appeared
essentially vain. But I have remembered that this very feeling of mine
would make as good a ground for a philosophy as any other, if I only had
the patience and audacity to work it out. This is what I hope to do in some
measure next year. I have already written a good deal, but in a loose and
disjointed manner. All needs rewriting.

I have come here to visit my father, and expect to remain until the middle
of August, when I shall go to England, and thence to America. I have been
well, seeing a good deel of Berenson & Carpenter at Berlin, as well as emper-
ors' funerals, and the rest of it. Hoping to hear from you, I am

Sincerely yours

G. Santayana

Address: Avila, Spain, until Aug 1ˢᵗ, then Brown Shipley & Co. London.

[1]George Herbert Palmer (1842–1933) was an American philosopher and moralist. In
1870 he became a Greek instructor at Harvard, and later translated Homer's *Odyssey*
(1884). He taught philosophy at Harvard (1872–1913) and published fifteen books. In
The Nature of Goodness (1903) Palmer distinguished extrinsic from intrinsic goodness
and maintained that the identifying mark of a human being is self-consciousness, the
moral aim of life being self-realization expressed through continuous self-develop-
ment. See *Persons*, 246–47.

[2]Wilhelm Max Wundt (1832–1920) was a German physiologist, psychologist, and
philosopher who founded the first experimental psychology laboratory at Leipzig in
1879. Besides *Grundzüge der physiologischen Psychologie* (1874), later translated by E. B.
Titchener as *Principles of Physiological Psychology* (1904), Wundt published philosophical
volumes.

To William James

7 August 1888 • Ávila, Spain   (MS: Houghton)

Avila, Aug 7, 88.

Dear Prof. James.

Many thanks for your letter, and for your expressions of interest. I have not seen anywhere that residents can't hold the Walker Fellowship, but if such be the case or even if it be thought that non-residents have a better claim to it, of course I am quite ready to resign. The doubt you express about my "fulfilling the purposes, etc" was a reason in my mind for returning to Harvard. I fancy that if I were there I should run less danger of being considered an unprofitable servant. Being a foreigner and coming from a rather different intellectual and moral <u>milieu</u>, I have a lighter and less conscience-stricken way of taking things, which produces the impression of idleness and frivolity in the absence of ocular proof that after all I do as much work as other people. You interpret my disillusions in the matter of philosophy rather too seriously. There is nothing tragic about them. I was drawn to philosophy in the beginning by curiosity and a natural taste for ingenious thinking, and my attachment to philosophy remains as firm as ever, as I said in my previous letters. These things never came to me as a personal problem, as a question of what was necessary for salvation. I was simply interested in seeing what pictures of the world and of human nature men had succeeded in sketching: and on better acquaintance I see reason to think that they are conventional and hieroglyphic in the extreme. But the interest in these delineations is no more destroyed for me by not trusting their result or ~~there~~ their method than the charm of a play is destroyed if it is not historical. Philosophy does not cease to be a field of human activity and as such to have its significance and worth, and I cannot see why one so inclined by temperament cannot make good use of his time in that study, as in the study of art or comparative religion. Renan[1] has said that no one can be a good historian of religion who has not been a believer and who is not a sceptic: the same may be true of philosophy. I therefore do not think that my present attitude unfits me to study philosophy or to teach it, although I can easily imagine that others may not be of my opinion in this respect. I will therefore not throw up the fellowship on the ground that I have had a moral and mental collapse, a conversion to the devil, as it were, that unfits me, as insanity might, to hold any official position. I have had nothing of the sort. My notions about the possibilities of human thought and knowledge have gradually changed, and I have become convinced that most of our scheme of doctrine is built on false or arbitrary axioms. But this has been no personal crisis, no inward transformation. There may have been moments when I have tired of certain authors, or certain problems, and in this mood I may have said something liable to be misunderstood. But the good authors, the sharp and radical thinkers, are still my delight and even my chief amusement, and I can imagine no more congenial task than to talk them over with other students. I have known all along that there was little chance of my being trusted anywhere with a professorship of philosophy: but I have taken this opportunity of study for its own sake and for mine, thinking that I could always live by teaching one thing or another, while I have not enough to live on without work.

This is frankly the way I feel about the matter. If it seems to you that under the circumstances it would be better to give up the fellowship, I am ready to do so. At any rate I intend to return to America, as it is a better country than this to get a living in, and for the present I can live with my mother. I shall probably arrive about Sept 15, when I hope to have the pleasure of seeing you.

Yours ever
GSantayana

[1]Joseph Ernest Renan (1823–92) was a French historian, essayist, and philologist who was interested in the evolution of languages and religions as manifestations of the developing human mind. His *Histoire des origines du Christianisme*, 8 vols. (1863–83), explains by a scientific historical method the birth and spread of Christianity.

To William Cameron Forbes
Wednesday [c. 1888 or 1889] • Roxbury, Massachusetts   (MS: Houghton)

26 Millmont St
Roxbury
<u>Wednesday</u>

Dear Cam.[1]

I am sorry I haven't been able to get out to-day. I was out, and didn't get your note till this evening. Tomorrow and Friday I have to be with a friend of mine who is passing through Boston, and on Monday I have arranged to go to Manchester to spend the day. But on Tuesday you may expect to see me in the 3.55 train, and I will stay and spend the night, as you kindly ask me to do. I hope you didn't think me awfully impatient and grasping to write so soon again, but you see I was anxious not to miss a glimpse of you before other things got in the way. Once in Cambridge one is lost, and any place more than a mile from Boston Common becomes inaccessible. I am looking forward to having you train my aesthetic eye on the good points of horses and dogs—I promise to make wonderful progress with a single lesson.

Yours ever

GSantayana

[1]William Cameron Forbes (1870–1959) was one of the models for Oliver Alden, the protagonist of *Puritan.* Spartan, puritanical, and outdoorsy, he coached the Harvard football team and was a member of the Harvard class of 1892. An administrator and diplomat, he served as U.S. governor of the Philippine Islands (1909–13) and as U.S. ambassador to Japan (1930–32). He was the grandson of Ralph Waldo Emerson. Santayana was a frequent guest at Naushon, an island in Buzzard's Bay, Cape Cod, that belonged to Cam's grandfather John Murray Forbes, and at the family estate in Milton, Massachusetts, an impending visit to which is announced in this letter. See *Persons,* 346–48.

To Charles Augustus Strong
[Before 1889?] • [Roxbury, Massachusetts?]   (MS: Rockefeller)

Thursday

Dear Strong

Thank you for this. I am pleased ~~with~~ that the reviewer[1] takes us seriously; but he seems to be exclusively occupied with one point.

I see Fuller[2] now and then—unsatisfactory mind: always seems to be really thinking of something else, like a woman. Yesterday he had a young French professor[3] in tow who said Einstein[4] was an absolutist, and that his theory should have been called Théorie de l'Invariance!

Yours ever

G.S.

[1]Unidentified.
[2]Benjamin Apthorp Gould "Bags" Fuller (1879–1956) was a member of the Harvard class of 1900. He pursued graduate study (Ph.D., 1906) with Santayana and later was appointed to the Harvard faculty.
[3]Unidentified.
[4]Albert Einstein (1879–1955), born in Germany, was an American theoretical physicist (known for his theory of relativity) who won the 1921 Nobel Prize.

To Charles Augustus Strong

29 January 1889 • Roxbury, Massachusetts   (MS: Rockefeller)

26 Millmont St.
Roxbury.

Jan • 29 • 89

Dear Strong.

You have brought upon yourself a letter of whose length I have no idea as yet; but you must not complain for if all evils are to be charged to their First Cause, this epistle is to be laid at your door. You have touched my most susceptible spring: still I am too much dulled and dried up by work— by work, I say,—to promise you any thing clever. But here goes.

You ask: Why should ideals be null in the sight of God simply because they all are involved in his nature? Just as, on pantheistic principles, error is involved in God's nature, yet for him exists as error, and is contrasted with a known truth, why should not in the same way moral ideals exist for God as approximations to an absolute ideal, which he recognized as the standard of value? That is your question, as I understand it. Now I will begin by confessing that to my mind pantheism is nothing but the atheism of a religious man: it is religious emotion in a world without gods. Hence I should at once admit that if there is a God he may regard a moral standard as absolute, and that we, in so far as we recognize his authority, will acknowledge God's standard as overruling ours. But for Spinoza there is in reality no God: there is no definite being whose moral or intellectual judgments we may look to as the fulfilment and ideal perfection of our own. The nature of things, for Spinoza, is indeterminate, or, rather, is nothing but the equal and uncaused reality of all existent things: hence ideals in his system have no greater authority than ₐthatₐ they derive from their social and psychological necessity. But you seem to me to be wrong in saying that the ideals are "null". They are perfectly valid as ideals, as directions of human aspiration; and their presence in us together with our allegiance to them is sanctioned by the nature of things. Thus Spinoza's own ideal of contemplative, scientific, piety, is perfectly valid: only it has no transcendent authority, no authority over other ideals in other minds.

And this Spinozistic doctrine seems to me true not only for a world without God, as his was, but even for a world with a God in it. Here is where you will probably not agree with me: you will say that a divine mind would essentially have authority in matters of truth and of right, as in all other matters. But I fail to understand how this authority can exist except by virtue either of a physical sanction or of an immanent agreement between God's judgments and the tendency of our own. Take the case of truth. You say God would see the truth; do you mean that there is a certain constitution of things with which our ideas more or less agree, and with which Gods ideas agree perfectly? In that case God would see the truth because his ideas would be representations of the same reality ∧as∧ our ideas stand for; God's mind would be the ideal of our mind. And his authority would derive from the immanent tendency in our minds to agree with him. In other words, because he is what we wish to be, because he understands what we strive to understand, there fore he is as we ought to be and therefore his thoughts are the truth. Now take the other supposition, and consider that God's thoughts are not representations of the same objects as ours, but that there is no external reality for his thoughts to agree with at all. Then God's thoughts become that objective reality which our thoughts represent; and the question of their truth is impossible, not because they are undeniably true, for they are not representative, but because they are the <u>facts</u> which our thought seeks to represent. And here again the authority of the facts is explicable: it is founded on a physical sanction. Unless our thoughts do agree with the reality life becomes impossible for us: we go mad, and the conduct grounded on these thoughts involves our ruin. So that only those survive who agree with God. But that apart from this physical sanction the thoughts of such a God have any authority over ours, I cannot concede. As facts, as the nature of things with which our thoughts deal, of course these divine thoughts are the truth, the reality: but if as thoughts they should be utterly different from our representation of them, yet our representation was in so far parallel to them as to guide our conduct rightly: then for the life of me I can't see why you should say that those divine thoughts were truer than my thoughts.

I have taken the more difficult subject on purpose: you can apply the same to the case of moral standards. Only in this case it is impossible to conceive an external object to which judgments should conform. Evidently the only possible criterion of a moral judgment is another moral judgment. And between them there can be only a physical judge: that is, only the actual impossibility of maintaining a moral ideal can do away with its authority. Authority is the essence of moral ideals: so long as they exist, they have authority; for this they do not derive but confer. Therefore a moral ideal is essentially and inevitably absolute: you can drop it, you can

make it disappear, but you cannot overrule it. This is the only interpretation of Kant's categorical imperative that does not make a crying absurdity
of it: which, however, was undoubtedly what Kant made of it. himself.

So much for insistence on the arbitrariness of ideals, which you hastily
call their nullity—as if my preferences for were null because I can't pretend
to enforce them in other men But you will doubtless say that I have not
answered your question: cannot God have a moral ideal? And I answer
that in the affirmative. Undoubtedly if as much above our passions as the
ends of space are beyond our thunderstorms there is a consciousness and
an emotion, these will contain some judgment of value, some sense of what
ought to be. And the various parts of this world may appear to God, if he
thinks of this world at all, as having different degrees of hideousness and
insignificance. He may have his preferences among us: but who can tell
what personage is his favorite hero? And by what test shall we decide
whether the standards of this exalted divinity are morally good? They may
not be comparable to ours at all: perhaps what God values in us is some
function of ours in the universe of which we have no conception and that
has no relation to those pleasures and pains, to those volitions, that are our
terrene standards of value. The fact that God may be a moral being does
not at once signify that the objects of his moral life are the same as ours:
and it is only on that supposition that his judgments would have any moral
significance for us. Who would venture to say that infinite varieties of life,
untold complications of interests and endeavors may not fill this infinite
space? But what have such possibilities to do with our ethics? Nothing,
absolutely nothing. The value of God as a moral authority lies in the identity of his judgment with our own: it lies in the belief that our moral judgments are shared by an immortal judge. Not the least particle of moral
guidance can such a belief give us: only a certain moral intensity in maintaining ideals that have such super-human indorsement. The only thought
that could give a moral ideal an absolute authority is that it was the only
existent ideal: that every where where ideals existed at all they were parts
and parcels of this. Then, in the absence of all competition, this ideal
would be absolute indeed: for as I have said it is the nature of ideals to be
absolute over those in whose minds they are present. If the same ideal
were present in all minds, that ideal would be alone absolute. And this is
perhaps what you are trying to believe: and you may believe it so long as
you don't pretend to know what that ideal is, so long as in some mystical
and self contradictory way you hope that the various ideals at war in yourself and in others are really one and the same ideal. But if you are ever

tempted to say, I know that single and absolute ideal: men that think they value something else are simply in illusion: I know their true interests better than they do themselves:—the moment you say that, you become a fanatic, and are guilty of impiety against all those ideal goods that are dear to men's hearts. For in truth their are many ideals, many absolute goods. The art of life is to realize as many of those we cherish as possible, and the science of ethics is ~~the~~ to consider how many of them are realisable together, and what are the conditions of the realization of each.

I have nothing of sublunary interest to impart. We go on with Kant and Lotze. I have been rather overpowered and Lotzified into an impossibility to think: but I have gone to see a few people, even gone to a ball, and I feel better for it. I expect to begin the final copy of my thesis in a few days: not that the rough draught is finished, but that I don't propose to make any complete rough draught. (I suppose this should be draft; but I should prefer the other sort: I am very thirsty and sleepy: so, good by.)

Ever sincerely yours
GSantayana

To Charles Augustus Strong

19 March 1889 • Roxbury, Massachusetts   (MS: Rockefeller)

---

26 Millmont St
Roxbury.

March 19, 89.

Dear Strong:

Just a word to wish you all joy, and a pleasant voyage. I am very sorry I can't go to the wedding, it would have been something to remember with pleasure.

Pray thank Miss Rockefeller for me for her kind and ingenious little note. I wonder how she found so much to say about such a little matter.

I hope to hear from you occasionally, and to get some notion of your multifarious studies.

With the very best wishes, I am
Ever yours
G. Santayana

To Henry Ward Abbot

26 July 1889 • Roxbury, Massachusetts   (MS: Columbia)

26 Millmont St.
Roxbury.

July 26. 89.

Dear Harry.

I don't wonder you didn't like my last letter. But you mustn't complain of rough handling in a serious tone, for that is what you indulge in yourself. I should never have written such a letter to anyone else. You, who are an analyser of character and motives after the manner of the novelists, may be able to answer a question that puzzles me: why do you manage to exasperate and at the same time to influence me more than anyone else?

I have been reading Tourgennef's "Dimitri Roudine."[1] I suppose you know it. Novels when they interest me, as this did, oppress me extraordinarily. They are good not because they are beautiful, but because they make one uncomfortable. Life seems so cheerless, so unideal. The good men are so unpoetic, the poetic people are so insufferable and absurd. Doubtless it is so in real life. But why repeat real life?—we have enough of it and to spare. In books, above all in fiction and poetry, (which are the same thing; that's ∧one reason∧ why my verses are not poetry: they create nothing:) in books, I say, I like to find what I like to think of, not what I am in the habit of observing. I like to think of Achilles; were I a painter or sculptor I should describe him:[2] but I don't like to think of "Dimitri Rudine," nor should I ever describe such a person.

I send you my last harpings on the old string.

Ever yours
GSantayana

Vale et Ave.[3]

The pagan, when he felt his days were done,
Drew o'er his swimming eyes a seemly veil,
Saying, Farewell, fair splendour of the sun!
Hail, Tartarus,[4] eternal darkness, Hail!

The dying Christian, through a mist of tears,
Strained his dim sight until he thought he saw
Heaven, the wage of all his straightened years,
The sanction manifest of awful law.

My soul was native to the Christian dream,
And in faith's faery garden oped her eyes;
The floating angels did her playmates seem,
On banks of incense in the purple skies.

When night o'erwhelmed the glories of that day
And drove my soul from her enchanted life,
She to the house of exile took her way,
Wrapped in her mantle, and disdaining strife.

Till, from the portals she beheld the morn
Gilding the vineyards of an earthly ~~veil~~ vale,
And cried, Farewell, ye paling ghosts forlorn!
Hail, living fire, kind light of heaven, Hail!

———

July 25, 89.

[1]Ivan Sergeyevich Turgenev (1818–83) was a Russian novelist whose masterpiece is *Fathers and Sons* (1862). *Rudin* (1855) is his story about the travails of Dmitri Nikolayevich Rudin who impressed people with high-minded talk that mirrored German idealist philosophers. He was unprepared for decisive action. When he tried to act, by participating in a revolt in Paris, he was shot dead. Rudin has been characterized as a superfluous man, unable to find a suitable cause or proper outlet for his energies.

[2]Achilles is the prototype of manly valor and beauty in Greek mythology. He was the hero of Homer's *Iliad* where he took part in the Trojan War and slew the Trojan hero Hector. Achilles had been dipped in the river Styx by his mother, which rendered him invulnerable except in the heel by which she held him. He was fatally wounded there by an arrow shot by Paris, Hector's brother. Santayana described Achilles in the three sonnets entitled "Before a Statue of Achilles," published in *The Harvard Monthly* (October 1897) and later in *Complete Poems*, 128–29.

[3]Farewell and Hail (*Complete Poems*, 423–24).

[4]In Greek mythology souls of the dead went to an underworld, Hades. Tartarus, below Hades, was a place of torment for the very wicked.

To Henry Ward Abbot

6 August 1889 • Roxbury, Massachusetts   (MS: Columbia)

26 Millmont St.
Roxbury.
Aug 6, 89.

Dear Harry.

Your answer to my question is satisfactory and flattering (in a way I like). Mrs. Patterson[1] also seems to be right; not that I expect or want you to be cleverer or more active, but that I expect you to be less common-place in your tastes and more open to generous emotions. You are not a Philistine: why then do you have the hardness the narrowness and the dog-matism of Philistia in your feelings? It exasperates me because I have always believed you were not really so: that the best in you was the real, and the worst the affectation and accidental dye. You may not influence me in the way of changing my ideas: I am not your disciple or (as you once wrote) your protégé. But you do make me do things I should not do of my own free will, as e.g. show you my verses. When I am with you I almost adopt your notions about my supposed literary rôle: I almost catch your tone. But my real feeling and conviction are quite opposed to that: I know what I want to do, and what I amount to. You think you encourage me, and in one sense you do: but you encourage me to be something worse than what I really am: that is what you do not see, and it disgusts and repels me that you should not see it. You would be better pleased if I acted like Fullerton. You do not see that I am of another type.

I must quarrel with your criticism of neo-paganism. In my case it may be true that it is forced (although I do not feel it so myself). I may not be able to free myself entirely from the oppression of a false idealism. But the question is a broad one: my lingering superstitions or yours are personal accidents. I protest against the notion that what is really joyous and lovely in life is for ever vitiated to all men because a fictitious and fanatical sys-tem has had great influence in the world. Your position is hardly tenable. You admit, do you not, that paganism is rational and satisfactory for men who have not been Christians? So that for our children, if we brought them up without Christianity, paganism would be natural and rational. That is, paganism is the human and spontaneous attitude of an intelligent and cul-tivated man in the presence of the universe. So that your consistent pes-simism is but the unnatural ~~effect~~ ^reaction^ after an unnatural excitement and strain. The Hebrew religion and its twin offspring, and more than all, the Hebraising sects of Christianity, represent a false moral interpretation of life, a weight of responsibility and a consciousness of importance, which human nature repudiates. The Jews had the incredible conceit of believing they had made a covenant with nature, by which the mastery of the earth and all the good things thereof were secured to them in return for fidelity to a certain social and religious organization. Freed from its religious and irrational nature this covenant might stand for something real. Nature does award her prizes in return for fidelity to certain ethical laws: only these laws are natural: they are variable according to circumstances, and discoverable only by experience and study of history. But a religion, as it developss, loses hold of the natural significance and justification of its first principles. The fiction grows, the truth dwindles. So with the Hebrew idea. From recognition of the conditions of worldly success it waxed into the assertion of an inscrutable inward law with transcendent and imaginary sanctions. The crushing weight of delirious exhaltation is still felt, especially in Protestant communities. Catholicism is rational in its morals: its superstitions are in the field of fancy and ∧emotional∧ speculation; in conduct it has remained rational, granting the reality of the conditions of life believed in. In fact I have never been well able to understand the moral superstition of conscience and duty. Only when reading ∧of∧ or seeing cases of insanity has it become clear to me. Alan Mason,[2] for instance, has moral delirium, a fearful belief in right and wrong, without external sanctions, and of pathological origin. A touch of this insanity is what pervades society. And will you pretend to assert that life is not worth living if we are not mad? that only superstitious terrors give it value? that actual goods are worthless and fictitious and imaginary goods—in which is no enjoyment, no peace, and no loveliness,—are alone valuable? I confess, that seems to me pure madness. The world may have little in it that is good: granted. But that little is really and inalienably good. Its value cannot be destroyed because of the surrounding evil. But the greatest of all evils is surely that lunacy that convinces us that this little good is not good, and subverts natural standards in favor of unnatural and irrational standards. It is a form of insanity. And you know how the insane tinge sometimes all their experiences with a pathological horror or emptiness. That is just what you would have us do in the name of consistency. It seems to me that even supposing that our illusions are pleasant and consoling (which is not the case with moral illusions, although it may be with purely imaginative and speculative fictions) the lesson of life is to give them up quietly and settle down, a sadder but a wiser man, on the new basis. And believe me, in respect to paganism, the new basis is the best basis. It admits more noble emotion, more justifiable ambition, more universal charity, than the old system. I cannot go on for ever: but I should like to show how we deceive ourselves in thinking that immortality, for instance, really added to our lives any value. An old man's enthusiasms, if he has any, are <u>naturally</u> for the world he leaves behind him not for himself. Cf. Gladstone.[3] F. Harrison[4] may be a fool, but positivism, if truly pagan, seems to me good. But Goethe is the real spokesman of neo-paganism. I follow him.

Yours ever GSantayana

[1]Unidentified.

[2]Alan Gregory Mason was a member of the Harvard class of 1886.

[3]William Ewart Gladstone (1809–98) dominated Britain's Liberal Party from 1868 to 1894. As chancellor of the exchequer he promoted free trade and fairer tax distribution. As four-time prime minister, he achieved notable reforms. His advocacy of Irish home rule ended his ministry. Gladstone was a powerful orator and a master of finance.

[4]Frederic Harrison (1831–1923) was an English jurist, historian, and sociologist. He co-founded the *Positivist Review* and was president of the English Positivist Committee. He wrote on law, politics, and literature, as well as biographies, a novel, and a long poem.

To Henry Ward Abbot

29 September 1889 • Cambridge, Massachusetts   (MS: Columbia)

---

29 Thayer.[1]

Cambridge

Sept 29. 89.

Dear Harry.

It is really very nice of you to ask me down again after my shabby treatment of you since my last visit. I meant to have looked you up at the Tremont House,[2] but somehow I didn't. Now I am really in a dreadful condition of slavery. Bowen[3] has resigned his place, and his course in the Cartesians[4] and Germans has been turned over to me of a sudden. I am expected to lecture every day, and what with reading, getting up the lectures, hunting for books in the library, and worrying over the slip-shod way in which after all the work is presented to the boys, I haven't a spare moment. I have, however, the consolation of feeling rich; I don't know how much I am to get for this second course, but I presume another $500, so that with my habits I shall have plenty. As soon as you return come to see me; come at some meal-time, and I will take you to 16 Oxford St. where I am at a little table with Baker, Carpenter, and Fletcher.[5] Also, if you write, tell me when your mother and sister are coming home, as I want to take the first chance I have of seeing them.

I can't write much more. I am sorry you are so despondent. You ought to be out here, or in some equivalent place, where life is really very pleasant, and the inner man enjoys various gentle delights. This way you have of wandering about in search of nothing is what depresses you. Go to Rome with your mother, get into some studio there, and paint. Or do something pleasant, that is work but work that can be done for its own sake, and is therefore also play. You preach to me about lack of ambition and discouragement about myself. Why, I marvel at my own audacity and impudence in talking ex tempore out of my inner consciousness to a few (a very few, viz. 5 and 6 respectively) boys about a lot of things I only half know. But you are really discouraged, really underestimate yourself. You ought to stand up for yourself. No one else will stand up for you if you don't. And its as easy as lying.[6] Convince yourself you are necessary in the world, and you will convince the world of your utility. You haven't self-sufficiency enough. That is why you are despondent. Cheer up, and try to enjoy the beauty and vanity of life and be happy in the pleasantness of the present moment. And, while we are in good health, the present moment has its pleasantness, if you only will see it. The trouble is we look for those gifts from the Hours which they don't bring us, and peevishly refuse those they lay at our feet. One brings a memory, and we ask it for a hope; another a pleasure, and we insist on a consolation. But there is time for all these things, as for sunny and rainy days in the year. Nothing is more foolish than not to enjoy the fair days when [*across*] they come, but insist they shall change places with the storms, which if we accept them, have also their beauty. But I must read Descartes life for my to-morrow's lecture; so good by, and come to see me as soon as possible.

Ever yours
GS.

[1]Thayer Hall in the Harvard Yard.

[2]In Boston.

[3]Francis "Fanny" Bowen (1811–90) was the Alford Professor of Natural Religion, Moral Philosophy, and Civil Polity at Harvard (1853–89). See *Persons*, 236.

[4]The Cartesians are followers of René Descartes (Renatus Cartesius) (1596–1650) who was a French philosopher, scientist, and mathematician often called the father of

modern philosophy. Descartes worked out the treatment of negative roots and a system of notation in algebra, originated Cartesian coordinates and curves, and founded analytic geometry. In his *Discourse on Method* (1637) Descartes describes a method of systematic doubt as the starting point for rational inquiry; in *Meditations on First Philosophy* (1641) he shows that one fact cannot be doubted: the existence of the doubter (*Cogito ergo sum*: I think, therefore I am). From this, Descartes reestablishes distinct ideas and beliefs in all he had previously doubted, utilizing the proofs for God's existence he offers along the way. *Principles of Philosophy* (1644) is a formal presentation of his views. Descartes's methodology makes epistemology the starting point of philosophical inquiry, and his mind-body dualism is central to discussions in the philosophy of mind.

[5]Possibly Charles Ruel Fletcher, Harvard class of 1886, or Jefferson Butler Fletcher (1865–1946), class of 1887.

[6]'Tis as easy as lying. *Hamlet*, III.ii.374.

To Charles Augustus Strong
22 July 1890 • Ávila, Spain   (MS: Rockefeller)

Avila, July 22, 90.

Dear Strong–

It was a great pleasure to get your letter. I have seldom read anything more fair and admirable than your arguments and statements. You are only mistaken in thinking I differ from you on the matter. But before saying any more on that subject, let me tell you what I have been doing.

In the Spring of '89, while I was writing my thesis for the doctor's degree, James proposed that I should give Phil 5 for him the next year, while he finished and published his Principles of Psychology. I accepted at once, for I believe in taking thought for the morrow, but not for the day after. This seemed an obvious thing to do for the present, and might prove a useful beginning for my work When the time came and I had met my class of five students a few times, Bowen resigned. The President[1] came to see me and asked me to take Phil 6 also. This increased my salary to $1000, and gave me one lecture a day for the year. I had only three men in 6. The work was not absorbing or fascinating, but it seemed to be fairly successful and I believe the impression I produced was not unfavorable on the whole. At any rate, I have been reappointed for next year, when I shall give Phil 5 again (reading Hobbes, beside Locke Berkeley & Hume)[2] and a new course on Lotze's Microcosmos,[3] which will not be hard for me, and the psychology of the single introductory course in philosophy now offered. This course, Phil 1 in the new arrangement, consists of three parts. Until Xmas Palmer lectures on logic, then until Easter I follow in psychology, and James winds up with metaphysics, or general problems. You see I shall be busy. As to my plans for the future, they are simply to take up and put up with what offers. I am content to go on with lectures at Harvard indefinitely, if they want me. If they don't, something else will probably present itself. Harvard has many attractions and advantages, the main one being the great freedom you enjoy. Royce last year annoyed me a good deal. I took a course he gave in Hegel's Phenomenologic[4] which was appalling, and he seemed to be bent on converting me to absolute idealism nolens volens.[5] But Royce, although sometimes such a bore, is a good and kind man, and very appreciative, and generous to me. With Palmer I get on well. We never discuss anything. I treat him as if he were a clergyman, and he is nice to me. With James I have much more sympathy, both personal and intellectual I think he is beginning to understand that I am not a dreamer and obscurantist, and that, in spite of certain literary leanings, I am capable of facing questions of fact and evidence without repugnance ~~and~~ or parti pris.[6] Everett[7] has also become a friend of mine. Peabody is the only member of the philosophical Committee that seems to think me dangerous and highly improper. The President looks upon me with favor, because as I am told, he thinks I may contribute to the college a little of that fresh air and blood of which it stands in so much need. It is really sad to see how mediocrity Germanised rules supreme there. For all these reasons I think my position at Harvard tolerably stable and honorable. I study to keep apart from the Germans. Royce is the only one I cannot avoid. I dined with Carpenter and Baker, of the English department, and with Fletcher, a graduate student of philosophy and a nice man. In the afternoon I walked with Boylston Beal or others of the unphilosophical, and I saw something of a number of undergraduates, men on the papers or family connections and friends. Altogether I had a good time, and enjoyed what I never had cared for before, the air and sunlight, food and drink, and the consciousness of life—rational and irrational—about me.

By the way, I saw your former chief Prof. Schurmann this winter. He came to sound the Cambridge philosophers on the subject of founding an American philosophical journal.[8] I was glad to see that his project met with universal discouragement. Since that time, however, Royce has afflicted me with the subject again, and even asked me if I would be willing to undertake the editorship. I gave an evasive answer, for I should not particularly object, if the thing were perpetrated at all, to have some influence in selecting the kind of ignorance and presumption that should appear in it. A little less Hegelian drivel might thus be administered to the feeble minded public. But I hope the plan may collapse. If anything is written in America worth publishing it can go into Mind,[9] which certainly has room for it. I do not attach great weight to Schurmann's objection to this plan, viz. that in two weeks a number of Mind is behind the times, and we must have a pure American truth, served hot every morning like the biscuits. Schurmann, indeed, appeared to me like a wise man of Philistia,[10] rhetorical, vulgar, and self-asserting.

I have not left room for much discussion of Ethics. I admit all you say about the inherent lack of authority in a "demand". All the stars laugh at a demand. I have no notion of making it sacred. And I also admit (and here I am glad to see we have been moving in the same direction) that it is by their consequences that the lawfulness of actions should be measured. Theirre is no practical seriousness in a system that poopoos consequences, and strings phrases ‸together‸ about self imposed, self evident principles. But I would have you observe, in excuse for my former insistence on demands as the basis of Ethics, that our judgments about good and bad consequences are inspired by instincts which may very properly be called our natural demands. The reason why I should not do a particular atrocity, e.g. maintain protection or Hegelianism, is the consequences. But why is poverty, the consequence of the one, or idiocy, the consequence of the other, an evil? Because of my natural demand, and that of my fellows, for wealth and for intelligence. And so it still seems to me, after heartily admitting all you say, that our actual and spontaneous demand for one kind of existence rather than another is the ultimate basis of all values.

I shall remain here until late in August. I sail from Liverpool on the Teutonii on Sept. 3. In London I saw Fullerton and Berenson. Fullerton is a great personage, and Editor of the London Times. Burke,[11] whom you may remember, is married to a widow with two children, but younger than himself in spite of her varied experiences. Lord Russell is also married,[12] and busy about engines and electric aparatus as usual. Johnson[13] has left Oxford and is to live in London among artists, at 20 Fitzroy St. I give you the address in case you care to go to see him if you are soon to be in England. I hope before long our paths may cross again, or still better meet and run on together. My best regards to Mrs. Strong. I hope she is quite well by this [*across*] time. Let me know your plans and movements, and if possible your thoughts as well.   Ever Yours   G. Santayana

[1]Charles William Eliot (1834–1926) began teaching at Harvard after his 1853 graduation. After study in Europe, he became chemistry professor at the Massachusetts Institute of Technology in 1865. He was appointed president of Harvard in 1869. In

1909, at the end of his tenure, Harvard had become one of the great universities of the world. Characteristic of his curricular reform was advocacy of the elective system and abolition of a required curriculum. Santayana saw Eliot's reform program as a movement away from traditional liberal education toward mere "preparation for professional life" and "service in the world of business." (*Persons,* 396)

[2]Thomas Hobbes (1588–1670) was an English philosopher who set forth a mechanistic rationalistic materialism. His *Leviathan* (1651) made him the first of the great English political theorists. John Locke (1632–1704) founded British empiricism. His empiricism was expanded by Berkeley and Hume, and men of the Enlightenment regarded him as the prophet of reason. George Berkeley (1685–1753) was an Irish English philosopher credited with founding the philosophical doctrine of subjective idealism–the theory that all qualities are known only in the mind, that matter does not exist apart from its being perceived, and that the observing mind of God makes possible the continued apparent existence of material objects. David Hume (1711–76) was an influential Scottish philosopher whose works include *Treatise of Human Nature, An Enquiry Concerning the Principles of Morals,* and *An Enquiry Concerning the Human Understanding.* An empiricist influenced by Newton, Hume wanted to apply the experiential method to the principles of the human mind to develop a science of human nature. He thought only naturalism could avoid the skeptic's argument and was an enemy of religion.

[3]*Microcosmus: An Essay Concerning Man and his Relation to the World* (1894).

[4]*Phenomenology of Mind* (1807).

[5]Whether willing or unwilling.

[6]Preconceived opinion.

[7]Charles Carroll Everett (1829–1900) was a theologian, author of *Science of Thought* (1869), and dean of the Harvard Divinity School (1878–1900).

[8]Jacob Gould Schurman (1854–1942) was a professor of Christian ethics and mental philosophy at Cornell (1886). He became dean of Cornell's School of Philosophy (1890) and later president of Cornell (1892). He believed in objective idealism and emphasized the totality of human experience in its social, historical, and institutional aspects. In 1892 the first general scholarly philosophical journal in America, the *Philosophical Review,* began publication at Cornell under his editorship. He served as minister to Greece and Montenegro, minister to China, and ambassador to Germany.

[9]*Mind: A Quarterly Review of Psychology and Philosophy,* originally published in London, later Edinburgh, now Oxford, was established in 1876 and is issued quarterly. Its editors have included George C. Robertson, G. F. Stout, G. E. Moore, and Gilbert Ryle.

[10]Philistia was an ancient country in southwestern Palestine that was the land of the Philistines.

[11]An Oxford friend of Frank Russell. See *Persons,* 299.

[12]Mabel Edith Scott (d. 1909), Frank Russell's first wife. Russell's marriage to her on 6 Feb 1890 was ill-fated: the couple lived together for three months.

[13]Lionel Pigot Johnson (1867–1902) was a Welsh poet and critic whom Santayana met at New College, Oxford. See *Persons,* 304–5.

To Charles Augustus Strong
10 August 1890 • Ávila, Spain   (MS: Rockefeller)

Avila, Aug 10, 90.

Dear Strong—

I am very glad to hear you are to be at Worcester. I shall hope to see you often. It is true I am one of those who don't wholly approve of Clark University,[1] or rather who don't approve of Clark but do approve of universities, and think it a pity there should be new foundations when the old are in such need of enlargement. Still, I understand Clark intends to be a sort of special school, and it will find its place I suppose. But I shall be glad to learn something about it by your experience.

You surprise me a little by your tone of discovery and enlightenment, because of the theory of the parallelism of body and mind. Of course the idea is admirable and the facts fit into it because it leaves room for them in the physical chain. Fictions also fit into it, because the whole psychical [*illegible*]sphere is there waiting to be filled by them. For facts, observable facts about which verifiable theories can be made, are all physical. Now you may argue that the cosmic order would be more beautiful and symmetrical if there were a chain of psychical facts, connected by psychical laws, running parallel to all the physical facts ultimately observable. But as far as my poor studies and observations go this argument a pulchriori[2] is not supported by any evidence. The few ~~physical~~ psychical facts we know, or can assume to exist without violence to common sense and convention, don't cover the physical order by any means. Take it nearest home. Our mental life is far from having an element corresponding in any way to every element of our bodily life. Consciousness is a local and occasional ebulition like the hiccough. What business have you, on the basis of some scattered phenomena (for such mental phenomena are, in comparison with physical) to invent an infinite universe of mind stretching over the whole of space and time and wherever matter is found? Why not be satisfied with confessing the ignorance we cannot avoid whether we confess it or not? The world we look out upon and live in is composed of matter in space; but by a process you know better than I, doubtless, how to describe, we discover that this whole apparition, ~~and~~ ˄with˄ the emotions that arise from it, is lodged and bound in one small part of the matter, in one spot of the space, which because of this singular quality is called my body. And a very natural anɸalogy leads us to suppose the same mental life to lodge in

the other similar bodies of our universe. But this anɲalogy by which alone
you get any parallelism at all, cannot carry you very far. For there is no
parallelism observed directly between my soul and body, ~~but~~ ˄for˄ my
mental life is a unique phenomenon, the one phenomenon, in fact; but
the parellism is between other supposed minds (and I assimilate mine to
the~~irs~~m out of courtesy) and bodies. In a word, you establish a parallelism
not between facts of the same category, of the same plane of existence,
but between objects and ejects, between facts and interpretations of facts,
between hypostatizations of the first degree and hypostatizations of the
second.

All this I say understanding you to mean a universal parallelism after
the fashion of Spinoza. If you mean only that no energy is spent on
thought, and that mind wherever it may appear, is an epiphenomenon, I
sympathize with you; but I think a matter of the transformation of energy
ought to be left for experiment to settle, and if no experiment can be made,
opinions are idle. It might turn out, if we entered the brain and visited it,
as Leibniz[3] suggests, as we should a mill,—it might turn out that here and
there a little energy dropped in or out; that some imponderable stream ran
a wheel in one place, and that in another place a motion was checked without any apparent cause. We might then reasonably infer that these exiʃts
and entrances of force into the physical world and out of it, corresponded
to those transitory flashes of existence which alone are observed in the
mental sphere. If we found no such breaks in the material universe, however, we ought, it seems to me, to be satisfied with adding our psychology
in occasional footnotes ˄to our physics,˄ where by chance be had found it
to belong. The mind would have to be treated as a parasite, if that can be
called a parasite which comsumes nothing of the substance on which it
lives. I doubt that your "science" of psychophysics has got within sight of
a solution of this question. If it has I beg to be informed, for although I
have no preferences in the matter and am quite as willing that the world
should have been made on the one plan as on the other, yet I am curious
to know what preferences the gods may have shown. Possibly—or is this
doubt too irrational for you—the gods don't run the world on a plan at all,
and our principles of intelligibility are not at all the principles of being.
The alternative we are discussing may not be a dilemma for nature, but she
may live on without laws or, what is the same thing, according to laws
beyond our comprehension.

I don't know whether all this is intelligible. I think I could make it so, if
it were worth while, but I suppose you will supply my lacunae yourself eas-

ily enough. What I mean is this merely. Aren't you in some danger of falling into the habit, so common among philosophers, of taking conceivability for proof? But when a theory is conceived and all logical and moral objections to it are cleared away or ridden over, your theory remains a mere idea one possibility out of the infinite possibilities of being. I ask for evidence that nature is really built so. Is there any?

You will say that you adopt your theory only as a good "way of learning the stuff of the universe." Very well; but if you adopt it too exclusively you will make other ways of classifying things repugnant and impossible for you; you may miss whole aspects of nature which to others are visible. To my mind there is only one way of learning the stuff of the universe, and that is to reject ~~none.~~ ₐno way of learning it.ₐ The universe is a sum of vistas: to talk of any one as adequate is like discussing from which mountain you can view the whole surface of the earth. The universe we deal with is human experience: beyond that ſno mythology, nay, not even psychophysics, can take us. And human experience includes many ways of viewing the world, it is, in fact, a vast succession of momentary ways of viewing it. And the object of our education is to instruct the mind in as many ways ~~and~~ as possible of absorbing experience. Why Greek studies, if not to prevent the loss by humanity of the memory of its happiest moment? Why philosophical studies, if not to increase our possibilities of comprehension, to increase our elasticity of mind? And it is a dream worthy only of the conceit and ignorance of a Hegel to imagine that we can reach one system inₐtoₐ which all others will flow like tributary streams, carrying all their wisdom with them. No, unhappily. The human mind can grow in wisdom, let us hope it may long grow in wisdom. But its greater wisdom will be the usuper of its lesser, the destroyer of all that went before. An old man may be wiser than a young man, or as frequently happens infinitely more foolish. But change is change, in whatever direction, and the young man's "way of learning the stuff of the universe" is necessarily different from the old man's. And the irreparable changes are more evident still in history. The only way of making our conception and idea of things better than those that others have had is to cultivate our susceptibility, to make ourselves sensitive to the greatest variety of impressions and quick with the greatest number of generalizations and abreviations of them. They are all good and no one is sufficient, simply because each excludes us from all the others.

Pardon this long letter. I hope we may soon talk these and others matters over. I expect to be about Cambridge on Sept. 15th. Then o*f*r there-
after I hope to see you there or in Boston.

Ever yours
GSantayana

[1]Clark University at Worcester, Massachusetts, was chartered in 1887 and opened in
1889 as a nonsectarian, coeducational school. It became one of the pioneer graduate
schools, specializing in education and psychology.
[2]On the basis of beauty.
[3]Gottfried Wilhelm Freiherr von Leibniz (1646–1716) was a German philosopher and
mathematician who was learned in science, history, and law.

To Alice Freeman Palmer
Sunday [1890–96] • Cambridge, Massachusetts   (MS: Chicago)

My dear Mrs Palmer[1]
    It would give me a great deal of pleasure to come to tea tomorrow and
meet Miss Monroe,[2] but I have an appointment in town—at the dentist's—
and hardly know when I shall get away. You will believe that if I don't turn
up, it will be very much against my inclination. With many thanks for your
kindness

Yours sincerely
GSantayana

7 Stoughton
Sunday

[1]Alice Freeman Palmer (1855–1902) was married to George Herbert Palmer of the
Harvard Philosophy Department. Prior to her marriage, she was a history professor
and then president of Wellesley College. Later she was dean of the women's department at the University of Chicago.
[2]Unidentified.

To Charles Augustus Strong

16 August 1891 • Ávila, Spain   (MS: Rockefeller)

Avila, Aug 16, 1891.

Dear Strong

Many thanks for your interesting article,[1] which has been forwarded to me here. As I have nothing of interest to say about myself or my doings—for I am here as usual on a visit to my father—I will plunge at once into some considerations a propos of your criticism.

Professor Case[2] is wholly unknown to me, and apparently I have no great reason to regret the fact. What you say is so obvious that I need hardly say I agree with it. Only when you get to the bottom of page 6, and make some assertions of your own, do I find any trouble in reproducing your thoughts. "In perception" you say "we have the certitude of a world beyond ourselves." "What matter is, we know not . . . . for we perceive only the simulaera[3] of things." "But what mind is, we know." "Reality which appears to us under the form of a material world." In this last phrase you seem to admit that phenomena are material in form: the matter of which we are ignorant can only be a supposed metaphysical substratum, not the parts of the material world. Our knowledge of mind is just of this nature: we don't know the "essential nature" of mind, if you believe there is any essence apart from appearance. We know parts of the psychical world, just as we know parts of the material world: both are phenomena we behold. I wonder at your assuming so boldly that there is a hidden reality of which physical phenomena are the symbols. It is possible, of course; but that is no reason for thinking it true. In perception we have no certitude of a world beyond ourselves, if you mean by ourselves the seat of phenomena. We see an extended world, with our bodies in the middle of it. We have the conception and (while this conception is unchecked) the belief that this extruded world exists eternally and independently. But experience teaches us that our conception of it is dependent on our senses and brain; i.e. that a certain constellation of physical phenomena is the condition of psychical phenomena. But all these discoveries are well within the apparent world—the physical world. For the material world is not a metaphysical object behind phenomena. It is the phenomenon itself. And mind, which you say we know directly, is nothing but the leavings and surplusage of the phenomenal object, those images (imagination and memory) which won't go to make a permanent and orderly conception of nature, and are therefore relegated to the sphere of mere appearances–i.e. appearances that don't count in life. The idea of mind is the counterpart of the idea of objective reality–this is a division which experience teaches us to make within the field of direct appearances. Our part is found to be valid for life and inter-communication–that is called the reality. Another part is found invalid and misleading–that is called the appearance, or the subjective world. But the stuff of both is exactly the same–sensations and conceptions–and in so far as they have a describable content at all, this content is spatial, so that all alike are ideas of matter. I should flatly deny that we know mind more directly than we know matter. What we have before us–what constitutes ofur vision–is a mass of ideas, all essentially spatial and material in form (with emotional qualities, to be sure, which, being useless as information, are all afterwards relegated to the subjective sphere.) By sifting and combining these ideas we gain conceptions of independent permanent things; and by contrast to these independent permanent things, we [*illegible*] call the fleeting and unclassified images ~~me~~ appearances or mental facts. Of course, if you mean by mind not any definite sphere of reality–not the subject-matter of psychology–but the transcendental self–the seat of all these sensations, conceptions, and beliefs–in fact, the world itself as a phenomenon–of course all we know is mental, it is phenomenal, it is a vision and a dream. But this is an utterly futile and idle reflection. It leads no where. I have no surety or hint of anything except as it appears and suggests itself to me now. But the moment I focus my attention, and look about to see what sort of a world I am dreaming about, I find nothing but matter, matter, matter, and mind as its occasional product and accompaniment.

In brief: if you mean by mind the transcendental consciousness–my consciousness now as the source and seat of all reality and truth for me– you have no business to suppose anything whatever beyond it, physical or psychical. If you mean by mind a certain class of objects or phenomena– objects which life and convention regards as invalid and merely personal– then ~~we~~ you are wrong in saying that we know mind more directly than matter, for it is only by making out the laws of matter that we fix the limits and differentiate the character of subjective facts.

You invoke the authority of Kant, and in the same breath bring out evidence about the nature of things in themselves. To my mind, Kant's great achievement is to show that we must dream our dream, that it is absurd to try to talk of any thing but the objects our faculties discover to us; and that the only relations between mind and matter we can make out at all, are the relations between various phenomena—between the empirical self and the objects in space and time. This relation, as you so clearly show, is being fast made out by experiment and study. It is a relation in which mind appears as the accompaniment of certain transformations of brain tissue; and that is all that is to be said about it.

You won't blame me if on such a subject I haven't been perfectly clear. I should be glad if what I say would call out some explanations from you, so that I might clarify my own thoughts on the matter.

I expect to be in Boston on Sept. 13. If you come at any time after that, don't fail to look me up. I shall be in the same room at Cambridge

Yours ever
GSantayana

[1]Unidentified.
[2]Possibly Thomas Case (1844–1925), whose works include *Physical Realism* (London and New York, 1888).
[3]Representations.

To Henry Ward Abbot

15 February 1892 [*postmark*] • Cambridge, Massachusetts (MS: Columbia)

7 Stoughton
Sunday

Dear Harry

I shall be very glad to come and dine with you on Thursday and meet Mr Silsbee. I once saw him for a moment at Mrs Don's, but he propbably doesn't remember me.[1]

I am very much pleased with what people have said of my verses lately, and I am making up my mind to try and publish more, finally following your advice of long ago. The reason is that having deteriorated and become worldly I want the world to think me a poet and philosopher; while I really had the temper of one I despised the world as it deserves. I also should like to have a reputation and a resource to back me in my academic life, which is resolutely unconventional, and which people may not always put up with. But I will never be a professor unless I can be one, as it were, per accidens. I would rather beg than be one essentially.—With many thanks,   Yours ever   G.S.

[1]Silsbee and Mrs. Don are unidentified.

To Isabella Stewart Gardner
26 February 1892 • [Cambridge, Massachusetts]   (MS: Unknown)

Impromptu[1]
Three things are infinite: the Sea
    Of griefs uncomforted unknown,
The laughter of the stars at me,
    And Music's woof of peal and moan—

With thanks for an unforgettable evening from
                                        G.Santayana

[1]This was written on a program from a musical event hosted by Mrs. John "Jack" (Isabella Stewart) Gardner (1840–1924), a wealthy woman of distinction who was a leader in Boston society. She and her husband patronized artists and musicians and collected old masterpieces in their home, which today is the Isabella Stewart Gardner Museum. The concert featured Ignace Jan Paderewski (1860–1941), Polish pianist, composer, and statesman. The program reads: MR. PADEREWSKI WILL PLAY PIANOFORTE PIECES BY BEETHOVEN, BACH, SCHUMAN, [sic] CHOPIN, AND A QUARTET FOR PIANOFORTE AND STRINGS BY BRAHMS   FEBRUARY TWENTY-SIXTH 1892.

To Josiah Royce
6 March 1892 • Cambridge, Massachusetts   (MS: Harvard)

7 Stoughton
March 6. 92.

Dear Prof. Royce

I have been waiting to thank you for your book, which I got long ago, until I had read enough in it to have some just sense of the value of the gift.[1] I perceive now that it is much more than a mere record to your lectures, as we heard them; a thousand things that one overlooked or forgot in the hearing stand out in the printed page and stick in the memory. It is marvellous to me that you should have been able to write a book so full of enthusiasm and humanity in circumstances of such external pressure and distraction. I have read the appendices with special care, and feel much enlightened by them not only in regard to Hegel, but even in regard to Kant. Many things that are vaguely before one are not made really known until one comes upon the just and brief expression of them.

It must be a great satisfaction to you to have brought into the world so attractive and inspiring a book, and I am grateful to you for having sent me a copy of it.

Always faithfully yours

GSantayana

[1] *The Spirit of Modern Philosophy: An Essay in the Form of Lectures* (1892).

To Isabella Stewart Gardner

29 March 1892 • [Cambridge, Massachusetts]   (MS: Unknown)

To

I. S. G.

a Lenten Greeting.

—

Sonnet[1]

—

They must find it sweet to pray
   Who like you have understood
   All the beauty of the good,
All the virtue of the gay.
By the thought that we are clay
   Is proud grief itself subdued;
   May the Spirit of the Rood[2]
In all sorrow be your stay!
Spring your pleasures will renew,–
   For the heart is merry after
Which to Heaven hath been true,–
And, more low for lenten calm,
   Then the music of your laughter
Will have joy as of a psalm

G.S.

March • 29 • 1892

[1] A later version was published in *Complete Poems*, 161.
[2] Cross or crucifix symbolizing the cross on which Christ died.

To Isabella Stewart Gardner
[Spring 1892 or 1894] • Cambridge, Massachusetts   (MS: Gardner)

Dear Mrs Gardner

Alas! I am not going to Venice at all, not even to Paris or Avila, but only to Mr. Davidson's school of philosophy in the Adirondacks.[1] Where else I may go, I hardly care, I am so disappointed at missing the many pleasures of being in Venice with you. But the obstacles are too great. I can't get off on the 28th of May, on account of my work not being over; the next steamer is on June 18,–too late! And any other way of going is impossible on account of the expense–as I am this year particularly impecunious. It was a great comfort in the midst of all this, to get the tickets for the concerts and think you had remembered me so kindly upon going away. I will send them back to Johns before the last concert, as you [*across*] wished. The first, or rather last, concert was very nice indeed–some delightful Mozart.– I felt a little confused when the orchestra looked up at me expecting to see something so much more interesting in that place. What a good place it is, too, to hear from! Conrad Slade[2] went with me, and was also much obliged for that pleasure to you. Will you give my love to Howard Cushing[3] when you see him, together with many regrets at not seeing him this summer.

Yours penitentially
GSantayana

[1]Thomas Davidson (1840–1900) was a Scottish-born American philosopher who came to Canada in 1866 and moved to the U.S. On an 1883 visit to London he founded the Fellowship of the New Life, out of which the Fabian Society developed. Later he established a summer school at his home in the Adirondacks (Hugo Münsterberg taught at this school the summer of 1894) as well as lecture classes for workers in New York City. He served as a tutor, traveled extensively in Europe, and wrote several books on philosophy and education.

[2]Conrad Hensler Slade (b. 1871), the most Nordic of Santayana's American friends, was a member of the class of 1893 and a sculptor. He "was content to live in Paris among poor artists and working people, with none of the comforts or social pleasures among which he had been bred." At Harvard, Slade had rowed with the varsity crew. Described by Santayana as "very good-looking in the expressionless, statuesque manner" and of a solitary, independent nature, Slade was one of the models for Oliver Alden in *Puritan*. Slade's personality and adventures also contributed to Santayana's conception of the *Puritan* character Mario Van de Weyer. See *Persons*, 383–84.

[3]Howard Gardiner Cushing (1869–1916) was a member of the Harvard class of 1891 and a painter. See *Persons*, 348–49.

To William Cameron Forbes
1 December 1892 • Cambridge, Massachusetts   (MS: Houghton)

Dec • 1 • 92

Dear Cam

I am delighted to hear you are going to Spain, and I hope you will not fail to stop at Avila and take this note to my sister. You will find her house very near the Fonda del Ingles,[1] to which you will go, I suppose, and any waiter will show you the way there or take the note. I shall be very glad to hear of your impressions of Spain and especially of Avila. I expect to go there myself in the summer, but probably not so early as to miss you when you come home.

Things are as usual. They have, however, raised my salary unasked to $1500, which makes me rich and happy for the time being, and consoles me for the approach of my twenty-ninth birthday.[2] We have snow on the ground now, but not enough to last until Christmas.

I wish I were travelling about with you, and hope you will have as delightful ₐaₐ time as you ought to under the circumstances.   Yours ever
GSantayana

[1]Inn of the Englishman.
[2]On his 16 December birthday, Santayana gave a dinner for his friends Robert "Bob" Barlow, Francis "Swelly" Bangs, Warwick Potter, Boylston Beal, James A. "Jay" Burden Jr., Julian Codman, and Gordon Bell. In a letter to Daniel Cory (11 Nov 1932) Santayana said the occasion was "one of the pleasantest memories of my life."

To Mary Augusta Jordan
19 December [1892] • Cambridge, Massachusetts   (MS: Smith)

My dear Miss Jordan[1]

Norman Hapgood[2] has kindly told me that you were to be at Mrs. Minot's[3] this week, and that you had some project about my going to Smith College during the next term for a visit. Will you let me know if I shall find you in on Thursday or Friday afternoon, and at what time? Hoping I may have the pleasure of seeing you, I am

Sincerely yours
GSantayana

7 Stoughton, Cambridge
    Dec. 19.

[1]Mary Augusta Jordan (1855–1941) was a member of the Smith College faculty (1884–1921).

[2]Norman Hapgood (1868–1937) was a member of the class of 1890 and edited *The Harvard Monthly.* He was editor of *Collier's Weekly* and later editor of *Harper's Weekly* and *Hearst's International.* Hapgood's autobiography, *The Changing Years,* was published in 1930; he wrote several books.

[3]Possibly Mrs. Charles Sedgwick Minot whose husband taught in the Harvard Medical School (1880–1914).

To Horatius Bonar Hastings
20 December [1892] • Cambridge, Massachusetts   (MS: Unknown)

Dec 20.

My dear Mr Hastings[1]

I shall be perfectly satisfied if you hand in your thesis after the vacation. I have given extra time in several cases, for a less weighty reason than yours.   Yours truly

GSantayana

[1]Horatius Bonar Hastings received an A.M. from Harvard in 1893.

To Sara Norton
Friday [1893] • Cambridge, Massachusetts   (MS: Virginia)

My dear Miss Norton[1]

I shall be delighted to come to dinner today at seven and to hear Prince Wolkonsky read his paper.[2] With many thanks for your kind note and invitation

Yours very truly
GSantayana

7 Stoughton
    Friday

[1]Sara Norton (b. 1864) edited her father's letters, *The Letters of Charles Eliot Norton* (1913).
[2]Prince Serge Wolkonsky (c. 1862–1937) was a Russian author and teacher whose first visit to the U.S. in 1893 included a series of lectures on Russian history at Boston's Lowell Institute.

To Hugo Münsterberg
Saturday [1893] • Cambridge, Massachusetts   (MS: Boston)

My dear Professor Münsterberg[1]

I am very glad to know that you are feeling well enough to return to the laboratory, and if I can be of any use upon Wednesday evening, I shall come with pleasure, and say a very few words. They will have to be very few indeed as my scanty knowledge of Mediaeval theories of the Will will not allow of more. In fact, I doubt that very much material exists for treatment. However, I will do what I can.

I wish I might have done something for you during your illness, following so close upon your bereavement,[2] but both Professor Royce and Dr. Wesselhaft[3] told me there was nothing to be done. But although I have done nothing to manifest it, I have indeed felt a great deal of sympathy for you and for Mrs Münsterberg in her sorrow and anxiety.

Believe me very truly yours

GSantayana

7 Stoughton
Saturday.

[1]Hugo Münsterberg (1863–1916) was a German-born psychologist and philosopher. At the instigation of William James, Münsterberg was persuaded to come from Germany to Harvard as professor of psychology in 1892 where he directed the psychological laboratory. His daughter, Margarete Anna Adelheid Münsterberg (b. 1889), wrote *Hugo Münsterberg, His Life and Work* (New York and London: D. Appleton and Co., 1922).
[2]The death of Mrs. Münsterberg's father.
[3]William Fessenden Wesselhoeft (1862–1943) was chief surgeon at the Massachusetts Memorial Hospital and clinical professor of surgery at the Boston University School of Medicine. He graduated from Harvard in 1884 and from the Medical School three years later.

To Horatius Bonar Hastings

14 April 1893 • Cambridge, Massachusetts   (MS: Santayana)

7 Stoughton
April 14 • 93

My dear Mr Hastings

Mr Henshaw[1] showed me yesterday the very careful and full notes you took in Phil. 8. Might I borrow them long enough to have them copied? They will be very useful to me as they are much more full than the brief headings from which I lectured I am thinking of publishing a little book[2] based on these discussions, so that your notes will be invaluable to me.

Yours very truly
GSantayana

[1]Oliver Bridges Henshaw (d. 1898) was a member of Harvard's class of 1893. The following year he received an A.M. at the University of California.
[2]*Beauty.*

To William Cameron Forbes

[Spring 1893] • Cambridge, Massachusetts   (MS: Houghton)

DELTA PHI CLUB.[1]

Dear Cam

I was delighted to get your letter and to know you had seen my sister and liked Avila of which I am very fond although it isn't an exciting place, as you may imagine. My sister has also written about your visit. She says she was sorry not to be able to ask you to stay at her house, but she thought that as no one but herself spoke English the situation might be a little uncomfortable. You were, she says, a great success with the boys,[2] who were delighted with your stamps. They pitied you very much for not speaking Spanish and being a heretic. However, they realized that it was more your misfortune than your fault. It is too bad you couldn't have come when I was there; we might have made some expeditions into the country. I sail on June 10th in the Fulda for Gibraltar. Guy Lowell is going too, but will not land with me, as he meets his family in Italy.[3]–This club is getting on very well; '95 is a great class, and I can even come down in the afternoon with a loaf of cake under my arm and get three or four fellows to have some tea. There is much talk now about the novel topic of panelling the room, also about the novel one of the first ten.[4] At this moment Julian, Austin Potter, and Hewitt Morgan are having lunch in the next room, Irving is looking at the Illustrated London News in Chalker Walker's long chair, and I am writing at the table by the window.[5] I now have my first breakfast (2 eggs and tea) in my room while I dress, and after my morning lecture come down here for a second breakfast or lunch, which I get at about twelve. Hoedke, our new man, is faithful, although a little slow and stupid, and too conversational. '94 is a poor class. Lincoln Davis and Percy Turnure are the only good men here, besides Bob Blake.[6] But '95, as I said before, is splendid, although they have one goat among the sheep, which is not much considering that there was one Judas among the twelve apostles.— Ever since my expedition to Naushon I have been developing a great fondness for the country, and now I try to get out of town every Sunday. Last Sunday Boylston Beal and I with two sophomores drove to Concord, had dinner, saw the sights, and drove back in great form, with splendid weather to favour us. I am going again to Groton with Warwick Potter,[7] and also to Amherst, for now I like to visit all sorts of colleges. Yale I think delightful, although it be heresy to say so, and Amherst is very pretty. Even Smith has its charms. I went to lecture there not long ago, and had a fine time. The girls were very attentive, and I took me to dinner and supper with them. Twenty eight girls, two matrons, and one man is a novel dinner party, but very charming I assure you. Before long I shall have to return there, for it would never do to have the dear things forget me altogether. The Annex is now quite a matter of course for your humble servant; we get along very nicely together. The Annex maid is not very learned; she is rather foolish and very sensitive, on the whole not at all dangerous.[8] You tell me nothing of your plans. Are you coming back soon, or has one any chance of seeing you in Europe this summer? I expect to reach England about the middle of August. Next year, at any rate, we must have some of our oldtime dinners. Your brother Edward is in the club now, as you know, and comes down a good deal.[9] He reminds me of you in some ways, and I hope we shall be good friends before long. It will take him a little while to feel quite at home here, I suppose; the men don't seem to be his most intimate friends, but it will not take them long to become so. Altogether the club is now very pleasant, and the bad luck of '93 and '94 is getting to be a thing of the past.

Yours as ever
GSantayana

[1]The Delta Phi Club, which occupied a house in Mount Auburn Street, was called the Gas House "because all its windows would be lighted up at once by the electricity that was then a novelty; so that it was called 'The Gas House' because of the absence of gas." (*Persons*, 349–50) It was originated by Thoron, Lyman, and Beal of Santayana's class of 1886. Santayana had no money for dues as an undergraduate and did not become a member until he returned from Germany in the fall of 1888. About 1898 it became a final club, changing its name to the Delphic Club.

[2]Susan had married Celedonio Sastre Serrano, a widower with six children.

[3]Guy Lowell (1870–1927) received degrees from Harvard (1892), Massachusetts Institute of Technology (1894), and École des Beaux-Arts in Paris (1899). A successful American architect and confirmed classicist, his designs include the New York County Courthouse.

[4]First ten refers to the method by which Harvard men from about 1880 to World War I were ranked socially and designated eligible for membership in clubs. "The whole membership from each class, either at the end of its sophomore or the beginning of its junior year, chose the first 'ten' from the next class; this 'first ten' chose the second, these two the third, and so on until the limit had been reached. Until 1904 the names were printed in the college and Boston papers in the exact order of their election, and the whole list served as an index of social rating." (*Harvard*, 423–24) See Santayana's "The Judgment of Paris or How the First-Ten Man Chooses a Club," *Complete Poems*, 492–96.

[5]Julian Codman (1870–1932), son of Lucy Sturgis and Charles Codman, was Santayana's student and a member of the Harvard class of 1892. Later a corporate and real estate lawyer, he was a leader in efforts to repeal Prohibition. Austin Potter (Harvard, 1895) was the brother of Warwick and Robert Burnside Potter. James Hewitt Morgan (d. 1909) was a member of Harvard's class of 1894. Alexander Duer Irving (1873–1941), Harvard class of 1895, became an insurance broker. Chalker was probably Brooks Walker, a member of Harvard's class of 1895.

[6]Hoedke is unidentified. Lincoln Davis (Harvard, A.B. 1894, M.D. 1898) taught anatomy and surgery at Harvard. Percy Rivington Turnure (Harvard, A.B. 1894) received the A.M. (1898) and M.D. (1898) from Columbia. Robert Parkman Blake died in 1914.

[7]Warwick Potter (1870–93), a student and friend of Santayana, was a member of the Harvard class of 1893. Warwick's unexpected death had a profound effect on Santayana (see *Persons*, 423). The four sonnets "To W. P." are in *Complete Poems*, 125–27.

[8]The Harvard Annex, organized by an association for Private Collegiate Instruction for Women (CIW), was located at 15 Appian Way. It opened in 1879 with courses taught by Harvard professors in their spare time. In 1894 the CIW received a state charter as Radcliffe College. (*Harvard*, 391–92) Students at the Harvard Annex were called Annex maids.

[9]Edward Waldo Forbes, a member of the Harvard class of 1895, received an LL.D. from the University of Pittsburgh (1927), served as director of the Fogg Art Museum, and was a Fellow of the American Academy.

To Louisa Adams Beal

3 July 1893 • Ávila, Spain   (MS: Houghton)

My dear Mrs Beal[1]

I can't resist the impulse to write you a few words to say how delighted I am with the news. You must feel very happy to see Boylston's long wish realised, and to have so charming a girl[2] become a member of the family. I only wish I were able to see you sooner, and hear all about this event, which is in one way a surprise, because I had no idea things had got so far already. I believed it would be ultimately, however. Boylston deserves to get the girl of his choice, even if she <u>is</u> the finest girl in Boston, and I was sure, if she had any sense, she would not refuse him. I am longing for my trip to come to an end, although it has been a very pleasant one, in order to get back to Boston and shake hands all round over this auspicious event.

Please give my regards to Mr Beal, who I am sure must feel a great satisfaction, too, and believe me

Yours very sincerely
GSantayana

Avila
July 3, '93

[1]James H. and Louisa Adams Beal were Boylston's parents.
[2]Elsie Grew, a cousin of the Sturgis family.

To Boylston Adams Beal

4 July 1893 [*postmark*] • Ávila, Spain   (MS: Houghton)

Dear Boylston

Nothing that could have happened would have given me the pleasure this news does. I got it yesterday in Madrid, through a letter of my sister's, to whom Mrs. Grew had written.[1] You must be very happy, dear old boy, I hoped this would happen, but didn't expect it so soon. I believed it would be, because I could see that your love for her was real and that she was too clever and sensible a girl to despise the chance to be happy, or not to find out what an angel you are. This is perfectly fine and makes me feel so un-Laodicean[2] that I should like to give three cheers for you both. I had not noticed anything amiss about you, except your early hours; of course for the present we renounce you, but everything has its time, and you must not say hard things about bachelorhood and its joys, which have a tenderness of their own which, <u>faute de mieux</u>[3] no doubt, I cling to still. You shall have a box all to yourself, as once before, and I shall have a beautiful long coat for the wedding. I want to write to Elsie, too, and have so many letters today that I stop here. God bless you.   G. S.

[1]Elizabeth Sturgis Grew, Elsie's mother.

[2]The Laodicean Club was founded at Harvard by Santayana and a group of friends, which included William Vaughn Moody and Norman Hapgood, "based on the idea that Paul was too hard on the church that was in Laodicea, when he attacked it for being neither hot nor cold, and that there was much to say for the balanced attitude of that seldom-praised institution." (Norman Hapgood, *The Changing Years* [New York: Farrar & Rinehart, 1930], 44.) "The Club, with Santayana as pope, was something of a lark." (Larzar Ziff, *The American 1890s: Life and Times of a Lost Generation* [London: Chatto & Windus, 1967], 311.)

[3]For want of something better.

To William Cameron Forbes
6 July 1893 • Ávila, Spain   (MS: Houghton)

Avila. July 6, 93.

Dear Cam

My sister has asked me to answer your letter for her, which she would have done long before this if she had not been full of things to attend to. Her husband has been laid up with a sprained ankle and to-day they go to the farm for the wheat harvest.[1] I am going to spend a day there next week, and get a glimpse of agriculture as it is. I expect to leave Avila about August 1st and go to the Pyrenees and Paris and reach London about the 15th I sail on September 3rd from Southampton. Write me if you are near London thru C/o Brown Shipley & Co.—My sister suggests the books on the list which I enclose.[2] There doesn't seem to be a great plenty of readable books in Spanish. People here read translations from the French. The <u>Episodios nacionales</u> are a lot of volumes; these mentioned in the list are perhaps the best. If you want an old but very amusing book, read the <u>Lazarillo de Tormes</u>.[3] I suppose your Spanish studies are on account of the West Indies and Honduras. I had no idea you were at it.—Guy Lowell and I came together to Gibraltar, and both managed to keep pretty well: I didn't miss a meal until the seventh day, which is a record for me. Guy is probably in Italy now; I have not heard from him since we separated at

Cordoba. The great piece of news is Boylston's engagement to Elsie Grew, which of course you have heard. It was not entirely a surprise to me, although I didn't expect it so soon. It is a splendid thing, and shows she is as sensible as she is charming.—I envy you at Cambridge. I was once there during the Eights' week, and had a fine time.[4] Here nothing interrupts the monotony of life, although this year I have the novelty of finding my sister in the midst of her queer new family. I am getting fond of them, and may have to adopt one of the boys. It is quicker than raising one, and cheaper.

[*across*]

    Yours ever

        GSantayana

[1]On 26 Nov 1892 Susan married Celedonio Sastre Serrano (c. 1840–1930) of Ávila, Spain. He was a landowner and lawyer.

[2]Unlocated.

[3]*Episodios nacionales* are the forty-six novels of Spanish history by Benito Pérez Galdós (1843–1920) which trace the country's development from the battle of Trafalgar to the restoration of the monarchy in 1875. *La vida de Lazarillo de Tormes* (1554), a picaresque novel by an anonymous author, is the fictional autobiography of the wily Lázaro, who describes his experiences with various masters he served. Written with vigorous realism and irony, *Lazarillo* was popular and inspired sequels.

[4]Eights were eight-oared racing boats or their crews at Cambridge University.

To Charles Augustus Strong

21 August 1893 • Ávila, Spain   (MS: Georgetown)

                                     Avila Aug 21. 93

Dear Strong

    Many thanks for your note and your offer to try to get me a room. Anything you think proper would please me, I am sure, and it would be an additional pleasure to meet Professor Shorey.[1] I should like a room beginning on the 12th or 13th of September until the 22nd or so. If you will write to me C/o Mrs F. G. Shaw,[2] 118 East 30th St. New York, I shall know what to do when I land, which will be on Sept 11th or 12th.—I have been delayed in Avila by the saddest of reasons, the illness and death of my father. He was seventy nine years old and very feeble, so that the loss is not unexpected, but none the less great and final. His age and the fact that I had lived little with him make me feel this less than most sons would, but the impression is still strong, all the more as it was the first death I had ever seen. I am now with my sister, who lives here with her husband and children, and leave to-morrow evening for London. I hope I may see you in New York or Chicago.

Yours faithfully   GSantayana

[1]Paul Shorey (1857–1934).
[2]Mrs. Francis George (Sarah Blake Sturgis) Shaw (1815–1902) was a sister of Santayana's mother's first husband: "by a pleasant arrangement that at once was established I too called her 'Aunt Sarah' and repeatedly stayed at her house in Staten Island or in New York." (*Persons*, 51)

To John Corbin

11 October 1893 • Cambridge, Massachusetts   (MS: Virginia)

My dear Mr Corbin[1]

You were very good to remember my interest in my little book, and to take so much trouble to get it back to me. I shall go to 23 H.[2] for it; I have just come from there, but Mr. Gillespie was out.[3] I don't want to wait till I find him before I thank you very sincerely for your kindness.

Please give my regards to Williams[4] when you see him and believe me

Very truly yours
GSantayana

Oct. 11. 93

[1]John Corbin, Harvard class of 1892, became a writer and drama critic.
[2]Hollis Hall is a dormitory in the Harvard Yard.
[3]Probably Robert McMaster Gillespie, a member of Harvard's class of 1892.
[4]Unidentified.

To William Cameron Forbes

9 December 1893 • Cambridge, Massachusetts   (MS: Houghton)

Dec • 9 • 93

DELTA PHI CLUB.

Dear Cam

Next Saturday, December 16, is my thirtieth birthday, and I wish all my friends to come and console me at a beer night here at ten o'clock. If you have no more attractive engagement, won't you come early and dine with me at half past six at the Colonial Club?[1] I have been hoping to see you

before this, but have been rather ill and full of engagements. I depend upon your coming, if not to dinner, at least afterwards, since nothing keeps up after twelve on Saturday night—   Yours as ever
GSantayana

[1]The Colonial Club, founded in 1890, was a Cambridge social and dining club at 20 Quincy Street. It maintained bowling alleys, a billiards room, and rooms for overnight visitors.

To Herbert S. Stone and Hannibal I. Kimball
11 December 1893 • Cambridge, Massachusetts   (MS: Virginia)

Dec • 11 • 93

Messrs Stone & Kimball[1]

Gentlemen.

I have looked over my manuscripts and think I shall be able to make a collection of suitable ~~peices~~ pieces that will fill at least sixty pages. There is a sequence of twenty sonnets, besides a few miscellaneous ones, and enough other stuff to fill up. The longest and, as I think, best poem is one which it may not be wise to print, as it is somewhat free in subject and expression.[2] I am myself indifferent to criticism on that score, but I conceive that it might be objectionable from your point of view. There are also a few translations, if you think them worth printing. I will write out a copy for you to inspect during the Xmas vacation. As regards a title, I should suggest Sonnets and other verses. I dislike fancy or botanical titles for books of verse. The get up I should also wish to be simple and dignified. If all this meets with your approval you can go ahead and announce the book.

Yours truly
GSantayana

[1]Herbert S. Stone and Hannibal Ingalls Kimball were Harvard men who set out to publish Harvard poets and writers. During its brief career, the firm of Stone and Kimball (later Herbert S. Stone and Co.) issued interesting and well-made volumes, including Santayana's first book, *Sonnets.* A study of this publishing venture is Sidney Kramer's *A History of Stone and Kimball and Herbert S. Stone and Co., with a Bibliography of Their Publications, 1893–1905* (Chicago: Norman W. Forgue, 1940).
[2]"Lucifer, A Prelude" occupies the last twenty-one pages of *Sonnets.*

To William Cameron Forbes
16 December 1893 • Cambridge, Massachusetts   (MS: Houghton)

Dec • 16 • 93

DELTA PHI CLUB.

Dear Cam

I am very sorry to hear that you are laid up, and I mean to come and see you during the vacation, when I suppose you will be up again. Dibblee has gone today.[1] He has been called to California because his father is not well. I am afraid it is something serious, although it is not given out as such. I wish you could be here tonight. Most of the old stagers have promised to come, and it will be real "setting party". Please thank your father[2] for his kind note, and get well quickly. It must be a nuisance to be tied up, but I suppose it is the only way under the circumstances.

Yours ever

GSantayana

[1]Albert "Bert" James Dibblee was a member of Harvard's class of 1893.
[2]William Hathaway Forbes (1840–97), called Colonel Forbes after his Civil War service, founded and was president of Bell Telephone Company (1878–87), directed several other companies, and was a horse breeder.

To Norman Hapgood
[16 December 1893] • Cambridge, Massachusetts   (MS: Unknown)

Dear Norman:

My answer must be also without any news of importance and with no other object than to get the pleasant illusion of a little confab with you. Today is my thirtieth birthday and I feel tolerably happy. The past has had its pleasures and the future will not be without its consolations.

As you know I made my peace with nature long ago, and I continue to feel that my vocation is found in the protest of quietness against an agitation which has not made out its rationality. Thought ought to lighten the burden of existence, to keep us from vanities, and square our accounts with the universe. The turgid thought that prevails in our day and generation is itself an unregulated passion, an imposition of the unnecessary, and an aggression against our natural contentment. It becomes clearer to me every day that both in teaching and living our need is simplification, measure and docility to the facts. How can such a spirit fail to lead us in the direction both of truth and of the greatest possible happiness?

GSantayana

To William Cameron Forbes
Tuesday [c. 1894 or 1895] • Cambridge, Massachusetts   (MS: Houghton)

Tuesday

DELTA PHI CLUB.

Dear Cam

Will you dine with me on Friday of this week at the Delta Phi at seven o'clock? Guy Murchie[1] will be here, and you must come and make him feel at home. Don't dress; even the rest of us won't. I expect to have only Julian, if he can come, and if not Hal Coolidge,[2] so that it will be your ideal Naushon party of last December.

Yours ever

GSantayana

[1]In 1895 Guy Murchie received his A.B. and his LL.B. from Harvard.
[2]Harold Jefferson Coolidge was a member of the Harvard class of 1892.

To Charles William Eliot
23 June 1894 • Cambridge, Massachusetts   (MS: Harvard)

7 Stoughton
June 23 '94

My dear Mr Eliot

I wish to express to you my regret that my whim in going to New London should have led to such unhappy results. I cannot apologise without hypocrisy for my way of carrying on the Examinations, even if a more suspicious attitude could have prevented this abuse. But I lament that I should have undertaken an office which evidently demanded another kind of person. I should be sorry to think that this mistake had contributed to bring annoyance to you or disrepute to the college.[1]

Yours very truly

GSantayana

[1]Santayana had been reprimanded by President Eliot for his lax manner of proctoring the examinations of the Harvard crewmen. The annual Yale–Harvard boat races are held in New London, Connecticut.

To Guy Murchie

[1 August 1894] • Cambridge, Massachusetts   (MS: Murchie)

---

7 <u>Stoughton</u>
<u>Wednesday</u>

Dear Murchie

I meant to have said this morning when I saw you how much I appreciate your invitation. It was very sweet of you to ask us, and we are both very sorry not to accept. Russell blamed me this morning for not having brought you to lunch to-day: but there may be another person here, a friend of his, and I thought you would find it pleasanter another day. Come on Friday to breakfast at 9.15 if you can, and we shall see how the weather is and arrange some expedition. We both leave on Saturday, Lord Russell for California and I for Cotuit[1] where I stay a fortnight so I shall hardly see you again until October

Yours sincerely
GSantayana

[1]Location of the Cape Cod country house of "Cousin Lucy" Lyman Paine Sturgis, daughter of Russell Sturgis (1805–87), and her husband Charles Russell Codman. Julian was their youngest son. See *Persons*, 357 and 361–63.

To Guy Murchie

20 November 1894 • Cambridge, Massachusetts   (MS: Murchie)

Dear Murchie

Here is a bad consequence of our talk of the other night. However, being "the only begetter of this ensuing sonnet,"[1] you should be presented with the child.   Yours ever

GS

You thought: "The vapourous world on which I gaze
Why is it beautiful? Why in the dome

Of silent heaven do the planets roam
In patient reckoning of the hallowed days?
Why do the resinous pine woods, the bays
Grey 'twixt the islets, or the pregnant loam
With keen sweet voices speak to me of home?
'Tis God within them hearkens to my praise."
To yours he may: to me the frozen sod
And barren stars are piteous, and no God
Called to me ever from the sullen sea.
Yet have I known him, in my soul apart
Worshiped him long, and found him in your heart.
What higher heaven should his dwelling be?[2]

~~Oct~~ November 20. 94.

[1]The dedication of Shakespeare's *Sonnets* (1609) reads 'TO THE ONLIE BEGETTER OF / THESE INSVING SONNETS / MR. W. H. ALL HAPPINESSE / AND THAT ETERNITIE / PROMISED BY / OVR EVER-LIVING POET / WISHETH / THE WELL-WISHING / ADVENTVRER IN / SETTING / FORTH /   T. T.'
[2]*Complete Poems*, 135.

To Guy Murchie
23 December [1894] • Cambridge, Massachusetts   (MS: Murchie)

Sunday morning
December 23.

Dear Guy

I was at the Bancroft's[1] last night and will give you an accurate description of all I saw. In the first place it was a smaller and more intimate gathering than I had expected, some forty or fifty people, and no supper, so that you had a pleasant feeling that every one had come from a genuine interest in the event. Captain Flack[2] had arrived that morning, and complained of the discomfort of the night journey from New York (or New York, as he called it.) His English is good but not very fluent. That fact as well as the trying situation may explain his seeming a little dull. I made a foolish attempt to amuse him. 'They say', said I, 'that in America all men are born free and equal and all women superior to the men'.–a joke from last year's Pudding play I think. He looked puzzled and said 'Do they say that?' He is a well built light haired man, of the type that looks very youthful at a distance but rather oldish near to, like Dean Briggs.[3] He is of

medium height, with a nice ugly face and altogether a naval appearance.–
Here is an incident not without interest. An old lady I was talking to
pointed out Miss Bancroft introducing Winslow Clarke to the happy man.
'How pathetic,' she cried, 'the old lover meeting the successful one.' I
knew nothing of such an affair but my dear gossip assured me it had been
an old quasi-understanding among all the family friends. If it is true, it
explains better why Clarke, whose friendship for me has been rather a
memory of late, insisted on my going to supper with him and Jim Putnam,[4]
as in the old days. We sat up until half past one over chicken sandwiches
devilled eggs, Camembert cheese, and beer, and talked of nothing but
their college adventures, without a word about the present marriage.–The
bride-to-be seemed very happy and gay, and looked better than at the
Gray's party.[5] I told her that as I was something of a wanderer too, I hoped
to meet her some day in an unexpected corner of the earth, and she was
very gracious and friendly in talking about that possibility. Mrs Bancroft
was beaming. Mr Bancroft was not, but sat in a chair and looked rather
unhappy.

You must enjoy yourself and get thoroughly well during these holidays.
It is very natural to be somewhat upset in one's senior year. One begins to
see the end of college days and the perplexities of the future make one
reflect. One discovers the difficulty of fancying any career that shall be
wholly satisfying, even in prospect. We have to learn to love the imperfect
for the beautiful things it contains, and that takes discipline. The alternative is to mistake the imperfect for the perfect, which to my mind is a much
sadder fate. But I am getting melancholy which is out of season. I meant
to send you a copy of the Apocryphal [across] Gospels for Christmas, but
the book had to be bound so that you will not get it until your return, when
I hope to see you full of the p. j. of y.[6]

Yours ever

G.S.

[1]John Bancroft was the son of the celebrated historian, Hubert Howe Bancroft
(1832–1918). [D. C.]
[2]Of the Royal Swedish Navy, fiancé of Miss Pauline Bancroft. [D. C.]
[3]Le Baron Russell Briggs, dean of Harvard (1891–1902) and dean of the Faculty of
Arts and Sciences (1902–25). [D. C.]
[4]Winslow Clarke and Jim Putnam were socially prominent Bostonians. [D. C.]
[5]Possibly Mr. and Mrs. John Chipman Gray; he (d. 1915) taught law at Harvard
(1869–1913).
[6]Perpetual joy of youth. (per Guy Murchie)

To Gertrude Stein

[1895 or 1896] • [Cambridge, Massachusetts?]   (MS: Beinecke)

My dear Miss Stein[1]

Friday evening is perfectly convenient, and you may expect me at 7.45 at Miss Yerxa's.[2]

If you don't think the subject too vast I should like to talk about 'Faith and Criticism'.

Yours very truly
GSantayana

[1]Gertrude Stein (1874–1946) attended Radcliffe where she studied psychology with William James and knew Santayana, then an instructor. After graduation (1897), she did graduate work in psychology at The Johns Hopkins University before abandoning scientific study for a literary career. Living in Paris after 1903, she influenced many writers and artists. Her writing has a repetitious, colloquially impressionistic style. She authored poems, stories, art criticism, operas, and autobiographical works.

[2]Unidentified.

To Charles Eliot Norton

28 February 1895 [*postmark*] • Cambridge, Massachusetts   (MS: Houghton)

My dear Mr Norton

I was very glad to see Mr Blaydes[1] yesterday, and to talk over with him things English and American. As I asked him to tell you, I had a class here at half past seven, and could not accept your kind invitation to dinner. I am very much obliged to you for it, as well as for sending me our Cambridge visitor

Yours very truly
GSantayana

7 Stoughton
  Thursday

[1]Unidentified.

To Macmillan and Co.
2 May 1895 • Cambridge, Massachusetts   (MS: New York)

Cambridge, Mass
May 2, 1895

Macmillan & Co

Gentlemen.

I beg to thank you for the copy of Marshall's <u>Aesthetic Principles</u> which I have just received.[1] It seems to be a very attractive and judicious little book and I have no doubt will be serviceable to classes studying the subject. My own class will not be held next year. The lectures which I have for three years given in the psychology of taste have now taken shape in a book,[2] which is practically finished, and which I had thought of submitting to you, in hopes you might find it convenient to publish it, as I think no other house would give it so acceptable a form or secure for it so good a public. My book is rather longer, more systematic and, I think, more philosophical than Marshall's: but it has the same general tendency of thought. I suspect, therefore, that you may not care to consider the publication of it; but if you do, I should be glad to send you the MS for inspection, ~~which~~ ₐ. It ₐ will be ready in a few weeks.

Yours truly

GSantayana

[1]Henry Rutgers Marshall's (1852–1927) *Aesthetic Principles*, lectures delivered at Columbia College in November and December 1894, was published by Macmillan and Co. in 1895.

[2]*Beauty*, Santayana's first published book of prose, was for many years the best seller of his works.

To Herbert S. Stone and Hannibal I. Kimball
4 June 1895 • Cambridge, Massachusetts   (MS: Virginia)

Cambridge
June 4, 95

Dear Stone & Kimball

Can you let me have two copies of the large edition of my verses? I have given the last I had away–to Fullerton, who has just been here–and should like to make one or two other gifts of it before I leave for Europe on June 22.–I also wanted to ask you whether the second edition is a <u>de facto</u> one, and whether it would be possible to add a number of sonnets– as many again, almost–and some other pieces in any future printing of the book. I shall have a good deal ready in the autumn, and if you saw your way to a really second edition, enlarged and improved, I should be very glad.[1]–Your removal to Chicago seems to have been auspicious, to judge from the prosperity of the Chap Book, which I receive with punctuality, and observe with interest.[2] I wish you were still here, however, for my own convenience and pleasure. If you publish me from Chicago, however, I shall feel like a poet of the future.

Yours very truly
GSantayana

[1] *Sonnets* was not a true second edition for it was printed from the plates of the original 1894 edition with revisions and the addition of the thirty sonnets of the Second Sonnet Sequence.

[2] A chap-book is a small book of ballads, tales, or tracts.

To William Cameron Forbes

18 June 1895 • Cambridge, Massachusetts   (MS: Santayana)

Cambridge
June • 18 • 95

Dear Cam

Thank you very much for your copy of <u>Life and Death</u>.[1] I like the verses more the more I read them and think about them, and I foresee that I shall end by writing an imitation of them in my own style, which, if ever done, I shall quickly send to you for your criticism. The change you made doesn't seem to me an improvement. It avoids the awkwardness of "well-coming", but it is less natural and expressive. The final words seem~~ed~~ tagged on, to the lines. But I like the movement of the thing as a whole, and above all the noble, chivalrous sentiment of it, which is worthy of you, dear Cam, and just like yourself. I am afraid my tricked-out version will have little of it. Be good to yourself this summer, and let me find you really well when I return in September, when I hope I may come out to Milton again to see you,. ~~which is~~ For the present my cry is Avila, Avila!

Yours ever   GSantayana

[1]In *Persons* (347), Santayana says: "One day … he showed me some verses of his about a young man dreaming that two goddesses, Life and Death, appeared to him and offered him their respective gifts: a sort of Puritan Judgment of Paris. The young man listens to their respective boasts and respective promises, and then says: I will choose Life, but on one condition: that I may afterwards reverse my judgment, and choose Death.

"The verses were not well composed, and I doubt that Cam has written any others; but the thought was so original, so wise, and so courageous, that nothing in Emerson has ever pleased me more. Think what an incubus life would be, if death were not destined to cancel it. … [T]he preference for life is, as Cam felt, a duty, as well as a natural sporting impulse; but it is a conditioned preference … ."

To Macmillan and Co.

19 June 1895 • Cambridge, Massachusetts   (MS: New York)

Cambridge
June 19 • 95

Messrs Macmillan & Co

Gentlemen:

This morning I sent you by express the manuscript of my book on Aesthetics "<u>The Sense of Beauty</u>" about which I had already written to you, and received from you a very kind and welcome reply. I leave on Saturday for Spain, sailing from New York on the Werra.[1] My address during the summer will be care of Brown Shipley & Co, London, but I shall be at Avila, in Spain, during July, and any communication sent to me there will reach me more directly. I shall of course be glad to hear from you as soon as possible. This book has been so long in preparation that I am eager to have the last uncertainties in regard to it over, and to feel that it is, as far as I am concerned, a thing of the past.

Yours very truly
GSantayana

[1]The steamship to Antwerp.

To Guy Murchie

3 September 1895 • London, England   (MS: Murchie)

NATIONAL LIBERAL CLUB,
WHITEHALL PLACE. S.W.

Sept • 3 • 95

Dear Guy

I have taken my passage for the eleventh in the 'Richmond Hill' which takes thirteen days to get from London to New York. The fare, however, is only ten guineas, and they say the ship is comfortable and empty. I join Russell tomorrow at Woodstock. My address until I sail is 87 Jermyn Street, and I hope if you feel like it you will write me a line to tell me your plans, and how soon you graduate from Coignet University.[1]

I have only a bad reason for writing tonight, which is the sonnet opposite. But you should forgive it, considering that it has (for us) a historical if not an aesthetic interest.

Your Chapman is not forgotten, but you must be patient; they are looking one up.[2]   Yours aff[y]   GS

Brévent[3]

O dweller in the valley, lift thine eyes
To where, above the drift of cloud, the stone
Endures in silence, and to God alone
Upturns its furrowed visage, and is wise.
There yet is being, far from all that dies,
And beauty, where no mortal maketh moan,
Where larger spirits swim the liquid zone,
And other spaces stretch to other skies.
Only a little way above the plain
Is snow eternal; round the mountains' knees
Hovers the fury of the wind and rain.
Look up, and teach thy noble heart to cease
From endless labour. There is perfect peace
Only a little way above thy pain.

———

The end of this sounds as if it had been inspired by Mrs Louise Chandler Moulton.[4] But it is written. Let it go.

[1]"In 1895 Santayana and I were in Europe. He came to see me at La Terrace par le Touvet (near Grenoble, France) where I was studying French at the Villa of M. Coignet. We started from La Terrace on a short walking trip (about 150 miles) … spending a night on Mont Brévent (opposite Mont Blanc)." (per Guy Murchie)

[2]George Chapman (c. 1559–1634) was an English dramatist and poet who is most famous as a translator of Homer's *Iliad* (1611) and *Odyssey* (1614–15). Chapman was immortalized in verse by John Keats's poem "On First Looking into Chapman's Homer."

[3]A version of this sonnet was published in *Hermit*, 123, and *Complete Poems*, 131.

[4]Ellen Louise Chandler Moulton (1835–1908), the "Duchess of Rutland Square" (South Boston), was a genteel poetess and author of *In the Garden of Dreams*. [D. C.]

To Lawrence Smith Butler

[1895–96?] • [New York, New York]   (MS: University Club)

---

49 West 44th Street

Dear Lawrence[1]

It is truly provoking, but I have to go to an early dinner in <u>Brooklyn</u>—something academic—and much as I want to see and hear you, it will be impossible tomorrow afternoon. I am very sorry. You must manage to be at something that I am going to—perhaps the Blair Fairchilds'[2] on Friday evening, else I don't see how I am to see you before I go, as all my regular dates are taken up. We must manage somehow, though, as it would be too absurd not to see you at all.

Yours ever

GSantayana

[1]Santayana met Lawrence Smith Butler (1875–1954) during an Atlantic crossing in June 1895. After graduation from Harvard in 1898, Butler studied at the Beaux Arts. A nephew of Stanford White, he too became an architect. He cultivated his fine tenor voice, studying with Jean de Reszke in Paris. But, like poor Oliver Alden [of *Puritan*], he could only sing what he felt and, hence, failed to become an artist vocally. See *Persons*, 381–82.

[2]Blair Fairchild (1877–1933), Harvard class of 1899, was a composer influenced by Widor and César Franck.

To Lawrence Smith Butler
Monday [1895–96?] • [New York, New York?]   (MS: University Club)

Dear Butler

I am very unlucky about seeing you. You won't see me on Thursday, as I go to Rice's wedding and then to a dinner. As I told you, my time is pretty much taken up until I leave, on Wednesday or Thursday of next week.

Could you by chance dine with me on Wednesday of this week, after your race? You may have some other plan, but if not, come to the Empire, and I will promise to take good care of you if, after your long training, the fumes should go to your head. It is the only evening I have now. Let me know if you will come, and at what time. Any hour is convenient for me.

I shall be in all day tomorrow, Tuesday, if you care to come in, but not in the evening. I am sorry you don't come to lunch.

Yours ever
GSantayana

Monday night.

To Lawrence Smith Butler
Thursday [1895–96] • Cambridge, Massachusetts   (MS: University Club)

7 S.
Thursday

Dear Butler

I was very much disappointed at not seeing you in New York. Won't you come in for a while this evening after the concert and have a temperance drink?

Yours ever
GSantayana

To Macmillan and Co.
3 October 1895 • Cambridge, Massachusetts   (MS: New York)

> 7 Stoughton
> Cambridge
> Mass

Oct • 3 • 95

Gentlemen.

I received a few days ago your polite note about my MS, but the MS itself has not arrived.[1] Would you be so kind as to see that it is sent me at once, as a further delay would be rather inconvenient for me

> Yours very truly
> GSantayana

[1]Macmillan and Co. declined to publish *Beauty*.

To Charles Augustus Strong
10 November 1895 • Cambridge, Massachusetts   (MS: Rockefeller)

> Cambridge
> Nov 10 '95

Dear Strong

I am delighted you thought of sending me your article,[1] not only because I shall enjoy reading it very much, but even more because it proves you have not forgotten an old friend in spite of such a long absence of communication between us. Are you again active at Chicago this winter? If so, do you see my Harvard friends there, and does the place continue to please you? I got such a favourable impression of it when I was there two years ago.[2] This summer I have been in Europe again, in Spain for a while, and afterwards with Loeser in Italy and Switzerland, coming back finally by way of England and an economical cattle steamer. It was interesting, but not all I should have wished in the way of a change of life. This may come before long, however as there seems to be a crisis coming on in my relations with Harvard, and I hardly expect to remain here after this year. I shall not unless they make me an assistant professor. My plan is to go to London for a year, and see what will turn up after that. The change of intellectual surroundings would do me a lot of good. Let me hear from you soon.

Yours ever

GSantayana

[1]Unidentified.
[2]See 21 Aug 1893.

To Guy Murchie
1 December 1895 • Naushon, Massachusetts   (MS: Murchie)

Sunday, 10 a.m.

Dec. 1 '95

NAUSHON.

Dear Guy

I am all alone here this morning and must write you a word simply because it is so beautiful a place that I want to tell you about it before the enthusiasm of the moment has time to cool. Cam Forbes, Harold Coolidge, Bert Dibblee, and I have come down for a couple of days, and the other three went off this morning at four o'clock in the launch to shoot duck, leaving me to sleep the sleep of the lazy; the weather is crisp clear and bracing, the water in all directions sparkling and blue, the woods ankle-deep in dead leaves, the crows caw away, the deer peep now and then from behind the bushes, and the sheep nibble what green grass they can still find among the moss and stubble. Just now a number of very philosophical kine are gazing at me through the windows. It is a lovely island; the harbour, beyond which one sees Wood's Hole, is like ~~these~~ those landscapes, all little hills and sheets of water, that the old masters like to put behind their Madonnas. I was here once before in winter and discovered how much more beautiful nature is then than in summer, at least to me. There is more variety of colour; all these browns, russets, yellows, and purples are blended in the subtleſst and ~~more~~ most interesting ways; there is an expression of sincerity, as it were, about the naked landscape that appeals to me immensely. There is more <u>truth</u> in this than in the season when every thing is mascarading in green. The articulation of the branches is also plainer now, and they are seldom really bare. At the entrance of the avenue to this house there are two elms which may some-day grow to be like those we admired, as you may remember, in front of the Lawrence's house at Groton.[1] They are as yet not very big; but I wish I could paint them as they looked yesterday, with their perfectly [*remainder missing*]

[1]The home of James Lawrence, son of Abbott Lawrence (1792–1855), on Farmer's Row in Groton, Massachusetts.

To Guy Murchie

12 March 1896 • Cambridge, Massachusetts   (MS: Murchie)

Cambridge
March, 12 '96

Dear Guy

The pen was literally in my hand to begin a letter to you when it was stopped by the arrival of your note and the new thoughts it suggested. It is pleasant to know that you are so well, and to know it directly from yourself. How I wish I could ride with you over those snowy ridges, where I suppose I shouldn't be much hurt if I was thrown a few times from the saddle. In time I should learn to stay on, if I had a sufficient incentive. When you come back (in a month or two n'est-ce pas?)[1] we can go away for a day or two into the country. You would make me very happy if you made up your mind to come and stay with me here, but I understand that it may not suit your plans. My visit to you on that Monday night was mal à propos,[2] and I felt it. You hadn't said Briggs[3] was to dine with you and I had come in hopes of having a good talk. You had done nothing to put me out, but it seemed necessary to get out as quickly as possible, as that was the second time that day that I had found myself stepping in inopportunely between you and your friends. I am sorry if I betrayed my chagrin. That is what you must mean by saying that I needn't have gone away without even saying goodbye. Of course I said goodbye; not very elaborately, to be sure, since you used to dislike leavetakings, but you may remember that I told you to come to see me again if you remained longer about Boston, and that in any case we should meet in the other world. Wasn't that saying goodbye with a vengeance?

I continue to hear about your courtship from all sorts of people. The general feeling is that you would be a lucky man, and that you are carrying on a determined campaign. Your friends, on the contrary, don't seem to like the idea, because they want you to work out your own salvation, and not make a lifelong choice before you know what you will be and what you will want. My own feelings are mixed. The match presents all the conditions which you know I desire for you; it seems ideal. Yet I have a lurking suspicion that your own reasons and deliberate choice are passive in the matter; that you are being overpowered with encouragement, and that possibly your senses are driving you where your judgment would not go. And besides I think marriage for you extremely risky. You have not the gift of being easily happy or of making others so. You are inconsequential, and the more one loves you the more one must suffer from such vacillations of your sympathy. And if you married simply from boyish inclination, because your senses drew you on and your heart was without defence, great unhappiness might come to you both in the future. It is a revenge the devil sometimes takes upon the virtuous, that he entraps them by the force of the very passion they have suppressed and think themselves superior to. It is hard for a young man like you to distinguish the charm of a particular woman from that of woman in general, to distinguish affinity from proximity. Russell's misfortunes all sprang from his inexperience in this respect, so that the danger of it is very present to my mind. If you could weather this storm, the very experience would strengthen you and enlighten you for the future; and after a few years of life among men and women you could go to the woman you would be proudest to call your own, and say, "I love you with my whole soul <u>and my whole mind</u>; I have chosen you from all the world." That is a man's love, which is a better and safer ~~one~~ thing than a boy's, and a kind you could offer, very likely, to this same girl when you came back to her with your character formed and your resolution made. It is the kind of love I should now feel for the woman of my choice, and the kind I feel for you too, dear Guy, who are a great deal more to me than any of my friends could be when I was a young fellow, and could not really know either myself or other men. There is resolution in this sort of love, it is the expression of character and not of chance. And I should wish you to come to it some day; it is worth waiting for. You will forgive this long sermon, and forget it if your mind is already made up. I have written all this because, if it happens to be in the line of your own reflections, it might help you a little towards clearness. If not, it will do no harm since you will pay no attention to it.

Of course you know that I sent Katharine Dexter[4] a little book in payment of our bet, and that she wrote me a very ingenious note of thanks, in which she pretended to apologize for having deceived me. I hope she is not really sorry for having been so frank with me about you, because I valued that frankness very highly, as a tribute to my friendship for you. I hope you will keep it up, and tell me any important news there may be as soon as possible, so that I may know what to hope for.

I have made a new and amusing friend in the person of Mr Robert Collier of New York, a graduate of the Jesuit college at Georgetown and a great sport. His father[5] is a sport also, keeps horses and hounds, hunts, is an intimate of Mrs Ladenburg,[6] and swims in money made by the publication of a series of dime novels and of I don't know what religious paper. My friend is living with his mother at the Empire, and deceives her into thinking he is at Harvard College, while he only comes out to Cambridge to see a friend of his and lounge about, until it is time to go to dinner and to the Hollis Street Theatre where one of the troupe is his present flame. This pleasant youth has been at Oxford, knows something of the lighter contemporary literature, and is lavish with invitations. He came originally to ask me for advice about entering Harvard, which he means to do next year, and about the best way of getting into the best clubs. I asked him in turn if he knew the meaning of the word 'swipe'; he said no, and wanted to hear the derivation of it. I told him decency wouldn't allow me to explain it that, but I described the thing at length, and when he went away he thanked me for having given him these hints about the social standards of the College.

Another episode: I went to see Mrs Toy[7] the other day and was taken short, having caught cold from a sharp wind that had just sprung up. I was obliged to leave, saying I wasn't feeling well. But the law of compensation would have it that the next morning I should get a note from the lady, inviting me to come and nurse myself at her house, where she would make me very comfortable. See, even I have a Mr James to take pity on my infirmities and put me up when I am ill. Of course I declined the offer, but I may actually go to spend a few days there in May, while I move my things from Cambridge to Longwood, where my mother lives. Mrs Toy is a very good friend of mine: her attentions are of the kind that make one feel a little flattered, a little grateful, and a little annoyed. You know the kind I mean, don't you?–the kind your friends are apt to impose upon you.

I don't know whether this letter fulfils the requirements which Copeland[8] has been telling us a good letter ought to satisfy; it should contain a picture, ₐandₐ an incident, and be written in a style that unites correctness with ease. I am afraid I have forgotten those precepts, in my haste to tell you some of the many things I have had no chance to talk to you about, or at least to talk about enough. In the immediate future I expect to lead a monotonous life and you will not hear from me. But write if you feel inclined, especially if anything is settled about your plans for the future.

Yours ever

GS

[1]Is it not?

[2]Inappropriate.

[3]Walter Motherwell Briggs was Murchie's roommate and a member of the class of 1895.

[4]The daughter of Mrs. Wirt Dexter, Katharine and Murchie did not marry each other but remained close friends.

[5]Robert Collier was the son of Robert Collier, founder and owner of *Collier's Weekly*. [D. C.]

[6]Mrs. Adolf Ladenburg (d. 1937) was a socially prominent New Yorker who inherited a large sum of money after her husband's disappearance in 1896.

[7]Nancy Saunders Toy (d. 1941) was married to Crawford Howell Toy (1836–1919), Hancock Professor of Hebrew and Oriental Languages at Harvard (1880–1909).

[8]Charles Townsend Copeland (1860–1952), Harvard's class of 1882, became Boylston Professor of English at Harvard. See *Persons*, 407, and *Harvard*, 402–3.

To Charles Scribner's Sons

19 March 1896 • Cambridge, Massachusetts   (MS: Princeton)

Cambridge Mass
March 19 '96

Messrs Charles Scribner's Sons[1]
    New York

Gentlemen

At the request of Mr Lord[2] I sent you some weeks ago a MS entitled "The Sense of Beauty." If it is not now being read, would you be kind enough to send it back to me, as I had promised some time ago to read a portion of it before a club in Philadelphia on April 22, thinking that by that time I should have got it back again. When I have selected and copied the portions I wish to read, I can send the MS back to you, if you still care to retain it.

Yours very truly

GSantayana

[1]Charles Scribner (1821–71) gave up law practice to found the publishing firm of Baker & Scribner in 1846. After his partner's death, the firm continued in Scribner's name. His son, Charles Scribner (1854–1930), served as president of the firm

(1879–1928) and then was chairman of the board. After 1878, the firm was known as Charles Scribner's Sons. The majority of Santayana's works were published by Scribner's..

[2]Unidentified.

To Herbert S. Stone and Hannibal I. Kimball
23 March 1896 • Cambridge, Massachusetts   (MS: Temple)

Cambridge Mass
March 23 1896

Messrs Stone & Kimball
   Chicago

Gentlemen

   Here are the corrections I should like to have made in the proposed new edition of my Sonnets, and also thirty new ones which if you think proper could be added to the series that opens the book. I suggest leaving out the title on p. 3 because it seems to be trying to peep over the top of the page. As the new sonnets form another sequence, I think it would be well to leave a blank page between them and the old ones. Possibly subtitles, 'First Series', 'Second Series', could be put on page 1 and on the new page 23. But I should like the numbering of the sonnets to be continuous, as in the manuscript.[1]

   I think this addition will reinforce the volume, if in no other way, at least by treating a subject which the sentimental missed in it before. At the same time the new matter will not change the general character of the book, and will be a further justification of the title. Hoping soon to hear from you on this subject I remain

Yours truly
GSantayana

[1]These changes were made.

To William Cameron Forbes
[Spring 1896] • Cambridge, Massachusetts   (MS: Houghton)

Dear Cam

   I sail in the <u>Parisian</u> from Montreal on June 27.[1] I am dreadfully busy, but must see you some how before I leave. Can't you come to the club dinner on Monday night? Boylston Beal and I are trying to get the old crowd together then for a last time.

Yours ever
GSantayana

Tuesday

¹Santayana sailed for Liverpool on 28 June, bound for a year of study at Cambridge University.

To Charles Scribner's Sons

5 May 1896 • Cambridge, Massachusetts   (MS: Princeton)

Cambridge Mass
May 5, 1896

Gentlemen.

I enclose a copy of the contract as you requested, with the sample page of the "Sense of Beauty." The first arrangement, No 1, seems to me too decidedly the best, and the lighter numeral you suggest would, I should think, further improve it. I like the page and print very much.

In respect to the suggestions made by your reader, I should be glad to change the title of the first part, to avoid the repetition he has noticed. Instead of "Definition of Beauty" we might then have "The Nature of Beauty," leaving "Definition of Beauty" for the last section in that Part. The main criticism he makes, however, is not one on which I could act, as he seems to me not to understand the generally accepted theory of which my treatment of the perception of beauty is only an example. The confusion of which he complains is nothing but the usual psychological point of view, which makes all qualities of objects projected sensations of ours, because it believes the ~~latter~~ former have no other origin or mode of existence. I could, perhaps, by adding a word of explanation or a comparison here and there to the text, make this point of view more explicit and clear; and I shall be glad to do so if you will send me back that part of the manuscript. My attempt to present the images of evil as a pure loss in art is one which I expect will not be generally regarded with favour; it is naturally, however, a thing which, as relatively original and essential to my view of the subject, cannot be given up without destroying the whole theory.

I expect to sail for England in about a month; my address there will be care of Brown Shipley & Co, London.

Yours very truly
GSantayana

To Charles Scribner's Sons

20 June 1896 • Cambridge, Massachusetts   (MS: Princeton)

Cambridge Mass
June 20 '96

Charles Scribner's Sons

Gentlemen.

I send you this morning the proof I have so far received. I have tried to make more paragraphs. If this could be done in the rest of the book before printing I suppose it would save trouble.

I sail from Montreal on June 27th in the S.S. Parisian. Any proof sent me after the receipt of this had better, therefore, go to London, Care of Brown Shipley & Co. I will try to send it back as soon as possible, so that the delay may not be unnecessarily great. I am very sorry it has to occur at all.

The putting of the headings of sections on the right hand side of the page was, I suppose, an accident. It looks much better, I think, as it is in §1.

Yours very truly
GSantayana

To Guy Murchie

27 June 1896 • Quebec, Canada   (MS: Murchie)

CHATEAU FRONTENAC.
QUEBEC. CANADA.

June 27 1896

Dear Guy

I can't resist the impulse to write you a line from here, because I am thinking of you, wishing you were here, and wondering where in the world you are. If your father sold the mine in Newfoundland and you bought a farm in New Brunswick, why are you in Newfoundland and not chez toi,[1] if, as they tell me now, you are in Newfoundland? I give it up: but of course it doesn't matter if in some way you are finding what will ultimate satisfy you. Let me know soon what is up, for now when I pass the sad shores of Newfoundland I shall never know whether to gaze upon them with moist eyes and wave a metaphorical handkerchief in that direction, or whether the Mecca lies rather behind my back. You see, in spite of th¢is then pursuit of vain knowledge, even the faithful need a little geography. We sail from here tomorrow, Sunday, morning. I like the place. The people are <u>peuple</u>. These are the long-sought peasants of America. I think it might be pleasant to live here: it would be like Europe, in the country. I have seen no one, however, that I know or that interests me since I left Boston: I have nothing to report as yet in the way of impressions, and this letter, in spite of the official look of the sheet, is not a regular communication, but a spontaneity by the way. But in Boston I saw a great many people during the last week—all I could in the intervals of moving and packing. Among others, I dined with Copeland at his invitation. We talked of Shakespeare and Stevenson,[2] and he grew eloquent on the subject of Lincoln; but you were not even mentioned! At the Perkins[3] wedding and on Class Day I saw many friends; on Tuesday I dined with Mrs Gordon Dexter and on Thursday with Mrs Wirt, so that on Wednesday Gordon Bell[4] said I was <u>ambi-dex trous</u>. I have, by the way, new impressions of Katherine Dexter, and if you should ever hear me talk again about anything that has to do with her, you will, I hope, find me more intelligent. Mrs Gordon has been very nice to me; she sent me a farewell present—Renan's <u>Ma soeur Henriette</u>.[5] I also saw Fred Winslow,[6] who came last Sunday to Cotuit to say goodbye. We parted at the water's edge, most poetically—but there the poetry stopped, and so must this letter, for I am in measurable danger of beginning another sheet. Goodbye, then, until I write again, and God bless you.

Yours aff^{ly}

GS

---

[1]At your place.

[2]Robert Louis Stevenson (1850–94) was a Scottish novelist, poet, and essayist. He is noted for the novels *Treasure Island* (1884), *The Strange Case of Dr. Jekyll and Mr. Hyde*, and *Kidnapped* (both published in 1886). His work is marked by power of invention, command of horror and the supernatural, and psychological depth.

[3]Unidentified.

[4]Mrs. Wirt Dexter and Mrs. Gordon Dexter were distinguished, charming Boston hostesses. Gordon Knox Bell (Harvard class of 1893) was a well-known wag. (per Guy Murchie)

[5]*My sister Henriette* was published first in 1862 in a limited edition of one hundred under the title *Henriette Renan. Souvenir pour ceux qui l'ont connue* (Henriette Renan. A Remembrance for Those Who Knew Her).

⁶Frederick Winslow, Harvard class of 1895, became a prominent Boston physician. .

To Charles Scribner's Sons
26 July 1896 • Oxford, England   (MS: Princeton)

26 Banbury Road
Oxford
July 26, 1896.

Messrs Charles Scribner's Sons
   New York

Gentlemen.

   I send you back today the corrected proof of my book pp 1–94, and galleys 64–127, which only reached me the day before yesterday. There are,
as you may see, still some errors in the page proofs, and I think I should
prefer to see the rest also. There needn't be the same delay, as you will be
able to send the rest by mail, which seems to be so very much quicker than
the express. I am very glad to see the comments you make on the margin
and hope you will be freer with them. I am conscious of my inexperience
in writing, and value your suggestions very much. Of course, as you will
see by these proofs, I am ready to stick by my phrases when I think them
just upon reflection.

   Why have the marginal titles been usually put on the right hand side?
The left seems the natural place but of course the other will do if there is
a practical reason for it, only there should be consistency throughout.

   Do you think a preface or index, or both, desirable?

   I shall probably remain at Oxford for some time, but care of Brown
Shipley & Co, London, will still be the safer address.

Yours very truly

GSantayana

To Conrad Hensler Slade
11 August 1896 • Oxford, England   (MS: Unknown)

26 Banbury Road,
Oxford
August 11, '96

Dear Conrad,

It is a long time since I got your good letter and even longer since I read one of yours to Andersen.[1] From them I know that you are getting on well. Walter Cabot[2] not long ago gave me news of you to the same effect. Now that I have come to a place where, having a geographical sense, I am conscious of being much nearer you, I must write and let you know it, as well as that in the course of the winter I expect to make you a long visit. My plans are as follows: Until October 1ˢᵗ I remain here—with the interruption of possible visits to friends—reading in the Bodleian[3] and writing hard. The "Marriage of Aphrodite"[4] is nearly finished, and shall be submitted to you in due time. It seems to me less amusing than I had hoped, but not wholly bad, and capable of publication, with some expurgations for the sake of our Alma Mater. At the beginning of October I go, if I am admitted, which is not yet formally done, to King's College Cambridge, for a term, possibly for more. My idea is to go on with my writing, but at the same time to see something of people, and if possible read a little Plato,[5] and see what the aesthetic religious and philosophical atmosphere in England is now-a-days. I should stay at Oxford, except that there is no way of getting into a college here which doesn't involve becoming an undergraduate again, which is impossible with my dignity and weight of years. But at King's they promise to take me in as a sort of honorary fellow—dining with the Dons[6] etc.—and so I may go there. King's is a good college. I have a friend there, Wedd,[7] whom I met in '87, and the place has, you know, the loveliest and grandest chapel in the world, where before long—if it were not heretical and I didn't have a moustache—you might see your good friend in his stall dressed in his surplice! In January, or (if I stay for a second term) in March, I expect to go to Paris, and there I should like nothing better than to live with you, if you can find room for me in or near your quarters, and I could spend my time lolling in your studio and adjuring you to idealize your models. Then I should like to go to Italy and if possible to Greece, returning to Paris, probably, on my way to America. I needn't be back there before September '97, when my courses begin again. But I am never going to live at Harvard again; I am to stay with my mother in Longwood for a year, and if I remain at Harvard after that, I can either stay on in Longwood or take rooms in Boston. The idea of living in Cambridge without friends is intolerable to me, but in Boston I should have the ladies to console me and a more normal life for a man of my age than at the university.

This place is lovely, and I wish I could tell you how much delight I get from wandering about in it and around it. The solitude increases the charm; the place ought to be deserted. The sunlight here does wonders with the towers, especially St. Mary's and Magdalen, the latter one of the most engaging and satisfying towers in the world. I wish I could paint it as it looks at about seven in the afternoon when one walks along the High;[8] the trees on either side frame in the picture, while the level sunlight gilds the eight pinnacles and the beautiful balustrade into the mellowest of golden grays. The stone gets gradually more mossy and rough as the eye follows the lines downward, and more clean white and silvery as it traces them up to the four gilt weather-vanes, that sparkle as they turn together majestically in the sun. That is the jewel of Oxford; but every where there are charming lanes and vistas, monastic seclusions for an amateur religion. I go often to evening prayers at Christ Church, and the more I hear them the more I am impressed with the diplomacy of the prayerbook; the non-committal dignity of it is worthy of a conference of the powers.—And then the country about is full of a quiet charm. If you follow the towpath up the river you come to Witham, if you follow it down to Iffley, both lovely villages, the latter for its church the former for everything. You never saw such nests of neatness and foliage; flint walls overgrown with ivy, thatched cottages with climbing rosebushes, little children half way between Kate Greenaway and Sir Joshua Reynolds,[9] and inns with very refreshing cider and bitters. And beyond the fields in both directions are low hills, which tempt you to a two-hours healthy walk almost every afternoon.—My luncheon is on the table and my pen is getting used up; but I have written enough to give you an idea of what I am about. I feel very free and happy and while my letter of credit holds out I am going to forget all about being—or rather not being—a professor.[10] Write to me soon and tell me what you are at work on, and everything else about yourself. My permanent address is care of Brown Shipley & C° London—

Yours ever
GSantayana

[1]Andreas Martin Andersen (1869–1902) was the artist who sketched Santayana's favorite portrait of himself. From Venice in November 1939 Santayana wrote on a print of this portrait: "Done in charcoal by the firelight in N⁰ 7, Stoughton Hall, in the Harvard Yard, where I lived as proctor, from 1890 to 1896. The artist, a young Norwegian who had studied in Paris, was cut off by an early death from a promising career."

[2]Probably Walter Mason Cabot who was a member of the Harvard class of 1894.

[3]The celebrated library at Oxford University, the Bodleian is famous for its collection of rare books and manuscripts.

[4]The title of this play was changed to *The Marriage of Venus*. It was published in *Testament* after Santayana's death.

[5]Plato (c. 427–347 B.C.) was a Greek philosopher who was the student of Socrates and the teacher of Aristotle. In the *Republic* the good life for the individual and the state founded on action governed by knowledge of the Theory of Forms, a sense of both the ideal and the individual that influenced Santayana's philosophy. Platonic Forms, stripped of ontological or moral status, provide a basis for understanding Santayana's notion of essence.

[6]A don is a head, tutor, or fellow in an English university.

[7]Nathaniel Wedd (1864–1940) was a tutor and lecturer in classics at King's College, Cambridge (1888–1940). He translated Euripides' *Orestes* in an English edition of 1895. He, along with another fellow of King's College, Lowes Dickinson, suggested that Santayana study there under a newly created category of "advanced student." Santayana took a year's leave of absence from Harvard and spent the academic year 1896–97 studying Plato. See *Persons*, 394, 436, and 438.

[8]The main street of Oxford.

[9]Kate Greenaway (1846–1901) was an English illustrator and watercolor painter famous for fanciful, humorous, delicately colored delineations of child life. Joshua Reynolds (1723–92) was an English portrait painter and a founding member of the Royal Academy. He is admired for his paintings of women and children.

[10]Santayana resolved to leave Harvard if he were not promoted soon after his return in 1897; he was promoted to assistant professor early in 1898. See *Persons*, 394–95.

To Guy Murchie

13 August 1896 • Oxford, England   (MS: Murchie)

~~P.S. You may send Fred Winslow this letter if you like. I shall hardly have time to write to him separately~~

Oxford
Aug. 13, 1896

Dear Guy

I have been waiting a long time before writing to you in hopes of knowing what I was going to do, but everything is yet unsettled, and I write now so that you won't think I am forgetting my promise. Let me give you a little account of my adventures hitherto.

The <u>Parisian</u> in which I sailed from Quebec was horribly overcrowded, and there was on board a thing called the Canadian Rifle Team. However, we arrived in Liverpool in eight days, and had seen some interesting bits of the St Laurence coast, and Belle Ilse, which had still a good deal of snow on it. Icebergs were there in plenty, but not large or very impressive. The shore of Ireland was of course a welcome sight, and really pretty, with patches of the liveliest green. We entered the harbour of Londonderry, and then skirted the cliffs they call the Giants' Causeway. There is a strangely delightful and exciting sensation when one sails in a large ship very near the land, especially when it is rocky and precipitous, as this was, and over-hangs your masts. From Liverpool I went straight to London, where I staid a few days, and then went with Russell to a place in the Hampshire downs, within sight of the sea, where he has bought a little cottage for his "cousin". Her mother was there to give respectability to the party. We staid four days, which I spent very pleasantly wandering about alone a good deal – Russell was suffering from a complaint that made walking impossible, and besides, it was well to leave the cousins together, as they only see each other once a week–. I walked about alone, then, or rather among the most prodigious quantity of rabbits, along charming dells and windy downs, and got my first whiff of liberty and nature. From Telegraph House, so the little cottage is called, having been once a signal station, by which messages went from Portsmouth to London, I went to Windsor where I spent a week with my friend Howard Sturgis.[1] The house was filled with people, a most entertaining and bewildering lot of them. There was a Mrs Sheridan, daughter of the American historian Motley, and at times also her husband, a descendant of the playwright,[2] but he was usually absent, attending to his stables and kitchen gardens at home. Although of such lit-erary ancestry these charming people are free from literature themselves. The husband spends his leisure–when not occupied as I said just now–in telling stories to make the married women laugh, and the unmarried ones listen. The wife meantime tells you with a sigh and a smile how sorry she is for the provincial millionaire who is about to marry her daughter. These lovers were also in the house, he a dapper nice little man of thirty nine with forty thousand pounds a year, she a lazy big society belle of some two and twenty, without the rudiments of anything but a colossal selfishness. There turned up at various times for a day or two, Story (Emma Eames' husband) a young Harcourt (son of Sir William) various relations of our host, whom I was glad to meet, and finally many people for single meals, including four Eton boys, and Tom Motley, father and son, whom you may have known at Harvard. The Eton boys were very nice, as were two masters who came another day to luncheon and the School itself, which I walked to repeatedly. One of these boys, the nicest perhaps, was Waldorf Astor, who reminded me of my friend Joe Hunt in his beardless days.[3] I also thought of you, because it seems to me that you were made to bring up such fine boys as these in the way they should go. If you only had had a little Anglican Churchiness about you, you would have drifted into that sort of thing very easily. But the clerical element seems necessary—it gives a little touch of the highest propriety with the least possible constraint. The more I see of the Church of England the more I admire it, not, you conceive, philosophically or as a thing possible for myself, but as a masterpiece of social diplomacy, by which everything passes off with a vague dignity, a sense of spiritual elevation is attained, and no harm is done. A real religion, on the other hand, raises the imagination to a higher power, but makes it inapt, and an encumbrance to a man in the business of this world.

From Windsor I came up here, where I have been living very pleasantly and methodically. I read in the Bodleian, which is an ideal place for that, and write a good deal. My rooms are small but comfortable, my food plain but excellent, my landlady efficient but invisible. For the afternoon I have three favourite walks, each I fancy of about seven miles. One is to Sandford and Iffley, one to Marston, and one to Wytham. When it rains or I feel less energetic I wander about the town and drop in for evening prayers at Christ Church. Now the boy-choir is broken up for the long vacation only the tenors and basses remain, and the anthem is usually in Latin. That gives the singing a monastic sound, and if I succeed in abstracting my attention from a few details in the foreground—such as the byicyclists and American tourists with their Baedekers[4] for breviaries—I can fancy myself in Oxford as it was meant to be. To complete the impression the choir does not pronounce Latin in the English but in the to me natural continental way. I remember these words, for instance: Non nobis, Domine, non nobis, sed nomini tuo sit gloria; and another day: Beati mortui morientes in Domino.[5] Hearing that, I couldn't help thinking of my friends Sanborn[6] and Warwick Potter who cared for these things too, and who would have been glad, I think, to be here with me to listen.—I should remain in Oxford indefinitely were it not that, being in a University town, every one says I ought to be in a college. I couldn't, however, join any college here except as an undergraduate, which is beneath my dignity and experience of life. At Cambridge on the other hand, as you know, the situation is different, and it is not unlikely that I may go to King's for next term. I have been corresponding with Wedd about it, but nothing is yet definitely arranged.

I see few people here, the Dyers[7] sometimes, and while the summer term was still going some Balliol people. Corbin, whom you perhaps remember as a poet-athlete in 92, was there, and introduced me to some dons and undergraduates—no one particularly interesting. I like this seclusion: I seldom even read the papers, so that when I do I am startled at the references to things I know nothing of. What, for instance, has Cleveland[8] been proclaiming about Cuba? Something outrageous, probably. Don't forget, dear Guy, that I know nothing about you either.   Yours aff^{ly}

G.S.

[1]Howard Overing Sturgis (1855–1920), a novelist, was the son of Russell Sturgis (1805–87), a wealthy Bostonian living in London, and his third wife, Julia Overing Boit. Howard, a cousin to Santayana's half brother and half sisters, was educated at Eton and Trinity College, Cambridge. Santayana first met Sturgis in 1889 at the Cotuit house of Lucy Sturgis Codman. Afterwards, Santayana made almost yearly visits to Sturgis's house, Queen's Acre, near Windsor Park.

[2]Mrs. Sheridan's father was John Lothrop Motley (1814–77), famous for his histories of the Netherlands under Spanish rule. Mr. Sheridan's ancestor was Richard Brinsley Butler Sheridan (1751–1816), an Irish-born English dramatist, orator, and statesman who wrote satirical comedies of manners.

[3]Emma Eames (1865–1952) was a soprano who sang with the Metropolitan Opera (1891–1901). William George Granville Venables Vernon Harcourt (1827–1904) was an English statesman, parliamentarian, Liberal leader, and supporter of Gladstone, as well as an international law expert. Thomas Motley received an honorary degree from Harvard in 1872 and was an instructor in farming (Bussey Institute, Harvard, 1870–95). His son, Thomas Motley, was a member of Harvard's class of 1896. Waldorf Astor (1879–1952) was an American-born member of the English House of Lords, graduate of Oxford University, and an influential Conservative politician. Joe Hunt is possibly Joseph Howland Hunt (d. 1924), a member of the Harvard class of 1892, who graduated from the École des Beaux-Arts in Paris.

[4]Karl Baedecker (1801–59) was a German publisher and founder of Baedeker guidebooks.

[5]"Not to us, Lord, not to us, but to your name be glory;" and "Blessed [are] the dead dying in the Lord."

[6]A poet, Thomas Parker Sanborn (1865–89) was a member of Santayana's Harvard class of 1886 who committed suicide. Santayana published two obituaries of Sanborn: the first in *The Harvard Monthly* 8 (March 1889): 35, and the second in the *Harvard College Class of 1886 Secretary's Report No. VII, Twenty-Fifth Anniversary, 1911* (Cambridge: University Press [1911?]), 200–201. See *Persons*, 187–88 and 191.

[7]Louis Dyer (1851–1908) graduated from Harvard in 1874 and took a B.A. at Oxford in 1878. A translator, editor, and writer in classical and Renaissance literature, he was

appointed lecturer in German and French at Balliol College, Oxford (1893–95). See
Persons, 231 and 487.

[8]Stephen Grover Cleveland (1837–1908) was twice President of the United States
(1884–88, 1892–96). The question about Cuba refers to Cleveland's stand on the 1895
revolt there. Though there was public sympathy for the revolutionists, Cleveland did
not grant official U.S. support. In 1896 he was not offered the Democratic nomination;
the more radical wing of the party nominated William Jennings Bryan instead.

To Hannibal Ingalls Kimball
20 August 1896 • Oxford, England   (MS: Columbia)

Oxford
Aug. 20. '96

My dear Mr Kimball

Two copies of the new edition of my Sonnets reached me here a few
days ago. Everything seems right about it; I like the cover very much better than that of the first edition. There is one misprint on page 51 last line
"worshipped." I can't think how that escaped all our eyes.

You wrote me some time ago that the account I had received contained
some mistake, but I have never received the corrected version. If I have
any assets which are now payable conveniently I should be glad of it, as I
am this year travelling without any income, and every little helps an empty
stomach.

Would you be likely to wish to print another small volume containing
two long dramatic poems called "The Hermit's Christmas"[1] and "The
Marriage of Aphrodite"? The first is a sort of religious legend, the second
a comedy, not wholly without savour, perhaps, but somewhat risqué in
theme and occasionally in treatment. Expurgations, however, might make
it pass muster on that score. I ask you because it is possible I may submit
the pieces to some publisher here, and if you cared for the American
rights, I should be glad to make that a condition of the agreement with
him. Of course you can't give an answer without seeing the MS, but you
might possibly have a preconception one way or the other which might
guide me.   Yours very truly

GSantayana

Address care of
Messrs Brown Shipley & Co
        London.

(over)

Will you kindly have copies of the new edition of the Sonnets sent to the
following addresses, with my compliments, and charge them to my
account?
A. C. Coolidge Esq[2]
        Ware Hall Cambridge.
Mrs C H Toy
        7 Lowell St Cambridge.

[1] *The Hermit of Carmel.*
[2] Archibald Cary Coolidge (1866–1928), Harvard class of 1887, taught history at
Harvard (1893–1928) and served as director of the Harvard University Library
(1910–28).

To Charles Scribner's Sons

29 September 1896 • Maidenhead, England   (MS: Princeton)

Maidenhead
Sept. 29 '96

Messrs Charles Scribner's Sons
    New York

Dear Sirs:

I am glad you are going on with the publication of the <u>Sense of Beauty</u>
without waiting for the last proofs, as there seems to be no error in them.
I enclose a list of people to whom I should like you to send copies with my
compliments, charging them to my account according to what may be
your usual practice. I suppose you will yourselves know what papers the
book had best be sent to; the following, I should say, should be among
them: in America. The Nation, the American Philosophical Review
(Cornell) The American Journal of Psychology, The Harvard Graduate's
Magazine. In England: Mind, the Saturday Review the Spectator, the
Academy. In France the Revue Critique, Revue Philosophique, Revue de
philosophie critique. In Germany: Vierteljahrschrift für wissenschaftliche
Philosophie, Litterarisches Centralblatt. I can think of no other important
ones at present, but will send you the names if they occur to me.

Yours very truly
GSantayana

^c/o Brown Shipley & Co
    London.

Please send copies of the <u>Sense of Beauty</u> with the author's compliments
to the following:

Professor Norton,	Shady Hill,	Cambridge,	Mass.
" Wm. James,	Irving St.	"	"
" Josiah Royce	" "	"	"
" G. H. Palmer	Quincy St	"	"
" C. C. Everett,	Garden S	"	"
Professor & Mrs C. H. Toy,	7 Lowell St.	"	"
The Delta Phi Club,	72 Mt Auburn St	"	"
John Corbin, Esq.	Dunster Hall	"	"
Mrs John L. Gardner,	152 Beacon St	Boston	"
Mrs Henry Whitman[1]	77 Mt Vernon St.	"	"
Howard Cushing Esq.	168 Beacon St	"	"
Miss Lowell[2]	118 E 30th St	New York	N.Y.
Norman Hapgood Esq,	New York Evening Post,	"	" "
Earl Russell,	Amberley Cottage, Maidenhead,		England.
Louis Dyer Esq,	68 Banbury Road, Oxford		"
Bernhard[3] Berenson ˄Esq.˄	^c/o Baring Bros. & Co London.		"
Miss Julia Robins[4]	" " " " " "		"
Charles Loeser, Esq,	^c/o Theodor Veit, Stuttgart,		Germany.
Professor Hugo	Münsterberg, Freiburg, Germany.		
J. T. Stickney, Esq .[5]	^c/o J. S. Morgan & Co, London,		England.
Wm. Morton Fullerton, Esq.	^c/o London Times, ",		".
Conrad Slade, Esq,	^c/o Périer Mercet & ^{cie} Paris,		France.

[1]Sarah Wyman Whitman (b. 1845) was married to Henry Whitman, a Boston wool
merchant and banker. She was well known in Boston for church work and as an interior decorator.
[2]Carlotta Russell Lowell.
[3]Berenson changed his name from Bernhard to Bernard.
[4]Unidentified.
[5]Joseph Trumbull "Joe" Stickney (1874–1904), Harvard class of 1895, studied for
seven years at the Sorbonne and was the first American to receive its *Doctorat des
Lettres.* He wrote *Dramatic Verses* (1902) and taught Greek at Harvard (1903–4).

To Boylston Adams Beal

10 October 1896 • Cambridge, England   (MS: Houghton)

1 Silver Street
Cambridge.

Oct. 10, '96

Dear Boylston.

Your good letter reached me two days ago at Elvington, Julian Sturgis's[1] place near Dover where I was spending a few drenching days. Many thanks for the news, of which the best part is what relates to your own plans. I am delighted that you are coming abroad to have such a gay winter, and that I may hope to meet you and Elsie in Italy in the Spring. The engagements you announce are indeed suitable. It is the marriage of bread with butter. None of the persons in question achieves the pungency of cheese. You speak of Guy Lowell. Could you send me his address and that of Bob Potter,[2] in Paris? I continually forget them, and now I want to send them my book, which I believe is on the point of appearing, if it has not already done so, and later I shall want to go and find them myself. I am only sorry Howard Cushing and I seem to be playing hide and seek. How is Austin, and Duer Irving, and Phil Dalton, and Palmer Welsh, and my other ΔΦ friends?[3] I should write them also a circular letter if I thought they would be interested in it.

Since my last, which you have seen, my movements have been few, but not without interest to me. I left Oxford early in September, after seeing both Frederic and Edwin Morgan[4] there, and went to Haslemere to visit young Bertrand Russell at his father-in-law's, Mr Pearsall Smith's.[5] This is a family of Philadelphia Quakers long settled, or unsettled, in England. When the old lady, who delivers temperance lectures and now has Armenia on the brain, goes off to Evangelize something, the old man at home takes the opportunity to dis-evangelize himself, and declare he is not a Quaker at all, but a Buddhist. For, he says, the suffering in the world is appalling, and the best thing we can hope for is extinction and peace. He has accordingly removed himself as far as possible from earth already by building a hen-coop, covered with glass, up in a tree, where he squats, and, I believe, spends the night. He directed me to the place through the woods, and I had the curiosity to climb up to it, not without imminent danger of transmigration. There are wires stretched all around a circular ladder, by way of balusters in which one is sure to get caught. Perhaps they symbolize the Veil of Maya. However that may be, the family is not uninteresting, and Bertrand Russell himself is very clever and nice. He is writing a book on the history of the fourth dimension, or, as he calls it, the "Foundations of Geometry".[6] Everything now-a-days turns out to be founded on its latest development. This I suppose is what is called final causes, or ends that are beginnings, or putting the cart before the horse. Sally Fairchild was also, to my surprise, at Haslemere, and I have met her several times since. She is staying now with Ellen Terry.[7] She seems to be a great success with the virtuous intellects over here, who take her seriously.–From Haslemere I went to Maidenhead, to the wicked Earl's, where I stayed some four weeks. It was a very happy time. I was much alone, as Russell is busy and often goes to the city; I read a good deal, wrote a little, and took long walks, as I believe I told you I did at Oxford. I made friends with Tubby the Dog, who was my constant companions on these peripatetic occasions. Among other things, I read George Merideth, The Egoist and Evan Harrington, and like them.[8] The style is not good in the former book, nor the plot, but the characters are well drawn: the latter reminds one in places of Thackeray and true wit.[9] Russell's affairs have been getting more and more perplexed. The Scotts,[10] beaten at every point, have finally exploded, and sent out 350 copies of a circular, full of most filthy and ridiculous details, printed out, charging Russell with b–[11] I mean, abusing all his servants ten years ago. Two of them have actually been bribed to sign the papers, and one to have a summons for an assault, committed at Winchester ~~ten~~ nine years ago, issued against Russell. This summons came as a surprise, and everything had to be prepared for the defence in a great hurry. It turned out, however, that at the time selected, June 18, 1887, both Burke and I were with Russell at Winchester, and he was staying at the College with Mr & Mrs Richardson.[12] With the testimony of other servants, that have remained faithful, it would have been possible to prove an alibi, and expose the malice of the accusation. The Scotts either got wind of this, or their counsel refused to act for them, for when yesterday we had all gone to Winchester, to the trial, and the Rev. Mr. Dickens, Vicar of St John's had come in his trap for us and driven us to the court, which was packed, and we,–a dozen of us a least,–had crowded it still more, the representative of the prosecution got up and said that to save the time of several gentlemen in the court, he would announce that the ~~case~~ action against Lord Russell had had to be abandoned, for it had been found that the spot where the offence was alleged to have been committed lay outside the limits of Winchester, and therefore beyond the jurisdiction of that court. Matthews, Russell's counsel thereupon got up melodramatically and with fearful grimaces and pregnant inflections of the voice, said he would make no comment, etc, but he was not surprised, not in the least surprised, etc, that the prosecution had dropped the case like a hot potatoe. Meantime Russell's solicitor had got hold of the publishers of the libels, who are willing to swear that Lady Scott paid them and instructed them, and have produced the list of 350 names, peers, judges, relations, and academic people, in Lady Scott's own hand, on her own scented note-paper, to whom the libels were sent. This connects Lady Scott with the publication, and a warrant for her arrest has by this time, I suppose, been issued. We now hope to get her at least two years' hard labour.[13]

After this bloodless victory at Winchester I came straight to Cambridge, to the rooms I had previously engaged. They seem pretty comfortable, the study particularly being cheerful, with running windows on two sides looking up and down the main street, in the very midst of things, so that I may not feel out of it. I have just got formal notice of my admission to King's with the standing of M.A. Wedd, my mentor, took me yesterday to dine in hall, which was of course very grand. with the old plate and the—not many—old portraits. One of Sir Horace Walpole[14]—the only "great" man the college has produced—has the place of honour, and he looks very smart indeed in his dim and gigantic canvass, with his wig, and his superflous drapery, floating about him in the breeze. Oscar Browning[15] was there, and talked absurd nonsense over his port, making everybody laugh, although at his own expense. The other people at the High Table, where I am now to dine when I dine in hall, may be divided into two classes; the parsons, shy, with shining red faces, and mellifluous voices, very awkward and very athletic creatures, and the Bohemians, comparatively dingy, hairy, and intelligent, no less fond of the good things of this world, only fond of a greater number of them. Of this type my friend Wedd—who has, so to speak, <u>Wedded</u> me to King's,—is the best example. He is a little man, with a shock of hair like a lap-dog, with no eyes, to speak of, a bushy moustache, a great laugh, and a self-effacing manner: a short man, not over-neat. He takes his liquour like a Trojan, and is writing a book on the trade routes of the Greeks and Romans, a vast work to occupy his life-time. Another youngish Don, a little less Bohemian, seemed rather interesting, but they haven't all turned up yet, and I will speak of them when I have got to know them better.

This afternoon I took my first walk in Cambridge, along the tow-path, to watch the fours row. There is great activity, and the way these fellows tug at their oars seems rather unscientific to a Harvard eye, but alas! not for that reason ineffective. The afternoon was lovely and the Cam, although ugly compared with the Isis,[16] was not without its charm. The blazers worn here certainly deserve the name, cherry, light vermillion, orange, and lemon yellow, not to speak of all sorts of blue. There is to be a football match next Saturday, when I hope to be initiated into the technicalities of an undeveloped Rugby game. The Chapel I have not yet visited: I am waiting until I get my cap and gown, to which I had no right until this evening, if I have it yet, not having matriculated. When I have them I will go often, as ¢that must be one of the greatest treats of life at King's.[17]

A dull letter, I am afraid, but it would not be better for being longer. So, farewell.

Yours ever   GSantayana

[1]Julian Russell Sturgis (1848–1904), son of Nathaniel Russell Sturgis, was a gentleman of leisure who occasionally wrote novels.

[2]Robert "Bob" Burnside Potter (c. 1869–c. 1936), Harvard class of 1891, became an architect. Santayana's poem entitled "Dedication of the first sonnets to a friend on the eve of his marriage" was written in honor of him. See *Complete Poems*, 263.

[3]Austin Potter, Alexander Duer Irving, Philip Spaulding Dalton (class of 1898), and Julian Palmer Welsh (class of 1897) were members of the Delta Phi Club.

[4]Frederic Grinnell Morgan (d. 1920) was a member of the class of 1891, and Edwin Vernon Morgan (1865–1934), a member of the class of 1890, was the U.S. minister to Brazil (1912–33).

[5]Bertrand Arthur William Russell (1872–1970) was educated at Cambridge and held a variety of posts there. He reacted against idealism with realism in *Principles of Mathematics* (1903). He adopted the alternative of logical constructions, substituting wherever possible constructions out of known entities for inference to unknown ones. Presentation of pure mathematics from logic exemplifies this policy. See his classic *Principia Mathematica* (co-authored with A. N. Whitehead, 1910–13). *Our Knowledge of the External World* (1914) applies Russell's logical constructionism to physical objects. Later Russell became interested in social and political issues, publishing *Marriage and Morals* (1929), *Education and the Social Order* (1932), and *New Hopes for a Changing World* (1951). He received the Nobel Prize for Literature in 1950. He married four times, and his first wife was Alys Pearsall Smith (1867–1951), the daughter of Hannah Tatum Whitall and Robert Pearsall Smith. They were married from 1894 to 1921. See *Persons*, 285–89, 439–44, 475–76, and 485–86.

[6]*An Essay on the Foundations of Geometry* (New York: Dover Publications, 1897).

[7]Sally Fairchild is unidentified. Dame Ellen (Alicia) Terry (1848–1928) was an English actress whose premier roles were Shakespeare's Portia, Olivia, and Beatrice.

[8]George Meredith (1828–1909) was an English novelist, poet, and critic who hated egotism and sentimentality and supported the intellectual equality of women. He believed in the medicinal quality of laughter, that comedy corrects the excesses of sen-

timentality, selfishness, and vanity. *The Egoist: a Comedy in Narrative* (London: C. Kegan Paul & Co., 1879) and *Evan Harrington* (London: Bradbury & Evans, 1861).

[9]William Makepeace Thackeray (1811–63) was an English novelist and satirist, known for his satirical and moralistic studies of upper- and middle-class English life. After failing as both a lawyer and painter, he achieved success as a contributor to various magazines and then wrote *The Yellowplush Correspondence* (1838), *The Paris Sketch Book* (1840), and *The Fitz Boodle Papers* (1842–43). He was on the staff of *Punch* (1842–51), to which he contributed satires published as *The Book of Snobs* (1848). With the publication of this book and his masterpiece *Vanity Fair* (1848), Thackeray won popular and critical recognition.

[10]Lady Maria Selina Burney Scott (d. 1909) and her daughter Mabel Edith. Bitter courtroom battles were fought between Russell and these women, whose sensational allegations gave Russell the "wicked Earl" title. Santayana testified on Russell's behalf at the 1897 trial held in London's Old Bailey, in which Russell accused his mother-in-law of libel.

[11]Buggery.

[12]Rev. G. Richardson was one of the masters at Winchester College, Russell's school. The Richardsons were fond of Russell. See *Persons*, 310.

[13]At the subsequent London trial Lady Scott was convicted of libel and sentenced to prison. Russell gives a full account of these proceedings in *My Life and Adventures* (London: Cassell, 1923).

[14]Horace Walpole (1717–97) was an English historian and fourth earl of Orford. His books include *Memoirs, Anecdotes of Painting in England* (1762–71), and *Correspondence*. His *The Castle of Otranto* (1764) is the first English Gothic novel.

[15]Oscar Browning (1837–1923) was a master at Eton (1860–75) and later held positions at Cambridge University. See *Persons*, 435–36.

[16]The Cam (or Granta) flows past Cambridge. Isis is the stretch of the Thames that flows past Oxford University.

[17]Santayana's meditations in the Chapel are recorded in his poem, "King's College Chapel," composed in November 1896. See *Complete Poems*, 169–73.

To James Edwin Creighton
15 October [1896] • Cambridge, England   (MS: Cornell)

King's College
Cambridge

Oct 15

Dear Mr Creighton[1]

I am ashamed to have kept Willmann's book so long, but the truth is, more pressing tasks and travelling have made me forget his existence for months at a time.[2] I haven't yet read half the book, which is rather dull, and if you could wait yet a little longer, I should be very much obliged, as I am only just settling here, and life is a series of interruptions. How long, by the way, would you like the review to be? The work, I fancy, is not a very important one, but the subject and the views are not uninteresting, and might suggest a good deal. Would you like something of an independent article, or merely a notice?

Yours very truly
GSantayana

My permanent address is
^c/o Brown Shipley & Co
    London.

[1]James Edwin Creighton (1861–1924) taught at Cornell University and coedited the Philosophical Review from 1892 to 1902 when he became sole editor. He was the American editor of Kantstudien (1896–1924). Creighton cofounded the American Philosophical Association and became its first president in 1902.
[2]Otto Willmann (1839–1920) was the author of *Geschichte des Idealismus.* Santayana reviewed volume two (*Der Idealismus der Kirchenväter und der Realismus der Scholastiker*) in *Philosophical Review* 6 (November 1897): 661–64.

To Josiah Royce
17 October 1896 • Cambridge, England   (MS: Harvard)

---

1 Silver Street
Cambridge

Oct. 17 '96

Dear Professor Royce

    You may have wondered at not hearing from me before this, and I should indeed have written if I could have given any clear account of myself earlier. Professor Palmer has probably told you that he saw me at Oxford. I spent most of the summer there with great joy, reading in the Bodleian, writing off a couple of articles I had on hand—on Cervantes and on the absence of religion in Shakespeare—and taking long walks.[1] The Dyers and a few stragglers at Balliol were the only people I saw often, as the place was of course deserted for the long vacation. I should very gladly have stayed on; but there seemed to be no possibility of joining any college with a proper status, and to live there without official relations is not a desirable thing. With great regret, therefore, I decided to come here, where an old acquaintance, Wedd, a classical man, has managed to get me into King's with the MA standing, so that I dine at high table, and meet the Dons daily on a friendly footing. People are much more hospitable and openhearted here, and there is more bustle and intellectual eagerness, so that I have much to comfort and congratulate myself with, in spite of the absence of a certain Oxonian distinction. My work is now definitely arranged, under Dr Jackson's advice. I am to hear his lectures on the Philebus, and those of Archer-Hind on the Phaedo, and to have an hour a week privately with Jackson on the Parmenides.[2] I have been reading a little Plato in the summer, and want to concentrate my attention on him for a while. Other things can follow later, if there is time for them. My stay here is indefinite as yet, and will be longer or shorter according to developments. I rather think I may stay two terms, that is, until the middle of March, and then go off to Paris and Italy, in search of old friends and new impressions.

I should be very glad to hear from you and to know how Harvard prospers, and especially the Department. My young friends write to me occasionally about College matters of a terrestrial and foot-ball plane, but I don't know what currents blow in the upper ether. Hoping they are all propitious to you, I am always   sincerely yours
GSantayana

[1]Miguel de Cervantes Saavedra (1547–1616) was a Spanish novelist, dramatist, and poet. His reputation as a great writer rests almost entirely on *Don Quixote* (1605) and the twelve short stories known as the *Novelas Ejemplares* (1613), even though his literary output was extraordinary. The articles Santayana refers to are "Cervantes (1547–1616)" in *A Library of the World's Best Literature: Ancient and Modern*, ed. Charles Dudley Warner (New York: The International Society, 1897), 8:3451–57 and "The Absence of Religion in Shakespeare" in *New World* (Boston, 1896), 5:681–91.
[2]Henry Jackson (1839–1921) was a Plato scholar, professor of Greek, and fellow of Trinity College (see *Persons*, 439). Richard Dacre Archer-Hind (1849–1910) translated Plato, including the *Phaedo* (1883). *Philebus*, *Phaedo*, and *Parmenides* are Platonic dialogues.

To Charles Scribner's Sons
22 October 1896 • Cambridge, England   (MS: Princeton)

King's College
Cambridge

Oct 22. 96

Dear Sirs:

I have your letter of the 13th but the two copies of the Sense of Beauty have not yet reached my hands. Thank you for despatching the 22 copies to my friends. I should be glad if you would send a copy also, on the same terms, to the European periodicals I mentioned, including the English weekly's, unless your plan of placing an edition in London is to be immediately realized. The sale of the book, as you say, may not be affected by these papers so much, but its reputation depends very largely on them, and that, of course, is what I am concerned about. You can use the four remaining copies assigned to me for this purpose, and charge the rest to my account.

As I am spending the winter in England it is not unlikely that I may occasionally wish to get another copy to give to a friend, or that enquiries may be made to me about the place where the book may be ordered from. Is there any bookshop in London where some copies may be found? I should think a half dozen copies might be easily sold in this town, if put in the window of a bookshop–Macmillan's, for instance–as my friends here would perhaps be curious to see it. Some might also be sent to Oxford, where I have acquaintances. ~~also.~~ This is, I daresay, what you mean by "placing an edition".

I am not sure that I mentioned the four English papers besides <u>Mind</u>– the Academy, Athenaeum, Spectator, and Saturday Review.

Yours very truly
GSantayana.

To William Cameron Forbes
1 November 1896 • Cambridge, England   (MS: Houghton)

^c/o Brown Shipley & Co
      <u>London</u>

King's College
Cambridge.

Nov. 1 '96

Dear Cam

Your delightful letter took me back to you very vividly and pleasantly, and made me wish I could see you, although you will understand that as far as your expeditions on the Merlin are concerned I much prefer the description to the reality. What you say about Phil Rhinelander[1] interests me particcularly. †go on on the other sheet. The two were stuck together as I wrote.† I tried to see him at Oxford this summer, but he was away most of the time, and when he did return I didn't know of it. I hope to see several of our old friends in Paris before long, but I shall miss Howard Cushing.

My life here is very pleasant. My rooms are cheerful and well-situated, although my landlady's aesthetic sense is not what I could wish, and her worsted roses under glass bells—now happily banished—are not what my eyes most love to feast upon. However, life is well-arranged. I dine in Hall at the High Table with the Dons, of whom I see a great deal also at other times. They are for the most part very quiet, cultivated, odd, youngish men. Most people here are shy, but very friendly and unaffected, easier to get on with than Oxford people if perhaps less interesting. As you might guess, I go often to watch the football "matches". The game as played in England is very pretty, especially the passing while on the run, by which the long gains are usually made. There is no interference—the men run far apart, for the sake of the passing—and, strangest of all, the ball belongs to neither side after a down but is thrown into the middle of a double turtle-back formation, and kicked ("heeled") about until one side or the other succeeds in making it slip out where its backs can pick it up and pass it for a run or kick. The art of tackling is almost unknown but men are hurt all the same. Our game is much more glorious and exciting, but this is very good in its way, and is hard, varied exercise. Every man has frequent chances to kick, and team work tells in the heeling and passing. It's too bad you didn't take a more responsible position in coaching this year. You probably have been called on by this time to do more than you expected when you wrote. My own exertions are all directed to Plato at present. I hear two lectures a week and have one hour in private with Jackson of Trinity, who is excellent, most stimulating and enlightening. It's hard stuff—Parmenides and Philebus—but very interesting to me on account of the deep logical and metaphysical questions involved. My Greek, too, is coming back in a rather reassuring manner, and I hope to be less ignorant in several ways than I was when the year began. I shall probably stay here till March, then go abroad.

Write again, and tell me something about Edward,[2] unless he is willing to write to me himself, which I should be very glad of.

Yours ever   GSantayana.

[1]Philip Mercer Rhinelander, Harvard class of 1891, received his B.A. (1896) and M.A. (1900) from Oxford. He later became a bishop in Pennsylvania.

[2]Edward Forbes.

To Carlotta Russell Lowell
11 November 1896 • Cambridge, England   (MS: Houghton)

King's College
Cambridge

<u>Nov. 11 '96</u>

Dear Lotta

Many thanks for both your notes. When I got the first I never expected a second, as it is the part of prudence to thank an author for his book before reading it, so as to avoid the necessity of lying about it afterwards. That you should have written both before and after is very gratifying, as it seems to mean that you liked the book better than you expected, and at any rate well enough to say something nice about it when this was no longer necessary. I am delighted that you found most of the book intelligible and interesting, and that you agreed with most of it. That is all I can now say for it myself, as there are already several things I should like to see put otherwise in it.

My life here is very pleasant and interesting, and perhaps a little luxurious. I try to chasten myself, however, with some tough Greek–the Parmenides and Philebus of Plato, which I am reading carefully–and with long walks among the clouds, which in this country come down to the surface of the land and especially of the water. The afternoons are very lovely, and the river with its many boats, blazers, byíciycles, and coaches on horseback is a gay and pretty sight. My friends at King's have the flavour of their Port, sweet, mellow, and with lots of body, and it will be hard not to get so fond of them as to miss them when I go. My plan is now to go to Paris for Christmas, when we have five weeks' holiday, and return here for the Lent term after which will come a little trip to Italy and in August, probably, America again.

Haven't the Russells[1] turned up? I should have been glad to have you meet, they are such nice people. He is mathematical and she humanitarian, but both are human at the same time.

You may tell Bob Barlow[2] that my idea of writing about morals is not abandoned, and that in fact some paragraphs are already set down, but it will take a long time yet to work out the scheme properly. It is a soberer subject than the "Sense of Beauty" and has to be constructed as solidly and compactly as possible, which means hard work. I also await the criticisms of the learned on my first flourish, in case they should contain useful hints. Remember me to Aunt Sarah[3] and your mother and believe me

Always sincerely yours

GSantayana

My address is Brown Shipley & Co
London.

[1]Bertrand and Alys.
[2]Robert Shaw Barlow (b. 1869), Harvard class of 1891, practiced law in New York, serving as assistant corporation counsel of the City of New York (1891–98). After returning to Boston in 1898, he continued to practice law. See *Persons*, 341–42.
[3]Sara Putnam Lowell (b. 1843) was the daughter of John Amory Lowell, wife of George Baty Blake, and aunt of Herbert Lyman. See *Persons*, 82 and 255.

To Henry Ward Abbot

19 November 1896 • Cambridge, England   (MS: Columbia)

King's College
Cambridge

Nov. 19 '96

Dear Harry

Many thanks for your good letter, which has only the defect of showing that you are not very happy, and continue to discourage yourself without definite reasons. The world is full of sad and unaccountable things, of which the most hopeless, perhaps, is that unfit persons like ourselves have been brought into it under circumstances that make real satisfaction impossible for us. However, when once the main thing is renounced, there are a variety of compensations and incidental pleasures to be found; and what makes me feel a little out of sympathy with your state of mind is that while you say you are without illusions you refuse your intelligence its entertainment and your will its hard earned peace. How can you say that the world is robbed of its moral beauty because that is not true which, if true, would make "love repine and reason chafe"? As for me, I quite agree that it is perdition to be safe when one ought to die for the truth; but I seek to give this last phrase a meaning, and not to make it simply an ebullition of irrational feeling, an Emersonian equivalent for "damn."[1] To die for the truth can only mean to die in the pursuit of a safe basis for living.

I did not stay at Oxford because there was no way of entering any good College there except as an undergraduate. Here I have M A standing, dine with the Dons, and read Plato with Jackson of Trinity, a very jolly old man. I go to Paris for the Christmas holidays and to Italy after the Lent term. In the Summer I expect to be still in Italy, possibly to go to Spain, and to be back in Boston in August or early September.

Give my best regards to your mother and believe me

Yours as ever

GSantayana

[1]Ralph Waldo Emerson (1803–82) was an American poet, essayist, and philosopher. In 1835, he settled in Concord, Massachusetts, and became the center of a major literary circle. Emerson wrote *Nature* (1836) and from 1842 to 1844 edited *The Dial.* His thought is characterized by its reliance on intuition as the way to a comprehension of reality. He was attracted to mystical Indian literature and philosophy.

To Charles Scribner's Sons

21 December 1896 • Paris, France   (MS: Princeton)

Paris Dec. 21. '96

Messrs Scribner's Sons
    New York

Dear Sirs

I received in due time the two copies of the "Sense of Beauty" which you originally sent me, and later your letter, announcing the sale of sheets to A & C Black.[1] I am much pleased with this and also with several notices of the book that have reached me.

Of the four copies which you say you are still keeping for me will you kindly have one sent to each of the following addresses:

Guy Lowell, Esq. 3 rue Soufflot
R B Potter, Esq. 3 rue St. Simon

Paris

The appearance and binding of the book seem to me very good and appropriate, and although, printed out and published, the writing seems hardly my own any more, it is perhaps no worse than that of most other people.

Yours very truly

GSantayana

C/o Brown Shipley & Co
    London.

[1] A. and C. Black published *Beauty* in London in 1896.

To Susan Sturgis de Sastre

14 January 1897 • Cambridge, England   (MS: Virginia)

King's College
Jan. 14, 1897

Dear Susie

Your good letter and the Calendar find me this morning with nothing to do, and I am going to take the opportunity of writing you a long letter and giving you an account of myself up to date. Let me say first, however, that I am very, very sorry about Celedonio's eyes, both for his sake and yours. Even if in the end the operation is successful, as no doubt it will be, there is the long anxiety, discomfort and expense to think of, and I see that the affair will involve a great deal of care and sorrow to the whole family. As to Eduardo's[1] smallpox, that would alarm me more if I didn't know from experience how lightly such a thing is thought of in Spain.[2] I infer that no one else in the family has caught it, and that he himself is quite well again.

My life here is as quiet as possible without any excitements or notable variations. The people are much to my mind, being refined, simple, and serious, but theirs is a slow fire and it takes a long time to get warm at it. Sometimes it seems as if the time for going away would come before I had really got into the ways of the place. I have made several valuable acquaintances, especially that of a man named Dickinson, a tutor at King's, who is the type of everything I like and respect in the way of intelligence and feeling.[3] I walk with him sometimes, and also with other young men, and we ask one another to lunch and breakfast, as is the custom in these parts. Dinner, as you know, is in Hall, and we go afterwards to a smoking room, where the papers are, to have coffee and perhaps a game of whist or chess; not that I play myself, as I prefer to do nothing when there is nothing to do. Perhaps what I shall carry away from this prolonged visit to England more than anything else will be a love for the fields and the country air: it was one of the dreadful lacks in our education that we had nothing of that, and I feel it now as a permanent incapacity and disadvantage; the last six weeks of Paris and London have made me feel the change, for already I miss the country, and feel the oppression of pavements and walls, and the need of space and silence. Oxford last summer was a paradise in that respect, and I shall never forget my long solitary walks about that lovely region. The river here in the boating season is also beautiful, with its willows and broad fields, and the crowds of students, in their bright blazers, and in every sort of athletic costume, moving about ∧on∧ the water and the banks. It is a very simple, youthful life every one leads here, and Harvard in comparison seems constrained and corrupt. It is also more interesting, I must confess, and this Cambridge to say the truth is very dull. I should have stayed at Oxford if it had been possible to enter any college there except as an undergraduate (which I could not become again with dignity at this late day.) Here they are beginning to admit graduates to advanced standing (I eat and live with the Dons, and am not subject to ordinary regulations) and therefore I had to come here or remain at Oxford unattached to the University, which would not have served my purpose. However, you mustn't think I am not satisfied with my experiment. I am: only more exciting and interesting surroundings could be imagined than these.

For the holidays I went to Paris and stayed most of the time (four weeks) with Guy Lowell and Joe Hunt. You may remember Guy Lowell as the man I went to Spain with some years ago; he is a son of the late Mr. Edward Lowell, whom I believe you know.[4] Joe Hunt is a son of the architect (now also dead).[5] Both are studying architecture, and live in an apartment near the Panthéon.[6] Above them are seven other American students, and all dine together in a very jolly way. They made me a temporary member of the concern (I paid for my share of the food, but was Guy Lowell's guest as to lodging.) It was very interesting to hear so much about the technique of architecture; you remember how you, being once interested in it for a feminine reason,[7] passed the taste on to me who have retained it ever since. I also learned a great deal about the ways of the Quartier Latin,[8] went much to the theatre, and learned to know and love Paris as I had never done before. But after all what I valued most in that very pleasant month was seeing so many old friends—their names would mean little to you, but they were young men I had had about me at Harvard at various times, and grown more or less fond of—and especially Bob Potter and his wife. This is the eldest of the three brothers of whom you have heard me speak, of whom the second, Warwick, died to the great sorrow of so many of us. It was delightful to me to see him again and find our old sympathies quite spontaneously revived. His wife, too, far from being a barrier between us, is the essence of sympathy, intelligence, and devotion. I am even on affectionate terms with the baby, the new Warwick; and altogether we have got on so well that it is arranged we shall go to Italy en famille in April.[9] Mrs Potter is to remain in Florence with the child and nurse, while Bob and I go on to Rome, stopping on the way at the more important places. We shall then return to Florence and Venice, and I expect to remain in Italy for some time after the Potters return to Paris, which will be about June 1ˢᵗ I can't tell yet whether I can arrange to go to Avila. We can discuss that later. The idea of Greece is definitely abandoned: I have neither time, money, nor energy for it, especially as Loeser, the person with whom I should have gone, has also given up the project. And to travel alone to a new country where I don't know the language or any of the inhabitants, even if that country is Greece, is now-a-days a prospect that does not tempt me. That is one reason why the idea of travelling with the Potters makes me so happy. I was going to Italy anyhow, but the possibility of being often alone in hotels or lodging-houses, without my books or a companionable fire, and with no one to discuss things with, seemed a little cheerless. I should have had to pick up travelling companions on the way, but that, you know, is a thing more easily done when one is not yet thirty three, and is less particular about other people and more amiable in oneself. I still expect to stay at Florence with Loeser and at Fiesole (close by) with Berenson, both art critics and old acquaintances of mine. Doubtless many other people will turn up, among them Boylston and Elsie Beal who will be on their way back from Egypt and Greece.–In Paris I saw Susie Minturn and her daughter Gertrude, at the house of her other daughter Edith Stokes, whose husband is studying architecture at the Beaux-Arts.[10]

I came back to London to do a very singular thing–to give evidence in a <u>cause célèbre</u>. My unfortunate friend Russell has been pursued by his wife with two great lawsuits already, which she has lost, of course, ~~and~~ as well as her reputation. But exasperated by this, Lady Scott, the mother-in-law, got up a most abominable libel on her daughter's husband, had it printed in a disreputable hole, and circulated it anonymously in all the clubs and other places where Russell could have friends. He had no choice but to have her arrested, as well as her accomplices, and as the publication of the libel was proved against them beyond doubt, they took the impudent course of asserting that all it contained was true. Then it ~~beg~~ became necessary to disprove the various stories the libel contained, and as one of them was put at a time–June 1887,–when I was with Russell at Winchester, my evidence as to what there occurred became useful. There were many complications in the case–as the death of one of the prisoners–and at last, after all had been done that was possible to ruin Russell's reputation—Lady Scott and her people threw up their case, and pleaded guilty. They were sentenced to eight months imprisonment, a year being the maximum the law allows in such a case. The matter thus ends, but it has been a most scandalous and disgusting affair, and even with the certainty of ultimate success, Russell and his friends have had to go through dreadful moments. It is not pleasant to hear one of one's best friends accused in public with the utmost art and deliberation, of all that is most shocking and dishonourable, and not to know how many people all over the world will hear only that accusation—never the disproof of it—and believe it. But the judge did his best to put things right in the end, and to vindicate Russell, who has shown a most admirable courage and patience through it all. But I shouldn't wonder if when Lady Scott comes out of prison she didn't do something even more desperate. His house was burned to the ground, not long ago, and there was for a moment some fear it might have been done at her instigation. That however seems not to have been the case, but anything of the sort, even an attempt on Russell's life, would not be surprising from such wicked and vindictive women. I never heard of such characters in life or in fiction.

I will send you a French book or two at once; not that I am a particularly good person to get novels, as I don't read them myself, and seldom remember the names of those I promise to read on my friend's recommendation.

Love to all, and a happy new year from your affectionate brother

GSantayana

[1]Eduardo Sastre González was the fifth son of Celedonio by his first wife. His name does not appear in Santayana's "will" letter of 14 Feb 1928, by which time Eduardo was presumably dead.

[2]During Santayana's first return visit to Spain, at age 19, he contracted smallpox: "They said they were relieved. I was better. It was only 'small-pox,' and a mild case." (*Persons*, 207)

[3]Goldsworthy Lowes Dickinson (1862–1932) was a fellow of King's College (1887–1932) and lecturer in political science (1896–1920). An agnostic interested in mysticism, his favorite subjects were Plato and the Greeks. A pacifist during World War I, he became president of the Union for Democratic Control, which advocated "peace without victory." His writings reflect both of these primary interests and include *The Greek View of Life* (1896) and essays dedicated to furthering the cause of peace. See *Persons*, 438.

[4]Edward Jackson Lowell (1845–94) was an American historian and member of Harvard's class of 1867. He authored *The Eve of the French Revolution* (1892).

[5]Richard Morris Hunt (1827–95) was an American architect and exponent of nineteenth-century eclecticism who studied at the École des Beaux-Arts in Paris. He was

one of the organizers of the American Institute of Architects, of which he became president in 1888. Many important public buildings were constructed from his designs, including the Tribune Building in New York which was one of the first elevator buildings, the old Lenox Library Building, the Naval Observatory in Washington, and the base of the Statue of Liberty.

[6]The Panthéon in Paris was designed by J. G. Soufflot and built 1764–81. Now it is a mausoleum for illustrious Frenchmen.

[7]In her youth in Boston, Susan was interested in John Putnam, an architect. [D. C.]

[8]For centuries the preserve of the university was the Old Latin Quarter on the left bank of the Seine.

[9]Elizabeth "Lily" Stephens Clare Fish married Potter in 1894. The daughter of Nicholas Fish (for years American minister at Brussels), she had been educated abroad, was charming, spoke French and German, and learned Italian in preparation for the spring 1897 trip through Italy. The Potters' sons were Warwick and Hamilton. See *Persons*, 379–81.

[10]Susie Minturn was a daughter of Francis George Shaw and his wife Sarah Blake Sturgis (1815–1902). Sarah Shaw was a sister of Santayana's mother's first husband. Isaac Newton Phelps Stokes (1867–1944) was an American architect, housing reformer, historian, and member of the Harvard class of 1891. He compiled *The Iconography of Manhattan Island* (6 vols., 1915–28).

To Hannibal Ingalls Kimball

31 January 1897 • Cambridge, England   (MS: Virginia)

King's College
Cambridge

Jan • 31 • '97

My dear Mr Kimball

May I ask you to send me two more copies of my Sonnets?

A poet, at least of my calibre, doesn't expect to make money out of his verses. But I confess I am puzzled and annoyed at the vicissitudes of my account with you. First I had a balance of $82; that was a mistake, and the true balance was $16; now a third account shows that I owe $5. Will you kindly explain this, and let me know what system we are going on in future. I agree, as I wrote before, to whatever seems to you likely to be most satisfactory all round, but I should like to know what that is.

Yours very truly
GSantayana

Address
C/o Brown Shipley & Co
London.

To Charles Scribner's Sons

1 February 1897 • Cambridge, England   (MS: Princeton)

2 Free School Lane
Cambridge
England

Feb 1, 1897

Dear Sirs.

Will you kindly send me the two copies of "the Sense of Beauty" which I understand you are still reserving for me? I meant to get some copies of the English edition to give to my friends here on my departure, but they have bound the book in such a frivolous and gaudy cover that I blush to present it to anyone in that dress. I now see from what awful possibilities your own care and good taste have preserved me.

Yours very truly
GSantayana

Messrs Charles Scribner's Sons
New York

To Josiah Royce

23 April 1897 • Florence, Italy   (MS: Harvard)

Florence
April 23 1897

Dear Professor Royce

I was very glad this morning to get your letter and to hear what the arrangements are for next year. The change from Phil I to Phil II is a gain for me, and gives me a more interesting and less exhausting task. The change of hour, however, in my morning course is very inconvenient, as I am never very fit in the early morning, and next winter, when I expect not to be living in Cambridge, it will involve getting up at an absurd hour. I don't see the justice of the argument that eleven o'clock is filled up. Who fills it up, and why shouldn't I be one of these, when that is the hour I have lectured at for seven years? I am sorry you have allowed yourself to be brow-beaten by the official sophistry, but I suppose there is no help for it now. As to Radcliffe, I think I can give the History of Philosophy half-course, if it comes in the second half year, but not the other. Repetition is not what it seems in a philosophical course, and I shall have enough to do with my new work, for which I am imperfectly prepared.

I am going back to King's for the Long Vacation to go on with my Plato. Italy is very delightful and I am with old friends, which makes even the dull places in the tourist's existence bearable. Loeser and Berenson are also here, and I see them sometimes.

It is very nice that Münsterberg has decided to come back; it relieves the rest of all anxiety about the laboratory. Otherwise, I ~~forsee~~ foresee that Cambridge will be the same as ever

Hoping to hear from you again I remain

Yours very sincerely

GSantayana

To Guy Murchie

17 July 1897 • Cambridge, England   (MS: Murchie)

King's College
Cambridge

July 17. 1897

Dear Guy

Your letter deserves an immediate answer, but can hardly have an adequate one, as I should have to cover a whole year of history and several of plans if I was to attempt to make up for such a long silence. You know already what I have been doing, although it is not true that I have been in Greece or Spain, but only in Italy for the months of May and April. The rest of the time I have spent here, with the avowed object of reading Plato, which I have done more in earnest, perhaps, than I myself expected. If you look at the elective pamphlet for ₐnextₐ year you will see that I am offering a course mainly in him. My teacher has been Dr Henry Jackson of Trinity, a splendid old man, who knows the text of Plato better, perhaps, than he knows Plato's mind, but who is a very inspiring and jolly guide to one's own reading. I have heard him lecture twice a week, and he has been good enough to give me an hour besides to myself, and I have read with him several of the hardest and most crucial of the dialogues. Besides this I have seen some, not many, people, and written some, not good, verses.

My pedestrian companion has been usually Morgan, who is at Trinity–Frederic Morgan, you know,–sometimes Wedd (whom you may remember) and the highly sympathetic and melancholy Dickinson of King's. The undergraduates here have little other charm than the great one of youth and innocence. There is a quietness and solidity about them that will make their Harvard cousins seem rather loud and rather cheap when I get back to them, but the great civic and manly virtue that prevails here gives people a sort of neutrality and dulness which will make me leave them without much regret. The place has not succeedinged in making me love it–not that it has tried–as Oxford did long ago, with a passion that increases with every view of her sacred and profane charms. I was there for a week in March and for four weeks in June, often amused by the people I met and always very happy when alone. In spite of the deep differences between you and me, here is something we have in common–the greater facility of being happy alone. Is it because we don't care enough for our fellows or because ~~they~~ we care for them too much? I know what most people would say, at least in respect to me, but I will give a much truer answer to the question, namely, that we are happier alone because our love of people is too great for their deserts and too little for our satisfaction. Nature deceives with more art, and never fetters the imagination so much as to bring about a disillusion afterwards. And then all her changes are due to our own inconstancy alone–which is the best sort of change–whereas people grow old and wicked as a matter of objective fact. These reflections, however, are parenthetical, and what I really meant to say was that at Oxford I saw George Griswold and F. Huidescoper;[1] and many of their friends, and in another direction the Delphic Dyer and his robust family, now increased by the addition of one daughter, consequent upon a fat inheritance from a father-in-law. So immediately do well regulated households illustrate the laws of Malthus.[2]

I am now at work on an exposition and defence of Plato's bad treatment of poets, whom, as you may know, he banished from his republic as trivial and demoralizing persons. There were solid reasons for that judgment even then–what would he have said of an age that believes in the moral dignity of a Wagner and a Browning?[3] At the same time–and the vulgar logician might see an inconsistency here–I am giving the finishing touches to my own Lucifer–now a prodigious tragedy in five fat acts, with melodramatic situations and lyrical episodes all designed to effect the purgation of souls by pity of the author and dread of having to peruse his complete works. That, as Aristotle says, is the true function of tragedy.

I wish you all joy in your summer solitudes. When you return to Cambridge you may find me wandering homelessly about the streets and the Colonial Club, where I dare say you also now dine. In that case we shall have many a chance of exchanging our impressions of the past two years. I am not to have a room in Cambridge, but to live in Longwood with my mother. There are several reasons for this: that three days in the week will thus be quite clear of interruptions and temptations; that it will be an economy; that it will mark more clearly the merely temporary status which I have, while they don't make up their minds about promoting me; and that it will make it easier for me than it was last year to give up Harvard altogether, if such is the final issue of things. I have had two Harvard lives already; this, if it lasts or not, must be a wholly different one. If they make me an assistant professor and I decide to stay indefinitely it will be time to look for a domicile, for I believe on the whole it would be better to live in Cambridge and do one's sharinge in maintaining or establishing the academic traditions of the place. I sail on September 2nd in the "Gallia" for Boston, and hope soon after my arrival to have the pleasure of seeing you. But I should prefer that it might be here, where there is space and quiet, and the most exquisite verdure. If you could only turn up for a paddle in the river or a cup of tea in this room, which being Wedd's, overlooks the Backs,[4] I should quite feel what I half feel already, that I am in a kind of dream.

If you write to Fred Winslow will you ask him to send me a line with his address? He sent me a little book with the promise of a letter many months ago. I answered to what I believed was his address in Newberry Street, to which I had sent other things before, but perhaps I got the number wrong.

Yours ever

GSantayana

[1]George Griswold was a member of Harvard's class of 1893, and Frederic Louis Huidekoper was a member of the class of 1896.

[2]Thomas Robert Malthus (1766–1834) was an English political economist. As curate of the Church of England, Malthus published *An Essay on the Principle of Population* (1798) in which the "Malthusian doctrine" was forwarded. It says that population increases in a geometric ratio while the means of subsistence increases in an arithmetic ratio, and that crime, disease, war, and vice are necessary checks on population.

[3]Robert Browning (1812–89) was an English poet noted for psychological insight into character and motivations, his abrupt but forceful colloquial English, and his perfection of the dramatic monologue in which the speaker reveals something of himself and sometimes reveals more than he realizes.

[4]The vast lawns behind the colleges leading down to the river Cam.

To Hugo Münsterberg

16 September 1897 • Brookline, Massachusetts   (MS: Boston)

75 Monmouth Street
Brookline

Sept. 16, '97

Dear Professor Münsterberg

Your charming little volume had by some oversight not been sent on to me, and I found it here only the other day on my arrival. I didn't know you also yielded sometimes to poetical temptation, and I have read your poems through with great delight. It seems to me—although I fear my judgment of German verse isn't worth much—that they breathe the spirit of the lovable and inspired Germany of pre-prussian days, and trAre truly ideal. What you have to say about America also hits me, especially that description of Yankee freedom—freedom to walk on the track! But you are too favourable to the ladies; they are so shrill. Thank you very much for sending me the book.

I am not living in Cambridge this year, but here at my mother's. Nevertheless I hope to have frequent opportunities of seeing you and Mrs Münsterberg. It is a great satisfaction to every one in these parts that you have decided to remain for good

Yours very truly
GSantayana

To Susan Sturgis de Sastre

18 October 1897 • Longwood, Massachusetts   (MS: Virginia)

Longwood
October •18 •1897

Dear Susie.

It occurs to me that you will be interested in hearing something about Edgar Scott, Maisie's fiancé.[1] He is a Philadelphian, very rich, and twenty seven or twenty eight years old. Although his health is in some respects not good he is a big and robust man, or at least was when I saw him some years ago. He was in the class of '93 at Harvard, but did not graduate, as the climate of Cambridge was not good for his weak lungs—this was the explanation I heard at the time from Warwick Potter, who was a good and ever-faithful friend of his. The gossips have given out others, but they may be regarded as false. He then went to Florida, and a year or two later bought a big steam yacht, the "Sagamore" in which he went around the world. It was on board this boat that Warwick died of cholera in October 1893. Edgar Scott and Bob Potter came back to America with the body, and Maisie, I remember, came alone from Philadelphia to New York to the funeral. As Warwick was no special friend of hers, it was clear that her interest in Edgar Scott and his experiences was what brought her there at that time. I don't know what he has been doing since, but the present administration has appointed him second secretary of the American embassy in Paris, where he now is. He is coming back in December if he can get leave of absence so soon, if not in February, when the wedding will take place, and they will go back to Paris immediately. The advantages of this match from a wordly point of view are great, and there seems to be an old affection also in the matter. The draw-backs are that Edgar Scott has not, it is thought, a good constitution, but has suffered some say from the lungs some from Bright's disease—just Uncle Robert's and Aunt Susie's maladies[2]—and that ~~their~~ there is drunkenness in his family, and a certain amount of wild oats in his own past. But the family seem to be pleased, and from what ∧old∧ Mrs Potter and Austin ∧her son∧ tell me of Edgar Scott, I have no doubt that he is as worthy of a good girl's affection, and as capable of making her happy, as nine tenths of our gilded youth.

I find things here quite as usual and everybody well. Living at home has great advantages, insuring quiet and freedom from interruptions for my reading and writing. At the same time, when I go to Cambridge, which is nearly every day, I have a chance to see a lot of different people and to propound philosophy ex-cathedra.[3] As to serious discussion of anything really interesting, that is impossible in this country, as there is here no cultivated public, only a few individuals with pronounced personalities, like Professors Norton and James, who don't lend themselves to easy conversation. I have to wait for my next visit to Europe, which I hope may be next summer, when I may come also to see you. People have been asking me about as usual, and I have been in Cotuit with the Codman's, at Beverley with Boylston & Elsie Beal, at Nahant with Robert and Ellen,[4] whose children are nice, and go next Sunday to Manchester to the John Sturgises,[5] where two of their English cousins, Margorie Sturgis (Harry's[6] eldest daughter) and Mildred Seymour[7] are staying. Grafton[8] and Howard Cushing will also be there, so we shall have a very distinguished house-party

Cam Forbes, whom you may remember at Avila, has just lost his father—a loss more than usually painful in his case as ~~their~~ there was the greatest sympathy and intimacy between father and son. He is coaching the football team this year and I see him often in Cambridge.—Julia Robins is here, but very poor and very unhappy, thinking of escaping again to Europe and, I suspect, of marrying some foreigner and joining the Catholic Church at last. How things come round in this world!—Give my love to Celedonio and the family

Your ever aff^{te} brother

George

[1]In 1898 Edgar Thomson Scott (c. 1870–1918), who attended Harvard in the early 1890s, married Mary "Maisie" Howard Sturgis (1872–1944), the daughter of Robert Shaw (1824–76) and Susan Brimmer Inches (d. 1900) Sturgis.

[2]Robert Shaw and Susan Inches Sturgis. Bright's affects the kidneys.

[3]From the chair, especially of a teacher; with the authority that comes from one's rank or office.

[4]Robert Shaw Sturgis (c. 1854–1921) was the fourth of Santayana's mother's five children by her first husband, George Sturgis. Robert managed Santayana's financial affairs. He and Ellen Gardner Hodges (d. 1918) married in 1890. They were the parents of George and Josephine Sturgis.

[5]Probably the wife, Frances Anne Codman Sturgis (d. 1910), and children of John Hubbard Sturgis (1834–88).

[6]Margery was the daughter of Mary Cecilia Brand (d. 1886) and Henry Parkman Sturgis (1847–94). She had three sisters and two brothers.

[7]Unidentified.

[8]Grafton Dulany Cushing was a member of Harvard's class of 1885.

To Charles William Eliot

1 December 1897 • Brookline, Massachusetts   (MS: Harvard)

~~COLONIAL CLUB~~
~~CAMBRIDGE~~

75 Monmouth St
Brookline
<u>Dec. 1. 1897</u>

Dear Mr Eliot

I see by the notice and the cheque I received this morning from the Treasurer that my salary for this year has been reduced to $1500 from $1750, which it was in 1895–1896. I venture to call your attention to the fact, as possibly the change was not intended.

You may remember that two years ago I spoke to the members of my department of my unwillingness to continue at Harvard unless there was some prospect of my promotion. I afterwards suggested taking a year away and returning for this other year with my former standing, in order that the Corporation's plans for the Philosophical Department, which I understood were not yet fully decided upon, might be arranged in the interval. I should naturally be glad to hear as soon as possible what the decision in regard to myself is likely to be, so that if I am not to remain here I may make other arrangements.

Yours very truly
GSantayana

To Charles William Eliot
4 December 1897 • Brookline, Massachusetts   (MS: Harvard)

---

75 Monmouth Street
Brookline
December 4, 1897.

Dear Mr Eliot

I am much obliged for your letter and the explanation it contains. I had no idea that the increase in my salary in 1895–6 was due to the fact that I offered a course in Ethics, numbered Phil. 15, which in a sense was a substitute for Professor Palmer's Phil 4, omitted that year. That course did not add to my hours of work, as it took the place of the one in Aesthetics which I had previously given; but it is true that the greater dignity of the subject, and the fact that it attracted a somewhat larger number of students, may be said to have increased my responsibilities. However, as I received no intimation that my salary was raised on that account, I supposed that the increase had followed in the normal course of events, and naturally expected to receive the same sum this year.

Phil. 20 f. was taken in October last by two graduates, Mr Montague and Mr Sheldon, but it was discontinued after a few weeks.[1] They are both anxious to prepare for the examination for the doctor's degree, and it seemed to them and to me that under the circumstances they could devote their time more to the purpose by taking other subjects than Scholastic philosophy.

Thanking you again for your letter, I am

Very truly yours

GSantayana

[1]William Pepperell Montague (1873–1953) was a Harvard educated philosophy professor whose system was developed in relation to scientific discoveries. His works include *The Ways of Knowing; or, The Methods of Philosophy* (1925), *Belief Unbound* (1930), and *The Ways of Things* (1940). Wilmon Henry Sheldon received his A.B. (1896) and Ph.D. (1899) at Harvard and taught philosophy at both Dartmouth and Yale.

To [Sara or Grace] Norton
10 January [1898 or 1907–1908] • Brookline, MA   (MS: Houghton)

75 Monmouth Street

Brookline

Dear Miss Norton[1]

Your kind note arrived when I was absent in New York else I should have answered it more promptly. I am very sorry that my answer, besides being belated, cannot be an acceptance, but I have an engagement for this evening which it is impossible for me to break.

With many thanks for your kind invitation

Yours sincerely

GSantayana

Jan. 10.

[1]Probably the daughter (Sara) but possibly the sister (Grace) of Charles Eliot Norton.

To Charles William Eliot
1 February 1898 • Brookline, Massachusetts   (MS: Harvard)

75 Monmouth Street

Brookline

Feb 1 1898

Dear Mr Eliot

Thank you very much for your letter informing me of my appointment as assistant professor. It is very gratifying to me that the University should have confidence enough in me to take this step, and I shall endeavour to do my best to justify its expectations.

Yours very truly

GSantayana

To William Roscoe Thayer
2 March 1898 • Cambridge, Massachusetts   (MS: Houghton)

52 Brattle Street
March 2 1898

Dear Mr Thayer[1]

Would my review of Berenson be signed?[2] If so, I am a little afraid of undertaking it, as he is an old friend of mine and not very tolerant of any diversity of opinion, however qualified with appreciation of what is brilliant and useful in his way of putting things. But if the contribution can be anonymous and I may have the Summer to write it in, I should be glad to have it entrusted to me, as I have the greatest interest in Berenson's books, and read them with considerable pleasure.

Yours very truly
GSantayana

[1]William Roscoe Thayer (1859–1923), Harvard A.B. 1881 and A.M. 1886, wrote *The Life and Letters of John Hay* (1915) and *Theodore Roosevelt: An Intimate Biography* (1919). He was editor of the *Havard Graduates' Magazine* (1892–1915) and was awarded the Litt.D. from Harvard in 1913.

[2]An unsigned review of Bernard Berenson's *Italian Painters of the Renaissance* (1897) appeared in the *Harvard Graduates' Magazine* 7 (September 1898): 29–35.

To Charles Scribner's Sons
17 March 1898 • Brookline, Massachusetts   (MS: Princeton)

75 Monmouth Street
Brookline Mass
March 17, 1898.

Charles Scribner's Sons
   New York

Dear Sirs

I beg to thank you for your favour of the 9th including a statement of the sale of the "Sense of Beauty," and a cheque for $36.90. I enclose in return a list of the errata[1] I have noticed, which are more, I am sorry to say, than those pointed out by our friend at Bowdoin.[2]

Yours very truly
GSantayana

[1]Unlocated.

[2]Unidentified.

To William Roscoe Thayer
7 July 1898 • [Windsor, England]   (MS: Houghton)

Address: Care of Brown Shipley & Co
London

July 7, '98

Dear Mr Thayer

Your note has just reached me here. I am sorry the article is not yet in your hands. It is begun, and I will send it on within a week.

If it is in time for your next number and you decide to print it I suppose I must trouble you to look at the proofs. If it has missed this issue, perhaps you will forward them to me, or let me see them later in Cambridge
                    Yours truly   GSantayana

To William Roscoe Thayer
14 July [1898] • Windsor, England   (MS: Kentucky)

Address
[C]/o Brown Shipley & Co
London
~~QUEEN'S ACRE,~~
~~WINDSOR.~~

July 14.

Dear Mr Thayer

Here is my review grown to such a length that perhaps it had better appear as a signed article. I think Berenson will find the pill sufficiently sugared, and anyhow I think it will do him good, if indeed he comes by it at all which is doubtful.

I hope I have not inconvenienced you by the delay.
                    Yours truly
                    GSantayana

To Charles Scribner's Sons

8 November 1898 • Cambridge, Massachusetts   (MS: Princeton)

52 Brattle Street
Cambridge Mass

Nov. 8, 1898
Messrs Charles Scribner's Sons
    New York

Dear Sirs:

I have a number of articles and essays, some in print and some in manuscript, which might, I should think, be put together in a volume.
Although the subjects are various there is a certain unity of method and
tendency in them all. They might be called "Studies in Poetry and
Religion."[1] The papers are on the Homeric hymns,[2] the absence of religion
in Shakespeare, Platonism in some Italian poets,[3] Emerson, the poetry of
barbarism (a study mainly of Browning and Whitman), the nature of
poetry, and some other similar topics.

I write to ask you if there is any probability of your wishing to undertake the publication and, if so, at what time it would be best to have the
MS in your hands. There is some work of revision to be done, which I
could hasten, if it were necessary, so as to bring out the volume at a
favourable season.

I am glad to see that the "Sense of Beauty" has continued to have a
small sale, and I hope it has paid expenses. The reviews I have seen have
been flattering, although all somewhat unsatisfactory to me on account of
their silence on what I regard as the essence of the book—namely, its philosophical position.

Yours very truly
GSantayana

---

[1]Published by Scribner's as *Interpretations*.
[2]Poems in the epic style modelled after the works of Homer, these hymns were presented by the poets before their recitation of Homer at public festivals. Thirty-three
poems are extant (among them hymns to Demeter, Pan, and Apollo). See
Interpretations, 21–22.
[3]See chapter V of *Interpretations*.

To Charles Scribner's Sons

9 February 1899 • Cambridge, Massachusetts   (MS: Princeton)

52 Brattle Street
Cambridge Mass

<u>Feb. 9, 1899</u>

Dear Sirs.

You are very good not to forget my promised "Studies in poetry and religion." The MS would be already in your hands but that, in looking over the pieces to arrange them for publication, I have become convinced that several of them have to be rewritten, as there are repetitions and incongruities in them as they now stand. I don't like to print what I have still a reasonable hope of improving materially, so I will ask you to give me a little more time—until the autumn, perhaps,—so that I may turn these papers into a more consecutive and consistent whole. The subject is really one throughout, and I want the effect also to be simple and clear.

My college work keeps me so busy now that I may not be able to do much before June, although a week or two of steady application would, I think, be enough for the revision and rearrangement which ~~is~~ are necessary.

Yours very truly
GSantayana

To Charles Carroll Everett

11 February 1899 • Cambridge, Massachusetts   (MS: Redwood)

52 Brattle Street
Cambridge

<u>Feb 11 '99.</u>

Dear Dr Everett

I shall be very glad to write an article about Professor Campbell's book for the <u>New</u> <u>World</u>.[1] You don't say when you would like to have it, so I hope the date is not too near, as I haven't read the book and should like to have time to digest it properly. Thank you very much for wishing to trust it to me.

Yours sincerely
GSantayana

[1]"Greek Religion," *The New World* 8 (Boston, September 1899): 401–17 is a review of *Religion in Greek Literature: A Sketch in Outline* (London and New York: Longmans, Green, and Co., 1898). This book was written by Lewis Campbell (1830–1908).

To Macmillan and Co.
25 February 1899 • Cambridge, Massachusetts   (MS: New York)

---

52 Brattle Street
Cambridge Mass

Feb. 25, '99

The Macmillan Company
New York

Dear Sirs,
It is true that I am at work on a book on a subject which is largely ethical, but the task is a great one and will not be finished, I am afraid, for some years. Scribner's Sons, as you may know, have published my "Sense of Beauty" and should in courtesy have the first option in the case of my other books, but if when the one you refer to is finished they should not care to undertake it, I should be glad to submit it to you.

Yours very truly
GSantayana

To Hugo Münsterberg
[Spring 1899] • Cambridge, Massachusetts   (MS: Boston)

Dear Münsterberg
A word to say good bye—I am sorry it is not in person—and to thank you for the very generous and friendly appreciation of my poetic venture. Lucifer has been so long in my thoughts that it is a relief to see him petrified in print, and to be free to turn to other projects. If there is anything in the book to give you pleasure the fact is a great satisfaction to me. There is nothing that does one more good than to be able to believe that the more inward and finer part of one's thinkings have not gone wholly astray.

Wishing you a happy and fruitful Summer
Yours sincerely
GSantayana

To Boylston Adams Beal
7 August 1899 • Oxford, England   (MS: Houghton)

Oxford
August 7 –99

Dear Boylston

It is just a month ago that you wrote me your good letter and I am ashamed not to have sent you my congratulations and thanks before this. But the fact was you didn't give me the first pleasure of hearing the news,[1] as I had heard it at Howard Sturgis's a few days before, so that I was not carried away by that impulse which would otherwise have made me answer at once. But you may be sure I was most glad to hear that all was well and that a young lady had appeared about whom it is natural to have such pleasant anticipations.

I have been leading my usual summer life here—in fact, I am afraid this Oxford pilgrimage is becoming a dangerously fixed habit—and have been adding ∧to∧ and amending my essays on poetry and religion which, as you may know, I hope to bring out in the autumn. The task has proved much more troublesome than I had expected, but it is almost done now. I leave tomorrow for London and Paris; after a week with the Potters at Sainte Marguerite I go on to Avila for a fortnight, and then return to sail from Cherbourg on September 13ᵗʰ. I have got some rather decorative Arundel prints[2] here which you must come to see when I have them put up. I have also been buying books—not my habit, as you know—to help me in my proposed translation of Aristotle's Metaphysics[3]–a French version, a German version and lots of commentaries.

My old acquaintance Fletcher of Christchurch (not the rowing man but the livery stable keeper)[4] is still here, and I have been playing whist in his rooms a good deal in the evening. He had a theatrical brother of his ∧with him∧ and a Scotchman named McGreggor,[5] whose only conversation was to say "Thank you". We made up an odd party, especially as none of us knew anything of the game. However, it was congenial in an animal sort of way, with candles and whisky and water.–Americans I have not seen much of, only Mrs Toy and two young women who were here with her, and two Harvard undergraduates who have come for me to show them Oxford—Montgomery Sears, Jr, and Bayard Cutting.[6] The latter is now Mr Choate's private secretary, as Joe Choate has been promoted to third secretary of legation and Spencer Eddy[7] has been transferred to Paris and—I presume—perfect happiness. In London I also saw Frederic Morgan who has been three years at the English Cambridge and was then on the point of leaving for his ancestral acres at Aurora, New York. He carried with ~~wh~~ him a whole tailor's and habberdasher's establishment and a junk shop of old furniture and things. They tell a story about him here which deserves a wider circulation. History was the subject of his "special research". Having failed to pass the examinations at the end of his second year and having been thrown over by the best coaches as a man who wouldn't work seriously, he saw the examinations of the third year coming on, and went to bury himself in the country to cram for them. But, alas! a few days before they were on, he reappeared among his astonished friends with his right arm in a sling. He had fallen from his bicycle and wouldn't be able to write his papers at all or to get a degree! What a calamity! But they say he was caught merrily putting on his collar with both hands, and there is no doubt he recovered very soon after the examinations were over. His English friends are also much amused at what they call his American accent—he has that—but the worst of it, they say, is his way of pronouncing A. You know how they say <u>assk</u> and <u>cann't</u> in his regions: he was bound to change all that, and so sent everybody into fits of laughter by talking about the <u>grahndeur</u> and <u>mahgnificence</u> of the <u>lahndscape</u>!

I shall not fail to give my sister your kind messages. She will be much interested in hearing of the new arrival.   Yours ever

GSantayana

[1]Of the birth of the Beals' daughter, Betty.

[2]Thomas Howard, 2d earl of Arundel (c. 1586–1646), was educated at Trinity College. The first great English patron of arts, he formed a collection of ancient sculptures which were given to Oxford University in 1667. The Arundel Society (founded in 1849 and discontinued in 1897) reproduced the works of famous artists. On 8 Jun 1947 Santayana wrote to Rosamond Sturgis: "The views you send me ... take me back to the day when I was daft on architecture and the arts generally–the 1890's–and when Pinturicchio in particular graced the space over my fireplace with a large Arundel print full of lovely horses, costumes, and early renaissance decorative architecture. It was a sort of breathing-tube to the old world from the depths of the flood."

[3]A project never realized.

[4]Harold John Fletcher (b. c. 1876) (see *Persons*, 493–97). The "rowing man" could have been Charles Ruel Fletcher, Harvard class of 1886, or Jefferson Butler Fletcher, Harvard class of 1887.

[5]Unidentified.

[6]J. Montgomery Sears Jr. was a member of the Harvard class of 1900. William Bayard Cutting Jr. (1878–1910) received his B.A. from Harvard in 1900. He served as secretary to the vice-consul in the American Consulate in Milan (1908-1909) and secretary of the American Legation, Tangier, Morocco (1909).

[7]Joseph Hodges Choate (1832–1917), Harvard class of 1852, had a legal career of over fifty years. In 1899 President McKinley appointed him ambassador to Great Britain, where he served for six years with distinction. In 1907 he headed the American delegation to the Second Hague Conference. Joseph Hodges Choate Jr. was a member of the Harvard class of 1897. Spencer Fayette Eddy also attended Harvard (class of 1896).

To William Cameron Forbes

[Autumn 1899–June 1904] • Cambridge, Massachusetts   (MS: Houghton)

---

60 Brattle Street

Cambridge

Dear Cam

I didn't answer your mysterious note of a week ago because I was expecting some further information about what you want me to do. As I have heard nothing more I write to say that I have no engagements for the end of next week and should be very glad to do in your agreeable company anything not contrary to law and morals, and not in the nature of giving lectures, writing poems, correcting blue-books, or reading theses for the degree of doctor of philosophy—all things of which I am weary almost unto death.

So, if what you have in mind is sufficiently frivolous and not too athletic, you may count on me.

Yours ever

G Santayana

To Charles Augustus Strong
[Autumn 1899–June 1904] • Cambridge, MA   (MS: Georgetown)

60 Brattle St
Cambridge

Dear Strong

Do you remember that you asked me to come to Lakewood[1] again in the Spring? If you are still of the same mind you may count on me for a short visit during the holidays which for me last from the 13th to the 19th of April. For the last part of the week I have engagements in New York and Philadelphia, but nothing would give me more pleasure than to spend Monday or Tuesday or both with you and, I hope, Mrs Strong.

Let me know if this is convenient, but be perfectly frank if there is any obstacle whatever, as I might perhaps see you in town or else in June, when I expect to be in New York again.

I have been reading more Fichte[2] and Hegel, but my inner self rebels increasingly against their empty pertinacity and shocking habit of covering a paradox with a truism, and making you believe the absurd under the guise of the self-evident. So I shall be kindly disposed to the things-in-themselves.

I have had a polite invitation to your academic festival, but on the 19th must be in Philadelphia, so cannot join you.

With best regards to Mrs Strong   Yours always
GSantayana

[1]Rockefeller estate in New Jersey.
[2]Johann Gottlieb Fichte (1762–1814), a German philosopher and political thinker, was an important influence in the development of German Romanticism. His philosophy was focused on the ethical. He developed the Kantian distinction of noumena and phenomena in his *Grundlage der gesammten Wissenschaftslehre* (Foundation of the complete theory of knowledge, 1794). He held that the essence of the universe is mind and that it posits the material world through a process called productive imagination.

To Charles Scribner's Sons

26 October 1899 • Cambridge, Massachusetts   (MS: Princeton)

60 Brattle Street
Cambridge, Mass.

Oct. 26. 1899

Messrs Charles Scribner's Sons
  New York

Gentlemen.

I am sending you today by express the MS of ten essays under the title "Interpretations of poetry and religion." You may remember that last winter I spoke to you of them and you kindly asked to see them when they were ready. The labour of fitting and patching them together has been longer than I expected, but here they are at last.

If you decide to publish the book, I wish you would tell me whether you think it well to add an appendix with the text of the rather numerous and important passages, for the most part verse, which I have translated and quoted in the essays. I should prefer to have such an appendix, as poetical translations can never be close or adequate, nor can what merits they may have be appreciated unless the original is at hand for comparison. But perhaps the expense and annoyance of printing so much in foreign languages—there is Greek, Italian, and a little French and Spanish—would be greater than the advantage gained.

"The dissolution of Paganism" (under the form of a review of Campbell's Religion in Greek literature) and the "Absence of religion in Shakespeare" have appeared in the "New World". The others have not been published, although the "Platonic love in some Italian poets" (although blushing under another name) was privately printed by a ladies' club in Buffalo, to which it was originally read![1] I am not sure whether the "New World" has any copyright, but I think not.

Yours very truly
GSantayana

---

[1]"Platonism in the Italian Poets" (Buffalo: Paul's Press, 1896) was written for the Contemporary Club and read on 5 Feb 1896. It was revised and reprinted in *Interpretations* (73–89).

To Mary Augusta Jordan

30 October 1899 • Cambridge, Massachusetts   (MS: Smith)

60 Brattle Street
Cambridge

~~No~~October. 30. 1899

Dear Miss Jordan

Words of encouragement are always pleasant and stimulating to those who make expeditions into comparatively solitary regions. Thank you very much for yours.

If John Burroughs[1] expresses the reaction of his so innocent mind on the subject of <u>Lucifer</u>, perhaps you will let me hear of it.

Yours gratefully
GSantayana

[1]Possibly John Burroughs (1837–1921), a prolific author who established the American nature essay as a literary type.

To Charles Scribner's Sons

15 November 1899 • Cambridge, Massachusetts   (MS: Princeton)

60 Brattle Street
Cambridge Mass
Nov. 15. 1899.

Messrs Charles Scribner's Sons
New York

Gentlemen:

I thank you very much for the generous terms, in every sense of the words, in which you undertake to publish the "Interpretations of Poetry and Religion". It seems to me also that this book will arouse more interest—doubtless more adverse criticism too—than did the other; but that, if it comes, will not ~~to~~ do you or me any harm.

I shall await with interest the proofs as you get them ready, and I will try to read them more carefully than I did ~~the~~ those ₌of the₌ "Sense of Beauty", into which a few errors crept in one way or another. I hope the disordered state of the <u>MS</u>–the result of various revisions–will not make trouble with the printers.

Believe me, with renewed thanks for your friendly appreciations,

Yours very sincerely

GSantayana

To Charles Scribner's Sons

11 December 1899 • Cambridge, Massachusetts   (MS: Princeton)

---

60 Brattle Street
Cambridge

Dec. 11. 1899.

Messrs Charles Scribner's Sons
New York

Dear Sirs:

I have at this moment no photograph of myself to send you. None has been taken for years and I confess I have some aversion to such things in general and particularly to their use as advertisements. But I am well aware of the reasons there are for conforming to custom in such matters, and I will try to get some reproduction made of a drawing a very clever young painter, Mr Andreas Andersen, made of me a few years ago, and send it to you. It is rather odd and now a trifle youthful, but I fancy those traits will not stand in the way of what is wanted.

I enclose the contract, and the corrected proof will follow.

Yours very truly

GSantayana

To [Sara or Grace] Norton

22 December 1899 • Cambridge, Massachusetts   (MS: Houghton)

60 Brattle Street
Dec. 22. '99

Dear Miss Norton

I am very sorry that I have another engagement for Sunday evening. It would have been a privilege—I don't say to help you entertain your strangers—but to be entertained so Christianly in their company.

Yours sincerely
GSantayana

To Josiah Royce

30 December 1899 • New York, New York   (MS: Harvard)

New York
December 30 '99

Dear Royce

Your letter reached me as I was about to start on a little trip for the holidays (including a glimpse of the Psychological Association meeting at New Haven) and I have not had an opportunity to answer before as I wished to answer, because I have to thank you at the same time for the pleasure I have had in reading your new book.[1] It seems to me to make your doctrine more approachable for those of us to whom it is not a native conviction, and the supplementary essay gives it more definition, I should say, than any of your previous works had done. Perhaps my own mind has been better prepared by dealing so much of late with Plato, and has been moving more than it once did in lines parallel to those of your philosophy. There are some questions I should like some day to ask you: I don't see, for instance, how the third and fourth conceptions escape a kind of realism in that they still seem to make one part of the system of things <u>representative</u> of other parts and of the whole, not included in the given part, and seen to be related to it only by a third person—the philosopher himself. For the <u>existence</u> of the completion of my life is no datum of my life itself, although the <u>demand</u> for that completion may be such a datum.

Of course I shall be glad to keep Phil. 4 A going until you return. How would it do for me talk to them about the ethics of political and religious parties in the nineteenth century, as an introduction to Contemporary controversies? I mean, merely to classify such tendencies as the clerical, (Catholic and Puritan,) Rousseau and the French revolution,[2] Romanticism, and Utilitarianism,–<u>Multum in parvo</u>[3]–but what else is to be expected of a philosopher?

I hope you will find James stronger. Remember me to him, and believe me, with best wishes for the New Year,

Yours sincerely

GSantayana

[1]*The World and the Individual,* 2 vols. (New York: Macmillan, 1900–1901).
[2]Jean Jacques Rousseau (1712–78) was a Swiss-born French philosopher, author, political theorist, and composer. His closeness to nature, sensitivity, individualism, rebellion against established social and political order, imagination, and glorification of emotions make him the father of French Romanticism. The leaders of the French Revolution of 1789 were influenced by his political ideas.
[3]Much in a little.

To William Morrow

[1900] • Cambridge, Massachusetts   (MS: Fales)

<u>60 Brattle Street</u>

Dear Mr Morrow[1]

I find it will be impossible for me to be at the dinner[2] tomorrow. I am very sorry, as I was looking forward to the occasion with much pleasure

Yours truly

GSantayana

[1]William Morrow was a member of the Harvard class of 1900.
[2]The annual dinner of *The Harvard Monthly.*

To Moncure Robinson

January 1900 • [Cambridge, Massachusetts]   (MS: Unknown)

Letter to M. R.[1]

Dear kindly host,
      The task in haste
  imposed—
To write in verse and in blank verse
  at that
Miltonic, massive, monumental,
  mouthed,
Explains this bread-and-butter
  letter's lateness. For
Accustomed as I am to tinkling
  rhymes
And toying with a facile muse,
  I lacked
Due inspiration and apprentice-
  ship
For noblest melodies; by which alone
The height and breadth of your
  great friendliness
Might equalled be, or the truth
  paralleled
Of my unfeignèd thanks. For
  which high theme
The inspiration of some stateliest
  muse,—
Some Louisa Cushing[2] of
  Parnassus Street—
Had first to be invoked;
  but she, alack,
In love with her affianced
  jack-an-apes
Grudgingly listened to my suit
  and granted
But few and halting phrases
  to my pen.
I left you, and the moving
  corridor
That threads its iron path on
  thundering wheels,
A noisy, dusty, hissing centi-

pede,
Received me and my chattels,
   in one hand
I held the long and much-
   stamped evidence
Of having paid, ere venturing
   to mount,
My fare to Charon[3] to trans-
   port me thence;
In the other hand the <u>New</u>
   <u>York Herald</u>'s yet
Close-folded, undeciphered
   oracles.
When one named Stewart
   of the Clan-o'-Forbes[4]
Greeted me; but with dim
   lack-lustre eye
And mouth far more in-
   clined to ope to yawn
Than to be reason's discreet
   instrument.
He had sat late that night
   And deeply drunk
More than was good. Yet
   had we chops together
Abstemious, tough, and cheap.
   There, too, appeared
One Warren Sturgis[5] and his
   frowsy bride,
Grotonians,[6] whom with
   damnèd heresies
And signs papistical and
   Tory sneers
I rudely shocked, and left to
   plume themselves,
Sweet cooing doves and Evan-
   gelical.
But chiefly Stimson of the
   grey-green eye

And grisly Van Dyk[7] beard beguiled
   an hour
With harmless gossip and the
   bookman's shop.
Thus we reached Boston,
   carpeted with snow
And whistling-cold. And from
   that moment on
The daily indistinguishable
   round
Of daily motions so hath
   swayed my soul
That I remember nought.
   That I have talked
I fear; that I have ate, I
   well believe,
And trust that I have slept;
   but in what sort
You can as probably divine
   as I.

Above the revolution of this
   scene
And flight of moments, floats
   the pleasant sense
Of days in Gotham,[8] lately
   spent with you;
Of your one sister, charming
   when first known
And when more known
   more charming; of the other[9]
Too little seen, alas, in those
   quick days;
Of the keen frost, the long
   straight avenue,
Between its beetling cliffs,
   glazed honeycombs
Of perpendicular stone; the
   genial fire,

The midnight drink, the shivering
   morning bath,
The Wilsons'[10] box, my hat, on
   Wilson's head
Removed, forgotten, missed
   and found again;
And Calve[11] in her spangled
   robe of black
With pink and yellow roses—
   all these things
And many slighter thoughts,
   unnamable
In this proud metre's high-laced
   eloquence,
Yet sizzle in my pot, the
   while I sit
Beside my hearth, and poke
   its vestal fires.
With this adieu, till
   Spring consent to blow
Or some auspicious moment
   bring you here,
Then shall we meet again
   and plan anew
How houses should be
   garnished. For the nonce
Farewell, and may all
   blessings follow you.

G.S.

January, 1900

[1]Moncure Robinson (d. 1920) was a member of the Harvard class of 1898 and a wealthy New Yorker.

[2]Unidentified.

[3]In Greek mythology Charon is the ferryman of Hades who transports the newly arrived dead across the Styx.

[4]Probably Charles Stewart Forbes, a member of Harvard's class of 1900.

[5]Possibly Sullivan Warren Sturgis, a member of Harvard's class of 1893.

[6]Referring to Groton School in Groton, Massachusetts.

[7]Sir Anthony Van Dyck (1599–1641) was a Flemish painter who is best known as a portrait painter.

[8]New York City.

[9]Robinson's sister, Augusta, married Philip Chetwynd. His other sister is unidentified.

[10]Unidentified.

[11]Emma Calvé (1866–1942) was a French operatic soprano who sang at the Metropolitan Opera in New York (1893–1904). Carmen was one of her famous roles.

To Charles Scribner's Sons

20 February 1900 • Cambridge, Massachusetts   (MS: Princeton)

60 Brattle Street
Cambridge Mass
Feb. 20. 1900

Messrs Charles Scribner's Sons

Dear Sirs:

Thank you very much for the six copies of <u>Poetry and Religion</u> which came a day or two ago. The appearance of the book seems most satisfactory. Let us hope the sale will be no less so.

The persons to whom I asked you to send copies in my name seem not yet to have received them. As I sent you the list some time ago, I mention the fact, in case it has been mislaid or escaped your notice. Otherwise there is, of course, no particular haste about the matter.

Very truly yours
GSantayana

To Elizabeth Ellery Sedgwick Child

5 April [1900–1905] • Cambridge, Massachusetts   (MS: Houghton)

Mr Santayana
regrets that he is not able, on account of a previous engagement, to accept
Mrs Child's
kind invitation for the evening of Wednesday April 9th

60 Brattle Street
   April 5th

[*Unsigned*]

To William James

Easter 1900 • Cambridge, Massachusetts   (MS: Houghton)

60 Brattle Street

<u>Easter 1900</u>

Dear James

Palmer has just sent me your delightful letter by which I see with joy that you are full of life again in this season of resurrection. May the revival be perennial for you and full of fruits! You must have thought me very unfeeling not to write and make personal inquiries during all these months; it has not been for lack of concern but merely from perplexity in finding the right moment and the right words, as well as from the knowledge of how little my platonic sympathies would count in the midst of the affection of your many friends. But I am as glad as any of them can be at the change for the better, and full of confidence that you underestimate the amount of energy that you will find again in yourself ere long.

I see that you have discovered me in the <u>Poetry</u> <u>&</u> <u>Religion</u> more than in my verses or the <u>Sense</u> <u>of</u> <u>Beauty</u> although I fancy there is no less of me in those other books. But there is more to come, and although I daresay you won't like the <u>Life</u> <u>of</u> <u>Reason</u> much better than you like my attitude hitherto, I think you will find that, apart from temperament, I am nearer to you than you now believe. What you say, for instance, about the value of the good lying in its <u>existence</u>, and about the continuity of the world of values with that of fact, is not different from what I should admit. Ideals would be irrelevant if they were not natural entelechies, if they were not called for by something that exists and if consequently their realization would not be a present and actual good. And the point in insisting that all the eggs at breakfast are rotten is nothing at all except the consequent possibility and endeavour to find good eggs for the morrow. The only thing I object to and absolutely abhor is the assertion that all the eggs indiscriminately are good because the hen has ~~hatche~~ laid them.

You tax me several times with impertinence and superior airs. I wonder if you realize the years of suppressed irritation which I have past in the midst of an unintelligible sanctimonious and often disingenuous Protestantism, which is thoroughly alien and repulsive to me, and the need I have ˄of˄ joining hands with something far away from it and far above it. My Catholic sympathies didn't justify me in speaking out because I felt them to be merely sympathies and not to have a rational and human backing; but the study of Plato and Aristotle has given me confidence and, backed by such an authority as they and all who have accepted them represent, I have the right to be sincere, to be absolutely objective and unapologetic, because it is not I that speak but human reason that speaks in me. Truly the Babel in which we live has nothing in it so respectable as to put on the defensive the highest traditions of the human mind. No doubt, as you say, Latinity is moribund, as Greece itself was when it transmitted to the rest of the world the seeds of its own rationalism; and for that reason there is the more need of transplanting and propagating straight thinking among the peoples who hope to be masters of the world in the immediate future. Otherwise they will be its physical masters only, and the Muses will fly over them to alight among some future race that may understand the gods better.

If I get to Europe this summer I shall hope to see you, but it is doubtful: I may stay here or go to Japan—a wholly new sphere for me where a friend who has gone before is tempting me to follow him.[1] I shouldn't like Japan very much, but I should like to have seen it.—Of things here you have better reporters than I, so I say no more. May Schott[2] be auspicious and all things physical and metaphysical go on well and rapidly.

Always sincerely yours

GSantayana

[1]Unidentified.
[2]Theodor Schott was a heart specialist at Nauheim, a spa in Germany where William James sought treatment.

To Charles Augustus Strong
16 April [1900] • Brookline, Massachusetts   (MS: Rockefeller)

---

75 Monmouth St
Brookline
<u>April 16</u>

Dear Strong

I am awfully sorry that I can't get off either for lunch or dinner today, and I am afraid I shall miss you this time altogether. It would be a great pleasure to see you, and I have a letter of James's (addressed to Palmer) with some rich things about my new book which it would amuse you to see, besides no end of James†onian†isms on other subjects. (The extra syl-

lables may not be right, but the subject deserves them!) He says my philosophy is "the perfection of rottenness", that he never read anything so
"imperturbably impudent," etc, etc.

I wish our vacations didn't coincide, for it is then that I have most
engagements for whole days and can be least depended on for casual visits. Next time give me a longer warning and I will keep a big place for a
talk on things in themselves and things in general.[1]

Yours sincerely
G Santayana

[1]See the letter from William James to George Herbert Palmer of 2 Apr 1900 in *The
Letters of William James*, vol II, (Boston: the Atlantic Monthly Press, 1920).

To Charles Augustus Strong
19 April 1900 • Brookline, Massachusetts   (MS: Rockefeller)

Brookline, April 19, 1900.

Dear Strong

I am delighted beyond measure that my little book should please you.
Thank you very much for all you say. It encourages me very much, coming from a person of your solid judgment and religious nature and education. If you find my book good, it can't be <u>rotten</u>. But I must attempt to
answer your criticism, so as to set myself right both with you and with my
own conscience. When I said that religion should give up its pretension to
be dealing with matters of fact, I meant, as you doubtless felt yourself, that
the religious machinery (gods, hell, heaven, grace, sacraments etc) was not
in the plane of fact but in the plane of symbols. But symbols are symbols
of fact; and in a sense poetry deals with matters of fact, and the better and
more poetical the poetry the more real and fundamental the facts with
which it deals. It is not artificial in the sense of being arbitrary. It is a representation of reality, according to the requirements of a part of reality, the
human imagination. And yet there is a plain sense in which it is right and
obvious to say that poetry does not deal with (I should have said, perhaps,
does not contain, does not constitute) matters of fact. Apollo is not a fact
in the same plane as the sun: yet the religion of Apollo "deals with" the
fact "sun".[1] Otherwise the religion of Apollo would be impossible; it would
have no basis and no subject-matter. So that all I mean by relegating religion to the sphere of poetry is to distinguish, as we should all do in poetry,

between the reality represented and the fiction by which that representation is made. Painting does not deal with flesh and hair, but with pigments; ϸyet by its manipulation of those pigments it represents, and, if you like, deals with, hair and flesh. Possibly the whole ambiguity might be removed by saying deals <u>in</u>, instead of deals <u>with</u>. But my book was not meant to be a creed, even for skeptics, and its definitions are not meant to have theological precision. They are "thrown at" ideas.

As to the "creed for skeptics" which you have <u>in petto</u>,[2] it is my own and I subscribe to it beforehand. Only it seems to me a philosophy, not a religion. The religious element in it is hardly, I should say, a survival; it is rather an incipient reconstitution of a poetic object, in response to the religious faculty that survives, as it always should, the destruction of its outgrown embodiments. Your "Universe", even if said not to be a person or essentially moral, is an imaginative entity, a poetic interpretation or symbol of the sundry forces known to science and life. For notice: every real object of attention every law of nature or habit of society which can constitute a rule (I should say rather a <u>condition</u>) of our conduct, is only an element in that dramatic character which you call the Universe, and whose intractable nobility and substantial lovableness you go on to describe. <u>It is pure poetry to regard the parts of the Universe as its Expressions</u>. Yet only by so regarding them, by forgetting that it is the idea "Universe" that is secondary and merely expressive of discursive experiences of your own, can you concentrate your cosmic emotions (and even your moral feeling, as you propose to do) on a single object called Deus sine Natura.[3] This synthesis no doubt corresponds to an objective system of forces, to a real dynamic continuity outside: but you have no right (except poetically and loosely, braving the unthinkable inconsistencies involved) to give that external system a moral physiognomy. Only its parts have moral characteristics, when they touch favourably or unfavourably the unfolding of human interests (or ∧of∧ such non-human interests as appeal to our sympathy.) You can't sum up the moral values of the parts of the Universe and say the result is the moral value of the Universe itself. For these moral values cancel one another and disappear into merely physical energies when you trace them back to their source. The good and evil in the world are not the world's merits and demerits, because by the time you have traced them back to the general laws from which good and evil alike flow, the laws have forfeited those ∧moral∧ characteristics. I disagree, then, with what you say about the credit for what is fair and good being due rather to the Universe than to us. It is as if you said vision belonged rather to the

Universe than to the animals in it, because of course the Universe gave the animals eyes, and not they to themselves. The Universe deserves no credit for our virtues until it acquires them—until it becomes ourselves. When the sympathy with moral ends begins to be a <u>principle</u> of action, moral values arise; there are none in the mere conditions of goodness, and the rain and the corn and sunshine are not moral objects. To regard them as such is really to make them gods; it is mythology; and to my mind your awe-inspiring, amiable, sympathetic and admonishing Universe is a mythological object. I value it as such; as such it is a religious idea, and a true one; but it is not a matter of fact. But by all means be a poet and write your creed. I will subscribe to it [*across*] with all my heart, for our new conception of reality requires just such an interpretation of it, in terms of its relation to our <u>Gemüth</u>[4]

     Yours   G. S.

[1]Apollo was a Greek god, the son of Zeus and Leto. As Phoebus Apollo, he came to be the god of light, but not properly of the sun. Called "the most Greek of Greek gods," he spoke for modern concepts of justice and human relations as opposed to the more primitive traditions.

[2]The Italian phrase (literally "in the breast") implies works that are in a developmental stage of composition.

[3]God without nature.

[4]Emotional nature.

To William Bond Wheelwright
12 May 1900 • Cambridge, Massachusetts   (MS: Unknown)

<u>60 Brattle Street</u>

Dear Mr Wheelwright[1]

    I am truly sorry that I can't accept your kind invitation for next Wednesday. I have a previous engagement which I mustn't break. It would have been a great pleasure to dine with you all and to hear some of those witty things which Lampy finds too good for the vulgar, and doesn't say in print.

    With many thanks

                 Your sincerely
                 GSantayana

May 12 1900

[1]William Bond Wheelwright (1879–1958), Harvard class of 1901, wrote for the *Lampoon* during his college years.

To Nathaniel Wedd
17 May 1900 • Cambridge, Massachusetts   (MS: King's)

Cambridge U.S.A
May 17 1900

Dear Wedd

After some hesitation I have decided to go to England as usual this summer and expect to be in London about July first. Won't you let me know
if you are at King's (as you said last year you might be) or elsewhere within
reach of London. My address is C/o Brown Shipley & Co, Founders Court
E.C.   Yours ever

GSantayana

To William Roscoe Thayer
29 May 1900 • Cambridge, Massachusetts   (MS: Houghton)

60 Brattle Street
Cambridge
May 29, 1900.

Dear Mr Thayer

I must write a word of thanks for your very kind and flattering letter,
and, having taken pen in hand for that purpose, I am tempted to add a
word suggested by your criticism. You say you find in "Poetry and
Religion" no definite statement of a creed. The reason is that I have none,
if by a creed we are to understand settled convictions upon matters of
which we can have no real knowledge. But my philosophic attitude, if I
may call it so, is definite enough, and I should think would have appeared
clearly on almost every page. My feeling is that we know and can know
nothing but our experience–our experience as it comes. All inferences
about its conditions, causes, or ultimate results is pure speculation in the
air. This ˄mass of˄ theory, a product of our intelligence or imagination,
has, however, different degrees of value. Sometimes it is in the air after the

manner of a bridge, touching the earth at both ends, so that our thought can pass over it from experience to experience. Such verified or practically sanctioned theory is science. Another part of our speculation only touches experience at one end, the point of its origin: it is in the air after the fashion of a captive balloon. In that case it is called metaphysics or theology, and is essentially a kind of poetry. While it is still relevant to experience, still a natural expression of the reflective imagination, it is good poetry, good religion, something morally significant although literally mythical, since we can never pass through it to any further experience or verify it in practice. But if our balloon gets loose altogether, if our poetry and religion cease to connect with life even in their origin and are not the interpretation or symbol of any thing real, then our fictions become absolutely vapid and without value of any sort. So I distinguish four stages of being–if I may call them so–1st actual experience, which is the only known or knowable "reality", 2nd science, which is valid and verifiable theory, 3rd good poetry and good religion, which contain ideas ∧(like the idea of a "person")∧ unverifiable but significant and relevant to the experience which has suggested them and which they represent in symbolic forms, and 4th bad poetry and bad religion, which is are neither useful in life nor truly expressive of it.

After this I need hardly say that I neither wish people to kiss the Pope's toe nor to be liberals, if liberalism in philosophy is to mean the tendency to ∧believe that∧ unverifiable hypotheses, if they are meagre and abstract enough, may be passed off for matters of fact. I want my metaphysics and religion to be good poetry, not bad and inadequete poetry. As I am not eager to smuggle it into the dark corners and fine interstices of reality (like our transcendental friends) I am glad to have it as full and interesting as possible, a real counterpart and idealization of life. Therefore I prefer Catholic ideas to Protestant, and Pagan ideas to Catholic: or, if you like, I would only accept Christianity as a form of Paganism. For in Paganism I see the only religion that tried to do justice to all life, and at the same time retained the consciousness that it was a kind of poetry.

I didn't mean to write such a long letter–but you have the stimulus of your own to blame for this prolixity.   Yours very truly
GSantayana

To Nathaniel Wedd
[July 1900?] • London, England   (MS: King's)

108 Jermyn Street
S.W.

Dear Wedd

I am so glad you are to be in town on the 11th. I expect to be here then. Look me up in the morning or let me know where to meet you. As doubtless you come to attend to something and may be busy at other times, I hope you will at least lunch and dine with me, when we can talk of Dionysius[1] and more modern matters.   Yours ever

GSantayana

[1]Dionysius the Elder (c. 430–367 B.C.) and the Younger (368–344 B.C.) were the tyrants of Syracuse. Dionysius of Halicarnassus was a first century B.C. Greek who wrote *Antiquities of Rome.* Saint Dionysius the Areopagite was the first bishop of Athens and a martyr. Perhaps Santayana meant to write Dionysus, who was, in Greek legend, god of fertility and wine, patron of song and drama, and son of Zeus and Semele.

To D. Appleton and Co.
2 October 1900 • Cambridge, Massachusetts   (MS: USC)

60 Brattle Street
Cambridge
Mass.

Oct. 2. 1900

Messrs D Appleton & Co
New York

Gentlemen,

Is it still possible to get copies of No. 87 of the Journal of Speculative Philosophy, the issue for September 1892?[1] If so, I should be glad if you would send me two copies. Perhaps you could also tell me, what would interest me very much, whether Mr Davidson carried out the plan which he speaks of in that number of the Journal, of translating the whole of Aristotle's Metaphysics. I ask because I have a project of that kind myself, and I should like to take advantage of his labours if they were at all considerable.

Yours truly
GSantayana

¹The *Journal of Speculative Philosophy*, the first philosophical journal in the English language, was founded by William Torrey Harris (1835–1909) in Saint Louis in 1867 and moved to New York in 1880. From 1867 to 1893 Harris edited this journal, which published some of Thomas Davidson's (1840–1900) works, which include *Aristotle and Ancient Educational Ideals* (1892).

To William Torrey Harris

9 October 1900 • Cambridge, Massachusetts   (MS: USC)

Cambridge. Mass
60 Brattle Street
October 9, 1900

Mr William T Harris
Washington.

Dear Sir.

Thank you very much for the two numbers of the Journal of Speculative Philosophy which you have forwarded, for which I enclose a cheque.

My translation of the Metaphysics is only just begun and I hardly dare to think when it may be finished. But I hope the day may come. A readable and trustworthy English version is certainly much needed

Yours truly
GSantayana

To William Torrey Harris

[19 October 1900] • Cambridge, Massachusetts   (MS: USC)

60 Brattle Street
Cambridge Mass

Dʳ WT Harris
Washington.

Dear Sir:

You are very kind to wish to make me a present of these two numbers of the Journal of Speculative Philosophy, and I thank you for them most sincerely. When I reach the twelfth book I expect to find Mr Davidson's version of great assistance. It will already be useful to my classes, whom I cannot expect to read Aristotle in the original.

The work of translation is going forward slowly. I find it very interesting and stimulating; if my enthusiasm holds I shall finish it within a year or two.

With renewed thanks

Yours very truly
GSantayana

To William Bond Wheelwright
3 November 1900 • Cambridge, Massachusetts   (MS: Unknown)

60 Brattle Street
Nov. 13, 1900

Dear Wheelwright

Won't you and Camprubi[1] come to dine with me tomorrow ₐWednesdayₐ at the Colonial Club at 6.30? I have been asked to give my verses[2] of the other night to the <u>Monthly</u>, but you may have them for the <u>Lampoon</u> if on second thoughts you don't think them too long and heavy. I never remember to have seen so long a piece in the <u>Lampoon</u>, and I hardly see how you can get it in. However, you shall be judge. I hope to have the MS back on Wednesday.

Yours sincerely
GSantayana

[1]José Augusto Luis Raimundo Aymar Camprubi received his A.B. from Harvard in 1901 and his S.B. in 1902. He was employed in 1914 in the Foreign Department of General Electric Company in New York City.
[2]"Young Sammy's First Wild Oats: Lines Read at the Thirtieth Anniversary of the Signet" was a satire on the Spanish-American War and contemporary American imperialism. (Santayana belonged to the Signet Society, a Harvard club.) This was published in the *Harvard Lampoon Supplement* 40 (20 Nov 1900): 1–4. [Reprinted with subtitle "Lines Written before the Presidential Election of 1900" in *Hermit*, 204–15.]

To Anna Boynton Thompson
9 November 1900 • Cambridge, Massachusetts   (MS: Radcliffe)

60 Brattle Street
Cambridge
Nov. 9th 1900

Dear Miss Thompson[1]

Professor Palmer tells me that you have some thoughts of reading Aristotle's Metaphysics with us. I should be most happy to have you join us, the technical conditions being fulfilled, as I understand, if you are a member of Radcliffe. We meet on Tuesday afternoon at two o'clock in my rooms, and the class consists only of Mr. Fuller, and Mr. Doroty[2] of the Episcopal Theological School. We have been translating privately, and bringing in a written version of a chapter or two a piece to each meeting. My plan is, the versions and their meaning having been discussed in common, to write out later a clean copy, and publish it. I should be very glad indeed of your cooperation in this work.

Yours truly
GSantayana

[1]After graduation from Girls High School in Boston, Anna Boynton Thompson (1848–1923) travelled in Europe for two years. She studied at Radcliffe College (B.A., 1898; M.A., 1899), Harvard (with Santayana and Royce), and Tufts College (Ph.D.). She taught at Thayer Academy in Braintree, Massachusetts, for forty-four years and chaired the history department for much of that time.
[2]Unidentified.

To Anna Boynton Thompson
12 November 1900 • Cambridge, Massachusetts   (MS: Radcliffe)

60 Brattle Street
Cambridge
Nov. 12. 1900

Dear Miss Thompson

The sort of work which you would wish to do would be of the greatest use in our undertaking, the more as it would supply the deficiencies of the rest of us. My purpose being largely practical—the desire to publish a useful translation—I cannot myself stop to investigate every point for its own sake. But the study of commentators and of such sources as there are would often throw light upon the text, even if it should at other times envelope it in darkness. If you wish to do the work, I should of course be most happy to profit by it, although I can hardly see in what sense you would be working "under my direction." You would be rather contributing notes and auxiliary matter to the study which we should be engaged in.

I will therefore leave it for you to do as you like. ˄and will gladly read the translations you may send me.˄ You can undertake the study of the Metaphysics or any part of it, and come to compare your results with ours whenever you like. That would not involve, I should think, attendance at the Seminary in a formal manner, although it would give us material assistance to have you join us when you had the time. Or you could occasionally meet me alone, as you suggest, and talk over any point that interested you particularly. Your method of working is so thorough, that it would be you rather than I that would be the instructor on those occasions.

I find Bonitz' Latin commentary and his German translation the most useful to control my version by: although I think a freer and fuller rendering if is often better in English than his literal translation.[1] We have got now to the middle of Book III or B; but there is no objection to your beginning where you like.   Yours truly
                                            GSantayana

[1]Hermann Bonitz (1814–88) wrote *Aristotelis Metaphysica* (1849), a two-volume Latin commentary. His translation, *Metaphysik*, was republished (Hamburg: Rowohlt) in 1966. The coauthors of this work were Hector Carballo and Ernesto Grassi.

To Charles Scribner's Sons
3 December 1900 • Cambridge, Massachusetts   (MS: Princeton)

---

60 Brattle Street
Cambridge Mass
Dec. 3. 1900

Messrs Charles Scribner's Sons
New York

Gentlemen:
I don't remember ever seeing a book of verse among your publications, but nevertheless it occurs to me to ask you whether you would care to look at a set of poems of very various sorts which I am getting together.[1] Stone

and Kimball—or Herbert S Stone, as the firm is now called—published my sonnets and <u>Lucifer</u>, and would very likely take the new volume also. But Chicago is a long way off and not a place from which it seems natural for my books to come, and my relations with you in respect to the <u>Sense of Beauty</u> and the <u>Interpretations</u> have been, for me, so entirely satisfactory, that I don't like to take steps towards any further publication without asking you whether you would be inclined to undertake it.

Yours very truly
GSantayana

[1] *Hermit.*

To Charles Scribner's Sons

10 February 1901 • Cambridge, Massachusetts   (MS: Princeton)

---

60 Brattle Street
Cambridge Mass
February 10, 1901

Messrs Charles Scribner's Sons
    New York

Gentlemen:

I sent you yesterday by express the verses of which I formerly wrote to you and which you encouraged me to submit to you. I have been retouching many of the pieces, which are juvenile, and hesitating about including others; in fact the whole group which is placed last, under the title, of <u>Convivial and occasional verses</u> gives me some qualms, although I have lopped off heads and tails unmercifully in the effort to make them discrete and presentable. Perhaps it would have been better to leave them unmutilated and unpublished; but I had a feeling that if printed here they might relieve the excessive idealism and religiosity of the first part of the little book, and keep people from rushing to the conclusion (to which some of my critics seem to have come) that the author is himself the <u>Hermit,</u> the <u>Lucifer,</u> or the innocent Platonist they read about. I suppose if those states of feeling did not appeal to me at all it would be unlikely that I should dwell on them so much; but at the same time that pure idealism by no means represents either my way of life or my speculative opinions; and I should be glad to give my little public some hint of that fact. Not that I wish them to form another or better idea of my personality, for that is just what I dislike; what I wish is to be taken as an artist, not as a man writing his confessions. So that a few perfectly sincere frivolities (of which I have a considerable stock) may serve to <u>dérouter</u>[1] the sentimentally impertinent reader.

I say this to explain my idea in preparing such a medley as what I am sending you. If you think any of the pieces, or the whole last group, had better be left out, pray say so with entire frankness.[2] I should sacrifice them without a pang, all the more as they would thereby be restored to their personal and far more pungent context; for of course most of these dinner-verses were originally full of personalities. I would rather not print anything for which an apology is necessary even in the form of a date given to show how young and clever the author was when he committed his indiscretions or perpetrated his crudities. If a thing is not worth saying now it is not worth saying at all: although a poet may well say a thousand things he does not wholly believe.

Yours very truly

GSantayana

[1]Lead astray.
[2]"Convivial and Occasional Verses: were included in *Hermit*, 161–234.

To James Edwin Creighton
16 April 1901 • New York, New York   (MS: Cornell)

New York

April 16 1901

Dear Sir

Your letter should have been answered before but had to follow me here from Cambridge. I shall be glad to write the notice of Martin's <u>Saint Augustin</u>[1] which you ask for, if you are willing to wait until Aug 1<u>st</u> for it.

Yours very truly

G Santayana

[1]Jules Martin (b. 1844) wrote *Doctrine Spirituelle de Saint Augustin* (Paris: P. Lethielleux) in 1901. Santayana's article appeared in the *Philosophical Review* 10 (September 1901): 515–26. It was reprinted with changes in *Religion*, 148–77.

To Harry Morgan Ayres

[Spring 1901 or 1902?] • [Cambridge, Massachusetts?]   (MS postcard:
Lango)

Final grade in Philosophy 10: —[1]

B

G.S.

[1]Harry Morgan Ayres (1881–1948) was a member of the Harvard class of 1902 and received his Ph.D. in 1908 (in philology). He became an associate professor of English at Columbia University in 1919.

To Alice Freeman Palmer

[June 1901?] • Cambridge, Massachusetts   (MS: Wellesley)

<u>60 Brattle Street</u>

Dear Mrs Palmer

It will give me great pleasure to celebrate so auspicious an occasion with you on Wednesday the 19<u>th</u>. I don't say that I will come to congratulate Mr Palmer, for we are all to be congratulated on his long and fruitful labour.[1]

With many thanks and pleasant expectations

Yours sincerely   GSantayana

[1]This letter has been dated June 1901 based on the Brattle Street address and on the publication of Palmer's book, *Field of Ethics, being the William Belden Noble Lectures for 1899* (1901). Possibly the occasion mentioned is a celebration of this publication.

To Charles Scribner's Sons
12 June 1901 • Cambridge, Massachusetts   (MS: Princeton)

60 Brattle Street
Cambridge
June 12 1901

₵Messrs Charles Scribner's Sons
New York

Gentlemen.

I send you at last the enclosed agreement[1] which I had mislaid. I hope this long delay has not put you to any inconvenience.

As to the title, I have a wholly new suggestion to make. The Phi Beta Kappa has asked me to read them some verses at their annual meeting in Cambridge, on the day after the Harvard Commencement, and I am at work on a piece to be called "Spain in America", in Spenſcer's measure, the idea being to moralise on the career of Spain in the New World, her exits and entrances, and what can remain over of definitive good and ill.[2] As the subject has some interest and the poem may be of considerable length (I shall not read it all!) it has occurred to me that it might be put in the front of the new volume, which might then be called "Spain in America and other poems". Perhaps that might attract more general attention and have, at the same time, a certain personal propriety even in respect to the other things in the book.

I believe it is customary not to announce the subject of Phi Beta Kappa poems beforehand, so I beg you to consider this note confidential–until June 27ᵗʰ.

I sail for Europe from New York on June 29ᵗʰ and if my M.S. is then at your office, perhaps you would let me have it for a few minutes, as I wish to make some substitutions in one or two of the pieces, preferably before they go to the printer.

My address during the summer–after June 29ᵗʰ–will be ᶜ/o Brown Shipley & Co 123ᐃ Pall Mall, London. In sending me the proof, it is unnecessary to inclose the M.S. as I never look at it, partly because I know the verses pretty well, and partly because the fresh impression made by the printed page helps me to see little faults and make the necessary changes. The mere proof can be easily sent by mail, and I will return it immediately so as not to make the delay any longer than it must be of necessity under the circumstances.

Yours very truly

GSantayana

[1]Unlocated.

[2]Santayana read fifteen stanzas of this poem in Sanders Theatre on 27 Jun 1901. These stanzas were printed in *The Boston Herald.* (See "Convivial and Occasional Verses," *Hermit,* 216–31.) Edmund Spenser (c. 1552–99) was a great English poet whose works include *The Faerie Queene.* The Spenserian stanza consists of eight five-foot iambic lines, followed by an iambic line of six feet, rhyming a b a b b c b c c.

To William Roscoe Thayer

[20 June 1901] • Cambridge, Massachusetts   (MS: Houghton)

---

60 Brattle Street

Dear Mr Thayer

    My ΦBK poem is probably coming out in the autumn in a new volume of verses which Scribner is publishing for me. I don't know whether they will like or dislike the idea of having the piece appear simultaneously in the Graduates' Magazine, but I will inquire and let you know. For my part I should be delighted, although I am not sure that you will not think it sins both in length and by obscurity. However, I don't expect to read it all, so that the audience will have only one cross to bear–   Yours very truly

GSantayana

To Charles Scribner's Sons

20 June 1901 • Cambridge, Massachusetts   (MS: Princeton)

---

60 Brattle Street

Cambridge

June 20, '01

Messrs Charles Scribner's Sons
New York

Gentlemen:

    M[r] Thayer of the Harvard Graduates' Magazine asks me if he may publish my Φ.B.K. poem in September. I have not given him a definitive answer, wishing first to refer the matter to you. You may remember that I was thinking of using the title, "Spain in America", for our new volume, and if that is to be done, I am not sure that it would be advisable to reprint the leading poem elsewhere. Or would it be rather a sort of advertisement for the book?

Yours very truly
GSantayana

To William Roscoe Thayer

25 June 1901 • Cambridge, Massachusetts   (MS: Houghton)

60 Brattle Street
June. 25. 1901

Dear Mr Thayer

Scribner seems to be disinclined to have the whole of my effusion published elsewhere, and I think myself that it would be long and unnecessary in the pages of the Magazine. Considerable extracts, however, will go to the daily press, and those of course would be at your disposal, if they helped you to fill a vacant page. But between the bits in the papers and the portentous whole in the book, I should think there was hardly room for an abridged version in your review. However, that is for you to decide.

I am sorry not to lend myself more unreservedly to your flattering idea, but you see ~~wh~~ how the matter stands.

Yours very truly
GSantayana

To Charles Scribner's Sons

[c. 25 June 1901] • Cambridge, Massachusetts   (MS: Princeton)

60 Brattle Street
Cambridge Mass

Charles Scribner's Sons.
New York

Gentlemen:

I was glad to get your letter of the other day and to know the view you took of the poems as a whole and of the occasional pieces in particular. The royalty of 10% you suggest is all I should have expected if I had thought of the matter at all. Of course my interest in publishing verses consists entirely in the desire to see them in my friends' hands and to be rid of that feeling of prolonged pregnancy which comes from having old things in MS when new things are in one's mind asking for their turn to be hatched. I only hope you will not suffer any loss by venturing to undertake their publication.

What you say about the title is very true, although it had not struck me before.[1] I will try to think of a better one, at least for the volume. Several suggest themselves to my mind, in view of what you say about a certain doctrinal and spiritualistic tendency in the ~~two~~ first ₍two₎ poems: but I dislike too poetical and pretentious a title as would be "The lessons of love", "The penances of love" or anything of that kind. "Christian Episodes" would perhaps be better, and would have the advantage of indicating the "objective" way in which I look, and should like the reader to look, at those little studies. But as the publication is not to be until the autumn, there is time for happier thoughts, as well as for some changes and corrections which begin to occur to me—most of them, however, slight enough to be made in the proof.

Yours very truly
GSantayana

[1]Scribner's editor, William Crary Brownell, rejected "Spain in America" as the title of Santayana's book of verse. He feared that public sentiment generated by the Spanish-American War (1898) might prejudice the book's success.

To Charles Scribner's Sons

26 June 1901 • Cambridge, Massachusetts   (MS: Princeton)

60 Brattle Street
Cambridge Mass
June 26 1901

Messrs Charles Scribners Sons
New York

Gentlemen.

I see that you put your trust decidedly in metaphysics, and I am heartily glad to concur in that preference. We will then put "<u>Spain in America</u>" at the end of the volume, among the occasional verses, and this is all the more fitting as now that the piece is finished I perceive that it is shorter more artificial and less grand than I had imagined it in its nebulous state.

I will follow your suggestion about the other matter also and only offer Mr Thayer the extracts which will also be given to the daily press, which usually gives a good deal of space to such poems. It will only be a part of what I shall read and a smaller part of what I have written.

A satisfactory title for those metaphysical love scenes has not yet occurred to me. Can you suggest something, or at least point to some good example ∧s∧ ?

Yours very truly
GSantayana

To William Crary Brownell

29 June 1901 [*postmark*] • New York, New York (MS postcard: Princeton)

Poems
New Poems
Christian Episodes and other poems.
The Hermit's Christmas and other poems
Dramatic and other poems.
<u>Scenes and Elegies and other poems</u>.
<u>A Hermit of Carmel</u> and other poems.[1]
A Hermit of Mount Carmel and other poems.
A meeting in ∧ ✝Mt. ✝∧ Carmel and other poems.

G.S.

¹Brownell drew lines through all the suggested titles except this one, which he circled and wrote alongside: "This is it."

To Susan Sturgis de Sastre
17 July 1901 • Oxford, England   (MS: Virginia)

<u>Oxford July 17, 1901</u>

Dear Susie

I have been in England a week or ten days, waiting to make definite plans for the summer before writing to you. They are hardly made yet, but on the point which most concerns you, whether I shall get as far as Avila or not in my wanderings, I may say that I don't think it likely. I must absolutely do some solid work, and unless I get fagged and bored, so that work becomes impossible, I mean to stay here and keep at it all summer, with the exception of some short visit to Howard Sturgis or some other friend near London. It is possible, however, that I may go in August to Paris, and in that case I should like very much to run on to see you, even if it were only for a short time. In fine, it is possible that I may turn up about the middle of August, but certainly not earlier. Of course you will here hear from me long before, so that you must not let the possibility of my coming interfere with any plans about <u>baños</u>¹ or anything else which you may have in mind.

I am sadly ignorant of all that has been going on at your house all this time, except that I gather that Antonia and Felisa² were in Alicante during the winter, and that Antonia's health was improved by the trip. How about Rafael's commission? Has he got it? What are the other boys about?³ I understand you and Celedonio are in good health and that the house is finished and satisfactory. I am very glad of it.

I staid in America unusually late this year and had a horrid time. The heat was unspeakable, and after my lectures were over I was bored and restless, longing to get away. What kept me was a function at the Phi Beta Kappa, where they had asked me to read some verses, and as that is locally regarded as an honour, I was obliged to accept and stay. But it will never happen again, so that in future years I may hope to have a longer vacation and more time for a visit to you.

Things at home are quite unchanged, as you may judge from the letters they write you. So are all my private affairs.

My return passage is taken from Southampton for September 18th so that I have half of that month to count on, in compensation for this decapitated July.

Give my love to Celedonio and the boys and write a line to you affectionate brother   George

[*across*] Address ^C/o Brown Shipley & Co. London.

[1]Bathrooms.
[2]Antonia was Celedonio's eldest child and only daughter. Felisa is unidentified.
[3]Rafael (d. 1940) was one of Celedonio's sons and was Santayana's walking companion when he visited Ávila. Celedonio's other sons were Antonio (d. 1928), Luis (d. 1937, Rafael's twin), Eduardo, and José "Pepe."

To Charles Scribner's Sons
19 July 1901 • Oxford, England   (MS: Princeton)

Oxford   July 19 1901

Messrs Charles Scribner's Sons
New York

Gentlemen

Mr. R. Brimley Johnson, a publisher about whom I know nothing, wrote me a few days ago asking me if I had any book in preparation which he might publish.[1] I answered him that I had nothing of the kind he meant (like the <u>Interpretations</u>) but that you were about to issue a volume of my verses, about an English edition of which you might or might not have any arrangements in view. I have now got the inclosed reply,[2] and send it on to you, in case you have nothing better to consider. I should think it would do no harm to send Brimley Johnson a proof of the new book and let him if he liked issue some copies in England. Or you might send me a duplicate proof to forward to him from here, when you despatch one to me. I suggest this, of course, only under the supposition that no plan for an English issue is already afoot.

I sent you before sailing a postal-card with a lot of possible titles for the new volume, some of which I hope seemed suitable.

Yours very truly
GSantayana

Address:
> ^C/o Brown Shipley & Co
> 123 Pall Mall
> London.

¹Reginald Brimley Johnson (1867–1932) published *Hermit* in London in 1902.
²Unlocated.

To James Edwin Creighton
21 July 1901 • Oxford, England   (MS: Cornell)

Oxford, July 21. 1901

Dear Sir

I am afraid this article on Saint Augustine is not the review I promised you, but the book proved too meagre and the subject too suggestive for me to carry out the original intention. Of course you will not feel in the least bound to print this, which both in manner and in length may not seem suitable for your *Review. Pray feel entirely free in the matter, and do not hesitate to reject the article altogether or to print the first pages only in the form of a notice. Should you decide to do the latter, however, I trust I may get the whole M.S. back, as it may be useful to me in other connections.

My address for the summer is ^C/o Brown Shipley & Co London. I shall be back at Harvard about September 25th

With apologies for the irregularity of this review, I remain

[*Unsigned*]

To William Archer
24 July [1901] • Oxford, England   (MS: British)

---

5 Grove Street¹
Oxford

July 24

Dear Sir,²

You will not get my photograph from Pach³–I am sorry you have taken the trouble to write to him. The many photographers I find in Oxford do not tempt me much more than he; but although I dislike the idea of having my face associated with my verses, I am writing to a friend in Paris, who has the photograph of a drawing made in '96 by Andreas Andersen which I am asking him to send you. It is a clever drawing, and as it represents a past and somewhat fantastic aspect of my humble personality, I object to it less than to a glaring photo. Moreover, it corresponds exactly to the date of the later sonnets.

If I am in town for more than a few hours I shall not fail to let you know. Thank you very much.

Yours faithfully
GSantayana

[1]Later renamed Magpie Lane.
[2]William Archer (1856–1924) was born in Scotland but worked in London as a drama critic and for various papers. In 1919 he assisted with the establishment of the New Shakespeare Company at Stratford-upon-Avon. He included a selection of Santayana's poems in his *Poets of the Younger Generation* (London and New York: John Lane, The Bodley Head, 1902), 373–84. Archer's commentary compared Santayana's powers as a sonneteer to those of Shakespeare.
[3]Unidentified.

To Susan Sturgis de Sastre

13 August 1901 • Oxford, England   (MS: Virginia)

Oxford, Aug. 13, 1901

Dear Susie

I have given up all idea of going even to Paris this year, and expect to remain here until I sail. It is a disappointment not to see you, but on the whole it seems best to put off that trip for another year, as I am in the midst of steady work and well and happy in this place. It has rained more or less lately so that the air is fresh and the country like an emerald. I drive about a good deal with some friends of mine, one of whom is a horse-dealer[1] and the other (his brother) an actor. The horse-dealer ~~has a ch~~ runs a coach and four to Blenheim twice a week and sometimes takes me when he is driving himself. You may think this very low company for a philosopher to keep, but you would be quite mistaken. He is a gentleman and in fact a great swell who has taken to keeping horses as the most congenial possible business. England is full of singular people of that sort. I have also been seeing something of Anglican monks who have a toy monastery[2] here where they work in the garden with an expression of self-conscious beatitude on their

faces. These contrasted types (I was introduced to the monks by the actor)
keep me amused when I need a little change from my books and papers,
so that I am having a good vacation and at the same time doing considerable work. England is not, as you naughtily say, the best possible world but
it is the best actual country, and a great rest after America.

What you say about Rafael makes me very sorry for the poor chap; he
must be feeling rather sore. Farming is a good thing, but I am afraid there
is not enough at Zorita[3] for so many candidates as you have at home. You
must tell us in your letters how the new projects for a <u>carrera</u> turn out.

Give my love to the family and tell them I hope to see them all next
year.   Your affectionate brother   George

[1]Harold Fletcher.
[2]The monastery of the Cowley Fathers. See *Persons*, 496–97.
[3]The location of Celedonio's farm about one hundred miles from Ávila.

To Charles Scribner's Sons
28 August 1901 • Oxford, England   (MS: Princeton)

<u>Oxford   Aug 28 1901</u>

Gentlemen

I am sorry if the "out" in the <u>Hermit</u> was due to my carelessness.
Apparently a page or two dropped out of the MS before I numbered the
sheets. I have no copy here, but send you a substitute which is perhaps no
worse than the original passage. I could only remember a few lines.

I shall be here until Sept. 18th when I sail for New York. After the 26th I
shall be back in Cambridge.[1]

Yours truly
GSantayana.

P.S. It is all right about Black. I only sent you Johnson's[2] letter that you
might take note of it if you had no other arrangement in view.

[1]Massachusetts.
[2]Adam and Charles Black were the publishers who issued *Interpretations* in England.

To Susan Sturgis de Sastre

15 September 1901 • Oxford, England   (MS: Virginia)

Oxford, Sept. 15, 1901.

Dear Susie

Many thanks for your nice letter and the news you give me about your-self and the family. If you have been having other guests it was perhaps as well that I did not break in upon you also. I had another temptation to travel, this time to Greece and Constantinople, and back by Buda-Pesth and Vienna. Three young men who were going suggested that I should join them, but the hope of accomplishing something here and the fear of spending more than Robert[1] would approve of kept me quiet. Robert is no doubt right about the possibility of getting a higher rate of interest for money in America. I should not be unwilling to sell the house in Avila[2] if anything could be got for it worth mentioning. I believe I wrote you this before, but I hardly expect that anyone would care to buy the house as an investment, while the people who would live in it would never have money to invest. I am not sorry to keep the house, as I may go and live in it myself some day, except that I am afraid it gives you a lot of trouble which it hardly repays. If you see a chance to sell it for what seems a fair price, do so by all means.

I see you look on MᶜKinley's end as a judgment of heaven. There were other people probably far more guilty in respect to the war, which I am afraid could not have been avoided in the end, given Spanish inefficiency and the sentimental and acquisitive instincts of the American public. The worst of this accident is that Rooseveldt is not a safe person;[3] but respon-sibility may sober him and he may be able to resist the machine better than a mere bell-wether like MᶜKinley.

I sail from Southampton in three days in the <u>Kronprinz Wilhelm</u>, and after one night in New York at the Potters' (with whom I travelled once in Italy) except to be at home again, about the 26ᵗʰ   With love to all   your affᵗᵉ brother

George

[1]Santayana's half brother.
[2]Santayana's father's house.
[3]William McKinley (1843–1901), the twenty-fourth president of the United States, advanced the interests of American commerce. Trouble with Spain ended in the Spanish-American War. McKinley asked Congress to declare war, though Spain hinted

at concessions to avoid it. Victorious, he demanded the Philippine Islands for the U.S. After his assassination, he was succeeded by Vice President Theodore Roosevelt (1858–1919), who had organized the Rough Riders. As president, Roosevelt championed the rights of the "little man," engaged in trust busting, and followed a policy of conservation of natural resources.

To Anna Boynton Thompson
1 October 1901 • Cambridge, Massachusetts   (MS: Radcliffe)

60 Brattle Street
Cambridge
October 1.

Dear Miss Thompson

I am very sorry that my slowness in answering your letter should have made you think I had taken offence at any thing said or not said in it. The delay was only due to this; that I don't yet know what form the seminary will take, or whether it will be given at all, and I was waiting in hopes of giving you in a few days a definitive answer.

Mr. Fuller, the only other person who has applied, and who translated several books of the Metaphysics last year, is also in somewhat uncertain health, but writes me that he will be in Cambridge again this week and will be ready to make some arrangement for work. I understand he wishes to take Books XI and XII. From what you wrote me last year I gathered that you would wish to begin at the beginning. You might do so for your private work, but I suppose at the meetings we should have to go on where we left off, at Book IV, I think. When I have seen Mr. Fuller I shall be able to make a more definite proposal.

Do you think of becoming a member of Radcliffe or would the Seminary be merely a private conversation between us three? This is not a point that in the least matters to me, but I ask you so as to be able to answer the question if it should be put to me in future.

I hope your health will give you no more trouble and that we may have the advantage of your cooperation   Yours sincerely
                GSantayana

To Charles Scribner's Sons

26 October 1901 • Cambridge, Massachusetts   (MS: Princeton)

60 Brattle St   Cambridge
October 26 1901

Messrs Charles Scribner's Sons
New York

Gentlemen:

I have not seen the proofs of the title page or table of contents for "A Hermit of Carmel", which I trust is not a sign that the book is not soon coming out.

I enclose a list[1] of persons to whom I should like copies to be sent, to be charged as usual to my account.

May I have also three copies each of the <u>Sense of Beauty</u> and the <u>Interpretations</u> to be sent to me here?–There are some misprints in both books. Is it worth while or possible to correct them at this late date? And there are already many changes I should like to make in the <u>Hermit</u>, such is the inconstancy of the poetic flame!

Yours very truly
GSantayana

[1]Unlocated.

To Anna Boynton Thompson

28 October 1901 [*postmark*] • Cambridge, Massachusetts   (MS: Radcliffe)

<u>60 Brattle St.</u>

Dear Miss Thompson

Mr Fuller writes me that his father is dying and consequently we shall have to give up our meeting tomorrow. I will send you word if Mr Fuller is not able to come the following week, as he is so important a member of our trio that I am not sure you would find it worth while to come in his absence. If you do not hear from me we shall meet as usual next week.

Yours sincerely
GSantayana

To Charles Scribner's Sons
29 October 1901 • Cambridge, Massachusetts   (MS telegram: Princeton)

Cambridge, Mass. 29.

Scribners,
   153 Fifth Avenue, Newyork.
Mistake seems of no consequence go on with publication
G. Santayna.

To Charles Scribner's Sons
30 October 1901 • Cambridge, Massachusetts   (MS: Princeton)

60 Brattle Street
Cambridge Mass
October 30 1901

Gentlemen.

I answered your letter by telegraph yesterday before I had received the copy of <u>The Hermit</u> which you were sending on. I found it this morning. The disagreement between the title page and the cover[1] seems to me a very small matter, and I am surprised you should take it so seriously. Perhaps a matter of title is more important in business than it seems to my impractical head. On the other hand I can't say I like the cover in itself, and I should be glad if the accident of a wrong article would lead you to have the rest of the edition bound more simply. The "fancy" lettering seems to me in doubtful taste—why have any at all?—and the croziered rose-window seems to hint at some occult meaning which escapes me. Does it symbolise my "mysticism"? In a word, I should have greatly preferred a perfectly simple and straightforward exterior (like the title-page, which seems to me admirable.)

I am much obliged for the six copies which you kindly promise and should be glad to get them here. In fact I shall have to ask for more, as my friends expect to get them gratis and with autograph dedications. Could you send me <u>ten unbound</u> copies, as well as the six you offer me? And if so will you kindly countermand the sending of the presentation copies ordered the other day, except ~~the~~ those ˄in the˄ ~~following~~ ˄enclosed˄ list, which is to be substituted for the one I sent you?

The general appearance of the book, in spite of what I say above, pleases me very much, and the inside has a very attractive look. As to the outside, may I suggest another change, in case the lettering is changed. It would seem enough to have my surname only on the back. There is no one else of the name, while the polyglot effect of both surname and cognomen might be avoided

Yours Ⅴvery truly   GSantayana

Please send copies of "A Hermit of Carmel"
with the Author's Compliments, to

Professor C. E. Norton,	Shady Hill,	Cambridge.	Mass
" Wm James,	Irving St	"	"
" Josiah Royce,	" "	"	"
" G. H. Palmer,	Quincy St	"	"
" Münsterberg,	7 Ware St	"	"
Delta Phi Club, 72 Mt Auburn S		"	"
Mrs C. H. Toy, 7 Lowell St		"	"
Mrs John L. Gardner, Green Hill		Brookline	"
Mrs Henry Whitman, 77 Mt Vernon St.		Boston	"
Mrs J. C. Gray, 186 Beacon St		"	"
Mrs Gordon Dexter, 171 Commonwealth Ave		"	"
Mr & Mrs R B Potter, 39 E. 28ᵗʰ St		New York	
King's College Library, Cambridge		England	
Howard Sturgis Esq. Queen's Acre, Windsor ".			
Miss Julia Robins, ᶜ/o Baring Bros & Co. London, Eng.			
J. T. Stickney, Esq. 3 rue Soufflot, Paris, France			
Dᵃ Susana Sturgis de Sastre, Avila, Spain.			
Blair Fairchild Esq. American Legation, Teheran, Persia.			

[1]The agreed upon title, *A Hermit of Carmel And Other Poems*, appears on the title page, but *The Hermit of Carmel and other Poems* appears on the spine and front cover.

To Anna Boynton Thompson
31 October 1901 • Cambridge, Massachusetts   (MS: Radcliffe)

October 31, 1901

Dear Miss Thompson

I am exceedingly sorry you came the other day to find me gone. My note ought to have arrived in time; had I had the least suspicion that it might not I should have telegraphed. But I am even more sorry that this incident should precipitate a decision on your part not to come any more. The journey must be fatiguing, I quite understand that. And the profit you can get by our discussions is perhaps a very small addition to what you would gather for yourself from the text and commentaries. But I myself find the friction of minds—even the comparison of ignorances—so much more profitable than "grubbing" alone, that I should regret for myself your deserting us altogether. Of course I shall be glad to read over ~~my~~ your translation and notes; and if you are not in haste to have them returned I hope to use ~~it~~ them in a revision of our last year's translation—which was too loose—which I have begun and which I hope will serve as the final rendering for publication.

Let us leave the matter in this form: you will send me the translation as you make it, and you will come to the meetings whenever you feel disposed, not regarding them as appointments hanging over you in all weathers, but merely as possibilities of making yourself useful.

Mr Fuller, whom I have not yet seen, expects to be here next week, but the movements of his family are always more or less uncertain and I don't know what plans they may make under these new circumstances—

Yours very truly

GSantayana

To Charles Scribner's Sons

4 November 1901 • Cambridge, Massachusetts   (MS: Princeton)

60 Brattle Street
Cambridge
Nov. 4, 1901

Gentlemen:

I enclose a list of such misprints or unfortunate expressions as I have noted in my books.[1] Most of them are trivial and if any considerable trouble or expense is involved in correcting the plates, I should not trouble about them. Those about which I feel some concern are those on pp. 58, 59 of "Poetry and Religion" and on pp. 74, & 129 in the "Hermit", especially this last page, where I am afraid an echo of Shelley's <u>Bridal Song</u>[2] made me write something which in this place is ridiculous.   Yours very truly

GSantayana

Corrections for "<u>Interpretations of
Poetry & Religion</u>".

page	line	for	read
10	17	,	[*delete symbol*]
	22	,	[*delete symbol*]
1~~3~~6	13	,	[*delete symbol*]
18	7 from bottom	only arises,	arises only
∧57∧ ~~22~~ ∧57∧	11	,	[*delete symbol*]
58	5 from bottom	nine	seven
	3 " "	"	"
59	8	"	"
64	8	nor	or
73	7	imminent ,	immanent
74	10 from bottom	,	[*delete symbol*]
134	21	"from the senses grow"	
	read	but a flattering show	
177	6	peversity	perversrity
184	5 from bottom	man	men
230	8 " "	pretence	pretense
286	6	where	when

Corrections for "A Hermit of Carmel"

page	line	for	read
39	last but one	praise	praised
58	6	after "remember"	–
74	5 from bottom	along.	away.
129	9	song	lay
	13	along.	away.
201	2	ages	age's
229	4 from bottom	"	[*delete symbol*]

[1]These corrections were never made by Scribner's. The corrections for *Interpretations* were made in the critical edition, and the corrected poems from *Hermit* appear in *Complete Poems*.

[2]Percy Bysshe Shelley (1792–1822) was an English Romantic poet whom Santayana admired. Santayana held regular meetings of undergraduates in his Harvard rooms for the purpose of reading poetry aloud. During 1910–11 the group read "only Shelley, from beginning to end, except *The Cenci*." Santayana wrote "Shelley or the Poetic Value of Revolutionary Principles" (*Doctrine*, 1913).
The closing stanza of Shelley's "A Bridal Song" reads:
Fairies, sprites, and angels, keep her!
Holy stars, permit no wrong!
And return to wake the sleeper,
Dawn, ere it be long!
Oh joy! Oh fear! what will be done
In the absence of the sun? …
Come along!
Before correction, the angel speaks the following lines in Santayana's "Resurrection":
She hath befooled thee long,
And fondly thought to smother
The sweet and cruel laughter of my song
Which the stars sing together, and the throng
Of seraphs ever shout to one another.
Come, heaven-chosen brother,
Dear kinsman, come along.

To Lawrence Smith Butler
28 November 1901 • Cambridge, Massachusetts   (MS: University Club)

---

60 Brattle Street
Nov. 28, 1901.

Dear Lawrence

Many thanks for your nice letter. It was a great pleasure to hear from you, although, to be sure, I knew you were safe at home, far from the wicked orgies of the Quartier latin. We miss you very much in Boston. Aren't you ever coming to visit your old friends? You should come and gather the chorus of praise which we are raising about the big room at the Union.[1] It is the only noble room in the college and will give many people here their first notion of what good architecture means in practice. Façades and towers and details are one thing, but a beautiful place to live in, noble in colour and proportions, is something new in these parts and, it seems to me, invaluable. The Union seems to be a great success socially and gastronomically—although the ubiquity of ice water is a trifle chilling. The place is much used and the dining room (where I often go to eat) is crowded. Architecturally only the large room is of much consequence, but the rest seems serviceable and inoffensive. As to the gates, we have been suddenly blessed with too large a family of them; they look as if they had been all hatched in a hurry and had not yet got any feathers and hardly knew what they had come into the world for. But when the trees grow and hang about them again and the crude colour is toned down, I think they will seem all right and fall into a natural place in the landscape. The terrace in front of Palmer's house puzzles me a little, but I suppose some great pavillion is to back it up some day. I like to imagine it there, flanked with a few poplars standing high against the sky. However, this being Thanksgiving we ought to be grateful for what we have received up to date, without relying too much on favours to come.

I expect to be in New York at Christmas and will surely look you up. I am going out of town for a part of the time, to my friend Professor Strong's, but I will write to you when I know my exact plans, so as not to miss seeing you.—I hope [across] your father will soon be well again. This long illness must have been a great anxiety to you all.

Yours affectionately   G.S.

[1]The Harvard Union on Quincy Street was erected in 1900–1902. It was intended to provide an attractive gathering place for students not wealthy enough to afford the luxuries of a club. Thus, an esprit de corps would be encouraged among the students at this common meeting place.

To Charles Scribner's Sons
4 December 1901 • Cambridge, Massachusetts   (MS: Princeton)

60 Brattle Street

Cambridge Mass

Dec. 4. 1901

Gentlemen.

I no longer have the Spectator's review of my <u>Sonnets</u> and of <u>Lucifer</u> but I have looked it up in the College library and copied the principal passages, which I enclose.[1] They could be fairly quoted in an advertisement since the rest of the notice does not qualify them. The comparison to Lucretius etc is highly absurd, but it may serve your turn, the public not knowing my little friend Haynes[2] to be the author.

If you are in want of favourable notices for the announcements you may wish to make, you might use William Archer's article, which appeared last winter in the ＾London＾ Daily Mail and which is to reappear in his book on "Poets of the Younger Generation". I don't know whether the book is yet out, nor have I the article.

Yours very truly

GSantayana

[1]Unlocated.
[2]Unidentified.

To Charles Augustus Strong
20 December 1901 • Cambridge, Massachusetts   (MS: Rockefeller)

60 Brattle Street

Dec. 20, 1901

Dear Strong.

Do you still want me to come and make you a visit during the Christmas holidays? If so, will you let me know what days would be most convenient? I am thinking of going to New York on the 26th and should like to make other engagements for the days when I am not to be with you. As I only get to N. Y. once or twice a year there is always a lot for me to do.

Yours ever

GSantayana

To Anna Boynton Thompson
20 December 1901 • Cambridge, Massachusetts   (MS: Radcliffe)

60 Brattle Street
Dec. 20. 1901

Dear Miss Thompson

Thank you very much for your monograph on Fichte.[1] I spent the greater part of yesterday over it, and learned at least one thing very important and satisfactory to my own mind, viz. that Fichte surely did not mean his transcendental machinery to preexist, but that it was an ideal construction residing only in the thought that conceives it. This interpretation, to which I was already inclined on account of a constitutional aversion to believing that great men teach absurdities, releiieves Fichte of the charge of having constructed a new mythology to take the place of the old, a mythology which surely would not have had the pictorial value of the traditional one. If, however, he was only making explicit the ideal terms and movements of thought, without, as you say, pretending to describe its creation, he becomes at once a friend, a person whose discoveries are as welcome as his candour is engaging. I see that I shall gain much light and encouragement from your presentation and from the interesting selections you have appended. What I have read of Fichte—which is little more than the <u>Wissenschaftslehre</u>[2]—has not yet made me get over a certain feeling of strangeness and elusiveness, as if I were listening to the confessions of a refracted sun-beam rather than of a two-legged man. But I am going to reread and to read on, and with your assistance hope to become more intelligent and sympathetic.

I wrote to Mr Dyer the day before yesterday and sent him your address so that if he chose he might answer to you directly.

With many thanks for your book

Yours sincerely
GSantayana

---

[1] *The Unity of Fichte's Doctrine of Knowledge* (Boston: Ginn, 1895), Radcliffe College monographs, 7.
[2] *Grundlage der gesammten Wissenschaftslehre.*

To Lawrence Smith Butler

21 December 1901 • Cambridge, Massachusetts   (MS: University Club)

60 Brattle Street
Dec 21 1901

Dear Lawrence

It was only last night that I heard you had lost your father, else I should have written before, because you know that my thoughts would turn ₐtoₐ you at such a moment. I hope to see you soon—I go to New York on Xmas day and will look you up at once—but as one is not always inclined or able to say at odd times what is most in one's heart, I will write you a word now. This is an irreparable loss for you but not a bitter one, because it is in the order of nature that we should survive our parents and your father has lived to see you all grown up and to leave his memory and influence always with you. That ought to be a consolation for you. This world is so ordered that we must, in a material sense, lose everything we have and love, one thing after another, until we ourselves close our eyes upon the whole. It is hard for the natural man to bear this thought, but experience forces it upon him if he has the capacity of really learning anything. We should not set our hearts, then, on a material possession of anything, but our happiness should be made to lie in this, that whatever we possess for a time should reveal the ideal good to us and make us better in ourselves. Your family life has been so ideally happy and united (at least so it impresses your friends) that it must be doubly sad to suffer this cruel change; but you cannot lose that past happiness altogether, because it was of the sort that brings happiness in memory and prepares one ₐforₐ meeting all the other events of life, sad and gay, in a right spirit, with a sense of what is truly good. The truly unfortunate are those persons—and how many of our friends are in this case!—who have never known anything worth living for, any noble and natural characters, any true happiness, or any beautiful thoughts and things. But those who have known such things and grown like them can never be truly unhappy because they carry the sweetness and truth within themselves which alone make ₐaₐ happiness that is worth having. Your nature and surroundings have opened this spiritual world to you more than to most people—that is why I have always cared for you so much—and that is a gift all the more to be grateful for in that it cannot be taken away.

Yours ever

GSantayana

To William Cameron Forbes

[1902–June 1904] • Cambridge, Massachusetts   (MS: Houghton)

<u>60 Brattle Street</u>

Dear Cam

Will you dine with me on Wednesday Feb. 12ᵗʰ at seven o'clock at the Harvard Union, where I am trying to get together a few of the old crowd? I hope very much you will not fail us.

Yours ever

GSantayana

I need not warn <u>you</u> not to dress.

To Charles Scribner's Sons

10 February 1902 • Cambridge, Massachusetts   (MS: Princeton)

60 Brattle Street

Cambridge Mass

Feb. 10, 1902

Gentlemen:

I have just received the enclosed letter[1] from Stone & Co, who published my <u>Sonnets</u>. I should be glad if you cared to take on the book, in which case we could make any arrangement which seemed to you fair about the payment for the plates. There is this complication: the book of <u>Sonnets</u> contains the first act of <u>Lucifer</u>, afterwards republished entire by Stone in a separate volume.[2] It would be better to get the rights to <u>Lucifer</u> simultaneously and then the two could be published in one volume, or the fragment of <u>Lucifer</u> omitted from the volume of <u>Sonnets</u>. I should not be sorry to let <u>Lucifer</u> disappear for a while; some day I may feel like revising it thoroughly and reproducing it in connection with a set of historical and philosophical plays[3] which I have been long at work on, but which I think it would need a wider reputation than I have at present to float in the literary market. They are things which may be liked if they are read, but which it would be extremely hard to get anyone to read spontaneously.

What answer would you suggest that I should make to Stone & Co?

Yours very truly

GSantayana

[1]Unlocated.
[2]*Lucifer*, 1899.
[3]Only two of these plays, *The Marriage of Venus: A Comedy* and *Philosophers at Court*, were published, both posthumously in *Testament*. Other plays by Santayana exist in manuscript.

To Charles Scribner's Sons

22 February 1902 • Cambridge, Massachusetts   (MS: Princeton)

Cambridge Mass
Feb. 22. 1902

Messrs Charles Scribner's Sons
New York

Gentlemen,

I have this morning had the pleasure of receiving your letter, chiefly concerning Stone's proposition, and gladly take note of your suggestions. As you will readily understand, I can have no object in buying the plates myself, even at a moderate price. The matter, therefore, may be allowed to rest.

As to a translations of Don Quixote, I am not the person to make recommendations, as I do not read them. But from casual examination I have always imagined that Shelton's was the best.[1] Its inaccuracies make little practical difference, while it has <u>verve</u> and an Elizabethan vocabulary. I could not possibly, with my present work, undertake to edit your edition, if that is what you propose; but if you merely desired an essay on Don Quixote to serve as an introduction, I might write one, although a paper of mine on much the same subject exists in that strange work "The World's Best Literature" under the head of <u>Cervantes</u>.[2] But if I reread Don Quixote—I have not read it for many years—very likely new impressions and ideas might suggest themselves which could be put down for the occasion. I should think, however, that an edition by a scholar—I am not one in Spanish literature or philology—would be a more honourable a production than a mere reprint with a casual preface.

Very truly yours
GSantayana

[1]Thomas Shelton (1601–c. 1650) translated *Don Quixote* into English c. 1620.
[2]"Cervantes (1547–1616)," *A Library of the World's Best Literature: Ancient and Modern*, ed. Charles Dudley Warner (New York: The International Society, 1897), 8:3451–57.

To Isabella Stewart Gardner

7 April [1902?] • Brookline, Massachusetts   (MS: Gardner)

---

75 Monmouth Street
Brookline
April 7

Dear Mrs Gardner

It was a delightful surprise to see your handwriting last night, when I got home and found your kind note and interesting present. It is very good of you to remember me. I haven't been very well for the last year, and busier every day, and more of a hermit, so that your message seems to bring me up again into the land of the living, and I hope soon to have got enough of my fleshly substance back to become visible in the polite world. Talking of hermits, it occurs to me that you may not have seen another collection of verses of mine with that title—my poetical wastepaper-basket and closing of accounts with the Muses. I send you a copy in case anything in it—perhaps the translation from Théophile Gautier[1]—may interest you. I am proud to see that you have placed my other verses on your honourable list. I wish they were more worthy but I was only a poet by youth, not by genius.

Believe me, with [*across*] many thanks,   Always sincerely yours
GSantayana

[1]Théophile Gautier (1811–72) was a French poet, novelist, and critic whose aesthetic creed influenced the Parnassians. The translation was of "L'Art," 156–59. See *Complete Poems*, 211–12, for eleven of the fourteen stanzas.

To Charles Scribner's Sons

21 April 1902 • Cambridge, Massachusetts   (MS: Princeton)

60 Brattle Street
Cambridge Mass
April 21 1902

Messrs Charles Scribner's Sons
New York

Gentlemen:

The list of corrections I sent you some time ago for the "Sense of Beauty" was copied from my original notes; I had forgotten that most of them had been made already. There remain, then, to my knowledge only those which I add on the inside page here.[1]

I am glad that the small but continued sale of the books warrants a reprint.

Yours very truly
GSantayana

[1]Unlocated.

To Charles William Eliot

29 May 1902 • Cambridge, Massachusetts   (MS: Harvard)

60 Brattle Street
May 29. 1902

Dear Mr Eliot

Professor Münsterberg told me some time ago that you had approved of assigning $50 to an assistant in Philosophy 10. Dr Rand[1] has been reading the theses for me. I find that the Bursar has no orders in the matter and he refers me to you for an endorsement.

I hope I am not giving you unnecessary trouble, but I do not know what the usual procedure is in such a case.

Yours very truly
GSantayana

[1]Benjamin Rand (1856–1934) received his A.B. from Harvard in 1879. He was a philosophy instructor there from 1897 to 1902; beginning in 1906 he served as librarian of the Philosophical Library.

To Charles Francis Mason

1 June 1902 • Cambridge, Massachusetts   (MS: Harvard)

---

60 Brattle Street
June 1 1902

To the Bursar of Harvard College[1]

Dear Sir:

Will you please pay to Dr Benjamin Rand, the fifty dollars which, I understand, have been assigned for an assistant in Philosophy 10 for this year.

Yours truly
GSantayana

[1]Charles Francis Mason (A.B., Harvard, 1882) was Bursar from 1888 to 1922.

To Benjamin Rand

3 July 1902 • Ávila, Spain   (MS: Harvard)

Avila, July 3, 1902

Dear Dr Rand

I have received word from the President's secretary about your money, and he says that if you will send in a bill to the Bursar approved by me the ₐPresidentₐ will also approve it, and then the Bursar can pay it. If you have not already done so, you might send in such a bill, with the order I formerly sent you which will do, I expect, as an endorsement.

I enclose a paper[1] that explains itself.   With best wishes

Sincerely yours
GSantayana

Address ^C/o
Brown Shipley & Co, London.

¹Unlocated.

To Charles Scribner's Sons
1 December 1902 • Cambridge, Massachusetts   (MS: Amherst)

---

60 Brattle Street
Cambridge Mass
Dec. 1, 1902

Gentlemen:

Your letter about Don Quixote has remained so long unanswered because I wanted to think the matter over and see if in some way it could be arranged. But I am afraid I shall have to excuse myself again from taking part in your project. It would be an interesting piece of work, but my own plans are so many, and some of them so well advanced towards realization, that it would be foolish to complicate the situation still further and postpone the real accomplishment of anything. I have been at work since 1896 on a philosophical book to be called <u>The Life of Reason</u>: I wish to finish this soon—if possible within a year.¹ That would be a great load off my back; and if by that time your arrangements for Don Quixote have not been made and you should still want me to help you, it is possible that I might fall into temptation—although even then it is doubtful whether I should not do better to attend to things nearer my own vocations. When I remember that in a few weeks I shall be thirty-nine years of age and have as yet done nothing but play with the foils, I begin to fear that I may never have a bout with the real enemy. So that, however regretfully, I must decline your alluring suggestions and stick to business.

Yours faithfully
GSantayana

¹The five books of *Reason* were published in 1905–6.

To Hugo Münsterberg

6 February 1903 • Cambridge, Massachusetts   (MS: Boston)

Dear Münsterberg

It is too bad that you should have come <u>five</u> times to Brattle Street: why not send me a line and I should have come to you? However, all is well. I will read a part of the old drama—a new part—with pleasure on Thursday the 26th, although I fear the end, without the beginning, will not be very interesting. And I shall enjoy at least the other parts of the symposium.

Thank you very much for your article with the table showing your classification of the sciences. I have read the former and studied the latter with great interest. I follow you almost everywhere, although in places I find some difficulty with the terms. Sometimes an alternative phrase has occurred to me, and I should like to show you my version, to learn whether it changes your thought or not. By the way, I have never written to you about your big and great book;[1] the questions and comments that arise in my mind are too <u>diffused</u>, too incidental, to be summed up in a letter, but I hope some day to write a long review and to submit it to you before it is published, to make sure that I have misinterpreted nothing.

Yours sincerely
GSantayana

Feb.6.1903

[1] *Die Amerikaner* (1903), 2 vols., trans. Edwin B. Holt (New York: McClure, Phillips, and Co., 1905).

To Sally Fairchild

23 February 1903 • Cambridge, Massachusetts   (MS: Houghton)

Cambridge
<u>Feb 23 1903</u>

Dear Miss Fairchild

Don't trouble to return Russell's Sermons[1] which I am sending you this morning. It occurred to me that ~~it~~ they might amuse you to when you remembered the author, and they are also not uninteresting as a document of the times.

I have not yet got over the pleasure of having seen you.

Yours sincerely

GSantayana

[1]John Francis Stanley Russell, while imprisoned in England for bigamy, composed a book of "Lay Sermons" which was subsequently published. Santayana's estimate of these was "applied sophistry ... in the service of ... prejudice or passion." (*Persons*, 475–76)

To Horace Meyer Kallen
20 March 1903 • Cambridge, Massachusetts   (MS: American)

60 Brattle Street

March 20 1903

Dear Mr Kallen[1]

Thank you very much indeed for the Japanese prints. I like them both, but especially the flowers, and I am going to try making them into a lamp-shade, so that they may please the eye both ~~ni~~by night and by day.

It was very kind of you to think of sending them to me and I greatly appreciate your friendly intention as well as the gift itself.

Yours sincerely

GSantayana

[1]Born in Germany, Horace Meyer Kallen (1882–1974) attended Harvard (A.B., 1903; Ph.D., 1908) and taught English at Princeton (1903–1905). From 1908 to 1911 he taught philosophy at Harvard and worked closely with both William James and Santayana. Later he taught at the University of Wisconsin and Columbia. Kallen was one of the founders of the New School for Social Research in New York City. A leading Zionist, he wrote books on philosophy, politics, and education.

To John Henry Wright
6 April 1903 • Cambridge, Massachusetts   (MS: Ohio)

60 Brattle St

April 6 1903

Dear Mr Wright[1]

F. S. Darrow[2] is an intelligent, painstaking student, who puts down what he hears quite accurately and has at the same time a good deal of spon-taneity and "temperament." I have no doubt he would not disgrace the

Norton Fellowship, although I should not have thought of him for such a place. I mean that he lacks a certain plasticity and literary sensitiveness which might be expected to lead to Greek Studies.

Yours sincerely

GSantayana

[1]John Henry Wright (1852–1908) was professor of Greek (1887–1908) and dean of the Graduate School of Arts and Sciences (1895–1908) at Harvard.

[2]Fritz Sage Darrow received his A.B., A.M., and Ph.D. from Harvard. He later was professor of Greek Language and Literature (1907–10) at Drury College in Springfield, Missouri.

To Susan Sturgis de Sastre

13 August 1903 • Oxford, England   (MS postcard: Sanchez)

CHRIST-CHURCH COLLEGE. OXFORD.

Torre de la catedral.

En esta torre está la escalera que se vé en otra fotografía.

Exterior del <u>Hall</u> ó refectorio que tambien se vé en otra targeta.[1]

<u>August 13 1903.</u>

Dear Susie.

I am leaving Oxford tomorrow for a few days to stay with Russell near Portsmouth. Here are some more views of this place—you see how picturesque it is. There are some twenty colleges, not all so grand as Christ-Church, of course, but each complete with its chapel, hall, and gardens. Love to all the family.   Yours aff[ly]   George

[1][*Translation of Spanish written under card's photograph:*]
Cathedral tower.
In this tower is the stairway one sees in the other photograph. [*Unlocated*]
Exterior of the <u>Hall</u> or refectory which one also sees on the other postcard.

To The Mayflower Club
26 October 1903 [*postmark*] • Cambridge, MA   (MS postcard: Houghton)

60 Brattle St.
Cambridge

I beg to acknowledge the receipt of your letter, inclosing fifty cents in stamps to pay for the messenger for Miss Lowell.

GSantayana

To Harry Norman Gardiner
20 November 1903 • Cambridge, Massachusetts   (MS: Smith)

60 Brattle Street
Cambridge Mass
Nov. 20, 1903

Dear Professor Gardiner[1]

Yes, I think I can promise to read a short paper at Princeton on December 29th or 30th on the 'Place of Aesthetics'. I have a suggestion to make which may excite discussion.

Thank you very much for your renewed offer about the Philosophical Association. My only doubt is whether I could often attend the meetings. I have only been once to the Psychological Association. However, we can speak of this when we meet.

Yours sincerely
GSantayana

[1]Born in Germany, Harry Norman Gardiner (1855–1927) taught philosophy at Smith College from 1884 to 1924. He wrote *Feeling and Emotion–A History of Theories* (1937).

To Horace Meyer Kallen

5 December 1903 • Cambridge, Massachusetts   (MS: American)

60 Brattle Street
Cambridge
Dec. 5, 1903

Dear Kallen

I see it has taken me more than a month to answer your letter, which I was really very glad to get. What you tell me is amusing, and makes me think that perhaps you are inwardly enjoying the horrors of Princeton. Of course Princeton is very far away—but we may ask, as the Westerner said on a similar occasion "Far away from <u>where</u>?"—and of course it is intensely provincial, as I hear President Harper[1] of the University of Chicago says New York and the whole East is, and notably Boston.[1] Why isn't it very nice to have class spirit and respect for professors? And why isn't it interesting to see puritanism and industrialism trying to express themselves in one philosophy? You shouldn't mind the ugly symbols in which these things are expressed; now-a-days we have no taste in symbols. We have to ignore them as we should the style of a telegram or the drawl of a preacher, and try to attend only to the thing signified, the force embodied. Doesn't Princeton embody a force? Isn't it a better place than Harvard, for instance, in which to study America? And America is something worth a lot of trouble to understand. If I thought I could quite succeed, I think I could be brought to sit for half an hour in President Wilson's[2] pink parlor, and to breathe a pretty strong scent of religiosity even for a whole year. You remember what Socrates said to his son about Xanthippe's bad temper?[3] "If people used equally bad language at one another on the stage, would that disturb you? Then why should bad language, uttered without malice, disturb you in the real world?" The religious people merely use a bad language; what they mean, if they only knew what it was, would be all right.

I may be idealizing Princeton out of sheer ignorance, but I am going to see at least the outside of it very soon. They have asked me to read a paper to the Philosophical Association there on December 29 or 30. Will you be there then? I very much hope you may, and that you will show me the architectural and other wonders of the place.

My book is unfinished and will not be out until something like a year from now. I mean to stay in this country next summer until it goes to the printer. Internally, it is getting on well; being enriched and better ordered. Hoping to see you soon,

Yours sincerely

G.S.

¹William Rainey Harper (1856–1906) wrote several texts on Hebrew language and literature. In 1886 he went to Yale to teach Semitic languages, resigning in 1891 to become the first president of the University of Chicago.

²Thomas Woodrow Wilson (1856–1924) served as president of Princeton University from 1902 to 1910. In 1912 he was elected twenty-eighth president of the United States.

³Socrates (469–399 B.C.) was a Greek philosopher who dedicated himself to combating scepticism and arousing love of truth and virtue. The Socratic method was to question someone, then show skillfully the inadequacy of the answer by further questions, all guiding toward a sounder answer. Xanthippe was Socrates' wife; she had a shrewish nature.

To Frederick James Eugene Woodbridge
16 December 1903 • Cambridge, Massachusetts   (MS: Columbia)

---

60 Brattle Street

Cambridge Mass

Dec. 16. 1903

Dear Professor Woodbridge¹

I regret very much having missed your visit; the fact is my rooms here are hardly where I live, so that I am seldom in. I hope you did not make more than one attempt to find me.

The difficulty in writing a review of Schiller's book, which obliges me to say no to your flattering request, is not the lack of time. Schiller is a personal friend of mine, to whom I owe many kindnesses.² His book on the other hand is one which I thoroughly dislike, not on grounds of abstract opinion so much as on account of a general confusion and irresponsibility which I find there. It would be impossible for me to write anything about it that I could print, or to print anything that I could honestly write.

Please forgive my incapacity to help you. It is not laziness.

Yours very truly

GSantayana

¹Frederick James Eugene Woodbridge (1867–1940) was a Canadian-born philosopher who, like his colleague John Dewey, was a professor at Columbia (1902–37). His influence is responsible for the revival in the United States of Aristotelian trends of thought. A self-described realist and naturalist, he argued that life and mind are prod-

ucts that develop in the natural world. Woodbridge cofounded (with Wendell T. Bush) the *Journal of Philosophy, Psychology, and Scientific Methods* (later *The Journal of Philosophy*) in 1904.

[2]Ferdinand Canning Scott Schiller (1864–1937) was a British pragmatist philosopher who was influenced by James. But Schiller focused on the personal aspect of thinking and regarded knowledge as relatively subjective. Schiller felt the British school had forgotten the truth of Protagoras that man is the measure of all things. The book was *Humanism: Philosophical Essays* (1903). As a member of Corpus Christi College, Oxford, Schiller had invited Santayana to dinner several times at the High Table in the College Hall. Santayana described him as having the "airs of a professed and shameless sophist" and was mortified when Schiller requested that Santayana write a letter recommending him for the chair of logic at Oxford. See *Persons,* 506–7.

To Jessie Belle Rittenhouse
19 February 1904 • Cambridge, Massachusetts   (MS: Rollins)

60 Brattle Street
Cambridge
Feb. 19, 1904

Dear Miss Rittenhouse[1]

I will not conceal the fact that I feel some repugnance at having my photograph and quite uninteresting handwriting appear to attract attention to my modest verses. I am not an American and hardly a poet; may I not be eliminated from your gallery? I am sure I should not be missed.

My sonnets are out of print; my other volumes of verse you may be able to get by writing to Stone of Chicago and to Scribners, the respective publishers.

If you insist on including me in your survey, and can find my verses somewhere to base your remarks upon, I should of course not be able to deny you the same photograph which Archer obtained—and maltreated. But I pray you to reconsider your intention and to relegate me to the camp of the wingless philosophers, where I belong.

Yours truly
GSantayana

[1]Jessie Belle Rittenhouse (1869–1948) was an American poet and anthologist. A founder of the Poetry Society of America, she published several books, including *The Door of Dreams* (1918), *The Lifted Cup* (1921), and *The Moving Tide: New and Selected Lyrics* (1939). Santayana is included in Rittenhouse's *The Younger American Poets* (Boston: Little, Brown & Co., 1904), 94–109.

To Jessie Belle Rittenhouse
2 March 1904 • Cambridge, Massachusetts   (MS: Rollins)

60 Brattle Street
<u>March 2 1904</u>

Dear Miss Rittenhouse,

I enclose a photograph (after a drawing by the late Andreas Andersen, made in 1∅896) and two stanzas from my translation of <u>l'Art</u>.[1]

Publication is self-alienation and I have no moral right to impede any plans you may have to operate on the <u>corpus</u> <u>vile</u> of my poor Muse.

Yours truly
GSantayana

From <u>l'Art</u> by
Théophile Gautier.

… All things return to dust
Save beauties fashioned well.
        The bust
Outlasts the citadel … . .

Chisel and carve and file,
Till thy vague dream imprint
        Its smile
On the unyielding flint.

GSantayana

[1]These stanzas are the handwriting sample mentioned in the last letter.

To Frederick James Eugene Woodbridge

7 March 1904 • Cambridge, Massachusetts   (MS: Columbia)

> 60 Brattle Street
> Cambridge Mass
> March 7. 1904.

Dear Professor Woodbridge

I shall be glad to review Sneath's books.[1] I have read his "Mind of Tennyson" and have the book, so you need not send it if you can find any other use for it.

But I should be glad to see the "Philosophy of Poetry".

> Yours sincerely
> GSantayana

[1]Elias Hershey Sneath (1857–1935) wrote *Philosophy in Poetry: A Study of Sir John Davies' Poem Nosce Teipsum* (1903) and *The Mind of Tennyson: His Thoughts on God, Freedom, and Immortality* (London: Archibald Constable, 1900). Santayana's review appeared in *The Journal of Philosophy, Psychology, and Scientific Methods* 1 (14 Apr 1904): 216–17.

To Hugo Münsterberg

2 May 1904 • Cambridge, Massachusetts   (MS: Boston)

> 60 Brattle Street
> May 2 1904

Dear Münsterberg

Perhaps I had better mention that I <u>have</u> seen a copy of the correspondence in question. Not suspecting what was up or that Miller[1] had anything to do with it I happened to meet him in the Yard and asked him if he knew what the meeting was about. He then said he would like me to read the correspondence that had passed between you, and he left a copy of it in my room later, which I have read and returned to him.

Naturally I am exceedingly sorry that such asperities should have embittered Miller's last year with us, and that you, too, should have found yourself involved in such a disagreeable controversy.

Where there is not a deep identity in traditions and character it is always better, I have found, to avoid intricate relations and to maintain a perfect independence of action. Otherwise there is sure to spring up some misunderstanding and perhaps some grave offence. Miller is sensitive, he feels isolated and weak, and he is jealous of his freedom. He must have suffered very much and something ought to be forgiven him.

I am glad to think that this affair may now be considered closed.

Yours sincerely
GSantayana

[1]Dickinson Sargeant Miller (1868–1963) studied philosophy at Harvard (A.M., 1892) and earned a Ph.D. (1893) from Germany's Halle-Wittenberg University. He taught in the Harvard philosophy department from 1899 to 1904. Miller wrote under the name R. E. Hobart.

To Charles Scribner's Sons

25 May 1904 • Cambridge, Massachusetts   (MS: Princeton)

60 Brattle Street
Cambridge Mass
May 25 1904

Messrs Charles Scribner's Sons
New York.

Gentlemen:

I am sending you a first installment of my <u>magnum opus</u> "The Life of Reason".[1] There are four more Books, which will follow in a few weeks if you ∧are∧ favourably disposed towards the idea of publishing them. I send this part ahead, as I am anxious to have all arrangements for publication made before I leave this country, as I am to be away for fifteen months.

This book is not like my former ones, a mere incidental performance. It practically represents all I have to say of any consequence, so that I feel a special interest in having it done in a way that shall express its own character and suggest the spirit in which I would have it read. My ideas may seem to you wrong, and of course I shall not insist on them if they prove to be really unreasonable; but if objections to them rest only on financial considerations, I should be inclined to run the risk and insure you against loss in any way that seems to you suitable, provided the liability is not beyond my means.

What I desire is chiefly this: that the five books be bound separately, making five small volumes, so that they may be easily held and carried about, and may also, at least eventually, be sold separately as well as in sets. The remaining parts are on Society, Religion, Art, and Science respectively, and might well be independent books. A system runs through them all, but there is no formal continuity; or only such as might well exist between three plays in a trilogy. The page might well be like that in the "Sense of Beauty" (better than in the Interpretations) or even ₄smaller and₄ more closely set: I don't think large print really attractive: I hate a sprawling page. A compact page with a rather generous margin would be my ideal; and in this margin might be the running summary I have provided. This might ~~also~~ be ₄instead₄, if you thought it better, at the upper corner of each page, or in an indentation (as in the Sense of Beauty). But in whatever form it appears it is a very important feature, because it is meant not merely to help the eye and carry along the thought over the details, but often to be a commentary as well as a summary and throw a side light on the subject.

The binding might be in more than one form: I should be glad to have the book as cheap as possible so that students might buy it. Why are hardly any books sold in paper covers in this country? Boards surely are a respectable garment, and seem to suggest that the body is more than the raiment. I confess, however, that I don't know what difference in price would be involved in different sorts of binding, and I should be much interested if you would tell me.

Proof would have to be sent to me abroad; but there is no need of sending the MS with it, and the delay, once the operation has begun, is insignificant.

I shall probably not sail until the middle of July and shall be once or twice in New York in the interval, when I could easily call upon you.

Yours very truly
GSantayana

[1] *Common Sense.*

To Isabella Stewart Gardner

[June or July 1904?] • Cambridge, Massachusetts   (MS: Gardner)

---

60 <u>Brattle Street</u>

Dear Mrs Gardner

Do you remember that you told me to come to Green Hill[1] for a Sunday? I have not forgotten it, and if this Sunday or next will do I should be delighted, as they are the last I spend in these parts before sailing.

I have been off during the last two Sundays according to semi-engagements of long standing, else I should not have taken so long to remind you of your delightful commands.

My work is all done—thank Heaven—so that I have nothing to do but amuse myself for a while. By the way, if you have made arrangements for these Sundays already, I might perhaps come on some week-day   Yours sincerely

GSantayana

[1]Mrs. Gardner's farmhouse in Brookline, Massachusetts.

To Charles Scribner's Sons

19 June 1904 • Cambridge, Massachusetts   (MS: Princeton)

Cambridge Mass
<u>June 19, 1904</u>

Messrs Charles Scribner's Sons
New York

Gentlemen:

I am much pleased that you find the <u>Life of Reason</u> so promising that you will publish it on the ordinary terms; I had supposed that would hardly be possible, because it will take years, I expect, for the edition to be sold out. However, you are the best judges in such a matter, and I gladly accept your proposition to give me the ten per cent. royalty. I had no desire to intervene in the publication, and much prefer that you should undertake it yourselves, seeing you are disposed to do so.

As to publishing serially, that is of no consequence to me, and any arrangement you think best will suit me. Indeed, in one way, I find the suggestion very convenient, as the revision I am now at work on is taking longer than I expected–the book had grown up in seven years, so that it was full of repetitions and inconsistencies–and I need not send you all the MS at once. The next three books–Reason in Society, Religion, and Art– I will entrust to you before I go abroad; they will be ready, and safer in your keeping, and you can go on with the printing at such intervals as you think suitable. The last book–Reason in Science–I can send to you later, and as it is in many ways the most important it will perhaps do no harm to meditate a little longer on it before giving it a final shape.

I have tried to make the books nearly equal in length, but the attempt has been a failure: the matter could not be pressed, and I hardly wished to expand it. Book II, IV, and V, will be shorte$d$r than I, and III (Religion) a little longer. At least, I think so, although I am not good at counting words.

I think you have already my address for next year ^C/o Brown Shipley & Co, 123 Pall Mall, London. ~~This~~ That will be my address after July 15.

Yours very truly
GSantayana

To Jerome Davis Greene
20 June 1904 • Cambridge, Massachusetts   (MS: Houghton)

60 Brattle St
June 20 1904

Mr Jerome D Greene[1]
Cambridge

Dear Sir:

Will you kindly make my excuses to the President and tell him I am exceedingly sorry not to be able to help in welcoming the Filipinos. I leave this afternoon for Oberlin, where I am to give an address on Wednesday morning.[2]

Yours very truly
GSantayana

[1]Jerome Davis Greene (1874–1959), Harvard class of 1896, served as secretary to Harvard's president (1901–1905). Later he became an executive officer of the Rockefeller Foundation. In 1916 he helped establish the Institute for Government Research (Brookings Institute).

²Santayana gave the commencement address, "Tradition and Practice," at Oberlin College in Ohio. This address was published in *Oberlin Alumni Magazine* 1 (October 1904): 4–14.

To Charles Scribner's Sons
18 July 1904 • Cambridge, Massachusetts   (MS postcard: Princeton)

<u>Cambridge Mass</u>
<u>July 18. 1904</u>

I am sending you Books II and III and half of Book IV of the "Life of Reason".

The other half of Book IV will be ready shortly and I will send it to you from England.

GSantayana

Address ᶜ/o Brown Shipley & Co. 123 Pall Mall, London.

To Celedonio Sastre Serrano
25 July 1904 • Plymouth, England   (MS postcard: Sanchez)

NORDDEUTSCHER LLOYD
BREMEN.

Plymouth[1]
<u>25 de julio</u>

Llegamos esta mañana con toda felicidad despues de un viaje de seis dias desde Nueva York. Escribiré desde Lóndres.

Jorge

[1]Translation:
We arrived this morning with great satisfaction after a voyage of six days from New York. I will write from London.

To Susan Sturgis de Sastre

[August 1904] • Ostende, Belgium   (MS postcard: Sanchez)

L'ESTACADE. ENTRÉE DU PORT OSTENDE

Many thanks for your letter. I am on ~~in~~ my way to Holland with two
friends Saturday   G.

To Celedonio Sastre Serrano

20 August 1904 • [Cologne, Germany?]   (MS: Sastre Martín)

Colonia, 20 de Agosto de 1904.[1]

Sr D. Celedonio Sastre Serrano
Avila.

Querido Celedonio: en vista de que el plazo en que se debe llenar la
hoja para el registro fiscal de edificios y solares termina en pocos dias, y
que yo no puedo llegar á Avila á tiempo para llenarla en persona, te
agradecería muchísimo que la llenaras y firmaras en mi nombre, en todo
lo que corresponde á mi casa sita en la Plaza de Santa Ana en esa ciudad.
Tu hermano que te quiere
Jorge Ruiz de Santayana

[1]Translation:
  Dear Celedonio: since the time limit for filling out the form for the fiscal registra-
tion of buildings and ancestral dwellings ends in a few days, and I can't arrive in Avila
in time to fill it out in person, I would appreciate it very much if you would fill it out
and sign in my name, everything concerning my house in the Plaza de Santa Ana in
that city.
Your brother who loves you

To Celedonio Sastre Serrano

27 August 1904 • Heidelberg, Germany   (MS: Sastre Martín)

Heidelberg, Baden.
27 de Agosto de 1904[1]

Querido Celedonio: en este momento recibo tu carta que ha dado varios rodeos antes de llegar á mis manos. Te agradezco mucho el interés que manifiestas en el asunto de la casa, que efectivamente se tasó muy alta, considerando la renta que puede producir. Si hubiese recibido la hoja declarativa á tiempo, yo la hubiera firmado con gusto, más por evitar la molestia que has tenido en firmarla tu en mi nombre que por el beneficio que pueda resultar. Comprendo que por la forma desees tener autorizacion previa de mi parte para ello, aunque ya sabes que la tienes para todo lo que te parezca conveniente. Por eso la incluyo, aunque no sé si está bien redactada.

En pocos dias espero llegar á Paris, desde donde volveré á escribir anunciado mi salida en direccion de España. Aqui ha llovido sin cesar durante cuatro dias, pero sin embargo lo hemos pasado bien, visitando el castillo y la población y algunos puntos muy pintorescos de la montaña que está cubierta de bosques.

Me alegraria que me pusierais dos letras á Paris, al <u>Hôtel du Quai Voltaire</u>, diciendome si se os ofrece alguna cosa por esas partes.

Tu hermano que te quiere
Jorge

[1]Translation:

Dear Celedonio: I have just received your letter which went a roundabout way before arriving in my hands. I thank you very much for the interest that you show in the matter of the house, that effectively is appraised very high, considering the income it can produce. If I had received the declarative form in time, I would have signed it gladly, more to avoid the bother which you had in signing it for me than for the benefit that may result. I understand that for the sake of convention you may wish to have previous authorization from me for it, though you already know you have it for everything which seems suitable to you. Therefore I include it, although I don't know if it is well drawn up.

In a few days I hope to arrive in Paris, from where I will write again announcing my departure for Spain. Here it has rained for four days without stopping, but nevertheless we have lived well, visiting the castle and the village and some very picturesque points of the forest-covered mountain.

I would be glad if you should write me two letters to Paris, at <u>Hôtel du Quai Voltaire</u>, telling me what I can bring you from there.

Your brother who loves you

To Charles Scribner's Sons
9 September 1904 • Paris, France   (MS: Princeton)

Paris, Sept. 9. 1904

Messrs Charles Scribners' Sons
New York

Gentlemen:

The proof of the first volume of the Life of Reason (the first part having been delayed) reached me some days ago, and I am sorry not to have been able to despatch it before today. I have revised the whole and am sending it to you all together.

The only thing I might add is in answer to your question about page headings. If these are needed, I should have "The Life of Reason", on the left hand page throughout, and on the right the chapter-title, or an abbreviation of it, as for instance in Chapter XII, sometimes "Flux in human nature" and sometimes "Constancy in human nature".[1]

The print in which the occasional quotations of verse are printed seems to me much too heavy. The lines look like advertisements.

I have restored the u's in "honour" etc, partly because I prefer them and partly because, if this book appears also in England, the other spelling would shock people too much. They will receive shocks enough from the substance without adding others in the manner.

I should certainly like to see the page-proof, if sending it does not involve too great a delay.

Yours sincerely
GSantayana

[1]The recto running head was published as 'Flux and Constancy'.

To Lawrence Smith Butler
17 September 1904 • Ávila, Spain   (MS: University Club)

Novaliches, 6.
Address: Avila, Spain

Sept. 17, 1904

Dear Lawrence

It was a great disappointment not to see you in Paris. I asked for you several times, but the <u>concierge</u> had no news. When you arrive please drop me a line and tell me if there is any chance of your wishing to come to Spain while I am here. Come if you possibly can. I could meet you at Burgos and we could take a turn to the North-west and South, including Portugal, and you could return by Madrid while I went out by way of Gibraltar. Or we could make any other ~~place~~ ₍trip₎ that suited our respective plans. Mine are vague, except that I must get to Sicily, Egypt, and Greece during the year.

I expect to be here about a fortnight; after that it will be safer to address ^c/o Brown Shipley & Co, London.

Yours aff^{ty}
GSantayana

To Charles Scribner's Sons
24 September 1904 • Ávila, Spain   (MS: Princeton)

Avila, Sept. 24th 1904

Messrs Charles Scribner's Sons
New York

Gentlemen:

In case you do not find it convenient to send me the page-proof of the <u>Life of Reason</u>, vol. I, I want to recommend the title-page to your special care. There is an error in it, I think: my impression is that in the motto from Aristotle[1] I wrote ἡ γὰρ τοῦ νοῦ ἐνέργεια ζωή, whereas it should be ἡ γὰρ νοῦ (without τοῦ), as in the title-pages to the other volumes.

I presume you have received the MS to Books II, III, and the first part of IV. Doubtless you acknowledged the receipt of them at the time, but the person in America who has charge of forwarding my letters probably didn't think that receipt material, and didn't send it on. I should like to be sure, however, that the M.S. arrived safely. I am employing what moments I can snatch from idleness to copy the rest of the M.S.

Yours very truly
GSantayana

Address:
^C/o Brown Shipley & Co.
   123 Pall Mall,
      London.

[1]For the activity of mind is life.

To Charles Scribner's Sons

21 October 1904 • Ávila, Spain   (MS: Princeton)

Avila, October 21, 1904

Messrs Charles Scribner's Sons
New York

Gentlemen:

The page proof of Book I of the <u>Life of Reason</u> I sent you from here some time ago; the galley-proof of Book II follows today, and I enclose the pages needed to supply a lost passage, and also another addition which it seemed well to make.

I can well understand that the delay in sending me ₍ₐ₎page-₍ₐ₎proof so far away is annoying, and if you think it safe, I am willing you should not do so. The page headings could in most cases be the exact title of the chapter. In chapter III called Industry, Government, and War, perhaps the title "Government" would serve the purpose.[1] Nevertheless, I should much rather see the page-proof, as that of volume I certainly needed further revision.

It occurs to me that you may intend to present me with some copies, as you have generously done on former occasions. As at present, however, I am on the wing, one copy is all that I should be able to take with me. If you will send me that, I shall be much obliged; and also if you will send copies to the addresses in the enclosed list.

I return a signed copy of the agreement[2] and remain

Yours very truly

GSantayana

P.S. Covers like that of the <u>Sense of Beauty</u> would be good, ₍ₐ₎unless some other dark colour fades less.₍ₐ₎ On the back there will hardly be room for everything. You might leave out, for one thing, my Christian name; and besides "The Life of Reason" it might suffice to have either "Common

Sense" or "Book I." I think it would be better, for the sale especially, if the titles of the Books—"Society", "Religion", "Art", etc, appeared on the back, together with a numeral to indicate the volume. If it is not too crowded, I should like the following lettering,

SANTAYANA

THE LIFE
OF REASON

I
REASON IN
COMMON
SENSE

SCRIBNERS[3]

[1]The running head of chapter III of *Society* reads: Industry, Government, and War.
[2]The pages, list, and agreement are unlocated.
[3]Santayana sketched the proposed spine of the volume. The publisher slightly altered this design.

To Goldsworthy Lowes Dickinson
22 November 1904 • Florence, Italy   (MS: King's)

Nov. 22. 1904

I TATTI,[1]
SETTIGNANO,
FLORENCE.

Dear Dickinson

I have been spending a few days here, at the Berensons', and leave today for Rome, where I shall be perhaps a fortnight at the Hôtel de Russie—with Loeser, who goes with me there. Are you by chance coming to Italy for Christmas and is there any likelihood that you should go to Greece in the Spring? I hope to be there then and should so much like to come across you in these regions, more congenial to the inner man than those in which we last met.

If Wedd is planning any such excursions, please ask him to let me know of it. My address is ᶜ/o Brown Shipley & Co, London.

Yours ever

GSantayana

P.S. I have been reading Moore's Principia Ethica[2] which I had not seen until I reached this house. I should more heartily agree with his logic if it were backed by some sense of the conditions in which it operates, some knowledge of human nature. His points ~~only~~ become cogent ₐonlyₐ when the speaker forgets himself and makes his assertions irresponsibly forthright and categorical. So taken—as ready-made accidental judgments—they may well be what Moore says they are in respect to their form. Their substance, however, needs to be transformed by experience and culture. How little <u>wisdom</u> these metaphysicians have, and how punctiform and scholastic their vision of things is apt to become when they live in colleges or dwell in an atmosphere of technical controversy. In its rather insignificant sphere, however, I agree with Moore's doctrine. Good is a unique predicate, quite distinct in meaning from pleasant, etc; but its application is intelligible, and what things are good can be decided only by asking what things make a difference to somebody. The inanimate "beautiful" universe Moore speaks of can be good only because it meets a <u>given</u> sense for harmony.

[1]Bernard and Mary Berenson's villa.

[2]George Edward Moore (1873–1958). Moore was a proponent of common sense who wrote *Principia Ethica* (1903). He began editing *Mind* in 1921 and was elected to a professorship of philosophy at Cambridge University in 1925. After his retirement from that post in 1939, he visited the United States, serving as visiting professor at various colleges and universities, including Smith, Princeton, and Columbia.

To Charles Scribner's Sons

22 November 1904 • Florence, Italy   (MS: Princeton)

Nov. 22. 1904

I TATTI,
SETTIGNANO,
FLORENCE.

Messrs Charles Scribner's Sons
New York

Gentlemen:

Please add to the list of addresses to which I have asked you to send copies of <u>The Life of Reason</u> the three following:

Dr Frederick Winslow
 29 Commonwealth Ave
  Boston Mass
Dr D. S. Miller
 University of Pennsylvania
  Philadelphia. Pa.
Dr R. B. Perry[1]
 Harvard College, Cambridge Mass

Yours very truly
GSantayana

[1]Ralph Barton Perry (1876–1957) was an American realist philosopher. He attended Princeton University (B.A., 1896) and received his M.A. (1897) and Ph.D. (1899) from Harvard. He briefly taught at Williams College and Smith College, and from 1902 to 1946 at Harvard, where, after 1930, he was the Edgar Pierce Professor of Philosophy. He was Hyde Lecturer at various French universities during 1921–22.

Susan Sturgis de Sastre

23 November [1904] • Rome, Italy   (MS postcard: Sanchez)

ROMA—S. PIETRO VEDUTO DAL PINCIO

Nov. 23.

Thanks for your letter. Loeser came on with me here last night. We are <u>en pension</u> at the Hôtel de Russie for a fortnight.

[*Unsigned*]

To Mary Whitall Smith Berenson
25 November 1904 • Rome, Italy

(MS: I Tatti)

<u>Hôtel de Russie</u>
<u>Rome, November 25, 1904.</u>[1]

The Loeserisms of Loeser the Son of Loeser (may prayer and peace be upon him!).

Know, O Lady[2] among all ladies, that Allah, the compassionate, the bountiful, had written our safe arrival at this City of the Devil, the seat of two quarrelling kings,[3] enemies to each other and to all the faithful. One is a dwarf, with an angry beard on his upper lip, who with difficulty was persuaded to abandon the impure condition of a bachelor, and now entertains his wife by reading to her books on the base and uncivil art of gunnery. How different from the generous husbands of Islam! The other king is an old man, living shut up in his palace, plotting with his grand vizier, Merridelvallah, how to circumvent his enemies and recover his lost territories; but the curse of God is upon him, and having vowed himself and his thousands of eunuchs and ten thousands of slave-girls to a hideous celibacy, he spends his days and nights adoring painted idols; and not being satisfied with those belonging to his own unholy religion, he has collected and preserved in his courts all the abominations worshipped of old by the heathen, even to the least remaining fragment of their false gods; which may Allah grind quickly into dust!

Having arrived at the city gates ~~and~~ ^we^ alighted from our litters, and Loeser lifted up his voice and said that we wished to walk to our kahn.[4] I enquired of him if he knew the way, and what might be the distance, for I saw that it had rained mightily and that the mud and the pools of water were deep. And he answered, By my Michael Angelos[5] but I do, and it is scarce seven parasangs.[6] Thereupon we proceeded on foot, going into the bye-lanes to view by the darkness the bungling and ponderous ornaments with which the unbelievers decorate the outside of their houses, as of their souls, leaving no joy within.[7] And we wandered long and far, not seeing ɸaught for the darkness save the glimmer of lamps, reflected from every wet stone, so that the stars which had deserted the heavens seemed to have come down to be trampled under foot and to pave this city. And Loeser spoke again, saying that the Kahn was the famous resort Russian Grand

Dukes and was unknown to Americans; but on arrival I heard the accent, from a thousand noses, which I have long heard beyond the sea, and I could not refrain from reciting the following verses:

The waves of the sea are many but their voice is ~~but~~ ∧as∧ one voice.

Men traverse them from West to East to find what they have left behind them. O my![7]

On the following day Loeser set out to visit the Souk and examine the Rome of the Quattrocento;[8] but when we opened our eyes, Íbehold, we had gone to see the statue of Garibaldi upon the Janiculum.[9]

Turning homewards wearily he declared that he would show me the fashionable tea-rooms where all the houris of paradise were assembled:[10] and the rooms were indeed pink, but the waiting-maid was the only living thing within them.

In a slum we passed a cobbler's shop where Loeser had once bought a pair of shoe-strings, and he lifted up his voice and said: This is the famous shop where every body buys shoe-strings. Amen.

As the houris of paradise had absented themselves from the tea-shop, Loeser said we should like to go the next day to the famous bar of the Grand Hôtel, where all the great diplomats, literateurs, artists, and scholars of the four nations were gathered together. When we reached the door, it was locked, and I trembled to think what secret conclave might be convened within, hatching great affairs. But Loeser undismayed knocked once, and twice; and at the third knocking ~~and~~ an old man in a white cap and apron opened the door. There was paper on the walls, and when we had sat down and been silent for an hour the old man brought us some cold black coffee. Presently a step was heard sounding through the empty corridor and a young man appeared, dressed as the stable-boys of unbelievers dress when they walk abroad on their private business, casting aside the robe of office; and Loeser stretched forth his hand and cried Tommy! Tommy, he said, was the famous bar-tender of the Grand Hôtel. And he inquired of Tommy where were all the diplomats and sages and poets; and Tommy said they ~~were~~ ∧met∧ now at the Cosmopolis, or, as the vulgar call it, the barber's shop.

All that.

But what further adventures Allah may have written for us I forbear to prophesy with rashness, ~~but~~ ∧and∧ seeing that the hour for luncheon has arrived, discretely, as is my wont, I am silent.

G.S.

[1]Santayana reread *A Thousand and One Nights* during a visit to the Berensons. In this letter Santayana imitates the style of this book in describing his first trip to Rome. See *Persons*, 218–19, 462.

[2]Mary Whitall Smith Berenson (1865–1945), sister to Logan Pearsall Smith, lived with Bernard Berenson for ten years before their marriage in 1900.

[3]King Victor Emmanuel III of Italy and Pope Pius X. The pope finally relinquished sovereignty over all Rome but the Vatican City in 1929.

[4]Their hotel.

[5]Santayana was skeptical of Loeser's claim that he owned original works of Michelangelo Buonarotti. See *Persons*, 218.

[6]Ancient Persian measurement in which one parasang equals about three and a half miles.

[7]"[B]ut I doubt that the first loud accents that I heard on arriving at the Hotel were those of a Russian Grand Duchess. She said simply: 'Oh my!'" (*Persons*, 219)

[8]A souk is a marketplace in the Muslim East. Literally, quattrocento means four hundred but is short for fourteen hundred (the fifteenth century).

[9]Giuseppe Garibaldi (1807–82) was an Italian patriot. On his statue on the Janiculum (a ridge running north and south, which was fortified in early times) overlooking Rome is engraved his famous cry *Roma o Morte* (Rome or Death).

[10]A houri is one of the dark-eyed virgins of perfect beauty that in Muslim belief live with the blessed in paradise.

To William James
29 November 1904 • Rome, Italy   (MS: Houghton)

Rome, Nov. 29, 1904

Dear Mr James

Thank you very much for your two articles[1] which have reached me here and filled an evening with very refreshing home-thoughts after the merciless biograph of mere phenomena which one gets in travelling. I am here with my old class-mate Loeser, whom you will remember, and who wishes me to send you his love. He has an eighteenth century statuette of Locke with he wishes to present to you, but neither he nor I are quite clear about the possibility of sending it free through the custom house. I tell you of it so that you may mentally give him credit for his good intentions in case the object itself should never reach you.

Since I left America I have had glimpses of England, Belgium, Holland, ₐGermanyₐ and France, beside six weeks with my sister in Avila and almost a month in Florence with the advantage of being near Loeser and Berenson. I am profoundly out of humour with "aesthetics", yet I have been feeling the new <u>douche</u>[2] of it which these friends of mine have drenched me with as a rather invigorating change; one gets so dry in America with no food for the senses, especially if one is obliged to pump up theory every day. From here I mean to go on to Naples and Sicily, Egypt and Greece—all new ground for me; and I hope to return in the autumn a new man, with a fresh supply of "pure experience" and a budding crop of new ideas.

Your articles—apart from ~~there~~ their intrinsic importance—have interested me particularly on account of a certain harmony which there is between what you make for and what I have fallen into myself. Doubtless you have from of old let seeds fall into my mind which have sprouted there into what I feel to be quite native convictions; and it comes to me now as a rather surprising happiness that I can invoke your authority in support of a great deal that I feared might seem rash in my opinions. It is the general attitude which Bergson[3] also encourages, although of course it may be turned in various ways and expressed in various vocabularies. What I don't quite understand in your way of stating the matter is whether the conceptual world has <u>only</u> its immediate status. Of course every conception, taken existentially, is a part of the flux, which as you say is largely chaotic in its immediacy; but things and truths have also a systematic and more or less static dimension. For instance, if a candle which was nine inches long when left burning in an empty room is found to be six inches long on the observer's return, was it ever really eight inches in length? Of course the eight-inch candle will ~~have~~ ∧draw∧ a potential sort of being ~~in~~ ∧from∧ the philosopher's views, themselves immediate experiences of his; the <u>conception</u> that the ∧candle∧ passed through that phase will be an absolute item in the universal inventory. But the question seems to me to be whether the eight-inch candle has <u>only</u> that imputed being; or rather whether imputed being is not what we mean by reality and the immediate flux itself by appearance. The forthright intellect seems to be the life of the mind, and what it rests in seems to be alone important, true, or efficacious. The eight-inch candle is something to be believed in, because in the material world which the intellect has discovered it is a needful element that counts and rewards our confidence in its reality. The materials which experience is composed of must therefore be credited with an existence which makes them material elements and gives them a mechanical order, since they exist <u>also</u> permanently, potentially, and beyond our range.

If this is what is implied in your views—and I conceive that it is—the result seems to be quite different from panpsychism[4] and far more rationalistic. According to panpsychism the eight-inch candle exists only by virtue of its inconceivable psychic substance, that mass of irrelevant experience of which a candle at best is but a remote symbol or effect. The real eight-inch candle is not eight inches long and is no candle at all. It is perhaps a conclave of politic worms electing an infallible pope to maintain that the universe is nothing but a musical composition. According to your view—if I understand it—and to mine, on the contrary, the material qualities of the candle themselves subsist, and it is a cylindrical white body that is really eight inches long at an assignable instant. The world of science, for us, then, would not be a mere fiction, but a real efficacious order discovered in the chaos of immediate experience, ₐa systemₐ consisting bodily of the given elements, but of course involving many more, and the longer subsistence of them. Am I right?

Please wish the various members of the department a happy new year in my name and believe me

Very sincerely yours
GSantayana

Address:
^C/o Brown Shipley & Co
   London

¹"Does Consciousness Exist?" and "A World of Pure Experience" were published in 1904 in *The Journal of Philosophy, Psychology, and Scientific Method.*
²Gush.
³Henri Bergson (1859–1941) was a French philosopher who taught at the Collège de France. His philosophy is complex, but the basic premise of his intellectual system is a faith in direct intuition as a means of attaining knowledge.
⁴Panpsychism is the theory according to which all objects in the universe, not only human beings and animals but also plants and even objects usually classified as inanimate, have an inner or psychological being.

To Benjamin Apthorp Gould Fuller
3 December 1904 • Rome, Italy   (MS: Houghton)

Rome. Dec 3. 1904

Dear Fuller

Your letter comes to remind me that a place I have often heard of called Harvard College actually exists: it seems from here a rather improbable myth; and quite an unnecessary complication in the world, that has a complete history already. I am glad that you take to your native country so well; I wonder why in a land where so much is potential the potential has not been allowed any place in philosophy, whereas an Aristotle, who lived in a finished world, made so much of the potential in his speculation. This is a sign, I suppose, that speculation is seldom a genuine expression of life, but rather a parasitic tradition expressing what is effete in the contemporary world.

Have you read Moore's principia ethica? The book seems to contain a grain of accuracy in a bushel of inexperience.

James has sent me two of his new articles from the Columbia Journal.[1] The one (or more) in Mind I have not yet seen. Dickinson writes to me from Cambridge. "I love W. James as a man. But what a singularly bad thinker he is!"

James' new statements do not seem to me to be bad insight, whatever may be thought of the logic of them. They point to materialism, which I believe may be destined before long to have a great rehabilitation. The material world is a fiction; but every other world is a nightmare.

Please wish Mrs Burnett[2] a merry Christmas. I am delighted that you have kept my rooms, as your brother's youthful energies might have been too much for it them. By the way, will you do me a favour, and in an idle moment cut off judiciously a bit of the red silk over my bed and send it to <u>Charles Loeser, 11 via Lamberttesca, Florence</u>? Loeser has promised to get me some more stuff of the same shade, to make a bed coverlet of, so that my dreams may be as genteel and sumptuous as possible.

I am enjoying myself hugely and reading a good deal more than usual. Friends of mine turn up at regular intervals, and the sun shines, and humanity smiles about me almost without hypocrisy. I feel at home.

Yours sincerely   G.S.

---

[1]*The Journal of Philosophy, Psychology, and Scientific Methods* (New York), issued fortnightly, was founded in 1904 by F. J. E. Woodbridge and W. T. Bush. In 1921 the name was changed to *The Journal of Philosophy*.

[2]Landlady at 60 Brattle Street, Cambridge, Massachusetts. [D. C.]

To Charles Scribner's Sons
3 December 1904 • Rome, Italy   (MS: Princeton)

Rome, Dec. 3. 1904.
Address: ^C/o Brown Shipley & Co
London.

Messrs Charles Scribner's Sons
New York:

Gentlemen:

Today I have sent you the second proof of <u>vol. II.</u> of the "Life of Reason", with the title page to <u>vol I</u>, ~~with~~ in which I see nothing to change except perhaps the date. As you do not inclose the title page or table of contents for <u>vol. II.</u> I am not sure whether you mean to bring it out at once. If so, please note that, owing to some pages being lost and a passage inserted, the M.S. table of contents for <u>vol. II.</u> does not exactly correspond to the marginal summary as it now stands. It should be made to do so.

I am much obliged to you for sending me the page-proof. There were certain words in it which I am glad to have had a chance to revise, beside a few—very few—printer's errors still remaining.

I am going to Sicily and Egypt this winter, so that if you mean to go on with <u>vol. III</u> at all soon, you had better count on a certain further delay in getting the proofs back from me.

Yours very truly
GSantayana

Please send copies of the <u>Life of Reason</u>, with the author's compliments, to the following:

Professor C. A. Strong,	Lakewood,	New Jersey.
" Norton,	Shady Hill	
" James,	95 Irving St	
" Royce	105 " "	
" Münsterberg	7 Ware St	
" & Mrs. Toy	7 Lowell St	Cambridge, Mass.
" Palmer	11 Quincy St	
Harvard Union Library	Quincy St	
Signet Society	Dunster St	
Delta Phi Club	9 Linden St	
A. G. Fuller, Esq	60 Brattle St	

Francis Bullard, Esq	3 Commonwealth Ave	
B. A. Beal, Esq.	108 Beacon St.	Boston, Mass
Mrs J. C. Gray	196 " "	
Mrs J. B. de Santayana[1]	75 Monmouth St	Brookline, Mass
Mr. Justice Holmes[2]	Washington, D.C.	

Mr. & Mrs R. Burnside Potter,   60 Fifth Ave.[3]   New York.
Earl Russell   Chichester
Hon. Bertrand Russell   Haslemere
Howard Sturgis Esq   Queen's Acre,   Windsor.
T. D. Roberts Esq[4]   Christ Church,   Oxford.   England
G. L. Dickinson Esq King's College,   Cambridge
King's College Library   Cambridge
Charles Loeser, Esq.   Via Lambertesca 11,   Florence   Italy.
Bernard Berenson, Esq. Settignano   Florence
Baron Albert von Westenholz[5]   Hamburg, 17,   Germany.

[1]His mother, Josefina Borrás de Santayana.
[2]Oliver Wendell Holmes (1841–1935), Harvard class of 1861, was appointed to the U.S. Supreme Court by President Theodore Roosevelt. He served there from 1902 until his death. He was a true liberal and greatly influenced many of the foremost lawyers and jurists.
[3]The correct address of Potter's architectural office was 160 Fifth Avenue.
[4]Thornton Delano Roberts, a member of Harvard's class of 1903.
[5]Santayana said Albert W. von Westenholz was "one of my truest friends. Personal affection and intellectual sympathies were better balanced and fused between him and me than between me and any other person." (*Persons*, 261–65) Santayana met the German aristocrat at Harvard, where Westenholz was a student, in the early 1900s.

To Mary Whitall Smith Berenson

8 December 1904 • Rome, Italy   (MS: Indiana)

Rome, Dec. 8, 1904.

Dear Mrs Berenson

I must thank you at last for sending me my washing which arrived safely I don't know how long ago. I was putting off writing *I* until I had accumulated a fresh lot of Loeserisms, but they have been flowing slowly of late, except that he has been threatening to leave me for the last week and now Mrs Baldwin[1] has arrived nobody knows what will happen.

I have put off going to Sicily until the spring and expect to sail for Port Said from Naples on December 28.

Settignano and all that belongs to it remain a bright spot in my memory.   Yours sincerely
                                        GSantayana

¹Unidentified.

To Charles Scribner's Sons
8 December 1904 • Rome, Italy   (MS: Princeton)

GRAND HÔTEL DE RUSSIE
ET DES ILES BRITANNIQUES
H. SILENZI
ROME

ROME, LE 8 décembre 1904

Messrs Charles Scribner's Sons
New York

Gentlemen:
    Please add to the list of names of persons to whom the "Life of Reason"
is to be sent (with my compliments) that of
W. Bayard Cutting Esq
    Nordhoff, California
                        Yours very truly
                        GSantayana

To Mary Whitall Smith Berenson
10 December 1904 • Rome, Italy   (MS: I Tatti)

Rome, Dec. 10. 1904¹

    The Wisdom of Loeser-ben-Loeser, Light of the Five Nations, and other
delectable fictions.

    Know, Thou Mistress of all the Arts, that once upon a time there lived
in a far country a poor philosopher, who had wasted his youth without the
delights of love and without receiving courteous entertainment from
princes or hearing the pleasant voices of poets. But it came to pass that the
fame of Loeser-ben-Loeser reached his ears and he said in his heart: Go

to: I will take ship and sail to that land of ancient poets and princes where Loeser-ben-Loeser abides, and he shall instruct my soul.

So the philosopher sold all his possessions and, putting a thousand dinars[2] of gold in his pouch, travelled by land and sea to the city of Loeser-ben-Loeser,[3] where, as no man knew his name, he was called l'Amico di Carlo.[4]

And when Loeser-ben-Loeser saw him approach, he welcomed him and taking him by the hand led to the divan beside him; and he bade Giuseppe, his grand-vizier, command the female slaves to make ready the banquet and to summon the Lady Chamier, whose hat was like the full moon, to discourse before them.

And when the feast was ended Loeser-ben-Loeser said: Know that there is in this city an old woman who lives in a tower: go and seek after her and when you have found her she will open the door unto you and lead you to her uppermost chamber. And there she will spread a small hard couch for you and set before you a small jug of cold water. And this she will not abstain from doing daily while you tarry with her; for that shall be your lodging.[5] And when you depart hence, you will reward her with a cast-off robe of honour and thirty shekels[6] of paper; and then her children shall wash their faces and her large white cat shall wear a string of pearls around its neck. And all things came to pass even as Loeser-ben-Loeser had said, so that l'Amico di Carlo marvelled greatly at his foresight and wisdom.

But when now l'Amico was about to depart Loeser-ben-Loeser said: I may not suffer you to go hence unattended. So he ordered his grand vizier to make ready a caravan, with bales of precious stuffs, morning shirts and evening shirts, and precious turbans, and abundance of shoes, and trousers in boxes of cedar, and bottles of divers unguents, and phials of perfume, and many gems of price. And having prudently provided all these things for his own use, he set forth in company with his friend, to do him honour; and when he was come to the City of Rome, the slaves and maid-servants at the kahn perceived that he was a wise man, having a knitted forehead and ten camels-loads of baggage.[7]

And when they had rested from their journey and spent fourteen days in continuous eating and drinking, and in seeing the sights of that city, Loeser-ben-Loeser bethought him to return to his own house: but there was a great feast in that city, to celebrate the fiftieth anniversary of a new title bestowed on a female deity, and many strangers gathered there to enjoy the occasion; and among these was a lady of four times fourteen years of age, beautiful as the moon in its last quarter; and she sent her eunuch to Loeser-ben-Loeser, who, after thrice kissing the earth between his hands, said: The lady Baldonina is here, and bids you follow me and feast with her this day. And Loeser-ben-Loeser hearing these words was marvellously delighted; and he arose straightway and followed the eunuch, leaving the ten camel-loads of luggage in the porter's hands. And he returned not until evening was fallen, when l'Amico beheld him approach with a quick step, and ~~his~~ with his robe of water-proof open and flying behind him: and he said: Behold the lady Baldonina and her daughter, like two full moons, are coming this night to sup with us at this kahn. Therefore wash your face and put on your robe of honour, while I hasten to command a special banqueting chamber to be made ready, with all manner of viands and sweetmeats and sherbets, together with copious cooled bottles of the strong drink of the Franks.[8] And the philosopher went quickly to his bath, but was not yet out of the barber's hands, not having donned his robe of honour—nor any other—when Loeser-ben-Loeser reappeared in greater haste than before. Behold the Lady Baldonina's eunuch was even now here; and he says that the Lady Baldonina's daughter is marvellous distempered and has locked herself in her own Chamber. And they come not to feast with us this night. But I commanded the ~~eunch~~ eunuch to kiss the ground between the Lady Baldonina's feet and to say: Loeser-ben-Loeser and his companion come this night in a golden palanquin[9] to bear the Lady Baldonina about the city, that she may view the illuminations and delight them with her beauty and the shafts of her keen wit, either of which would extinguish all the lights which the unbelievers can kindle before their idols. So make haste that we snatch a morsel—for the feast is countermanded, all but one cooled bottle of the strong drink of the Franks, to give us courage.

Hearing these words L'Amico was not wholly displeased; for having risen that morning before the sun, to miss no part of the festivities, he was remarkably hungry and thirsty, and not averse to being borne in a golden palanquin, rather than to walk longer upon his feet.

But Loeser-ben-Loeser was thinking of the Lady Baldonina, and relished not his soup: and of the fish he said it was ~~noisesome~~ noisome to leave the carcase upon a salver before one, and had it carried away, though perhaps l'Amico would liked a second help. And when a filet of beef appeared with peas and potatoes, Loeser-ben-Loeser was about to spirit it away, waving to the slave to remove it: but l'Amico hastened to protest that even beef and peas and potatoes might on occasion be excellent; and then Loeser-ben-Loeser himself took three slices. But he said that to do so was not good: for it was not the strong drink of the Franks that went to one's head, but the solid food one had with it. Wherein the science of Loeser-ben-Loeser doth well appear, and remaineth a guide to all succeeding bibulous men. And a letter from the chief architect that was building Loeser-ben-Loeser's summer palace having at that moment arrived, in which it was expressly declared that the walls, without being rebuilt, would not support the quattrocento arches designed for the stairs, he who is the light of the five nations said that the vegetable then before him was most indigestible, and informed the attendant that he and his friend had no appetite for the roast and salad.

They therefore went at once into the street, where, as no golden palanquin was in attendance, Loeser-ben-Loeser said they would proceed in a more ordinary conveyance to the Lady's door, and there take one of the golden palanquins that would be in waiting. And as only one vehicle with one horse, with knees bent almost in the attitude of prayer, was then visible, they took this, and reached the kahn where the Lady was lodged. She bade them welcome, and disappeared to don the veils that, to vulgar eyes, were to conceal her charms, and to ~~our~~ ₐotherₐ eyes her wrinkles. They waited some brief hours, lost in meditation; and when she reappeared she was leading by the hand her younger daughter, like a crescent moon, but large enough to fill a place in a golden palanquin. And Loeser-ben-Loeser said: βWe shall now be conveyed to the top of the Piazza stairs; and thence we will proceed on foot to view the celebrations. And the Lady Baldonina murmured that she had on satin slippers, and that it had rained all day. But Loeser-ben-Loeser had superior wisdom. He had with incredible foresight refused to dismiss the slave that had brought him and his friend thither: for seeing that no golden palanquins were to be seen anywhere, he foresaw that even that humble conveyance would please the Lady, who would, he knew, have satin slippers on her feet–a benediction to all true believers. So he and his friend, the lady and her daughter, compressed themselves as best they could, and, clinging to one another, reached their destination.

Here Loeser-ben-Loeser magnanimousₐlyₐ Í released the one-horse slave, giving him honourable payment; and though, owing to the lateness of the hour, the illuminations were for the most part extinguished, they all proceeded to pace the public streets and squares. But when Loeser, vaunting the charms of popular life, said they should walk the whole length of the Corso, the lady Baldonina, consenting as it seemed, nevertheless of her own motion cried "Cocher",[10] arresting a passing cab. And the four again placed themselves, like four roses in one bowl, within that merchantable conveyance, the Lady prudently admonishing her daughter and saying "Prends le bras de M. Loeser pour ne pas tomber."[11]

But Loeser-ben-Loeser directing the hired slave cried in a loud voice—go to the Piazza di Spagna. And the slave answered: I kiss the earth before my master, but we are at this moment in no other place. ~~Kow~~ Knowest thou not, said the wise man, wroth not without cause, that Spain and Venice are the same thing, and that when I say one I necessarily mean the other!

But when they had reached ~~this~~ their destination, as there was nothing in particular to do there, they directed the slave to return to the Lady's kahn. This time Loeser-ben-Loeser—may his prudence never forsake him—did not forget to dismiss the varlet; for he bade the porter pay him three lire. And when, having bidden the ladies farewell, he was departing on foot to his own hostel, l'Amico suggested that the three lire had not been restored to the porter, who would subtract them, doubtless, from the lady's treasury. That, cried the wise one, he would do in any case. So let it be. Thus the Lady Baldonina profited (without knowing it) by not having a golden palanquin ∧on∧ that day.

[*Unsigned*]

[1]This is a sequel to his 25 Nov 1904 letter.
[2]An ancient gold coin used in some Muslim countries.
[3]Loeser was living in Florence near the Uffizi Palace. Santayana mistakenly gave the year of this 1904 visit to Loeser as 1905 in *Persons* (219).
[4]The Friend of Charles.
[5]"My room was indeed in a tower; there were 149 stone steps with hardly a door to pass on the way up: my choice room did have a bed in it, but the loggia was bitterly cold in those sunless mornings. This didn't matter, however, since there was no breakfast. My woebegone landlady had no idea of coffee, milk, or rolls, and her tea, in an open broken old dish, was half dust." (*Persons*, 219)
[6]An ancient unit of weight equal to about half an ounce.
[7]In London Loeser "lived in the Burlington Hotel, behind the Arcade, amid a great lot of leather portmanteaux and hat-boxes." (*Persons*, 218)
[8]The Franks were a group of Germanic tribes which settled along the Rhine and later moved into Gaul. After 870 the kingdom of the West Franks became France; that of the East Franks became Germany.
[9]An enclosed litter or sedan chair.
[10]Driver.
[11]Take Mr. Loeser's arm so as not to fall.

To Celedonio Sastre Serrano

1 January 1905 • Port Said, Egypt   (MS postcard: Sanchez)

PORT-SAID. PANORAMA.

1 de enero 1905[1]

Esta mañana hemos llegado á Puerto Said sin novedad. La travesía desde Nápoles ha durado tres dias. Salgo en este momento para el Cairo.   Jorge

[1]Translation:
This morning we have arrived in Port Said without incident. The crossing from Naples has taken three days. I leave right now for Cairo.

To James Hazen Hyde

5 January 1905 • Cairo, Egypt   (MS: Unknown)

C/o Brown Shipley & Co.,
   London.

Cairo, Jan. 5th 1905.

Dear Hyde:—[1]
   When I got your telegram, forwarded to me by post to Naples, I hardly knew what your proposal involved and although naturally much flattered at receiving it, I thought it well to wait for your letter, which would give me more particulars.
   This has just reached me. If the lectures had been only eight, like those given at Cambridge, it struck me at once that I might find a suitable and interesting subject—Philosophy in America. Now that I know the formidable nature of the business it is harder for me to find a subject. Nevertheless, it is too glorious and congenial an opportunity to miss, and I accept your proposal gladly, trusting as I think it over that the right subject and method of treatment may occur to me. As you can imagine, I labor under a personal disadvantage in this matter in that I am not an American, and yet shall be expected to represent, in a sense, American ways of seeing things. It will of course be impossible for me to disguise a certain external or foreign quality in my treatment of things Anglo-Saxon, and this foreignness, while it may make what I say more easily intelligible to French people, will doubtless prevent me from arousing any such warm interest as I understand Wendell has aroused. In other words, you must

not expect me to be a popular success: but I will try to appeal to that unenthusiastic faculty, the intellect, of which the French have so much, and I may perhaps interest a smaller number of people more deeply.

"Philosophy" and "Aesthetics", which you suggest, are subjects much too large and universal. What would you think of "English Poetry", or, to borrow a title of President Eliot's "English Contributions to Civilisation", in which I should of course include the American, and should be thinking largely of moral habits and characteristic types of English thought, ending, perhaps, with a lecture on William James!

"Contemporary Philosophy in England and America" might be a better way of announcing the same general topic.

It is a very fine impulse in you that prompts these innovations, and a somewhat cosmopolitan person like me may perhaps appreciate even more than others the need there is of better mutual understanding among men, now that religion and distance may be said to no longer divide them. How glad I would be if someone would explain these Arabs to me, but nobody can, least of all they themselves.

You may then count on me for your project, and believe me,

Sincerely yours,

GSantayana

[1]James Hazen Hyde (1876–1959), Harvard class of 1898, whom Santayana refers to in *Persons* as "Caleb" Hyde, was president of Le Cercle Français during his undergraduate days. Hyde established the exchange professorship between Harvard and the Sorbonne of which Barrett Wendell was the first appointed in 1904–5 to lecture in English at Paris, and Santayana the second, in 1905–6. (See *Harvard*, 375 and 432, and *Persons*, 411–12.)

To Benjamin Apthorp Gould Fuller

11 January [1905] • Luxor, Egypt   (MS: Houghton)

ANGLO-AMERICAN NILE STEAMER & HOTEL COMPANY,
CHIEF OFFICE, SHARIA BOULAC, CAIRO,
(GRAND CONTINENTAL HOTEL BUILDINGS)

January 11th 1904[1]
near Luxor on the Nile

Dear Fuller

There is a plan afoot which, if it is realised, will keep me in Europe for still another year. In that case, you may keep my rooms if you want them;

if you don't, may I ask you to let me know, so that I may write to the landlord's agent giving them up.

I am ˄at this moment˄ going up the Nile with an impossible party of
tourists, conscious of being no less grotesque myself than the rest of them.
So many labour-saving-machines have left us no time for anything, else I
should like to travel long in the East and yield for a time to its fascinations.
People here seem to realise something of Faust's dream, to be young in
body and old in spirit. What an amusing place the world would be to such
a creature. We sometimes speak of regretting lost illusions. What a silly
idea! We may well regret lost powers, but the loss of illusions is an
unmixed benefit. It leaves you free face to face with the facts and autho-
rises you to profit by every real opportunity. The trouble is that, the Life
of Reason being so largely in abeyance, people do not ordinarily lose their
illusions till they have lost their passions, and then the real world, when
they see it for the first time as it is, seems to them stale, not because it is
real but because they are played out.

I may perhaps go to Jerusalem and Damascus before returning to
Europe. The donkey is losing its terrors for me and I now generally ride at
the head of the party. Think what a party it must be!   Yours
                                                              GSantayana

[1]Santayana mistakenly dated this letter 1904.

To Celedonio Sastre Serrano
13 January [1905] • Luxor, Egypt   (MS postcard: Sanchez)

LOUXOR–COLONNADES DU GRAND TEMPLE

13 de enero.[1] Seguimos nuestro viaje sin novedad.   Jorge

[1]Translation:
We continue our voyage without incident.

To Susan Sturgis de Sastre

25 January [1905] • Cairo, Egypt   (MS postcard: Sanchez)

CAIRE.

Jan. 25th   Got back here today from Upper Egypt and am installed at Morgan's in safety.

[*Unsigned*]

To Charles Scribner's Sons

25 January 1905 • Cairo, Egypt   (MS: Princeton)

Jan. 25. 1905

KASR-EL-DOUBARAH
CAIRO

Messrs Charles Scribner's Sons
New York

Gentlemen:

Your letter of the 6th has just reached me here. I am rather sorry that the publication of the "Life of Reason" has been put off so long, although I quite understand that the trouble came from my being so far away. As to the independent title of each volume, that is not of any consequence from my point of view. Apart from the common heading "The Life of Reason" which I understand you have retained, the volumes will be kept together well enough by their individual titles, which are obviously meant to go together–"Reason in Common Sense", "in Society" etc. Merely leaving out the number of the volume or of the book will make no difference in the continuity of the work, especially as in the three later books I am still able to put in a phrase or two pointing to the next one in order. This reference forward happens to exist already in the first two books. That each book may be <u>read</u> apart from the others, as you say, was part of my original plan and I am glad you are taking steps to bring this result about.

Yours very truly
GSantayana

To Susan Sturgis de Sastre

4 February [1905] • Tel Aviv-Yafo, Israel   (MS postcard: Sanchez)

JAFFA   THE SEA-SHORE

Feb. 4th   First glimpse of Asia.

My visit to Egypt has been a great success and I am in high spirits for what is coming.

[*Unsigned*]

To Susan Sturgis de Sastre

10 February [1905] • Jerusalem, Israel   (MS postcard: Sanchez)

FRONT OF THE HOLY-SEPULCHRE.

Feb. 10th   I have been delayed here by heavy rains which make the roads almost impassable. However I hope to start

INTERIOR OF THE HOLY SEPULCHRE WITH ORNAMENTS.   JERUSALEM.

Feb. 10 (Continued).

in a few days for Damascus by carriage with a dragoman that Cook[1] has furnished me, a nice old man. Jerusalem reminds me of Avila.   G.S.

[1]Thomas Cook & Son, the British agency.

To Susan Sturgis de Sastre

17 February [1905] • Jerusalem, Israel   (MS: Virginia)

Jerusalem, February 17, 1904[1]

Dear Susie

The rains during the first week I spent here were so heavy that it was impossible to do the usual sight-seeing, and they have left the roads in such a state that it seemed imprudent to start on a long driving-tour such as I had planned. The other day when several of us went to Jericho and the Dead Sea two of our carriages got stuck in deep mud, and the horses had to be taken out while we waded to terra firma and help was brought to pull out the carriage∧s∧. Such incidents, which do no harm in a short excursion when the town is hard by, might be serious in the wilds, when no halting place for the night might be within reach after a delay of several hours. I am therefore starting tomorrow morning for Damascus by way of Jaffa and Beyrout, a journey wholly by rail and steamboat. From Damascus I return to Beyrout and sail thence again for Athens <u>via</u> Smyrna. I expect to reach Greece about March 1st and you may address me there for a month or two directly, to the <u>Hôtel Grande Brétagne, Athènes</u>; if I don't like that place and go elsewhere I will let you know by the swift picture-post-card.

The impression which the Holy Land makes on the traveller must depend more even than in other places on his point of view and his expectations. There are no ruins of architectural importance. Every thing has been rebuilt at various periods, and now the town is a conglomerate of all sorts of buildings, chiefly shabby and modern. The shrines, at the Holy Sepulchre (which contains the supposed site of Calvary as well) and at Bethlehem, etc, are generally caves, hung with many small lamps, and enclosed in a more or less imposing church. These churches are cut up into sections belonging to the various confessions, the Greeks usually having the lion's share. To make Jerusalem satisfactory as a place of pilgrimage one would have to possess unlimited faith in the traditions identifying the various spots, and even then I am not sure that much is gained for devotional purposes by knowing that the cross was planted here or there. The Catholic convents and hospices are numerous here and in good order; the Dominicans have a pretty bran-new church and college and the Franciscans and Carmelite₍s₎ also have various establishments. There is a very large religious hostlery, where French brothers receive pilgrims at eight francs a day; it is well built in white stone with two elaborate chapels and other signs of prosperity. The older part of the town is inhabited by the Moslems and Jews, the latter very numerous and divided into Spanish and German Jews; the Spanish section still speaks a corrupt Castillian. The Moslems are themselves of various nations: Ara₍i₎bic is the language of the country, but Turkish is that of the government, and the Beduins, Turks, Syrians, and negroes are strangely jumbled together. A shepherd I met in a country walk spoke to me <u>in English</u> and two other peasants in Italian. French, not very pure, is spoken by all the educated natives and most shop-keepers. Costumes are no less mixed. The country people still look Biblical, and from their flowing white robes and bare feet you pass by insensible degrees to complete European dress, modified only by the Fez or <u>tarbush</u> which most natives still wear. Apart from this museum of humanity what has interested and pleased me most has been the landscape. It is arid and hilly, the slopes being often quite covered with loose stones and ledges of rock peeping through the surface; but there are also many olive-trees, and the deep gorges and dry beds of torrents make the scene most wild and varied. I had no idea how easily one can dominate the whole country; from the Mount of Olives, for instance, you not only can see the Dead Sea but you can see quite across it, as if it were a pond at your feet, while the mountains of Moab on its eastern shore rise high up before you, like a wall of stone that you might touch with a long stick. From hills only a little higher you can at the same time see the Mediterranean; so that the ancient Jews could from a single mountain-top view the whole land of promise. What an influence this intimate familiarity with their country must have had on their intense patriotism. With most nations their country is only an idea, but for the Jews it was a sensible and tangible place, like one's own house and garden.

The site of the Temple is still magnificent and a very pretty round ámosque occupies the place where the altar for burnt-offerings stood in antiquity, just before the door of the Temple. The rest of the enormous platform once occupied by the temples of Solomon and Herod is now bare; only a few stone kiosques and arches, and a few trees rise above the immense pavement. Around stand several modern minarets and an old Christian basilica, somewhat "restored" and turned into another mosque. Those who are not Moslems are only permitted to visit these places on stated days and accompanied by a <u>cavass</u> or <u>gend'arme</u> from the consulate: Jews are never allowed to come in at all: this is because the Moslems also hold the Temple of Solomon sacred. They venerate some Christian shrines as well, for instance, the supposed site of the ascension, in which they believe; but they are indifferent to all that relates to the passion because the Koran says that Christ was never really crucified, but that a man resembling him was executed in his place, while he was translated like Elijah into heaven and will not die until the end of the world; after which he will rise again, and at the last judgment will stand on the Mount of Olives while Mohammed stands on the hill of the Temple; a rope will be stretched between and those souls that are able to pass over it will be saved, while those who fall in the transit will be lost. This last is not in the Koran, but is a popular conception.

I am perfectly well and feel well pleased with my journey so far, which is not so very expensive—about seven dollars a day since I came to the Orient, all included. I have been talking Spanish a great deal here with the South Americans [across] that fill this hotel. They are for the most part from

Buenos Aires and bubble over with self-satisfaction in their country.   Love
to all from   G.S.

¹Santayana mistakenly dated this letter 1904.

To Susan Sturgis de Sastre

20 February [1905] • Baalbek, Lebanon   (MS postcard: Sanchez)

BAALBEK, VUE GÉNÉRALE DE L'ACROPOLE

Feb. 20. Came here today from Beyrout over the Lebanon which is covered with snow. Fine Roman ruins

[*Unsigned*]

To Susan Sturgis de Sastre

25 February 1905 [*postmark*] • Beirut, Lebanon   (MS postcard: Sanchez)

DAMAS, ET LE BARADA
SOUVENIR DE LA SYRIE

Beirut.
Feb. 25.
I sail today for Smyrna where I change ship for Athens. Damascus (which
you see here) is very interesting on account of the people and the costumes, but I could find no good photographs of the streets. All well.

[*Unsigned*]

To [Susan Sturgis de Sastre]

27 February [1905] • Vathi, Samos, Greece   (MS postcard: Sanchez)

PORT DE VATHY, CAPITALE DE SAMOS

Feb. 27. 1904¹
Vathi, Samos

Our steamer, a French one, has stopped here for the day after a good voyage of thirty six hours from Beirut and I have landed to take a walk and a
look about the town, which is very picturesque and Italian-like. On the

voyage we have been all the time in sight of mountains, often covered with snow. The coast of Syria under Mount Lebanon (where

SOUVENIR DE SAMOS

Beirut is) and that of Asia Minor along the Mediterranean are very high and magnificent and only need a little admixture of trees to make them perfect. This town (Vathi) is the first Greek place I have seen—for it is an autonomous Greek principality under nominal Turkish suzerainty,—and the people speak Greek. There is nothing but the language and landscape, however, and an occasional head, to remind one of antiquity. Tomorrow Smyrna. Love to all.

[*Unsigned*]

¹Santayana mistakenly dated this postcard 1904.

To Wallace de Groot Cecil Rice
3 March 1905 • Athens, Greece   (MS: Newberry)

Hôtel Minerva
Athens, March 3, '05

Dear Sir¹

No letters have reached me for three weeks while I was making a tour in Syria, and that is the reason I have not answered you before. Of course it will be only an honour and a pleasure to me that you should use my "Ode"² for your athletic symposium. Thank you, too, for the "Flying Sands" which don't take long enough in running—if I may mix sand-metaphors like the blameless Longfellow.³ You seem to me to combine a great many things which go to make a poet's soul—affectionate familiarity with nature, sincere reflection, and metrical sense. Perhaps, however, the age we live in is too cold a winter for even the best of us to do more than chirp a little, lest the tradition should be altogether lost, until the Spring sets somebody really singing.

My publishers have the copyright, as you doubtless know, and are reported to be somewhat chary of permissions to reprint; in this case, however, they can have—generous souls!—no pecuniary interest in the matter; and you may appeal to my wish, if need be.

Yours very truly
GSantayana

[1]Wallace de Groot Cecil Rice (1859–1939), Harvard class of 1883, was admitted to the bar but gave up law for a career as a literary and dramatic critic, writing for newspapers and magazines. His books include *Under the Stars* (1898) (with Barrett Eastman) and *The Flying Sands* (1898).
[2]"Athletic Ode," originally written for an O.K. Club dinner at Harvard in the 1890s, was published in 1905 in Rice's *The Athlete's Garland: A Collection of Verse of Sport and Pastime* (19–23), in *Hermit* (185–91), and in *Complete Poems* (146–49).
[3]Henry Wadsworth Longfellow (1807–82) was a poet best known for his works *Hiawatha, Evangeline, The Children's Hour,* and *The Courtship of Miles Standish.* He graduated from Bowdoin College and began his teaching career there as a professor of modern languages. He later became a professor at Harvard and lived primarily in Cambridge for the remainder of his life.

To Susan Sturgis de Sastre
3 March [1905] • Athens, Greece   (MS postcard: Sanchez)

ATHENES   VUE DE LYCABETTE
March 3rd
I have arrived here safely and established myself at the <u>Hôtel Minerva</u> for 10 francs a day. Athens is very pleasing.

[*Unsigned*]

To William James
4 March 1905 • Athens, Greece   (MS: Houghton)

Athens, <u>Hôtel Minerva</u>
<u>March 4, 1905.</u>
Dear Mr James
    Thank you very much for your amusing letter.[1] Why didn't the Messiah come this year and leave me the more congenial task of being a Paul to him and reducing his doctrine to dead dogmas and metaphysical Hellenisms? It is not too late, and if you are so well (which I am happy to hear) why shouldn't you stay in France for next year and leave it for me to follow, if need be, on the year after-next, or even later? My book, in spite of its five volumes, is not good to turn into lectures: it is <u>too concise!</u> My

idea is rather to review my contemporaries, which I neglect in the book altogether, and to take for a subject "Contemporary philosophy in England and America." Hyde says you may wish to take that subject, or something like it, yourself, and if so, I could of course easily find a new title. I suspect, however, that you would be looking forward in your treatment, while I should be looking back—at least as far as Jonathan Edwards[2] and the statuetted Locke. Scoo that even with the same theme we might make too sufficiently different symphonies to delight the Parisian ear with.

I have just arrived here from Palestine and Damascus, where I have received the usual impressions; I am staying here for two months, so that I look for the pleasure of doing a little peripatetic philosophy, under your distinguished guidance,[3] on its native heath—a heath being all there is left to philosophise over.

I hope you will like Spain and find it worth the inconveniences it will put you to.

Yours sincerely
GSantayana

---

[1]James had written to Santayana on 8 Feb 1905, urging him to accept the Hyde lectureship in France for the following autumn and winter: "I cannot believe, considering where you already are, and that your book [*Reason*] is ripe for being made into lectures, that you will refuse such an opportunity. I can't conceive a better man for our university to put forward among the first. The plan between Eliot and Hyde is to make <u>me</u> the lecturer the next year, 1906–7, and I am feeling so hearty again that I don't say nay. You the Baptist! I the Messiah! (That's the way it looks to my wife!) Pray write to me again and tell me how the whole thing is looking at your end." [D. C.]

[2]Jonathan Edwards (1703–58) was an American theologian and philosopher. His early thought was idealistic (under Locke's influence), and his theology was Calvinistic, emphasizing the supremacy of God.

[3]James later joined Santayana in Athens. [D. C.]

To Charles Scribner's Sons

30 March 1905 • Athens, Greece   (MS: Princeton)

^C/o Brown Shipley & Co
   123 Pall Mall
      London

                                             Athens
                                             <u>March 30, 1905</u>

Messrs Charles Scribner's Sons
New York

Gentlemen:

From various persons who have written to acknowledge the receipt of "The Life of Reason" I know that the first two volumes are safely out. They have not reached me, however, and I should naturally be glad to see them. Please send me a copy, if you have not done so already. You may remember that I asked you to send me only one; perhaps that is the reason I haven't got any. There is another copy which I fear, on account of a mistake of mine, may have gone wrong. It should have been addressed to Mr. & Mrs R. Burnside Potter, 160 Fifth Ave. New York. I am afraid I put down <u>60</u>, so that the books may have come back to you. The Potters now live in 73^{<u>rd</u>} Street, I think, but as they have moved there since I left America I don't know the number. The other address, of course, is Mr Potter's office.

If you mean to get out a further volume or two this year or even next year, I am sorry to say that you will continue to have the annoyance of sending the proof abroad. It is arranged that I shall be in Paris next winter, to give the Hyde lectures which Mr Wendell has inaugurated this season, and which you have doubtless heard of. Paris, however, is a good deal nearer than Egypt, and the circumstances may have this advantage for the sale of my book, that my name will probably be in the American papers more than it would have been for more glorious but less notorious achievements.

Your notice of "The Life of Reason" in the "Book Buyer" seems to me splendid—most flattering, naturally, but at the same time, even if it be not becoming in me to say so, essentially <u>just</u>. At least the critic has quite understood my intentions.

                         Yours very truly
                         GSantayana

To Charles Scribner's Sons
15 April 1905 • Athens, Greece   (MS: Princeton)

<u>Athens April 15. 1905</u>

Messrs Charles Scribner's Sons
New York.

Gentlemen:

I have your note of March 24<u>th</u> in which you tell me you sent me one copy of "The Life of Reason", for which I beg to thank you although it has not yet reached my hands.

I have sent you today, in two packages, the M.S. of the rest of "Reason in Art", which I hope will arrive safely. "Reason in Science" is not quite copied out, as I have been making a general revision of that volume, but it will doubtless be ready by the time your printers have finished the other parts. If there should be any special hurry about it, I could at any moment send you the earlier chapters, which are ready. As I have no great confidence in South-European post-offices (knowing the perfidious character of the Spanish one) I prefer to wait till I get to England—about June 1<u>st</u>—if there is no urgency in the matter.

Yours very truly
GSantayana

^c/o Brown Shipley & Co
London.

To Susan Sturgis de Sastre
[Spring 1905] • Corinth, Greece   (MS postcard: Sanchez)

SOUVENIR DE CORINTHE
VUE DE VIEUX CORINTHE AVEC
ACROCORINTHE

Easter
<u>Monday</u>

I have climbed this mountain this morning—an hour and a half up and one hour down. There is a small church and a <u>fiesta</u> on the top. A great many peasants in their best.

[*Unsigned*]

To [Susan Sturgis de Sastre]
29 April [1905] • Nauplia, Greece   (MS postcard: Sanchez)

<u>Nauplia, 29 of April</u>.   Yesterday I came here to begin a little tour of inspection in Greece, before leaving it for Constantinople. This town is beautifully situated, as you may judge by this card, and last night presented a very curious spectacle. It was the Greek Good Friday. After a long chanted office in the church, a procession started through the town, every one carrying a lighted candle. The chief object carried was a sort of cenotaph made of flowers with candles stuck all over it. It represents the tomb of your Lord. This town has Venetian balconies everywhere, and they were filled with people also holding candles and in many places calcium lights as well. There was a guard of soldiers with reversed arms and a military band playing funeral airs. The sight was most striking, especially as rockets and fire-crackers were going off in every direction! The Greeks seem to take Holy Week very gaily; in church absolutely nobody seemed to be praying or doing anything but attending a public function. Yet every one seemed perfectly happy and much interested in what was going on. There was a sort of adoration of the cross, only instead of a crucifix people kissed an embroidered cloth—as images <u>in bulk</u> are not allowed in the Greek Church. The day after tomorrow I go to Delphi.

[*Unsigned*]

To Susan Sturgis de Sastre
19 May [1905] • Constantinople, Turkey   (MS postcard: Sanchez)

ROUMELI HISSAR, BOSPHORE, CONSTANTINOPLE.
19 de mayo. Hoy salgo para Buda-Pesth, y espero llegar á Lóndres en diez días. Sigo entusiasmado con este pais.[1]

[*Unsigned*]

[1]Translation:
May 19. Today I leave for Budapest, and hope to arrive in London in ten days. I continue to be excited with this country.

To Susan Sturgis de Sastre

27 May 1905 [*postmark*] • Nürnberg, Germany   (MS postcard: Sanchez)

NÜRNBERG, DER SCHÖNE BRUNNEN NACH SEINER WIEDERHERSTELLUNG.

Today, May 27th I am here in the heart of Germany. The place is undoubtedly quaint and mediaeval but oh, so insipid! I leave tomorrow morning for London–25 hours.

[*Unsigned*]

To Charles Eliot Norton

5 June 1905 • London, England   (MS: Houghton)

London, June 5th 1905

Dear Mr Norton

No letter which I have received about my book has given me more satisfaction than yours.[1] As you have never divided justice from kindness, it is hard not to believe that your approval is justified, even when expressed in such flattering and partial terms. I hoped that you would like the general intent and moral ideal that underlies all I say, although probably many arguments and tenets which I have ventured to propound may seem to you precarious and needlessly metaphysical. I am compelled, however, to use the tools of my trade and cannot altogether escape the controversial traditions in which I have been trained, much as I should have preferred, if Nature had consented, to be a purer humanist. Nevertheless, some may be led in this way out of the fog and shown how the speculative instinct may be tamed and turned to moral uses in supporting and refining practical understanding.

With many thanks for your very kind letter I am   Sincerely yours
GSantayana

[1]Norton wrote Santayana on 23 Apr 1905 after reading *Reason*: "If I were writing to a layman in philosophy like myself I should not hesitate to speak of the extraordinary range of your thought, the admirable ordering of it in a consistent system, its striking originality, and the display in it of the union of remarkable power of imagination with not less remarkable faculty of the understanding ... . Now that you are away from Cambridge I know not where to look for anyone who is truly meditating on the problems of life. Contemplation is an unfamiliar practice. Nobody seems to feel the need,

or to say 'So many hours must I contemplate'. The University is given over to facts, and regards thoughts with suspicion.—Come back soon, to redress the balance!"

To Charles Augustus Strong
20 June 1905 • Richmond, England   (MS: Rockefeller)

^c/o Brown Shipley & Co
London

Richmond
June 20 1905

Dear Strong

Let me hasten to thank you for your letter and your article[1] and to tell you what they fill my mind with before it all evaporates and I am quite empty again—for the older and more set one gets the sooner do new ideas run off and leave nothing but the old ones standing. How fresh and receptive you are, by the way, and how you prance about manfully in the contemporary arena! You make me feel like a senile hermit in comparison, revolving his own dogmas in a melancholy soliloquy. I wish I had read Moore's article,[2] without which it is hard to see ∧look at∧ your∧s∧ article with the right focus. I have read—nay, studied—his Principia Ethica, however, and perhaps with that clue, and the one furnished by Russell's Philosophy of Mathematics,[3] I may guess at his position/∧, which I agree with.∧

The detail of your reasoning, and your psychological analysis, seems to me right. I think, without exception, but there is an underlying assumption of yours which I reject, and thence comes whatever divergence there may be between us. (I speak of your article, not of your criticism of my book.) You say that immediate existence consists of feelings. What is denoted by "feeling"? Is it mere existence? Is it a characteristic or locus different from anything given in the immediate facts themselves? Obviously it must be, ∧according to you,∧ since the facts themselves, as they exist, have no psychological nature. Their qualities are all their own, and material; their locus is only their own locus ∧medium∧, and "objective". To call them feelings either means nothing—for they are ex hypothesi existences—or it means something illegitimate; viz. that they belong to personal lives, being observations made by Strong & Co. You seem to me both to admit and to forget that the latter proposition is secondary, and impossible until the equally intellectual proposition has been accepted that the environment of

Strong and Co. is material, independent, permanent, and causal in respect to their experiences ∧[*across*] Data cannot be said to be feelings until what they stand for is known to be things. Toothache would not be a feeling if there were no teeth. It would be a devil.∧ In other words, facts do not belong to psychology before they belong to physics, but only after; and psychology is really a part of physics, as I have so often said to you before. Psychology transfers the immediate to a conceived medium, the life of some individual, some body's mind. Physics transfers the immediate, with many supplements, to another conceived medium, the permanent and mechanical system of nature. You have no right, in calling the primary existences feelings, to assume that they belong à priori to the psychic stream. The flux is the flux of things, and men are a part of them. You say yourself that the relation of subject and object exists only for thought. That seems to me to give your whole case away, for if calling primitive facts feelings means anything it must mean that they exist for a subject, that they are some body's feelings. In that case the fallacy of calling them primary is obvious, since to be feelings it is requisite that they be not things, i.e. that the qualities ~~proper to~~ ∧inherent in∧ them be not their real qualities, but ∧that they contain mere∧ pictures of those qualities; as the feeling of a white ship is not a white ship, since it cannot float in water or be seen at a distance or have any other of the natural dynamic relations of white ships. In fine, it seems to me that while your insight and intention is right, you are handicapped by a perverse psychological Berkeleyan phraseology, and the assumption that what exists is prima facie mental, which I should say was the opposite of the truth.

As to your comments on my book, I am naturally pleased and flattered that you should like it, and that you should not say it is unintelligible, as many people—philosophers—have said. Naturally I am not convinced by your criticisms, which seem to me near-sighted. And it saddens, though it no longer surprises, me to hear that I am a phenomenalist. James informed me that I was a disciple of Schiller, which was even worse. Imagine how salutary for one's vanity, when one thought one was reconciling Plato and Democritus,[4] purging Aristotle and humanising Spinoza, to be brought suddenly down to hard contemporary fact and know that one was the companion of loudest clown in the sophistical circus! But I am chastened enough, I hope, not to mind, and to believe that these optical illusions will cancel one another in time, and leave a fair average image of one's intent in the mind of anyone who may read one at a greater distance. I hope the public, if it notices me at all, will not misunderstand me so much as the philosophers, do. The latter, catching the whiff of any stock doctrine in one's pages, at once attribute the whole stock doctrine so suggested to their minds to the unhappy author. Because I point out continually the empirical ground and origin of our beliefs, you say I am a phenomenalist; but it is not I that made valid physical knowledge arise by observation and be tested by experiment. So I say constantly that religion is imaginative and symbolic; but that is not a dogmatic piece of scepticism. It is a conviction gained by living in the world, coming to close quarters with more than a single sect, and reading, with my eyes open, Homer the Bible and the Summa Theologiae.[5]–But enough of egotism. I mustn't fill any more sheets, and there is hardly room in this one to thank you for your invitation to your Château,[6] [across] which I hope to accept later in the Summer. With best regards to Mrs Strong and a great desire for more discussion with you, I remain   Yours ever   G. S.

[1]Unidentified.
[2]Unidentified.
[3]Bertrand Russell's *Principles of Mathematics* was published in 1903.
[4]A materialist, Democritus (c. 460– c. 370 B.C.) was a Greek philosopher who held that the world was made up of tiny particles, imperceptible to the sense but indivisible and indestructible. Consequently, the true nature of things can be discovered only by thought, for sense perceptions are confusing.
[5]*Summa Totius Theologiae* (c. 1265–74) is a major philosophical treatise by Saint Thomas Aquinas. A summary of theology, it is the doctrinal basis for all such teachings in the Roman Catholic Church. It applies the methodology of Aristotelian logic to problems of Christian doctrine.
[6]At Compiègne, France.

To Charles William Eliot
23 June 1905 • Richmond, England   (MS: Harvard)

---

^c/o Brown Shipley & Co
    London.

Richmond
June 23 1905

Dear Mr Eliot

You are no doubt perfectly well informed of the arrangements which Mr. J. H. Hyde has been making with me about lectures to be given by me in Paris next winter, but as I have had no official communication with you, perhaps it is as well that I should formally ask for your authorisation, and that of the Corporation, for the plan proposed.

My lectures, arranged like those of Mr. Wendell, are to be on "Contemporary philosophy in England and America." Mr. Hyde offers to pay half my ordinary salary, and gives me to understand that my leave of absence on half-pay will be continued for the year 1905–1906, by the College. I should be glad to know that this arrangement is definitely approved.

My holiday and travels have passed very pleasantly. I got as far as Assouan in Egypt, and Damascus and Constantinople in the other direction, and spent two months in Athens. The proofs and correction of my new book kept me busy at recurring intervals. I am now thinking of my next year's task, for which I have to do a great deal of reading. I shall probably go before long to my sister's in Spain, and remain there until it is time to go to Paris.

From Professor James, who was with me ~~from~~ for a time in Greece, and by letters from other friends, I hear good news concerning Harvard finances, and about the establishment of our department in Emerson Hall.

Believe me, with sincere regard,

Yours very truly

GSantayana

To Robert Calverley Trevelyan
25 June 1905 • Richmond, England   (MS: Trinity)

Richmond

<u>June 25 1905</u>

Dear Mr Trevelyan[1]

I have just finished reading the "Birth of Parsival"[2] and must not let the moment pass without writing a line to thank you for the pleasure it has given me to read it, as well as for your kindness in sending me the book and its predecessors. You must have thought it strange and rude of me not to have acknowledged them before, but you will forgive me if I am able to make clear the somewhat mixed instinct that kept me silent so long. Your poems seem to me the best, the most pleasing, that are being written in these days, and it has not been for want of compliments (which would have been sincᵣeere) to pay you that I have said nothing. The truth is that I have fallen out of love with poetry and feel a kind of incompetence in speaking of it, as one might in the case of ₐaₐ sweetheart that had jilted one. I seem to see in what I read the author's intention rather than his achievement. I have written enough verse, and dreamt of enough poetry, to know how agreeably the images, the music, the dramatic effects of a work smile upon us in the planning. It is easy to recognise these imaginative joys behind other people's work as well: and there is little poetry that, to a sympathetic and pliant reader, is not full of beauties. But beyond these dreamful and, if I may say so, pathological merits, the question seems to me to confront us: What has this composition accomplished? Is it <u>viable</u>? Is it a stone in any habitable and homelike edifice in which the human imagination can come and dwell? Are we, by our retrospective literary fables, doing more than indulge a sort of school-boy's day-dream, dealing with nothing real, with nothing that can beautify or colour pertinently the lives we must lead? Is not our whole imaginative labour one hollow anachronism, encouraged by a mere coterie of dilettanti, and made possible by a pathetic incapacity to face our own world and feel the true eloquence and passion of our lives?—I do not say all this in order to dissuade you—heaven forbid!—from writing more, but only to excuse myself for having so little to say at all relevant to your performance. My appreciation is choked by these scruples. I am out of tune with the singers!

Yours sincerely   GSantayana

[1]Robert Calverley Trevelyan (1872–1951) was an English poet and translator of the classics.
[2]London and New York: Longmans, Green, 1905.

To Susan Sturgis de Sastre
28 June [1905] • Box Hill, England   (MS postcard: Sanchez)

BURFORD BRIDGE HOTEL.

Boxhill, near Dorking, Surrey.
<u>June 28.</u>

Dear Susie.

I send you this batch of cards so that you may have an idea of the pretty place I have come to. I moved yesterday from Richmond, where I had been discovered by two friends and also somewhat disturbed by the noise in the town, really a suburb of London. This place is only 23 miles from the capital, yet very rural. The hotel (see the back of this card) is quite in

DORKING.   HIGH STREET.

the country, at the foot of a high hill, and beside a little river. I have persuaded the landlady to give me an old card-table to write on, on which I
can stretch my elbows and spread my papers. I think I may stay here two
or three weeks. The people are quiet, though too numerous, and the
omnipresent motor-car drops its crowds in for tea on pleasant afternoons.
However it is much more secluded than Richmond.

Deep Dene (see next card) is a house

THE DEEPDENE, DORKING

belonging to one of the old duchesses of Marlborough (there are two
beside the young one) and the fine garden is open to the public until four
o'clock, when I suppose the great have their afternoon tea. There are one
or two other big houses with parks in the immediate neighbourhood, and
a nice town of one street, like so many in England.

My plans are somewhat changed and I am thinking of coming to make
you a visit in October. My lectures don't begin, I find, until November 15.
After sending off

BOXHILL.   THE ZIGZAGS.

the manuscript of my last volume (which I am still copying out) I may go
to Hamburg to stay with my friend Westenholz at a new country-house
he has built himself. From there I should go to Paris and make Strong (a
fellow-professor of philosophy) another visit. He has a château—a modest one, he says—at Compiègne, and four empty spare rooms, and wants to
convert me to his matter-is-mind philosophy.

I have begun reading English books for my lectures. They are rather
absurdly simple, after Greek and German metaphysics.

Love to all from your loving brother

G. S.

To Charles Scribner's Sons
28 June 1905 • Box Hill, England   (MS: Princeton)

^C/o Brown Shipley & Co
London
Boxhill, Surrey
June 28 1905

Dear Sirs:
  Will you please send a copy of "The Sense of Beauty" a copy of "Interpretations of Poetry & Religion", and copies of the volumes of "The Life of Reason" now out to the address below, and add it to the list of addresses to which the forthcoming volumes of the L. of R. are to be sent, with the author's compliments?
                    Yours very truly
                    GSantayana

Monsieur C. Cestre[1]
  7 rue Le Nôtre
    Dijon, France.

[1]Charles Cestre (1871–1958) received his Ph.D. from Harvard in 1897, where he taught French one year and was an exchange English professor for one year. In 1909 he began teaching English and literature at Bordeaux (France). His many works include *Un grande université américaine, l'université Harvard* (1899) and *La révolution française et les poètes anglais (1789–1809)* (1906).

To Charles Scribner's Sons
1 July 1905 • [Box Hill, England]   (MS: Princeton)

^C/o Brown Shipley & Co
London.
                                        July 1, 1905

Messrs Charles Scribner's Sons
New York.

Dear Sirs:
  I forgot in my message of the other day to include the "Hermit of Carmel" among my books, to be sent to M. C. Cestre, 7 rue Le Nôtre, Dijon, France.

I see by the proofs of "Reason in Art"–despatched today–that you intend to bring out this volume, and I presume "Religion" as well, in September. Will it be contrary to you∧r∧ plan to postpone the fifth volume until a later date? I find myself horribly entangled in a recasting of it which I have undertaken, partly under the influence of certain comments on vol. I which prove to me that my intention in the book, and my meta-physical views, are not clearly expressed there. I am trying to make clearness doubly clear in volume 5; but the process is extremely difficult and I should be glad not to be hurried. The first part is ready, however, if you want it; and the whole could be got ready in a few weeks.

Yours very truly
GSantayana

To Charles Augustus Strong

20 July 1905 • Box Hill, England   (MS: Rockefeller)

Address
^C/o Brown Shipley & Co
   123 Pall Mall
     London

Box Hill, Surrey
July 20, 1905

Dear Strong,

Thank you for your post-card. I count indeed on paying you a visit, but should like to leave it for as late a date as is consonant with your plans. When do you leave for America? My idea is to go first to Hamburg to see a friend who, like you, is living in the country in a place he assures me is most suitable for work. From there I should go to Paris, when I could immediately come to you. After you left, I meant to go to Spain, leaving only an interval sufficient for finding my winter quarters and leaving most of my belongings there. As Spain is not attractive before October, I should like to leave my visit to you, say, for the middle of September, if you were still at Compiègne; but I will come earlier if your <u>villegiatures</u>[1] comes sooner to an end.

In my fifth volume, which I am now revising, I have added a note about your philosophy (not mentioning you). Lest there be any misrepresenta-tion I copy it here and beg you to point out anything that is wrong. Of course you must not ask me to leave out the joke; but apart from that I will change anything. The text has been saying that the philosophy of mind is in hopeless confusion since "it is not settled whether mind means the form of matter, as with the Platonists, or the effect of it, as with the materialists, or the seat and ˄false˄ knowledge of it, as with the transcendentalists, or perhaps after all, as with the pan-psychists, means exactly matter itself." Here follows the note: "The monads of Leibniz could justly be called minds, because they had a dramatic destiny and the most complex experience imaginable was the state of but one monad, not an aggregate view or effect of a multitude in fusion. But the recent improvements on that system take the latter turn. Mind-stuff or the material of mind is supposed to be contained in large quantities within any known feeling. Mind-stuff, we are given to understand, is diffused in a medium corresponding to apparent space (what else would a real space be?), it forms quantitative aggregates, its transformations or aggregations are mechanically governed, it endures when personal consciousness perishes, it is the substance of bodies, and, when duly organised, the potentiality of thought. One might go far for a better description of matter. That any material must be material might have been taken for an axiom; but our idealists, in their eagerness to show that "Gefühl ist Alles",[2] have thought to do honour to the spirit by forgetting that it is an expression and wishing to make it a stuff.

There is a further circumstance showing that mind-stuff is but a bashful name for matter. Mind-stuff, like matter, can be only an element in any actual being. To make a thing or a thought out of mind-stuff you have to rely on the system into which that material has fallen. The substantial ingredients, from which an actual being borrows its intensive quality, do not contain its individuating form. This form depends on ideal relations subsisting between the ingredients, relations which are not feelings but can be rendered only by propositions."

To this note is reduced the chapter I had written about "Natural philosophy in quest of substance": for I find that to keep volume five within limits I must reject everything not strictly falling under its title "Reason in Science". A chapter on "Transcendentalism" which I love like the apple of my eye is also sacrificed: so that when I have had a good rest and am back in Cambridge I may begin to rival you other prolific article-writers out of the slaughtered innocents born to bloom in the L. of R.

I have found a (somewhat vulgar) retreat here among the hills between Surrey and Sussex, and am making rapid progress with my work. As a relaxation I am reading Mill's Logic.[3] What bad logic—but what good feeling and good scholarship and pure wisdom! He is a sort of steadier and four-footed James.

President Eliot writes me that they have collected $2,400,000 for increasing our Harvard salaries. It [*across*] sounds magnificent, but I believe it doesn't b́ amount to $500 a piece.   Yours ever   G.S.

[1]Rural retreats.
[2]Sensation is everything.
[3] *System of Logic.*

To Charles Augustus Strong

26 July 1905 • Box Hill, England   (MS: Rockefeller)

address: ᶜ/o Brown Shipley & Co
          London.

                                              Box Hill, Surrey
                                              July 26 1905

Dear Strong,

Please excuse this sheet of fool's cap: I have no frivolous note-paper at hand and the contents are going to justify the pomposity—and perhaps the name—of the medium.

I had no notion that in submitting my innocent foot-note to your previous censorship I was asking you to aid me in any attack upon your doctrine. Perhaps, if you would only allow me my language, your doctrine is ₍would be₎ almost my own. What I wanted was, not to misreprent you. Now, my prudence seems to have its reward, for apparently I <u>did</u> misrepresent you in supposing that you made human thought "a view or result of much mind-stuff in fusion." Your correction, if I understand it, brings up a point quite new to me. Mind-stuff contains relations between its own parts; and adding these relations together you get a sort of continuum given within mind-stuff, although the total landscape is only represented, and not within mind-stuff anywhere in an absolute sense. The partners hold hands, so to speak, but no one contains the whole minuet. Is this your idea? If so, it seems to me you are jumping from the frying-pan into the fire. For the "extensity" of sensations, or their essential lapse, is a character <u>of their object</u>; and this is a material character. If the extensity of a sensation can be predicated of mindstuff itself, then mind-stuff is extended! You would not maintain that, I suppose; yet how can you avoid it? Your inclusion of relations within mind-stuff either lifts mind-stuff into mind, its object acquiring the relations observed and it itself being lifted to a transcendental sphere and made an act of apperception or (as my book will call it) an intent; or else this inclusion reduces it more obviously than ever to matter. Isn't this what Bergson, (t̶r̶whom I am surprised to hear you invoke, when his dichotomy of <u>Matière et Mémoire</u>[1] is all on my side) tries to do, making the immediate material, and the reflective possession or representation of it spiritual and eternal—which is more than I can agree to. However, with many thanks for this information, I hasten to correct my foot-note and will make it read: "a certain bulk of sentiency c̶o̶n̶t̶a̶i̶n̶i̶n̶g̶ ̶a̶n̶d̶ ᴧin flux,ᴧ illustrating spatial and temporal relations, a̶s̶ ̶w̶e̶l̶l̶ ̶a̶s̶ ᴧand not merelyᴧ representing them."[2] Is this better? There will be time to make further corrections, if I have gone wrong. I will also correct the phrase about "doing honour to f̶e̶e̶l̶i̶n̶g̶ ᴧspirit,ᴧ" and substitute "thinking to give spirit a more congenial basis by making it its own stuff, thereby forgetting that spirit is a̶n̶ expressio̶n̶ve and, being expressive a̶n̶d̶ ̶s̶p̶i̶r̶i̶t̶u̶a̶l̶, must have a different status from that of its basis or subject-matter." The style suffers: but I, too, am ready to make any sacrifice of personality on the altar of truth. I may, however, think of a better wording than that above.

Where I can't accept your criticism is in respect to the word matter. Why should Berkeley's ignorance of Aristotle be allowed to infect more generations? Matter is in a way approached from without, since it is potential and inferred, as every substance must be, including mind-stuff, or as truth is. But it means the surd in things, the existential strain that makes them be here and now, in this quantity and with this degree of imperfection. I have a previous note on the use of this word, too long to quote. You will see it when [*across*] the book appears, for on this subject I know what I am talking about and speak quite deliberately.

I am glad you will remain at Compiègne through September. I will write from Hamburg when I know the date of my departure and shall very probably be able to come before September 15.

Yours ever   G. S.

[1] *Matière et mémoire*, Paris, 1896.
[2] See *Science*, page 115.

To William James
27 July 1905 • Box Hill, England   (MS: Houghton)

Box Hill, Surrey
July 27 1905

Dear Mr James

I have just re-read, or read for the first time in some cases, the series of articles you have been good enough to send me. They have given me new light on many points—most important of all on the relation of "Humanism" to "Truth". It is perfectly clear that opinions are not all equally good on pragmatic principles, since some fulfil their pledges with advancing experience while others do not. I am inclined to think that you would meet with less misapprehension and hostility on this score if you gave out, in dogmatic form, how you conceive "the final system of reality" (which you assume on page 3 of the article on "Experience of Activity") to be made up. I imagine ∧you would say∧ it is a historical system, its substance being feelings which may or may not be appropriated by persons. It would remain to work out a physics of these feelings, and to show how proposition might be essentially true or false descriptions of this historical flux.

I have got a clearer notion, I think, than I had when we talked in Athens, of what makes my way of seeing things puzzling to you—a mystery, you called it. You expect me to look at everything as I look on the things I don't believe in—religious myths, e.g.—which can have, of course, a symbolic or pragmatic truth. My nature, on the other hand, compels me to believe in something in quite a different sense, and this something is, in my view, double—material nature with its animation on the one hand, and logical or mathematical forms on the other. These are discovered by us, starting from sensation, and, in the first case, are tested by pragmatic standards. But we look to them in order to understand the origin of our experience (or its standard in signification) and I, for one, heartily accept them in that rôle. So I embrace materialism on pragmatic grounds—and on transcendental grounds also. The prohibition to believe which, in some expressions of it, pragmatism seems to impose, as if every opinion had to be symbolic and had to be superseded, is what [*across*] I object to. It is too Hegelian. History, at least, must have a definite constitution, apart from the pragmatic value of knowing it.

With renewed thanks,   Yours sincerely   GSantayana

To Charles Augustus Strong
14 August 1905 • Volksdorf, Germany   (MS: Rockefeller)

Volksdorf, bei Hamburg
Aug 14, 1905

Dear Strong.

Your last letter has given me much to ruminate over—at first I couldn't understand all your points but I think that I do now. When you say that "extensity" is not extension, and that it belongs to sensation and not to the object felt, I recognise a Jamesianism; but it seems to me that if we distinguish the fact of feeling from the content of it, the former being a psychic event and the latter a material element, "extensity" is altogether absent from the first; a landscape has extensity, but my seeing the landscape has none. The difference between a landscape and infinite geometrical space, I understand; the latter being constructed; but the extensity of something which is a psychic fact and not the object represented or discovered there, is beyond me. Are you not running about in a circle trying to escape from natural things and forced nevertheless to find behind your back what you are removing from before your eyes? Of course I use "mind" for what is distinguishably psychic, non-extended, imponderable, neither north, east, south, or west of any other mental fact. But the extensity of James's belly-ache is decidedly under his waistcoat, and is in truth nothing at all but the projection or overlaying of one vague physical object, in which pain is felt, into the region covered by another physical object, better defined, in which pride, perhaps, is taken. But to say that the pain, apart from the idea or object called the belly, is extended seems to me as capritious capricious and silly as to say that the pride I take in my waistcoat is an extended, rounded, and many-buttoned pride. I agree with you that sensation and emotion are the subject-matter of psychology, quite as much as reflection or thought; but sensation, to be distinguished from <u>what</u> is felt, has to lose its material properties and cease to be extended, coloured, heavy, measurable, lockable in chests, or preservable through time. In a word the occasions of knowledge are mental but the objects of knowledge are not.

I hope you don't mind my having sent so many books ahead. I think I shall be in Paris by September 1<u>st</u> and I could come to you at any time after that.   Yours ever

GSantayana

Address: ^c/o Baron Albert v. Westenholz
         Hamburg, 17.

To Charles Scribner's Sons
21 August 1905 • Volksdorf, Germany   (MS: Princeton)

                                        Volksdorf bei
                                            Hamburg

<u>Aug 21 1905</u>

Messrs Charles Scribner's Sons.
Gentlemen:
    On the back is the revised list of addresses to which I should like copies of vols. III & IV of "The Life of Reason" to be sent when they appear. You may disregard the old list altogether, and any additions or corrections that I may have to make can be attached to this list.
    I understand that you twice sent me copies of vols I & II, but I received neither consignment. My banker in London assures me that he has never seen them. Perhaps if you will let me know when vols. III & IV are to appear I could send you my direct address for the moment, so that there may be less likelihood of losing the books on the way.
    The other consignments you made of the first two volumes all seem to have reached their destination, as I have had acknowledgements in every case but two (now omitted from the list).
    If you think it better, I could ask Constable[1] to send the three sets addressed to England, but I should a little prefer that the American copies should be sent, so as to make the volumes uniform. I have not seen the English copy.   Yours ʃvery truly
                                        GSantayana

Address
    ^c/o Brown Shipley & Co
        London.

Professor Norton–	Shady Hill–	Cambridge,	Mass.
" James	Irving Street–	"	"
" Royce	" "	"	"
" Palmer–	Quincy "	"	"
" Münsterberg–	Ware "	"	"

Professor & Mrs Toy–   7 Lowell   "   "   "
Dᴿ R. B. Perry   18 Little's Block   "   "
A. G. Fuller Esq   60 Brattle St   "   "
Delta Phi Club   9 Linden St   "   "
Harvard Union   Quincy St   "   "
Francis Bullard Esq   3 Commonwealth Ave Boston,   Mass
Mrs. J. B. de Santayana 75 Monmouth St   Brookline,   Mass
Professor C. A. Strong   Lakewood   New Jersey
Dᴿ D. S. Miller,   University of Pennsylvania,   Philadelphia.
King's College Library, King's College,   Cambridge,   England
G. L. Dickinson Esq   "   "   "   "
Bernhard Berenson Esq,   I Tatti, Settignano, Florence, Italy.
Hon. Bertrand Russell,   Bagley,   Oxford,   England.
Baron Albert von Westenholz,   Hamburg 17,   Germany
Monsieur C. Cestre,   7 rue Le Nôtre,   Dijon,   France.

¹Santayana's London publisher.

To Charles Augustus Strong
[29 August 1905] • Volksdorf, Germany   (MS: Rockefeller)

<u>Volksdorf, Tuesday</u>

Dear Strong

The intricacies of your last letter have discouraged me and made me put off answering it until I am afraid it is getting almost too late to warn you of my approach. I expect to leave Hamburg on Friday, sleep that night at Cologne and start again at 10 a.m on Saturday, reaching Compiègne, I hope, some time in the late afternoon. If anything should upset this plan I will telegraph. I had no idea Compiègne was so far from Paris when I suggested going to Paris first. As it is, your idea of leaving Paris until later seemed far better. And I hope you will feel like "doing" some cathedrals with me near Compiègne. I see it is thick with them thereabouts. <u>Au revoir</u>, then, on Saturday.   Yours,

G.S.

[*across*] P.S. I should also warn you that I have gray hair and a sort of French beard, lest you should set your <u>dogues</u> upon me when I approach the draw-bridge of your castel.

To Susan Sturgis de Sastre

3 September [1905] • Compiègne, France   (MS postcard: Sanchez)

COMPIÈGNE.—LE CHÂTEAU DES AVENUES, FAÇADE PRINCIPALE

Sept 3$\underline{\text{rd}}$ Yesterday I arrived here, where I am in this house, once occupied by Queen Isabella.[1] All well except Mrs. Strong.[2]

[Unsigned]

[1]Isabella II (1830–1904), Queen of Spain (1833–68), succeeded her father Ferdinand VII under the regency of her mother. Her ascension was challenged by her uncle Don Carlos, resulting in the Carlist Wars. Deposed in 1868, Isabella went into exile in France. The château at Compiègne was often a royal residence.

[2]Elizabeth had suffered a stroke shortly after her marriage to Strong (c. 1889) and died on 14 Nov 1906. See *Persons*, 375.

To Charles Scribner's Sons

9 September 1905 • Compiègne, France   (MS: Princeton)

Compiegne

ₐSept.ₐ ~~August~~ 9$\underline{\text{th}}$ 1905

Messrs Charles Scribner's Sons
New York

Gentlemen:

If the presentation copies of vols. III, & IV of "The Life of Reason" have not yet been sent out, will you kindly alter the two following addresses?

Dr D. S. Miller– 312 South 10th Street, Philadelphia.

Professor C. A. Strong,

^{C}/o Morgan Harges & Co

31 Boulevard Haussmann, Paris

And will you kindly add to the list the following:

Howard Sturgis Esq

    Queen's Acre

        Windsor, England.

                    Yours very truly
                    GSantayana.

Address

^c/o Brown Shipley & Co
    London

To Susan Sturgis de Sastre

14 September [1905] • Compiègne, France   (MS postcard: Sanchez)

BEAUVAIS.—LA CATHEDRALE.

<u>Compiègne</u>.

September 14.   Yesterday Mrs. Strong's doctor who was returning to Paris, took us here in his automobile. I am staying a week longer.

[*Unsigned*]

To Susan Sturgis de Sastre

26 September 1905 [*postmark*] • Paris, France   (MS postcard: Sanchez)

I have got both your letters and will attend to your rubber-bag, etc. It looks as if nothing would interrupt my journey and arrival on the 2nd unless I should find an irresistible bull-fight going on at Burgos or Valladolid, in which case I will telegraph or write. Strong came here today and went on to Aix-les-Bain for the waters.

COMPIÈGNE.—LA PLACE DE L'HÔTEL-DE-VILLE

Hôtel Foyot.   Paris.   Sept. 26.   I leave here Friday morning.

[*Unsigned*]

To Charles Scribner's Sons
26 September 1905 • Paris, France   (MS: Princeton)

Hôtel Foyot– Paris
Sept 26 1905

Messrs Charles Scribner's Sons
New York.

Gentlemen–
Volumes I and II of "The L. of R" reached me safely at last a few days ago, and I have also received your two subsequent notes. I will endeavour to reform about the photograph, but as I leave tomorrow for six weeks in Spain there may still be a short delay before I submit to the operation. I will try having it done in Avila, but the result may not be satisfactory.

Thank you for the books and the previous account. It was quite right to send the cheque to my (half-)brother, Mr Sturgis, in Boston.

If you get this before vols III and IV are sent abroad you might address my copy here, Hôtel Foyot, Paris, to avoid the apparent dangers of Brown Shipley & Co–who assure me the loss of the other volumes was not their fault–and the dangers, which I had always supposed more real, of the Spanish post-office. They will keep the books here until my return.

Yours very truly
GSantayana

P.S. I am sending you Chapters IX and X of volume V. to be added to your accumulating M.S. There is one more chapter which is not quite ready, but you will receive it, I hope, in a week or two, so that you can safely begin the printing of volume V. if it is for any reason expedient to do so.

To Charles Augustus Strong
3 October [1905] • Ávila, Spain   (MS: Rockefeller)

Novaliches 6,
Avila
October 3$^{\underline{rd}}$

Dear Strong
Your telegram reached me just as I was leaving Paris and until I arrived here (yesterday) I have not had a peaceful hour in which to write to you.

By this time you are doubtless at Compiègne again and, I hope, feeling the good effects of Aix-les-Bains.

In the train—endless hours of it—I have been reading Ribot on the English psychologists[1] and sometimes finding things that reminded me of our debates about psychologism, the immediate,[2] and all the rest of it. I am afraid I was not very sympathetic, nor clear, in my objections to your doctrines. The fact is I have grown rather impatient of minute philosophising. It seems idle, unless the points discussed are really scientific and *I* could be decided by evidence, in which case discussion is premature. But a new way of stating my general objection to a world behind the scenes has occurred to me: I don't know whether it will makes things much clearer, but here it goes.

Suppose the "Being of the brain" were really mind-stuff, and the observed body a figment of imagination, as your theory demands. To every situation in the material world a certain group of psychic existences would correspond—or a certain mass of them, if they are inwardly "continuous" in some way I can't understand. Now, what would justify the assertion that the body was a phenomenon of <u>that</u> mass of mind-stuff, rather than of any other, or of none at all? What meaning is there in saying that we perceive mind-stuff <u>as</u> body? We perceive body; what relevance has the underlying mind-stuff to that object?

The alternative which I prefer is to say that the question merely is whether that body is animated or not; if it is animated, you may well say that the psychic existence emanating from it is the reality of it <u>to itself</u>; it is, rather, the appearance of it to itself. The pertinence of these animating feelings to the body is given in them—since they represent the body pictorially and are interested in its pictured fortunes. The relevance of this pictured body to the body perceived by a third person is the ideal identity of the situation in which that body finds itself in both pictures. A and B agree, for instance, in that A was born on Monday and B on Tuesday: and this agreement—when carried out so as to define determinate facts in the world known to both, and to determine them similarly—constitutes the relation, wholly ideal, which makes my propositions about the world relevant to your propositions about it.

But I can't see how mind-stuff discoursing about nothing, and I discoursing about bodies (which you assert for a reason I don't understand to be perceptions of <u>that</u> mindstuff) have anything to do with each other.

In a word, two worlds are a world too much.

I am sending you my politic discourse to them at Oberlin.[3] It may amuse you. Let me know how you are getting on at Cannes.

Yours ever   G.S.

[1]See 7 Dec 1905.
[2]Seven pages entitled "The Immediate" in Santayana's hand follow this letter.
[3]See 20 Jun 1904.

To Benjamin Apthorp Gould Fuller
5 October 1905 • Ávila, Spain   (MS: Houghton)

Avila, October 5 1905

Dear Fuller

I write–breaking my habitual silence, to which I hope you have got used and indifferent–to ask you to do me several favours. One is to look at my copy of "Interpretations of Poetry and Religion," and see if there are errata marked on the fly-leaf at the back, and if there are, to send the book to Charles Scribner's Sons, 153–157 Fifth Ave, N.Y. They have asked me for any corrections in view of a new edition.

Favour no. 2. Will you be an angel and send me to the <u>Hôtel Foyot, rue Tournon, Paris,</u> the following books, if you can conveniently pick them out of the heap–I don't know if they still sit on the shelves or have been compelled to yield to your own aids to wisdom.

Spencer's First Principles.

Green's Prolegomena.

Ward's Naturalism & Agnosticism.[1]

They are books for which I have a qualified admiration and I don't think it necessary to possess two copies of each. But I need them for reference in preparing my winter's lectures. In payment for your trouble and the postage I will send you a Christmas present when I reach Paris. It shall be Bergson's books, if you haven't got them; if not, something else which you must select.

A letter which I got from you long ago gave me a very cheerful impression in respect to your state of mind and to things in general at Harvard. I trust that happiness is still unclouded, and that fat salaries and intelligent students are beginning to prevail–by students I mean candidates for the Ph.D. for the blameless tribe of moderate geniuses known as undergraduates no doubt ebbs and flows as sweetly as ever. Your letter also contained an interpretation of the Life of Reason which seemed original; what my own is may be a little clearer in the two volumes which I hope you have lately received; and it will be made quite unequivocal in the last volume, to appear in the Spring. Some people say I am a pragmatist and some say I am not. On the whole, I agree with the latter, as pragmatism seems to involve a confusion between the test and the meaning of truth. I have been reading Mill, and the psychologism of his theory[2] repels me so much that I am sure I can't belong to any school which feels at home in it. Mill is a sort of ponderous and sober James. His temper and learning are admirable; his heart is in the right place; and his love of the good is honest. But his logic is a minus quantity, and the survival of dogma, psychological and theological, makes his conclusions pathetically personal and altogether unstable.

With best wishes

Yours ever

GSantayana

^C/o Brown Shipley & Co
London

[1]*First Principles* by Herbert Spencer, 2d ed. (London: Williams and Norgate, 1867). Thomas Hill Green (1836–82) was an English neo-Hegelian philosopher who asserted that consciousness made knowledge possible, thus setting idealism against prevailing empiricism and sensationalism. Santayana's copy of *Prolegomena to Ethics* (Oxford: Clarendon Press, 1890) is at Georgetown University. James Ward (1843–1925) was an English philosopher and psychologist. In 1897 he was elected to the chair of logic and mental philosophy at Cambridge, which he held for the rest of his life. *Naturalism and Agnosticism* (2 vols.) was published in London and New York by Macmillan Co. in 1899. This work was based on the Gifford lectures he delivered before the University of Aberdeen in the years 1896–98.

[2]Psychologism is the term first used in Germany in the nineteenth century to designate the philosophical trend defended by J. F. Fries and F. E. Beneke against the dominant Hegelianism. Later that century psychologism was defended in the field in which it would seem most foreign–logic and mathematics. In Mill's *A System of Logic* it is stated that introspection is the basis of the axioms of mathematics and the principles of logic; in Mill's *Examination of Sir William Hamilton's Philosophy*, logic is classified under psychology and distinguished from it as the part from the whole or art from science. Both of these books are in Santayana's library at Georgetown.

To Charles Scribner's Sons
5 October 1905 • Ávila, Spain   (MS: Princeton)

Avila, Oct 5 1905

Messrs Charles Scribner's Sons
New York

Gentlemen:

I have your note of Sept. 21st in which you ask for corrections for a new issue of my "Interpretations". There are doubtless some verbal ones that I should be glad to make, but unfortunately my copy, in which they may be marked, is in America. I will ask Mr A. G. Fuller, who is living in my Cambridge rooms, to send you the volume, if he finds there are <u>errata</u> indicated in the fly-leaf, as I expect there are. You might return the volume to him at 60 Brattle St, Cambridge, Mass.

As to the two slips in the new volumes, one is certainly a bad one, and Chinese or "blameless Chinese" should certainly stand for Liliputians, though the theory of the universe may not be appreciably improved by the change. As to calling the retina a part of the skin, the license was perhaps intentional—I don't remember the passage now—as my point was that sight was only a highly speciallisised sort of touch, and that one part of the sensitive surface in our bodies may assume the function of another part under stress of necessity. However, I shall note the passage when I have leisure to re-read the volume and mark the <u>errata</u> in it. I suppose the corrections cannot be made now.

It is gratifying that a new issue of the "Interpretations" should be required. Perhaps the comparative failure of that book—at least in America, for I hear that in England it is not procurable—may be somewhat remedied by reflected notoriety, coming from my big book.[1]

Yours very truly
GSantayana

Address:
^{C}/o Brown Shipley & Co
    123 Pall Mall
        London

[1] *The Life of Reason.*

To Charles Scribner's Sons
11 October 1905 • Ávila, Spain   (MS: Princeton)

Avila, Oct. 11. 1905

Messrs Charles Scribner's Sons
New York

Gentlemen:

   Yesterday I sent you the last chapter of "Reason in Science" completing the MS of the "Life of Reason". I hope the various parts sent before have arrived and that the last volume is complete.

   Inclosed is a photograph[1] of me made here, which I sen*t*d in compliance with your request.

                    Yours very truly
                    GSantayana

[1]Unlocated.

To Susan Sturgis de Sastre
16 November 1905 [*postmark*] • Paris, France   (MS postcard: Sanchez)

PARIS.–VUE PANORAMIQUE DU PONT ALEXANDRE III, VERS LES INVALIDES

I am sending you the Paris "Woman's Home Journal" and a German paper I got to see what they said about Alfonso.[1] The Marquesa has written.

[*Unsigned*]

[1]Alfonso XIII (1886–1941) was King of Spain until 1931 when he went into exile in Rome after the republicans won the election.

To William James
5 December 1905 • Paris, France   (MS: Houghton)

Hôtel Foyot, Paris
December 5 1905

Dear Mʳ James

I am very grateful for your letter: I feel how <u>generous</u> it is, and how like you. I may say something about my book–in reply–if there is room at the end, but first let me answer your questions about the Sorbonne lectures.

As you may imagine my experience has been, so far, wholly unlike Wendell's. He seems to have grasped with avidity every opportunity to see things and to know people, and seems to have lectured as if he was borne on a bubbling wave of international enthusiasm. I have come, thinking only of my subject, seeing only my personal friends, having only official relations with officials, and keeping away as much as possible from the American colony. Naturally I have enjoyed a great quiet, and am ~~not~~ spending very little nervous energy on my work. The lectures themselves I find delightful to give–immensely <u>easy</u>. The Amphithéâtre Richelieu[1]– which holds 800–is about half full. The acoustics are admirable and it is not too hot. The audience–fully half ladies, mostly Americans–is sympathetic. One feels that not everything is fully understood; those that have ears, let them hear, has to be one's motto. But every one is attentive, and I find improvisation easy in that <u>milieu</u>.

Of course, even if you wished to take things as I am taking them, it would be impossible. You are too famous; every one here speaks of no one in America but you; you would have enormous audiences and a host of invitations, all of which you would find it impracticable to refuse. Nevertheless, I don't see why you shouldn't refuse the American (the most persistent) set of them; and the French people, if I may trust my impression and experience so far, are perfectly willing to let one alone. Pierre Janet[2] has asked me to dinner–three weeks ahead–but none of the other Frenchmen I have met has even called on me, or suggested that I should call on him. Of course, I repeat, it would be otherwise with you: but my experience will show you that, in the abstract, people here have no Hyde-Wendell idea of the momentousness of this affair. In all frankness–since you ask me to tell you everything–no one–<u>no one</u>, American or French– mentions Wendell here without an ambiguous smile. He evidently made a damned–Wendell of himself. The Hyde foundation has been a success;

audiences have been found; the idea of lectures in English is fashionable and politically opportune. But it is an incident lost amid a thousand others, a thing of importance to half a dozen persons. Paris could live without it, and if a man likes the undertaking, as I do, from the purely personal, academic, scholarly point of view, he ought to attempt it. It is a delightful and a moderate task. The freedom of speaking in a foreign language among foreigners—I mean the intellectual <u>room</u>—is exhilarating. You can say what is <u>really true</u>. You needn't remember that you are in Cambridge, or are addressing the youth entrusted to your paternal charge. I have never felt so grown up as I do at the Sorbonne; after our atmosphere, this is liberty. I am sure that—apart from the first lecture when the ice had to be broken—I am lecturing better than I ever did before; and the audience is appreciative and lets itself be carried along.

All this may not help you very much to make up your mind about coming next year or not. It is hard for me to imagine exactly what points would be decisive to your mind. I can see no reason, however, why a winter here (except for the dark, chill climate and constant drizzle) shouldn't be as profitable and pleasant as one in Cambridge. Two lectures a week on a subject of which your mind was already full, wouldn't be a great strain; and if you hardened your heart a little against the impertinent homage of the public, I don't see why you shouldn't find this a good opportunity for writing down your thoughts.

I have spent, as you may have heard, some weeks with Strong at Compiègne. We had many, rather unsatisfactory, discussions about idealism and mind-stuff. He tells me you are a convert to his theory: is this serious? I should think the same empirical reserve or abstention which makes you rebel against my materialistic Platonism would make you rebel against his reversible universe, perfectly concave and perfectly convex, matter lined throughout with mind. It is a scholastic artifice, <u>n'est-ce pas</u>? It is not science, nor nature, nor moral truth. Strong himself, let me add, seemed to me more heroic and admirable than ever and I enjoyed renewing our old friendship. I have left no room for more [*across*] but if there is anything you wish I had touched on that I have left out, pray ask.   Yours sincerely G.S.

[1]Armand Jean du Plessis, duc de Richelieu (1585–1642), known as Cardinal Richelieu, served as chief minister to Louis XIII (1624). A patron of the literary arts, he founded the Académie française (1635).

[2]Pierre Janet (1859–1947), a French physician and psychologist, contributed to the knowledge of mental pathology and hysteria by the use of hypnosis. He also founded automatic psychology and first described psychasthenia (the incapacity to resolve doubts or uncertainties or to resist irrational phobias, obsessions, or compulsions).

To William James
6 December 1905 • Paris, France   (MS: Houghton)

Hôtel Foyot
Paris, Dec 6. 1905

Dear Mr James—

I forgot yesterday to answer one of your questions, which I remember may be of importance to you. The lectures are at five o'clock in the afternoon on Tuesdays and Saturdays. I have no doubt they would change the hour for you if you wished. To everything they say "comme vous voudrez,"[1] and things here, as in England, seem to go by prerogative. You could also give as many or as few lectures as you chose—the Great Hyde consenting.

Another omission. Blood's poem,[2] after about six readings, has become intelligible to me, and I like the thought very much, also the diction, but the <u>composition</u> is deplorable. Why can't people begin and end, and give one some indication of what they are talking about? As to the Tychism[3] of it, it seems to me a good surface philosophy, a good expression of consciousness and the look of the flux. Of course what must be, if it must be, would never be <u>known</u> beforehand; and the machinery that may actually support our feelings doesn't deprive them of their dramatic novelty and interest, any more than the printed <u>dénoument</u> of a novel, extant in the last chapter, takes away from the dreamful excitement of perusing it and of wondering what will come next.

Now that I am launched I will say a word about some of the criticisms in your letter. You are very generous; I feel that you want to give me credit for everything good that can possibly be found in my book. But you don't yet see my philosophy nor my temper from the inside; your praise, like your blame touches only the periphery, accidental aspects presented to this or that preconceived and disparate interest. The style is good, the tone is supercilious, here is a shrewd passage, etc, etc. And you say I am less hospitable than Emerson. Of course. Emerson might pipe his wood-notes and chirp at the universe most blandly his genius might be tender and profound and Hamlet-like, and that is all beyond my range and contrary to my purpose. I am a Latin, and nothing seems serious to me except politics, except the sort of men that your ideas will involve and the sort of happiness they will be capable of. The rest is exquisite moonshine. Religion in particular was <u>found out</u> more than too hundred years ago, and it seems to me intolerable that we should still be condemned to ignore the fact and to give the parsons and the "idealists" a monopoly of indignation and of contemptuous dogmatism. It is they, not we, that are the pest; and while I wish to be just and to understand people's feelings, whereever they are at all significant, I am deliberately minded to be contemptuous toward what seems to me contemptible, and not to have any share in the conspiracy of mock respect by which intellectual ignominy and moral stagnation are kept up in our society. What did Emerson know or care about the passionate insanities and political disasters which religion, for instance, has so often been another name for? He could give that name to his last personal intuition, and ignore what it stands for and what it expresses in the world. It is the latter that absorbs me; and I care too much about mortal happiness to be interested in the charming vegetation of cancer-microbes in the system—except with the idea of suppressing it.

A more technical point. You say "activity" can be spiritual only. Is your activity, or sense of activity, not rather an ἐνέργεια[4] than a δύναμις?[5] Of course I should be the first to agree that activity, in the sense of actuality and conscious stress, belongs only to ∧this∧ consciousness or even to the rational and reflective energy of thought. But <u>efficiency</u>, in the sense of ~~actual~~ ∧regular∧ predictable contiguity with other specific events, belongs only to δύναμις, to the potential (= the potent.) In a dream there is the sense of activity, ~~their~~ there is commotion and actualization, ἐνέργεια: but there is no δύναμις, no material efficacy, save through the underlying metabolism in the brain; the story in the dream stops short; its purposes evaporate. This may be contrary to common sense, meaning ordinary ways of expressing oneself; but it seems to me quite of a piece with common sense of a progressive sort, with science. It might be contrary to common sense to say that the sun is larger than the earth, but not to common sense applied to the full situation. So this doctrine seems to me reasonable in its method and result, though as yet paradoxical in its language.

I have read practically no reviews of my book so that I don't know if any one has felt in it something which, I am sure, is there. I mean the <u>tears</u>. "Sunt lachrimae rerum, ac mentem mortalia tangunt."[6] Not that I care to moan over the gods of Greece, turned into the law of gravity, or over the stained-glass of cathedrals broken to let in the sunlight and the air. It is not the past that seems to me affecting, entrancing, or pitiful to lose. It is the ideal. It is that vision of perfection that we just catch, or for a moment embody in some work of art, or in some idealised reality: it is the concomitant inspiration of life, always various, always beautiful, hardly ever expressible in its fulness. And it is my adoration of this real and familiar good, this love often embraced but always elusive, that makes me ʈdetet the Absolutes and the dragooned myths by which people try to cancel the ˄passing˄ ideal, or to denaturalise it. That is an inhumanity, an impiety, that I can't bear. And much of the irritation which I may betray and which, I assure you is much greater than I let it seem, comes of affection. It comes of exasperation at seeing the only things that are beautiful or worth having treated as if they were of no account.

I seldom write to anyone so frankly as I have here. But I know you are human, and tolerant to anything, however alien, that smells of blood. [*across*]

                    Always sincerely yours   GSantayana

[1] As you wish.
[2] *Reveries of One* by Benjamin Paul Blood (1832–1919), an American poet and philosopher.
[3] For Aristotle, tyche (chance) is what happens exceptionally and yet fulfills a purpose, distinct from a spontaneous accident. In Greek mythology Tyche is the goddess of luck or chance.
[4] Actuality.
[5] Potentiality.
[6] "E'en here the tear of pity springs / And hearts are touched by human things." Conington's translation from Vergil's *Aeneid*, 1.462.

To Susan Sturgis de Sastre

6 December 1905 [*postmark*] • Paris, France   (MS postcard: Sanchez)

PARIS.–L'EGLISE SAINT-SULPICE.

Dec. 6. Thanks for your letter. The lectures are going on well, and my too faithful friend has left for Naples. I have others here, and too many invitations.   G.S.

To Susan Sturgis de Sastre

7 December 1905 [*postmark*] • Paris, France   (MS postcard: Sanchez)

PARIS.–LE PONT DES ARTS ET L'INSTITUT.

Dec 7.   If I left Ribot's book, "La psychologie anglaise contemporaine"[1] in Avila, could you send it to me here? I meant to have brought it along, but apparently forgot it.–This is a foot-bridge over the Seine by which I

usually cross. The Louvre is on this side of it.–I went to an American dinner party last night and was bored to death. A French lunch tomorrow, etc.

J

[1]Théodule Armand Ribot (1839–1916) was professor of psychology at the Sorbonne
and director of the psychological laboratory at the Collège de France. This was his first
book and was published in Paris in 1870.

To George Herbert Palmer
13 December 1905 • Paris, France   (MS: Boston)

Paris, Dec. 13, 1905

Dear Mr Palmer

As the chief part of your recent letter (being about my book) didn't
seem to require an answer, I have been forgetting that what you said about
your own book[1] did; but I believe I had already written to you about it,
saying I should be much obliged if you would keep the volumes, as you
suggest, until my return, as here I have not only a sufficient load materially, but also too many occupations and distractions to leave me a quiet
hour for poesy and piety of George Herbert's somewhat remote sort. It
must have been a rare pleasure and consolation to you to do this labour of
love and to recover familiarly the habits and thoughts of so congenial and
refined a spirit.

My lectures here are going on pleasantly and well before a moderate
audience composed in a large part of American ladies.

On another sheet[2] (taking time by the fore-lock) I send you my proposal
for courses next year, which I suppose will soon have to be determined
upon. Now that Perry is a professor and the author of a book[3] ad hoc, it
seems to me that he ought to go on with Phil 1,b, which he will carry on
much better than I should or ever did. However, I am ready, of course, if
it must be, to take my share of that heavy and (as it seems to me) unnecessary burden. Could I be relieved of it, there are several half-courses or
seminaries that I might offer instead–beside the problematical Aristotle I
mention.

With best regards

Yours sincerely

GSantayana

[1] *The English Works of George Herbert, newly arranged and annotated and considered in relation to his life* (1905). George Herbert (1593–1633) was an English religious poet whose works are some of the finest of metaphysical poetry.
[2] Unlocated.
[3] *The Approach to Philosophy* (1905).

To Susan Sturgis de Sastre

13 December 1905 [*postmark*] • Paris, France   (MS postcard: Sanchez)

PARIS.—EGLISE SAINT-ETIENNE-DU-MONT.

Dec. 13.

Thank you very much for the psychology-book which arrived today. For two days we have had brisk, almost clear weather, but this morning it is wet again. This church (near here) shows how un-Parisian Paris can be.

[*Unsigned*]

To Celedonio Sastre Serrano

25 January 1906 • Paris, France   (MS: Sastre)

Paris, 25 de enero, 1906[1]

Querido Celedonio: tuve mucho gusto en recibir á su tiempo tu carta del 27 de diciembre—parece imposible que se haya pasado un mes entero desde esa fecha. Por ella, y por otra anterior de Susana, comprendo que no hay fundado motivo para que no venga Rafael á Paris. Para mi será una verdadera satisfaccion, tanto por el gusto que tendré en verle, cómo por la ocasion que su presencia me ofrecerá de ver lo que no he visto en Paris, ó de volver á ver lo que mas me ha gustado. Estando solo, tiene uno ménos humor, sobre todo para las expediciones un poco largas, cómo la de Versalles ó la de Fontaînebleau, puntos que aún no he visitado.

Mis conferencias siguen su curso sin contratiempo de ningun género. El público ha disminuido algo, cómo era de esperar, pero todavia acuden unas doscientas personas, en gran parte señoras americanas. Pienso terminar las conferencias en Paris el dia 17 de ~~febrero~~ ₐmarzoₐ, y enseguida empesar mi vᴅiage redondo por las provincias; no se ha decidido todavia en que forma he de hacer ese viage, pero desea Hyde (el fundador de las conferencias, que está actualmente en Paris) que vaya por lo menos á nueve universidades. En ese caso debo despachar dos ó tres de ellas antes de la pascua de resurrección, para que me quede tiempo despues de las vacaciones para las restantes.

De salud sigo bien. El tiempo ha cambiado en estos últimos dias. Por fin hemos visto el sól; pero en cambio hace bastante frio.

Cariñosos recuerdos á todos de tu hermano   Jorge

[1]Translation:

Dear Celedonio: I was very pleased to receive in due course your letter of December 27–it seems impossible that an entire month has passed since that time. From this letter and the earlier one from Susana, I understand that there is no reason why Rafael can't come to Paris. For me it will be a real satisfaction, as much for the pleasure I will have in seeing him, as for the occasion that his presence will offer me of seeing things that I haven't seen in Paris, or of seeing again that which is most enjoyable to me. Being alone, one has less fun, especially for longer expeditions like that to Versailles or to Fountainebleau, places I have not yet visited.

My lectures continue on course without setback of any kind. The public has diminished somewhat, as was expected, but still some two hundred people come in, mainly American ladies. I plan to finish the lectures in Paris the 17th of March and to begin at once my round trip through the provinces; I still have not decided the route I have to make for this trip, but Hyde (founder of the lectures, that actually are in Paris) wants me to go to at least nine universities. In that case I ought to finish two or three of them before Easter, so that time remains to me after the vacations for the rest.

I continue to be healthy. The weather has changed in these last days. Finally we have seen the sun; but on the other hand it is rather cold.

Fond memories to all from your brother

To Benjamin Apthorp Gould Fuller
29 January 1906 • Paris, France   (MS: Houghton)

Hôtel Foyot. Paris
Jan. 29. 1906

Your criticism, my dear Fuller, of my third volume[1] has this defect, which I want to point out to you while the sense of it is still hot within me. You make an <u>insincere</u> objection. Of course there <u>might</u> be any number of finite gods making for righteousness, as there certainly are some natural and human forces making for it. But do you believe there are? In remote parts of nature we may well conjecture that some good is pursued and perhaps attained by beings inconceivable to us. But are these the gods of that living religion which you think I ignore? Of course the gods of actual reli-

gion are very confused and impossible monsters; but their essential func-
tions, when discriminated and made articulate, seem to me to be reducible
to the two I have insisted upon in my book. These are the <u>rational</u> values,
the eternal sources and sanctions of what is sane in religious madness. The
madness itself, in its psychological or dramatic texture, cannot be included
in the life of reason, though of course it may be referred to in a description
of that honourable fraction of our existence; nor do I think that I have left
this madness altogether uncharacterised.—As to my injustice to the Neo-
Platonists—of whom Plotinus is of course the best and the most Hellenic[2]—
I am more inclined to plead guilty, because I know little at first hand about
them, and you, in the full blush of your recent erudition, might easily
refute me with quotations selected <u>ad hoc</u>. I know that Plotinus, as against
even Gnostic Christians,[3] stood for what he <u>called</u> natural and political
goods; but nature and society were by that time transfused with a mystical
solvent which rendered his official allegiance to them, I imagine, largely
deceptive. And his followers made this illusion more transparent and quite
let the ascetic cat out of the bag.

You may have all of my furniture that pleases you. You will do me a
favour by getting these impedimenta out of my way and out of my mind.
[*across*] Here all goes well. Hyde has arrived and is very nice to me. The
Frenchmen are dulcet and disappointing, but I am having altogether a
delightful time.   Yours ever   G. S.

[1]*Religion.*

[2]Neoplatonism absorbed virtually all nonmaterialist and religious doctrines of earlier
systems. It is the only significant school of antiquity since the beginning of the fourth
century, a school that undertook to satisfy all intellectual and religious aspirations of
man. In the nineteenth century Platonism became sharply distinguished from
Neoplatonism. Plotinus (c. 204–c. 270) was a Greek philosopher of Neoplatonism.
Plotinus's treatises were arranged into Enneads (groups of nine), written during the last
seventeen years of his life. Hellenism is the culture, ideals, and pattern of life of Greece,
as represented in Athens at the time of Pericles; any modern attempt to revive Greek
ideals is called Hellenism.

[3]Gnosticism was a religious and philosophic movement from the Hellenistic era. Its
fundamental doctrine was that salvation was to be obtained through knowledge rather
than through faith or good works. The movement had a great effect on early
Christianity by forcing the new religion to define doctrines in declaring Gnosticism
heretical.

To Charles Scribner's Sons
29 January 1906 • Paris, France   (MS: Princeton)

Hôtel Foyot
rue de Tournon
Paris

Jan. 29, 1906

Messrs Charles Scribner's Sons
New York.

As I presume the fifth volume of "The Life of Reason" will be out soon, I send you a list of persons to whom I wish you would have it sent. If you still have the list I sent you for vols III & IV, you can follow that whereever the present one does not give a new or an added address.

I shall be in Paris, at this hôtel, until March 17ᵗʰ After that I go on a tour of provincial universities and my safest address will be Brown Shipley & Co. London

Yours very truly
GSantayana

Prof. Norton	Shady Hill	
" Palmer	Quincy St	
" James	Irving St	
" Royce	"	Cambridge
" Münsterberg	Ware St	Mass
" Perry	Appian Way	
" & Mrs Toy	7 Lowell St	
A. G. Fuller, Esq.	60 Brattle St	
Francis Bullard, Esq.	3 Commonweath Ave. Boston Mass	
Mrs. J. B. de Santayana	75 Monmouth St Brookline, Mass.	
Hon. Bertrand Russell,	Oxford.	
G. L. Dickinson Esq,	King's College Cambridge	England
King's College Library.	Cambridge	
Bernard Berenson Esq,	I Tatti, Settignano	Florence, Italy
Professor C. A. Strong.	Hôtel du Parc,	Cannes France
Delta Phi Club,	Linden St.	
Harvard Union,	Quincy St	Cambridge, Mass

W. Bayard Cutting, Esq. Villa Guardamunt St. Moritz, Switzerland.
R. Burnside Potter, Esq   123 East 73rd St,   New York, N.Y.

Please send a copy of "Reason in Science" with the author's compliments, to the above addresses.   G.S.

To Susan Sturgis de Sastre
11 February 1906 [*postmark*] • Paris, France   (MS postcard: Sanchez)

PARIS—PANORAMA DU JARDIN DES TUILERIES

Feb. 11. Thanks for your letter. I have heard nothing from Rafael directly, but he will be welcome on any day. If he hasn't yet started when this arrives, you might tell him, in case by any accident I shouldn't meet him at the Station, to take a cab and come to the Foyot and ask for me. As I don't know when he is to arrive, I might easily have an engagement at that moment, say for dinner, if he took the later train.   G. S.

To Susan Sturgis de Sastre
1 March 1906 [*postmark*] • Paris, France   (MS postcard: Sanchez)

PARIS—LE SACRÉ-CŒUR DE MONTMARTRE

March 1.   This morning I get yours of the 27th We are well. Rafael yesterday bought a suit for fifty seven francs. There were some slight alterations to make, so that he is going this afternoon again to try it on & to pay for it. Last night we went to an "emotional" play–<u>Le maître des Forges</u>"[1]– at which everybody cried and blew his nose. Rafael seems to have enjoyed it hugely.–The expense of having him here is turning out to be less than I expected, as we dine a good deal in the <u>Duval</u>[2] establishments which I never went to when alone. Rafael finds all the waitresses very pretty (whatever their age) in their white caps. I am having my portrait painted by Miss Swan, who lives with Mildred Minturn.[3] It was her idea; if it is a success I will have photographs made, for the benefit of the family–

GS

---

[1] *The Iron Master* by Georges Ohnet (1848–1918).
[2] A chain of inexpensive restaurants in Paris.
[3] Swan and Minturn are unidentified.

To Susan Sturgis de Sastre

1 April 1906 [*postmark*] • Lyon, France   (MS postcard: Sanchez)

NANCY.–HÔTEL DE VILLE (XVIIIE SIÈCLE)

Lyon. April 1. Am stopping here over Sunday on the way to Montpellier. My lecture at Nancy was crowded but hardly anybody understood English! I have had no news of Rafael's journey. I hope all went well.

G.S.

To Susan Sturgis de Sastre

3 April [1906] • Montpellier, France   (MS postcard: Sanchez)

1905   MONTPELLIER–LA CATHÉDRALE & LA FACULTÉ DE MÉDECINE

April 3.–It is delightful here in Montpellier. I think constantly of Avila & Greece. It is Spring at last.   GS.

To Charles Scribner's Sons

4 April [1906] • Montpellier, France   (MS: Princeton)

GRAND CAFÉ AMÉRICAIN
MADAME FLOUTIER
PROPRIÉTAIRE
9, RUE MAGUELONE
MONTPELLIER

MONTPELLIER, LE 4 avril

✝Pray excuse a traveller's stationer[*torn*]

Messrs Charles Scribner's Sons
New York

Gentlemen:

Some time ago I received your letter about the general success of "The Life of Reason" and it gave me great satisfaction. The copies of vol. 5. had previously reached me safely. My brother has also forwarded your half-yearly account, for which I beg to thank you as well.

Please have "Reason in Science" sent to the two following addresses, if they were not included in the list already used: Howard Sturgis, Esq.

Queen's Acre, Windsor, England and Monsieur C. Cestre, 26 rue de St Pothin, Dijon, France.

It is naturally most gratifying to me that my long book should receive so much recognition and should have such a respectable company of buyers. I have not read many reviews, as I find little profit in doing so as a rule; but two sent me by their authors Mr. Bliss Carman's in the Saturday literary supplement to the N. Y. Tribune,[1] and Professor Dewey's in "Science"[2] are very flattering indeed, and could furnish excellent sentences to quote in an advertising sheet. Doubtless you have taken note of them already.

An adequate philosophical criticism is not to be expected at once; the whole book has only just been ₐputₐ before the public, and the last volume is perhaps the most important from a theoretical point of view. Professor Dewey's notice covers the first two volumes only; so the desultory references in Dickinson's article in the "Independent Review."[3] Dickinson might write a review of the whole; I will ask him to do so. He does not agree with me, being too sentimental and (as I think) half-hearted ~~to do so~~ ₐfor thatₐ; but he is very keen and competent, and the divergence would give his appreciations a greater air of impartiality and more authority. He is a great friend of mine, however, as the inner circle might as well know.

Yours very truly
GSantayana

C/o Brown Shipley & Co.
    London.

[1]William Bliss Carman (1861–1929), Canadian-born member of the Harvard class of 1888, was a prolific poet whose books include *Low Tide on Grandpre: A Book of Lyrics* (1893), three books with Richard Hovey, and more than twenty volumes of poetry. Carman's review of *Reason* was in the *New York Times Saturday Review of Books* (27 Jan 1906): 45–46.

[2]John Dewey (1859–1952) was an American philosopher and educator long associated with Columbia University. His philosophy (instrumentalism) is related to pragmatism. In education he argued for learning by experience, motivated by the student's need. His review of *Common Sense* and *Society* was published in *Science* (9 Feb 1906): 223–25.

[3]Goldsworthy Lowes Dickinson comments on *Common Sense* and *Society* in "The Newest Philosophy" 6 (1905): 177–90.

To Hugo Münsterberg
11 April 1906 • Cannes, France   (MS: Boston)

April 11, 1906.

HÔTEL DU PARC
CANNES, A. M.

Dear Münsterberg,

I have come here to spend a part of my easter holiday with my friend Strong. My provincial lectures, of which I have given those at Nancy, and at Montpellier, has been very pleasant so far for myself, but as an audience who really understands English is not easy to find, I have been reduced rather to a phonetic machine, with the function of emitting interesting if unintelligible sounds. The audiences nevertheless have been large and religiously attentive, while the rectors and other professors have shown me every possible courtesy.

I enclose a letter from Cattell[1] which explains itself up to a certain point, although I suppose they would not have made me an offer which they could not have expected me to accept, unless they had something else in the background. I have answered, accordingly, refusing for the moment, but paving the way for any future offer which (as I have reason to think) they may have up their sleeve. Very likely you are better informed about the situation at Columbia than I am, or even than Strong is, and might give me some useful advice.

Yours most sincerely
GSantayana

[1]James McKeen Cattell (1860–1944) was professor of psychology at the University of Pennsylvania and at Columbia University (1891–1917). He established and edited the *Psychological Review* and was owner and editor of *Science* and *Scientific Monthly*. The letter is unlocated.

To Susan Sturgis de Sastre
11 April 1906 [*postmark*] • Cannes, France   (MS postcard: Sanchez)

CANNES.—BOULEVARD DE LA CROISETTE

April 11.   Today I get your letter and Celedonio's. I have also received one from Rafael, some time ago. Cannes is almost tropical and I am living in luxury (with Strong) but in an atmosphere of invalids. I am going to Avignon in about a week—on my way to Toulouse, where I am due to lecture on May 1ˢᵗ.   GS.

To Susan Sturgis de Sastre
24 April 1906 [*postmark*] • Nîmes, France   (MS postcard: Sanchez)

NÎMES.—LE PONT DU GARD.

April 25.   I have come here from Avignon this afternoon and am having tea in the open air very pleasantly. It is the best Roman aqueduct I have yet seen.   G.S.

To Susan Sturgis de Sastre
25 April 1906 [*postmark*] • Orange, France   (MS postcard: Sanchez)

ORANGE.—LE THÉÂTRE ROMAIN

Orange, April 25.   Yesterday, when I sent you two cards,[1] I made a mistake in the date. It was Tuesday the 24ᵗʰ Today I have come here to see this Roman theatre and a Roman triumphal arch, very interesting technically. It is nice & <u>cool</u>.

[*Unsigned*]

[1]Second card is unlocated.

To Susan Sturgis de Sastre
29 April 1906 • Toulouse, France   (MS: Virginia)

GRAND HÔTEL & HÔTEL TIVOLLIER
TOULOUSE
RUE DE METZ

TOULOUSE, LE <u>29 avril</u> 190<u>6</u>

Dear Susie:

    I got your letter yesterday afternoon when I was leaving Carcassonne. It is raining this morning, so I take the opportunity to answer at once.

    1ˢᵗ   I don't know what newspaper-cuttings about my book they have been sending you. I have repeatedly begged them not to send me any, and they have finally stopped doing so; the reviews I have seen—one or two excepted—are quite incompetent and often written by people who have not even read a page of the book through. It is not worth paying any attention to what they say.—As to my teaching Strong "Catholic metaphysics", you must understand that my own philosophy—no es muy Católica;[1] it is independent of religion altogether, and looks at religion merely as at a historic and human fact—more or less appealing or beneficent, as the case may be. You have seen all you probably care to see of this attitude in my "Interpretations of poetry and religion". The attitude of my new book is exactly the same; but of course it deals with many other subjects as well as with religion.

2nd   Why should you be worried at Rafael's going to "Mauriscot"? If he is to be long at Cartago isn't it much better that he should be normally settled there, with a domestic circle of his own, and smaller Rafaelitos to think about? He told me something about the affair: that you haven't seen the girl is nothing against her; you may see only too much of her some day. If you knew her and didn't like her, it might be something to complain of, although it would have to be put up with all the same.

3rd   Mr. Rockefeller[2] is not a lunatic; he is, I understand, a little timid, and doubtless has detectives to protect him against "cranks" that might loiter about his house. But he is comparatively well, and has a new wig to make him beautiful; and he is coming to spend seven weeks at Compiegne this Summer with the Strongs. Mrs. Rockefeller comes with him; they are going to travel under an assumed name, to protect themselves from begging letters and indiscrete curiosity. Strong tells me that he has written an essay on the duties of rich men, which he is going to read some Sunday afternoon to his father-in-law. It points out that very large fortunes are truly "trusts"; and that instead of being left to individuals of one's family they should be made into public funds, administered by some trustees of distinction, for the benefit of the community at large.—It is easy to give this generous advice when one is a philosopher, [across] and one's only daughter[3] is sure, in any case, of being well provided for. Strong himself is growing much more luxurious; I think the old man has given him a million dollars, and it is beginning to tell. Strong refers to it by saying that he "has some money in the bank"—à propos of having his book well printed. I send you a letter of his,[4] so that you may judge of him for yourself. It is a terrible life he leads, as his wife is like a child, hopelessly ill, yet apparently not going to die for the present.

Love to Celedonio and the family from   George

[1] Is not very Catholic.

[2]John Davison Rockefeller (1839–1937) was an industrialist and philanthropist married to Laura Celestia Spelman. Their children were "Bessie," Alice, Alta, Edith, and John D. Jr. His Standard Oil Company dominated the U.S. oil-refining industry, and he founded the University of Chicago (1892). His philanthropies promote public health and further science.
[3]Margaret (1897–1985) was the Strongs' only child.
[4]Unlocated.

To Charles Augustus Strong

29 April 1906 • Toulouse, France   (MS: Rockefeller)

GRAND HÔTEL & HÔTEL TIVOLLIER
TOULOUSE
RUE DE METZ

TOULOUSE, LE <u>29 Avril</u> 190<u>6</u>

Dear Strong

I, too, under the influence of your effusion, received last night on my arrival here, have been composing verses in my dreams. Here is all I can now remember:

> This philosophic waste of ink
> Comes of not saying what you think,
> Forgetting what a fool might know,
> And proving (sic) what isn't so.

As to the soul fortified by having lived before the days of James, Dewey and Schiller, I thought it was Clough.[1]

> It fortified the soul of Clough
> That Truth, though bid, was safe enough:
> But how it tickles James & Co
> That, what seems true, is always so!

What is this foolishness but a clear consequence of the damnable sensualism of Berkeley, in which we have all been brought up? I have no prejudice against Berkeley, but he is a damnable engine of Satan. The three things to which my inspired oracle attributes the waste of ink are conspicuous and fundamental in his philosophy. He doesn't say what he thinks when he declares that an idea can be like nothing but an idea, for he thinks—being capable of thinking—that an idea may be like a thing. He forgets what a fool might know that the image of a man may have only one leg, one arm, and one ear, ^while^ the <u>real</u> man has two of each. And he proves that every ~~perception~~ ^idea^ is caused by the desire to have it,— having it already or not having it yet, take your choice of absurdities!

If I felt that you were washed quite clean of this sophistry, I should have more confidence in your "mind-stuff."

I am glad you had a nice time, and only a slight indigestion, at Marseille. At Carcassonne and Avignon[2] I also had a good time, and no indigestion at all, in spite of the doubtful food. The cold has set me up. I didn't go to Vaucluse to poetise about Laura[3] because it was raining rather too much to shed tears in comfort over spiritual tragedies. I went straight to Carcassonne instead, but only after seeing Orange and the Pont du Gard.[4] Great pragmatists, those Romans, because They believe^d^ in <u>intelligence</u> and <u>geometry</u>.

Yours ever
G.S.

[1]Arthur Hugh Clough (1819–61) was an English poet and friend of literary figures.
[2]Carcassonne in southern France is a medieval walled city which was restored in the nineteenth century. Avignon, in southeast France, was papal property until 1791. Its landmarks include a papal palace and the Basilica of Saint Peter.
[3]Vaucluse, in southeast France, was made famous by Petrarch, who lived there. Laura was the beloved of Petrarch and the subject of his lyrics. He first saw her in the church of Saint Claire at Avignon; she died twenty-one years later on the same date. Poets since have used the name Laura to denote an idealized lady to whom they address their love lyrics.
[4]Orange, in southeast France near Avignon, has a Roman amphitheater still in use. The House of Orange is the reigning dynasty of the Netherlands. The Pont du Gard is a perfectly preserved aqueduct built in 19 B.C. across the Gard River near Remoulins in southern France, to supply Nîmes with water. It has three tiers of arches, the lowest of which is used as a road bridge.

To Susan Sturgis de Sastre

5 May 1906 [*postmark*] • Toulouse, France   (MS postcard: Sanchez)

TOULOUSE—NEF DE L'EGLISE ST- SERNIR

May 5. Today I leave for Pau, on my way to Bordeaux. Last night I dined at the rector's here, and had a good time. There was an African explorer, who talked well. Much rain.

[*Unsigned*]

To Frederick James Eugene Woodbridge
5 May 1906 • Toulouse, France   (MS: Columbia)

^C/o Brown Shipley & Co
123 Pall Mall
London.

Toulouse, May 5, 1906

Dear Mr Woodbridge

I send you the inclosed communication to be published, if you think fit, among the "ⴋDiscussions" in your Journal.[1] If it would take too long to send me a proof, may I ask you to look it over? I am afraid the printer's reader might make me say things more foolish than I mean, as for instance, by transforming "beatifying" in § 2 into "beautifying".

I was very much flattered by Professor Dewey's review of my first two volumes, and, in general, also by Moore's: but his desire to make a "pragmatist" of me has nettled me a little: hence this effusion.

Yours sincerely
GSantayana

[1]"The Efficacy of Thought," *The Journal of Philosophy, Psychology, and Scientific Methods* 3 (1906): 410–12 is a response to Moore's two-part review of *Reason* in the same journal, 3 (12 Apr 1906): 211–21, and 5 (16 Aug 1906): 469–71. Moore responded to Santayana with "The Function of Reason" (1906): 519–22. Addison Webster Moore (1886–1930) was a philosopher who taught at the University of Chicago. He allied himself with the school of instrumental pragmatism (created by Dewey).

To [Susan Sturgis de Sastre]
8 May [1906] • Pau, France   (MS postcard: Sanchez)

PAU.–VUE SUR LA CHAÎNE DES PYRÉNÉES.

Pau, May 8th   I have found this place just what I wanted–delightfully warm and sunny, not too crowded, the gardens in full flower, snow mountains in sight, and nothing to do but stroll and scribble. These three days I have spent mostly in the parks, sitting on some bench, and either reading the papers or writing in my note-book things suggested by my recent discussions with Strong. It has been very nice and restful. Pau is a much more wonderful place than I remembered it to be–most luxuriant and grand at the same time. This photograph [*across*] doesn't do the view justice, as the mountains are much higher & nearer than they look here.

[*Unsigned*]

To Hugo Münsterberg
10 May 1906 • Bordeaux, France   (MS: Boston)

Bordeaux, May 10, 1906

Dear Münsterberg

At the same time with your long letter of April 23, I get one from Cattell (who seems to have been in communication with you on the subject) proposing that I should go to New York for two days in the week, giving four hours of lectures, and receiving $1500. Your proposal is less definite, but I infer that what you would suggest is that I should give all my eight hours at Harvard in the other four days. Such an arrangement, I need hardly say, is out of the question. I am accordingly writing to Cattell that I could accept his offer only if my work at Harvard were greatly reduced, (by "greatly reduced" I mean reduced to one course) but that as this does not seem to be contemplated by you, who speak, I presume, "by authority", I am obliged to decline.

When I wrote to you before I supposed you would have heard that they had a new professorship at Columbia in <u>Kulturgeschichte</u>,[1] and that my name had been mentioned for it; but I understand it has since been filled by one of their own professors of history. This is what I meant by something which, I had reason to think, might be in the background.

No acceptable proposal being before me, then, I see no use in discussing what I might do if there was one. I am much obliged for your account of my position at Harvard, moral and material. There is nothing in it, however, altogether new to me, except the fact that it has only just been decided that I shall some day be a professor. I had supposed that point decided when, thanks largely to your friendly efforts, my appointment as assistant professor was made. After ten years of this, I supposed a full professorship followed as a matter of ~~ye~~ course; and while it is usual, no doubt, to grant the promotion somewhat earlier, even if millions have not been just subscribed for "increase of salaries and promotions," I rather expected that, in my case, reasons would be found for postponing action to the last possible moment. But I never doubted that the promotion would come; and as I don't need the money, I was willing enough to wait—not, I confess, without a certain amusement.

Thank you for arranging my courses as I wished and for the news of James.

My tour is going on pleasantly and audiences come, though not always to get more than a phonetic exercise. The rectors and deans, as a rule, are charming.

Yours very sincerely
GSantayana

[1]Cultural history.

To Susan Sturgis de Sastre

11 May 1906 • Arcachon, France   (MS postcard: Sanchez)

ARCACHON.—VUE DAN LES DUNES.
May. 11, 1906.

I have come here for a few days of quiet between lectures.

[*Unsigned*]

To Hugo Münsterberg

16 May 1906 • Bordeaux, France   (MS: Boston)

Bordeaux, May 16, 1906

Dear Münsterberg

Your second letter, which reached me last night, does not change the aspect of affairs. The arrangement you propose—with assistants relieving me of my work on Fridays—does not attract me, and we will therefore stick to my work as arranged and give up all thoughts of Columbia.

I should be sorry if this little affair—ending in smoke—had caused you unnecessary trouble and inconvenience. At least it may have made us all a little more conscious of our sentiments toward one another—which may prove useful on occasion.

I have been spending four days in the pine woods of Arcachon, very much enjoying the silence.

People here are very hospitable, so that my time is rather taken up.

Yours very sincerely
GSantayana

To Susan Sturgis de Sastre

18 May 1906 [*postmark*] • La Rochelle, France   (MS postcard: Sanchez)

LA ROCHELLE.–L'HÔTEL-DE-VILLE.–LA COUR.

La Rochelle, May 18. I have come here on the way to Caen, after rather a weary time at Bordeaux–three nights out to dinner speaking French. By the way, if I left my pass-port (in a red pocket-book in my desk) you might send it to me someday. It is always well to have it in case of registered letters. Tomorrow I go on to Angers.

[*Unsigned*]

To Susan Sturgis de Sastre

22 May 1906 [*postmark*] • Caen, France   (MS postcard: Sanchez)

CAEN–L'ABSIDE DE L'ABBAYE-AUX-HOMMES

Caen, May 22.

Dingy old town with fine Gothic churches. Rain and cold. I go back to Paris the day after tomorrow.   G.S.

To Mr. Helder

28 May 1906 • Paris, France   (MS: Virginia)

Paris, May 28 1906

Dear Mr Helder[1]

Your question about "Strong defences" for individual immortality puzzles me a good deal–I can think of none.

As to my personal opinion on the subject, you will find it expressed at length in the last two chapters[2] of volume III of my book on "The Life of Reason"–the volume (which can be got separately) on "Reason in Religion". But you will get little comfort out of it.

Yours truly
GSantayana

[1]Unidentified.
[2]Chapter XIII is "The Belief in a Future Life," and chapter XIV is "Ideal Immortality."

To Charles Augustus Strong
28 May 1906 [*postmark*] • Paris, France   (MS: Georgetown)

Quai Voltaire, <u>May 28</u>

Dear Strong
The shades of two rectors have intervened between me and the vision of a week in Paris and I leave tomorrow morning for Lille, whence I go directly to Dijon. You will not find me here when you come. I am very sorry.

Thank you for the errata. How shocking some of them are!
Yours ever
G.S.

To Susan Sturgis de Sastre
5 June 1906 • Dijon, France   (MS postcard: Sanchez)

DIJON.—ECLUSE DE LARREY.

<u>Canal de Bourgoque</u>.   5 de junio, 1906.

[*Unsigned*]

To Susan Sturgis de Sastre
10 June 1906 [*postmark*] • Morez, France   (MS postcard: Sanchez)

MOREZ (JURA).—VUE GÉNÉRALE, PRISE DU BECHET.
10 de junio. $He pasado aquí la noche. J[1]

[1]Translation:
June 10.   I have spent the night here.

To Susan Sturgis de Sastre

12 June 1906 [*postmark*] • Col de la Faucille, France (MS postcard: Sanchez)

COL DE LA FAUCILLE–ALT. 1323 M.

June 12.   I am going down this afternoon from here (after spending two nights at the Inn you see above) to Geneva, on my way to Lyons. Nice weather.

[*Unsigned*]

To Susan Sturgis de Sastre

19 June 1906 [*postmark*] • Grenoble, France   (MS postcard: Sanchez)

GRENOBLE–QUAI XAVIER-JOUVIN ET LE Sᵀ-EYNARD

Grenoble, June 19ᵗʰ   I came to this charming place yesterday from Lyons. Lyons was hot, and I was pursued by official people, so that I couldn't call my soul my own. Here they don't know I have arrived, and I am happy! It is all swift rivers high hills and nice gardens by the water.   G.S.

To Charles William Eliot

23 June 1906 • Grenoble, France   (MS: Harvard)

Grenoble, June 23, 1906

Dear Mʳ Eliot

The series of lectures which I have been giving in France, ended here yesterday. The year has been a delightful one for me personally,–except that my health has not been quite so good as usual; together with the previous twelvemonth of travel, it has given me a very refreshing change of scenes and of companionships. Even in respect to my philosophic interests, I have found a great deal that is new to me, and interesting, in the movement of French speculation, which is very active at present and is carried on in a most critical and open-minded spirit, as well as with a solid foundation in scholarship.

My impressions about the value of the Hyde lectureship are rather too complex to be expressed in a letter; I have accordingly written the accompanying memorandum.[1] It represents my sincere opinion upon this undertaking, when reflected on in cold blood. It might give a wrong impression, however, of my personal satisfaction at the reception I have met with both from officials and from the public. The post I have held is a delightful one; the question is whether the general advantages of maintaining such a lectureship are not largely factitious.

Mr Hyde has seen this memorandum and, I believe, has kept a copy of it.

With sincere regards
Yours very truly
GSantayana

Address:
  ^c/o Brown Shipley & Co
    123 Pall Mall
    London.

[1]Located in the Harvard University Archives.

To Susan Sturgis de Sastre

28 June 1906 [*postmark*] • Paris, France   (MS postcard: Sanchez)

PARIS—NOTRE DAME

Paris, June 28.   The friends I was to join, now my lectures are over, have given out on account of bad health. I have come here in despair, but find Paris charming in spite of the heat. I may stay here two or three weeks at the Hôtel du Quai Voltaire.

[*Unsigned*]

To Susan Sturgis de Sastre

9 July [1906] • Évian, France   (MS postcard: Sanchez)

ÉVIAN-LES-BAINS
RETOUR DE PÊCHE

Evian, Savoie.   July 9.   We have come here across the lake from Glion for an excursion. I expect to start for Avila on Friday, going by Lyon-Toulouse-Bayonne and arriving on Monday at 11:30 a.m.–It has rained a great deal since I got here.

[Unsigned]

To Charles William Eliot
7 August 1906 • Compiègne, France   (MS: Harvard)

Compiègne

August 7, 1906

Dear Mr. Eliot.

I had already heard that Coolidge[1] was coming to France next winter, but I am glad to learn that Professor James still thinks of undertaking the lectures during the following year. I should certainly advise Coolidge not to go to nine provincial universities, as I did; it would be better, in my opinion, to go only to Lyons and Bordeaux, where he might well give several lectures to audiences that would appreciate them.

I have received no invitation to take a permanent place at Columbia; what was offered was a position for one year, as substitute for Professors Fullerton and Strong. This position I could have accepted only if I had leave of absence from Harvard, which it would be unreasonable to ask for after having obtained it for two years in succession. It is true that a rumour reached me at the same time that a permanent and well-endowed professorship at Columbia might possibly be offered to me; but the place was filled, I believe, by the promotion of one of their own professors. Thus nothing remained for me to consider seriously in the matter.

After this long holiday I am looking forward with pleasure to taking up my regular work.

Yours very sincerely
GSantayana

[1]Archibald Cary Coolidge.

To Susan Sturgis de Sastre
20 August 1906 [*postmark*] • Windsor, England   (MS postcard: Sanchez)

THE LONG WALK, WINDSOR.

Windsor, Aug. 20–This is my favourite walk here.–I weathered the Channel the other day although it was rather rough. Howard looks very well. Five Seymours are at the house. They are nice.

[*Unsigned*]

To Susan Sturgis de Sastre
24 August 1906 [*postmark*] • Brighton, England   (MS postcard: Sanchez)

BRIGHTON, OLD STEINE GARDENS.

–August 24–   I am at the hotel you see at the right edge of this card.– Brighton is nice and lazy and the weather good.   GS

To Reginald Chauncey Robbins
15 September 1906 • Brookline, Massachusetts   (MS: Houghton)

> 75 Monmouth Street
> Brookline
> 15–9–1906

Dear Robbins[1]

On getting back to this country I find your "Poems of Personality" with your kind note of Dec. 8. The other books had reached me in due season in various parts of the world, but without your address, so that I believe I have never thanked you for them. The "Love Poems" I read through, many parts more than once, and found them full of <u>experience</u>; and, what is perhaps less germane to poetry but very appealing to me, full of learning and of historical imagination. I look forward with great pleasure to this new volume.[2]

You are, in your poetry, one of those volcanic minds that overwhelm me a little with the rumblings, smoke, and precipitancy of their effusions. It is not always easy for me to translate such hints and indirections, and such unexplained fervours, into the plain prose that is all I can understand.

Nevertheless, I feel the presence in your poetry of something that inspires respect—experience, depth, heroism, readiness to face reality, whatever it may turn out to be. It is largely fed, and greatly pregnant. If it lacks articulation, after the manner that I am in the habit of looking to, that is perhaps because it has a great future, because it announces ways of feeling and acting which are only now dawning on the world.

I am very much flattered by your desire that I should not be altogether a stranger to your view of life.

With many thanks for all three volumes I am

Sincerely yours

GSantayana

[1]Reginald Chauncey Robbins (1871–1955) was a writer who took his A.B. from Harvard in 1892 and then did graduate work there.

[2]*Poems of Personality* (1904) and *Love Poems* (1903) were published by Riverside Press in Cambridge, Massachusetts.

To Charles Augustus Strong
[Mid-November 1906] • [Unknown]   (MS: Georgetown)

Dear Strong

I am here until midnight and if you care to see me I will come at any time that suits you. You have my sincerest sympathy.[1] G.S.

[1]This note is on the back of Santayana's calling card. It may refer to the 14 November death of Strong's wife, Elizabeth "Bessie".

To Charles Scribner's Sons
21 November 1906 • Brookline, Massachusetts   (MS: Princeton)

75 Monmouth St
Brookline Mass
Nov 21 1906

~~COLONIAL CLUB.~~

Messrs Charles Scribner's Sons
Gentlemen:

Please have a copy of vols. III and IV (Religion and Art) of "The Life of Reason" sent to

Mrs R. Burnside Potter

The New Weston
33 East 49ᵗʰ St
New York,
and charged to me.

You asked some time ago for a list of <u>errata</u> in "The Life of Reason". I have one that I can send–unhappily a rather long one–but if the possible reprint is not to be made soon, it might be better to keep it a while longer, as new errors are pointed out to me from time to time by various people, and I suppose the correction ought to be as thorough as possible.

I don't mean to make any changes in the text, except of clerical errors, on the principle of Musset "lorsqu'on change sans cesse au passé pourquoi rien changer"?[1] When I am converted I will make my recantation in a new book and not spoil the old one.

Yours very truly
G.Santayana

[1]Since we are constantly changing, why try to change what is past?

To Charles Augustus Strong
5 December 1906 • Brookline, Massachusetts   (MS: Rockefeller)

December 5 1906
75 Monmouth Street
Brookline

COLONIAL CLUB

Dear Strong

Thank you very much for your note and for the "Temps", which I spent the whole morning yesterday in reading. It took me back to the interesting politics of France, which I hear nothing of in these parts, although of course they take the "Temps" and the "Times" at the library, and I might read it all up if I had the persistency required. Brisson[1] makes out a good case for his immediate measures and shows a fair spirit. Perhaps the fundamental question at issue, however, would need a wider historical and political treatment. The Republicans seem to be vying with the Socialists at present to see who can do more to keep the Catholic "culte" going. Is that their ultimate ideal?

James asked me the other day to go and hear his lecture on "Pragmatism and Truth", which he said would go over the heads of most of his audience, and he wished to have a few intelligent people to talk to. So flattered, of course I went; but I was disappointed. He made some concessions: logical truth is eternal, and prior to the discovery of it, he says: naturally he doesn't dwell much on that point. Furthermore it appears that even material truth may belong to unimportant ideas; but who would care for <u>such</u> truth? So that the distinction seems to be accepted, though not made explicitly, between truth simple and pragmatic value or practical importance in ideas. After these concessions, James went on to repeat the old confusions and to protest against the want of imagination of those who take "Pragmatism" at its word. This lecture will not do what James says it is meant to do: it will not clear the air.

Did I ever thank you for the duds which I left at Compiègne and which you [*across*] were good enough to send on? It was hardly worth the trouble, but I am much obliged, and have one more shirt to my back.   Yours ever

G.S.

[1]Possibly Eugène Henri Brisson (1835–1912), a French historian.

To Charlotte Edith Taussig
29 December 1906 • Brookline, Massachusetts   (MS: Unknown)

---

75 Monmouth Street
Brookline, Mass.
Dec. 29, 1906

Miss Charlotte E. Taussig[1]
Dear Madam

My regular engagements, I am sorry to say, will not allow me to have the pleasure of addressing your club this winter. I am able to give but few lectures away from Cambridge, and those only in this corner of the country.

With high appreciation of the compliment your invitation involves, I remain

Yours very truly
GSantayana

[1]Miss Charlotte Edith Taussig (1876–1963) attended Smith College and Washington University in Saint Louis. She wrote poetry and the play "Thus Conscience Does Make Cowards of Us All." She frequently read papers at the Wednesday Club.

To Isabella Stewart Gardner

Tuesday [c. 1907 or 1908] • Brookline, Massachusetts   (MS: Gardner)

75 Monmouth St
Brookline

Tuesday

Dear Mrs Gardner

I am so sorry that you have chosen <u>next</u> Sunday, as I have promised–it is the only engagement I have!–to go and spend the weekend at Sherborn with young Fuller, my philosophical colleague, and a metaphysical house-party.

It is very good of you to ask me, and I shall soon find my way to Green Hill to thank you again in person.

Yours sincerely
GSantayana

To Charles Augustus Strong

2 January 1907 • Brookline, Massachusetts   (MS: Rockefeller)

75 Monmouth St
Brookline Mass
Jan 2 1907

Dear Strong,

Are you established at the Buckingham? If so, will you kindly ask if they can let me have a room for Monday night, Jan 7th; it will be the first of my trips, which will be five in number a week apart: after Jan. 28th I mean to stay in New York for the whole week, until my following lecture.

I hope you are beginning your work auspiciously and that you and Margaret will have a happy new year.

Don't take the trouble to answer; I will turn up at six o'clock on Monday afternoon in any case, and hope to see you then.

Yours ever
GSantayana

To Hugo Münsterberg

13 January [c. 1907 or 1908] • Brookline, Massachusetts   (MS: Unknown)

> 75 Monmouth Street,
> Brookline
> Jan. 13

Dear Professor: Thank you very much for your kind letter, and the invitation for next Tuesday, at seven o'clock, which it will give me great pleasure to avail myself of.

I am sorry you should have taken the trouble to hunt for this house. Much as I should like to see you, I don't expect any of my friends to come so far. Don't think it necessary to stand on such formalities as returning visits.[1] Thanking you again, I remain,

> Yours very sincerely
> GSantayana

P.S. I have not thanked you for "Also Sprach Zarathustra",[2] which arrived safely, and which I have read with pleasure. The title is also good, although I don't see that there is anything very new at bottom, or very philosophical, in the new ethics. Has it, for instance, any standard of value by which we can convince ourselves that the <u>Uebermensch</u>[3] is a better being than ourselves? I should like some day to hear your own opinion of this ideal.

[1] Santayana rarely received visitors at his mother's house.
[2] *Thus Spoke Zarathustra* (1883–92) is the philosophical poem by Friedrich Nietzsche.
[3] Superman or demigod.

To Miss Levy

2 February 1907 • New York, New York   (MS: Barnes)

> THE BUCKINGHAM
> FIFTH AVE & 50TH ST.
> NEW YORK.

> February 2 1907

Dear Miss Levy[1]

I am very sorry that you have made so many arrangements for February 12, but I feel even less able than when I wrote the other day to undertake any more speaking on that day. These trips to New York have proved very fatiguing, and I am not myself; never shall I undertake such a peregrination again. Of course, not being able to address your club, it would be an imposition for me to come to dinner, and I must beg you to excuse me from both engagements, which were made under a misunderstanding.

Perhaps you might get some other speaker to take my place, so as not to need to countermand your notices.

I owe you most humble apologies for having encouraged you to go so far, but I really had no idea of what was being done, and it all seems to have been transacted by magic and without my knowledge.

Yours very truly
GSantayana

[1]Unidentified.

To Charles William Eliot

16 February 1907 • Brookline, Massachusetts   (MS: Harvard)

---

75 Monmouth Street
Brookline
Feb. 16, 1907

COLONIAL CLUB.

Dear Mr Eliot

At a meeting of the Philosophical Division held this afternoon a question came up about a proposed course of mine which it was agreed should be submitted to you for decision.

Some time ago Professor Schofield[1] asked me if I would offer some course in his department. I answered "Yes", and suggested one on "Three philosophical poets—Lucretius Dante, and Goethe"—a half-course in which the conception of the world and the moral sentiment of the three should be described and compared. Professor Schofield accepted this idea. Now the Philosophical Department seems to be of opinion that this half-course should be given under their auspices, and not in the department of comparative literature. They add that if a part of my work is to lie in another department, a part of my salary too should be regarded as coming from that quarter, and a corresponding sum should be set free for the uses of the philosophical division.

To me it is a matter of indifference in which part of the pamphlet my proposed course figures, except that it is meant for the student of literature rather than for the technical philosopher, and that the requirement of a previous course in philosophy (usually made in offering our philosophical courses) would be out of place in this instance. Should I withdraw my offer made to Professor Schofield and should the proposed course be announced under the head of philosophy?

At our meeting this afternoon it was voted, as Professor Perry will doubtless report to you, that the Corporation be asked to appoint a well-known professor to fill Professor James's[2] place. I concur heartily in this desire, but if such an appointment were made "over my head" and previous to my own promotion, I should not regard my position as satisfactory.

Yours sincerely   GSantayana

[1]William Henry Schofield (1870–1920) was a Canadian who received his Ph.D. from Harvard in 1895 and who, as a member of the faculty, introduced courses in the Scandinavian languages and founded the Department of Comparative Literature (*Harvard*, 374).

[2]William James retired from Harvard in 1907.

To Charles Scribner's Sons
18 February 1907 • Brookline, Massachusetts   (MS: Princeton)

---

75 Monmouth Street
Brookline, Mass
Feb. 18, 1907.

Messrs Charles Scribner's Sons
New York

Gentlemen:

Mr. Alexander Jessup[1] has asked me to beg you for permission to reprint my translation of Alfred de Musset's Souvenir in an English version of the French poet's works which he is to issue. I assume that you can have no objection to his doing so. It might even serve as an advertisement to the defunct volume in which it originally appeared.[2]

I am awaiting your semi-annual report with interest, to see if a second edition of the Life of Reason is likely to be demanded. I am reserving the list of emendations—all slight, but numerous—which ought to be made, and, if you think well of the idea, I should like to write a short preface to the new edition, describing more explicitly the character of the work and of my reserved philosophic creed—not expressed there because not required by my conception of the book.[3] Critics, and the sophisticated part of the public, seem to have been misled by these omissions, beginning by the friendly, and I daresay useful, advertisement prepared by yourselves in which my philosophy is called a kind of "Pragmatism". Mr. Dickinson also put me in the same class, so that the fault evidently lay in my not stating explicitly enough that this book—long as it is—represents, to my mind, but a very casual and human aspect of the universe.

I have lost Mr Jessup's address, which you doubtless know, so that if you would signify your decision about the <u>Souvenir</u> directly to him, I should be much obliged.

Yours very truly
GSantayana

[1]Alexander Jessup (b. 1871) translated several French writers, but no book on Musset was located.

[2]The translation "From Alfred de Musset: *Souvenir*" was composed during the 1880s. It was published in *The Harvard Monthly* (March 1890) and afterwards in *Hermit*. The translation was included in vol. 2 of *The Complete Writings of Alfred de Musset*, ed. Emily Shaw Forman and Marie Agathe Clark (New York: Edwin C. Hill, 1907). It also appears in *Complete Poems*, 198–204.

[3]The second edition was published by Scribner's in 1922 and by Constable in 1923. It included a new preface.

To Charles William Eliot
19 February 1907 • Brookline, Massachusetts   (MS: Harvard)

75 Monmouth Street
Brookline
February 19, 1907

Dear Mr Eliot

Thank you for your reply to my enquiry about the proposed course. I am writing to Schofield giving him your reasons for the decision arrived at.

I am sorry our Department cannot be fortified at present—it was a Platonic wish on our part more than an expectation. What you say about promotions is naturally very welcome, and I am glad that they may be expected to extend eventually to other members of the department as well as to myself.[1]

Yours sincerely
GSantayana

[1]Santayana had been an assistant professor for nine years before being promoted to full professor in 1907. See *Persons*, 395.

To Charles William Eliot

21 February 1907 • Cambridge, Massachusetts   (MS: Harvard)

February 21, 1907

COLONIAL CLUB.

Dear Mr Eliot

As the Philosophical Department wished my proposed course to figure in their list, while I had agreed with Schofield that it should be a course in Comparative Literature, it occurred to me that the point had better be submitted to you, as the most competent and impartial authority in such a matter. I quite understood that you did not mean to impose your decision as absolutely final, but it becomes so in virtue of the fact that we were appealing to you as a sort of umpire. Personally I had a feeling that in the Department of Comparative Literature the course would be in a freer and less pretentious atmosphere, and might attract a new type of men to philosophy; but there are advantages in the other arrangement, and I am quite satisfied to abide by your suggestion, especially as it coincides with the views of my colleagues in the Philosophical Department.

I am much obliged to you for the kind interest you have taken in the matter.

Yours sincerely
GSantayana

To Mr. Overton

1907 • [Cambridge, Massachusetts?]   (MS: Unknown)

1907

To Mr. Overton,[1]

The parcel containing Mr. Young's[2] copies of my books have arrived ... will send the packages back as soon as I have written something in each volume—an operation which will be entertaining but which with my slow wits may take some time. Some of the books are printed on a paper which causes ink to spread ... in these cases I suppose it will be better for me to write on a separate sheet of paper and paste it in. I can't understand why Scribners has no copies of "Interpretations of Poetry and Religion" as I received their semi-annual statement showing that they had many bound volumes on hand. It may be a reprint but identical with the first edition, even the printing errors not being corrected. If Mr. Young doesn't mind a soiled copy I should be glad to send you mine. The same applies to my "Sense of Beauty," which is not on your list, the current reprint of which contains clinical corrections. If you wish to have my works complete you should add "Lucifer, a Theological Tragedy" printed by Herbert S. Stone & Co. Chicago, 1899. The copyright is now by Duffield[3] N.Y. As to the "Life of Reason," all the volumes are of the first edition which is not yet exhausted. The volumes were published seriatim, which accounts for the change in date. Thank you for the interesting copy of "The Throne."[4]

Yours truly,

G. Santayana

[1]Probably an employee of Charles Scribner's Sons.
[2]Mr. Young of Minneapolis is unidentified but was a collector who sent authors copies of their own works and asked them to inscribe these with dedications.
[3]Duffield & Company of New York published *Sonnets* in 1906.
[4]Unidentified.

To Horace Meyer Kallen
[Spring 1907?] • Cambridge, Massachusetts   (MS: American)

Dear Kallen

I am very much ashamed—but I clean forgot that you were to lunch with me yesterday and stayed stupidly at the Colonial Club, where I was reading the <u>Times</u>.

If this doesn't reach you in time for lunch today (Tuesday), won't you come tomorrow at 12.30 to the Union?

With many apologies

GSantayana

To Harold Witter Bynner

[17 May 1907] • Cambridge, Massachusetts   (MS: Houghton)

<u>Friday</u>

COLONIAL CLUB.

Dear Bynner[1]

I shall be here on Monday at 12.30 and hope very much you will turn up.

Your note reached me this morning too late to answer for today.

Yours sincerely
GSantayana

[1] A member of Harvard's class of 1902, Harold Witter Bynner (1881–1968) was an American playwright, satirist, and translator. He served as editor and literary advisor for several magazines. He taught briefly at the University of California and afterward traveled in the Orient where he developed a keen interest in Chinese poetry. *The Jade Mountain* (1929) was the first volume of Chinese verse to be translated by an American. Later Bynner became interested in the poetry of Native Americans.

To Harold Witter Bynner

[20 May 1907?] • Cambridge, Massachusetts   (MS: Houghton)

Monday

COLONIAL CLUB
CAMBRIDGE

Dear Bynner

Will you forgive me for not appearing today? I have been called away by a family occasion—a bothersome piece of business—and have to be in town when I should like to be here.

Let me know when you are in Cambridge again—

With many apologies

Yours sincerely
GSantayana

To Charles Augustus Strong

28 May 1907 • [Cambridge, Massachusetts?]   (MS: Rockefeller)

C/o Brown Shipley & Co
123 Pall Mall
May 28 1907

Dear Strong

Thank you very much for your letter which I was delighted to get. The winter—in spite of its climatic and other horrors—has passed quickly, so quickly that I am surprised to find myself at the end of it without having written to you. I am sailing on June 13 for Hamburg and after a week spent there I expect to make my way towards Avila. Would you be likely to be in Paris at the end of August or early in September? If so it might be better for me not to attempt to reach you at Glion in July, as that détour would delay very much my arrival at Avila; nevertheless, if you are not to move from there before September, I may be able to manage it by coming down through Germany and then cutting across by Lyons to Bordeaux, where I could connect with the fast train to the South.

It is very nice to have progressed so far with your book.[1] A synopsis is more than a composition—it is an Idea! It will be most interesting and profitable for me to read it over and discuss it with its distinguished author.

I am longing to get away—as you were when in New York—being still bothered by my cold and conscious of having lectured ill and accomplished nothing all this winter. But I have pleasanter prospects for next year and hope to pick up a little during the holidays.   Yours ever
G.S.

[1]Strong's books include *Why the Mind Has a Body* (1903), *The Origin of Consciousness* (1918), *Essays in Critical Realism* (1920), *The Wisdom of the Beasts* (1921), *A Theory of Knowledge* (1923), *Essays on the Natural Origin of the Mind* (1930), and *A Creed for Sceptics* (1936).

To Horace Meyer Kallen

6 June 1907 [*postmark*] • Brookline, MA   (MS postcard: American)

Sorry to hear you are laid up. I will come to Cambridge tomorrow or Saturday, and I will bring you my notebook, with marks, etc. in Phil 10, and talk over the exam. paper.[1] If you are declared well and dismissed before I arrive, please leave word where I may find you.

G. S.

75 Monmouth St
  Brookline, June 6.

    [1]Kallen was Santayana's graduate assistant.

To Horace Meyer Kallen

11 June 1907 • Brookline, Massachusetts   (MS: American)

---

75 Monmouth St
Brookline
June 11 1907

Dear Kallen

Here is something by way of compensation for your work in Phil. 10. In the old days when B. Rand used to read blue-books for me I used to give him fifty cents for each, but it would be an insult to put you in the same class, even if wages hadn't gone up in the interval. However, if there is any fraction over the regulation scale, pray spend it in Germany on cakes and ale–I mean on Bier and Pfannkuchen–which I thought excellent thought-food in my day.

I hope you have really got out of the infirmary and will not allow the cares of this world and the next to keep you any longer awake o'nights.

Yours sincerely
GSantayana

C/o Brown Shipley & Cº
  123 Pall Mall, S.W.

To Charles Augustus Strong

23 June 1907 • Hamburg, Germany   (MS: Rockefeller)

Hamburg, June 23 1907.

Dear Strong

Your letter was awaiting me here when I arrived yesterday after a pretty good voyage. I think it will be better for both of us that I should go to

Glion; it will be much more suitable for philosophical discussions, and I think pleasanter. If my calculations are right I shall be able to get there about the fifth of July; but I will send you word during my journey, which is probably to be through Berlin, Weimar, Frankfort, and Bâle,[1] of the progress I make and of the exact time of my arrival.

Perhaps early in September, or late in August, when I pass through Paris on my way to England, you might join me there for another interview; Glion sounds most attractive, and I am looking forward to the scene and the good company there, but I sha'n't be able to stay more than just a week, as otherwise my trip to Spain would be too much delayed.

I shall be most interested in what you are planning for Margaret, and I hope talking the matter over with me may help you to decide just what is best for her, although I don't see what a crusty old bachelor can be expected to supply in the way of wisdom about the education of young ladies.

The title of Bergson's new book,[2] which I hear for the first time, seems to be, like the substance of it, just yours reversed. I have no doubt it is most ingenious and contains good thinking in his private categories; but since I saw Bergson I have no serious interest in his productions. He is a disguised Jew, and might as well be a learned Jesuit, for all the genuine humanism or free philosophy that is to come out of ~~it~~ ∧him.∧ He will speak the language of the liberal world when he thinks it may conduce to de-liberalising it, but that is all. So his science will be studious and ingenious, and he may call attention to real speculative problems and mere residual possibilities—like indeterminism—but it will be fundamentally perverse, scholastic, and retrograde.

We had a truly "liberal" mind with us in Cambridge for a while this winter—Gilbert Murray[3] of Oxford—who lectured with great éclat about early Greek poetry and culture—Homer and what preceded. It was both in substance and in manner very much to my mind, although he takes, on the technical Homeric question, a radical view which I had not before been inclined to, and on which I am yet much in doubt. But the feeling for moral progress, for the cleansing and rationalizing of human society, was very fine and clear in him, so much clearer than in our canting professional moralists. But being English, or rather Scotch, he has to have some private isms, and is a Vegetarian, a Tee-totaller, a Pro-Boer,[4] a Woman~s~ Suffragist, etc, etc.

I am being called to go out—I am staying at the old Baroness's until this afternoon when we go to Westenholz's cottage at Volksdorf[5]—so that I have to cease philosophising for the moment.

I bring my three volumes of Dante–did I ever thank you for the last?–
which I am reading and rereading with pleasure, but with an increasing
sense of the vast amount of subsidiary knowledge which is required for a
thorough understanding of the allusions, and often of the intention of a
passage. The total upshot, however, which is what concerns me at present,
is tolerably plain.

Yours ever
G.S.

[1]Bâle (Basel), in northern Switzerland, borders France and Germany.
[2]*L'Évolution créatrice* (Paris, 1907). Translated as *Creative Evolution* (New York, 1911).
[3]George Gilbert Aimé Murray (1866–1957) was a British classical scholar who was
born in Australia. In 1908 he was appointed regius professor of Greek at Oxford. He
wrote books on English politics but is best known as a Greek scholar and as a translator of Greek drama.
[4]The Boer War (1899–1902) was the culmination of a conflict between the British and
the Boers (South Africans of Dutch descent), both of whom had interests in South
Africa.
[5]See *Persons*, 262–64.

To Susan Sturgis de Sastre
2 July 1907 • Weimar, Germany   (MS postcard: Sanchez)

WEIMAR   RESIDENZ-SCHLOSS.
2 de julio,   1907 Palacio del Gran-Duque.

[*Unsigned*]

To Charles Augustus Strong
17 July 1907 • Ávila, Spain   (MS: Rockefeller)

Address,   Novaliches, 6
                   Avila, July 17, 1907
Dear Strong

I got here without mishap on Monday morning and found my sister and
her family flourishing. It is pleasantly warm–not more–and there are some
clouds. As it hasn't rained since May, the natives are not sorry to see them
and hope–despairingly–that there may be a shower.

James's book[1] has not arrived yet, so that my reading in that direction is interrupted, but I found Calvin's Institutes[2] awaiting me here—in a German translation which sounds like a pious, warm, hearty sermon of the seventeenth century—and I have devoted these two mornings to it—reading in bed, where I have my chocolate, in a manner that I fear is incongruous, voluptuous, and inspired of Satan. I am learning something nevertheless, and am delighted that the idea of reading Jonøathan Edwards and Calvin came into my head, as it is opening a new world to me, at least, a much clearer and more genuine vista into a vague old world I had always heard about. "Righteousness"—almost the opposite of rational "justice"—will always be a clearer concept for me henceforth.

Your psychology of cognition has been a good deal in my mind, and some other day I may write you my second thoughts about it. I am afraid I was a very stubborn and unsympathetic listener to your exposition, but the reason is not that I have any dislike for your ₐultimateₐ views but only that your dichotomies do not coincide with the lines of cleavage I seem to see in things, and so confuse me and constantly slip again out of my mind.

Let me herear something about your journey and first impressions of the Engadine.[3] I hope you will like it as well as Glion and the Lake, of which I have a much pleasanter memory myself. In passing by Pau, I remembered you [*across*] and felt quite confident that the place would please you. It is most verdant and lovely.   Yours ever   G.S.

---

[1]William James, *Pragmatism: A New Name for Some Old Ways of Thinking* (New York: Longmans, Green, and Co., 1907).

[2]John (Jean Cauvin) Calvin (1509–64) was a French Protestant reformer whose theological doctrines had tremendous influence, particularly in the Puritan religion of England, Scotland, and later America. Calvinism as a religious system recognized only the Bible as a source of knowledge and authority in questions of belief. Calvin's major work was the *Institutes of the Christian Religion* (1536), originally addressed to King Francis I of France in defense of the French Protestants. *Institutes* provides a systematic presentation of the lines of thought found in Calvin's other mature works.

[3]Engadine, the upper part of the Inn River valley in eastern Switzerland, is the location of many tourist and health resorts.

To Harold Witter Bynner
29 September 1907 • Brookline, Massachusetts   (MS: Houghton)

75 Monmouth St
Brookline
Sept. 29, 1907

Dear Mr Bynner

I found your volume only the day before yesterday when I got back from Europe, and was waiting to thank you until I had had time to read a little in it.[1] A glimpse has convinced me that I shall find it interesting—you seem to have allowed the humorous and the enthusiastic to relieve one another in your Ode,[2] where otherwise the great danger would have been to sound hollow. And I am looking forward with pleasure also to the other poems.

If you come to Cambridge, don't forget to look me up.

With many thanks for having remembered me,

Yours sincerely
GSantayana

[1] *Young Harvard, and Other Poems* (New York: Frederick A. Stokes Co., 1907).
[2] "Ode to Harvard" includes these lines about Santayana: "The Spanish poet-philosopher whose eye would so beguile / That you'd see no more his meaning, but the flaring altar-oil / That was burning as for worshippers inside."

To William Roscoe Thayer
7 October 1907 • Brookline, Massachusetts   (MS: Houghton)

75 Monmouth Street
Brookline

October 7, 1907

~~COLONIAL CLUB~~
~~CAMBRIDGE~~

Dear Mr Thayer

I am a little ashamed not to accede at once to your request, but I have been living for some time so far from things of local and present interest that I really can't think of anything to write about for your magazine. Perhaps it is that I am pumped dry and that nine lectures a week contrive to keep me so. All summer I have been trying to write an article about

Professor James's last philosophy, but I can't find the right tone nor disentangle my ideas.

It is very pleasant to know that you have been interested in the "Life of Reason". Let me deprecate, however, your calling it a system of the universe. It is only a review of human experience, and even that is too large a title. Had I been sure of living until sixty and of being wiser then, I should have left the review of human experience until I had fairly gathered at least the experience of one life. But speculation has to anticipate, and when we allow ourselves that license it is hard to control the extent to which we shall indulge in it.

Please tell Professor Norton that I have no system of the universe—only glimpses of the history of man.

Yours very truly
GSantayana

To William James
19 October 1907 • Cambridge, Massachusetts   (MS: Houghton)

October 19 1907

COLONIAL CLUB
CAMBRIDGE

Dear Mr James

Thank you very much for the tickets to Lutoslawsky's lectures.[1] I had no idea that wandering luminary had drifted back to this country.

By your handwriting on the envelope I infer that you have arrived in Cambridge, and I am looking forward to seeing you soon and hoping to hear your opinion of Bergson's new book, which I know you admire. Your long letters to Strong, some of which I read this summer, were very interesting but not always clear to me, and I should like to have a chance to ask you some questions quietly on those subjects. It seems terribly hard to get a common vocabulary and to keep the same realities in mind as one's interlocutor, when one is discussing this terrible Erkenntniss Theorie.[2] I failed to get anywhere with Strong, though we talked for days and days on the same questions.

I haven't thanked you for the copy of "Pragmatism" which made my philosophical pabulum at Avila this summer. I appreciated getting it very much.

Yours sincerely
GSantayana

[1]Wincenty Lutoslawski (1863–1954) was a philosopher whose works include *The Origin and Growth of Plato's Logic, with an Account of Plato's Style and of the Chronology of His Writings* (London and New York: Longmans, Green, and Co., 1897).
[2]Theory of knowledge.

To Harry Morgan Ayres

21 October 1907 • Brookline, Massachusetts   (MS: Dykeman)

---

75 Monmouth Street
Brookline
Oct 21 1907

COLONIAL CLUB
CAMBRIDGE

Dear Sir[1]

It will give me great pleasure to speak to the Modern Language Conference on Monday evening, February tenth, and I thank you for giving me a date so long ahead, and not asking at once for an exact subject. When the time approaches, it will be possible to think up something that may be of interest to the Conference and to its classifcal guests and I should be glad if you would suggest any subject that may have occurred to you. If left to myself I might perhaps tend a little too much to trespass on metaphysics.

Yours very truly
GSantayana

[1]This letter was found in a copy of *Matter* that previously belonged to Ayres.

To Charles Scribner's Sons

13 November 1907 • Brookline, Massachusetts   (MS: Princeton)

75 Monmouth Street
Brookline. Mass
Nov. 13, 1907.

~~COLONIAL CLUB~~
~~CAMBRIDGE~~

Messrs Charles Scribner's Sons

Gentlemen:

When I suggested writing a preface for the "Life of Reason", I thought a new edition was likely to be issued, in which a few verbal corrections might also be made. As the copies to be bound now are still a part of the first edition, the new preface seems less called for. I am also somewhat in doubt whether any short paper could help much towards straightening matters out. Perhaps an independent small volume would attract more attention and prove more satisfactory. I am meditating one, but can hardly say yet whether it will ever be written, or when. If, however, you your-selves think a preface added now would be of advantage, I could easily write one.

Yours very truly
GSantayana

To Charles Augustus Strong

16 December 1907 • Brookline, Massachusetts   (MS: Rockefeller)

December 16 1907
75 Monmouth St
Brookline

~~COLONIAL CLUB~~
~~CAMBRIDGE~~

Dear Strong

You will find me here at any time you come and very glad to see you, too. I have been too busy with Dante to think of anything else, but now he is finished, and I am hoping for a little more time for other things. I sha'n't go to Ithaca, however; I wish you joy of your discussion, but it will not be about Truth, but about the various dynamic consequences of having various kinds of false ideas.

So you are dégoûté de[1] New York? I don't know how serious that is, for I have been dégoûté de Cambridge for the last ten years and it looks as if I might be here for ten years more. However, I suppose under the circumstances you will go abroad again for the Summer. It looks as if I might go too, after all, as my brother seems to be giving up the idea of going himself. In that case, we might meet again in Paris, or thereabouts. Or you might come and try Oxford for a while, where I should probably spend a part of the holidays.

Give my compliments to Margaret and to Miss Laurenson.[2] I suppose Margaret will have a nice Christmas with her cousins and her aunts. Children have such "full lives" nowadays that one doesn't have to think of amusing them but if anything of providing an occasional rest-cure for their little nerves.

I shall look for you about New Years—

Yours ever   G.S.

[1] Disgusted with.
[2] Unidentified.

To Charles Augustus Strong

[Before March 1908] • [Brookline, Massachusetts]   (MS: Rockefeller)

75 Monmouth St
Brookline

Dear Strong

I will call for you at the Parker House tomorrow, Wednesday, at about two o'clock, so that we may have the whole afternoon before us. If the weather is good and you are not tired, we can take a walk until the sun goes down, and then you can read me your paper on Pragmatic Truth or Wooden Iron.

I am sorry that, when you come to Boston, I cannot be more hospitable, but my mother is not able to see anyone, and her house is too small for us to have separate compartments. And I am even without a club—except at Cambridge—but on Thursday, at least, you must dine with me at a restaurant. We will try to imagine we are in Paris. Au revoir.   G.S.

To William James
Thursday [c. 1908] • Brookline, Massachusetts   (MS: Houghton)

75 Monmouth Street
Brookline

Dear Mr James

I find your note here when it is too late to profit by it. I am very sorry, not so much for not gratifying Mr Gordon's[1] morbid desire to look upon the Devil, as for not giving him a chance to make the sign of the cross over me (or whatever is the Old South equivalent) and perhaps drive the Father of Lies out of me into some dumb and non-literary animal where he wouldn't do so much harm.

I will come in some afternoon soon—I have no rooms in Cambridge now—in hopes of seeing you and Mrs James—and also perhaps your son "Billy" with whom I dined very pleasantly in Paris not long ago.[2]

With many thanks and regrets

Yours sincerely
GSantayana

Thursday

[1]Unidentified.
[2]William James Jr. (1882–1961) was one of the Jameses' four sons.

To William James
7 January 1908 • Cambridge, Massachusetts   (MS: Houghton)

Jan • 7 • 1908

COLONIAL CLUB
CAMBRIDGE

Dear Mr James

Thank you very much for these documents.

Aren't you and Strong talking at cross purposes? And isn't the doctrine of your little paper quite different from the usual pragmatism—that opinions are true if they work satisfactorily? I don't think I shall publish anything at present on this subject. It is too kaleidoscopic for me, and I shouldn't know what I was talking about.

Yours sincerely
GSantayana

To Horace Meyer Kallen

10 January 1908 • Cambridge, Massachusetts   (MS: American)

Jan. 10, 1908

COLONIAL CLUB
CAMBRIDGE

Dear Kallen.

Your two letters have arrived almost together, and have given me a great deal of pleasure. You seem to be very active in mind and in body. Your thesis[1] will shape itself as everything does in this world—and is as likely to be better as to be worse than what you may have ˄originally˄ projected. Only one thing—besides your hints of uncertain health—is a bad sign: you idealise <u>us</u>, which means that you have not learned to idealise <u>them</u>. Perhaps, when you are here again, the tables will be turned. I notice that Fuller, who was rather irritated and sore when he left Oxford, now thinks of that place with some kindness. Of course, you have been there too short a time, and under too great intellectual pressure, for the same associations to have been formed. London and Toynbee Hall[2] will make you ultra-socialistic. As I am a socialist myself, I have no objection to that in theory; but in practice—let me warn you—I don't like other socialists, and in the case of Molière's Misanthrope[3] whose opinions were blamed by himself, so soon as he heard them from other people. But that, while it may raise a laugh at his expense or at mine, is really a proof of honesty on our part: for in socialism, as in logic, the <u>intent</u> is all. And a man may be a socialist, like Plato, for the love of aristocracy and to spread a greater pedestal for the <u>perfect</u> man, or he may be a socialist out of pity and vicarious ambition for the <u>common</u> man. In the ideal, at least, we should begin by cleansing the inside of the cup.

Your functionless Rector rather interests me, and your young friend with the Orthodox Aunt has a good chance to learn what life is. Does she want him to take orders? I don't know, talking of orders, whether you have heard that Miller has become a high-Church divine.[4] He means, however, to go on teaching philosophy (having failed in the practice of it) and meantime to exert his influence to liberalise the Church. Under the circumstances it is safe to bet on the Church.

James is inconceivably active explaining his Protean Pragmatism—which, as it gains in clearness, seems to lose its radical quality.   With best wishes

Yours sincerely   G.S.

[1] *Notes on the Nature of Truth* (Ph.D., 1908).
[2] Toynbee Hall, the first social settlement, was named for Arnold Toynbee (1852–83), an English economic historian and reformer.
[3] Molière, pen name of Jean Baptiste Poquelin (1622–73), was a French comic dramatist. His unhappy marriage to Armande Béjart provided the experience that led to his writing *Le Misanthrope* (1666).
[4] Dickinson Miller.

To Horace Meyer Kallen
5 February 1908 • Cambridge, Massachusetts   (MS: American)

February 5, 1908

COLONIAL CLUB
CAMBRIDGE

Dear Kallen

Thank you for your long and amusing letter. I am glad to know you have all the explosive forms of socialism behind you. In what I said—not very seriously—I may have forgotten how much experience you have for your years, or for anybody's years. It will be interesting to hear from you, when you come back, what the Babel of tendencies is amongst the reformers of the day.

You shouldn't have shocked the Aristotelian Society with good doctrine couched in bad language. Next time you tell the story say "blooming" or "bally"—every one will understand what the original was, and be delighted, but the sense of propriety will not be wounded by an unveiled oath. The figleaf is more useful in language than in sculpture—for language forces itself on the attention whereas the eye may pretend not to perceive every part of what is presented to it.

Your experience with Moore[1] is like my experience with Bergson: I thought him a great man, one of those whom we admire without feeling called upon to agree or disagree, since they seem to be above controversy, like the poets. But when I saw Bergson, and felt what his inspiration was, that he was a little cowed advocate of irrational prejudices and stubborn misunderstandings, feigning and acting the part of an impartial, subtle, liberal thinker—then all the charm vanished even from his written words, and I hear the cracked voice of the sectary and the whine of the reactionary in every syllable. Moore is doubtless much more offensive, because he is arrogant and brutal, whereas Bergson is suavity itself. I don't know what the general effect of Moore's system is: how does he attach existence to Being? But I like the clearness with which he holds to the <u>intent</u> of thought and avoids those psychological sophisms to which we all, brought up under the blight of idealism, remain so prone. For that lesson I am willing to forgive him all his narrowness and general incapacity. I have no doubt he is a most disagreeable and unfair person. But he is one from whom we can learn something, which is more than can be said of most contemporary writers. Russell is far better known to me, both personally and as a writer, and I feel as if I agreed with him pretty thoroughly, inspite of all differences in temperament and in knowledge. At least, disagreements with Russell don't trouble me, because I feel them to be due to <u>additional</u> insights, now on his part now on mine: while disagreements with a haphazard person like James are more annoying, because they come from focussing things differently, from being <u>schief</u>.[2] You may be quite right in thinking that I agree almost entirely with what James means: but I often hate what he says. If he gave up subjectivism, indeterminism, and ghosts there would be little in "pragmatism", as it would then stand, that I could object to. Of course, pragmatism in a wider sense involves an ethical system, because we can't determine what is useful or satisfactory without, to some extent, articulating our ideals. That is something which James doesn't include in philosophy. Dewey is far better in that respect, and I notice he even begins to talk about the <u>ideal object</u> and the <u>intent</u> of ideas! What a change from those "Logical Studies" in which there is nothing but social physiology!

My brother has decided to remain in this country next summer, so that I am going to Europe as usual—very likely to spend a part of the Summer at Oxford. Have you discovered any good landlady with remote, cell-like lodgings? My haunt at 5 Grove Street[3] has its charms, but I shouldn't mind something more country-like and cheerful for a change.

My health is better; only rheumatism left in one knee. But I am not very fit for lecturing: I am stale and confused, and [*across*] seem to be remembering rather than thinking when I talk. It is a horrid feeling.   Yours sincerely

G.S.

[1]George Edward Moore.
[2]Cockeyed.
[3]The three-story stucco house still stands at what is now No. 5 Magpie Lane in the heart of Oxford.

To George Herbert Palmer
8 February 1908 • Cambridge, Massachusetts   (MS: Wellesley)

February 8, 1908

COLONIAL CLUB

CAMBRIDGE

Dear Professor Palmer

Thank you for letting me know how far you got in Phil. A. I shall keep it in mind, as a large proportion of the men in Phil. B. will doubtless come from your course. My plan, however, had been to begin at once with Descartes, and I think I shall stick to that plan. It makes a simple and radical beginning, and strikes at once the key-notes of naturalism and subjectivism which are to sound all through the symphony. There will be occasions—as in discussing Leibniz's theodicy,[1] for instance—where I may nevertheless feel the need of going back and saying something about Neo Platonic and Mediaeval systems. I have found, however, that our students do not take readily to those forms of speculation. They o ˄logy˄ seem˄s˄ unreal to them and it is only with great pains and with partial success that they can be made to feel the vitality and grandeur which was in ~~them~~ it. I have just had an occasion to notice this again in Phil. b, when I spoke about Dante. The assistants in Phil. B, whom I consulted the other day, also advised me not to attempt any elaborate introduction, but to plunge in at once into the particular systems. It gives them something positive to take hold off from the start.

Yours sincerely

GSantayana

---

[1]Leibniz's philosophical book *Essais de Théodicée sur la bonté de Dieu, la liberté de l'homme et l'origine du mal* was published in 1710.

To Conrad Hensler Slade
4 March 1908 • Brookline, Massachusetts   (MS: Unknown)

> 75 Monmouth Street
> Brookline Mass
> March 4 1908

Dear Conrad,

A great weight is lifted off my mind. My brother has decided to remain in America this summer, a decision which leaves me free to do what I like, and you know what that must be. My passage is taken for June 18 eastward and September 10 westward, in the Hamburg-American Kaiserin and Deutschland respectively. First I go to England; but before July is far advanced I hope to be in Paris. If you are going to some idyllic place and would not think me an intruder, I might join you for a month or so. We might read—I am deep in history now, Gibbon, Curtius,[1] etc.—and sketch. Perhaps you might give me a few lessons in drawing, or you might paint my portrait and immortalize us both. About September first it is not impossible that I may go to Heidelberg—it is the only place in Germany that tempts me back—to an international philosophic congress that is to meet there. I should see in the flesh a lot of ugly old men whose names I have seen in print all my life; and then I might go to Hamburg to make my friends[2] there a few days' visit before sailing for my Peru—that is what Cambridge is getting to be to my mercenary mind.

When you get this send me a card with your surest address—I am never sure what it is—and I will forward you the first volume of the Arabian Nights,[3] which I have read twice, once at sea and once on cold winter nights, and which has made both wildernesses turn for the moment into enchanted oases. And it is so funny! Only at times my Hellenic political conscience rebels against this irresponsible, unintellectual way of feeling life—all changes and surfaces and prodigies. Send me the second volume that I may have read it when I see you, and be ready to buy the next.

> Yours affly,
> GSantayana

---

[1]Edward Gibbon (1737–94) was an English historian who wrote *Decline and Fall of the Roman Empire*, 1776–83, as well as his autobiography. Ernst Robert Curtius (1814–96) was a Greek scholar famous for his excavations at Olympia (1875–80). He was a professor at Göttingen and Berlin.
[2]Baron Albert von Westenholz and his sister, Mathilde.

[3]Santayana owned the sixteen-volume *Le Livre des Mille Nuits et Une Nuit* (*A Thousand and One Nights*), trans. J. C. Mardrus (Paris, 1918).

To Charles Augustus Strong
4 March 1908 • Cambridge, Massachusetts   (MS: Rockefeller)

March 4, 1908

COLONIAL CLUB

CAMBRIDGE

Dear Strong

Münsterberg has been talking to me about the international congress at Heidelberg next Summer and has almost persuaded me to go to it. Do you expect to be there? I suppose so, as you are a leading member, according to the document I have just received. I forget whether I have already told you that, my brother having decided not to go to Europe this year, my liberty of action has been restored to me, and I have taken my passage for June 18 eastward and September 10 westward—both in Hamburg-American ships. My idea now is to spend only two or three weeks in England, cross in July to Paris, and, if I go to Heidelberg, sail direct from Hamburg, which will enable me to make my friends there a visit of three or four days.

Our collegague Perry has had appendicitis and, as the operation had been unaccountably delayed, has been in a dangerous condition. The last news is favourable, however, and he is declared to be well out of danger.

Has Rome, I wonder, lost none of its last year's charms? I envy you very much; although in this half of the year, being less busy, I am having a good time reading. I have begun Gibbon—of whom I had read long ago only, I think, the volume on Christianity—and am enjoying the book immensely. I am also deep in Greek history. Grote,[1] whom I tried first, is too <u>indigeste</u> and unideal; now I am giving Curtius a trial. When I finish Gibbon, I mean to take up Burckhardt's Renaissance.[2]

When is the first installment of your book going to reach me?

Yours ever   G.S.

[*across*] Love to Margaret: I hope she and Miss Lawrenson are well and happy.

[1]George Grote (1794–1871), banker, was MP for the City of London (1832–41) and was in favor of the reform movement. His famous *History of Greece* (1846–56) was published in eight volumes. His other works include studies of Plato and Aristotle.

²Jacob Burckhardt (1818–97) was a Swiss historian principally known in Britain for his work *Die Kultur der Renaissance in Italien* (1860, trans. as *The Civilization of the Renaissance in Italy*), a survey which discusses the arts, politics, and philosophy. This book propounds the view that at this time man, previously 'conscious of himself only as a member of a race, people, party, family or corporation' became aware of himself as 'a spiritual *individual*'.

To Isabella Stewart Gardner

[Late May or early June 1908] • Cambridge, MA   (MS: Gardner)

Thursday

COLONIAL CLUB
CAMBRIDGE

Dear Mrs Gardner

I am so sorry, but I have promised to spend Sunday the 7ᵗʰ with some friends in the country, and must miss the pleasure of lunching with you on that day. But I hope to find you some afternoon before I leave for Europe, which is not for a fortnight yet.

It is a surprise to me that my old lecture has appeared,[1] but it is all the more of a satisfaction if it at all interests you. I was afraid it had turned out somewhat abstruse and pretentious. It was "made to order" which is not a good method–at least with me.

Thank you very much for writing.

Yours sincerely
GSantayana

[1]"Sculpture" appeared in the *New England Magazine* 38 (March 1908): 103–11.

To Charles Augustus Strong

2 June 1908 • Cambridge, Massachusetts   (MS: Rockefeller)

June 2ⁿᵈ 1908

COLONIAL CLUB
CAMBRIDGE

Dear Strong

I am very sorry your health has not been satisfactory and that your book has progressed so slowly. The article, which I have read carefully, seems to put things in the same way as did your verbal explanations, and

I am still a little bewildered by your epistemological trinity. I understand Plotinus' trinity[1] better, I think, which I have been read- about a little of late. You know, I suppose, where I diverge from you in the analysis of cognition. Your "subject" seems to me to stand for two things—the bodily organs and the mental state. The mental state, however, includes what you call "content", and also includes what I call "intent". It is a transitive energy employed on definable terms (the "content") and projecting these terms (if you like) into an object; but this projection is merely the positing or seeing of the content in its own medium (in space, if it be an image of spatial qualities, in musical regions, if it be a sensation of sound) without any consciousness of the sensation as such or of the act of projecting it.

What you call "content," however, is not merely a sensation (a part of the psychological "subject") but also a quality of what you call the "object". If you don't admit this, it is clear that the true and independent object will be unknowable. The object we have any occasion believe in is an object describable by the "content" of our experience. As Aristotle says (I have quoted this to you often) the sensibility of the organ and the sensible character of the object are <u>one and the same in act</u>; it is only in there potentiality, or in their conditions, as we might say, that they are double. Now these conditions are themselves existences, and actual in their respective ways. But neither the subjective condition of cognition—the brain—nor the objective condition—the other parts of nature, distant from the brain or anterior to its present state, as in memory—are necessarily like the act in which they come together. What they are in their potentiality may be representable, not in the "content" elicited by their common act, but in ~~what is~~ ∧another "content,"∧ actualized in another cognition altogether. Your crucial case of introspection or memory of sensation as such †most memory is of things, not of "contents"† is one in which it might seem that "content" and "object" almost coincided in character, and knowledge was consequently literally true. But I suspect what makes cognition, even in this case, is just the difference between the present and the past state, the memory of the toothache and the toothache in its pulsing ignorance. So that perhaps it is always the secondary qualities of objects that appear in the "content"; the primary qualities (which of course appear in the content of <u>some</u> congition, else they could not be known) are always, perhaps, read betweeen the lines of the "content" by trained minds only, who can conceive the object as it is, or was, and not as subjective sense or subjective, legendary memory happens to picture it for the moment. In other words, the object is like the content, not of the moment in which the object is first given, but of the moment in which it is critically recast and intelligently imagined.

This, of course, plays nicely into the hands of your theory, since mind-stuff is just such an ulterior, critical conception of what the real object must be. My objection to your revision of sensuous beliefs about ~~what~~ reality, does not rest on the amount of transformation which you demand in vulgar notions. I am not a materialist for love of the vulgar, but from distrust of them. Transform sensuous conceptions of things as much as you please, and I shall applaud and, if possible, follow you. But don't transform vulgar reality into a reality without coherence, a substance incapable of bringing any order out of chaos. Don't revert to the most vulgar, most sub-human, most chaotic sort of appearance and say—"This is the reality I pine for, this is my true world!" I suspect that would be no world and no reality at all, but only the thinnest and flimsiest miasma of sentiency, remaining altogether incapable of breeding anything, much less the better instances and the occasions of its own self. Reality is, I believe, more like our best than like our worst ideas.

My plans are unchanged, and I shall hope to see you in Paris about July 15. It will hardly be possible for me to get to Glion, so we must make the most of the café de la Régence.

My affectionate regards to Margaret whom I hope to see tall and rosy.

Yours ever
GSantayana

Address
^C/o Brown Shipley
    London.

---

[1]Plotinus divided Plato's realm of intelligibles into three: the One (highest principle, or cause), the Intelligence (intellect, spirit, mind), and the Soul (some souls remain unembodied; others descend into bodies).

To Charles Augustus Strong
5 July 1908 • Windsor, England   (MS: Rockefeller)

July 5, 1908
QUEEN'S ACRE,
WINDSOR.

Dear Strong

Just a line to say I expect to be at the Quai Voltaire on Saturday evening, July 11ᵗʰ and hope you will turn up then or soon after, as I am off at once to Brittany to see the Potters from whence I shall make for Spain without returning to Paris—that is, until late in August.

Are you going to the Heidelberg congress? I am in doubt, and your plans would influence mine in this matter.

I have spent a day with Bertie Russell. Moore also turned up. He is a most agreeable surprise, not ugly or ferocious, as I had expected, but young, silent, and nice-looking. Both Russell and he seem to be favourably disposed towards your system.

Yours ever
G.S.

To Bertrand Arthur William Russell
6 July 1908 • Windsor, England   (MS: McMaster)

July 6, 1908
QUEEN'S ACRE,
WINDSOR.

Dear Russell

Here is your article with James's comments, both of which are entertaining, but I can't help thinking that "pragmatism" still requires a fair historical elucidation. It seems to be a mixture of old saws and half-born intuitions, the most fundamental of them being, perhaps, despair concerning attainable truth, or agnosticism.

It was a real pleasure to see Moore who is so different from what I expected, so young, shy, and nice-looking, instead of ugly, old, and aggressive, as for some reason I had imagined him.

Kind regards to Mrs Russell.

Yours sincerely
GSantayana

To Susan Sturgis de Sastre

11 [July?] 1908 [*postmark*] • Cherbourg, France   (MS postcard: Sanchez)

CHERBOURG.—LA PLACE DIVETTE.

Viernes, 4 de la tarde.

En este momento nos embarcamos.[1]

[*Unsigned*]

[1]Translation:
Friday, 4 in the afternoon.
We are leaving now.

To Susan Sturgis de Sastre

18 July 1908 • Concarneau, France   (MS postcard: Sanchez)

CONCARNEAU—L' "ATLANTIC HÔTEL" ET LE VIVIER, VUS DE LA MER

July 18ᵗʰ

If you have anything to tell me, write to the <u>Hôtel de France</u>, <u>Nantes</u>, where I shall be next Sunday, the 26ᵗʰ. Here, in Brittany, I shall get no letters, as I have had everything sent to Avila.—This is across a bay from the Potter's villa, where I go this morning by boat.

[*Unsigned*]

To Susan Sturgis de Sastre

25 July 1908 [*postmark*] • Quimper, France   (MS postcard: Sanchez)

VUES PRINCIPALES DU RÉSEAU D'ORLÉANS
STATUE DU ROI RENÉ (ANGERS)

Quimper. Friday.

I am still hoping to reach Avila on Tuesday the 28ᵗʰ at half past eleven by the Sud-Express. You may expect me unless you hear to the contrary

[*Unsigned*]

To Charles Augustus Strong

[August 1908?] • Avignon, France   (MS postcard: Georgetown)

LE PONT DU GARD

I arrived safely last night, though the journey was rather tedious.—It is delightfully cool here this morning—I hope you are having a good rest and not writing too many slips, which might involve making a few of them.—I am carrying away a delightful souvenir of Cannes, in spite of not having been quite well there. You must attribute my bad humour at certain moments to biliousness and not to aversion to mind-stuff, which is an excellent thing when rightly used—that is, when turned into <u>mind</u>. Elsewhere it seems to be that paradoxical thing—"luminous" <u>mud</u>.

This place is very shabby.   G. S.

To Susan Sturgis de Sastre

18 September 1908 • New York, New York   (MS: Virginia)

<u>Friday Sept. 18, 1908</u>

HOTEL MANHATTAN
HAWK & WETHERBEE
MADISON AVE. & 42<u>ND</u> ST.
NEW YORK.

Dear Susie

We have had a very bad passage, after the first day, with rough seas and rain, yet I was only seasick on the second day, with a little discomfort again at the end on account of the violent motion. I spent most of the time with a Mexican named Manuel Sanchez Carmona,[1] who says he is descended from the conquerors and is very pro-Spanish and an enthusiastic admirer of Don Alfonso, by whom he was received and who, he says, <u>vale mucho mas</u>[2] than D. Porfirio Diaz, the president of Mexico, although the latter is, he agrees, a great man.[3] He has drawn such a pleasant picture of the City of Mexico for me that he has given me some desire to visit it. One might even spend a summer there very agreeably, it seems.

I am taking the ten o'clock train this morning for Boston.

The enclosed[4] will give you some notion of the last day or two at sea, and of the delay in landing which made me miss the five o'clock train yesterday and stay here overnight, as there was no comfortable berth in the midnight train, and I needed a rest. The storm was very amusing in its way, on account of people tumbling and things smashing; almost every one was up and well, as it was towards the end of the voyage and the ship rolled, not pitched, which is a less insidious motion.

Love to Celedonio and the rest of the family.

In Paris I saw a lot of my friend Slade, the painter-sculptor; otherwise amused myself alone.

Your aff^{te} brother

G.S.

[1]Unidentified.

[2]Much more influential.

[3]José de la Cruz Porfirio Díaz (1830–1915) was a Mexican statesman who gained prominence in support of Benito Juárez and the liberals in the war against Maximilian. He rose against the government of Lerdo de Tejada in 1876 and remained in power as president until 1911.

[4]Unlocated.

To Charles Augustus Strong

24 September 1908 • Cambridge, Massachusetts   (MS: Rockefeller)

September 24, 1908

COLONIAL CLUB
CAMBRIDGE

Dear Strong

So you are off again! I understand, I envy. I almost admire; but at the same time I am a little sorry, because doubtless you have felt many jars, had many perplexities to surmount, and find no decision and no prospect altogether satisfactory. However, let us hope (and my hope is belief in this case) that this is the best move for the present, at least. Paris, during the week I spent there just after you left, was perfectly delightful, in spite of its being the Empty Month of September. Slade kept me company, and was good company. I saw a most amusing play—amiably immoral, or rather tenderly frank—called Chant de Cygne,[1] as well as other less interesting things.– I hope your voyage will ₍have₎ proved better than mine in the opposite direction. We had horrid weather and I was seasick for one whole day, and not comfortable on various other occasions. A Mexican whom I came upon at the very moment of leaving Paris, talked to me all the way to New York, it seemed almost without interruption, as we sat together at table and in the smoking room; but this too-muchness had its good side, because he taught me a good deal about his country, and left me with some inclination, such as I had never felt before, to visit that part of Spanish America.

My Summer otherwise was quite as usual. I found my sister pretty well, and everything normal in her household,—except one maid, who suddenly went stark mad.

With best wishes for you and Margaret for the season

Yours as ever

GSantayana

[1] *Song of the Swan.*

To Edward Joseph Harrington O'Brien
[September 1908–January 1912] • Cambridge, MA   (MS: Denson)

3 Prescott Hall
COLONIAL CLUB
CAMBRIDGE

Dear Mr. O'Brien:[1]   We are besieged at this moment by <u>soi-disant</u>[2] philosophers from all over the country, and I shall not be my own master until Saturday. If you could come to tea then or on Sunday, at about four o'clock, I should be delighted to see you.

Perhaps you would explain to me then some of the things you refer to in your letter, which I don't quite understand. The tempests of the Olympians to not reach my catacomb.

Yours very truly

GSantayana

[1]Born in Boston, Edward Joseph Harrington O'Brien (1890–1941) was a poet, editor, anthologist, and critic.
[2]Self-styled.

To William Roscoe Thayer
10 October 1908 • Cambridge, Massachusetts   (MS: Houghton)

3 Prescott Hall
Cambridge
Oct. 10, 1908

Dear Mr Thayer

There is a drawing of me done by the late Andreas Andersen (who married Miss Olivia Cushing)[1] some ten or twelve years ago, when I used to write verses. It is very clever and penetrating, and if you wish me to figure as a poet, I should think you would prefer this drawing to a photograph of my present self.

However, if you would rather have me as I look now, I will get one of our Cambridge photographers to let me sit for him, as the likeness taken last year for the Senior class album is really too vile.

There is another possibility. A Mrs Rieber[2] of California did two oil sketches of me last winter, and said she was going to have one of them photographed. Perhaps I might get that for you, if you liked.

What poetry has Woodberry[3] written? Who else, besides him and Moody,[4] are you counting as Harvard poets? Do you exclude Bliss Carman, McCullough, Witter Bynner, Arthur Ficke, and Hermann Hagerdorm?[5]

Yours sincerely

GSantayana

P.S.   You see I have taken rooms again in Cambridge.

[1]Olivia was the sister of Howard Gardiner Cushing.

[2]Winifred Smith Rieber was the wife of a former student of Santayana, Charles Henry Rieber (Ph.D., 1900). She had been engaged to paint a group portrait of James, Palmer, Royce, Santayana, and Münsterberg. The philosophers disagreed, resulting in Santayana's posing alone. (See *Santayana*, 204–5.)

[3]George Edward Woodberry (1855–1930), Massachusetts critic, poet, and literary scholar, was professor of comparative literature at Columbia University (1891–1904). His poetry books include *The North Shore Watch* (1890) and *Heart of Man* (1899).

[4]William Vaughn Moody (1869–1910) graduated in 1893 and taught English at the University of Chicago. He published dramas and poems. His play *The Great Divide* was an important advance in American drama. *The Faith Healer* was produced in Cambridge (1909) and in New York (1910). His early death cut short a promising career, for he was a thinker as well as a conscientious artist.

[5]Hugh McCullough (c. 1872–1902) was a member of the Harvard class of 1894 who wrote *Quest of Herakles and Other Poems* (1894). Arthur Davison Ficke (1883–1845), Harvard class of 1904, was a poet and regular contributor to the *New York Times*.

Hermann Hagedorn (1882–1964), member of the Harvard class of 1907, was a New York author known for his many books about Theodore Roosevelt. Other works include *Poems and Ballads* (1912) and *This Darkness and This Light: Harvard Poems, 1907–1937* (1938).

To William Roscoe Thayer
6 November [1908] • Cambridge, Massachusetts   (MS: Houghton)

3 Prescott Hall
Cambridge
Nov. 6th

Dear Mr Thayer

It will give me great pleasure to lunch with you on Thursday the 19th and to meet Signor Ferrero.[1] You are very good to wish to include me in so distinguished a party.

With many thanks
Yours very truly
GSantayana

[1]Possibly Guglielmo Ferraro (1871–1942), who was an Italian historian and man of letters whose best-known works deal with Roman history.

To Francis Bullard
7 November 1908 • Cambridge, Massachusetts   (MS: Virginia)

3 Prescott Hall
Cambridge
November 7, 1908

Dear Frank

I hope you are having a good rest and enjoying the country in this fine wintry weather.

Your theory about that copy of my verses is interesting and ingenious, and I don't think it improbable. On the ~~stop~~ spot I have composed the following decima, which shall be written in the book whenever you like.

What frail sympathy long past
Linked a lost name to my name
On this page? What parting came,

That no pang of it should last?
The leaf torn, the volume cast
To the hawkers of the town
Tell the tale; till bending down
You redeemed the rumpled sheaf,
You who from man's dust and grief
Know to pluck his starry crown.

Now that the inscription is done, it may perhaps be safe to suggest a less sentimental hypothesis: namely, that some high-souled female gave my book on some occasion to a less soulful relation, who, tearing out the inscription, and not thinking the verses good enough to pass on the next Christmas to a different aunt, sold them for waste paper.

I heard James's first lecture in his new course yesterday. It has good passages describing the state of mind of sundry classes of persons, but no coherence and, so far, no thought.

To-morrow, and on later occasions, I expect to see Berenson who is here, and who always stimulates and amuses me.

I have a rather cheerful little room here; come and see it and me when you get back.

Yours affectionately
G.S.

To Isabella Stewart Gardner

[15 November 1908] • Cambridge, Massachusetts   (MS: Gardner)

3 Prescott Hall
Cambridge
Sunday

Dear Mrs Gardner

Thank you very much for wishing to include me in so charming a little party. I will come with great pleasure.

You say "a <u>week</u> from tomorrow, Sunday Nov. 22nd", and I shall understand it is the twenty second, unless I hear to the contrary. Don't trouble to write yourself again, as I am to see the Berensons tomorrow, and they will tell me which date it is.

You may observe that I have quitted my hermitage in Longwood for a new cell in Cambridge, but although a monk may have to change his cowl now and then, it is harder for him to change his solitary habits.

Thank you again for your kind invitation.

Yours sincerely

GSantayana

To Horace Meyer Kallen

10 December 1908 • Cambridge, Massachusetts   (MS: American)

December 10, 1908

COLONIAL CLUB

CAMBRIDGE

Dear Kallen.

Perhaps when you get this you will already have left Oxford, unless you are staying there during the holiday's to work on your thesis. The excitements of term-time will probaby have left you little freedom of mind to plod contentedly at an appointed task—and yet those are our happiest days. Jours de travail, [*illegible*] says Musset, seuls jours où j'ai vécu.[1]—I am a little sorry, though not surprised, that your impressions of Oxford are so censorious. It is getting to seem as if no one liked Oxford except me—and I don't. You talk as if you had ~~expept~~ expected to find ˄free˄ learning and philosophy there. You forget that it is a Christian place, founded by pious Queens and Bishops to save their own souls and those of other people. The quality of the salvation required has changed somewhat in five hundred years, but the tradition has not been broken, and the place is still scholastic on principle. They assume that they have long since possessed the Truth and the Way. Now, that may be an illusion; but what makes Oxford the best, if not the only, place in which an ideal of education can be acquired, is that, if we don't possess the Truth and the Way, we need to possess them. Until we do, and become ourselves what Oxford thinks it is, we can have no peace, no balance, no tradition, and no culture. It is inevitable, I know, and it is right, to be impatient at a premature or too narrow harmony: but how much more horrible is the disease we suffer from in America where the very idea of harmony and discipline are lost, and every ideal is discredited <u>a priori</u>!

I have heard from Roberts. He is a 7 King Edward Street, and complains of nothing. There is no need of looking him up unless you feel inclined.

Thank you very much for your interest in my health. I am much touched that you should think of it. My cold and the weather have been having their common vicissitudes, but I am not worse. Dante has kept me too busy to attend to anything else, or to amuse myself. In the Spring I hope for a many-sided rejuvenation.

Barrett Wendell never comes across me without talking much about you: he thinks a great deal of your letters. Write to me also when you can.

Yours   G.S.

[1]Days of work, the only days in which I have lived.

To Mary Williams Winslow
25 December 1908 • Cambridge, Massachusetts   (MS: Houghton)

---

3 Prescott Hall
Cambridge
Dec. 25, 1908

Dear Mrs Winslow[1]

Thank you very much for the most amusing book I have read for a long time—I devoured it all last night, and laughed aloud at the fat lady who had to lift food above the horizon. But I can't help thinking the author would be funnier if he well less satirical and more good-natured?. What is the use of judging the simple-minded rich by the complicated and obsolete standards of chivalry?

I suppose I ought to address my thanks to Fred also, but I can't help feeling it is you that did it, for though the hand is the hand of Esau the ribbon is the ribbon of Jacob.

I was sorry not to see you ₔtheₔ last time I came and that the young lady upstairs[2] seemed to be finding the world inexplicable in some particular. Time will bring the "higher optimism".

Yours sincerely
GSantayana

[1]Mary Williams Winslow and her husband were among Santayana's best friends during his later years in Boston.
[2]Polly, their baby daughter.

To Unidentified Recipient
[c. 1909 or 1910] • [Cambridge, Massachusetts]   (MS: Houghton)

Even in those days, when subjects and ideas gave out,[1] we had learned to appeal to the eternal idyl: a man and a girl for the picture, and for the words, anything. Memorial Hall soup and the puddles in the Yard gave a family likeness to every number, so that the reader, however startled by the novelties of the issue, could always reassure himself that Lampy was the same old Lampy still. May he long prosper, and amid his new glories[2] keep something of his careless and unworldly youth, when he took "Vanitas"[3] for a motto.

G. Santayana

[1]For the cartoons Santayana drew for the *Harvard Lampoon* during his undergraduate years.
[2]The new *Harvard Lampoon* Building was erected in 1909 on Mount Auburn Street.
[3]Untruth, a pun on the Harvard motto "Veritas," truth.

To Isabella Stewart Gardner
13 January 1909 • Cambridge, Massachusetts   (MS: Gardner)

3 Prescott Hall
Cambridge
Jan 13 1909

Dear Mrs Gardner

Mrs Berenson tells me that you are thinking of going to my lecture on the 28ᵗʰ It will be so nice to see you there, and I shall feel less lost before a strange audience, and less foolish for saying things that perhaps no one would understand—at least, as I meant them.

I am having two tickets sent you from New York, in case there is anyone with you who wants to come too.

I caught a sidelong glimpse of you at the tennis court last Saturday. The Coolidges[1] have added a charming feature to Cambridge, I think, by building this court. It is just the sort of thing we need to give us a little more distinction.

Yours sincerely
GSantayana

¹Mr. and Mrs. Archibald Coolidge.

To Isabella Stewart Gardner
19 January 1909 • Cambridge, Massachusetts   (MS: Gardner)

3 Prescott Hall
Cambridge
Jan. 19, 1909

Dear Mrs Gardner

I am so sorry that I sha'n't have the pleasure of seeing you in my audience at the Plaza. Of course the evening is an impossible time for lectures at this season. I didn't know myself, when I talked to the Berensons about it, that the hour would be 8.30, else I should have warned every body.

I sincerely wish I might be at the opera with you, instead of discoursing to the lecture-goers. But such is fate.

Yours sincerely
GSantayana.

Thank you for the tickets.

To Charles Augustus Strong
10 February 1909 • Cambridge, Massachusetts   (MS: Rockefeller)

3 Prescott Hall
Cambridge
Feb 10 1909

COLONIAL CLUB
CAMBRIDGE

Dear Strong

A tragic despatch in the papers (which a friend cut out and sent to me yesterday) informs me that you are in this country, or such fragments of you as are not "chewed up". I hope the thing has been exaggerated and that it has not proved very painful. I suppose mad Brazilians are not like mad dogs.

It happens that I am going to New York on the 19th to stay until the 22nd Let me know where you are, so that I may look you up. I expect to be at the Manhattan Hotel to sleep, and at the Knickerbocker Club for odd moments during the day and for meals when I am alone. It will be very nice to see you, and hear about your travels and the state of your book. And last, but not least, it will be nice to see Margaret once more.

Yours ever
GSantayana

To Charles Augustus Strong
[February 1909] • Cambridge, Massachusetts   (MS: Rockefeller)

3 Prescott Hall
Cambridge

COLONIAL CLUB
CAMBRIDGE

Dear Strong

I had just written to you when I got your letter. I am glad your condition is not so sad as the papers gave one to understand.

As to the School, I know nothing, but Mrs James and the other ladies here will tell you all you need to know. I am sorry that I can't come to see you on Sunday, but perhaps you will lunch with me on Monday (Margaret, too, if she is with you—we have a ladies' room here!) I should be very glad. Otherwise, I could look you up in the afternoon. The evenings are all filled up next week, I am sorry to say, and I leave on Friday, as I told you in my former note, for New York.

I should have said that the reason I can't come on Sunday is that I am to be in Worcester, talking to an Art Society. J'ai failli[1] preaching a sermon at Mr Garver's Church[2] that morning. He ask me to do so!

It will be very nice to see you again.

Yours
G.S.

[1]I nearly ended up.

[2]Austin Samuel Garver (1847–1918) of the Second Parish Church of Worcester wrote *Aristotle's Theory of Art: A Sketch* (Worcester, Mass., 1915) and *Greek Archaeology* (1904).

To Robert Underwood Johnson
14 March 1909 • Cambridge, Massachusetts   (MS: Academy)

3 Prescott Hall
Cambridge
Mass

March 14, '09

Dear Sir[1]

Your communication of February 9th has only just reached me, owing to negliglence in forwarding it from my old address.

I need hardly say that I feel it a great honour to have been elected a member of the Institute.[2]

Perhaps I ought to add that I am not an American citizen, and that I am not sure whether, in strictness, that fact should not be an obstacle to my figuring in the lists of the Institute.

Yours very truly
GSantayana

Mr R U Johnson

[1]Robert Underwood Johnson (1853–1937) was an American editor and poet. He was associate editor of *Century Magazine* (1881–1909) and secretary of the American Academy of Arts and Letters.

[2]Santayana was elected to the National Institute of Arts and Letters (later called the American Academy and Institute of Arts and Letters) on 5 Feb 1909 and resigned on 10 Mar 1911. He was elected a foreign honorary member in 1943.

To Susan Sturgis de Sastre
18 March 1909 • Cambridge, Massachusetts   (MS: Virginia)

March 18, 1909

COLONIAL CLUB
CAMBRIDGE

Dear Susie

It is several months since I last wrote to you, but as I know you get regular news of the family from Robert and Josephine, I don't make a point of sending my bulletin as well. Nothing much has happened, except that Robert seems to be really going to Europe, and that, during the last week or ten days, Mother has been ailing a little, although she is now better, and about in the same condition as before her cold, or whatever it was—for I saw no particular evidences of anything definite. We had a "trained nurse" for three or four days. It was much better for Mother, as her little meals were prepared nicely, given to her with a certain authority, so that she took them, as well as her medicines, and she slept with her <u>window open</u>, which of course helped to prevent her feeling ill and faint in the morning, which is one of the chief troubles she had. But now that she is more or less herself again, and comes down to the dining room as usual, they have sent the nurse away, and we shall return to the old routine. For Josephine, the nurse was evidently a nuisance at first. Josephine was more nervous and anxious than ever, and hardly could sleep. But after two or three days, she seemed to me to be calming down, and if the nurse (or somebody like her) had stayed, I think Josephine would have learned to put off her responsibility for a while now and then, and to sleep and take an outing with more peace of mind. Robert and I have told her so: but she persists in being vague and conditional in all she says about taking a nurse or maid, and it will have to be postponed until mother has another ill turn. Poor Josephine is naturally looking thinner and yellower than ever, and is pretty nervous; although, luckily, she is not at all unhappy or sad. On the contrary, Mother's mental weakness seems to strike her as something humorous and appealing, like the first notions of a young child; and she doesn't seem to be troubled about the future. What keeps her on the <u>qui vive</u>[1] is whether Mother has sneezed, or worked longer than usual at her knitting, or breathed hard in her sleep, as if complaining. The great fundamental situation doesn't seem to weigh on Josephine at all. Is this merely that she is too much taken up with details to consider things in the gross, or is it that she is resigned to the ultimate issue, and pleased to give herself up to pious little cares in the meantime? Mother is now distinctly more feeble, both in mind and body, than she was when I arrived in the autumn. But she is without pain and almost without discomfort: and I see no reason why she shouldn't remain in this condition for an indefinite time, perhaps for years. It is for Josephine that the situation seems to me grave; how can she stand months and months of continually watchfulness, night and day, with no distractions, hardly any fresh air, no appetite, and very little sound sleep? I hope she will soon convince herself that a nurse is needed, just as one would be needed for a baby, and that she will learn to throw off a part of her cares. What may contribute to this is that Mother is really quite indifferent to who is with her, and if her little wants were being attended to, she would never notice whether Josephine had been away for five hours or for five minutes.

As to myself, I am much more settled and comfortable than I was when I last wrote. My rooms are satisfactory: pupils and other friends come to see me very often—I have tea ready for them every day from four to half-past five—and, best of all, I have been to New York twice and had a real change which amused and refreshed me remarkably. An old friend—Moncure Robinson—got me rooms, a whole apartment, at Sherry's,[2] the very fashionable hotel at which he lives. I went out to lunch, dinner, and supper after the opera, every day, and on Sunday, even to breakfast. I saw a lot of very gay people. Their conversation is amusing and very risqué, but their manners are simple and excellent, and, for a change, I thought them delightful. One of the ladies I saw most was Mrs Ralph Ellis, a sister of Ward Thoron's wife. The most interesting, however, was Mrs John Jacob Astor,[3] who is a very Parisian sort of beauty, about forty, with grey hair, but a girlish figure, and a superficial interest in things intellectual, covering a fond[4] of sadness and of physical dissatisfaction. Her marriage was mercenary and has proved unhappy, and her boy, now about sixteen, tried to set fire to his school, and seems to promise nothing good for the future. This lady is one of the very few whom I look forward to seeing again when the occasion presents itself, and of keeping as a permanent link with the world. Of course she knows that she has made an impression on me, and she likes the idea. She has asked me to dinner since I came back, but I am not young and foolish enough to travel a day and a night for the pleasure of sitting for one hour next to any woman, no matter how charming.

My other friend Mrs Bob Potter has been for a day in Boston. Her mother died suddenly and she came to America to arrange her affairs. I hear that she has inherited $300,000; it is probably much less, but it will help the Potters to live more as they like. They are now in Athens, and I expect, as Bob has given up his business in New York, that they will be in Europe most of the time in future This is very nice for me, because it will help me to see them when I leave this country myself; and of course, in leaving it, I am far from wishing never to see my American friends again. It is only their country that I am longing to lose sight of. As a matter of fact, I have made my best American friends abroad, like Boylston Beal and the Potters, and I shall be able to see them as often, and to much greater advantage there than in Boston or New York. This is also true of my new flame, Mrs Astor.

Is there any "modernist" movement or party in Spain? I have been reading Loisy, Tyrrell, Paul Sabatier (who is a Protestant, but a great friend of the "Modernists)[5] as well as the Pope's Encyclical "Pascendi" and other documents. As I expect to be here this summer, I have agreed to give two lectures on the religious situation in Catholic countries before the parsons that come to the summer school here, and I am anxious to get any general information that I can. What I read at Avila in the "Lectura Dominical", though little, is going to be a help. Of course, I know what the theoretic position of the Church and of her enemies is; but what these ignorant parsons want to hear is what are the tendencies of popular feeling. Are there any socialistic Catholics like Murri[6] in Spain? If you have any pamphlets or books that deal with this subject I should be much obliged if you would send them to me. Quite apart from my lectures, which will have to be very superficial, the subject interests me in itself. I believe I have always been a "modernist"; only it never crossed my mind that such an attitude was compatible with being a practical Catholic, much less a priest. How can they be so blind?–   Love to Celedonio and the family, with a [across] great deal for yourself   from   George

[1]Lookout.

[2]Louis Sherry (1856–1926) was a New York City restaurateur, confectioner, and host who catered to the wealthy.

[3]John Jacob Astor (1864–1912), fourth of this name in the U.S., drowned in the *Titanic* disaster. His second wife was Madeleine Talmage Force, and their son was the fifth of the name.

[4]Depth.

[5]Alfred Firmin Loisy (1857–1940) was a French biblical critic who became the leader of Catholic modernism. His teachings were condemned by the Holy See, and he was excommunicated. George Tyrrell (1861–1909), a modernist theologian, joined the Society of Jesus in 1880. He was dismissed from his order in 1906 for what were considered unorthodox publications. Paul Sabatiér (1858–1940) was a French clergyman and historian who studied the life of Saint Francis of Assisi.

[6]Romolo Murri (1870–1944) was an Italian whose works include *La filosofia nuova e l'enciclica contro il modernismo* (1908) and *Della religione della chiesa e dello stato: considerazioni* (1910).

To Susan Sturgis de Sastre

19 April 1909 • Cambridge, Massachusetts   (MS: Virginia)

April 19, 1909.

COLONIAL CLUB
CAMBRIDGE

Dear Susie

Thank you for your letter.–Mother, as you know, is getting on nicely, and we now have a nurse, Sarah Quinn, permanently established in the house. She is elderly, Irish, and Catholic, so that she eats in the kitchen and gets on with the other servants. She also prepares and serves Mother's food, does her room, sits there when Josephine is away, and makes herself as useful as she can, although Josephine doesn't give her a chance to take charge as much as she would like, and as would be advisable for Josephine's sake. They tell me that Mother is apt to be drowsy and somewhat restless in the morning, but in the afternoon, when I usually see her, she is placid and cheerful, busy with knitting or playing with cards, or folding papers and things. The only thing that is a little troublesome is that she thinks very often that she is not at home, and wants to go out to find her family–her father and mother,[1] I think she means. But, with a little coaxing, she forgets this notion, and settles down again, quite happy in her armchair.

You must have been sorry, and perhaps alarmed, to hear that Robert has given up his trip. It is a case of tender feeling on his part. There is no reason to think that Mother will not be as she is now at the end of the Summer; but as she seems to like to see Robert, he feels that he had better stay. It is a natural sentiment, and I confess I thought it a little queer, considering Robert's character, that he should have planned to go away now. Of course, Mother forgets that he has come to see her as soon as he is gone, so that it makes no <u>steady difference</u> to her; but she seems to recognise him when he comes–that is, she is glad to see him, although she doesn't conceive that he is her son. Sometimes I think she imagines he is uncle Robert; but Josephine thinks I am wrong in this.

What you and Celedonio say about Mrs Astor has made me laugh a great deal. Do you suppose Jack Astor, after his wife has been amusing herself in every capital of Europe for twenty years, surrounded by all sorts of dandies, lady-killers, and <u>roués</u>, would suddenly develope homicidal jealousy of a bald, gray, near-sighted, and rheumatic professor of philosophy? Besides, the lady is not said to have actual lovers, and, if she had had them, might be expected to renounce them out of respect to her gray hairs. As to her husband, I didn't see him in New York; they never go about together, and are supposed to be practically separated, although nominally they live in the same house. I dare say he has another ménage also.

My rheumatism is much better; only a little weakness in the right knee left. I take phosphate of sodium every morning, which is supposed to be like Carlsbad water, and it agrees with me very well, regulating the bowels as well as helping the rheumatism.

Since Robert is to stay, there is no reason why I should ₍n't₎ go: so that I have taken passages from N.Y. to Liverpool for July 14, and from Liverpool to N.Y. for September 18, in the big new Cunarders,[2] where I find there are also single cabins to be had. I am sorry not to go to Avila, but the holiday is short, and I am thinking of spending it again chiefly at Oxford, where I have the Bodleian library to consult, and Bertrand Russell, the Earl's brother, to talk philosophy with. I am sailing so late on account of my lectures on pr[*illegible*] "Modernism", which are to be on July 8 and 9. You ask me what "Modernism" is precisely. It is not anything precise; but as a general tendency, it consists in accepting all the rationalistic views ₍current or₎ possible in matters of history and science, and then saying that, in a different sense, the dogmas of the Church may still be true. For instance, all miracles, including the Incarnation and Resurrection, are denied to be historical facts; but they remain, in some symbolic sense, theological truths. That is, they are normal ways in which religious imagination has expressed itself; and people ought to go on, in their devotions, using those expressions, just as they go on using a language or a style of dress that has naturally established itself. The Modernists say they are not Protestants, in that they wish to keep the whole doctrine and organisation of the Church, and to develope it further, rather than to lop off parts of it. But they are free-thinkers, since they regard that whole doctrine and organisation as simply a human growth, symbolic only, and changeable. They also say (but this is a plain inconsistency) that there is a peculiar providence or Holy Spirit guiding the Catholic Church in its development, such as does <u>not</u> guide the Mahomedans or the Buddhists. This, however, is rejected by Paul Sabatier, a Protestant friend and defender of the Modernists.—Theologically considered, Modernism is untenable, like every theory of double truths; but I don't know how far it may express the filtering in of rationalism into the seminaries and among the clergy.— Thank you for the <u>Lectura Dominical</u> of which one number has arrived so far. I didn't mean you to send it, as even if it mentions the subject, it will give a very one-sided view of it. But I am always glad to read [*across*] a little lively Spanish, and to get some hint of what is going on.   Love to all from   George

[1]José Borrás y Bufurull of Reus and Teresa Carbonell of Las Palmas. See *Persons*, 30–35.
[2]A steamship line.

To Charles Augustus Strong
18 July 1909 • At sea   (MS: Rockefeller)

^{C}/o Brown Shipley & Co
123 Pall Mall

July 18
1909.
At Sea

CUNARD R.M.S. "MAURETANIA".

Dear Strong

You may be surprised to see that, at this late date, I am on my way to England. My brother changed his plans, and as my mother is pretty well, I decided after all to take my usual outing. However, I hardly expect to leave England, so that I am afraid I sha'n't see you unless by some fortunate chance you have finally run off your beaten track and ventured across the Channel. Why don't you come for a change? It has often seemed to me that you might like England very much if you only went there a little oftener.

Please give my best regards to Margaret–I suppose she is such a young lady that I ought'n't to send her my "love", unless it is the uncle-like sort of love which I am now in the habit of dispensing to young people.–Let me have a word from you–

Yours   GSantayana

To Susan Sturgis de Sastre
7 August 1909 • Chichester, England   (MS: Virginia)

August 7th 1909.

M·R

TELEGRAPH HOUSE,
CHICHESTER.

Dear Susie

Your letter of the 3rd has just reached me here, where I came on Wednesday, the 4th. The house[1] has been rebuilt since I was last here and now has a tower with an extensive view, including the Ilse of Wight in the far distance. We are on the crest of high domelike hills, called Downs, and out of sight of all habitations. There isn't much quiet, however; for there are seven dogs, one cat, and three automobiles, a pumping-engine for water, another for electric light, and a general restlessness in the household. Russell is absorbed in business (he is now president of the Humber Motor-Car Company) and in politics, while his wife[2] is given over to woman-suffrage, dogs, and gardening. I send you her portrait (published for political purposes) which she has just presented me, and ˄I˄ write on her note-paper,[3] so that you will get a good impression of her personality. You may remember she is Irish, and has two other husbands living. Russell's other wife, by the way, and her mother Lady Scott, have both died this year.

Reports about the troubles at Barcelona have been sensational here at first, and now are more credible.[4] I will send you the Weekly Times on Monday, when I return to London, and any daily paper which seems interesting. The situation at Melilla[5] is what will cause, I am afraid, more trouble in the end, as it will be hard to circumscribe the operations, or to find a trustworthy and permanent authority in the country with which to make peace.

Josephine has not sent me even a post-card since I left, and I am without news, except what you give me. Was young Josephine[6] decidedly ill, or do you refer only to her "car-sickness"? I am sorry Celedonio is not quite rid of his annoyance in the eye; perhaps if his general condition is improved by the waters of Calzadilla the irritation in the eye will also disappear—As to the London especialist for hernia, of course if he were a real specialist he would not advertise, nor would he live in E.C., that is, in the East City, or oldest business portion of London, where no one resides, all the houses being offices. I hope the interest Luis[7] takes in this is not due to his suffering any bad turn at present.

At Howard's I heard little about the family and saw only Mildred Seymour, who has been ill but is now recovered. Her mother seems to be happy in her new marriage, and the children are partly reconciled to her Falle–as her husband's name is. On the other hand Harry and his wife[8] seem to have disagreed and to live more or less [*across*] apart. Her father (the novelist Merideth) died recently, and I suppose left her some money.– Teddy Seymour is controller to the Duchess of Albany's household, & his wife lady in waiting.–I think that is all I have heard by way of news.

Your affec^{tion} brother   George

[1]John F. S. Russell called his house, located on the South Downs near Harting, Petersfield, in Hampshire, Telegraph House, abbreviated to T. H. See *Persons*, 469–70.

[2]Countess "Mollie" (Marion Cooke Cumbermould) was Russell's second wife (Mrs. Sommerville when he married her). Santayana describes her in *Persons* (476–81) as "a fat, florid, coarse Irishwoman of forty [in 1895], with black curls, friendly manners and emotional opinions." Their 1900 Nevada marriage was legal according to American but not English law, and Russell spent three months in jail as a bigamist. They legally married in England in October 1901. After fifteen years of marriage, he and Mollie divorced.

[3]Her notepaper bore a coronet above her initials.

[4]Spain was engaged in a Moroccan war. The government instituted conscription, setting off a general strike, and a workers' revolution against the monarchy began in Barcelona.

[5]General Marina, after a hard campaign, occupied the massif of Gorongon and the hinterland of Melilla, and the Spaniards made themselves masters of the whole region between Oned Kert and Monlonya.

[6]Josephine Sturgis, daughter of Santayana's half brother, Robert.

[7]Luis Sastre González.

[8]Henry Parkman Sturgis married his second wife, Marie Eveleen Meredith, on 17 Jul 1894. They had two daughters.

To Susan Sturgis de Sastre

10 August 1909 • London, England   (MS postcard: Sanchez)

TOWER BRIDGE, LONDON.

London, Aug 10. '09.

Last night I got your letter with one from Josephine inclosed. Thank you very much. I also got a card from Josephine direct, dated the 28th of July. They were well.–It is very warm here, and I expect to leave for Oxford in a day or two, as soon as I can despatch with the tailor.

[Unsigned]

To Charles Augustus Strong

10 August 1909 • London, England   (MS: Rockefeller)

Address: ^c/o Brown Shipley & C°
                                123 Pall Mall S.W.

                                                109 Jermyn St. S.W.
                                                August 10 1909

Dear Strong

Of course I don't know whether Mrs Sidgwick[1] is now in Cambridge (where I presume she lives) or on a holiday. At Oxford they have a University Extension Session now running, which is what is making me hesitate about going there at once, although I expect I shall do so on Friday or Saturday of this week. When there, I shall look for lodgings for myself, and if I see or hear of anything that might suit you, I will make a note of it.

As to recommendations for a School for Margaret, I should think the best way would be to <u>write</u> to Mrs. Sidgwick, or to any other person you wish to consult. It is much easier than seeing them personally and for this purpose, I should think, more satisfactory.

Bertrand Russell and his wife (Mrs Russell,[2] you may remember was a person I thought would know what you had in mind for Margaret) are now on the Continent. Their address is Bagley Wood, Oxford, and I believe they will be back there before the end of this month.

I am most interested in your change of plan. My own feeling about life in England has changed a little in these last years—I find it somewhat <u>less</u> attractive than I did—but this is due, I think, to no change in the place but only to a greater restlessness or vacancy in my own mind, which makes a more amusing environment more pleasant. In a word—England is a place where one is easily <u>bored</u>; so that one must bring one's resources and habits with one. In this <u>boring</u> quality, I include the people, much as I admire them zoologically and in themselves: but they don't <u>amuse</u> <u>me</u>.

However, I still think England would suit you in many ways, and, on the whole, you would fine more people who would discuss philosophy with you than anywhere else

Yours ever

G.S.

[1] Eleanor Mildred Balfour Sidgwick (1845–1936), widow of Henry Sidgwick, was influential in founding Newnham College (a college for women at Cambridge) and was principal there from 1892 to 1910.
[2] Alys Smith Russell.

To Charles Augustus Strong

13 August 1909 • London, England   (MS: Rockefeller)

109 Jermyn Street S.W.
Friday, Aug. 13, 1909

Dear Strong

You will get a letter or telegram from me on Monday morning, telling you where I have engaged rooms for you in Oxford, and my own address there. (I haven't engaged rooms at a hotel ∧for myself,∧ and hope to take lodgings at once, and to be established when you arrive.) Please telegraph back the train you will come by, and I will meet you at the Station. The best trains are as follows:

	Leave Paddington	Arrive in Oxford
	9.50	11.15
	10.20	11.42
p.m.	1.45	3.3
	4.55	6.9
	6.15	7.32
	7.30	8.45

The two last have a restaurant car, so that you may dine in the train, if you think that a pleasure.

If I have luck in Oxford this afternoon, and settle everything, I will write at once, so that you may know of more definite arrangements the moment you reach London.

I shouldn't wonder if you found it inconvenient to start for Oxford on Monday. The heat in London has been great, but it may have moderated by that time, and you and Margaret may like to take a look about before you leave town.

If you want to go to the theatre, or rather to some show, let me recommend the Hippodrome (to which you can take Margaret) where there is a thrilling American piece, and some other good turns. Mrs Preedy & the Countess[1] at the Criterion (<u>not</u> before nine o'clock) is rather amusing, but slightly <u>risqué</u>.—On Sunday, Hampton Court[2] is the only resource. The most comfortable & [*across*] quickest way of getting there is to take a "taxi". Bargain with the driver for the whole trip.   G.S.

[1]*Mr. Preedy and the Countess: An Original Farce in Three Acts* by Richard Claude Carton.
[2]Hampton Court Palace, built in 1515 by Cardinal Wolsey, was a royal residence until the time of George II. It has an art gallery and public gardens.

To Charles Augustus Strong
[13 August 1909] • Oxford, England   (MS: Rockefeller)

Friday evening
THE EASTGATE HOTEL,
OXFORD.

Dear Strong

I have engaged three rooms for you at the Randolph Hôtel, which you probably remember, for Monday. You might have had them also in this little place, but so diminutive, and so queer, that I thought it best to go to the big American sort of place. I have not seen the rooms, but asked that two at least should be adjoining, as I suppose there is a lady in some capacity travelling with you.—This is badly expressed, but you know what I mean—Margaret's governness or nurse.

After much wandering I have taken lodgings for myself at 16 Turl Street, or <u>The Turl</u>, as it is usually called. All the most attractive quarters are infested with extensionist women, but they go in ten days and then, if I am not pleased with my place, I can find something more satisfactory.

I hope your journey has been comfortable in spite of the heat. Today we have had a shower here, and it is much cooler.

Telegraph to me to 16 Turl-Street by which train you will come on Monday.

Yours ever
G.S.

To Charles Augustus Strong

2 September 1909 • Oxford, England   (MS: Rockefeller)

16 Turl Street   Oxford
September 2, 1909

Dear Strong

Thank you very much indeed for "Orphans",[1] which I am delighted to have. It was very kind of you to send it, and it will now accompany me on my walks, to keep me company at tea, or at any moment when the grass is dry enough to sit on and the sun warm enough to allow one to stop.

Two or three further persons whom I have questioned have spoken well of St Felix;[2] I think you have probably done the best thing possible in choosing it. At Windsor, where I spent last Sunday, Howard Sturgis and his sister,[3] who is the mother of two nice girls,[4] also recommended highly two smaller schools, with thirty or forty girls only, which you may think it worth while to make a note of, in case any difficulty should present itself at the larger place and you should wish to make a change. They are Miss Weiser's, Northlands, Englefield Green, Surrey, and Miss Browning's, The Beehive, Bexhill-on-Sea, very near Hastings.

Yesterday I went to lunch at Bagley Wood and saw both Russell and Moore. The conversation, however, didn't get very technical, as there were other people present, including four ladies. We (I chiefly) talked a little about Bergson of whom Russell apparently has read nothing and Moore only half a book–the <u>Évolution créatrice</u>, and whom both equally dislike. Moore is writing an article[5] on the definition of the term "mental" and Russell's second volume[6] is ready for the press. He says it is the most elementary book ever written on mathematics. Both say that Perry & C⁰'s denial of psychic existence is unintelligible and unintelligent. They laugh at the notion that this is an application of their own philosophy[x]. I felt some relief, after the unsatisfactory issue of our late discussions at the "Randolph", to know that the original "new realists" admit the idealistic view of psychology or, if you prefer, of autobiography. In your book you yourself often spoke of mental facts and mental processes. Would you reject those conceptions now?   <u>Bon voyage</u>
Yours ever   G.S.

[across] [x] I gathered yesterday that they are pronounced idealists of Leibniz' type. Moore said "The monad is what the atom <u>really is</u>."

[1]Unidentified.
[2]Saint Felix School, Southwold, is in Suffolk East in England.
[3]Lucy Lyman Paine Sturgis Codman.
[4]Misses Anne Macmaster Codman and Susan Welles Codman.
[5]Unidentified.
[6]*Principia Mathematica*, 3 vols., written with Alfred North Whitehead (Cambridge, 1910–13).

To Susan Sturgis de Sastre
14 September 1909 • Oxford, England   (MS postcard: Sanchez)

TOM TOWER, CHRISTCHURCH.

Oxford, Sept. 14, 1909

I am sending you three volumes of "Jean Cristophe" by Rolland,[1] a book which has made some stir. There are four other volumes out (which I haven't read) and more to come. Don't read "L'adolescent", it is commonplace and coarse, but begin with "La Révolte." "La Foire" is a cruel picture of Paris.

[*Unsigned*]

[1]Romain Rolland (1866–1944) was a French author whose magnum opus is the ten-novel series *Jean Christophe* (1904–1912). He received the 1915 Nobel Prize in literature. His pacifism led to self-imposed exile in Switzerland until 1938.

To Wendell T. Bush
14 November 1909 • Cambridge, Massachusetts   (MS: Columbia)

3 Prescott Hall
Nov. 14, 1909

~~COLONIAL CLUB~~
CAMBRIDGE

Dear Mr. Bush[1]

Perhaps it would be better that some one else should review the translation of Croce, as I read and reviewed the book when it first came out, and hardly can notice it again without rereading it, which I hardly care to do.[2] It seems to be having a vogue which is unusual for a purely scholastic aesthetic; but his is polemical, and that gives it some spice.

I am writing my lectures on Lucretius, etc, and looking forward with pleasure to the delivery of them.   Yours sincerely

GSantayana

[1]Wendell T. Bush (1867–1941) received an M.A. from Harvard (1908) and a Ph.D. from Columbia. He was professor of philosophy at Columbia University and editor of *The Journal of Philosophy, Psychology, and Scientific Methods.*
[2]Benedetto Croce (1866–1952) was the best-known Italian philosopher of the twentieth century. The first volume of his philosophy of the spirit was *Estetica come scienza dell' espressione e linguistica generale* (1902). Douglas Ainslie translated this work as *Aesthetic as Science of Expression and General Linguistic* (London: Macmillan, 1909). Santayana's review of this book, "Croce's Aesthetics," appeared in the *Journal of Comparative Literature* 1 (1903): 191–95. (Reprinted in *The Idler and his Works* [1957], 108–15.)

To William Roscoe Thayer
22 December 1909 • Cambridge, Massachusetts   (MS: Houghton)

---

3 Prescott Hall
Dec. 22, 1909

Dear Mr Thayer

I am sorry to have missed the pleasure of seeing you and ~~of~~ to have given you the trouble to write.

I went to the Boston Latin School throughout my school days, remembering even old Mr. Gardner, the head master.[1]

I have not been naturalised in this country, but still travel with a Spanish passport.

I don't know what points you wish to notice, but I should think more important for my "poetry" than my school before College was my school after–Berlin, with a term at Oxford and–much later–a year at Cambridge.

Yours sincerely
GSantayana

[1]Francis Gardner was headmaster when Santayana began Boston Latin School in the autumn of 1874. See *Persons*, 148–49.

EDITORIAL
APPENDIX

Textual Commentary

I. Summary Statement of Textual Principles and Procedures

A. *The Works of George Santayana* and Editorial Scholarship

The volumes of *The Works of George Santayana* are unmodernized, critical editions of George Santayana's writings. This "unmodernized" edition retains original and idiosyncratic punctuation, spelling, capitalization, and word division in order to reflect the full intent of the author as well as the initial texture of the work. It is a "critical" edition because it allows the exercise of editorial judgment in making corrections, changes, and choices among authoritative readings. The editors' goals are to produce texts that accurately represent Santayana's final intentions regarding his works and to record all evidence on which editorial decisions have been based.

The other volumes of *The Works of George Santayana* pertain typically to materials composed by Santayana that he intended for publication and dissemination in a printed form. For these writings there may exist a holograph manuscript, a typescript, printers' proofs, two or more editions, and multiple impressions of editions. In such cases the term "critical edition" indicates the task of comparing these various forms of the text in order to ascertain and perpetuate the author's "final intentions" regarding his work. With letters, however, where the original handwritten document is generally the only form of the text, the editors pursue a different goal. Since they aim to provide the reader with a literal, or diplomatic, text, their task lies in correctly reading and transcribing the text.

Santayana probably never intended his correspondence to be published, and did not write letters as he wrote works for publication. The intent of this volume is to present the letters in a form that will give the reader an experience comparable to reading the original letter. Therefore, these published letters are, as much as possible, exact copies of the handwritten master. That is, they are diplomatic transcriptions, reproducing all of the characteristics of the autograph letters, including misspellings, mispunctuation, grammatical errors, slips of the pen, and such alterations as cancellations and insertions. The printed form of the letters adheres to the characteristics of the originals in all of these particulars. The exceptions to this practice of exact transcription and reproduction are the lineation, pagination, and nonsemantic features of the letter which Santayana did not intend to carry any meaning.

The editors subscribe to the view of modern epistolary scholarship that "a scholarly edition should not contain a text which has editorially been corrected, made consistent, or otherwise smoothed out. Errors and inconsistencies are part of the total texture of the document and are part of the evidence which the document preserves relating to the writer's habits, temperament, and mood." (G. Thomas Tanselle, "The Editing of Historical Documents," *Studies in Bibliography* 31 [1978]: 48.)

B. Transcribing, Editing, and Typesetting

Transcribing, editing, and typesetting *The Works of George Santayana* is done electronically and results in computer files. They are the basis of the book, which is produced with QuarkXPress, a commercial electronic typesetting program. The initial transcription of a copy-text (the document on which the critical text is based) includes typesetting codes for all the text elements, including chapter headings, subheadings, marginal headings, standard paragraphs, extracts, poetry lines, footnotes, and the like. In the letters edition, the copy-text is almost always a holograph manuscript, and transcriptions also include codes indicating authorial alterations of the text (deletions, insertions, and other corrections). Each transcription receives at least two independent sight collations against the copy-text to assure its accuracy. Computer files of the corrected copy-text transcription serve as the basis for the Critical Edition.

In addition to the copy-text, the front matter, the textual notes, appendixes, references, and index are assembled in computer files. This material is also proofed twice. Various software programs aid the editors in locating, counting, and compiling material needed in making editorial decisions. They are used to identify patterns of punctuation and spelling and all line-end hyphens in the copy-text. A "Word Book" indicating Santayana's usage and spelling of problematic words also is placed in a computer file for reference.

The computer files of the letters text and all related materials are then imported into QuarkXPress, a desktop publishing program that uses style sheets to format the various aspects of the letters text (headings, dates, signatures, footnotes, etc.), or the textual notes, or appendixes. These are printed and checked against copy with typesetting codes to ensure that all stylistic changes (italics, superscript, strikeouts) were made correctly. Use of the QuarkXPress program enables the editors to send proofed pages to MIT Press for printing. The pages are set up to match the font style and size of the volumes already published in *The Works of George Santayana*. This procedure eliminates the need for galleys and enables the staff to convert page and line numbers referred to in the textual notes from copy-text to critical edition before sending files to the press. MIT returns printed pages to the edition for final checking, but not a complete collation. Finally, before the book is printed, a thorough check of the blueprints (contact prints of the negatives) is made, focusing principally on line and page endings.

The technology of desktop typesetting employed in *The Works of George Santayana* greatly facilitates the editing and publication process. Significantly, once the letter is transcribed in a computer file, the integrity of that text is maintained throughout the editing process. Except for the incorporated emendations, the final critical edition text is identical to the original copy-text transcription. Hence, not only do the editors of *The Works of George Santayana* have direct control over the printing process, but also the integrity of the critical edition text is safeguarded by this technology.

II. Composition and Characteristics of Santayana's Letters

A. Letter-Writing a Part of Santayana's Daily Routine

George Santayana lived in an era when people regularly wrote letters. The telephone did not come into common use until the first decade of the twentieth century, and Santayana did not like using it (especially during the latter part of his life when he suffered from deafness which made even tête-à-tête conversation very difficult and use of the telephone impossible). Like his contemporaries, therefore, he wrote letters. He corresponded regularly with members of his family, friends, former students, his publishers, editors of periodicals publishing his essays and reviews, his colleagues in the Harvard philosophy department, readers of his books, authors who sent him copies of their productions, and others. He was a prompt and conscientious letter writer and generally answered correspondence sent to him within a few days of receipt.

Santayana's day was organized in a way that facilitated letter writing. Living primarily in hotels, he led his life according to a regular schedule. Rising about seven, he breakfasted in his room and spent the morning working on his literary and philosophical writings. He stopped work about noon, shaved, bathed, dressed, and normally went to a restaurant for his main meal of the day. He spent the rest of the afternoon walking (his sole form of exercise), usually stopping for an hour or two in good weather to sit on a park bench and read, for which purpose he bought cheap editions of books to cut up and carry in his coat pocket. In the early evening, he returned to his hotel and had supper served in his room. The rest of the evening was devoted to correspondence and to reading until going to bed between ten and eleven o'clock. This invariable routine—carried on wherever Santayana happened to be, whether traveling or at home—resulted in the production of a prodigious number of books, poems, plays, essays, magazine and journal articles, an autobiography, literary criticism, a best-selling novel, and more than 3,000 letters.

B. The Composition Process

Most of Santayana's letters were written with black ink on white notepaper. In later years, in Rome, he favored cross-hatch ruled paper (like graph paper) for his letters as well as for some of his writings for publication. He wrote everything by hand, and his writing instrument was almost always a steel nib in a wooden holder. During the last years of his life, someone gave him a fountain pen; but it did not work properly and he quickly abandoned it, reverting to his habitual writing tools. A few of Santayana's letters are typewritten, but these were either copied by a professional typist engaged by him for the purpose or by the recipient from the handwritten original. Santayana never learned to type, nor did he, like Henry James, purchase a typewriter and hire a typist to take dictation.

Santayana referred to his handwriting as "commonplace," but it is anything but that. It is, in fact, quite beautiful. The characters are well-shaped, and the words, in nearly all instances, clear and legible. While the handwriting is almost calligraphic, it is also admirably simple and unadorned; there are no flourishes or other indications of self-conscious penmanship. Neither is there much revision in Santayana's letters. Some contain authorial cancellations and insertions of words or phrases, but this is unusual. More often an alteration corrects a misspelling or a false start.

C. Chronology of the Letters

The earliest extant letter by Santayana was written in Spanish to his half sisters, Susan and Josephine Sturgis, in 1868, when Santayana was five or six years old.[1] It is remarkable in terms of its quality of personal objectivity and self-knowledge. The next earliest is that of 21 August 1882 to John Galen Howard, Santayana's classmate and recent fellow graduate of the Boston Public Latin School. But the beginning of the regular progression of extant letters commences in the late summer and fall of 1886, with those to his Harvard classmates, Henry Ward Abbot and Ward Thoron, and continues to 3 August 1952 to Daniel Cory, probably Santayana's final letter, written a few weeks before his death.

Not including the earliest letter referred to above, those accumulated in this comprehensive edition cover a period of almost three quarters of a century. As would be expected, there are fewer letters surviving from the earlier times than from the later. However, there are letters representative of virtually every period of Santayana's long life.

D. The Languages of Santayana's Letters

Santayana knew several languages, but except for letters written to relatives and friends in Spain (including a formal letter in Spanish of 28 December 1913 to Miguel de Unamuno) and one letter in Italian, to Dino Rigacci (Charles Augustus Strong's manservant at the Villa Le Balze at Fiesole) of 29 April 1945, his correspondence is in English. There may well have been some letters in French. For instance, it is likely that Santayana wrote to Marie Chassarant, for many years the *bonne* at Strong's apartment at 9 Avenue de l'Observatoire in Paris, or to her husband, Edmond; but no letters to the Chassarants have been located.

E. Destroyed or Unlocated Letters

The loss of Santayana's letters to his mother (written in Spanish) is particularly regrettable. In the last months of her life, Josefina Borrás, who had always been so astute, suffered from some form of dementia. Three months before her death on 5 February 1912, Santayana, in going through her papers and clearing out her desk, gathered together all the letters he had written to her and burned them. This event is reported in the 7 November 1911 letter to his sister Susan, and though he says that in reading over his letters to his mother he found them very impersonal and learned nothing from them that he did not perfectly remember, they might have revealed something regarding the immensely important—and largely negative—relationship between mother and son. Similarly, Santayana's letters to his father (also in Spanish) have not been located and probably have not survived. (However, Santayana, who habitually destroyed letters after reading or answering them, did preserve the ones that his father had written to him. Those letters are in the Rare Book and Manuscript Library of Columbia University.)

The reader familiar with Santayana's life and career will perhaps be disappointed not to find letters to certain persons with whom one would expect Santayana to have corresponded. In some cases, letters known to have been written to such persons have been destroyed or otherwise lost; in others there is no evidence that such correspondence did, in fact, occur.

A frustrating example of unlocated letters is that represented by the substantial batch that Santayana is reported to have written to his Harvard classmate, William Morton Fullerton. After graduation, Fullerton, an avid student of the French language and of French history and culture, went to Paris where he lived virtually all the rest of his life. At the age of twenty-five, he was foreign correspondent for the *Times* of London and later a writer for *Le Figaro*. He was also the author of a number of books on contemporary politics. Fullerton led a colorful personal life. He became an intimate friend of Henry James's and, for a time, the lover of Edith Wharton. A bisexual, Fullerton had numerous adventures with both men and women. Four of Santayana's letters to Fullerton have been located at the Humanities Research Center of the University of Texas at Austin and are included in the present collection. But many more letters (contemporary with these Texas letters, i.e., 1887–88, written while Santayana was a graduate student in Germany) were reported to have been seen on Fullerton's desk, in his Paris office, by his cousin Hugh Fullerton for many years director of the American Hospital at Neuilly. Fullerton died in the same year as Santayana; and, in the early 1970s, an independent American scholar and writer living in Paris, Dr. Marion Mainwaring, tracked down Fullerton's missing papers. Though there were many important documents relating to Fullerton's life, no Santayana letters were among them.[2] The four letters to Fullerton are unique among Santayana's writings for their Rabelaisian and scatological character and humor. It is a great pity that others, if indeed they existed, have not been located.

Two major modern American poets, T. S. Eliot and Wallace Stevens, were students at Harvard during Santayana's tenure there. Eliot, as a philosophy student, had been Santayana's pupil, and Stevens and Santayana had known one another sufficiently to compose rival sonnets.[3] Yet, there is no real evidence that Santayana wrote to either one. Mrs. Valerie Eliot, who edited and published her late husband's correspondence, informed William Holzberger that she could find no letters from Santayana to Eliot. Likewise, Holly Stevens wrote him that, to her knowledge, there was no exchange of letters between Santayana and her father.[4] Santayana did, however, exchange letters with Harvard historian Samuel Eliot Morison. Shortly after Professor Morison's death on 15 May 1976, Holzberger was told by Morison's secretary that she was unaware of any letters by Santayana among Morison's papers.

Santayana corresponded with a number of other persons for whom no letters have been located. Only six letters have been found of the many that Santayana must have written over the years to John Francis Stanley, the second Earl Russell. Given the significance of this relationship–Santayana, particularly the young Santayana, was fascinated by Russell–the loss of the other letters is most regrettable for they surely would have illuminated the nature of one of Santayana's most profound attachments. None of the letters that Santayana wrote to his friend Baron Albert von Westenholz have been located. Santayana knew the Hamburg aristocrat from the time of the latter's student days at Harvard until his suicide on 5 August 1939. Over the years, Westenholz's name was invariably included in the lists of persons that Santayana sent to his publishers to receive complimentary copies of his books. In *Persons and Places,* Santayana describes Westenholz as a hopeless neurotic, but he also says that Westenholz was exceptionally intelligent and, with Bertrand Russell and Trumbull Stickney, one of the three best-educated persons he had known.[5]

Other known correspondents whose Santayana letters have not been located, include Jacques Duron, the French lycée teacher and student of Santayana's philosophy whose book, *La pensée de George Santayana: Santayana en Amérique* (Paris: Librarie Nizet, [1950]), is an important critical analysis of Santayana's writings. Santayana did not like Duron,[6] but letters to him would doubtless contain important comments on Santayana's philosophy. Also unlocated are letters to the English novelist Gerald Bullett, with whom, Santayana told Cory, he enjoyed "a pleasant correspondence" during the early 1930s.[7] Robert S. Fitzgerald, the American classicist, poet, and translator of Homer and Virgil, received several letters from Santayana. Fitzgerald was a close friend of Robert Lowell, and he accompanied Lowell on a visit to Santayana in Rome. One of Santayana's letters to Fitzgerald survives (5 June 1949), but, according to a letter that Fitzgerald wrote to William Holzberger on 3 December 1978, there were others that Fitzgerald, in his words, "filed all too carefully."[8] One of these lost letters was ostensibly about an English translation of Sophocles' *Oedipus Rex* which Fitzgerald had collaborated on. A final example of unlocated correspondence is that of the "long literary letters" that Santayana said (in a letter to another Boston friend)[9] he used to write, "in my callow days," to a young woman by the name of Julia Robins, who later converted to Roman Catholicism and became an eccentric Boston spinster. Surely these letters to Miss Robins—who hinted that Santayana had been in love with her, and included him in a list of "geniuses I have known"—would be most interesting and are an unfortunate loss. A list of unlocated letters of which the editors are aware is included in the Editorial Appendix.

III. Publication History of the Letters

A. Earliest Publications

A few hundred of Santayana's letters have appeared, in whole or in part, in a number of periodicals and books. In the January 1924 issue of *The American Mercury,* in her article "Santayana at Cambridge," Margaret Münsterberg included a letter from Santayana to her father, Hugo Münsterberg, Santayana's colleague in the Harvard philosophy department. A letter to the editor of *The Harvard Monthly* appeared in the June 1937 issue of that periodical of whose editorial board Santayana had been a founding member. In his popular column of literary criticism, "As I Like It," in *Scribner's Magazine* of June 1936, Yale English professor William Lyon Phelps included letters he had received from Santayana. The 7 March 1936 issue of *The Saturday Review of Literature* contains a letter by Santayana commenting on *The Last Puritan.* Other periodicals containing letters include *Commonweal* (October 1952, to Cyril Clemens) and *The Atlantic Monthly* (August 1955, a selection made by Daniel Cory of letters not included in his 1955 Scribner's edition). Several letters also appeared in various books, including those to William James in Ralph Barton Perry, *The Thought and Character of William James* (1938), and in the autobiographies of William Lyon Phelps, *Autobiography with Letters,* and Logan Pearsall Smith, *Unforgotten Years,* both published in 1939. Earlier biographical books about Santayana containing letters are George Washburne Howgate, *George Santayana* (1938), Mossie May Wadington Kirkwood, *George Santayana: Saint of the Imagination* (1961), and Bruno Lind, *Vagabond Scholar* (1962). Daniel Cory's *Santayana: The Later Years: A Portrait with Letters* (1963) makes effective use of many letters to Cory in describing important events in Santayana's life and the history of their friendship. Recipients of the letters, editors of periodicals, and authors of books on Santayana recognized the quality and interest of the letters and were desirous of putting them before the public, but it was not until 1955 that a book-length collection of Santayana's letters became available.

B. The 1955 Scribner's Edition of *The Letters of George Santayana*

The first volume of Santayana's letters was collected and edited by Daniel Cory and published by Charles Scribner's Sons in 1955. It appears, however, that Cory was not the first person to consider seriously the idea of putting together an edition of Santayana's letters. In the 5 October 1936 letter to Benjamin Schwartz, we learn that Schwartz had evidently written suggesting that he and Justus Buchler prepare an edition. These two young New York scholars had edited a volume of Santayana's lectures, essays, and reviews published earlier that year by Scribner's under the title *Obiter Scripta* (incidental writings). In a letter to Schwartz, Santayana expressed his satisfaction with the volume and said that it demonstrated their competence in understanding his philosophy. But he stated that a collection of his letters would be premature, and that if Schwartz or Buchler should wish to undertake such a task, they should wait until after his death. He went on that Schwartz was young, had not known him personally, and was frankly not "the person to assume, as yet, that sort of responsibility towards the public and towards my reputation." Furthermore, he said that he had already chosen an executor to preside over his literary estate, Daniel Cory, "and it would naturally fall to him to collect my correspondence, as well as to edit my remaining manuscripts, if he thought it advisable."

The project for a collection of Santayana's letters began in the autumn of 1952 when, in a 21 October letter to Daniel Cory, Scribner's editor John Hall Wheelock suggested the undertaking of such a project.[10] Cory agreed to edit the collection and write an introduction for it, and he and Wheelock worked together at the task of gathering the letters. They wrote to individuals and took advertisements in various literary publications, including *The Times Literary Supplement,* the *Saturday Review of Literature, The New York Times Book Review,* the *New York Herald Tribune,* the *Harvard Alumni Bulletin,* the *Columbia Alumni News,* and the journal of the Modern Language Association. Letters soon began arriving from persons who had seen the advertisements; and those individuals, as well as others who had been contacted directly, began telling friends who had also corresponded with Santayana about the project, and by 4 April 1954 Cory could write to Wheelock that he had collected almost a thousand letters.[11] While working on the 1955 edition, Cory lived in Cambridge, Massachusetts, where he was recipient of the fellowship that Santayana, by bequest, had endowed at Harvard. But he also traveled to the libraries of Columbia and Yale, and probably to the Library of Congress. He and Wheelock were determined to produce a single-volume collection for which, as Cory put it, a "merciless selection" would have to be made among the assembled letters. Eventually Cory submitted 328 letters for inclusion in the volume, but the total number was reduced by Wheelock to 296. Cory completed his introduction and the manuscript of the letters volume was sent to the Scribner's production department on 11 February 1955. By 13 May Wheelock began sending Cory galley proofs for checking, and publication of the volume was scheduled for early October. Cory was to see both galley and page proofs. Constable bought sheets from Scribner's and also issued a volume of the letters in London the same year.

The Scribner's edition of *The Letters of George Santayana* is a handsome and well-made volume and an excellent selection of Santayana's letters. Cory and Wheelock made every effort to present the 296 letters to 86 recipients (constituting a wide variety of persons) as Santayana wrote them. A deliberate effort was made to preserve Santayana's spellings (American in the earlier letters and British in the later ones) and punctuation. Except for a few mistranscriptions from the holographs, the text of the 1955 edition is accurate. Several excisions were made by Cory either to omit what he regarded as irrelevant or unsuitable material and conserve space, or, on the advice of Scribner's attorney, Horace S. Manges, to avoid the possibility of libel suits.[12] Cory supplied a minimum of footnote information and a brief (seven pages) introduction in which he provided biographical information about Santayana's early life and Harvard career and pointed out that the letters should "dispel some current misconceptions about Santayana."[13] Toward the end of his *Introduction,* Cory observed that the catholicity of Santayana's interests and thought represented in the letters provided something for everybody: "for the poet, for the metaphysician, for the literary critic, for the historian of culture who is interested in every wind of doctrine." He concluded by declaring many of the letters to be "of a very high literary order." "Our attention," he wrote, "is arrested by a *beauty of expression welling from a profundity of observation.*"[14]

IV. The Comprehensive Edition of Santayana's Letters

A. Origins and Development

The project for a comprehensive edition of Santayana's letters was originated by Daniel Cory. His association with Santayana began in 1927, when Cory, age twenty-two, was living in England, having left Columbia University before completing an undergraduate degree. Columbia was always the place where Santayana was most admired, and there Cory had discovered Santayana's philosophy and had been inspired by his splendid literary style. It was after Cory had sent Santayana (who in 1927 was sixty-three and living in Rome) a copy of an essay that he had written on Santayana's philosophy that Cory had an opportunity to meet the philosopher in person. Impressed by the acuteness of the impecunious young man's insights into his philosophy, Santayana offered to pay Cory's expenses for a visit to Rome. The meeting occurred in Santayana's rooms in the Hotel Bristol, in the Piazza Barberini, early in April. The elderly philosopher and the young student began a friendship and professional association that continued for the rest of Santayana's life. Shortly after their first meeting, Santayana engaged Cory to serve as a literary secretary or assistant, reading his manuscripts and advising him on technical and compositional elements. This relationship—with many separations and interruptions—lasted until Santayana's death, on 26 September 1952. Santayana bequeathed to Cory his remaining unpublished manuscripts—and the rights to his literary properties generally—and named him his literary executor. Cory placed Santayana's manuscripts in four university libraries that were to become principal centers for Santayana manuscript materials: the Butler Library at Columbia University, the Houghton Library at Harvard University, the Humanities Research Center at the University of Texas at Austin, and the Alderman Library at the University of Virginia. He also began editing and publishing the essays, poems, and plays not published during Santayana's lifetime.

In a letter to William G. Holzberger dated Brunnenburg, Tirolo di Merano, Italy, 17 September 1970, Cory mentioned the idea of "a new and more definitive edition of the Letters." Although he may earlier have conceived of such a collection, it was, evidently, about this time that he began seriously to contemplate such a project. Early in July 1971, Cory began to make arrangements with an American university press for a new and enlarged edition of Santayana's correspondence. He then had on hand about 700 letters not included in the Scribner's volume, and a new two-volume edition was envisaged. He hoped to complete a finished manuscript by 31 October 1973, but he did not live to see this original delivery date. Had he done so, however, either the completion date would have had to be extended, or a two-volume selected edition would have been published, because neither Cory nor anyone else knew then just how many of Santayana's letters actually existed. Cory anticipated locating perhaps a few hundred more, but certainly he would have been astounded had he known that more than three times as many letters existed than had as yet been located.

At the same time William Holzberger was working on a critical edition of Santayana's poetry (published as *The Complete Poems of George Santayana* by the Bucknell University Press in 1979), and in the lengthy *Introduction* to that book, Holzberger quotes from several unpublished letters, which he had gathered while doing his research. Cory read a draft of this introduction and wrote Holzberger indicating that he needed help with the job of locating and collecting Santayana's letters. In December 1971, Holzberger sent Cory a list of approximately four hundred unpublished letters that he had located in twenty-one libraries. Cory was overwhelmed by the unexpectedly large number. Then sixty-seven years old, and despairing of ever finishing such a huge project alone (much less in two years time), Cory entered into a collaboration with Holzberger to produce the new edition.

A division of labor was established: Holzberger drew up a list of editorial principles to guide the work and assumed responsibility for editorial matters. Cory began transcribing the 398 pieces of unpublished correspondence that he had received from Santayana as well as copies of numerous others he had collected. Cory also began contacting additional individuals, whom he believed likely to have received letters from Santayana, and he planned to write an introduction. It was agreed that all of the photocopies and transcriptions should be collected in Holzberger's hands.

In March 1972 Daniel Cory was awarded a Guggenheim Fellowship, but the stipend was smaller than he had expected, and he was forced to cancel his plans to come to America to work on the project. Another disappointment to Cory at this time was that Robert Lowell (known familiarly as "Cal" to Cory and other personal friends) had not responded to his written appeals for copies of the important letters that he believed Santayana had written to the poet.[15] Then, at the beginning of April 1972, Cory began suffering from chest pains. A Merano physician diagnosed the condition as angina pectoris. Cory was not especially alarmed, thinking that giving up cigars and steep mountain hikes would avoid more serious developments. He and Holzberger planned to meet to discuss and work on the edition in Merano in August. He continued to feel unwell, however, and on 14 June wrote to Holzberger that he and his wife were planning to take two weeks' vacation in Venice, and that he regretted not being able "just now to pull my full weight in the editorial shell." Four days later while seated at his desk in their apartment in Brunnenburg Castle, in Tirolo di Merano, Daniel Cory suffered a fatal heart attack.

Cory's sudden and unexpected death occurred before he had opportunity to do much more than begin transcribing his own letters from Santayana and odd batches to various recipients. Later that summer, William Holzberger met with Margot Cory at Brunnenburg. Mrs. Cory, succeeding her husband as literary executor, approved the idea of continuing work on the letters edition. She afterwards transcribed the remaining letters and was helpful in locating additional originals in Europe. Later, in the spring of 1976, Holzberger spent a week with Mrs. Cory in Rome conferring on the edition. She provided invaluable information about Santayana's relationship with many individuals, including the long and close friendship that Santayana had with her husband.

William Holzberger continued the search for Santayana letters, adding to the collection, annotating the letters, and preparing them for publication. Early in 1977 he joined the project initiated by members of the Society for the Advancement of American Philosophy to produce a critical edition of all of Santayana's writings. Herman J. Saatkamp Jr. had been asked by the Society to organize the project and serve as General Editor. Holzberger was selected to serve as Textual Editor and, with Saatkamp, coeditor of the individual volumes. Subsequently, it was decided to incorporate the letters edition into the Critical Edition of *The Works of George Santayana*. From that time on, the full staff and resources of the Santayana Edition was devoted to the task of locating additional letters, both in the United States and Europe, keying the entire collection into the computer, researching, reviewing, and refining footnote annotation, and preparing the letters materials for publication as Volume V of *The Works of George Santayana*.

B. Locating and Collecting the Letters

The search for Santayana's letters, begun by Daniel Cory in the early 1950s and continued by the present editors until virtually the time of publication of this comprehensive edition, has resulted in the location of more than three thousand pieces of correspondence. These include letters, notes, postcards, and a few telegrams and cablegrams; the texts of all of these are contained in this edition. As indicated above, Daniel Cory's method of locating and collecting the letters was to publish advertisements in leading journals and reviews, to visit libraries known to contain principal collections of Santayana manuscript materials, and to write to individuals who he believed might have corresponded with Santayana. Later, in the 1970s, William Holzberger consulted both the first and second editions of *American Literary Manuscripts: A Checklist of Holdings in Academic, Historical, and Public Libraries, Museums, and Authors' Homes in the United States*[16] to generate a list of institutions reported as holding Santayana manuscripts. Letters of inquiry were sent to libraries at sixty-three institutions. In addition, fresh advertisements for Santayana letters were run in a number of leading literary publications, including *The Times*

Literary Supplement (London), *The New York Times Book Review, The New York Review of Books,* and *American Literature.* Letters of inquiry were sent to more than fifty individuals believed to have received correspondence from Santayana. Also, scholars familiar with this project have kept an eye out for Santayana letters in the course of their researches, and this has resulted in the acquisition of several valuable pieces of correspondence that otherwise might not have been acquired. This continuous effort to locate Santayana letters in the libraries or files of institutions and in the possession of private individuals has resulted in the location and acquisition of over two thousand more letters than the original thousand that Daniel Cory and John Hall Wheelock had accumulated at the time the selection was made for the 1955 Scribner's edition.

The title of the present edition, *The Letters of George Santayana,* is the same as that of Cory's selected edition. It is the best title for such a collection because it suggests comprehensiveness without implying absolute completeness. Although every effort has been made to locate and acquire all of Santayana's letters, that remains a goal impossible to achieve. We know (as described above) that Santayana himself destroyed the letters he had written to his mother; and he made references to other letters that remain unlocated. However, this comprehensive edition is as complete as many years of work can make it, and it certainly represents the principal corpus of Santayana's correspondence.

C. Arrangement of the Letters

The letters are arranged chronologically, from earliest (to Susan and Josephine in 1868) to latest (to Daniel Cory, 3 August 1952), a period of about eighty-three years. This chronological progression, together with division of the letters into books of approximately equal size, constitutes the sole organizing principle for the edition.

Except for the period covered in the first two books (1868–1920), Santayana's history is not clearly marked either by a sequence of periodic residences or dominating events. Therefore, any division of Santayana's life and letters into episodes seemed artificial and undesirable. Because of the gap between the earliest extant letter and the next earliest one (21 August 1882) and the fact that, as would be expected, fewer of the early letters have survived, the first book covers a much longer period than subsequent books. The organization of the letters in Volume V of *The Works of George Santayana* is as follows: Book One, [1868]–1909; Book Two, 1910–1920; Book Three, 1921–1927; Book Four, 1928–1932; Book Five, 1933–1936; Book Six, 1937–1940; Book Seven, 1941–1947; and Book Eight, 1948–1952.

V. Editorial Principles and Procedures

A. Transcription of the Letters

1. Transcribing the Texts from Photocopies of the Original Holograph Letters

The majority of letters of this edition were collected in the 1950s, '60s, and '70s, before the computer was in common use. Therefore, all but a few hundred were originally transcribed on the typewriter. Wherever possible, exact typewritten transcriptions were made from photocopies of the original holograph letters. The letters included in Cory's 1955 Scribner's edition were carefully collated against photocopies of the originals. Persons responding to Cory's advertisements, and many other individuals to whom he had written directly, lent Cory their original Santayana letters or sent him photocopies of those letters, from which Cory made typewritten transcriptions. Fifty-four letters to twenty-eight recipients included in Cory's 1955 Scribner's edition could not subsequently be located in library collections or elsewhere, and the published version is copy-text for these. Many of these letters are, presumably, still in the hands of the recipients or their descendants. Also, published forms in periodicals or books are copy-text for a number of Santayana's letters for which holograph originals are not available. Of the letters transcribed subsequent to the publication of the 1955 edition, 93 letters to 19 recipients were transcribed by Daniel Cory himself and 339 letters to 19 recipients (including 282 letters to Daniel Cory) were transcribed by Mrs. Cory. Of these letters we do not have photocopies of the holographs of 30 letters to 9 recipients transcribed by Daniel Cory and 12 letters to 12 recipients transcribed by Margot Cory. Typewritten transcriptions of those 42 letters were made by the Corys from handwritten copies of the letters that had been made earlier by Mrs. Cory. Together with the 296 letters from the 1955 edition, the total number of letters transcribed by the Corys is 728. All other transcriptions were made by members of the editorial staff of the critical edition.

The letters for which original holographs have not been located by the present editors are noted as '(MS: Unknown)' in the headnote. The texts of twelve letters to Daniel Cory are taken from handwritten copies of the original holographs made several years earlier by Margot Cory.[17]

The essential principle guiding transcription was to record everything that Santayana wrote on the holograph. This meant that any revisions that Santayana made—cancellations and insertions—were recorded. The symbols originally used to indicate authorial revisions were those customarily employed during the period of the 1950s through the 1970s: angle brackets ($</>$) were used to indicate cancellations and arrows ($\uparrow\downarrow$) to indicate insertions. Later, these editorial symbols were changed to others more natural and less arbitrary.

2. Plain-Text Transcription

The text of this edition of Santayana's correspondence is referred to as "plain text" by the editors of Mark Twain's letters (1988–). "Plain text," the Twain editors point out, stands in contrast to the two principal types of transcriptions of texts: "clear text" and "genetic text".[18] Transcriptions in "clear text" are devoid of editorial symbols; information regarding authorial revisions is provided in footnotes or in appropriate sections of the editorial appendix. Transcriptions in "genetic text," however, through the use of arbitrary symbols (such as angle brackets and arrows), profess to show any and all revisions that the author made on the holograph. The concept of "plain text" is to represent authorial revisions by signs more natural and less arbitrary, thus making a clearer and more immediately intelligible text for the reader. A "plain-text" transcription uses "type-identical" signs which are essentially identical with their handwritten counterparts.

Cancellations: single-character words, or single characters within words, cancelled on the holograph letter are indicated by slash marks. For example at 15 February 1892 to Henry Ward Abbot ('pro/bably') where Santayana wrote the 'b' over the 'p', or at [Spring 1893] to William Cameron Forbes ('/took') where 't' was written over 'I'. Cancellation of two or more characters as words, word fragments, or within words are indicated by a horizontal rule through the cancelled matter. See examples at 20 November 1894 to Guy Murchie ('~~Oct~~ November') where 'Nov' was written over 'Oct', at 18 October 1897 to Mrs. Celedonio (Susan) Sastre ('~~their~~ there') where the 're' was written over the 'ir', and at 5 October 1905 to Charles Scribner's Sons ('special~~lis~~ised') where 'ise' was written over 'lis'.

Insertions of single characters, word fragments, words, or phrases are indicated by the use of inferior carets. See for example the letter of 26 July 1889 to Henry Ward Abbot ('that's ‚one reason‚ why'), or 4 August 1915 to Benjamin Apthorp Gould Fuller ('with you‚r‚ friends'), or that of 18 January 1910 to Charles Scribner's Sons ('make any ‚great‚ changes'). Both linear and marginal insertions are indicated in this way, with marginal insertions noted in the textual note.

Cancellations within Insertions: are indicated by the combined use of slashes or horizontal rules and inferior carets (27 February 1917 to Charles Scribner's Sons, 'to correct ‚~~them~~‚').

It should be remembered that although plain-text transcriptions, through the employment of type-identical signs, bear a greater resemblance to the original handwritten letters than do transcriptions using the traditional editorial symbols, they are not in fact type facsimiles of the holograph letters. Plain-text transcriptions do not reproduce the original lineation, pagination, or any non-verbal characteristics of the manuscript unless the author intended them to bear meaning. (The purpose of plain text is not to reproduce the holograph letters pictorially, in the way of facsimiles.) The plain-text transcriptions of Santayana's letters in this edition are intended to represent the original holograph letters in type in such a way that any revisions are immediately identifiable and the texts completely legible.

Other signs used in this edition for transcribing the letters include:

⊦ ⊦ Broken brackets: indicate matter bracketed by Santayana on the holograph.

[ ] Editorial brackets: enclose editorial descriptions (in italic type) or text inadvertently omitted by Santayana on the holograph letter.

* or ˣ Asterisks or superscript 'x': designate Santayana's footnotes.

¹ Superscript numerals: indicate editorial footnotes.

Typewritten transcriptions of the letters' texts received two initial collations against photocopies of the original holograph letters to insure that the text of the holograph letter had been duplicated exactly, including any errors (in spelling or punctuation) or omissions. First, the transcription was collated against the photocopy of the holograph letter by the typist who made the transcription (that person always being a member of the staff of the letters edition, or, in the case of Daniel and Margot Cory, someone intimately connected with the edition). Next, the typewritten transcription was collated by William Holzberger. All letters included in Cory's 1955 Scribner's selection, for which original holograph letters could be located, have been carefully collated against photocopies of the originals and corrected where necessary.¹⁹ Later, when the computer, with all of its advantages for editorial scholarship, became available, all letters previously transcribed on the typewriter were, in the 1980s and early 1990s, transferred to computer files. Where possible, this transfer of the text of the letters from typewritten transcription to computer file was done on the Kurzweil electronic scanner, although many letters had to be keyed into the computer by hand. This, of course, required additional collations of the letters placed in computer files against photocopies of the originals in order to insure accuracy of their texts.

All of Santayana's letters that could be located are included in this edition. Following the exact transcription of the letters texts, certain standardizations (described below) were next introduced during the editorial process. The editors, by means of plain-text transcriptions, have attempted to represent the original holograph letters as nearly as an efficient printed format will allow. The goal has been to enable the reader to simulate the experience of reading the original holograph letters. To this end, the texts of the letters have not been altered: misspelled words are left uncorrected; no changes are made in grammar; and (except in rare instances, where meaning would otherwise be obscured) punctuation is neither altered, added, nor deleted. These occurrences are listed in the textual notes and marked '[*sic*]'. Accidentally repeated words are removed from the text, and this emendation is noted in the textual notes. Santayana very often did not close a paragraph with final punctuation, particularly at the end of a letter. This has not been altered, and since it is so common, the editors chose not to note every instance in the textual notes. The texts of Santayana's letters are represented in their original form.

3. Santayana's Spelling

Santayana generally preferred British spelling forms, although American spellings are common in his early letters and manuscripts. No effort has been made to standardize spelling; words are reproduced as Santayana wrote them. He was a good speller, and only rarely misspelled a word. (A curious exception is his repeated misspelling of the word 'parliament', in which he regularly metathesizes the 'ia' to 'parlaiment'.)

4. Editorial Omissions from the Letters Text

All letters are included in full, without editorial omissions. Mrs. Cory had requested that one complete letter to her husband be omitted from the collection. That is a letter from Santayana to Daniel Cory of 9 September 1933. That letter is not among the originals of the letters to Cory at Columbia University, and its location, if indeed it still exists, is not known. The present editors of the comprehensive edition of Santayana's letters have not seen it and have no idea of what it contains.

5. Letters in Languages Other Than English

The comprehensive edition of Santayana's letters contains forty-six items of correspondence by Santayana written in a language other than English. Santayana wrote in Spanish to members of the family of his half sister, Susan (her husband, and her stepsons and their wives in Ávila). There is also a formal letter in Spanish to Miguel de Unamuno. There is one letter in Italian to Dino Rigacci of 29 April 1945. Letters written in a language other than English appear in the original language of composition in the letters text, with a fairly literal English translation given in a footnote.

6. Recipients, Provenances, Addresses, and Dates

A headnote is added to each letter, indicating the recipient, date and place of composition, and manuscript location:

To Mary Williams Winslow
25 December 1908 • Cambridge, Massachusetts   (MS: Houghton)

A key to the location is found in the *List of Manuscript Locations*. 'MS: Houghton' means that the original holograph letter is in The Houghton Library, Harvard University. The textual notes give more information about particular collections. If the correspondence is a postcard or telegram, that will be indicated following 'MS'.

To Susan Sturgis de Sastre
13 August 1903 • Oxford, England   (MS postcard: Sanchez)

Also, an effort has been made to identify many, if not all, recipients with short biographical footnotes.

Dates editorially supplied are placed in square brackets, uncertain dates being followed by a question mark. When the letter is written on printed stationery, the printed address is included in small capitals. No account is taken of envelopes, except when used to establish the date of a letter, the recipient thereof, or Santayana's address. If a letter is dated by a postmark that date is given in the header followed by '[*postmark*]'.

7. Standardizations

Words underlined in the original holograph letter are underlined in the text; however, parts of the dateline underlined in the original letter are not underlined in transcription unless significant. Double underlining is reproduced in the text, but instances of more than double underlining are described in the textual notes.

8. Santayana's Punctuation

The letters are generally conscientiously punctuated. But certain marks of punctuation used by Santayana have always troubled his editors, partly because of the difficulty of determining the specific mark of punctuation represented in his handwriting, and also because of certain idiosyncratic usages. For instance, Santayana's colon and semicolon are frequently indistinguishable. That, of course, is characteristic of many writers' handwritten manuscripts; but sometimes Santayana also used the colon where the semicolon is generally called for (as shown in his published writings for which he had read and approved proofs). Daniel Cory said that Santayana once told him that this unorthodox use of the colon was due to a habit of "thinking in opposition." The procedure of the present editors has been to read a colon where clearly indicated on the holograph letter and commensurate with Santayana's habitual usage; but where the punctuation mark is unclear on the holograph and is situated where a semicolon would be standard usage, we have read the mark as a semicolon. (Thus, our practice sometimes differs from Cory's, in *Letters* (1955) and *The Later Years* (1963), where he has in certain instances read colon and we have read semicolon.)

One or two other punctuation problems have bedeviled Santayana's editors. Santayana's period frequently resembles a hyphen, and it has been read, by Daniel Cory and Bruno Lind, as a dash. Santayana's dashes, however, are generally longer than this "sliding period," which perhaps resulted from writing rapidly with an old-fashioned holder-and-nib-type pen. Santayana also appears to vacillate in the letters between the British custom of placing on-line punctuation either inside or outside of quotation marks depending upon whether or not the on-line punctuation is part of the meaning of the matter quoted, and the American practice of uniformly placing it inside except for semicolons and colons, which are always placed outside the quotation marks. In every clear instance, we place the on-line punctuation either inside or outside the quotation marks, according to where it occurs on the holograph letter. However, when—as often happens—the on-line punctuation falls directly beneath the quotation marks, we place it inside the quotation marks. Except for this practice, no effort has been made to standardize the form.

9. Signatures

The usual signature on the letters is the writer's standard 'GSantayana'. The early form of his signature was 'G. Santayana' (as found, for instance, on the holograph of the letter to William James of 28 January 1888). Later, he dropped the period following the first initial, carrying the stroke from the G to join the first letter of his last name.

B. Editorial Footnotes to the Letters

The policy of the present edition of Santayana's letters regarding footnotes is essentially to limit them to supplying factual information likely to make the letter more intelligible or meaningful to the reader. However, some effort has been made in the case of letters dealing with events of great historical importance (e.g., the First and Second World Wars, or the Spanish civil war) to provide historical information that will help the reader place the letter in the historical context and for that reason perhaps better understand it. This principle of a fuller understanding has also informed our practice in regard to providing translations of foreign words or expressions in footnotes. Santayana read and spoke several languages, and he makes frequent use of words, phrases, or quotations in the letters from these languages, including Greek, Latin, French, German, Italian, and Spanish. In order to facilitate the fullest possible understanding of the letters, we have included translations of foreign terms and phrases in the footnotes except in those instances where the foreign term or phrase is very commonplace or its meaning completely obvious. English translations of titles of books or articles in foreign languages are also provided in the footnotes if the work was translated.

Footnotes composed by Daniel Cory that provide special information are included, followed by his bracketed initials '[D. C.]'. We have made fairly extensive use of information about Santayana's life supplied by Daniel Cory in his book, Santayana: *The Later Years: A Portrait With Letters* (New York: George Braziller, 1963), frequently quoting directly from the book in footnotes.

The procedures for identifying persons mentioned in Santayana's letters follow a standard routine. Names are first checked in authoritative dictionaries and encyclopedias (including the *Dictionary of American Biography*, the *Encyclopedia of Philosophy*, *The Oxford Companion to American Literature*, *The Oxford Companion to English Literature*, and the *Quinquennial Catalogue of the Officers and Graduates of Harvard University, 1636–1925*) and also in the "WorldCat" database of "FirstSearch" in the Online Computer Library Center (OCLC). Leads to more specialized literature are followed, which in turn provide the bases for the identification in the footnotes to the letters. In some instances no reference can be found, which is noted as "unidentified" in the footnotes and index.

Lists of errata in Santayana's published works, included by him in, or with, a letter to his publishers, are included in the text of the letter. Such information may be useful to the reader of these letters in correcting his or her own copies of Santayana's works.

W.G.H.

H.J.S.

Notes

[1]See footnote 2 of this letter on page 3.

[2]For an account of Dr. Mainwaring's discovery of the missing Fullerton papers see R. W. B. Lewis, *Edith Wharton: A Biography* (New York: Harper & Row, 1975), 540–43.

[3]Stevens's and Santayana's sonnets were, respectively: "Cathedrals Are Not Built Along the Sea" and "Cathedrals by the Sea."

[4]Letters to William G. Holzberger from Valerie Eliot of 28 April 1976 and Holly Stevens of 27 April 1976.

[5]*Persons and Places,* 442.

[6]See Santayana's letters to Daniel Cory of 16 and 26 September 1936.

[7]See 7 June 1932 to Cory.

[8]Robert S. Fitzgerald to William G. Holzberger, 3 December 1978.

[9]See 6 April 1918 to Mrs. Frederick (Mary) Winslow.

[10]Wheelock to Cory, 21 October 1952, Scribner Archives, Princeton University Library.

[11]Cory to Wheelock, 4 April 1954, Scribner Archives, Princeton University Library.

[12]Per letter from Horace S. Manges to Wheelock, 28 January 1955. Scribner Archives, Princeton University Library.

[13]Daniel Cory, Introduction to *The Letters of George Santayana*, xxx.

[14]Ibid., xxxi.

[15]Nor did Lowell later respond to subsequent written appeals from Cory's widow, Margot, nor, later still, from William Holzberger. It was only in the spring of 1976 that Holzberger, while visiting with Richard Ellmann, at New College, Oxford, was informed by Ellmann, who knew Lowell, that the poet rarely answered letters from anyone, but that if spoken to directly might well be entirely cooperative. Holzberger managed to speak to Lowell over the telephone at his home in Maidstone, Kent, where the poet was then living with his third wife, Lady Caroline Blackwood. Lowell was very enthusiastic about his letters and agreed to write to the librarians at the Houghton Library, making his letters from Santayana (which were then sealed) available for inclusion in the comprehensive edition. The following year, 1977, Robert Lowell, who had been suffering for some time from physical and mental illnesses, died suddenly in a New York taxi-cab.

[16]Edited by Professor J. Albert Robbins, Chairman of the Committee on Manuscript Holdings, American Literature Section, Modern Language Association of America (Athens, Georgia: University of Georgia Press, 1977). The editors are grateful for the kind assistance provided by Professor Robbins in 1977 before the second edition of *American Literary Manuscripts* had gone to press.

[17]These twelve letters, the holograph originals of which are not among the rest of Santayana's letters to Cory in Columbia University's Rare Book and Manuscript Library, are dated 18 Nov 1927; 13 Jun 1933; 2 Sep 1933; 5 Dec 1934; 7 Dec 1934; 9 Jun 1935; 26 Sep 1935; 20 Sep 1936; 14 Oct 1937; 30 Apr 1938; 11 May 1938; and 18 May 1938. Similarly, we have not been able to locate the original holograph of the letter to Cory of 13 Sep 1950 and have had to transcribe the extract from it printed in *Santayana: The Later Years* (1963).

[18]*Mark Twain's Letters*, ed. Edgar Marquess Branch, Michael B. Frank, and Kenneth M. Sanderson (Berkeley: University of California Press, 1988), Vol. 1, xxvi-xxvii, and xlv, footnote 1.

[19]All letters by Santayana printed previously to this comprehensive edition, for which photocopies of the holograph originals have been obtainable, have been checked and transcriptional and typographical errors therein have been corrected for the text of this edition.

Short-Title List

The following short-title list includes the works most frequently cited in the footnotes.

Primary Sources

Character *Character and Opinion in the United States: With Reminiscences of William James and Josiah Royce and Academic Life in America.* New York: Charles Scribner's Sons; London: Constable and Co. Ltd.; Toronto: McLeod, 1920.

Complete Poems *The Complete Poems of George Santayana: A Critical Edition.* Edited by William G. Holzberger. Lewisburg, PA: Bucknell University Press; London: Associated University Presses, 1979.

Dialogues *Dialogues in Limbo.* London: Constable and Co. Ltd., 1925; New York: Charles Scribner's Sons, 1926.

Dominations *Dominations and Powers: Reflections on Liberty, Society, and Government.* New York: Charles Scribner's Sons; London: Constable and Co. Ltd, 1951.

Egotism *Egotism in German Philosophy.* New York: Charles Scribner's Sons, 1915; London and Toronto: J. M. Dent & Sons Limited, 1916.

Genteel *The Genteel Tradition at Bay.* New York: Charles Scribner's Sons; London: "The Adelphi," 1931.

Hermit *A Hermit of Carmel and Other Poems.* (New York: Charles Scribner's Sons, 1901; London: R. Brimley Johnson, 1902).

Gospels *The Idea of Christ in the Gospels; or, God in Man: A Critical Essay.* New York: Charles Scribner's Sons; Toronto: Saunders, 1946.

Interpretations *Interpretations of Poetry and Religion.* New York: Charles Scribner's Sons; London: Black, 1900. Critical edition edited by William G. Holzberger and Herman J. Saatkamp Jr. Cambridge, MA: The MIT Press, 1989. (Footnotes refer to critical edition page numbers.)

Puritan *The Last Puritan.* London: Constable and Co. Ltd., 1935; New York: Charles Scribner's Sons, 1936; Critical edition edited by William G. Holzberger and Herman J. Saatkamp Jr. Cambridge, MA: The MIT Press, 1994. (Footnotes refer to critical edition page numbers.)

Letters *The Letters of George Santayana.* Edited by Daniel Cory. New York: Charles Scribner's Sons; London: Constable and Co. Ltd., 1955.

Reason *The Life of Reason: or, the Phases of Human Progress.* Five volumes. New York: Charles Scribner's Sons; London: Constable and Co. Ltd, 1905–1906.

Common Sense	*Introduction and Reason in Common Sense.* Volume 1, 1905.
Society	*Reason in Society.* Volume 2, 1905.
Religion	*Reason in Religion.* Volume 3, 1905.
Art	*Reason in Art.* Volume 4, 1905.
Science	*Reason in Science.* Volume 5, 1906.

Essays   *Little Essays: Drawn From the Writings of George Santayana by Logan Pearsall Smith, With the Collaboration of the Author.* New York: Charles Scribner's Sons; London: Constable and Co. Ltd., 1920.

Lucifer   "Lucifer, A Prelude." In *Sonnets and Other Verses.* Cambridge and Chicago: Stone and Kimball, 1894. With changes becomes Act I of *Lucifer: A Theological Tragedy.* Chicago and New York: Herbert S. Stone, 1899.

Truce   Revised limited second edition published as *Lucifer, or the Heavenly Truce: A Theological Tragedy.* Cambridge, MA: Dunster House; London: W. Jackson, 1924.

Obiter   *Obiter Scripta: Lectures, Essays and Reviews.* Edited by Justus Buchler and Benjamin Schwartz. New York: Charles Scribner's Sons; London: Constable and Co. Ltd., 1936.

Persons   *Persons and Places: Fragments of Autobiography.* Critical edition edited by William G. Holzberger and Herman J. Saatkamp Jr. Cambridge, MA: The MIT Press, 1986.

Background   *Persons and Places: The Background of My Life.* New York: Charles Scribner's Sons; London: Constable and Co. Ltd., 1944.

Span   *The Middle Span.* New York: Charles Scribner's Sons, 1945; London: Constable and Co. Ltd., 1947.

Host   *My Host the World.* New York: Charles Scribner's Sons; London: Cresset Press, 1953.

Platonism   *Platonism and the Spiritual Life.* New York: Charles Scribner's Sons; London: Constable and Co. Ltd., 1927.

Poems   *Poems: Selected by the Author and Revised.* London: Constable and Co. Ltd., 1922; New York: Charles Scribner's Sons, 1923.

Testament   *The Poet's Testament: Poems and Two Plays.* New York: Charles Scribner's Sons, 1953.

Realms   *Realms of Being.* Four volumes. New York: Charles Scribner's Sons; London: Constable and Co. Ltd., 1927-1940.

Essence	*The Realm of Essence: Book First of Realms of Being,* 1927.
Matter	*The Realm of Matter: Book Second of Realms of Being,* 1930.
Truth	*The Realm of Truth: Book Third of Realms of Being.* Scribner's, 1938; Constable and Toronto: Macmillan Company, 1937.
Spirit	*The Realm of Spirit: Book Fourth of Realms of Being,* 1940.

Realms (1 vol.)   *Realms of Being.* One-volume edition, with a new introduction by the author. New York: Charles Scribner's Sons, 1942.

Scepticism   *Scepticism and Animal Faith: Introduction to a System of Philosophy.* New York: Charles Scribner's Sons; London: Constable and Co. Ltd., 1923.

Beauty   *The Sense of Beauty: Being the Outlines of Aesthetic Theory.* New York: Charles Scribner's Sons; London: A. and C. Black, 1896. Critical edition edited by William G. Holzberger and Herman J. Saatkamp Jr. Cambridge, MA: The MIT Press, 1988. (Footnotes refer to critical edition page numbers.)

Soliloquies   *Soliloquies in England and Later Soliloquies.* New York: Charles Scribner's Sons; London: Constable and Co. Ltd., 1922.

Sonnets   *Sonnets and Other Verses.* Cambridge and Chicago: Stone and Kimball, 1894.

Turns   *Some Turns of Thought in Modern Philosophy: Five Essays.* New York: Charles Scribner's Sons; Cambridge: Cambridge University Press, 1933.

Poets   *Three Philosophical Poets: Lucretius, Dante, and Goethe.* Cambridge, MA: Harvard University Press; London: Oxford University Press, 1910.

Doctrine   *Winds of Doctrine: Studies in Contemporary Opinion.* New York: Charles Scribner's Sons; London: J. M. Dent & Sons Limited, 1913.

Other Works

Years   Cory, Daniel. *Santayana: The Later Years: A Portrait with Letters.* New York: George Braziller, 1963.

Santayana   McCormick, John. *George Santayana: A Biography.* New York: Alfred A. Knopf, 1987.

Harvard   Morison, Samuel Eliot. *Three Centuries of Harvard 1636–1936.* Cambridge, MA: Harvard University Press; London: Oxford University Press, 1936.

Shakespeare   *The Works of William Shakespeare.* Edited by William A. Wright, 9 vols. New York: AMS Press, 1968 rpt. of 1891–1893 edition.

Textual Notes

Numbers on the left (i.e. 3.2) refer to Critical Edition pages and lines (Volume V, Book One). Line numbers refer to the text of the letters themselves. No heading or editorial footnotes are included in the count. The virgule (/) between words on the right of the bullet indicates a line break in the copy-text.

■ [1868] • Susan and Josephine Sturgis • Ávila, Spain

■*Copy-text:* MS, collection of Adelaida Sastre, Ávila, Spain. ■*Previous publication: Azafea* 1 (University of Salamanca, 1985): 359. This letter was originally transcribed by Pedro García Martín who indicates that it was found between the pages of one of Susan's books. ■*Emendations and textual notes:*

3.2	Londres Lo • Londres / Lo [*sic*]

■ 21 August 1882 • John Galen Howard • Roxbury, MA

■*Copy-text:* MS, Banc Mss 67/35 c, reproduced courtesy of The Bancroft Library, University of California, Berkeley. ■*Previous publication:* none known. ■*Emendations and textual notes:*

4.17	Comedia • [*sic*]
4.22	for more • [*sic*]

■ 9 June [1885] • Charles Eliot Norton • Cambridge, MA

■*Copy-text:* MS, George Santayana Collection (#6947), Clifton Waller Barrett Library, Special Collections Department, University of Virginia Library. ■*Previous publication:* none known. ■*Emendations and textual notes:* none.

■ 16 August 1886 • Henry Ward Abbot • Göttingen, Germany

■*Copy-text:* MS, George Santayana Papers, Rare Book and Manuscript Library, Columbia University. ■*Previous publication: Letters,* 1–3. ■*Emendations and textual notes:*

6.11	~~in~~ to • ['to' *over* 'in']
6.15	avow~~d~~edly • ['e' *over* 'd']
6.28	chan~~g~~ce • ['c' *over* 'g']
6.30	~~of~~ over • ['over' *over* 'of']
6.32	excep~~ts~~t • ['t' *over* 'ts']

■ 16 August 1886 • Ward Thoron • Göttingen, Germany

■*Copy-text:* MS, George Santayana Papers (bMS Am 1542), by permission of the Houghton Library, Harvard University. ■*Previous publication:* "A Psalm of Travel" in *Complete Poems,* 191; *Letters,* 3–4. ■*Emendations and textual notes:*

| 8.18 | deed • [*sic*] |
| 9.7 | L~~iee~~e • ['e' *over* 'ee'] |

■ 27 August 1886 • Henry Ward Abbot • Göttingen, Germany

■*Copy-text:* MS, George Santayana Papers, Rare Book and Manuscript Library, Columbia University. ■*Previous publication: Letters,* 5–8. ■*Emendations and textual notes:*

11.4	one's • [*sic*]
11.7	~~see~~ look • ['look' *over* 'see']
11.12	~~ones~~ his • ['his' *over* 'ones']
11.19	~~gi~~selling • ['se' *over* 'gi']
11.19	birthright • birth- / right
11.21	~~on~~another • ['a' *over* 'on']
11.33	[*illegible*]my • ['m' *over unrecovered character*]
12.3	some o~~f~~ld • ['l' *over* 'f']
12.12	¢Epicurean • ['E' *over* 'e']

■ 9 September 1886 • William Morton Fullerton • Dresden, Germany

■*Copy-text:* MS, Harry Ransom Humanities Research Center, University of Texas, Austin. ■*Previous publication:* none known. ■*Emendations and textual notes:*

14.1	irresistably • [*sic*]
14.14	whilome • [*sic*]
14.16	comit • [*sic*]

■ 6 October 1886 • Henry Ward Abbot • Berlin, Germany

■*Copy-text:* MS, George Santayana Papers, Rare Book and Manuscript Library, Columbia University. ■*Previous publication:* none known. ■*Emendations and textual notes:*

15.17	somehow • some- / how
15.23	going attend • [*sic*]
15.24	~~if~~ should • ['sh' *over* 'if']
15.31	something • some- / thing
15.31–32	yourself? are • [*sic*]
16.1	dis/appointment • [*Santayana's slash*]
16.11	gr[*illegible*]ive • ['ive' *over* 'r' *and unrecovered characters*]

■ 1 November 1886 • Henry Ward Abbot • Berlin, Germany

■*Copy-text:* MS, George Santayana Papers, Rare Book and Manuscript Library, Columbia University. ■*Previous publication:* none known. ■*Emendations and textual notes:*

16.28	anything • any- / thing
17.8	afternoon • after- / noon
17.11–12	anti-Hegelianism • anti- / Hegelianism
17.13	something • some- / thing
18.29 and 30–31	i̶t̶ he • ['he' *over* 'it']
20.19	s̶ceases • ['c' *over* 's']
20.32	anyones • [*sic*]
21.4	animal culae • [*sic*]

■ 9 November 1886 • Herbert [Lyman] • Berlin, Germany

■*Copy-text:* MS unlocated. Published version is copy-text. ■*Previous publication: Complete Poems,* 506–21. ■*Emendations and textual notes:*

32.3	Shakespere • [*sic*]
34.19	fragant • [*sic*]

■ 12 December 1886 • Henry Ward Abbot • Berlin, Germany

■*Copy-text:* MS, George Santayana Papers, Rare Book and Manuscript Library, Columbia University. ■*Previous publication: Letters,* 8–11. ■*Emendations and textual notes:*

37.20	pro̶fbably • ['b' *over* 'f']
38.21	pre-Rap̶ahaelitism • ['h' *over* 'a']

■ 9 January 1887 • William James • Berlin, Germany

■*Copy-text:* MS, George Santayana Papers (bMS Am 1092.9), by permission of the Houghton Library, Harvard University. ■*Previous publication: Letters,* 12–13. ■*Emendations and textual notes:*

41.19	everything • every- / thing
41.27	thin̶kgs • ['g' *over* 'k']
42.13	that cozy • [*sic*]

■ 16 January 1887 • Henry Ward Abbot • Berlin, Germany

■*Copy-text:* MS, George Santayana Papers, Rare Book and Manuscript Library, Columbia University. ■*Previous publication: Letters,* 14–17. ■*Emendations and textual notes:*

43.23 and 25	n̶Nothing • ['N' *over* 'n']
43.34	buz • [*sic*]
44.15	overburdened • over- / burdened
44.24–25	ghost-and-faery-blind • ghost-and- / faery-blind
45.3	self-existent • self- / existent
45.21	point, and • ['a' *over* '.']
46.19	m̶hour • ['ou' *over* 'm']

■ 5 February 1887 • Henry Ward Abbot • Berlin, Germany

■*Copy-text:* MS, George Santayana Papers, Rare Book and Manuscript Library, Columbia University. ■*Previous publication: Letters,* 18–21. ■*Emendations and textual notes:*

48.3	A̸With • ['W' *over* 'A']
48.10	less ine[*illegible*]vitable • ['vit' *over unrecovered characters*]
48.28	self-existent • self- / existent
48.34	existen̸ce • ['c' *over* 't']
49.9	~~one~~ three • ['three' *over* 'one']
49.20	there • [*sic*]
49.24	the made • [*sic*]
49.28	be cause • be / cause [*sic*]

■ 17 February 1887 • Henry Ward Abbot • Berlin, Germany

■*Copy-text:* MS, George Santayana Papers, Rare Book and Manuscript Library, Columbia University. ■*Previous publication:* none known. ■*Emendations and textual notes:*

50.9	others • [*sic*]
50.20	Catechism) To • [*sic*]
50.28	~~tru~~and • ['and' *over* 'tru']
51.19	[*illegible*]around • ['a' *over unrecovered character*]
51.21	underexposed • under- / exposed
52.5	straightway • straight- / way
53.15	ressources • [*sic*]
54.6	~~on~~ to • ['to' *over* 'on']
54.11	anything • any- / thing
54.28	~~He~~ It • ['It' *over* 'He']
54.30	~~he~~ it • ['it' *over* 'he']
55.5	thereupon • there- / upon
55.15	~~it~~ we ḫmust have • ['we' *over* 'it' *and* 'm' *over* 'h']
55.24	~~an object~~ ₐa meansₐ • ['a means' *above* '~~an object~~']

■ 21 February 1887 • William James • Berlin, Germany

■*Copy-text:* MS, George Santayana Papers (bMS Am 1092.9), by permission of the Houghton Library, Harvard University. ■*Previous publication: Letters,* 21–23. ■*Emendations and textual notes:*

56.14	historal • [*sic*]
56.16	Schopenhauerians • [*sic*]
57.3	ὄντως ὄγ • [*sic*]
57.8	anything • any- / thing
58.4	correspondance • [*sic*]

■ 23 March 1887 • Henry Ward Abbot • London, England

■*Copy-text:* MS, George Santayana Papers, Rare Book and Manuscript Library, Columbia University. ■*Previous publication:* none known. ■*Emendations and textual notes:*

59.3	~~than~~ ∧besides∧ • ['besides' *above* '~~than~~']
59.28	little ɸfor • ['f' *over* 'o']
60.5	~~made~~ ∧cut∧ • ['cut' *above* '~~made~~']
60.35	mortels • [*sic*]
60.35	kalleidoscope • [*sic*]
61.11–12	and the fact • and the / the fact
61.19	~~their~~ there • ['re' *over* 'ir']
61.30	is question • [*sic*]

■ 23 April 1887 • Henry Ward Abbot • Oxford, England

■*Copy-text:* MS, George Santayana Papers, Rare Book and Manuscript Library, Columbia University. ■*Previous publication:* none known. ■*Emendations and textual notes:*

62.18	notebooks • note- / books
63.16	∧a∧ sane ~~men~~ man • ['a' *in margin*; 'a' *over* 'e' *in* 'man']
63.16	∧his∧ • [*in margin*]
63.29	~~ourselves~~ ∧our feelings∧ • ['our feelings' *above* '~~ourselves~~']
64.11	~~the~~ his • ['his' *over* 'the']
64.21	bɏut • ['u' *over* 'y']
64.29	otherwise • other- / wise
64.31	exhilirating • [*sic*]
65.11	not do • [*sic*]
65.23	~~peice~~ piece • ['ie' *over* 'ei']
65.32	a least • [*sic*]

■ 24 April 1887 • Ward Thoron • Oxford, England

■*Copy-text:* MS, George Santayana Collection (#6947), Clifton Waller Barrett Library, Special Collections Department, University of Virginia Library. ■*Previous publication: Letters,* 23–24; *Complete Poems,* 192–93. ■*Emendations and textual notes:* none.

■ 30 April 1887 • Henry Ward Abbot • Oxford, England

■*Copy-text:* MS, George Santayana Papers, Rare Book and Manuscript Library, Columbia University. ■*Previous publication:* none known. ■*Emendations and textual notes:*

| 68.15–16 | ~~lose~~ ∧lose∧ • ['lose' *above* '~~lose~~'] |
| 68.26 | ɰshall • ['sh' *over* 'w'] |

■ 11 May 1887 • William James • Oxford, England

■ *Copy-text:* MS, George Santayana Papers (bMS Am 1092.9), by permission of the Houghton Library, Harvard University. ■*Previous publication: Letters,* 25–26. ■*Emendations and textual notes:*

69.9	~~it~~ they • ['they' *over* 'it']
69.13	"Rechtsphilosophie" • "Rechts- / philosophie"
69.29	Mc Donnald • Mc / Donnald [*sic*]

■ 17 May 1887 • George Pierce Baker • Oxford, England

■ *Copy-text:* MS, Yale Collection of American Literature, Beinecke Rare Book and Manuscript Library, Yale University. ■*Previous publication:* none known. ■*Emendations and textual notes:*

71.13	without • with- / out
71.18	to longer • [*sic*]

■ 20 May 1887 • Henry Ward Abbot • Oxford, England

■ *Copy-text:* MS, George Santayana Papers, Rare Book and Manuscript Library, Columbia University. ■*Previous publication:* none known. ■*Emendations and textual notes:*

73.16	epicurianism • [*sic*]
73.19–20	living ,(and • ['(' *over* ',']
74.4	~~their~~ there • ['ere' *over* 'eir']
74.6–7	~~it~~ the • ['the' *over* 'it']
74.9	have • [*sic*]
74.32	~~g~~digestion • ['d' *over* 'g']
75.10	~~does not~~ doesn't • ['n't' *over* 'not']
75.16	fellow-man • fellow- / man
75.20	~~chose~~ choose • ['ose' *over* 'se']
76.14	to-morrow • to- / morrow

■ 27 May 1887 • Henry Ward Abbot • Oxford, England

■ *Copy-text:* MS, George Santayana Papers, Rare Book and Manuscript Library, Columbia University. ■*Previous publication:* none known. ■*Emendations and textual notes:*

77.7	~~chose~~ choose • ['ose' *over* 'se']
78.3 and 4	self-control • self- / control
78.6	allow • ['w' *over unrecovered character*]
78.14	~~beleive~~ believe • ['ie' *over* 'ei']
78.17	effect • [*sic*]
78.21	~~are~~ is • ['is' *over* 'are']

■ 29 May 1887 • Henry Ward Abbot • Oxford, England

■*Copy-text:* MS, George Santayana Papers, Rare Book and Manuscript Library, Columbia University. ■*Previous publication:* a portion of the letter is in *Letters*, 26–27; a different version of the poem entitled "At the Church Door" is included in *Complete Poems*, 418–21. ■*Emendations and textual notes:*

79.12	~~their~~ there • ['re' *over* 'ir']
79.17	~~is~~ only • ['on' *over* 'is']
79.18–19	however • how- / ever
80.12	~~lost~~ plucked • ['luck' *over* 'lost']
80.12	~~made~~ built • ['built' *over* 'made']
80.12	ⱥour • ['our' *over* 'a']
81.20	yeild • [*sic*]
81.34	Makⱥing • ['ing' *over* 'e']

■ 18 June 1887 • Henry Ward Abbot • London, England

■*Copy-text:* MS, George Santayana Papers, Rare Book and Manuscript Library, Columbia University. ■*Previous publication:* a revised verse "Sweet are the days we wander with no hope" became Sonnet XIII of the Sonnets Series First in *Sonnets*, 15, and is also included in *Complete Poems*, 97. ■*Emendations and textual notes:* none.

■ 10 July 1887 • William Morton Fullerton • Ávila, Spain

■*Copy-text:* MS, Harry Ransom Humanities Research Center, University of Texas, Austin. ■*Previous publication:* none known. ■*Emendations and textual notes:*

83.14	~~their~~ ₐitsₐ • ['its' *above* '~~their~~']
83.15	ꬵto • ['t' *over* 'f']
83.23	condiseration • [*sic*]
83.24	sixpense • six- / pense [*sic*]
83.27	think • [*sic*]
83.29	things⫽"! • [' " ' *over* '!']
83.33	irrationel • [*sic*]
84.5	thinks • [*sic*]
84.9	that Boston • [*sic*]
84.31	American • [*sic*]

■ 31 August 1887 • William Morton Fullerton • Ávila, Spain

■*Copy-text:* MS, Harry Ransom Humanities Research Center, University of Texas, Austin. ■*Previous publication:* none known. ■*Emendations and textual notes:*

85.5–6	you optimist • [*sic*]
85.14	collectionₐ honors • [*sic*]
85.17	tⱥwo • ['wo' *over* 'o']
85.17	ɏso • ['s' *over* 'y']
86.1, 2, and 4	arⱥk • ['k' *over* 'c']
86.7	breeches • [*sic*]

86.23	Davids • [*sic*]
86.27	th∉ose • ['ose' *over* 'e']
86.30	Loch's daughters • [*sic*]
86.36	t̶o̶ for ['for' *over* 'to']
87.1	influencial • [*sic*]
87.2–3	s̶o̶m̶ which • ['which' *over* 'som']
87.4	ẁthat • ['t' *over* 'w']
87.9	∉in • ['in' *over* 'e']
87.22	arr∤ogance • ['o' *over* 'a']
87.23	FEEL! • [*triple underline*]
87.25	something • some- / thing
87.30	m̸by • ['b' *over* 'm']
88.4	him, (the • ['(' *over* '.']
88.17	something • some- / thing

■ 18 December 1887 • William James • Berlin, Germany

■*Copy-text:* MS, George Santayana Papers (bMS Am 1092.9), by permission of the Houghton Library, Harvard University. ■*Previous publication: Letters*, 27–29; Ralph Barton Perry, *The Thought and Character of William James*, vol. 1 (Boston: Little, Brown, and Company, 1935), 401–2. ■*Emendations and textual notes:*

89.15	metaphysical • meta- / physical
89.19	t̶h̶e̶i̶r̶ these • ['se' *over* 'ir']
90.26–27	something • some- / thing
90.27	fellowship • fellow- / ship

■ 28 December 1887 • William Morton Fullerton • Berlin, Germany

■*Copy-text:* MS, Harry Ransom Humanities Research Center, University of Texas, Austin. ■*Previous publication:* none known. ■*Emendations and textual notes:*

92.5	bad The • [*sic*]
92.20–21	t̶h̶e̶ this • ['is' *over* 'e']
92.23	currupted • [*sic*]
92.38	Mastibation. • [*sic*]
93.8	h̶i̶m̶ her • ['er' *over* 'im']
93.12	disavantage • [*sic*]
93.14	On∮e • ['e' *over* 's']
93.29	Minots • [*sic*]
93.30	particularl • [*sic*]
93.34	by I know • [*sic*]

■ 28 January 1888 • William James • Berlin, Germany

■*Copy-text:* MS, George Santayana Papers (bMS Am 1092.9), by permission of the Houghton Library, Harvard University. ■*Previous publication: Letters*, 29–30; Ralph Barton Perry, *The Thought and Character of William James*, vol. 1 (Boston: Little, Brown, and Company, 1935), 404–5. ■*Emendations and textual notes:*

94.4	article of the • [*sic*]
94.9	scholarship • scholar- / ship
94.13	fellowship • fellow- / ship
94.19	now-a-days • now- / a-days
94.21	contempory • [*sic*]

■ 3 July 1888 • William James • Ávila, Spain

■*Copy-text:* MS, George Santayana Papers (bMS Am 1092.9), by permission of the Houghton Library, Harvard University. ■*Previous publication: Letters*, 30–31; Ralph Barton Perry, *The Thought and Character of William James*, vol. 1 (Boston: Little, Brown, and Company, 1935), 405–6. ■*Emendations and textual notes:*

95.15	therefore • there- / fore
95.18	without • with- / out
96.11	alchymist • [*sic*]
96.25	deel • [*sic*]

■ 7 August 1888 • William James • Ávila, Spain

■*Copy-text:* MS, George Santayana Papers (bMS Am 1092.9), by permission of the Houghton Library, Harvard University. ■*Previous publication: Letters,* 32–33. ■*Emendations and textual notes:*

97.23	~~there~~ their • ['ir' *over* 're']
98.9	anywhere • any- / where
98.9–10	professorship • professor- / ship

■ [c. 1888 or 1889] • William Cameron Forbes • Roxbury, MA

■*Copy-text:* MS, George Santayana Papers (bMS Am 1364), by permission of the Houghton Library, Harvard University. ■*Previous publication:* none known. ■*Emendations and textual notes:* none.

■ [Before 1889?] • Charles Augustus Strong • [Roxbury, MA?]

■*Copy-text:* MS, Box 6, Folder 87, The Papers of Charles Augustus Strong, Rockefeller Archive Center, Sleepy Hollow, New York. ■*Previous publication:* none known. ■*Emendations and textual notes:*

99.12	~~with~~ that the • ['that the' *over* 'with']

■ 29 January 1889 • Charles Augustus Strong • Roxbury, MA

■*Copy-text:* MS, Box 6, Folder 87, The Papers of Charles Augustus Strong, Rockefeller Archive Center, Sleepy Hollow, New York. ■*Previous publication:* none known. ■*Emendations and textual notes:*

100.9	any thing • any / thing [*sic*]
101.7	Gods ideas • [*sic*]
101.8	∧as∧ • [*in margin*]

101.12	there fore • there / fore [*sic*]
102.3	it. himself. • it. / himself. [*sic*]
102.6	men But • men / But [*sic*]
102.29	super-human • super- / human
102.31	every where • every / where [*sic*]
103.5	their are • [*sic*]

■ 19 March 1889 • Charles Augustus Strong • Roxbury, MA
■*Copy-text:* MS, Box 6, Folder 87, The Papers of Charles Augustus Strong, Rockefeller Archive Center, Sleepy Hollow, New York. ■*Previous publication:* none known. ■*Emendations and textual notes:* none.

■ 26 July 1889 • Henry Ward Abbot • Roxbury, MA
■*Copy-text:* MS, George Santayana Papers, Rare Book and Manuscript Library, Columbia University. ■*Previous publication:* the poem enclosed with this letter is in *Complete Poems*, 423–24. ■*Emendations and textual notes:*

104.11	Tourgennef's "Dimitri Roudine." • [*sic*]
104.21–22	"Dimitri Rudine," • [*sic*]
105.10	~~veil~~ vale • ['al' *over* 'eil']

■ 6 August 1889 • Henry Ward Abbot • Roxbury, MA
■*Copy-text:* MS, George Santayana Papers, Rare Book and Manuscript Library, Columbia University. ■*Previous publication: Letters*, 33–35, excerpt. ■*Emendations and textual notes:*

106.35	~~effect~~ ‸reaction‸ • ['reaction' *above* '~~effect~~']
107.12	developss • [*sic*]
107.15	inscrutible • [*sic*]
107.16	exhaltation • [*sic*]
107.34	sometimes • some- / times

■ 29 September 1889 • Henry Ward Abbot • Cambridge, MA
■*Copy-text:* MS, George Santayana Papers, Rare Book and Manuscript Library, Columbia University. ■*Previous publication:* none known. ■*Emendations and textual notes:*

109.18	its • [*sic*]
109.30	Descartes • [*sic*]

■ 22 July 1890 • Charles Augustus Strong • Ávila, Spain
■*Copy-text:* MS, Box 6, Folder 87, The Papers of Charles Augustus Strong, Rockefeller Archive Center, Sleepy Hollow, New York. ■*Previous publication:* none known. ■*Emendations and textual notes:*

110.12	work When • work / When [*sic*]

110.19	Locke Berkeley & Hume • Locke / Berkeley & Hume [*sic*]
111.4	something • some- / thing
111.13	intellectual I • [*sic*]
111.31 and 112.6	Schurmann • [*sic*]
111.39	drivle • [*sic*]
112.3	Schurmann's • [*sic*]
112.13	The~~ir~~re • ['re' *over* 'ir']
112.26	Teutonii • [*sic*]

■ 10 August 1890 • Charles Augustus Strong • Ávila, Spain

■*Copy-text:* MS, Box 6, Folder 87, The Papers of Charles Augustus Strong, Rockefeller Archive Center, Sleepy Hollow, New York. ■*Previous publication:* none known. ■*Emendations and textual notes:*

114.12	fit • ['t' *over unrecovered characters*]
114.14	[*illegible*]sphere • ['sphere' *over unrecovered characters*]
114.32	~~and~~ ₐwithₐ • ['with' *above* '~~and~~']
114.35	an∅alogy • ['a' *over* 'o']
115.1	an∤alogy • ['a' *over* 'n']
115.3	~~but~~ ₐforₐ • ['for' *above* '~~but~~']
115.5	parellism • [*sic*]
115.6	the~~irs~~m • ['m' *over* 'irs']
115.25	chance be • [*sic*]
115.27	comsumes • [*sic*]
116.12	~~none.~~ ₐno way of learning it.ₐ • ['no way of learning it' *above* '~~none.~~']
116.15	∮no • ['n' *over* 's']
116.27	usuper • [*sic*]
116.35	abrevations • [*sic*]
117.1–2	others matters • [*sic*]
117.2	o∤r • ['r' *over* 'f']

■ Sunday [1890–96] • Alice Freeman Palmer • Cambridge, MA

■*Copy-text:* MS, Poetry Magazine Papers, Department of Special Collections, The Joseph Regenstein Library, The University of Chicago. ■*Previous publication:* none known. ■*Emendations and textual notes:* none.

■ 16 August 1891 • Charles Augustus Strong • Ávila, Spain

■*Copy-text:* MS, Box 6, Folder 87, The Papers of Charles Augustus Strong, Rockefeller Archive Center, Sleepy Hollow, New York. ■*Previous publication:* none known. ■*Emendations and textual notes:*

119.11	o∤ur • ['u' *over* 'f']
119.16	[*illegible*] call • ['call' *over unrecovered characters*]
119.32	~~we~~ you • ['yo' *over* 'we']

■ 15 February 1892 [*postmark*] • Henry Ward Abbot • Cambridge, MA

■*Copy-text:* MS, George Santayana Papers, Rare Book and Manuscript Library, Columbia University. ■*Previous publication:* none known. ■*Emendations and textual notes:*

120.17   pro*p*bably • ['b' *over* 'p']

■ 26 February 1892 • Isabella Stewart Gardner • [Cambridge, MA]

■*Copy-text:* MS unlocated. Copy on microfilm in the Archive of American Art, Smithsonian Institution, New York City, is copy-text. ■*Previous publication:* none known. ■*Emendations and textual notes:* none.

■ 6 March 1892 • Josiah Royce • Cambridge, MA

■*Copy-text:* MS, Josiah Royce Papers, courtesy of the Harvard University Archives. ■*Previous publication:* none known. ■*Emendations and textual notes:* none.

■ 29 March 1892 • Isabella Stewart Gardner • [Cambridge, MA]

■*Copy-text:* MS unlocated. Copy on microfilm in the Archive of American Art, Smithsonian Institution, New York City, is copy-text. ■*Previous publication:* a different version is in *Sonnets*, 60, and *Complete Poems*, 161. ■*Emendations and textual notes:* none.

■ [Spring 1892 or 1894] • Isabella Stewart Gardner • Cambridge, MA

■*Copy-text:* MS, Isabella Stewart Gardner Museum Archives, Boston. ■*Previous publication:* none known. ■*Emendations and textual notes:*

123.11   Johns • [*sic*]

■ 1 December 1892 • William Cameron Forbes • Cambridge, MA

■*Copy-text:* MS, George Santayana Papers (bMS Am 1364), by permission of the Houghton Library, Harvard University. ■*Previous publication:* none known. ■*Emendations and textual notes:* none.

■ 19 December [1892] • Mary Augusta Jordan • Cambridge, MA

■*Copy-text:* MS, Smith College Archives. ■*Previous publication:* none known. ■*Emendations and textual notes:* none.

■ 20 December [1892] • Horatius Bonar Hastings • Cambridge, MA

■*Copy-text:* MS unlocated. Photocopy of original in the collection of Harriet Fitzgerald, Washington, DC, is copy-text. At one time original was with Paul C. Richards Autographs, Brookline, MA (not located). ■*Previous publication:* none known. ■*Emendations and textual notes:* none.

■ Friday [1893] • Sara Norton • Cambridge, MA

■*Copy-text:* MS, George Santayana Collection (#6947), Clifton Waller Barrett Library, Special Collections Department, University of Virginia Library. ■*Previous publication:* none known. ■*Emendations and textual notes:* none.

■ Saturday [1893] • Hugo Münsterberg • Cambridge, MA

■*Copy-text:* MS, Department of Rare Books and Manuscripts, by courtesy of the Trustees of the Boston Public Library. ■*Previous publication:* none known. ■*Emendations and textual notes:*

126.10   Wesselhaft • [*sic*]

■ 14 April 1893 • Horatius Bonar Hastings • Cambridge, MA

■*Copy-text:* MS, collection of the Santayana Edition. This letter was with the book of notes taken by Mr. Hastings in Santayana's Philosophy 8 class which was given to the Edition by Paul Hastings. ■*Previous publication:* none known. ■*Emendations and textual notes:*

127.7   lectured I • lectured / I [*sic*]

■ [Spring 1893] • William Cameron Forbes • Cambridge, MA

■*Copy-text:* MS, George Santayana Papers (bMS Am 1364), by permission of the Houghton Library, Harvard University. ■*Previous publication:* none known. ■*Emendations and textual notes:*

128.20   *I*took • ['t' *over* 'I']

■ 3 July 1893 • Louisa Adams Beal • Ávila, Spain

■*Copy-text:* MS, George Santayana Papers (MS Am 1371.8), by permission of the Houghton Library, Harvard University. ■*Previous publication:* none known. ■*Emendations and textual notes:* none.

■ 4 July 1893 [*postmark*] • Boylston Adams Beal • Ávila, Spain

■*Copy-text:* MS, George Santayana Papers (MS Am 1371.8), by permission of the Houghton Library, Harvard University. ■*Previous publication:* none known. ■*Emendations and textual notes:* none.

■ 6 July 1893 • William Cameron Forbes • Ávila, Spain

■*Copy-text:* MS, George Santayana Papers (bMS Am 1364), by permission of the Houghton Library, Harvard University. ■*Previous publication:* none known. ■*Emendations and textual notes:* none.

■ 21 August 1893 • Charles Augustus Strong • Ávila, Spain

■*Copy-text:* MS, George Santayana Collection, Special Collections Division, Georgetown University Library. ■*Previous publication:* none known. ■*Emendations and textual notes:*

132.22   seventy nine • [*sic*]

■ 11 October 1893 • John Corbin • Cambridge, MA

■*Copy-text:* MS, George Santayana Collection (#6947), Clifton Waller Barrett Library, Special Collections Department, University of Virginia Library. ■*Previous publication:* none known. ■*Emendations and textual notes:* none.

■ 9 December 1893 • William Cameron Forbes • Cambridge, MA

■*Copy-text:* MS, George Santayana Papers (bMS Am 1364), by permission of the Houghton Library, Harvard University. ■*Previous publication:* none known. ■*Emendations and textual notes:*

133.17   birthday • birth- / day

■ 11 December 1893 • Herbert S. Stone and Hannibal I. Kimball • Cambridge, MA

■*Copy-text:* MS, George Santayana Collection (#6947), Clifton Waller Barrett Library, Special Collections Department, University of Virginia Library. ■*Previous publication:* none known. ■*Emendations and textual notes:*

134.9   ~~peices~~ pieces • ['ie' *over* 'ei']

■ 16 December 1893 • William Cameron Forbes • Cambridge, MA

■*Copy-text:* MS, George Santayana Papers (bMS Am 1364), by permission of the Houghton Library, Harvard University. ■*Previous publication:* none known. ■*Emendations and textual notes:*

135.9   be real • [*sic*]

■ [16 December 1893] • Norman Hapgood • Cambridge, MA

■*Copy-text:* MS unlocated. Published verison is copy-text. ■*Previous publication:* *Letters,* 35–36. ■*Emendations and textual notes:*

136.3   GSantayana • [*not present*]

■ Tuesday [c. 1894 or 1895] • William Cameron Forbes • Cambridge, MA

■*Copy-text:* MS, George Santayana Papers (bMS Am 1364), by permission of the Houghton Library, Harvard University. ■*Previous publication:* none known. ■*Emendations and textual notes:* none.

■ 23 June 1894 • Charles William Eliot • Cambridge, MA

■*Copy-text:* MS, C. W. Eliot Papers, courtesy of the Harvard University Archives.
■*Previous publication: Letters,* 36. ■*Emendations and textual notes:*

136.18   cannot • can- / not
136.18–19   without • with- / out

■ [1 August 1894] • Guy Murchie • Cambridge, MA

■*Copy-text:* MS, collection of Guy Murchie Jr. ■*Previous publication:* none known.
■*Emendations and textual notes:* none.

■ 20 November 1894 • Guy Murchie • Cambridge, MA

■*Copy-text:* MS, collection of Guy Murchie Jr. ■*Previous publication: Letters,* 37; sonnet only in *Complete Poems,* 135. ■*Emendations and textual notes:*

137.20   vapourous • [*sic*]
138.13   ~~Oct~~November • ['Nov' *over* 'Oct']

■ 23 December [1894] • Guy Murchie • Cambridge, MA

■*Copy-text:* MS, collection of Guy Murchie Jr. ■*Previous publication: Letters,* 37–39.
■*Emendations and textual notes:*

138.17   Bancroft's • [*sic*]
139.6   quasi-understanding • quasi- / understanding
139.13   Gray's • [*sic*]

■ [1895 or 1896] • Gertrude Stein • [Cambridge, MA?]

■*Copy-text:* MS, Yale Collection of American Literature, Beinecke Rare Book and
Manuscript Library, Yale University. ■*Previous publication:* none known.
■*Emendations and textual notes:* none.

■ 28 February 1895 [*postmark*] • Charles Eliot Norton • Cambridge, MA

■*Copy-text:* MS, C. E. Norton Papers (bMS Am 1088), by permission of the
Houghton Library, Harvard University. ■*Previous publication:* none known.
■*Emendations and textual notes:* none.

■ 2 May 1895 • Macmillan and Co. • Cambridge, MA

■*Copy-text:* MS, Macmillan Company Records, Rare Books and Manuscripts
Division, The New York Public Library, Astor, Lenox and Tilden Foundations.
■*Previous publication:* none known. ■*Emendations and textual notes:* none.

■ 4 June 1895 • Herbert S. Stone and Hannibal I. Kimball • Cambridge,

MA

■*Copy-text:* MS, George Santayana Collection (#6947), Clifton Waller Barrett Library, Special Collections Department, University of Virginia Library. ■*Previous publication:* none known. ■*Emendations and textual notes:* none.

■ 18 June 1895 • William Cameron Forbes • Cambridge, MA

■*Copy-text:* MS, collection of the Santayana Edition. The letter is tipped into Forbes's copy of *The Middle Span.* ■*Previous publication:* none known. ■*Emendations and textual notes:*

142.22	on, to • ['t' *over* '.']
142.28	you,. • ['.' *over* ',']

■ 19 June 1895 • Macmillan and Co. • Cambridge, MA

■*Copy-text:* MS, Macmillan Company Records, Rare Books and Manuscripts Division, The New York Public Library, Astor, Lenox and Tilden Foundations. ■*Previous publication:* none known. ■*Emendations and textual notes:* none.

■ 3 September 1895 • Guy Murchie • London, England

■*Copy-text:* MS, collection of Guy Murchie Jr. ■*Previous publication: Letters,* 39–40; a version of the sonnet entitled "Mont Brévent" is in *Hermit,* 123, and *Complete Poems,* 131. ■*Emendations and textual notes:*

144.6	however • how- / ever

■ [1895–96?] • Lawrence Smith Butler • [New York, New York]

■*Copy-text:* MS, The University Club Library, New York. ■*Previous publication:* none known. ■*Emendations and textual notes:*

145.8	somehow • some- / how

■ Monday [1895–96?] • Lawrence Smith Butler • [New York, New York?]

■*Copy-text:* MS, The University Club Library, New York. ■*Previous publication:* none known. ■*Emendations and textual notes:* none.

■ Thursday [1895–96] • Lawrence Smith Butler • Cambridge, MA

■*Copy-text:* MS, The University Club Library, New York. ■*Previous publication:* none known. ■*Emendations and textual notes:* none.

■ 3 October 1895 • Macmillan and Co. • Cambridge, MA

■*Copy-text:* MS, Macmillan Company Records, Rare Books and Manuscripts Division, The New York Public Library, Astor, Lenox and Tilden Foundations. ■*Previous publication:* none known. ■*Emendations and textual notes:* none.

■ 10 November 1895 • Charles Augustus Strong • Cambridge, MA

■*Copy-text:* MS, Box 6, Folder 88, The Papers of Charles Augustus Strong, Rockefeller Archive Center, Sleepy Hollow, New York. ■*Previous publication:* none known. ■*Emendations and textual notes:* none.

■ 1 December 1895 • Guy Murchie • Naushon, MA

■*Copy-text:* partial MS, collection of Guy Murchie Jr. ■*Previous publication: Letters,* 40–41. ■*Emendations and textual notes:*

148.20–21	~~these~~ those • ['ose' *over* 'ese']
148.25	subtle/st • ['st' *over* 'r']
148.25	~~more~~ most • ['st' *over* 're']
148.28	mascarading • [*sic*]
149.1	Lawrence's • [*sic*]

■ 12 March 1896 • Guy Murchie • Cambridge, MA

■*Copy-text:* MS, collection of Guy Murchie Jr. ■*Previous publication: Letters,* 41–44. ■*Emendations and textual notes:*

149.13	<u>n'est</u>-ce pas • <u>n'est</u>- / ce pas [*sic*]
150.24	~~one~~ thing • ['thing' *over* 'one']
151.18	~~it~~ that • ['that' *over* 'it']

■ 19 March 1896 • Charles Scribner's Sons • Cambridge, MA

■*Copy-text:* MS, Author Files I, Box 130 of the Scribner Archives, Manuscripts Division, Department of Rare Books and Special Collections, Princeton University Libraries. ■*Previous publication:* none known. ■*Emendations and textual notes:* none.

■ 23 March 1896 • Herbert S. Stone and Hannibal I. Kimball • Cambridge, MA

■*Copy-text:* MS, Special Collections, Temple University Libraries. ■*Previous publication:* none known. ■*Emendations and textual notes:* none.

■ [Spring 1896] • William Cameron Forbes • Cambridge, MA

■*Copy-text:* MS, George Santayana Papers (bMS Am 1364), by permission of the Houghton Library, Harvard University. ■*Previous publication:* none known. ■*Emendations and textual notes:* none.

■ 5 May 1896 • Charles Scribner's Sons • Cambridge, MA

■*Copy-text:* MS, Author Files I, Box 130 of the Scribner Archives, Manuscripts Division, Department of Rare Books and Special Collections, Princeton

University Libraries. ■*Previous publication:* none known. ■*Emendations and textual notes:*

154.22   l̶a̶t̶t̶e̶r̶ former • ['former' *over* 'latter']

■ 20 June 1896 • Charles Scribner's Sons • Cambridge, MA
■*Copy-text:* MS, Author Files I, Box 130 of the Scribner Archives, Manuscripts Division, Department of Rare Books and Special Collections, Princeton University Libraries. ■*Previous publication:* none known. ■*Emendations and textual notes:* none.

■ 27 June 1896 • Guy Murchie • Quebec, Canada
■*Copy-text:* MS, collection of Guy Murchie Jr. ■*Previous publication:* none known. ■*Emendations and textual notes:*

156.1   will ultimate satisfy • [*sic*]
156.5   thₑis • ['is' *over* 'e']
156.17   Perkins • [*sic*]
156.20   Katherine • [*sic*]

■ 26 July 1896 • Charles Scribner's Sons • Oxford, England
■*Copy-text:* MS, Author Files I, Box 130 of the Scribner Archives, Manuscripts Division, Department of Rare Books and Special Collections, Princeton University Libraries. ■*Previous publication:* none known. ■*Emendations and textual notes:* none.

■ 11 August 1896 • Conrad Hensler Slade • Oxford, England
■*Copy-text:* MS unlocated. Published version is copy-text. ■*Previous publication:* Letters, 45–47. ■*Emendations and textual notes:*

158.11   October 1ˢᵗ • October 1st
159.24   Witham • [*sic*]
159.30   two-hours • [*sic*]
159.36   Cᵒ • Co
159.38   GSantayana • [*not present*]

■ 13 August 1896 • Guy Murchie • Oxford, England
■*Copy-text:* MS, collection of Guy Murchie Jr. ■*Previous publication: Letters,* 47–50. ■*Emendations and textual notes:*

161.6   St Laurence • [*sic*]
161.6   Belle Ilse • [*sic*]
161.7   Icebergs • Ice- / bergs
161.35   thirty nine • [*sic*]
162.29   foreground • fore- / ground

162.29–30	by̸icyclists • ['i' *over* 'y']
163.1	undergraduate • under- / graduate

■ 20 August 1896 • Hannibal Ingalls Kimball • Oxford, England

■*Copy-text:* MS, George Santayana Papers, Rare Book and Manuscript Library, Columbia University. ■*Previous publication:* none known. ■*Emendations and textual notes:*

164.11	every little • [*sic*]

■ 29 September 1896 • Charles Scribner's Sons • Maidenhead, England

■*Copy-text:* MS, Author Files I, Box 130 of the Scribner Archives, Manuscripts Division, Department of Rare Books and Special Collections, Princeton University Libraries. ■*Previous publication:* none known. ■*Emendations and textual notes:*

165.24	Graduate's • [*sic*]
165.27	wissenschaftliche • wissen- / schaftliche

■ 10 October 1896 • Boylston Adams Beal • Cambridge, England

■*Copy-text:* MS, George Santayana Papers (MS Am 1371.8), by permission of the Houghton Library, Harvard University. ■*Previous publication:* none known. ■*Emendations and textual notes:*

168.15	companions • [*sic*]
168.16	Merideth • [*sic*]
168.25	~~ten~~ nine • ['nine' *over* 'ten']
168.26	everything • every- / thing
168.35	a least • [*sic*]
168.38	~~case~~ action • ['action' *over* 'case']
169.20	grand. with • [*sic*]
169.23	superflous • [*sic*]
169.35	liquour • [*sic*]
170.8	football • foot- / ball
170.12	₵that • ['t' *over* 'C']

■ 15 October [1896] • James Edwin Creighton • Cambridge, England

■*Copy-text:* MS, Creighton Club Records (#3887), Division of Rare and Manuscript Collections, Cornell University Library. ■*Previous publication:* none known. ■*Emendations and textual notes:* none.

■ 17 October 1896 • Josiah Royce • Cambridge, England

■*Copy-text:* MS, Josiah Royce Papers, courtesy of the Harvard University Archives. ■*Previous publication:* none known. ■*Emendations and textual notes:* none.

■ 22 October 1896 • Charles Scribner's Sons • Cambridge, England

■*Copy-text:* MS, Author Files I, Box 130 of the Scribner Archives, Manuscripts Division, Department of Rare Books and Special Collections, Princeton University Libraries. ■*Previous publication:* none known. ■*Emendations and textual notes:*

174.2–3   English weekly's • [*sic*]

■ 1 November 1896 • William Cameron Forbes • Cambridge, England

■*Copy-text:* MS, George Santayana Papers (bMS Am 1364), by permission of the Houghton Library, Harvard University. ■*Previous publication:* none known. ■*Emendations and textual notes:*

174.32   particcularly • partic- / cularly [*sic*]

■ 11 November 1896 • Carlotta Russell Lowell • Cambridge, England

■*Copy-text:* MS, George Santayana Papers (bMS Am 1542), by permission of the Houghton Library, Harvard University. ■*Previous publication: Letters,* 50–51. ■*Emendations and textual notes:*

176.20   byicjycles • ['i' *over* 'y' *and* 'y' *over* 'i']
177.2   Sarah • [*sic*]

■ 19 November 1896 • Henry Ward Abbot • Cambridge, England

■*Copy-text:* MS, George Santayana Papers, Rare Book and Manuscript Library, Columbia University. ■*Previous publication:* none known. ■*Emendations and textual notes:* none.

■ 21 December 1896 • Charles Scribner's Sons • Paris, France

■*Copy-text:* MS, Author Files I, Box 130 of the Scribner Archives, Manuscripts Division, Department of Rare Books and Special Collections, Princeton University Libraries. ■*Previous publication:* none known. ■*Emendations and textual notes:* none.

■ 14 January 1897 • Susan Sturgis de Sastre • Cambridge, England

■*Copy-text:* MS, George Santayana Collection (#6947), Clifton Waller Barrett Library, Special Collections Department, University of Virginia Library. ■*Previous publication: Letters,* 51–55. ■*Emendations and textual notes:*

179.11   smallpox • small- / pox
179.22   sometimes • some- / times
181.17   thirty three • [*sic*]
182.3   months imprisonment, • [*sic*]

■ 31 January 1897 • Hannibal Ingalls Kimball • Cambridge, England

■*Copy-text:* MS, George Santayana Collection (#6947), Clifton Waller Barrett Library, Special Collections Department, University of Virginia Library. ■*Previous publication:* none known. ■*Emendations and textual notes:* none.

■ 1 February 1897 • Charles Scribner's Sons • Cambridge, England

■*Copy-text:* MS, Author Files I, Box 130 of the Scribner Archives, Manuscripts Division, Department of Rare Books and Special Collections, Princeton University Libraries. ■*Previous publication:* none known. ■*Emendations and textual notes:* none.

■ 23 April 1897 • Josiah Royce • Florence, Italy

■*Copy-text:* MS, Josiah Royce Papers, courtesy of the Harvard University Archives. ■*Previous publication:* none known. ■*Emendations and textual notes:*

185.9   ~~forsee~~ foresee • ['esee' *over* 'see']

■ 17 July 1897 • Guy Murchie • Cambridge, England

■*Copy-text:* MS, collection of Guy Murchie Jr. The last four lines of the letter were transcribed by him. ■*Previous publication: Letters,* 56–58. ■*Emendations and textual notes:*

186.9   succeed~~ing~~ed • ['ed' *over* 'ing']
186.19   deserts • [*sic*]
186.25   Huidescoper • [*sic*]
186.28   father-in-law • father- / in-law
187.15   shar~~ing~~e • ['e' *over* 'ing']

■ 16 September 1897 • Hugo Münsterberg • Brookline, MA

■*Copy-text:* MS, Department of Rare Books and Manuscripts, by courtesy of the Trustees of the Boston Public Library. ■*Previous publication: Letters,* 58–59. ■*Emendations and textual notes:*

188.7   sometimes • some- / times
188.10   ~~tr~~Are • ['Are' *over* 'tr'] [*sic*]

■ 18 October 1897 • Susan Sturgis de Sastre • Longwood, MA

■*Copy-text:* MS, George Santayana Collection (#6947), Clifton Waller Barrett Library, Special Collections Department, University of Virginia Library. ■*Previous publication: Letters,* 59–61. ■*Emendations and textual notes:*

188.25–26   twenty seven or twenty eight • [*sic*]
189.15   wordly • [*sic*]
189.19   ~~their~~ there • ['re' *over* 'ir']
189.23   nine tenths • [*sic*]

189.28	<u>ex-cathedra</u> • <u>ex-</u> / <u>cathedra</u> [*sic*]
189.34	Codman's • [*sic*]
189.35	Beverley • [*sic*]
189.37	Margorie • [*sic*]
190.2	~~their~~ there • ['re' *over* 'ir']

■ 1 December 1897 • Charles William Eliot • Brookline, MA

■*Copy-text:* MS, C. W. Eliot Papers, courtesy of the Harvard University Archives. ■*Previous publication:* none known. ■*Emendations and textual notes:* none.

■ 4 December 1897 • Charles William Eliot • Brookline, MA

■*Copy-text:* MS, C. W. Eliot Papers, courtesy of the Harvard University Archives. ■*Previous publication:* none known. ■*Emendations and textual notes:* none.

■ 10 January [1898 or 1907–1908] • [Sara or Grace] Norton • Brookline, MA

■*Copy-text:* MS, Norton Family Papers (bMS Am 1088.1), by permission of the Houghton Library, Harvard University. ■*Previous publication:* none known. ■*Emendations and textual notes:* none.

■ 1 February 1898 • Charles William Eliot • Brookline, MA

■*Copy-text:* MS, C. W. Eliot Papers, courtesy of the Harvard University Archives. ■*Previous publication:* none known. ■*Emendations and textual notes:* none.

■ 2 March 1898 • William Roscoe Thayer • Cambridge, MA

■*Copy-text:* MS, The Papers of William Roscoe Thayer (bMS Am 1081), by permission of the Houghton Library, Harvard University. ■*Previous publication:* none known. ■*Emendations and textual notes:* none.

■ 17 March 1898 • Charles Scribner's Sons • Brookline, MA

■*Copy-text:* MS, Author Files I, Box 130 of the Scribner Archives, Manuscripts Division, Department of Rare Books and Special Collections, Princeton University Libraries. ■*Previous publication:* none known. ■*Emendations and textual notes:* none.

■ 7 July 1898 • William Roscoe Thayer • [Windsor, England]

■*Copy-text:* MS, The Papers of William Roscoe Thayer (bMS Am 1081), by permission of the Houghton Library, Harvard University. ■*Previous publication:* none known. ■*Emendations and textual notes:* none.

■ 14 July [1898] • William Roscoe Thayer • Windsor, England

■*Copy-text:* MS, George Santayana Papers in the Radin Collection, Library of W. Hugh Peal, University of Kentucky Libraries, Lexington. ■*Previous publication:* none known. ■*Emendations and textual notes:* none.

■ 8 November 1898 • Charles Scribner's Sons • Cambridge, MA

■*Copy-text:* MS, Author Files I, Box 130 of the Scribner Archives, Manuscripts Division, Department of Rare Books and Special Collections, Princeton University Libraries. ■*Previous publication:* none known. ■*Emendations and textual notes:* none.

■ 9 February 1899 • Charles Scribner's Sons • Cambridge, MA

■*Copy-text:* MS, Author Files I, Box 130 of the Scribner Archives, Manuscripts Division, Department of Rare Books and Special Collections, Princeton University Libraries. ■*Previous publication:* none known. ■*Emendations and textual notes:*

196.16   i̶s̶ are • ['are' *over* 'is']

■ 11 February 1899 • Charles Carroll Everett • Cambridge, MA

■*Copy-text:* MS, Redwood Library and Athenaeum, Newport, Rhode Island. ■*Previous publication:* none known. ■*Emendations and textual notes:* none.

■ 25 February 1899 • Macmillan and Co. • Cambridge, MA

■*Copy-text:* MS, Macmillan Company Records, Rare Books and Manuscripts Division, The New York Public Library, Astor, Lenox and Tilden Foundations. ■*Previous publication:* none known. ■*Emendations and textual notes:* none.

■ [Spring 1899] • Hugo Münsterberg • Cambridge, MA

■*Copy-text:* MS, Department of Rare Books and Manuscripts, by courtesy of the Trustees of the Boston Public Library. ■*Previous publication:* none known. ■*Emendations and textual notes:* none.

■ 7 August 1899 • Boylston Adams Beal • Oxford, England

■*Copy-text:* MS, George Santayana Papers (MS Am 1371.8), by permission of the Houghton Library, Harvard University. ■*Previous publication:* none known. ■*Emendations and textual notes:*

198.27   Christchurch • [*sic*]

■ [Autumn 1899–June 1904] • William Cameron Forbes • Cambridge, MA

■*Copy-text:* MS, George Santayana Papers (bMS Am 1364), by permission of the Houghton Library, Harvard University. ■*Previous publication:* none known. ■*Emendations and textual notes:* none.

■ [Autumn 1899–June 1904] • Charles Augustus Strong • Cambridge, MA

■*Copy-text:* MS, George Santayana Collection, Special Collections Division, Georgetown University Library. ■*Previous publication:* none known. ■*Emendations and textual notes:* none.

■ 26 October 1899 • Charles Scribner's Sons • Cambridge, MA

■*Copy-text:* MS, Author Files I, Box 130 of the Scribner Archives, Manuscripts Division, Department of Rare Books and Special Collections, Princeton University Libraries. ■*Previous publication:* none known. ■*Emendations and textual notes:* none.

■ 30 October 1899 • Mary Augusta Jordan • Cambridge, MA

■*Copy-text:* MS, Smith College Archives. ■*Previous publication:* none known. ■*Emendations and textual notes:*

203.3   ~~No~~ October • ['Oct' *over* 'No']

■ 15 November 1899 • Charles Scribner's Sons • Cambridge, MA

■*Copy-text:* MS, Author Files I, Box 130 of the Scribner Archives, Manuscripts Division, Department of Rare Books and Special Collections, Princeton University Libraries. ■*Previous publication:* none known. ■*Emendations and textual notes:*

203.22   ~~to~~ do • ['d' *over* 't']
203.24   ~~the~~ those • ['ose' *over* 'e']
204.3   renewed • re- / newed

■ 11 December 1899 • Charles Scribner's Sons • Cambridge, MA

■*Copy-text:* MS, Author Files I, Box 130 of the Scribner Archives, Manuscripts Division, Department of Rare Books and Special Collections, Princeton University Libraries. ■*Previous publication:* none known. ■*Emendations and textual notes:* none.

■ 22 December 1899 • [Sara or Grace] Norton • Cambridge, MA

■*Copy-text:* MS, Norton Family Papers (bMS Am 1088.1), by permission of the Houghton Library, Harvard University. ■*Previous publication:* none known. ■*Emendations and textual notes:*

205.4   another • an- / other

■ 30 December 1899 • Josiah Royce • New York, New York

■*Copy-text:* MS, Josiah Royce Papers, courtesy of the Harvard University Archives. ■*Previous publication:* none known. ■*Emendations and textual notes:*

205.26	seen • [*sic*]
206.2	me talk • [*sic*]
206.4–5	, (Catholic and Puritan,) • [*parentheses over commas*]

■ [1900] • William Morrow • Cambridge, MA

■*Copy-text:* MS, Fales Library, New York University. ■*Previous publication:* none known. ■*Emendations and textual notes:* none.

■ January 1900 • Moncure Robinson • [Cambridge, MA]

■*Copy-text:* MS unlocated. Published version is copy-text. ■*Previous publication: Complete Poems,* 524–28. ■*Emendations and textual notes:*

209.1   Van Dyk • [*sic*]

■ 20 February 1900 • Charles Scribner's Sons • Cambridge, MA

■*Copy-text:* MS, Author Files I, Box 130 of the Scribner Archives, Manuscripts Division, Department of Rare Books and Special Collections, Princeton University Libraries. ■*Previous publication:* none known. ■*Emendations and textual notes:* none.

■ 5 April [1900–1905] • Elizabeth Ellery Sedgwick Child • Cambridge, MA

■*Copy-text:* MS, George Santayana Papers (bMS Am 1922), by permission of the Houghton Library, Harvard University. ■*Previous publication:* none known. ■*Emendations and textual notes:* none.

■ Easter 1900 • William James • Cambridge, MA

■*Copy-text:* MS, George Santayana Papers (bMS Am 1092.9), by permission of the Houghton Library, Harvard University. ■*Previous publication: Letters,* 61–62; Ralph Barton Perry, *The Thought and Character of William James,* vol. 2 (Boston: Little, Brown, and Company, 1935), 320–21. ■*Emendations and textual notes:*

212.12	underestimate • under- / estimate
212.30	past • [*sic*]

■ 16 April [1900] • Charles Augustus Strong • Brookline, MA

■*Copy-text:* MS, Box 6, Folder 88, The Papers of Charles Augustus Strong, Rockefeller Archive Center, Sleepy Hollow, New York. ■*Previous publication:* none known. ■*Emendations and textual notes:* none.

■ 19 April 1900 • Charles Augustus Strong • Brookline, MA

■*Copy-text:* MS, Box 6, Folder 88, The Papers of Charles Augustus Strong, Rockefeller Archive Center, Sleepy Hollow, New York. ■*Previous publication:* none known. ■*Emendations and textual notes:*

215.3	b̸yet • ['y' *over* 'b']
215.30	non-human • non- / human

■ 12 May 1900 • William Bond Wheelwright • Cambridge, MA

■*Copy-text:* MS unlocated. Published version is copy-text. ■*Previous publication: The Harvard Lampoon Centennial Celebration, 1876–1973*, comp. Martin Kaplan (Boston: Little, Brown, and Company, 1973), 144, in facsimile. ■*Emendations and textual notes:*

216.20	vulgar, and • ['a' *over* ',']

■ 17 May 1900 • Nathaniel Wedd • Cambridge, MA

■*Copy-text:* MS, King's College Library, King's College, Cambridge. ■*Previous publication:* none known. ■*Emendations and textual notes:* none.

■ 29 May 1900 • William Roscoe Thayer • Cambridge, MA

■*Copy-text:* MS, The Papers of William Roscoe Thayer (bMS Am 1081), by permission of the Houghton Library, Harvard University. ■*Previous publication:* none known. ■*Emendations and textual notes:*

218.19	i̶s̶ are • ['are' *over* 'is']
218.24	metaphysics • meta- / physics
218.25	inadequete • [*sic*]

■ [July 1900?] • Nathaniel Wedd • London, England

■*Copy-text:* MS, King's College Library, King's College, Cambridge. ■*Previous publication:* none known. ■*Emendations and textual notes:* none.

■ 2 October 1900 • D. Appleton and Co. • Cambridge, MA

■*Copy-text:* MS, Special Collections, University of Southern California. ■*Previous publication:* none known. ■*Emendations and textual notes:* none.

■ 9 October 1900 • William Torrey Harris • Cambridge, MA

■*Copy-text:* MS, Special Collections, University of Southern California. ■*Previous publication:* none known. ■*Emendations and textual notes:*

220.13	trustworthy • trust- / worthy

■ [19 October 1900] • William Torrey Harris • Cambridge, MA

■*Copy-text:* MS, Special Collections, University of Southern California. ■*Previous publication:* none known. ■*Emendations and textual notes:* none.

■ 3 November 1900 • William Bond Wheelwright • Cambridge, MA

■*Copy-text:* MS unlocated. Published version is copy-text. ■*Previous publication: The Harvard Lampoon Centennial Celebration, 1876–1973,* comp. Martin Kaplan (Boston: Little, Brown, and Company, 1973), 144, in facsimile. ■*Emendations and textual notes:*

221.11	Nov. *1*3, • ['3' *over* '1']
221.13	tomorrow • to- / morrow

■ 9 November 1900 • Anna Boynton Thompson • Cambridge, MA

■*Copy-text:* MS, Anna Boynton Thompson Papers, Schlesinger Library, Radcliffe College, Cambridge, Massachusetts. ■*Previous publication:* none known. ■*Emendations and textual notes:*

222.11	a piece • [*sic*]

■ 12 November 1900 • Anna Boynton Thompson • Cambridge, MA

■*Copy-text:* MS, Anna Boynton Thompson Papers, Schlesinger Library, Radcliffe College, Cambridge, Massachusetts. ■*Previous publication:* none known. ■*Emendations and textual notes:*

223.7	like. ₐand • [*sic*]
223.10	whenever • when- / ever
223.11	Seminary • [*sic*]
223.16	Bonitz' • [*sic*]
223.18	if is • ['s' *over* 'f']

■ 3 December 1900 • Charles Scribner's Sons • Cambridge, MA

■*Copy-text:* MS, Author Files I, Box 130 of the Scribner Archives, Manuscripts Division, Department of Rare Books and Special Collections, Princeton University Libraries. ■*Previous publication:* none known. ■*Emendations and textual notes:* none.

■ 10 February 1901 • Charles Scribner's Sons • Cambridge, MA

■*Copy-text:* MS, Author Files I, Box 130 of the Scribner Archives, Manuscripts Division, Department of Rare Books and Special Collections, Princeton University Libraries. ■*Previous publication:* none known. ■*Emendations and textual notes:* none.

■ 16 April 1901 • James Edwin Creighton • New York, New York

■*Copy-text:* MS, Creighton Club Records (#3887), Division of Rare and Manuscript Collections, Cornell University Library. ■*Previous publication:* none known. ■*Emendations and textual notes:* none.

■ [Spring 1901 or 1902?] • Harry Morgan Ayres • [Cambridge, MA?]

■*Copy-text:* MS postcard, collection of John W. Lango, New York. ■*Previous publication:* none known. ■*Emendations and textual notes:* none.

■ [June 1901?] • Alice Freeman Palmer • Cambridge, MA

■*Copy-text:* MS, Wellesley College Library, Special Collections. ■*Previous publication:* none known. ■*Emendations and textual notes:* none.

■ 12 June 1901 • Charles Scribner's Sons • Cambridge, MA

■*Copy-text:* MS, Author Files I, Box 130 of the Scribner Archives, Manuscripts Division, Department of Rare Books and Special Collections, Princeton University Libraries. ■*Previous publication:* none known. ■*Emendations and textual notes:*

227.4	₵Messrs • ['M' *over* 'C']
227.12	Spen₵cer • ['c' *over* 's'] [*sic*]

■ [20 June 1901] • William Roscoe Thayer • Cambridge, MA

■*Copy-text:* MS, The Papers of William Roscoe Thayer (bMS Am 1081), by permission of the Houghton Library, Harvard University. ■*Previous publication:* none known. ■*Emendations and textual notes:* none.

■ 20 June 1901 • Charles Scribner's Sons • Cambridge, MA

■*Copy-text:* MS, Author Files I, Box 130 of the Scribner Archives, Manuscripts Division, Department of Rare Books and Special Collections, Princeton University Libraries. ■*Previous publication:* none known. ■*Emendations and textual notes:*

228.17	ʃ20 • ['2' *over* '1']

■ 25 June 1901 • William Roscoe Thayer • Cambridge, MA

■*Copy-text:* MS, The Papers of William Roscoe Thayer (bMS Am 1081), by permission of the Houghton Library, Harvard University. ■*Previous publication:* none known. ■*Emendations and textual notes:* none.

■ [c. 25 June 1901] • Charles Scribner's Sons • Cambridge, MA

■*Copy-text:* MS, Author Files I, Box 130 of the Scribner Archives, Manuscripts Division, Department of Rare Books and Special Collections, Princeton University Libraries. ■*Previous publication:* none known. ■*Emendations and textual notes:*

230.18   ~~two~~ first ˄two˄ • [*transposition by Santayana*]

■ 26 June 1901 • Charles Scribner's Sons • Cambridge, MA

■*Copy-text:* MS, Author Files I, Box 130 of the Scribner Archives, Manuscripts Division, Department of Rare Books and Special Collections, Princeton University Libraries. ■*Previous publication:* none known. ■*Emendations and textual notes:*

231.4   Scribners • [*sic*]

■ 29 June 1901 [*postmark*] • William Crary Brownell • New York, New York

■*Copy-text:* MS postcard, Author Files I, Box 130 of the Scribner Archives, Manuscripts Division, Department of Rare Books and Special Collections, Princeton University Libraries. ■*Previous publication:* none known. ■*Emendations and textual notes:* none.

■ 17 July 1901 • Susan Sturgis de Sastre • Oxford, England

■*Copy-text:* MS, George Santayana Collection (#6947), Clifton Waller Barrett Library, Special Collections Department, University of Virginia Library. ■*Previous publication:* none known. ■*Emendations and textual notes:*

232.15   ~~here~~ hear • ['ar' *over* 're']
232.16   anything • any- / thing
233.6–7   to you affectionate • [*sic*]

■ 19 July 1901 • Charles Scribner's Sons • Oxford, England

■*Copy-text:* MS, Author Files I, Box 130 of the Scribner Archives, Manuscripts Division, Department of Rare Books and Special Collections, Princeton University Libraries. ■*Previous publication:* none known. ■*Emendations and textual notes:* none.

■ 21 July 1901 • James Edwin Creighton • Oxford, England

■*Copy-text:* MS, Creighton Club Records (#3887), Division of Rare and Manuscript Collections, Cornell University Library. ■*Previous publication:* none known. ■*Emendations and textual notes:*

234.11   ɼReview • ['R' *over* 'r']

■ 24 July [1901] • William Archer • Oxford, England

■*Copy-text:* MS, 45295, f. 44, Department of Manuscripts, The British Library, London. ■*Previous publication:* none known. ■*Emendations and textual notes:* none.

■ 13 August 1901 • Susan Sturgis de Sastre • Oxford, England

■*Copy-text:* MS, George Santayana Collection (#6947), Clifton Waller Barrett Library, Special Collections Department, University of Virginia Library. ■*Previous publication: Letters,* 63. ■*Emendations and textual notes:*

235.22	gentleman • gentle- / man
235.26	self-conscious • self- / conscious

■ 28 August 1901 • Charles Scribner's Sons • Oxford, England

■*Copy-text:* MS, Author Files I, Box 130 of the Scribner Archives, Manuscripts Division, Department of Rare Books and Special Collections, Princeton University Libraries. ■*Previous publication:* none known. ■*Emendations and textual notes:* none.

■ 15 September 1901 • Susan Sturgis de Sastre • Oxford, England

■*Copy-text:* MS, George Santayana Collection (#6947), Clifton Waller Barrett Library, Special Collections Department, University of Virginia Library. ■*Previous publication:* none known. ■*Emendations and textual notes:*

237.6	Buda-Pesth • [*sic*]
237.23	Rooseveldt • [*sic*]
237.26	<u>Kronprinz</u> • <u>Kron</u>- / <u>prinz</u>
237.28	except • [*sic*]

■ 1 October 1901 • Anna Boynton Thompson • Cambridge, MA

■*Copy-text:* MS, Anna Boynton Thompson Papers, Schlesinger Library, Radcliffe College, Cambridge, Massachusetts. ■*Previous publication:* none known. ■*Emendations and textual notes:*

238.7	seminary • [*sic*]
238.11	somewhat • some- / what
238.20	Seminary • [*sic*]

■ 26 October 1901 • Charles Scribner's Sons • Cambridge, MA

■*Copy-text:* MS, Author Files I, Box 130 of the Scribner Archives, Manuscripts Division, Department of Rare Books and Special Collections, Princeton University Libraries. ■*Previous publication:* none known. ■*Emendations and textual notes:* none.

■ 28 October 1901 [*postmark*] • Anna Boynton Thompson • Cambridge, MA
■*Copy-text:* MS, Anna Boynton Thompson Papers, Schlesinger Library, Radcliffe College, Cambridge, Massachusetts. ■*Previous publication:* none known. ■*Emendations and textual notes:* none.

■ 29 October 1901 • Charles Scribner's Sons • Cambridge, MA
■*Copy-text:* Telegram, Author Files I, Box 130 of the Scribner Archives, Manuscripts Division, Department of Rare Books and Special Collections, Princeton University Libraries. ■*Previous publication:* none known. ■*Emendations and textual notes:*

240.5	Santayna • [*sic*]

■ 30 October 1901 • Charles Scribner's Sons • Cambridge, MA
■*Copy-text:* MS, Author Files I, Box 130 of the Scribner Archives, Manuscripts Division, Department of Rare Books and Special Collections, Princeton University Libraries. ■*Previous publication:* none known. ■*Emendations and textual notes:*

240.21	straightforward • straight- / forward
240.28	~~the~~ those ˄in the˄ ~~following~~ ˄enclosed˄ • ['ose' *over* 'e'; 'in the' *in margin*; 'enclosed' *above* 'following']
241.7	V̶very • ['v' *over* 'V']

■ 31 October 1901 • Anna Boynton Thompson • Cambridge, MA
■*Copy-text:* MS, Anna Boynton Thompson Papers, Schlesinger Library, Radcliffe College, Cambridge, Massachusetts. ■*Previous publication:* none known. ■*Emendations and textual notes:*

242.7	understand • under- / stand
242.14	~~it~~ them • ['them' *over* 'it']

■ 4 November 1901 • Charles Scribner's Sons • Cambridge, MA
■*Copy-text:* MS, Author Files I, Box 130 of the Scribner Archives, Manuscripts Division, Department of Rare Books and Special Collections, Princeton University Libraries. ■*Previous publication:* none known. ■*Emendations and textual notes:*

243.11	something • some- / thing
243.18	1$\cancel{3}$6 • ['6' *over* '3']
243.20	˄57˄ ~~22~~ ˄57˄ • ['57' *over* '22'; *then struck through and* '57' *written in left margin*]
243.29	177 6 • [*sic*] [*should read* '6 from bottom']
243.29	perve$\cancel{s}$rsity • ['rs' *over* 's']

■ 28 November 1901 • Lawrence Smith Butler • Cambridge, MA

■*Copy-text:* MS, The University Club Library, New York. ■*Previous publication:* *Letters,* 64–65. ■*Emendations and textual notes:*

245.1   Quartier latin • [*sic*]
245.10   dining room • dining / room

■ 4 December 1901 • Charles Scribner's Sons • Cambridge, MA

■*Copy-text:* MS, Author Files I, Box 130 of the Scribner Archives, Manuscripts Division, Department of Rare Books and Special Collections, Princeton University Libraries. ■*Previous publication:* none known. ■*Emendations and textual notes:* none.

■ 20 December 1901 • Charles Augustus Strong • Cambridge, MA

■*Copy-text:* MS, Box 6, Folder 88, The Papers of Charles Augustus Strong, Rockefeller Archive Center, Sleepy Hollow, New York. ■*Previous publication:* none known. ■*Emendations and textual notes:* none.

■ 20 December 1901 • Anna Boynton Thompson • Cambridge, MA

■*Copy-text:* MS, Anna Boynton Thompson Papers, Schlesinger Library, Radcliffe College, Cambridge, Massachusetts. ■*Previous publication:* none known. ■*Emendations and textual notes:*

247.10   releiieves • ['ie' *over* 'ei']
247.13   however • how- / ever

■ 21 December 1901 • Lawrence Smith Butler • Cambridge, MA

■*Copy-text:* MS, The University Club Library, New York. ■*Previous publication:* *Letters,* 65–66. ■*Emendations and textual notes:* none.

■ [1902–June 1904] • William Cameron Forbes • Cambridge, MA

■*Copy-text:* MS, George Santayana Papers (bMS Am 1364), by permission of the Houghton Library, Harvard University. ■*Previous publication:* none known. ■*Emendations and textual notes:* none.

■ 10 February 1902 • Charles Scribner's Sons • Cambridge, MA

■*Copy-text:* MS, Author Files I, Box 130 of the Scribner Archives, Manuscripts Division, Department of Rare Books and Special Collections, Princeton University Libraries. ■*Previous publication:* none known. ■*Emendations and textual notes:* none.

■ 22 February 1902 • Charles Scribner's Sons • Cambridge, MA

■ *Copy-text:* MS, Author Files I, Box 130 of the Scribner Archives, Manuscripts Division, Department of Rare Books and Special Collections, Princeton University Libraries. ■ *Previous publication:* none known. ■ *Emendations and textual notes:*

250.18	undertake • under- / take
250.27	reprint • re- / print

■ 7 April [1902?] • Isabella Stewart Gardner • Brookline, MA

■ *Copy-text:* MS, Isabella Stewart Gardner Museum Archives, Boston. ■ *Previous publication:* none known. ■ *Emendations and textual notes:*

251.14	wastepaper-basket • waste- / paper-basket

■ 21 April 1902 • Charles Scribner's Sons • Cambridge, MA

■ *Copy-text:* MS, Author Files I, Box 130 of the Scribner Archives, Manuscripts Division, Department of Rare Books and Special Collections, Princeton University Libraries. ■ *Previous publication:* none known. ■ *Emendations and textual notes:* none.

■ 29 May 1902 • Charles William Eliot • Cambridge, MA

■ *Copy-text:* MS, C. W. Eliot Papers, courtesy of the Harvard University Archives. ■ *Previous publication:* none known. ■ *Emendations and textual notes:* none.

■ 1 June 1902 • Charles Francis Mason • Cambridge, MA

■ *Copy-text:* MS, C. W. Eliot Papers, courtesy of the Harvard University Archives. ■ *Previous publication:* none known. ■ *Emendations and textual notes:* none.

■ 3 July 1902 • Benjamin Rand • Ávila, Spain

■ *Copy-text:* MS, C. W. Eliot Papers, courtesy of the Harvard University Archives. ■ *Previous publication:* none known. ■ *Emendations and textual notes:* none.

■ 1 December 1902 • Charles Scribner's Sons • Cambridge, MA

■ *Copy-text:* MS, William Crary Brownell Papers (Box 1, Folder 15), Amherst College Archives. ■ *Previous publication:* none known. ■ *Emendations and textual notes:*

254.13	anything • any- / thing

■ 6 February 1903 • Hugo Münsterberg • Cambridge, MA

■ *Copy-text:* MS, Department of Rare Books and Manuscripts, by courtesy of the Trustees of the Boston Public Library. ■ *Previous publication:* none known. ■ *Emendations and textual notes:*

255.9   everywhere • every- / where

■ **23 February 1903** • Sally Fairchild • Cambridge, MA
■*Copy-text:* MS, George Santayana Papers (bMS Am 1542), by permission of the Houghton Library, Harvard University. ■*Previous publication:* none known. ■*Emendations and textual notes:*

255.24   i̶t̶ they • ['they' *over* 'it']
255.24   to when • [*sic*]

■ **20 March 1903** • Horace Meyer Kallen • Cambridge, MA
■*Copy-text:* MS, American Jewish Archives, Cincinnati, Ohio. ■*Previous publication:* none known. ■*Emendations and textual notes:*

256.8   n̶i̶by • ['by' *over* 'ni']

■ **6 April 1903** • John Henry Wright • Cambridge, MA
■*Copy-text:* MS, Ohio Historical Society, Columbus. ■*Previous publication:* none known. ■*Emendations and textual notes:*

257.1   Fellowship • Fellow- / ship

■ **13 August 1903** • Susan Sturgis de Sastre • Oxford, England
■*Copy-text:* MS postcard, collection of Paloma Sanchez Sastre, Madrid, Spain. ■*Previous publication:* none known. ■*Emendations and textual notes:*

257.9   targeta • [*sic*]

■ **26 October 1903** [*postmark*] • The Mayflower Club • Cambridge, MA
■*Copy-text:* MS postcard, George Santayana Papers (bMS Lowell 19.2), by permission of the Houghton Library, Harvard University. ■*Previous publication:* none known. ■*Emendations and textual notes:* none.

■ **20 November 1903** • Harry Norman Gardiner • Cambridge, MA
■*Copy-text:* MS, Smith College Archives. ■*Previous publication:* none known. ■*Emendations and textual notes:* none.

■ **5 December 1903** • Horace Meyer Kallen • Cambridge, MA
■*Copy-text:* MS, American Jewish Archives, Cincinnati, Ohio. ■*Previous publication:* none known. ■*Emendations and textual notes:*

259.11   York and the • York and / and the

■ 16 December 1903 • Frederick James Eugene Woodbridge • Cambridge, MA
■ *Copy-text:* MS, *Journal of Philosophy* Records, Rare Book and Manuscript Library, Columbia University. ■ *Previous publication:* none known. ■ *Emendations and textual notes:* none.

■ 19 February 1904 • Jessie Belle Rittenhouse • Cambridge, MA
■ *Copy-text:* MS, Rollins College, Department of Archives and Special Collections. ■ *Previous publication:* none known. ■ *Emendations and textual notes:*

261.6   handwriting • hand- / writing
261.10   Scribners • [*sic*]

■ 2 March 1904 • Jessie Belle Rittenhouse • Cambridge, MA
■ *Copy-text:* MS, Rollins College, Department of Archives and Special Collections. ■ *Previous publication:* none known. ■ *Emendations and textual notes:*

262.5   19896 • ['8' *over* '9']

■ 7 March 1904 • Frederick James Eugene Woodbridge • Cambridge, MA
■ *Copy-text:* MS, *Journal of Philosophy* Records, Rare Book and Manuscript Library, Columbia University. ■ *Previous publication:* none known. ■ *Emendations and textual notes:*

263.8   "Philosophy of • [*sic*]

■ 2 May 1904 • Hugo Münsterberg • Cambridge, MA
■ *Copy-text:* MS, Department of Rare Books and Manuscripts, by courtesy of the Trustees of the Boston Public Library. ■ *Previous publication:* none known. ■ *Emendations and textual notes:* none.

■ 25 May 1904 • Charles Scribner's Sons • Cambridge, MA
■ *Copy-text:* MS, Author Files I, Box 130 of the Scribner Archives, Manuscripts Division, Department of Rare Books and Special Collections, Princeton University Libraries. ■ *Previous publication:* none known. ■ *Emendations and textual notes:* none.

■ [June or July 1904?] • Isabella Stewart Gardner • Cambridge, MA
■ *Copy-text:* MS, Isabella Stewart Gardner Museum Archives, Boston. ■ *Previous publication:* none known. ■ *Emendations and textual notes:* none.

■ 19 June 1904 • Charles Scribner's Sons • Cambridge, MA
■ *Copy-text:* MS, Author Files I, Box 130 of the Scribner Archives, Manuscripts Division, Department of Rare Books and Special Collections, Princeton

University Libraries. ■*Previous publication:* none known. ■*Emendations and textual notes:*

267.12	shorte∉r • ['r' *over* 'd']
267.16	~~This~~ That • ['at' *over* 'is']

■ 20 June 1904 • Jerome Davis Greene • Cambridge, MA

■*Copy-text:* MS, George Santayana Papers, by permission of the Houghton Library, Harvard University. ■*Previous publication:* none known. ■*Emendations and textual notes:* none.

■ 18 July 1904 • Charles Scribner's Sons • Cambridge, MA

■*Copy-text:* MS postcard, Author Files I, Box 130 of the Scribner Archives, Manuscripts Division, Department of Rare Books and Special Collections, Princeton University Libraries. ■*Previous publication:* none known. ■*Emendations and textual notes:* none.

■ 25 July 1904 • Celedonio Sastre Serrano • Plymouth, England

■*Copy-text:* MS postcard, collection of Paloma Sanchez Sastre, Madrid, Spain. ■*Previous publication:* none known. ■*Emendations and textual notes:* none.

■ [August 1904] • Susan Sturgis de Sastre • Ostende, Belgium

■*Copy-text:* MS postcard, collection of Paloma Sanchez Sastre, Madrid, Spain. ■*Previous publication:* none known. ■*Emendations and textual notes:*

269.2	~~in~~ my • ['my' *over* 'in']

■ 20 August 1904 • Celedonio Sastre Serrano • [Cologne, Germany?]

■*Copy-text:* MS, collection of Señora Eduardo Sastre Martín, Madrid, Spain. ■*Previous publication:* none known. ■*Emendations and textual notes:*

269.10	agradecéría • [*sic*]

■ 27 August 1904 • Celedonio Sastre Serrano • Heidelberg, Germany

■*Copy-text:* MS, collection of Señora Eduardo Sastre Martín, Madrid, Spain. ■*Previous publication:* none known. ■*Emendations and textual notes:*

270.11	poc∉os • ['o' *over* 'a']

■ 9 September 1904 • Charles Scribner's Sons • Paris, France

■*Copy-text:* MS, Author Files I, Box 130 of the Scribner Archives, Manuscripts Division, Department of Rare Books and Special Collections, Princeton University Libraries. ■*Previous publication:* none known. ■*Emendations and textual notes:*

271.2	Scribners' • [*sic*]
271.11	throughout • through- / out
271.20	page-proof • page- / proof

■ 17 September 1904 • Lawrence Smith Butler • Ávila, Spain

■*Copy-text:* MS, The University Club Library, New York. ■*Previous publication:* none known. ■*Emendations and textual notes:*

272.9   ~~place~~ ₐtripₐ • ['trip' *above* '~~place~~']

■ 24 September 1904 • Charles Scribner's Sons • Ávila, Spain

■*Copy-text:* MS, Author Files I, Box 130 of the Scribner Archives, Manuscripts Division, Department of Rare Books and Special Collections, Princeton University Libraries. ■*Previous publication:* none known. ■*Emendations and textual notes:* none.

■ 21 October 1904 • Charles Scribner's Sons • Ávila, Spain

■*Copy-text:* MS, Author Files I, Box 130 of the Scribner Archives, Manuscripts Division, Department of Rare Books and Special Collections, Princeton University Libraries. ■*Previous publication:* none known. ■*Emendations and textual notes:* none.

■ 22 November 1904 • Goldsworthy Lowes Dickinson • Florence, Italy

■*Copy-text:* MS, King's College Library, King's College, Cambridge. ■*Previous publication:* none known. ■*Emendations and textual notes:*

275.8	points ~~only~~ become cogent ₐonlyₐ when • [*transposition by Santayana*]
275.9–10	forthright • forth- / right
275.12	however • how- / ever

■ 22 November 1904 • Charles Scribner's Sons • Florence, Italy

■*Copy-text:* MS, Author Files I, Box 130 of the Scribner Archives, Manuscripts Division, Department of Rare Books and Special Collections, Princeton University Libraries. ■*Previous publication:* none known. ■*Emendations and textual notes:* none.

■ 23 November [1904] • Susan Sturgis de Sastre • Rome, Italy

■*Copy-text:* MS postcard, collection of Paloma Sanchez Sastre, Madrid, Spain. ■*Previous publication:* none known. ■*Emendations and textual notes:* none.

■ 25 November 1904 • Mary Whitall Smith Berenson • Rome, Italy

■*Copy-text:* MS, Bernard Berenson Archive, Villa I Tatti, Harvard University Center for Italian Renaissance Studies, Florence Italy. ■*Previous publication:* none known. ■*Emendations and textual notes:*

277.10	uncivil • un- / civil
277.21	~~and~~ ∧we∧ • ['we' *above* '~~and~~']
277.28	outside • out- / side
277.30	ȼaught • ['a' *over* 'o']
277.33	resort Russian • [*sic*]
278.4	~~but~~ ∧as∧ • ['as' *above* '~~but~~']
278.8	Quattrocento • Quattro- / cento
278.8	ȴbehold • ['b' *over* 'l']
278.11	tea-rooms • tea- / rooms
278.15	shoe-strings • shoe- / strings
278.19	literateurs • [*sic*]
278.32	~~were~~ ∧met∧ • ['met' *above* '~~were~~']
278.36	~~but~~ ∧and∧ • ['and' *above* '~~but~~']
278.37	discretely • [*sic*]

■ 29 November 1904 • William James • Rome, Italy

■*Copy-text:* MS, George Santayana Papers (bMS Am 1092.9), by permission of the Houghton Library, Harvard University. ■*Previous publication: Letters*, 67–69; Ralph Barton Perry, *The Thought and Character of William James*, vol. 2 (Boston: Little, Brown, and Company, 1935), 396–97. ■*Emendations and textual notes:*

279.5	home-thoughts • home- / thoughts
279.9	with he • [*sic*]
280.8	~~there~~ their • ['ir' *over* 're']
280.24	~~have~~ ∧draw∧ • ['draw' *above* '~~have~~']
280.24–25	~~in~~ ∧from∧ • ['from' *above* '~~in~~']
280.32	eight-inch • eight- / inch
280.39 and 281.1	panpsychism • pan- / psychism

■ 3 December 1904 • Benjamin Apthorp Gould Fuller • Rome, Italy

■*Copy-text:* MS, George Santayana Papers (bMS Am 1603.3), by permission of the Houghton Library, Harvard University. ■*Previous publication: Letters*, 69–70. ■*Emendations and textual notes:*

282.15	rehabilȴitation • ['i' *over* 'a']
282.19	~~it~~ them • ['them' *over* 'it']

■ 3 December 1904 • Charles Scribner's Sons • Rome, Italy

■*Copy-text:* MS, Author Files I, Box 130 of the Scribner Archives, Manuscripts Division, Department of Rare Books and Special Collections, Princeton

University Libraries. ■*Previous publication:* none known. ■*Emendations and textual notes:*

283.8 ~~with~~ in which • ['in' *over erased* 'with']

■ 8 December 1904 • Mary Whitall Smith Berenson • Rome, Italy
■*Copy-Text:* MS, H. W. Smith Papers, Lilly Library, Indiana University, Bloomington. ■*Previous publication:* none known. ■*Emendations and textual notes:* none.

■ 8 December 1904 • Charles Scribner's Sons • Rome, Italy
■*Copy-text:* MS, Author Files I, Box 130 of the Scribner Archives, Manuscripts Division, Department of Rare Books and Special Collections, Princeton University Libraries. ■*Previous publication:* none known. ■*Emendations and textual notes:* none.

■ 10 December 1904 • Mary Whitall Smith Berenson • Rome, Italy
■*Copy-text:* MS, Bernard Berenson Archive, Villa I Tatti, Harvard University Center for Italian Renaissance Studies, Florence, Italy. ■*Previous publication:* none known. ■*Emendations and textual notes:*

286.32   forehead • fore- / head
286.32   camel$-loads • ['-' *over* 's']
287.5   camel-loads • camel- / loads
287.7   ~~his~~ with • ['with' *over* 'his']
287.33   ~~noisesome~~ noisome • ['ome' *over* 'esome']
287.35   would liked a second help. • [*sic*]
288.3   remain$eth ['eth' *over* 's']
288.18   ~~our~~ ∧other∧ • ['other' *above* '~~our~~']
288.22   ₿We • ['W' *over* 'B']
288.25   foresight • fore- / sight
288.27   anywhere • any- / where
288.37   nevertheless • neverthe- / less
289.5   ~~Kow~~ Knowest • ['no' *over* 'ow']
289.9   ~~this~~ their • ['eir' *over* 'is']

■ 1 January 1905 • Celedonio Sastre Serrano • Port Said, Egypt
■*Copy-text:* MS postcard, collection of Paloma Sanchez Sastre, Madrid, Spain. ■*Previous publication:* none known. ■*Emendations and textual notes:* none.

■ 5 January 1905 • James Hazen Hyde • Cairo, Egypt
■*Copy-text:* MS unlocated. A typescript, courtesy of the Harvard University Archives, is copy-text. ■*Previous publication:* none known. ■*Emendations and textual notes:*

290.5	^c/o • c/o
290.24	foreigness • [*sic*]
291.20	GSantayana • G. Santayana

■ 11 January [1905] • Benjamin Apthorp Gould Fuller • Luxor, Egypt
■*Copy-text:* MS, George Santayana Papers (bMS Am 1603.3), by permission of the Houghton Library, Harvard University. ■*Previous publication: Letters*, 66–67, 'To A. S. FULLER January 11TH 1904'. ■*Emendations and textual notes:*

291.24	1904 • [*sic*]
292.5	labour-saving-machines • labour- / saving-machines
292.5	anything • any- / thing

■ 13 January [1905] • Celedonio Sastre Serrano • Luxor, Egypt
■*Copy-text:* MS postcard, collection of Paloma Sanchez Sastre, Madrid, Spain. ■*Previous publication:* none known. ■*Emendations and textual notes:* none.

■ 25 January [1905] • Susan Sturgis de Sastre • Cairo, Egypt
■*Copy-text:* MS postcard, collection of Paloma Sanchez Sastre, Madrid, Spain. ■*Previous publication:* none known. ■*Emendations and textual notes:* none.

■ 25 January 1905 • Charles Scribner's Sons • Cairo, Egypt
■*Copy-text:* MS, Author Files I, Box 130 of the Scribner Archives, Manuscripts Division, Department of Rare Books and Special Collections, Princeton University Libraries. ■*Previous publication:* none known. ■*Emendations and textual notes:* none.

■ 4 February [1905] • Susan Sturgis de Sastre • Tel Aviv-Yafo, Israel
■*Copy-text:* MS postcard, collection of Paloma Sanchez Sastre, Madrid, Spain. ■*Previous publication:* none known. ■*Emendations and textual notes:* none.

■ 10 February [1905] • Susan Sturgis de Sastre • Jerusalem, Israel
■*Copy-text:* MS postcard, collection of Paloma Sanchez Sastre, Madrid, Spain. ■*Previous publication:* none known. ■*Emendations and textual notes:* none.

■ 17 February [1905] • Susan Sturgis de Sastre • Jerusalem, Israel
■*Copy-text:* MS, George Santayana Collection (#6947), Clifton Waller Barrett Library, Special Collections Department, University of Virginia Library. ■*Previous publication: Letters*, 71–73. ■*Emendations and textual notes:*

294.13	1904 • [*sic*]
295.3 and 4	Beyrout • [*sic*]

295.22	bran-new • [*sic*]
295.24	hostlery • [*sic*]
295.29	Ara₌ᵢ₌bic • [*sic*]
295.30	Beduins • [*sic*]
296.15	ⱥmosque • ['m' *over* 'a']

■ 20 February [1905] • Susan Sturgis de Sastre • Baalbek, Lebanon

■*Copy-text:* MS postcard, collection of Paloma Sanchez Sastre, Madrid, Spain. ■*Previous publication:* none known. ■*Emendations and textual notes:*

297.4	Beyrout • [*sic*]

■ 25 February 1905 [*postmark*] • Susan Sturgis de Sastre • Beirut, Lebanon

■*Copy-text:* MS postcard, collection of Paloma Sanchez Sastre, Madrid, Spain. ■*Previous publication:* none known. ■*Emendations and textual notes:*

297.13	photographs • photo- / graphs

■ 27 February [1905] • [Susan Sturgis de Sastre] • Vathi, Samos, Greece

■*Copy-text:* MS postcard, collection of Paloma Sanchez Sastre, Madrid, Spain. ■*Previous publication:* none known. ■*Emendations and textual notes:*

297.16	1904 • [*sic*]
297.19	thirty six • [*sic*]
297.20	Italian-like • Italian- / like
298.7	suzerainty₌– • ['–' *over* ',']

■ 3 March 1905 • Wallace de Groot Cecil Rice • Athens, Greece

■*Copy-text:* MS, The Newberry Library, Chicago. ■*Previous publication:* none known. ■*Emendations and textual notes:* none.

■ 3 March [1905] • Susan Sturgis de Sastre • Athens, Greece

■*Copy-text:* MS postcard, collection of Paloma Sanchez Sastre, Madrid, Spain. ■*Previous publication:* none known. ■*Emendations and textual notes:* none

■ 4 March 1905 • William James • Athens, Greece

■*Copy-text:* MS, George Santayana Papers (bMS Am 1092.9), by permission of the Houghton Library, Harvard University. ■*Previous publication: Letters,* 73–74. ■*Emendations and textual notes:*

300.7	S̶c̶o̶o • ['o' *over* 'co']
300.8	too • [*sic*]

■ 30 March 1905 • Charles Scribner's Sons • Athens, Greece

■*Copy-text:* MS, Author Files I, Box 130 of the Scribner Archives, Manuscripts Division, Department of Rare Books and Special Collections, Princeton University Libraries. ■*Previous publication:* none known. ■*Emendations and textual notes:* none.

■ 15 April 1905 • Charles Scribner's Sons • Athens, Greece

■*Copy-text:* MS, Author Files I, Box 130 of the Scribner Archives, Manuscripts Division, Department of Rare Books and Special Collections, Princeton University Libraries. ■*Previous publication:* none known. ■*Emendations and textual notes:* none.

■ [Spring 1905] • Susan Sturgis de Sastre • Corinth, Greece

■*Copy-text:* MS postcard, collection of Paloma Sanchez Sastre, Madrid, Spain. ■*Previous publication:* none known. ■*Emendations and textual notes:* none.

■ 29 April [1905] • [Susan Sturgis de Sastre] • Nauplia, Greece

■*Copy-text:* MS postcard, collection of Paloma Sanchez Sastre, Madrid, Spain. ■*Previous publication:* none known. ■*Emendations and textual notes:*

303.15   anything • any- / thing

■ 19 May [1905] • Susan Sturgis de Sastre • Constantinople, Turkey

■*Copy-text:* MS postcard, collection of Paloma Sanchez Sastre, Madrid, Spain. ■*Previous publication:* none known. ■*Emendations and textual notes:*

303.22   Buda-Pesth • [*sic*]

■ 27 May 1905 [*postmark*] • Susan Sturgis de Sastre • Nürnberg, Germany

■*Copy-text:* MS postcard, collection of Paloma Sanchez Sastre, Madrid, Spain. ■*Previous publication:* none known. ■*Emendations and textual notes:* none.

■ 5 June 1905 • Charles Eliot Norton • London, England

■*Copy-text:* MS, C. E. Norton Papers (bMS Am 1088), by permission of the Houghton Library, Harvard University. ■*Previous publication: Letters,* 75. ■*Emendations and textual notes:*

304.14   however • how- / ever
304.15   cannot • can- / not

■ 20 June 1905 • Charles Augustus Strong • Richmond, England

■*Copy-text:* MS, Box 6, Folder 89, The Papers of Charles Augustus Strong, Rockefeller Archive Center, Sleepy Hollow, New York. ■*Previous publication:* none known. ■*Emendations and textual notes:*

305.13	~~see~~ ∧look at∧ • ['look at' *above* '~~see~~']
305.16	Philosophy of Mathematics • [*sic*]
305.16–17	position/∧, which I agree with.∧ • [',' *over* '.' *and* 'I agree with.' *in margin*]
305.18	seems • [*sic*]
306.18	~~proper to~~ ∧inherent in∧ • ['inherent in' *above* '~~proper to~~']
306.20	cannot • can- / not
306.35	of loudest • [*sic*]
307.1	philosophers/ do. • ['d' *over* '.']

■ 23 June 1905 • Charles William Eliot • Richmond, England

■*Copy-text:* MS, C. W. Eliot Papers, courtesy of the Harvard University Archives. ■*Previous publication:* none known. ■*Emendations and textual notes:*

308.14	~~from~~ for • ['or' *over* 'rom']

■ 25 June 1905 • Robert Calverley Trevelyan • Richmond, England

■*Copy-text:* MS, courtesy of the Master and Fellows, Trinity College, Cambridge. ■*Previous publication:* none known. ■*Emendations and textual notes:*

308.31	sinc~~re~~ere • ['ere' *over* 're']
309.11	school-boy's • school- / boy's

■ 28 June [1905] • Susan Sturgis de Sastre • Box Hill, England

■*Copy-text:* MS postcard, collection of Paloma Sanchez Sastre, Madrid, Spain. ■*Previous publication:* none known. ■*Emendations and textual notes:*

309.27	somewhat • some- / what
310.5	quiʇet • ['e' *over* 't']
310.6	motor-car • motor- / car
310.8	Deep Dene • [*sic*]
310.24	matter-is-mind • matter-is- / mind

■ 28 June 1905 • Charles Scribner's Sons • Box Hill, England

■*Copy-text:* MS, Author Files I, Box 130 of the Scribner Archives, Manuscripts Division, Department of Rare Books and Special Collections, Princeton University Libraries. ■*Previous publication:* none known. ■*Emendations and textual notes:* none.

■ **1 July 1905** • Charles Scribner's Sons • [Box Hill, England]

■*Copy-text:* MS, Author Files I, Box 130 of the Scribner Archives, Manuscripts Division, Department of Rare Books and Special Collections, Princeton University Libraries. ■*Previous publication:* none known. ■*Emendations and textual notes:* none.

■ **20 July 1905** • Charles Augustus Strong • Box Hill, England

■*Copy-text:* MS, Box 6, Folder 89, The Papers of Charles Augustus Strong, Rockefeller Archive Center, Sleepy Hollow, New York. ■*Previous publication:* none known. ■*Emendations and textual notes:*

312.29	<u>villegiatures</u> comes • [*sic*]
313.22	mind-stuff • mind- / stuff
313.37	somewhat • some- / what

■ **26 July 1905** • Charles Augustus Strong • Box Hill, England

■*Copy-text:* MS, Box 6, Folder 89, The Papers of Charles Augustus Strong, Rockefeller Archive Center, Sleepy Hollow, New York. ■*Previous publication:* none known. ■*Emendations and textual notes:*

314.17	~~is~~ ∧would be∧ • ['would be' *above* '~~is~~']
314.17	misreprent • [*sic*]
314.23	mind-stuff • mind- / stuff
314.24	part$\cancel{s}$ners • ['n' *over* 's']
314.31	within mind-stuff • within mind- / stuff
315.4	Bergson, (~~tr~~whom • ['(' *over* ',' *and* 'w' *over* 'tr']
315.9–10	~~containing and~~ ∧in flux,∧ • ['in flux,' *above* '~~containing and~~']
315.10–11	~~as well as~~ ∧and not merely∧ • ['and not merely' *above* '~~as well as~~']
315.13	~~feeling~~ ∧spirit∧ • ['spirit' *above* '~~feeling~~']
315.15	expressi~~on~~ve • ['ve' *over* 'on']

■ **27 July 1905** • William James • Box Hill, England

■*Copy-text:* MS, George Santayana Papers (bMS Am 1092.9), by permission of the Houghton Library, Harvard University. ■*Previous publication: Letters,* 76–77. ■*Emendations and textual notes:* none.

■ **14 August 1905** • Charles Augustus Strong • Volksdorf, Germany

■*Copy-text:* MS, Box 6, Folder 89, The Papers of Charles Augustus Strong, Rockefeller Archive Center, Sleepy Hollow, New York. ■*Previous publication:* none known. ■*Emendations and textual notes:*

317.24	waistcoat • waist- / coat
317.25	many-buttoned • many- / buttoned

■ 21 August 1905 • Charles Scribner's Sons • Volksdorf, Germany

■*Copy-text:* MS, Author Files I, Box 130 of the Scribner Archives, Manuscripts Division, Department of Rare Books and Special Collections, Princeton University Libraries. ■*Previous publication:* none known. ■*Emendations and textual notes:*

| 318.23 | s̸very • ['v' *over* 's'] |
| 319.12 | Settiɲgnano • ['g' *over* 'n'] |

■ [29 August 1905] • Charles Augustus Strong • Volksdorf, Germany

■*Copy-text:* MS, Box 6, Folder 89, The Papers of Charles Augustus Strong, Rockefeller Archive Center, Sleepy Hollow, New York. ■*Previous publication:* none known. ■*Emendations and textual notes:*

| 319.31 | castel • [*sic*] |

■ 3 September [1905] • Susan Sturgis de Sastre • Compiègne, France

■*Copy-text:* MS postcard, collection of Paloma Sanchez Sastre, Madrid, Spain. ■*Previous publication:* none known. ■*Emendations and textual notes:* none.

■ 9 September 1905 • Charles Scribner's Sons • Compiègne, France

■*Copy-text:* MS, Author Files I, Box 130 of the Scribner Archives, Manuscripts Division, Department of Rare Books and Special Collections, Princeton University Libraries. ■*Previous publication:* none known. ■*Emendations and textual notes:* none.

■ 14 September [1905] • Susan Sturgis de Sastre • Compiègne, France

■*Copy-text:* MS postcard, collection of Paloma Sanchez Sastre, Madrid, Spain. ■*Previous publication:* none known. ■*Emendations and textual notes:* none.

■ 26 September 1905 [*postmark*] • Susan Sturgis de Sastre • Paris, France

■*Copy-text:* MS postcard, collection of Paloma Sanchez Sastre, Madrid, Spain. ■*Previous publication:* none known. ■*Emendations and textual notes:*

| 321.10 | bull-fight • bull- / fight |

■ 26 September 1905 • Charles Scribner's Sons • Paris, France

■*Copy-text:* MS, Author Files I, Box 130 of the Scribner Archives, Manuscripts Division, Department of Rare Books and Special Collections, Princeton University Libraries. ■*Previous publication:* none known. ■*Emendations and textual notes:*

| 322.8 | tomorrow • to- / morrow |

■ 3 October [1905] • Charles Augustus Strong • Ávila, Spain

■*Copy-text:* MS, Box 6, Folder 89, The Papers of Charles Augustus Strong, Rockefeller Archive Center, Sleepy Hollow, New York. ■*Previous publication:* none known. ■*Emendations and textual notes:*

323.11	will makes • [*sic*]
323.35	mind-stuff • mind- / stuff

■ 5 October 1905 • Benjamin Apthorp Gould Fuller • Ávila, Spain

■*Copy-text:* MS, George Santayana Papers (bMS Am 1603.3), by permission of the Houghton Library, Harvard University. ■*Previous publication: Letters,* 77–78. ■*Emendations and textual notes:*

324.9	fly-leaf • fly- / leaf

■ 5 October 1905 • Charles Scribner's Sons • Ávila, Spain

■*Copy-text:* MS, Author Files I, Box 130 of the Scribner Archives, Manuscripts Division, Department of Rare Books and Special Collections, Princeton University Libraries. ■*Previous publication:* none known. ■*Emendations and textual notes:*

326.17	speciallisised • ['ise' *over* 'lis']

■ 11 October 1905 • Charles Scribner's Sons • Ávila, Spain

■*Copy-text:* MS, Author Files I, Box 130 of the Scribner Archives, Manuscripts Division, Department of Rare Books and Special Collections, Princeton University Libraries. ■*Previous publication:* none known. ■*Emendations and textual notes:*

327.8	sen*t*d • ['d' *over* 't']

■ 16 November 1905 [*postmark*] • Susan Sturgis de Sastre • Paris, France

■*Copy-text:* MS postcard, collection of Paloma Sanchez Sastre, Madrid, Spain. ■*Previous publication:* none known. ■*Emendations and textual notes:* none.

■ 5 December 1905 • William James • Paris, France

■*Copy-text:* MS, George Santayana Papers (bMS Am 1092.9), by permission of the Houghton Library, Harvard University. ■*Previous publication: Letters,* 78–80; Ralph Barton Perry, *The Thought and Character of William James,* vol. 2 (Boston: Little, Brown, and Company, 1935): 399–401. ■*Emendations and textual notes:*

328.18	everything • every- / thing
328.25	Nevertheless • Never- / theless
329.3	without • with- / out

■ 6 December 1905 • William James • Paris, France

■*Copy-text:* MS, George Santayana Papers (bMS Am 1092.9), by permission of the Houghton Library, Harvard University. ■*Previous publication: Letters*, 81–83; Ralph Barton Perry, *The Thought and Character of William James*, vol. 2 (Boston: Little, Brown, and Company, 1935): 401–3. ■*Emendations and textual notes:*

330.19	<u>dénoument</u> • [*sic*]
330.31	Hamlet-like • Hamlet- / like
330.35	too hundred years • [*sic*]
331.4	whereever • [*sic*]
331.22	~~their~~ there • ['re' *over* 'ir']
331.35	sunlight • sun- / light
332.2	ʇdetest • ['d' *over* 't']

■ 6 December 1905 [*postmark*] • Susan Sturgis de Sastre • Paris, France
■*Copy-text:* MS postcard, collection of Paloma Sanchez Sastre, Madrid, Spain.
■*Previous publication:* none known. ■*Emendations and textual notes:* none.

■ 7 December 1905 [*postmark*] • Susan Sturgis de Sastre • Paris, France
■*Copy-text:* MS postcard, collection of Paloma Sanchez Sastre, Madrid, Spain.
■*Previous publication:* none known. ■*Emendations and textual notes:* none.

■ 13 December 1905 • George Herbert Palmer • Paris, France

■*Copy-text:* MS, Department of Rare Books and Manuscripts, by courtesy of the Trustees of the Boston Public Library. ■*Previous publication: Letters*, 83–84.
■*Emendations and textual notes:*

333.12	somewhat • some- / what
333.25	seminaries • [*sic*]

■ 13 December 1905 [*postmark*] • Susan Sturgis de Sastre • Paris, France
■*Copy-text:* MS postcard, collection of Paloma Sanchez Sastre, Madrid, Spain.
■*Previous publication:* none known. ■*Emendations and textual notes:* none.

■ 25 January 1906 • Celedonio Sastre Serrano • Paris, France
■*Copy-text:* MS, collection of Adelaida Sastre, Ávila, Spain. ■*Previous publication: Azafea* 1 (University of Salamanca, 1985): 359–60. ■*Emendations and textual notes:*

334.13	fundado • [*sic*]
334.22	~~febrero~~ ₍marzo₎ • ['marzo' *above* '~~febrero~~']
334.22	enseguida • [*sic*]
334.23	vɟiage • ['i' *over* 'a'] [*sic*]
335.1	viage • [*sic*]

■ 29 January 1906 • Benjamin Apthorp Gould Fuller • Paris, France

■ *Copy-text:* MS, George Santayana Papers (bMS Am 1603.3), by permission of the Houghton Library, Harvard University. ■*Previous publication: Letters,* 84–85. ■*Emendations and textual notes:* none.

■ 29 January 1906 • Charles Scribner's Sons • Paris, France

■ *Copy-text:* MS, Author Files I, Box 130 of the Scribner Archives, Manuscripts Division, Department of Rare Books and Special Collections, Princeton University Libraries. ■*Previous publication:* none known. ■*Emendations and textual notes:*

337.9	whereever • [*sic*]
337.24	Commonweath • [*sic*]

■ 11 February 1906 [*postmark*] • Susan Sturgis de Sastre • Paris, France

■ *Copy-text:* MS postcard, collection of Paloma Sanchez Sastre, Madrid, Spain. ■*Previous publication:* none known. ■*Emendations and textual notes:* none.

■ 1 March 1906 [*postmark*] • Susan Sturgis de Sastre • Paris, France

■ *Copy-text:* MS postcard, collection of Paloma Sanchez Sastre, Madrid, Spain. ■*Previous publication:* none known. ■*Emendations and textual notes:*

338.13	fifty seven • [*sic*]
338.14	afternoon • after- / noon
338.15	–La maître des Forges" • [*sic*]

■ 1 April 1906 [*postmark*] • Susan Sturgis de Sastre • Lyon, France

■ *Copy-text:* MS postcard, collection of Paloma Sanchez Sastre, Madrid, Spain. ■*Previous publication:* none known. ■*Emendations and textual notes:* none.

■ 3 April [1906] • Susan Sturgis de Sastre • Montpellier, France

■ *Copy-text:* MS postcard, collection of Paloma Sanchez Sastre, Madrid, Spain. ■*Previous publication:* none known. ■*Emendations and textual notes:* none.

■ 4 April [1906] • Charles Scribner's Sons • Montpellier, France

■ *Copy-text:* MS, Author Files I, Box 130 of the Scribner Archives, Manuscripts Division, Department of Rare Books and Special Collections, Princeton University Libraries. ■*Previous publication:* none known. ■*Emendations and textual notes:*

340.16–17	~~to do so~~ ‸for that‸ ; • ['for that' *above* '~~to do so~~']

■ 11 April 1906 • Hugo Münsterberg • Cannes, France

■*Copy-text:* MS, Department of Rare Books and Manuscripts, by courtesy of the Trustees of the Boston Public Library. ■*Previous publication:* none known. ■*Emendations and textual notes:*

341.5	easter • [*sic*]
341.6–7	lectures, . . . has • [*sic*]
341.16	background • back- / ground

■ 11 April 1906 [*postmark*] • Susan Sturgis de Sastre • Cannes, France

■*Copy-text:* MS postcard, collection of Paloma Sanchez Sastre, Madrid, Spain. ■*Previous publication:* none known. ■*Emendations and textual notes:* none.

■ 24 April 1906 [*postmark*] • Susan Sturgis de Sastre • Nîmes, France

■*Copy-text:* MS postcard, collection of Paloma Sanchez Sastre, Madrid, Spain. ■*Previous publication:* none known. ■*Emendations and textual notes:*

342.4	April 25 • [*sic*]

■ 25 April 1906 [*postmark*] • Susan Sturgis de Sastre • Orange, France

■*Copy-text:* MS postcard, collection of Paloma Sanchez Sastre, Madrid, Spain. ■*Previous publication:* none known. ■*Emendations and textual notes:* none.

■ 29 April 1906 • Susan Sturgis de Sastre • Toulouse, France

■*Copy-text:* MS, George Santayana Collection (#6947), Clifton Waller Barrett Library, Special Collections Department, University of Virginia Library. ■*Previous publication: Letters,* 85–87. ■*Emendations and textual notes:*

343.26	father-in-law • father- / in-law

■ 29 April 1906 • Charles Augustus Strong • Toulouse, France

■*Copy-text:* MS, Box 6, Folder 89, The Papers of Charles Augustus Strong, Rockefeller Archive Center, Sleepy Hollow, New York. ■*Previous publication:* none known. ■*Emendations and textual notes:*

345.2	~~perception~~ ∧idea∧ • ['idea' *above* '~~perception~~']

■ 5 May 1906 [*postmark*] • Susan Sturgis de Sastre • Toulouse, France

■*Copy-text:* MS postcard, collection of Paloma Sanchez Sastre, Madrid, Spain. ■*Previous publication:* none known. ■*Emendations and textual notes:* none.

■ 5 May 1906 • Frederick James Eugene Woodbridge • Toulouse, France

■*Copy-text:* MS, *Journal of Philosophy* Records, Rare Book and Manuscript Library, Columbia University. ■*Previous publication:* none known. ■*Emendations and textual notes:*

346.7   ⌀Discussions • ['D' *over* 'd']

■ 8 May [1906] • [Susan Sturgis de Sastre] • Pau, France

■*Copy-text:* MS postcard, collection of Paloma Sanchez Sastre, Madrid, Spain. ■*Previous publication:* none known. ■*Emendations and textual notes:*

347.1   photograph • photo- / graph

■ 10 May 1906 • Hugo Münsterberg • Bordeaux, France

■*Copy-text:* MS, Department of Rare Books and Manuscripts, by courtesy of the Trustees of the Boston Public Library. ■*Previous publication:* none known. ■*Emendations and textual notes:* none.

■ 11 May 1906 • Susan Sturgis de Sastre • Arcachon, France

■*Copy-text:* MS postcard, collection of Paloma Sanchez Sastre, Madrid, Spain. ■*Previous publication:* none known. ■*Emendations and textual notes:* none.

■ 16 May 1906 • Hugo Münsterberg • Bordeaux, France

■*Copy-text:* MS, Department of Rare Books and Manuscripts, by courtesy of the Trustees of the Boston Public Library. ■*Previous publication:* none known. ■*Emendations and textual notes:*

348.17   rel̶e̶iieving • ['ie' *over* 'ei']

■ 18 May 1906 [*postmark*] • Susan Sturgis de Sastre • La Rochelle, France

■*Copy-text:* MS postcard, collection of Paloma Sanchez Sastre, Madrid, Spain. ■*Previous publication:* none known. ■*Emendations and textual notes:* none.

■ 22 May 1906 [*postmark*] • Susan Sturgis de Sastre • Caen, France

■*Copy-text:* MS postcard, collection of Paloma Sanchez Sastre, Madrid, Spain. ■*Previous publication:* none known. ■*Emendations and textual notes:* none.

■ 28 May 1906 • Mr. Helder • Paris, France

■*Copy-text:* MS, George Santayana Collection (#6947), Clifton Waller Barrett Library, Special Collections Department, University of Virginia Library. ■*Previous publication:* none known. ■*Emendations and textual notes:*

349.16   defen̸ces" • ['c' *over* 's']

■ 28 May 1906 [*postmark*] • Charles Augustus Strong • Paris, France

■*Copy-text:* MS, George Santayana Collection, Special Collections Division, Georgetown University Library. ■*Previous publication:* none known. ■*Emendations and textual notes:*

350.6   tomorrow • to- / morrow

■ 5 June 1906 • Susan Sturgis de Sastre • Dijon, France

■*Copy-text:* MS postcard, collection of Paloma Sanchez Sastre, Madrid, Spain. ■*Previous publication:* none known. ■*Emendations and textual notes:* none.

■ 10 June 1906 [*postmark*] • Susan Sturgis de Sastre • Morez, France

■*Copy-text:* MS postcard, collection of Paloma Sanchez Sastre, Madrid, Spain. ■*Previous publication:* none known. ■*Emendations and textual notes:*

350.16 $He • ['H' *over* 'S']

■ 12 June 1906 [*postmark*] • Susan Sturgis de Sastre • Col de la Faucille, France

■*Copy-text:* MS postcard, collection of Paloma Sanchez Sastre, Madrid, Spain. ■*Previous publication:* none known. ■*Emendations and textual notes:*

351.3   Lyons • [*sic*]

■ 19 June 1906 [*postmark*] • Susan Sturgis de Sastre • Grenoble, France

■*Copy-text:* MS postcard, collection of Paloma Sanchez Sastre, Madrid, Spain. ■*Previous publication:* none known. ■*Emendations and textual notes:*

351.7 and 8   Lyons • [*sic*]

■ 23 June 1906 • Charles William Eliot • Grenoble, France

■*Copy-text:* MS, C. W. Eliot Papers, courtesy of the Harvard University Archives. ■*Previous publication: Letters,* 87. ■*Emendations and textual notes:*

351.20   open-minded • open- / minded

■ 28 June 1906 [*postmark*] • Susan Sturgis de Sastre • Paris, France

■*Copy-text:* MS postcard, collection of Paloma Sanchez Sastre, Madrid, Spain. ■*Previous publication:* none known. ■*Emendations and textual notes:* none.

■ 9 July [1906] • Susan Sturgis de Sastre • Évian, France

■*Copy-text:* MS postcard, collection of Paloma Sanchez Sastre, Madrid, Spain. ■*Previous publication:* none known. ■*Emendations and textual notes:* none.

■ 7 August 1906 • Charles William Eliot • Compiègne, France
■ *Copy-text:* MS, C. W. Eliot Papers, courtesy of the Harvard University Archives.
■ *Previous publication:* none known. ■ *Emendations and textual notes:*

353.9   Lyons • [*sic*]

■ 20 August 1906 [*postmark*] • Susan Sturgis de Sastre • Windsor, England
■ *Copy-text:* MS postcard, collection of Paloma Sanchez Sastre, Madrid, Spain.
■ *Previous publication:* none known. ■ *Emendations and textual notes:* none.

■ 24 August 1906 [*postmark*] • Susan Sturgis de Sastre • Brighton, England
■ *Copy-text:* MS postcard, collection of Paloma Sanchez Sastre, Madrid, Spain.
■ *Previous publication:* none known. ■ *Emendations and textual notes:* none.

■ 15 September 1906 • Reginald Chauncey Robbins • Brookline, MA
■ *Copy-text:* MS, George Santayana Papers (bMS Am 1426), by permission of the Houghton Library, Harvard University. ■ *Previous publication:* none known. ■ *Emendations and textual notes:*

354.21   overwhelm • [*sic*]

■ [Mid-November 1906] • Charles Augustus Strong • [Unknown]
■ *Copy-text:* MS, George Santayana Collection, Special Collections Division, Georgetown University Library. ■ *Previous publication:* none known. ■ *Emendations and textual notes:*

355.13   midnight • mid- / night

■ 21 November 1906 • Charles Scribner's Sons • Brookline, MA
■ *Copy-text:* MS, Author Files I, Box 130 of the Scribner Archives, Manuscripts Division, Department of Rare Books and Special Collections, Princeton University Libraries. ■ *Previous publication:* none known. ■ *Emendations and textual notes:* none.

■ 5 December 1906 • Charles Augustus Strong • Brookline, MA
■ *Copy-text:* MS, Box 6, Folder 89, The Papers of Charles Augustus Strong, Rockefeller Archive Center, Sleepy Hollow, New York. ■ *Previous publication:* none known. ■ *Emendations and textual notes:*

357.4   Furthermore • Further- / more

■ 29 December 1906 • Charlotte Edith Taussig • Brookline, MA
■ *Copy-text:* MS unlocated. Typed transcription by William G. Holzberger is copy-text. ■ *Previous publication:* none known. ■ *Emendations and textual notes:*

357.28   GSantayana • [*not present*]

■ Tuesday [c. 1907 or 1908] • Isabella Stewart Gardner • Brookline, MA
■*Copy-text:* MS, Isabella Stewart Gardner Museum Archives, Boston. ■*Previous publication:* none known. ■*Emendations and textual notes:*
358.6   weekend • week- / end

■ 2 January 1907 • Charles Augustus Strong • Brookline, MA
■*Copy-text:* MS, Box 6, Folder 90, The Papers of Charles Augustus Strong, Rockefeller Archive Center, Sleepy Hollow, New York. ■*Previous publication:* none known. ■*Emendations and textual notes:* none.

■ 13 January [c. 1907 or 1908] • Hugo Münsterberg • Brookline, MA
■*Copy-text:* MS unlocated. Published version is copy-text. ■*Previous publication:* Margaret Münsterberg. "Santayana at Cambridge," *The American Mercury* 1 (Jan 1924): 72. ■*Emendations and textual notes:*
359.12   GSantayana • G. Santayana.

■ 2 February 1907 • Miss Levy • New York, New York
■*Copy-text:* MS, collection of Catherine Barnes. ■*Previous publication:* none known. ■*Emendations and textual notes:*
359.27   undertake • under- / take

■ 16 February 1907 • Charles William Eliot • Brookline, MA
■*Copy-text:* MS, C. W. Eliot Papers, courtesy of the Harvard University Archives. ■*Previous publication:* none known. ■*Emendations and textual notes:*
360.23   half-course • half- / course
360.28   another • an- / other
361.8   afternoon • after- / noon

■ 18 February 1907 • Charles Scribner's Sons • Brookline, MA
■*Copy-text:* MS, Author Files I, Box 130 of the Scribner Archives, Manuscripts Division, Department of Rare Books and Special Collections, Princeton University Libraries. ■*Previous publication:* none known. ■*Emendations and textual notes:* none.

■ 19 February 1907 • Charles William Eliot • Brookline, MA
■*Copy-text:* MS, C. W. Eliot Papers, courtesy of the Harvard University Archives. ■*Previous publication:* none known. ■*Emendations and textual notes:* none.

■ 21 February 1907 • Charles William Eliot • Cambridge, MA

■ *Copy-text:* MS, C. W. Eliot Papers, courtesy of the Harvard University Archives. ■ *Previous publication:* none known. ■ *Emendations and textual notes:*

363.10   understood • under- / stood

■ 1907 • Mr. Overton • [Cambridge, MA?]

■ *Copy-text:* MS unlocated. Handwritten transcription by David Wapinsky taken from a copy of the original made by James Lowe, an autograph dealer, is copy-text. Mr. Wapinsky states that Mr. Lowe had left out a few phrases, some of which were returned when Wapinsky looked at part of the original. However, he did not see the first page nor an exact date. ■ *Previous publication:* none known. ■ *Emendations and textual notes:*

363.23   parcel … have • [*sic*]
364.3   Scribners • [*sic*]

■ [Spring 1907?] • Horace Meyer Kallen • Cambridge, MA

■ *Copy-text:* MS, American Jewish Archives, Cincinnati, Ohio. ■ *Previous publication:* none known. ■ *Emendations and textual notes:* none.

■ [17 May 1907] • Harold Witter Bynner • Cambridge, MA

■ *Copy-text:* MS, George Santayana Papers (bMS Am 1891), by permission of the Houghton Library, Harvard University. ■ *Previous publication:* none known. ■ *Emendations and textual notes:* none.

■ [20 May 1907?] • Harold Witter Bynner • Cambridge, MA

■ *Copy-text:* MS, George Santayana Papers (bMS Am 1891), by permission of the Houghton Library, Harvard University. ■ *Previous publication:* none known. ■ *Emendations and textual notes:* none.

■ 28 May 1907 • Charles Augustus Strong • [Cambridge, MA?]

■ *Copy-text:* MS, Box 6, Folder 90, The Papers of Charles Augustus Strong, Rockefeller Archive Center, Sleepy Hollow, New York. ■ *Previous publication:* none known. ■ *Emendations and textual notes:*

366.14   Lyons • [sic]

■ 6 June 1907 [*postmark*] • Horace Meyer Kallen • Brookline, MA

■ *Copy-text:* MS postcard, American Jewish Archives, Cincinnati, Ohio. ■ *Previous publication:* none known. ■ *Emendations and textual notes:*

366.25   notebook • note- / book

■ 11 June 1907 • Horace Meyer Kallen • Brookline, MA

■*Copy-text:* MS, American Jewish Archives, Cincinnati, Ohio. ■*Previous publication:* none known. ■*Emendations and textual notes:*

367.13   However • How- / ever

■ 23 June 1907 • Charles Augustus Strong • Hamburg, Germany

■*Copy-text:* MS, Box 6, Folder 90, The Papers of Charles Augustus Strong, Rockefeller Archive Center, Sleepy Hollow, New York. ■*Previous publication:* none known. ■*Emendations and textual notes:*

368.20   it ‸him.‸ • ['him.' *above* 'it.']

■ 2 July 1907 • Susan Sturgis de Sastre • Weimar, Germany

■*Copy-text:* MS postcard, collection of Paloma Sanchez Sastre, Madrid, Spain. ■*Previous publication:* none known. ■*Emendations and textual notes:*

369.10   Gran-Duque • Gran- / Duque

■ 17 July 1907 • Charles Augustus Strong • Ávila, Spain

■*Copy-text:* MS, Box 6, Folder 90, The Papers of Charles Augustus Strong, Rockefeller Archive Center, Sleepy Hollow, New York. ■*Previous publication:* none known. ■*Emendations and textual notes:*

370.7   Jonøathan • ['a' *over* 'o']
370.18   herear • ['ar' *over* 're']

■ 29 September 1907 • Harold Witter Bynner • Brookline, MA

■*Copy-text:* MS, George Santayana Papers (bMS Am 1629), by permission of the Houghton Library, Harvard University. ■*Previous publication:* none known. ■*Emendations and textual notes:* none.

■ 7 October 1907 • William Roscoe Thayer • Brookline, MA

■*Copy-text:* MS, The Papers of William Roscoe Thayer (bMS Am 1801), by permission of the Houghton Library, Harvard University. ■*Previous publication:* none known. ■*Emendations and textual notes:* none.

■ 19 October 1907 • William James • Cambridge, MA

■*Copy-text:* MS, George Santayana Papers (bMS Am 1092.9), by permission of the Houghton Library, Harvard University. ■*Previous publication:* none known. ■*Emendations and textual notes:*

372.19   Lutoslawsky's • [*sic*]
372.28   <u>Erkenntniss Theorie</u> • [*sic*]
372.29   anywhere • any- / where

■ 21 October 1907 • Harry Morgan Ayres • Brookline, MA

■*Copy-text:* MS, collection of King Dykeman, Fairfield, Connecticut. ■*Previous publication:* none known. ■*Emendations and textual notes:*

373.13   classifcal • ['c' *over* 'f']

■ 13 November 1907 • Charles Scribner's Sons • Brookline, MA

■*Copy-text:* MS, Author Files I, Box 130 of the Scribner Archives, Manuscripts Division, Department of Rare Books and Special Collections, Princeton University Libraries. ■*Previous publication:* none known. ■*Emendations and textual notes:* none.

■ 16 December 1907 • Charles Augustus Strong • Brookline, MA

■*Copy-text:* MS, Box 6, Folder 90, The Papers of Charles Augustus Strong, Rockefeller Archive Center, Sleepy Hollow, New York. ■*Previous publication:* none known. ■*Emendations and textual notes:*

375.16   New Years • [*sic*]

■ [Before March 1908] • Charles Augustus Strong • [Brookline, MA]

■*Copy-text:* MS, Box 6, Folder 90, The Papers of Charles Augustus Strong, Rockefeller Archive Center, Sleepy Hollow, New York. ■*Previous publication:* none known. ■*Emendations and textual notes:*

375.22   afternoon • after- / noon

■ [c. 1908] • William James • Brookline, MA

■*Copy-text:* MS, George Santayana Papers (bMS Am 1092.9), by permission of the Houghton Library, Harvard University. ■*Previous publication:* none known. ■*Emendations and textual notes:* none.

■ 7 January 1908 • William James • Cambridge, MA

■*Copy-text:* MS, George Santayana Papers (bMS Am 1092.9), by permission of the Houghton Library, Harvard University. ■*Previous publication:* none known. ■*Emendations and textual notes:*

376.24–25   anything • any- / thing

■ 10 January 1908 • Horace Meyer Kallen • Cambridge, MA

■*Copy-text:* MS, American Jewish Archives, Cincinnati, Ohio. ■*Previous publication:* none known. ■*Emendations and textual notes:*

377.29   however • how- / ever

■ 5 February 1908 • Horace Meyer Kallen • Cambridge, MA

■*Copy-text:* MS, American Jewish Archives, Cincinnati, Ohio. ■*Previous publication:* none known. ■*Emendations and textual notes:*

379.10	inspite • [*sic*]	

■ 8 February 1908 • George Herbert Palmer • Cambridge, MA

■*Copy-text:* MS, Wellesley College Library, Wellesley, Massachusetts. ■*Previous publication:* none known. ■*Emendations and textual notes:*

380.8	stick to that • stick to / to that
380.12	nevertheless • neverthe- / less
380.14	The⫫o‸logy‸ • ['o' *over* 'y']

■ 4 March 1908 • Conrad Hensler Slade • Brookline, MA

■*Copy-text:* MS unlocated. Published version is copy-text. ■*Previous publication:* *Letters*, 88. ■*Emendations and textual notes:*

381.30	GSantayana • [*not present*]

■ 4 March 1908 • Charles Augustus Strong • Cambridge, MA

■*Copy-text:* MS, Box 6, Folder 90, The Papers of Charles Augustus Strong, Rockefeller Archive Center, Sleepy Hollow, New York. ■*Previous publication:* none known. ■*Emendations and textual notes:*

382.16	collegague • ['a' *over* 'g']
382.28	Lawrenson • [*sic*]

■ [Late May or early June 1908] • Isabella Stewart Gardner • Cambridge, MA

■*Copy-text:* MS, Isabella Stewart Gardner Museum Archives, Boston. ■*Previous publication:* none known. ■*Emendations and textual notes:*

383.8	fortnight • fort- / night

■ 2 June 1908 • Charles Augustus Strong • Cambridge, MA

■*Copy-text:* MS, Box 6, Folder 90, The Papers of Charles Augustus Strong, Rockefeller Archive Center, Sleepy Hollow, New York. ■*Previous publication:* none known. ■*Emendations and textual notes:*

384.2	read- about • read- / about [*sic*]
384.15	occasion believe • [*sic*]
384.18-19	there potentiality • [*sic*]
384.25–26	~~what is~~ ‸another "content,"‸ • ['another "content,"' *above* ~~what is~~]
385.15	anything • any- / thing

■ 5 July 1908 • Charles Augustus Strong • Windsor, England
■*Copy-text:* MS, Box 6, Folder 90, The Papers of Charles Augustus Strong, Rockefeller Archive Center, Sleepy Hollow, New York. ■*Previous publication:* none known. ■*Emendations and textual notes:* none.

■ 6 July 1908 • Bertrand Arthur William Russell • Windsor, England
■*Copy-text:* MS, The Bertrand Russell Archives, McMaster University Library. ■*Previous publication:* none known. ■*Emendations and textual notes:*

386.23   half-born • half- / born

■ 11 [July?] 1908 [*postmark*] • Susan Sturgis de Sastre • Cherbourg, France
■*Copy-text:* MS postcard, collection of Paloma Sanchez Sastre, Madrid, Spain. ■*Previous publication:* none known. ■*Emendations and textual notes:* none.

■ 18 July 1908 • Susan Sturgis de Sastre • Concarneau, France
■*Copy-text:* MS postcard, collection of Paloma Sanchez Sastre, Madrid, Spain. ■*Previous publication:* none known. ■*Emendations and textual notes:*

387.12   Potter's • [*sic*]

■ 25 July 1908 [*postmark*] • Susan Sturgis de Sastre • Quimper, France
■*Copy-text:* MS postcard, collection of Paloma Sanchez Sastre, Madrid, Spain. ■*Previous publication:* none known. ■*Emendations and textual notes:*

387.18   Sud-Express • Sud- / Express

■ [August 1908?] • Charles Augustus Strong • Avignon, France
■*Copy-text:* MS postcard, George Santayana Collection, Special Collections Division, Georgetown University Library. ■*Previous publication:* none known. ■*Emendations and textual notes:* none.

■ 18 September 1908 • Susan Sturgis de Sastre • New York, New York
■*Copy-text:* MS, George Santayana Collection (#6947), Clifton Waller Barrett Library, Special Collections Department, University of Virginia Library. ■*Previous publication:* none known. ■*Emendations and textual notes:*

388.22   pro-Spanish • pro- / Spanish

■ 24 September 1908 • Charles Augustus Strong • Cambridge, MA
■*Copy-text:* MS, Box 6, Folder 90, The Papers of Charles Augustus Strong, Rockefeller Archive Center, Sleepy Hollow, New York. ■*Previous publication:* none known. ■*Emendations and textual notes:*

389.25   Chant de • [*sic*]

389.26   ₐhaveₐ • [*in margin*]

■ [September 1908–January 1912] • Edward Joseph Harrington O'Brien •
Cambridge, MA

■*Copy-text:* MS, collection of Alan Denson, New Deer, Scotland. The letter is
taped inside the 1899 copy of *Lucifer* purchased by Mr. Denson. ■*Previous publica-*
tion: none known. ■*Emendations and textual notes:*

390.17   bes¢ieged • ['i' *over* 'e']
390.17   soi-disant • soi- / disant
390.23   to not • [*sic*]

■ 10 October 1908 • William Roscoe Thayer • Cambridge, MA

■*Copy-text:* MS, The Papers of William Roscoe Thayer (bMS Am 1081), by permission of the Houghton Library, Harvard University. ■*Previous publication:* none
known. ■*Emendations and textual notes:*

391.11   photographers • photo- / graphers
391.19   Hagerdorm • [*sic*]

■ 6 November [1908] • William Roscoe Thayer • Cambridge, MA

■*Copy-text:* MS, The Papers of William Roscoe Thayer (bMS Am 1081), by permission of the Houghton Library, Harvard University. ■*Previous publication:* none
known. ■*Emendations and textual notes:*

392.6   Signor • [*sic*]

■ 7 November 1908 • Francis Bullard • Cambridge, MA

■*Copy-text:* MS, George Santayana Collection (#6947), Clifton Waller Barrett
Library, Special Collections Department, University of Virginia Library. ■*Previous*
publication: none known. ■*Emendations and textual notes:* none.

■ [15 November 1908] • Isabella Stewart Gardner • Cambridge, MA

■*Copy-text:* MS, Isabella Stewart Gardner Museum Archives, Boston. ■*Previous*
publication: none known. ■*Emendations and textual notes:*

393.29   twenty second • [*sic*]

■ 10 December 1908 • Horace Meyer Kallen • Cambridge, MA

■*Copy-text:* MS, American Jewish Archives, Cincinnati, Ohio. ■*Previous publication:*
none known. ■*Emendations and textual notes:*

394.12   holiday's • [*sic*]
394.16   impressions • im- / impressions
394.21   somewhat • some- / what
395.1   is a 7 King • [*sic*]

■ 25 December 1908 • Mary Williams Winslow • Cambridge, MA

■*Copy-text:* MS, George Santayana Papers (MS Am 1352), by permission of the Houghton Library, Harvard University. ■*Previous publication:* none known. ■*Emendations and textual notes:*

395.19	he well less • [*sic*]
395.19	good-natured?. • [‘.’ *over* ‘?’]
395.26	upstairs • up- / stairs

■ [c. 1909 or 1910] • Unidentified Recipient • [Cambridge, MA]

■*Copy-text:* partial MS, George Santayana Papers (bMS Am 1542), by permission of the Houghton Library, Harvard University. ■*Previous publication:* none known. ■*Emendations and textual notes:* none.

■ 13 January 1909 • Isabella Stewart Gardner • Cambridge, MA

■*Copy-text:* MS, Isabella Stewart Gardner Museum Archives, Boston. ■*Previous publication:* none known. ■*Emendations and textual notes:* none.

■ 19 January 1909 • Isabella Stewart Gardner • Cambridge, MA

■*Copy-text:* MS, Isabella Stewart Gardner Museum Archives, Boston. ■*Previous publication:* none known. ■*Emendations and textual notes:* none.

■ 10 February 1909 • Charles Augustus Strong • Cambridge, MA

■*Copy-text:* MS, Box 6, Folder 90, The Papers of Charles Augustus Strong, Rockefeller Archive Center, Sleepy Hollow, New York. ■*Previous publication:* none known. ■*Emendations and textual notes:* none.

■ [February 1909] • Charles Augustus Strong • Cambridge, MA

■*Copy-text:* MS, Box 6, Folder 90, The Papers of Charles Augustus Strong, Rockefeller Archive Center, Sleepy Hollow, New York. ■*Previous publication:* none known. ■*Emendations and textual notes:*

| 398.25 | He ask • [*sic*] |

■ 14 March 1909 • Robert Underwood Johnson • Cambridge, MA

■*Copy-text:* MS, George Santayana Papers, Archives of the American Academy of Arts and Letters, New York. ■*Previous publication:* none known. ■*Emendations and textual notes:*

| 399.7 | negliglence • [*sic*] |

■ 18 March 1909 • Susan Sturgis de Sastre • Cambridge, MA

■*Copy-text:* MS, George Santayana Collection (#6947), Clifton Waller Barrett Library, Special Collections Department, University of Virginia Library. ■*Previous publication: Letters*, 89–92. ■*Emendations and textual notes:*

400.1	whatever • what- / ever
400.20	something • some- / thing
401.32	future This • future / This [*sic*]
402.3	"Modernists) • [*sic*]
402.14	I believe • [*damage emended*]

■ 19 April 1909 • Susan Sturgis de Sastre • Cambridge, MA

■*Copy-text:* MS, George Santayana Collection (#6947), Clifton Waller Barrett Library, Special Collections Department, University of Virginia Library. ■*Previous publication: Letters*, 92–94. ■*Emendations and textual notes:*

404.34	Mahomedans • [*sic*]

■ 18 July 1909 • Charles Augustus Strong • At sea

■*Copy-text:* MS, Box 6, Folder 90, The Papers of Charles Augustus Strong, Rockefeller Archive Center, Sleepy Hollow, New York. ■*Previous publication:* none known. ■*Emendations and textual notes:*

405.21	ought'n't • [*sic*]

■ 7 August 1909 • Susan Sturgis de Sastre • Chichester, England

■*Copy-text:* MS, George Santayana Collection (#6947), Clifton Waller Barrett Library, Special Collections Department, University of Virginia Library. ■*Previous publication:* none known. ■*Emendations and textual notes:*

406.8	Ilse • [*sic*]
406.9	domelike • dome- / like
406.33	especialist • [*sic*]
407.8	Merideth • [*sic*]
407.11	affec^{tion} • [*sic*]

■ 10 August 1909 • Susan Sturgis de Sastre • London, England

■*Copy-text:* MS postcard, collection of Paloma Sanchez Sastre, Madrid, Spain. ■*Previous publication:* none known. ■*Emendations and textual notes:* none.

■ 10 August 1909 • Charles Augustus Strong • London, England

■*Copy-text:* MS, Box 6, Folder 90, The Papers of Charles Augustus Strong, Rockefeller Archive Center, Sleepy Hollow, New York. ■*Previous publication:* none known. ■*Emendations and textual notes:*

408.13	note of it. • note of / of it.

408.31   fine more • [*sic*]

■ 13 August 1909 • Charles Augustus Strong • London, England

■*Copy-text:* MS, Box 6, Folder 90, The Papers of Charles Augustus Strong, Rockefeller Archive Center, Sleepy Hollow, New York. ■*Previous publication:* none known. ■*Emendations and textual notes:*

410.2   Hippodrome • Hippo- / drome
410.3   Mrs Preedy • [*sic*]

■ [13 August 1909] • Charles Augustus Strong • Oxford, England

■*Copy-text:* MS, Box 6, Folder 90, The Papers of Charles Augustus Strong, Rockefeller Archive Center, Sleepy Hollow, New York. ■*Previous publication:* none known. ■*Emendations and textual notes:*

410.18   governness • [*sic*]

■ 2 September 1909 • Charles Augustus Strong • Oxford, England

■*Copy-text:* MS, Box 6, Folder 90, The Papers of Charles Augustus Strong, Rockefeller Archive Center, Sleepy Hollow, New York. ■*Previous publication:* none known. ■*Emendations and textual notes:*

411.15   Englefield • Engle- / field

■ 14 September 1909 • Susan Sturgis de Sastre • Oxford, England

■*Copy-text:* MS postcard, collection of Paloma Sanchez Sastre, Madrid, Spain. ■*Previous publication:* none known. ■*Emendations and textual notes:*

412.3   "Jean Cristophe" • [*sic*]

■ 14 November 1909 • Wendell T. Bush • Cambridge, MA

■*Copy-text:* MS, *Journal of Philosophy* Records, Rare Book and Manuscript Library, Columbia University. ■*Previous publication:* none known. ■*Emendations and textual notes:* none.

■ 22 December 1909 • William Roscoe Thayer • Cambridge, MA

■*Copy-text:* MS, The Papers of William Roscoe Thayer (bMS Am 1081), by permission of the Houghton Library, Harvard University. ■*Previous publication:* none known. ■*Emendations and textual notes:* none.

Report of Line-End Hyphenation

In quotations from the present Critical Edition, no line-end hyphens are to be retained except the following.

3.fn1	good-looking	256.7–8	lamp-shade
17.11–12	anti-Hegelianism	257.14–15	Christ-Church
44.24–25	ghost-and-faery-blind	281.3–4	eight-inch
109.19–20	self-sufficiency	286.4–5	Loeser-ben-Loeser
116.15–16	psycho-physics	286.30–31	maid-servants
130.25–26	un-Laodicean	298.19–20	sand-metaphors
158.20–21	now-a-days	317.18–19	belly-ache
159.21–22	non-committal	328.31–32	Hyde-Wendell
169.34–35	over-neat	336.8–9	Neo-Platonists
181.28–29	mother-in-law	339.21–22	half-yearly
184.29–185.1	half-course	352.24–25	Lyon-Toulouse-Bayonne
189.39–40	house-party	361.9–10	well-known
201.16–17	things-in-themselves	382.11–12	Hamburg-American
208.4–5	much-stamped	385.3–4	mind-stuff
216.7–8	awe-inspiring	401.5–6	half-past
225.10–11	dinner-verses	403.18–19	arm-chair

Chronology

William G. Holzberger

This chronology is based upon various sources of information about Santayana's life and work, including his autobiography, entitled *Persons and Places: Fragments of Autobiography,* originally published in three volumes as *Persons and Places, The Middle Span,* and *My Host the World* (in 1944, 1945, and 1953 respectively); his letters; the biography by Daniel Cory, entitled *Santayana: The Later Years;* and my conversations with Cory. It is also indebted, however, for its dating of Santayana's transatlantic journeys and other travels, to a large printed map of Europe sent to me by Santayana's grandnephew, Don Eduardo Sastre Martín, on which, in the early years of the twentieth century, Santayana carefully inscribed, in red ink, the dates of his voyages, the names of the transatlantic steamships on which he travelled, and the routes that he followed.

1847 or 1848

Agustín Ruiz de Santayana (c. 1814–93), George Santayana's father, is appointed Governor of Batang in the Philippines.

1849

On 22 August Josefina Borrás (c. 1826–1912), George Santayana's mother, marries George Sturgis (1817–57) of Boston, aboard a British warship at anchor in Manila Bay. They have five children, but only three survive to adulthood (Susan Parkman, 5 June 1851; Josephine Borrás, in 1853; and Robert Shaw, in 1854). The other two (Joseph Borrás, who was called Pepín, born in 1850, and James Victor, in 1856) die in infancy.

1856

Josefina and George Sturgis, with their surviving children, visit America. They sail from Manila to Boston aboard the *Fearless,* a journey of ninety days. Agustín Santayana is also aboard, on leave from his post at Batang and bound for Spain via America and England.

1857

George Sturgis dies in Manila at the age of forty. His brother, Robert Sturgis, gives Josefina ten thousand dollars.

1858

Josefina Sturgis sails for Boston from Manila. Her youngest child, James Victor, aged one year and seven months, dies on the journey, in London. Josefina and her three surviving children remain in Boston for three years.

1861 or 1862

Josefina and her children return to Spain. They live in Madrid with the parents and family of Mercedes de la Escalera y Iparraguirre.

1862

In Madrid Josefina Borrás Sturgis marries Agustín Santayana (whom she had known during their years in the Philippines).

1863

On 16 December, at No. 69, Calle Ancha de San Bernardo, Madrid, George Santayana is born. (He retains his Spanish citizenship throughout his life.)

1864

Santayana is christened Jorge Agustín Nicolás, on 1 January, in the parish church of San Marcos, Madrid. The first name is given by the godmother, his twelve-year-old half sister, Susan (Susana), who chooses the first name of her own father, George Sturgis.

1866

Santayana's parents and the four children move from Madrid to Ávila. Afterwards, Santayana's half brother, Robert, is sent to live in Boston.

1868 or 1869

Santayana's mother, with Susan and Josephine, leaves Ávila for Boston, in obedience to her first husband's wish that his children be brought up in America. George Santayana, age five, is left with his father in Spain.

1872

In his ninth year, Santayana and his father leave Spain in June, bound for America where the boy is to be raised and educated. They sail from Liverpool on 4 July on the Cunard steamer *Samaria*. Santayana's first American residence is his mother's house at No. 302 Beacon Street, where his father remained for several months before returning permanently to Ávila. Santayana attends his first American school, Miss Welchman's Kindergarten on Chestnut Street.

1873–74

During the winter of 1873–74, Santayana is at the Brimmer School, the public grammar school of the district. In the autumn of 1874, he transfers to the Boston Public Latin School, where he spends eight school years.

1876

Santayana travels to Philadelphia with his half brother, Robert, to see the Centennial Exhibition.

1880

In June Santayana, age sixteen, is awarded the Poetry Prize at the Boston Latin School for his poem "Day and Night." He regards the event as his "emergence into public notice." During the '80s Santayana regularly attends mass at the Church of the Immaculate Conception in Boston.

1881–82

Santayana's senior year at the Boston Latin School. He becomes founding editor of the *Latin School Register,* the student paper, in which he anonymously publishes poems. In the autumn of 1882, he matriculates at Harvard College. Throughout his undergraduate years, he lives in room No. 19, Hollis Hall, the Harvard Yard. On weekends he visits his mother, who now lives in Roxbury, Massachusetts. During this freshman year, he discovers Lucretius's *De Rerum Natura,* which he studies in Latin, but he fails algebra and does poorly in his course in Greek, taught by Louis Dyer, whose book, *The Gods in Greece,* is to influence him considerably. In the Greek course, he reads the *Bacchae* of Euripides, from which he takes his personal motto: Τὸ σοφὸν οὐ σοφία which, in translation, becomes the second line of his famous Sonnet III: "It is not wisdom to be only wise." He becomes cartoonist for the *Harvard Lampoon.*

1883–84

Santayana's sophomore year at Harvard. In June 1883, at the age of nineteen, he makes his first return to Spain to visit his father, sailing alone from New York to Antwerp and travelling from there to Ávila by train. He also visits relatives in Catalonia, where, at Tarragona, he contracts a mild case of smallpox. Nevertheless, he manages to see a number of major Spanish cities and also visits Lyons and Paris. Returning to America in October, from Antwerp, he resumes his studies at Harvard. At first he is advised by a skeptical William James against going in for philosophy. At the Church of the Immaculate Conception, he meets Ward Thoron, who becomes his closest friend during their undergraduate years.

1884–85

Santayana's junior year at Harvard. He is initiated into two undergraduate societies, the O.K. (on 22 April 1885) and the Hasty Pudding.

1885

He becomes a founding member of the editorial board of *The Harvard Monthly,* the avant-garde college literary magazine founded by classmate Alanson Bigelow Houghton. The first issue of October 1885 carries a sonnet by Santayana, and he continues to publish poems in the *Monthly* until 1903.

1885–86

Santayana's senior year at Harvard. He meets Charles Augustus Strong, who had come from the University of Rochester to study philosophy for a year at Harvard. Together they found the Harvard Philosophical Club. They are awarded jointly, by the Harvard Philosophy Department, the Walker Fellowship for graduate study in Germany. The stipend of five hundred dollars is to be divided between them. The issue of *The Harvard Monthly* for April 1886 contains what is to be Santayana's most anthologized poem, his Sonnet III, beginning, "O World, thou choosest not the better part!" He is introduced to John Francis Stanley, 2d Earl Russell ("Frank"), age twenty, who is visiting America after being "sent down" from Balliol College, Oxford, in May 1885 for an alleged misdemeanor. Russell, elder brother of philosopher Bertrand Russell, becomes Santayana's most admired friend and the model for Jim Darnley of Santayana's novel, *The Last Puritan* (1935). Santayana's Bachelor of Arts degree is awarded *summa cum laude* and *in absentia,* Santayana having sailed for Cherbourg after taking his last examination. In July 1886 he returns for the second time to Ávila, where he spends the summer with his father. In mid-August he is at Göttingen, Germany, and later that autumn (September) spends four to six weeks at Dresden. He also journeys to London, visiting that city for the first time, in company with Strong. They sail from the port of Bremen in northern Germany. In October 1886 Santayana is in Berlin for the start of the winter semester.

1887

In late March (at the close of the winter semester at Berlin) Santayana and Strong travel to England for a holiday. Santayana spends two days with Earl Russell aboard the latter's steam yacht *Royal,* sailing down the Thames from Reading to London. In April Santayana first visits Oxford, where, through Earl Russell, he meets poet Lionel Johnson, then a student at New College. On 18 June Santayana is in London. He visits Winchester, Russell's school, in company with the young nobleman. On 20 June he views the procession for Queen Victoria's Jubilee (the fiftieth anniversary of her reign) from a room in Buckingham Palace Road engaged for the occasion by John D. Rockefeller. The company includes Rockefeller's eldest daughter, Elizabeth ("Bessie"), and Charles Augustus Strong, to whom she had become engaged that spring. During the summer, Santayana makes his third return to Spain. He is in Ávila July and August. On 2 September he takes a ship from Malaga to meet his sister, Susana, on Gibraltar for a few weeks to tour southern Spain before returning to Germany. From that autumn until the following spring, Santayana continues his graduate studies at Berlin. (His December address in Berlin is Pottsdamerstrasse 123^{III}.) The current German psycho-physiological approach to the study of philosophy is uncongenial to Santayana; also he is apprehensive about writing a doctoral dissertation in German. He decides to return to Harvard to complete his doctoral program.

1888

He joins Earl Russell at Valence, France, on 2 June for a seventeen-day canal journey through Burgundy aboard the *Royal.* On 18 June they reach Paris, where Santayana leaves Russell. In August, following his summer stay in Ávila, he visits Russell at his house, Broom Hall, situated at Teddington. After over two years abroad, Santayana returns to America, sailing from Liverpool to Boston on the *Catalonia.* Josiah Royce rejects the suggestion of Schopenhauer as the subject of Santayana's dissertation, recommending Lotze instead. Until the following autumn (1889), Santayana lives with his mother in her house in Roxbury, Massachusetts, working on his doctoral dissertation.

1889

Santayana completes his dissertation on *Lotze's System of Philosophy* and is awarded Master of Arts and Doctor of Philosophy degrees by Harvard University. During the summer he stays with Julian Codman and his family at Cotuit, on Cape Cod, where he meets the novelist Howard Sturgis, cousin to his relations. That autumn, at the rank of instructor in philosophy, he begins his twenty-two-year teaching career at Harvard. During the academic year 1889–90, Santayana lives in rooms in Thayer Hall in the Harvard Yard. He becomes an honorary member of several college clubs, including the Delta Phi or "Gas House" (later the Delphic), the Zeta Psi (called "The Spee"), and the Signet Society. He meets Henry Adams at the historian's home in Washington, D.C., where he is taken by Ward Thoron.

1890

In June Santayana sails from New York for Liverpool. During the summer he first visits Queen's Acre, novelist Howard Sturgis's home near Windsor Park, England, which he is to visit almost yearly until Sturgis's death in 1920. He spends part of July and August in Ávila. Sailing from Liverpool on 3 September on the *Teutonic,* Santayana returns to America and moves into rooms at No. 7, Stoughton Hall, the Harvard Yard, where he will spend six winters. About this time he begins his "Poetry Bees": regular meetings held in his rooms with a group of student friends for the purpose of reading aloud from the celebrated poets. This practice is continued for several years before being discontinued and is revived in 1910–11, with Conrad Aiken as the leading light among the student members. Also, at about this time, Santayana, William Vaughn Moody, Norman Hapgood, Boylston Beal, and others, as a lark, found the Laodicean Club at Harvard, and Santayana is elected "Pope" by the membership.

1891

Santayana sails from Boston to Liverpool in June aboard the *Cephalonia*. He makes his first visit to Telegraph House (or "T.H."), Earl Russell's estate on the South Downs in Hampshire, England, where Santayana is to be a regular visitor until 1923. He visits Ávila in August and returns to Boston in September.

1892

Santayana spends the summer in Cambridge, Massachusetts. In the autumn he makes his first visit to Yale, where he is invited by William Lyon Phelps to watch the Harvard-Yale football game. Santayana is writing "nothing but poetry" at this time. On 26 November his half sister, Susana, then forty-one, marries Celedonio Sastre of Ávila, a widower with six children. On 16 December, Santayana's twenty-ninth birthday, he gives a dinner party for a group of Harvard friends: "one of the pleasantest memories of my life."[1]

1893

On 10 June Santayana sails from New York for Gibraltar on the *Fulda*.[2] Crossing to Tangiers, he meets the American painter John Singer Sargent on board ship. During the summer, he is in Ávila, where he witnesses his father's death at seventy-nine. He leaves Ávila on 22 August for London and returns to New York, sailing from Southampton on 3 September. He spends two weeks with Strong in New York on his arrival. Back in Cambridge in October, he learns of the death of the closest of his younger friends, Warwick Potter (who had graduated from Harvard that spring), from cholera in the harbor of Brest during a voyage aboard a friend's yacht. The body is returned to New York, where Santayana attends the funeral. He writes the four "To W. P." sonnets. About this time he is approached by Herbert S. Stone and Hannibal Ingalls Kimball, young Harvard men who offer to publish a collection of his poems. He also attends the New York wedding of Robert Burnside Potter, Warwick's elder brother. At the end of this year Santayana undergoes his *metanoia*, or fundamental change of heart, resulting in a renunciation of the world. This is brought about by a combination of disconcerting events, including Susana's marriage, his father's pathetic death, Warwick Potter's death, the end of youth (signaled by his thirtieth birthday), and the prospect of an undistinguished career and life in Protestant America.

1894

Santayana remains in Cambridge, Massachusetts, for the summer. Earl Russell, en route to San Francisco, spends a week with him in Cambridge. Santayana's first book, *Sonnets and Other Verses,* is published by Stone and Kimball in Cambridge and Chicago.

1895

In Cambridge, Massachusetts, until June, Santayana again sails from New York to Gibraltar on the *Werra*. During the summer, he visits Earl Russell at his "ugly villa" at Maidenhead, England, and meets Mrs. Marion Sommerville, who is later to divorce her husband and become Russell's second wife ("Countess Mollie"). During this summer, Santayana also travels in Italy with Charles Loeser and makes a one-hundred-fifty-mile walking tour through France to Switzerland with Guy Murchie. He returns to Cambridge in late September, sailing from London to New York on a cattle steamer.

1896

Santayana's first book-length prose work is published by Scribner's: *The Sense of Beauty: Being the Outlines of Aesthetic Theory*. The second edition of *Sonnets,* containing the thirty new sonnets of the *Second Sonnet Series,* also is published by Stone and Kimball in this year. Andreas Martin Andersen makes his charcoal drawing, which becomes Santayana's favorite portrait of himself. On 28 June Santayana sails from Quebec on the *Parisian,* bound for Liverpool and a year's leave of absence from Harvard. He plans to spend a year in advanced study at Cambridge University. Late July through early September, he is in Oxford. Early in October he visits Bertrand Russell at Haslemere, England; in September he begins a four-week stay in Maidenhead, England. He also appears in court in Winchester on 9 or 10 October to testify on behalf of Frank Russell against whom charges were brought by the Earl's estranged first wife, Mabel Edith, and her mother, Lady Lena Scott. Afterwards, Santayana goes immediately from Winchester to Cambridge, where he is admitted as an advanced student to King's College, with the standing of Master of Arts. His Cambridge friends include Nathaniel Wedd, G. Lowes Dickinson, Bertrand Russell, G. E. Moore, and J. M. E. McTaggart. He studies Plato under the direction of Henry Jackson of Trinity College. That December Santayana testifies on behalf of the "wicked Earl," as Russell's notorious court-room adventures caused him to be designated by the journalists, at the trial of Lady Scott and her codefendants for libel, held at the Old Bailey in London. They are convicted and sentenced to eight months at hard labor, but Russell intercedes to reduce the severity of Lady Scott's punishment. Santayana spends the Christmas holidays in Paris with club acquaintances at Harvard, who are studying at the Beaux Arts.

1897

In January Santayana returns to King's College, Cambridge, England. He spends April and May travelling in Italy with Mr. and Mrs. Robert Burnside Potter, visiting Florence, Venice, and Rome. On 22 June, in company with the Rockefellers (as in 1887), Santayana views Queen Victoria's Diamond Jubilee procession (the sixtieth anniversary of her reign) from a room in Picadilly taken by John D. Rockefeller for the occasion. During the summer, Santayana sees Lionel Johnson again, in Earl Russell's London rooms in Temple Gardens. His study at King's College is finished during July and August, and, after fifteen months abroad, he returns on 2 September 1897 to Boston from Liverpool in the *Gallia*. He resumes his teaching duties at Harvard and lives with his mother in her house in Longwood, Brookline, Massachusetts, walking to classes.

1898

Despite Harvard President Charles William Eliot's disapproval, early in the year Santayana is promoted from instructor to assistant professor for a five-year period at an annual salary of two thousand dollars. The promotion is endorsed by William James, Hugo Münsterberg, and Santayana's other colleagues in the philosophy department. He takes up permanent residence on Brattle Street in Cambridge to "do one's share in maintaining or establishing the academic traditions of the place."[3] In June he sails to England for his summer holiday abroad, but he is dismayed by the ignominious defeat of the Spanish fleet at Manila Harbor and Santiago in the Spanish-American War. He returns in September, sailing from Liverpool to New York.

1899

Santayana's *Lucifer,* a mythological tragedy, is published in Chicago and New York by H. S. Stone. Santayana sails from New York to Southampton in June and spends the summer at Oxford completing work on the manuscript of *Interpretations of Poetry and Religion.* He visits the Robert B. Potters at Sainte Marguerite and then spends two weeks with Susana and her family in Ávila before sailing to Quebec from Liverpool in September.

1900

Santayana spends the summer abroad, sailing in June from New York to London. He visits a number of cities in France, including Chartres, Orleans, and Toulouse, and then settles in Oxford for most of the time. Returning to America from Southampton in September, he moves into rooms at No. 60, Brattle Street, Cambridge, Massachusetts, where he continues to live until mid-1904. He meets Baron Albert von Westenholz ("one of my truest friends" [*Persons,* 261]) when the young German aristocrat appears at Harvard. *Interpretations* is published by Scribner's in New York and A. & C. Black in London.

1901

Publication of the last collection of new poems by Santayana, *A Hermit of Carmel and Other Poems,* in New York by Scribner's (and in London by R. B. Johnson in 1902). Henceforth, Santayana writes little poetry, concentrating

instead on philosophy. He spends the summer abroad, sailing for England in
July and returning in September.

1902

Santayana again spends the summer abroad, sailing in June from New York
to Southampton and returning from London in September.

1903

Santayana is reappointed assistant professor for a second five-year period,
at the same annual salary of two thousand dollars. Again the summer is spent
abroad, with Santayana sailing from New York to Southampton in June. In
mid-August he leaves Oxford for Portsmouth, to visit Earl Russell. He returns
to Cambridge, Massachusetts, from Hamburg in September.

1904–6

Santayana spends twenty-seven months abroad, including his only sabbatical leave (1904–5), travelling in Europe and the Middle East. In mid-July 1904
he sails from New York to Plymouth, England. That September, he sends the
last batch of manuscript for *The Life of Reason* to the publishers and then sets
out from Paris for his "first real travels." He visits Rome and Venice with
Charles Loeser. After spending a few weeks at Naples in December, he visits
Pompeii; then goes on to Sicily, where, at Syracuse, he reads the first proofs of
The Life of Reason. He returns from Sicily to Naples and sails for Greece. He is
in Egypt in January 1905 and travels by boat up and down the Nile. From
Egypt he travels to Palestine and Tel Aviv, spending three weeks at Jerusalem.
He visits Damascus and Baalbeck, then travels from Beirut to Athens and
through Greece, which, in its modern form, disappoints him. He sails from
Piraeus to Constantinople, concluding his odyssey with Budapest and Vienna.
Never again will he travel "for the sake of travelling." (*Persons,* 467) While still
in the East in 1905, Santayana is invited by Harvard to become Hyde Lecturer
at the Sorbonne for 1905–6; he accepts, thus extending his holiday for a second year. During this period he lectures on philosophical subjects at Paris and
the provincial universities. The five volumes of *The Life of Reason; or, the Phases
of Human Progress* are published during 1905–6 by Scribner's in New York and
Constable in London. Santayana rejects an offer of a position on the philosophical faculty of Columbia University. He returns to America in September
1906, sailing from Southampton to New York, and resumes his teaching duties
at Harvard.

1907

Santayana is promoted from assistant professor to full professor, and his
salary is doubled to four thousand dollars per year. In June he sails from New
York to Hamburg and returns to Boston from Liverpool in September.

1908

Santayana sails from Boston to Plymouth in June and spends time in England and France before returning to Boston from Cherbourg in September.

1909

Santayana is elected to membership in the National Institute of Arts and Letters (later the American Academy and Institute of Arts and Letters). He spends the summer in Europe, sailing in July, from Boston to Liverpool, on the *Lusitania,* and returning from Liverpool in September aboard the *Mauretania.*

1910

In February Santayana delivers a course of lectures, on "Three Philosophical Poets," at Columbia University. On 13 April he addresses the Century Club in Chicago, and from 14 April to about 24 April, he repeats his course of six lectures on the "Three Philosophical Poets" at the University of Wisconsin at Madison. These lectures constitute the book *Three Philosophical Poets: Lucretius, Dante, and Goethe* published later in the year by Harvard University Press, in Cambridge, Massachusetts, and by the Oxford University Press, in London. Santayana sails from Boston to Liverpool aboard the *Lusitania* in June, and he makes his penultimate transatlantic crossing in September, sailing from Hamburg on the *Kaiserin Augusta Victoria.*

1911

In April Santayana delivers his final lecture at Harvard. He receives an honorary Doctor of Letters degree from the University of Wisconsin. From Madison, he travels to the University of California at Berkeley, where, beginning in June, he teaches in the six-week summer session and has his only experience of the American West.

1912

Santayana makes his final transatlantic crossing (thirty-eighth), sailing aboard the *Olympic* from Boston on 24 January, bound for Plymouth and a holiday in Europe. He plans to return to Harvard in September 1913, but in fact he has left America for good. On 5 February Santayana's mother dies. His share of the inheritance, coupled with his savings, enables him to resign his professorship, which he does with a letter to Harvard President Abbott Lawrence Lowell of 6 June. In February he visits Cambridge University, where, as Bertrand Russell's guest, he sleeps in the clock tower of Trinity College. During the spring he lives in Spain with Mercedes de la Escalera (an old family friend) in her home in Madrid. At this time, Santayana's bronchitis becomes chronic, and he suffers from it periodically during the rest of his life. In May, he moves into C. A. Strong's Paris apartment at No. 9, Avenue de l'Observatoire, which, until his settlement in Rome in 1928, becomes his principal residence. At this time, his sister Josephine Sturgis is taken to Spain by her brother Robert, where she will remain permanently.

1913–14

Winds of Doctrine: Studies in Contemporary Opinion is published by Scribner's in New York and Dent in London. Santayana is in Ávila during December 1913 and spends the period January through May 1914 in Seville. He is back at Strong's Paris apartment in June. In July Santayana crosses the English Channel "to do some shopping, and see a few friends,"[4] travels to London, and early in August, to Cambridge. World War I breaks out, and Santayana returns to Oxford, where he remains essentially throughout the war, until the end of April 1919. During this period he often visits Earl Russell at Telegraph House. At Oxford Santayana also becomes friends with Robert Bridges, the poet laureate, and, through Bertrand Russell, with Lady Ottoline Morrell, whose Manor House at Garsington (near Oxford) is at this time a gathering place for the British literati.

1915

The controversial *Egotism in German Philosophy* is published by Scribner's in New York (and, in 1916, by Dent in London). Santayana is accused by his critics of writing propaganda.

1918

During the winter Santayana gives the Third Annual Henriette Hertz Lecture, before the British Academy in London. The lecture is published as "Philosophical Opinion in America," in the *Proceedings of the British Academy* for 1917–18, and later appears, in 1920, as chapter five of *Character and Opinion in the United States.*

1919

Robert Bridges tries unsuccessfully to persuade Santayana to remain in England. He wishes to arrange a lifetime membership for him in one of the Oxford colleges with which Bridges is affiliated, Corpus Christi or New College. Santayana is still considering a permanent residency in Oxford, but wants to travel for at least a year. At the end of June, after considerable difficulties obtaining a French visa, Santayana returns to Strong's Paris apartment to write. He declines an offer from Professor Wendell T. Bush to lecture at Columbia. In late November he accompanies a crippled Strong to his Villa Le Balze at Fiesole near Florence.

1920

During this year Santayana begins his practice of passing the winters in Rome, but continues to spend the summers in Paris, Ávila, Glion, at Lake Geneva, or Cortina d'Ampezzo. *Little Essays: Drawn From the Writings of George*

Santayana by Logan Pearsall Smith, With the Collaboration of the Author is published by Constable in London and Scribner's in New York. *Character and Opinion in the United States: with Reminiscences of William James, and Josiah Royce, and Academic Life in America* is published by Constable in London, Scribner's in New York, and McLeod in Toronto. His work continues on *Soliloquies* and *Realms of Being.*

1921

Santayana spends the winter months in Spain (Toledo and Madrid) concentrating on his writing. Several of the English soliloquies are published separately in the *The Dial,* the *The Athenaeum,* and the *Journal of Philosophy.* At the end of March he returns to Paris, and in October travels to Rome.

1922

After a winter in Rome organizing the *Realms of Being,* Santayana spends the summer in Paris working on the manuscript of *Scepticism and Animal Faith. Soliloquies in England and Later Soliloquies* and the revised second edition of the five volumes of *The Life of Reason* are published by Constable and Scribner's (*Life of Reason* by Constable in 1923).

1923

The introduction to Santayana's system of philosophy, *Scepticism and Animal Faith,* and the last collection of Santayana's poetry to appear during his lifetime, *Poems: Selected by the Author and Revised,* are published by Scribner's and Constable. Santayana has by now changed his mind about retiring permanently in England, partly because of the winter climate and partly because of his dissatisfaction with the current tone of life there. On his penultimate visit to England, Santayana delivers the Herbert Spencer Lecture at Oxford (entitled *The Unknowable* and published by the Clarendon Press). He makes final visits to Cambridge and to "T.H.," where Earl Russell is now alone, his third wife, the novelist "Elizabeth" (Mary Annette Beauchamp, widow of the German Count von Arnim) having left him in 1918.

1924

Santayana declines Professor George Herbert Palmer's invitation to read the Phi Beta Kappa poem at the Harvard Commencement exercises. A revised version of his tragedy (originally published in 1900) is published as *Lucifer; or the Heavenly Truce: A Theological Tragedy,* by Dunster House, at Cambridge, Massachusetts.

1925

Publication of *Dialogues in Limbo,* by Constable in London (and by Scribner's in New York in 1926).

1926

Santayana writes a short preface to the 1926 reprint of *Winds of Doctrine* (New York: Scribner's; London: Dent). During the summer, in a room in the Hotel Cristallo, in Cortina d'Ampezzo, he composes, "at one stretch," (*Persons,* 529) *Platonism and the Spiritual Life.* That autumn Santayana begins the annual practice of spending all or part of the months of September and October in Venice, staying at the Hotel Danieli, en route back to Rome from Cortina.

1927

Early in April, Santayana meets Daniel Cory, age twenty-two, who has come from England at Santayana's invitation to meet the philosopher in Rome. In August Santayana officiates as a "substitute papa"[5] at the wedding of Margaret Strong (daughter of C. A. Strong and Elizabeth Rockefeller) to George Cuevas, in Paris, by giving the bride away. Publication of the first volume of Santayana's system of philosophy: *The Realm of Essence: Book First of Realms of Being,* by Scribner's in New York and Constable in London.

1928

Early in January Santayana declines the offer, from President Abbott Lawrence Lowell of Harvard, of the Norton Chair of Poetry for 1928–29. His half sister Susana dies in Ávila, on 10 February, in her seventy-seventh year. At the end of August, Strong gives up his Paris apartment, in which, for many years, Santayana has lived as Strong's guest. Early in September, Santayana makes a penultimate visit to Spain. Avoiding Ávila, he goes to Mercedes de la Escalera in Galicia to ascertain the state of mental and physical health of his sister Josephine, who is living with Mercedes, and to advise her regarding her will. About this time, at a suggestion from his nephew, George Sturgis, Santayana begins composing his autobiography.

1929

By the first of September Santayana has finished work on the manuscript of *The Realm of Matter.* Again settled at the Hotel Bristol in Rome, in October he begins work on *The Realm of Truth.*

1930

Celedonio Sastre Serrano, husband of the late Susana, dies in Ávila on 12 May. At the end of May Santayana makes his final visit to Spain, in order to settle the affairs of his surviving sister, Josephine, as well as his own. He gives his father's house in Ávila to the Sastre brothers, Celedonio's sons. After his return to Rome, Josephine dies in Ávila, on October 15, at the age of seventy-seven. *The Realm of Matter: Book Second of Realms of Being* is published, by Scribner's in New York and Constable in London, and "A Brief History of My Opinions" appears in volume two of *Contemporary American Philosophy: Personal*

Statements, edited by George P. Adams and William P. Montague, and published by Macmillan in New York.

1931

John Francis Stanley, 2d Earl Russell, dies at Marseilles on 3 March at the age of sixty-five. Santayana reverses his intention to visit Ávila in the spring or summer, both because of disinclination and the worsening political unrest in Spain, presaging the impending civil war. *The Genteel Tradition at Bay* is published by Scribner's in New York and by the Adelphi in London. In December Santayana receives and declines the offer to become William James Professor of Philosophy at Harvard.

1932

Santayana attends the philosophical congress commemorating the tercentenary of Spinoza's birth, held at The Hague on September 6–10, where he delivers a lecture on *Ultimate Religion* (published in *Septimana Spinozana,* by Martinus Nijhoff, at The Hague, in 1933). He also goes to London, where he attends a meeting held there to commemorate the tercentenary of the birth of John Locke. On 19 October he gives an address on "Locke and the Frontiers of Common Sense" which becomes the first of five essays constituting *Some Turns of Thought in Modern Philosophy* (published in England by the Cambridge University Press and in New York by Scribner's in 1933).

1933

Evelyn Tindall, an Englishwoman who is secretary for the British Legation to the Holy See in Rome, is first mentioned as typing Santayana's manuscripts. Beginning with *The Last Puritan,* she continues her work with Santayana for almost twenty years.

1934

On 31 August Santayana completes work on his novel, *The Last Puritan: A Memoir in the Form of a Novel.* Begun in the early 1890s as a story of college life, the work has been in progress for more than forty years.

1935

In the spring Santayana declines the invitation of President James Bryant Conant and the Harvard Tercentenary Committee to attend the Commencement exercises in June and receive an honorary Doctor of Letters degree. He also declines the subsequent offer to receive, together with sixty other scholars, an unspecified honorary degree to be presented at Harvard during the summer. He regards these offers as merely grudging recognition of his achievement by official Harvard. *The Last Puritan* is published by Constable in London (on 17 October) and by Macmillan in Toronto. The

Scribner's edition, published in New York in 1936, becomes a Book-of-the-Month Club bestseller.

1936

The first six volumes of the Triton Edition of *The Works of George Santayana,* Scribner's deluxe limited edition of the collected writings in fifteen volumes, are published in New York. Santayana writes a general preface and autographs sheets which are placed at the front in volume one. (The remaining nine volumes are published during the period 1937–40.) *Obiter Scripta: Lectures, Essays and Reviews,* edited by Justus Buchler and Benjamin Schwartz, and *Philosophy of Santayana: Selections From the Works of George Santayana,* edited by Irwin Edman, are published by Scribner's (*Obiter* is also published by Constable). During June and July, Santayana makes a final visit to Paris.

1937

On 29 May Santayana's favorite grandnephew, Roberto Sastre (son of José ["Pepe"] and Isabel Sastre) is killed while fighting on the Falangist side in the Spanish civil war. *The Realm of Truth: Book Third of Realms of Being* is published in London by Constable (and in New York by Scribner's in 1938).

1938

The first book-length biography, *George Santayana,* by George Washburne Howgate is published in Philadelphia by the University of Pennsylvania Press.

1939

World War II breaks out in Europe. Santayana is refused a regular long-term visa by the Swiss officials and decides to remain in Italy. Daniel Cory stays with him at Cortina d'Ampezzo until the end of August. (Their next meeting will be at the Blue Sisters' nursing home in Rome, early in September 1947, eight years later.) In the autumn, the Hotel Bristol in Rome, Santayana's home for many years, is closed for reconstruction. Santayana decides to spend the winter of 1939–40 in Venice, a decision that, because of the severe cold and dampness of Venice in winter, he afterward regrets. In September he learns of the suicide of his friend Baron Albert von Westenholz.

1940

On 23 January, at Florence, Charles Augustus Strong dies at the age of seventy-seven. *The Realm of Spirit: Book Fourth of Realms of Being* is published by Scribner's in New York and Constable in London. *The Philosophy of George Santayana,* volume two of The Library of Living Philosophers, Paul Arthur Schilpp, Editor, is published in Evanston by the Northwestern University Press. The book, composed of critical essays by several hands, contains also Santayana's rejoinder entitled "Apologia pro Mente Sua."

1941

Santayana spends the summer at Fiuggi, returning to Rome in the Autumn. The Hotel Bristol being closed, he lives for a time in the Grand Hotel. Now seventy-seven years old, he finds looking after himself more difficult and, on 14 October, moves into a nursing home operated by the Blue Sisters of the Little Company of Mary, an order of Roman Catholic Irish nuns. The large establishment is situated in the Via Santo Stefano Rotondo, atop the Celius (*Monte Celio*), one of Rome's seven hills. This is to be Santayana's last home, where he will live for almost eleven years.

1942–43

The manuscript of *Persons and Places,* the first volume of Santayana's autobiography, is refused by the Italian postal authorities. Scribner's editor John Hall Wheelock, and Irish poet Padraic Collum, with the cooperation of American and Vatican diplomatic officials, succeed in spiriting the manuscript across national lines and ultimately to New York. Cut off by the war from correspondence with America and England, Santayana continues to write his autobiography and works on the manuscript of *Dominations and Powers,* a book composed of essays written over a great many years.

1944

Like *The Last Puritan,* in 1936, *Persons and Places* becomes a Book-of-the-Month Club bestseller. On 20 December George Sturgis, Santayana's nephew and financial manager, dies of a heart attack.

1945

The second volume of Santayana's autobiography is published as *The Middle Span,* the title being supplied by editor Wheelock of Scribner's. Santayana is awarded the Nicholas Murray Butler Medal by Columbia University.

1946

The Idea of Christ in the Gospels; or, God in Man: A Critical Essay is published by Scribner's in New York and Saunders in Toronto.

1947

Daniel Cory spends nearly two months with Santayana in Rome, living in a room opposite Santayana's in the Blue Sisters' establishment. He finds Santayana completely deaf in one ear. On 13 October Santayana gives Cory the manuscript of his *Posthumous Poems,* inscribing a personal dedication. These unpublished poems and translations, which Santayana had begun revising and transcribing at the end of the war, are published in *The Poet's Testament,* in 1953, edited by Cory and John Hall Wheelock.

1948

Dialogues in Limbo, With Three New Dialogues is published in New York by Scribner's.

1949

Cory spends the months of April and May helping Santayana with his work on the manuscript of *Dominations and Powers.* They agree that henceforth Cory should spend the winters in Rome. Cory returns to Rome at the end of October and remains there until the end of April 1950. In December 1949 Cory consults Santayana's physician, Dr. Luigi Sabbatucci about Santayana's persistent cough and recent loss of appetite. He interprets the doctor's circumspect answers as suspicion of serious illness.

1950

Artist Lino S. Lipinsky de Orlov does his series of pencil portraits of Santayana in August 1950. Cory returns to Rome from England in early October 1950 and remains there until early May the following year. He assists Santayana with the final checking and correction of the proofs of *Dominations and Powers,* and they complete this labor by the beginning of the New Year. In mid-October 1950 Robert Lowell and his wife, novelist Elizabeth Hardwick, visit Santayana in Rome.

1951

Dominations and Powers: Reflections on Liberty, Society, and Government, Santayana's last book published during his lifetime, is issued by Scribner's in New York and Constable in London. Santayana receives another visit from Robert Lowell early in the year, and Cory spends about nine months [c. September 1951–May 1952] with Santayana in Rome. They spend the autumn collaborating on the revised one-volume edition of *The Life of Reason* (originally published in five volumes in 1905-6, the new edition is published by Constable in London and Scribner's in New York in 1954). Cory observes that Santayana's deafness is increasing and that his vision, never good, is impaired by cataracts.

1952

On 4 June Santayana falls on the steps of the Spanish Consulate in Rome, where he had gone to renew his passport. He is taken to the nursing home in a taxi by officials of the Consulate. The effects of the fall include three broken ribs, a bleeding head wound, and patches of pneumonia on the lungs. Cory, hastily summoned from England by the Sisters, remains with Santayana until the end of June. Dr. Sabbatucci is amazed by Santayana's recovery. While recuperating, Santayana receives, as a present from George Salerno (a young American journalist, who had met Santayana while a soldier in the occupation forces), a copy of the poems of Lorenzo de' Medici. Santayana decides to spend the summer translating Lorenzo's lengthy pastoral *Ombron and Ambra,* and he works at this task into the summer, until increasing blindness and illness make further labor impossible. By the third week of August, Santayana becomes desperately ill. Cory arrives in Rome on 8 September and is told by Dr. Sabbatucci that Santayana is dying of stomach cancer. On 26 September, after much suffering, Santayana dies. His wish to be buried in unconsecrated ground in a Catholic cemetery is frustrated by the lack of such a section in Rome's Campo Verano. The Spanish officials intercede and, on 30 September Santayana's body is interred in the Tomb of the Spaniards. At the graveside, Daniel Cory reads aloud Santayana's poem, "The Poet's Testament."

1953

The third volume of Santayana's autobiography, entitled (by the publisher) *My Host the World,* is published in London by the Cresset Press, and in New York by Scribner's. *The Posthumous Poems,* together with two early plays, are published by Scribner's as *The Poet's Testament: Poems and Two Plays.*

1955

The Letters of George Santayana, a selection of two hundred and ninety-six letters to eighty-six recipients, edited by Daniel Cory, is published by Scribner's.

Notes

[1]Letter to Daniel Cory of 11 November 1932.

[2]On page 36 of volume 3 of Scribner's edition of *Persons and Places,* entitled *My Host the World* (1953) (and also on the holograph manuscript itself), Santayana's second visit to Gibraltar is described as follows "... I returned there in 1891, this time from America, and crossed to Tangiers. ..." On page 37, he observes that he was again at Gibraltar "two years later." Evidently, the date of 1891 is a slip, for on the map referred to above in the headnote to this chronology Santayana has indicated that in June of 1893, and again in June of 1895, he sailed from New York to Gibraltar, on the *Fulda* and the *Werra,* respectively. The map also indicates that in June 1891 he sailed from Boston to Liverpool aboard the *Cephalonia.* Santayana had left the map in Spain many years before, and therefore did not have it by him while composing his autobiography in Rome during the 'Forties.

[3]Letter to Guy Murchie of 17 July 1897.

[4]Letter to Mary Williams Winslow of 16 August 1914.

[5]Letter to Boylston Adams Beal of 21 November 1927.

Addresses

The following list of addresses is drawn from the place and date-lines and from the contents of Santayana's letters, from information provided in his autobiography, *Persons and Places*, and from other biographical sources. The list includes addresses where Santayana stayed for long and short periods, and it includes trips and visits to various places. Santayana's habit of changing residence with the seasons, however, complicates the task of accounting for his addresses, and this list, containing estimations as well as gaps and omissions, does not pretend to be complete. It is, nevertheless, reasonably accurate, and used in conjunction with the Chronology serves to inform the reader as to where Santayana was and what he was doing at a given time. The names of clubs at which Santayana dined and from which he wrote letters, but at which he did not actually reside (e.g., the Colonial and Delta Phi Clubs in Cambridge, Massachusetts, or the National Liberal Club in London, England) are not included in this list. Indented dates indicate temporary absence from a permanent address.

1863–66

69 Calle Ancha de San Bernardo, Madrid, Spain

1866–72 (June)

Ávila, Spain (father's house)

1872 (15 July)–**1881–82** (Winter)

302 Beacon Street, Boston, Massachusetts (mother's house)

1881–82 (Winter)–**1882** (September)

26 Millmont Street, Roxbury, Massachusetts (mother's house)

1882 (September)–**1886** (May)

Room no. 19, Hollis Hall, Harvard Yard, Cambridge, Massachusetts

1883 (June–September)

Visit to Spain; trips to Lyon and Paris, France

1886–1912

Spends each summer in Europe

1886 (July–early August)

Ávila (father's house)

(early August)
Visits to Paris and Cologne en route to Göttingen, Germany

(12 August to end of August)
c/o Fräulein Schlote, 16 D Obere Karspüle, Göttingen

(September)
c/o Frau Sturm, Werder Strasse 6, Dresden, Germany

(Autumn 1886)
Visit to London

1886   (October)–**1887** (February)
Schiffbauerdamm, 3^{II}, Berlin, Germany

1887   (late March)
Two-day boat trip down Thames, from Reading to London, visits to Windsor, Eton, and Winchester, England

(21 April–May)
Oxford, England

(June)
87 Jermyn Street, St. James, London, England

(July–August)
Ávila (father's house)

(early September)
Trip to Gibraltar and tour of southern Spain

1887   (1 November)–**1888** (mid-March)
Potsdamerstrasse 123^{III}, Berlin

1888   (June)
Canal journey through Burgundy, visit to Paris

(July–August)
Ávila (father's house)

1888   (August)–**1889** (August)
26 Millmont Street, Roxbury, Massachusetts (mother's house)

1889   (September)–**1890** (Spring)
Room no. 29, Thayer Hall, Harvard Yard

1890   (Summer)
Visit to Queen's Acre, Windsor, England (Howard Sturgis's house), and Ávila

1890   (Autumn)–**1896** (June)

Room no. 7, Stoughton Hall, Harvard Yard

1893 (Summer)
Visit to Gibraltar and Ávila, Spain

1895 (22 June–late September)
Summer abroad: Spain, Italy, France, Switzerland, England

1895 (December)
Naushon Island, Buzzard's Bay, Cape Cod, Massachusetts (John
Forbes's house)

1896   (27 June)
Chateau Frontenac, Quebec, Canada

(July–September)
26 Banbury Road, Oxford, England

(September)
Visit to Amberley Cottage, Maidenhead, England (villa of John
Francis Stanley, 2d Earl Russell)

(October–December)
King's College (1 Silver Street), Cambridge, England

(December)
Trip to Paris

1897   (January–June)
King's College (2 Free School Lane), Cambridge, England

(July–August)
Gibbs Hall (Fellows' Building), King's College, Cambridge,
England (Nathaniel Wedd's rooms)

1897   (September)–**1898** (Spring)
75 Monmouth Street, Longwood, Brookline, Massachusetts
(mother's house)

1898   (Spring)–**1899** (Spring)
52 Brattle Street, Cambridge, Massachusetts

1899   (June–August)
Summer at Oxford, visits to France and Spain

1899   (Autumn)–**1904** (June)
60 Brattle Street, Cambridge, Massachusetts

1900 (Summer)
France, 108 Jermyn Street, London, England, and Oxford

1901 (July–September)
Oxford, England (5 Grove Street, now Magpie Lane)

1902 and **1903**

Summers in Europe

1904   (July)–**1906** (September)
Twenty-seven months abroad: sabbatical leave and Hyde Lecture
program

1904 (July–September)
Travels in England, Belgium, Holland, Germany, and France

(24 September–October)
Ávila (sister Susana's house)

(November)
Villa I Tatti, Settignano, Florence, Italy (the Bernard Berensons'
villa)

(25 November–8 December)
Grand Hôtel de Russie et des Iles Britanniques, Rome, Italy

1905 (January–August)
Traveling in the Middle East and Europe

(January) Egypt
(February) Israel and Lebanon
(March and April) Greece
(May) Turkey, Hungary, and Germany
(June and July) England
(August) Germany (visits Baron Albert von Westenholz)

1905 (September)–**1906** (June)
Hyde Lecturer at the Sorbonne and at French provincial
universities, Paris address: Hôtel Foyot, Rue de Tournon

(September) Compiègne
(October–mid-November) Ávila (Susana's house)
(April) Lyon, Montpellier, Cannes, Nîmes, and Orange
(29 April–5 May) Toulouse
(May) Pau, Bordeaux, Arcachon, La Rochelle, and Caen
(June) Dijon, Morez, Lyon, and Grenoble

1906   (mid-September)–**1908** (mid-June)
75 Monmouth Street, Longwood, Brookline (mother's house)

1907 (January)
Lectures in New York City

1907 (mid-June–mid-September)
Summer abroad: Germany, Switzerland, Spain

(18 September)

Arrival from Europe in New York City: Hotel Manhattan

1908   (mid-June–mid-September)
Summer abroad: England, France; visit to Queen's Acre, Windsor,
in July (Howard Sturgis's house)

1908   (mid-September)–**1912** (January)
Room no. 3, Prescott Hall, Harvard Yard

1909 (mid-July–mid-September)
Summer in England; visit in August to Telegraph House ("T.H."),
Chichester, Hampshire, England (John Francis Stanley, Second
Earl Russell's house)

1910 (February)
New York City

(April)
Visits Chicago, Illinois, and lectures at the University of Wisconsin,
Madison

(8 June– 17 September)
Summer abroad; visit to Ávila

1911 (mid-June–end of August)
University Club, San Francisco, California

1912   (29 January)
On board the R.M.S. *Olympic*

(February)
Visits to Queen's Acre, Windsor, and to Trinity College, Cambridge

(20 February)
7 Bennet Street, St. James, London

(28 February)
Hotel du Quai Voltaire, Paris

(March and early April)
Serrano 7, Madrid, Spain (Mercedes de la Escalera's house)

(May–August)
9, Avenue de l'Observatoire, Paris (Charles Augustus Strong's
apartment becomes Santayana's principal residence [except during
the period July 1914–August 1919] until the end of August 1928.)

(September–November)
Travels in Italy (Milan, Bologna, Naples, Palermo) with an extend
ed stay in Rome

1912   (30 November)–**1913** (early January)

Villa I Tatti, Settignano, Florence

1913   (February–mid-March)
French Riviera: Nice and Monte Carlo

(mid-March–April)
Serrano 7, Madrid

(May–mid-July)
9, Avenue de l'Observatoire, Paris

(3 July)
Hotel de Ville, Brussels, Belgium

(mid-August–October)
66 High Street, Oxford

(November)
45 Chesterton Road, Cambridge, England

(December)
Ávila (Susana's house)

1914   (January–mid-May)
Hotel la Peninsular, Seville, Spain

(mid-May–June)
9, Avenue de l'Observatoire, Paris

(27 July)
Euston Hotel, London

(2–3 August)
Red Lion Hotel, Cambridge, England

(5 August)
Visit to Queen's Acre, Windsor

(16 August)
Oxford, England

(late August–11 October)
3 Ryder Street, London

(12 October–14 December)
45 Chesterton Road, Cambridge

1914   (14 December)–**1915** January)
Old Ship Hotel, Brighton, England

1915   (February–April)
45 Chesterton Road, Cambridge

(May)

66 High Street, Oxford

1915   (June)–**1919** (April)
22 Beaumont Street, Oxford (main residence during World War I)

1915 (September)
Visits London, Lewes, and North Luffenham, England

1915 (October)
Visit to Bournemouth, England

1917 (February–March)
6 Park Street, Torquay, Cornwall, England

1918 (Winter)
Trip to London

1919   (end of April)
Trip to London

(13–16 and 20–25 June)
Richmond Hill Hotel, Richmond, Surrey, England

(16–20 June)
Trip to London

(July–November)
9, Avenue de l'Observatoire, Paris

1919   (December)–**1920** (20 January)
Villa Le Balze, Fiesole, Florence, Italy (Charles Augustus Strong's villa)

1920   (20 January–early May)
Hotel Minerva, Rome

(during 1920)
Final visit to Queen's Acre, Windsor

(May 1920)
Florence

(early June–September)
9, Avenue de l'Observatoire, Paris

(October)
Ávila, Spain (Susana's house)

1920   (late October)–**1921** (3 January)
Hotel Castilla, Toledo, Spain

1921   (3 January–7 March)

Serrano 7, Madrid, Spain

(end of March–end of October)
9, Avenue de l'Observatoire, Paris

(early November)
Villa Le Balze, Fiesole, and afterwards the Hotel Royal, Rome

1921   (15 November)–**1922** (22 April)
Hotel Marini, Rome

1922   (24 April–11 October)
9, Avenue de l'Observatoire, Paris (part of June and early October
spent in the Hôtel du Palais Royal)

1922   (25 October)–**1923** (8 May)
New York Hotel, Nice, France

1923   (mid-May–mid-September)
9, Avenue de l'Observatoire, Paris

(mid-September–31 October)
Penultimate visit to England: London, Cambridge, Chichester,
Oxford, Bath, and Dover

(6 November–mid-November)
Villa Le Balze, Fiesole, Florence

1923   (mid-November)–**1924** (6 May)
Hotel Bristol, Rome

1924   (6 May–mid-June)
Hotel Bauer-Grünwald, Venice, Italy

(mid-June–29 September)
Hotel Cristallo, Cortina d'Ampezzo, Italy

(30 September–mid-October)
Villa Le Balze, Fiesole, Florence

1924   (late October)–**1925** (1 June)
Hotel Bristol, Rome

1925   (1–22 June)
Paris

(23 June–mid-July)
Ávila (Susana's house)

(mid-July–September)

9, Avenue de l'Observatoire, Paris

1925   (October)–**1926** (June)
        Hotel Bristol, Rome

1926   (end of June–1 October)
        Hotel Cristallo, Cortina d'Ampezzo

        (1–10 October)
        Hôtel Royal Danieli, Venice

1926   (10 October)–**1927** (5 June)
        Hotel Bristol, Rome

1927   (6 June–mid-September)
        9, Avenue de l'Observatoire, Paris

        (mid-September to mid-October)
        Hôtel Royal Danieli, Venice (except for four days in Padua)

1927   (17 October)–**1928** (10 June)
        Hotel Bristol, Rome

1928   (11 June–end of August)
        9, Avenue de l'Observatoire, Paris (Strong gives up the apartment at
        the end of August 1928.)

        (early September)
        Trip to Oporto, Portugal, and Bayona, Spain

        (6–21 September)
        Hotel Continental, Vigo, Spain

        (22 September)
        Santiago de Compostela, Spain

        (early October)
        Grand Hotel Miramare & de la Ville, Genoa, Italy

        (3–16 October)
        Villa Le Balze, Fiesole, Florence

1928   (16 October)–**1929** (May)
        Hotel Bristol, Rome

1929   (early June–mid-September)
        Hôtel Victoria, Glion-sur-Territet, Switzerland

        (mid-September–20 October)
        Villa Le Balze, Fiesole, Florence

1929   (November)–**1930** (20 May)

Hotel Bristol, Rome

1930   (22 May–15 June)
A brief stay at the Hôtel Royal Haussmann, Paris. After final visit to
Ávila, a return to the Royal Haussmann.

(16–22 June)
Pavillon Henri IV, Saint Germain-en-Laye, France

(early July)
Hôtel Foyot, Paris

(11 July–23 September)
Hôtel Vouillemont, 15, rue Boissy d'Anglas, Paris

(end of September–21 October)
Villa Le Balze, Fiesole, Florence

1930   (21 October)–1931 (10 June)
Hotel Bristol, Rome

1931   (11–22 June)
Hôtel Royal Danieli, Venice

(22 June–11 September)
Hotel Miramonti, Cortina d'Ampezzo

(12–17 September)
Hôtel Royal Danieli, Venice

(18 September–23 October)
Hôtel de Londres, Naples, Italy

(23 October–end of December)
Hotel Bristol, Rome (except during the first week of December in
the Anglo-American Nursing Home, 311 via Nomentana)

1931   (1 January)–1932 (22 June)
Hotel Bristol, Rome

1932   (23 June–early July)
Hôtel Royal Haussmann, Paris

(July–August)
Hôtel des Réservoirs, Versailles, France

(1–5 September)
Hôtel Royal Haussmann, Paris

(6–10 September)

Hôtel des Indes, The Hague, Netherlands

(11 September–20 October)
7 Park Place, St. James, London (final visit to England)

(21–24 October)
Dover, England

(25 October–early November)
Paris

1932   (8 November)–**1933** (20 June)
Hotel Bristol, Rome

1933   (22 June–early September)
Hotel Miramonti, Cortina d'Ampezzo

(6 September–20 October)
Hôtel Royal Danieli, Venice

1933   (20 October)–**1934** (19 June)
Hotel Bristol, Rome

1934   (20 June–16 July)
Villa Le Balze, Fiesole, Florence

(18 July–11 September)
Miramonti-Majestic Hotel, Cortina d'Ampezzo

(12 September–17 October)
Hôtel Royal Danieli, Venice

1934   (20 October)–**1935** (28 May)
Hotel Bristol, Rome

1935   (29 May–17 June)
Hôtel Royal Danieli, Venice

(18 June–10 September)
Grand Hotel Savoia, Cortina d'Ampezzo

(10 September–15 October)
Hôtel Royal Danieli, Venice

1935   (16 October)–**1936** (3 June)
Hotel Bristol, Rome

1936   (4 June–11 August)
Savoy-Hotel, rue de Rivoli, Paris

(12 August–21 September)

Hôtel Victoria, Glion-sur-Montreux, Switzerland

1936   (22 September)–**1937** (14 June)
Hotel Bristol, Rome

1937   (15–16 June)
Hôtel Royal Danieli, Venice

(17 June–13 September)
Grand Hotel Savoia, Cortina d'Ampezzo

1937   (14 September)–**1938** (17 June)
Hotel Bristol, Rome

1938   (18–20 June)
Hôtel Royal Danieli, Venice

(20 June–13 September)
Grand Hotel Savoia, Cortina d'Ampezzo

1938   (14 September)–**1939** (18 June)
Hotel Bristol, Rome (Autumn 1939: Hotel Bristol closed for
reconstruction)

1939   (19–21 June)
Milan and Venice

(22 June–3 September)
Grand Hotel Savoia, Cortina d'Ampezzo

1939   (4 September)–**1940** (19 June)
Hôtel Royal Danieli, Venice

1940   (9 June–6 July)
Hotel Ampezzo, Cortina d'Ampezzo

(6 July–11 September)
Grand Hotel Savoia, Cortina d'Ampezzo

(11 September–end of September)
Hôtel Royal Danieli, Venice

1940   (end of September)–**1941** (c. 20 June)
Grand Hôtel, Rome

1941   (c. 20 June–12 September)
Palazzo della Fonte, Fiuggi, Italy

(12 September–14 October)

Grand Hotel, Rome

1941   (14 October)–**1952** (26 September)
Calvary Hospital, Clinic of the Little Company of Mary, 6, Via
Santo Stefano Rotondo, Rome

Manuscript Locations

Academy	American Academy of Arts and Letters, New York NY
American	American Jewish Archives, Hebrew Union College-Jewish Institute of Religion, Cincinnati OH
Amherst	Amherst College Library, Amherst MA
Antiquarian	American Antiquarian Society, Worcester MA
Barnes	Catherine Barnes, Philadelphia PA
Beinecke	The Beinecke Rare Book and Manuscript Library, Yale University, New Haven CT
Berkeley	The Bancroft Library, University of California at Berkeley
Bidwell	David Bidwell, Geneva, Switzerland
Bodleian	The Bodleian Library, Oxford University, England
Boston	Department of Rare Books and Manuscripts, Boston Public Library, Boston MA
Bowdoin	Bowdoin College Library, Brunswick ME
Bowling Green	Western Kentucky University, Department of Library Special Collections, Bowling Green
British	The British Library of the British Museum, London, England
Brooklyn	Brooklyn College Library, Brooklyn NY
Brown	The John Hay Library, Brown University, Providence RI
Cambridge	University Library, Cambridge University, England
Castelli	Enrico Castelli Gattinara di Zubiena
Chicago	The Modern Poetry Library, University of Chicago Library, Chicago IL
Columbia	Butler Library, Columbia University, New York NY
Congress	The Library of Congress, Washington DC
Constable	Constable and Co. Ltd., London, England
Consulate	Spanish Consulate, Rome, Italy
Cornell	Cornell University Library, Ithaca NY
Dartmouth	Baker Memorial Library, Dartmouth College, Hanover NH

DeKalb	The University Libraries, Northern Illinois University, DeKalb
Denson	Alan Denson, Aberdeenshire, Scotland
Dickson	Mr. Carl Byron Dickson, Doswell VA
Duke	William R. Perkins Library, Duke University, Durham NC
Dykeman	King Dykeman, Fairfield University, Fairfield CT
Fales	Elmer Holmes Bobst Library, Fales Library, New York University, New York City
Fitzgerald	Robert Stuart Fitzgerald
Florida	University of Florida Library, Gainesville
Gardner	Isabella Stewart Gardner Museum, Boston MA
Georgetown	Lauinger Library, Georgetown University, Washington DC
Gerber	William Gerber, Washington DC
Gilmour	Mervyn D. Gilmour, Portadown, Northern Ireland
Harvard	Harvard Archives, Harvard University, Cambridge MA
Houghton	The Houghton Library, Harvard University, Cambridge MA
Howgate	Mrs. George W. Howgate
Huntington	The Henry E. Huntington Library, San Marino CA
Indiana	The Lilly Library, Indiana University, Bloomington
I Tatti	Villa I Tatti, Settignano, Italy
Kansas	University of Kansas Libraries, Lawrence
Kentucky	University of Kentucky, Lexington
King's	King's College Library, Cambridge University, England
Lamont	Collection of Lamont family papers
Lango	John W. Lango, New York NY
Leeds	Leeds University Library, The Brotherton Collection, Leeds, England
Lipinsky	Lino S. Lipinsky de Orlov
Lockwood	Lockwood Memorial Library, State University of New York at Buffalo
Loyola	Loyola University Library, Chicago IL
Macksey	Richard A. Macksey, Baltimore MD
McMaster	Mills Memorial Library, Bertrand Russell Archives, McMaster University, Hamilton, Ontario, Canada
Merriam	John McKinstry Merriam

Michigan	Bentley Historical Library, The University of Michigan, Ann Arbor
Minnesota	University of Minnesota Libraries, St. Paul
Morgan	The Pierpont Morgan Library, New York NY
Mumford	Lewis Mumford
Munitz	Milton Karl Munitz
Murchie	Guy Murchie Jr.
Newberry	The Newberry Library, Chicago IL
New York	The New York Public Library, New York City
North Carolina	University of North Carolina at Chapel Hill
Northwestern	Northwestern University Library, Evanston IL
Ohio	Ohio Historical Society, Columbus
Oregon	University of Oregon Libraries, Eugene
Penn	The Charles Patterson Van Pelt Library, University of Pennsylvania, Philadelphia
Pennsylvania	The Pennsylvania State University Libraries, University Park
Princeton	Department of Rare Books and Special Collections, Princeton University Libraries, Princeton NJ
Provincial	Provincial Archives, Province of St. Albert the Great, Chicago IL
Radcliffe	The Schlesinger Library, Radcliffe College, Cambridge MA
Reading	The Library, University of Reading, England
Redwood	The Redwood Library and Athenaeum, Newport RI
Rigacci	Dino Rigacci
Riverside	Rivera Library, University of California, Riverside
Rockefeller	Rockefeller Archive Center, Sleepy Hollow NY
Rollins	Rollins College, Winter Park FL
Salamanca	University of Salamanca, Casa Museo Unamuno, Salamanca, Spain
Sanchez	Paloma Sanchez Sastre, Madrid, Spain
Santayana	Santayana Edition, Indianapolis IN
Sastre	Sra. Rafael (Adelaida Hernandez) Sastre, Ávila, Spain
Sastre Martín	Sra. Eduardo Sastre Martín, Madrid, Spain
Scotland	National Library of Scotland, Edinburgh
Smith	Smith College Archives, Northampton MA

Smithsonian	National Portrait Gallery, Smithsonian Institution, Washington DC
Sommer	Melvin L. Sommer
Sorbonne	Universites de Paris, Bibliotheque de la Sorbonne, France
Southern	Morris Library, Southern Illinois University at Carbondale
Spiegler	Mrs. Charles (Evelyn) Spiegler, Forest Hill NY
Stanford	Stanford University Libraries, Stanford CA
Stroup	Timothy Stroup, Annandale NY
Sturgis	Robert Shaw Sturgis, Weston MA
Syracuse	Syracuse University Library, Syracuse NY
Temple	Temple University Libraries, Philadelphia PA
Texas	Harry Ransom Humanities Research Center, University of Texas at Austin
Thompson	Samuel Martin Thompson
Tisch	Arthur Tisch, Palm Beach Gardens FL
Trinity	Trinity College Library, Cambridge University, England
UCLA	University of California at Los Angeles
Union	Union College Library, Schenectady NY
University Club	The University Club, New York NY
USC	University of Southern California Library, Los Angeles
Vermont	University of Vermont Libraries, Burlington
Viereck	Peter Robert Edwin Viereck, South Hadley MA
Virginia	Alderman Library, University of Virginia at Charlottesville
Wellesley	Wellesley College Library, Wellesley MA
Wheeler	Samuel Wheeler, Storrs CT
Williams	Williams College Archives and Special Collections, Williamstown MA
Yale	Manuscripts and Archives, Yale University Library, New Haven CT
YIVO	YIVO Institute for Jewish Research, New York NY

List of Recipients

Book One, [1868]–1909

Abbot, Henry Ward

Archer, William

Ayres, Harry Morgan

Baker, George Pierce

Beal, Boylston Adams

Beal, Louisa Adams (Mrs. James Beal)

Berenson, Mary Whitall Smith (Mrs. Bernard Berenson)

Brownell, William Crary

Bullard, Francis

Bush, Wendell T.

Butler, Lawrence Smith

Bynner, Harold Witter

Charles Scribner's Sons

Child, Elizabeth Ellery Sedgwick

Corbin, John

Creighton, James Edwin

D. Appleton and Company

Dickinson, Goldsworthy Lowes

Eliot, Charles William

Everett, Charles Carroll

Fairchild, Sally

Forbes, William Cameron

Fuller, Benjamin Apthorp Gould

Fullerton, William Morton

Gardiner, Harry Norman

Gardner, Isabella Stewart (Mrs. John Gardner)

Greene, Jerome Davis

Hapgood, Norman
Harris, William Torrey
Hastings, Horatius Bonar
Helder, Mr.
Howard, John Galen
Hyde, James Hazen
James, William
Johnson, Robert Underwood
Jordan, Mary Augusta
Kallen, Horace Meyer
Kimball, Hannibal Ingalls
Levy, Miss
Lowell, Carlotta Russell
Lyman, Herbert
Macmillan and Company
Mason, Charles Francis
The Mayflower Club
Morrow, William
Münsterberg, Hugo
Murchie, Guy
Norton, Charles Eliot
Norton, Sara
Norton, [Sara or Grace]
O'Brien, Edward Joseph Harrington
Overton, Mr.
Palmer, Alice Freeman (Mrs. George Palmer)
Palmer, George Herbert
Rand, Benjamin
Rice, Wallace de Groot Cecil
Rittenhouse, Jessie Belle
Robbins, Reginald Chauncey
Robinson, Moncure
Royce, Josiah
Russell, Bertrand Arthur William
Sastre Serrano, Celedonio

List of Unlocated Letters

The following is a list of letters by George Santayana which were known to exist, but have not been located by the editors.

To Mr. and Mrs. Jack Ames
Prior to 12 Jun 1936   In 21 Jun 1936 to George Sturgis
To Sarah Ripley (Mrs. Jack) Ames
c. 23 Jul 1936   In 23 Jul 1936 to George Sturgis
To Henri Bergson
Prior to 13 Sep 1911   In 13 Sep 1911 to Charles Augustus Strong
To John Berryman
c. 21 Jan 1951   In 21 Jan 1951 to Robert Lowell
To David and Carol Bidwell
10 Feb 1950   In 11 Feb 1950 to Raymond Bidwell
To Josephine Sturgis Bidwell
January 1945   In 13 Jan 1945 to Rosamond Sturgis
7 Jun 1945   In 7 Jun 1945 to Raymond Bidwell
c. 20 Mar 1946   In 22 Mar 1946 to Raymond Bidwell
To Emile Boutroux
Prior to 21 Dec 1916   In 21 Dec 1916 to John Jay Chapman
To Wendell T. Bush
8 Nov 1914   Mentioned in letter from Bush of 23 Nov 1914
4 Jul 1915   Mentioned in letter from Bush of 23 Aug 1915
To Lawrence Smith Butler
September 1941   Mentioned in Sturgis Family Papers, Houghton Library
To James McKeen Cattell
c. April 1906   In 11 Apr 1906 to Hugo Münsterberg
c. May 1906   In 10 May 1906 to Hugo Münsterberg
To James Bryant Conant
Prior to 14 Apr 1934   In 14 Apr 1934 to George Sturgis
To Daniel MacGhie Cory
9 Sep 1933   (In a letter to William G. Holzberger, Mrs. Cory asked that this letter not be included, the editors never received copy, and it is not at Columbia.)

To George and Margaret de Cuevas
Dates unknown   Two mentioned in 11 Mar 1940 to Cory

To Durant Drake
c. 21 Jul 1917   In 21 Jul 1917 to Charles Augustus Strong
c. 21 Sep 1917   In 21 Sep 1917 to Charles Augustus Strong
c. 3 Oct 1917   In 3 Oct 1917 to Charles Augustus Strong
c. 21 Oct 1917   In 21 Oct 1917 to Charles Augustus Strong
c. 10 Dec 1917   In 10 Dec 1917 to Charles Augustus Strong

To Mr. Hoppin Duffield & Co.
Date unknown   In 21 Mar 1922 and 13 May 1922 to Constable &
Company

To Jacques Duron
20 Sep 1933   Cited in Duron's *La Pensée de George Santayana*, 87
6 Feb 1939   Cited in Duron's *La Pensée de George Santayana*, 518

To Josephine Sturgis Eldridge
Prior to 3 Nov 1922   In 3 Nov 1922 to George Sturgis

To Françoise
c. 5 Aug 1914   In 5 Aug 1914 to Charles Augustus Strong
c. 9 Aug 1914   In 9 Aug 1914 to Charles Augustus Strong
c. 20 Aug 1917   In 20 Aug 1917 to Charles Augustus Strong
c. 30 Apr 1919   In 30 Apr 1919 to Charles Augustus Strong

To George Grady
Date unknown   (A letter to George Grady of 25 Jul 1949 is in Special
Collections/Morris Library, Southern Illinois University, and the librarian
knew of the existence of a second letter to Grady which was sold to a
private collector.)

To Carl Sadakichi Hartmann
c. 3 Nov 1922   In 3 Nov 1922 to George Sturgis

To Leslie W. Hopkinson
c. 2 Apr 1940   In 2 Apr 1940 to Nancy Saunders Toy

To Alanson Bigelow Houghton
Two mentioned in 31 Aug 1887 to William Morton Fullerton

To John Galen Howard
Prior to 21 Aug 1882   In 21 Aug 1882 to Howard

To the editor of the *Hudson Review*
Date unknown.   In 17 Apr 1952 to John Hall Wheelock

To Otto Kyllmann
Telegraph of 26 Aug 1935   Mentioned in letter to Kyllmann of same date

To Pierre de Chaignon la Rose
c. 8 Mar 1929   In 8 Mar 1929 to Maurice Firuski
After 10 Mar 1930   In 10 Mar 1930 to Maurice Firuski

To Bruno Lind (Robert C. Hahnel)
c. 31 Jul 1951   In 3 Oct 1951 to Lind

To Herbert Lyman
16 Aug 1940   Mentioned in Sturgis Family Papers, Houghton Library

To Manageress of St. James's
Prior to 25 Aug 1932   In 25 Aug 1932 to Daniel MacGhie Cory

To Marie
c. 10 Dec 1920   In 10 Dec 1920 to Charles Augustus Strong
c. 10 Apr 1922   In 10 Apr 1922 to Charles Augustus Strong

To William Pepperell Montague
c. 28 Mar 1921   In 28 Mar 1921 to Charles Augustus Strong

To Samuel Eliot Morison
c. 10 Mar 1930   In 10 Mar 1930 to Maurice Firuski

To Andrew Joseph Onderdonk
10 Jan 1940   Mentioned in Sturgis Family Papers, Houghton Library

To James Bissett Pratt
c. 14 Sep 1917   In 14 Sep 1917 to Charles Augustus Strong

To Thornton Delano Roberts
Date unknown   In 3 Oct 1951 to Bruno Lind (Robert C. Hahnel)

To José Rodriguez Feo
Date unknown   Mentioned in biographies of Wallace Stevens

To Mr. Roelker
c. 10 Apr 1931   In 10 Apr 1931 to Curt John Ducasse

To Arthur Kenyon Rogers
c. 14 Sep 1917   In 14 Sep 1917 to Charles Augustus Strong

To Celedonio Sastre Serrano
3 Dec 1928   In 4 Dec 1928 to George Sturgis

To George Frederick Stout
13 Feb 1912   In 14 Feb 1912 to George Herbert Palmer
23 Feb 1912   In 23 Feb 1912 to George Herbert Palmer

To Charles Augustus Strong
c. 23 Apr 1920 [telegram]   In 23 April 1920 to Strong
c. 8 Jan 1929   In 19 Jan 1929 to Daniel MacGhie Cory

To Margaret Strong
c. 3 Sep 1912   In 3 Sep 1912 to Charles Augustus Strong
c. 3 Oct 1916   In 3 Oct 1916 to Charles Augustus Strong
c. 13 Jan 1917   In 13 Jan 1917 to Charles Augustus Strong

To Carol Sturgis (2d wife of George Sturgis)
Date unknown   In 10 Mar 1945 to Raymond Bidwell (Written shortly after
the death of George Sturgis, probably early 1945.)

To George Sturgis

Postcard between 8 Jun and 17 Jul 1939   In 17 Jul 1939 to George Sturgis

To Josephine Sturgis (sister)

12 Dec 1914   In 14 Dec 1914 to Susan Sturgis de Sastre

Prior to 28 Mar 1915   In 28 Mar 1915 to Susan Sturgis de Sastre

Prior to 29 Jun 1915   In 29 Jun 1915 to Susan Sturgis de Sastre

To Susan Sturgis de Sastre

13 Aug 1903   13 Aug 1903 to Susan mentions another postcard sent on this date

24 Apr 1906   25 Apr 1906 to Susan mentions two postcards sent on 24 Apr 1906

24 Sep 1912   Companion to another postcard of 24 Sep 1912

30 Sep 1912   Companion to another postcard of 30 Sep 1912

28 Oct 1913   Companion to another postcard of 28 Oct 1913

To Unidentified Recipients

Prior to 7 Feb 1934   In 7 Feb 1934 to Charles P. Davis

Prior to 1 Jan 1936   In 1 Jan 1936 to Otto Kyllmann

To James Ward

January or early February 1912   In 14 Feb 1912 to George Herbert Palmer

To Bentley Wirt Warren

Correspondence mentioned in 31 May 1933 to George Washburne Howgate

To Luciano Zampa

c. 14 Sep 1919   In 14 Sep 1919 to Joseph Malaby Dent

INDEX

Colophon

*This book was designed and set in Baskerville.
It was printed on 50-pound acid-free recycled paper
and bound in Holliston Roxite B-51545 cloth
by Edwards Brothers Incorporated.*

Box Hill, Surrey
July 27 1905 —

Dear Mr James

I have just re-read, or read for
the first time in some cases, the series
of articles you have been good enough to
send me. They have given me new light
on many points — most important of all
on the relation of "Humanism" to "Truth".
It is perfectly clear that opinions are not
all equally good on pragmatic principles,
since some fulfil their pledges with advancing experience while others do not. I
am inclined to think that you would meet
with less misapprehension and hostility on
this score if you gave out, in dogmatic
form, how you conceive "the final system
of reality" (which you assume on page 3 of
the article on "Experience of Activity") to be
made up. I imagine, you would say, it is a historical
system, its substance being feelings which
may or may not be appropriated by persons.
It would remain to work out a physics
of these feelings, and to show how propos-